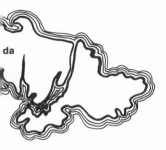

da

5 0 5 10

Nautical Miles

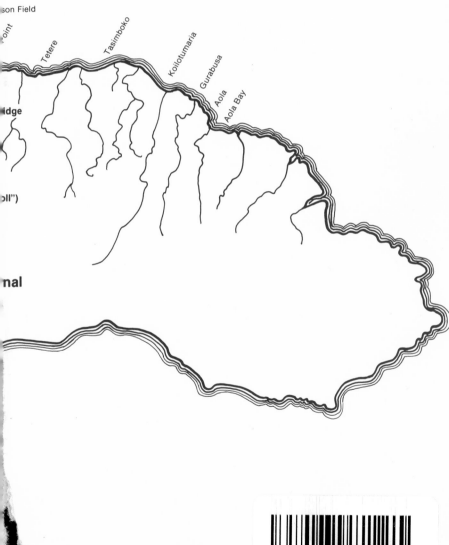

nbottom Sound

son Field

oint

Tetere

Tasimboko

Koilotumaria

Gurabusa

Aola

Aola Bay

idge

oll")

nal

Shots Fired
in
Anger

Shots Fired in Anger

Revised & Expanded
Second Edition

*A Rifleman's View of the War in the Pacific, 1942-1945,
Including the Campaign on Guadalcanal and
Fighting with Merrill's Marauders
In the Jungles of Burma*

by

Lieutenant Colonel John B. George

Drawings by Hideo and Melissa Leith

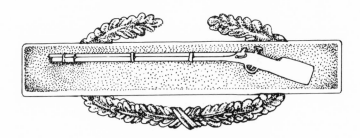

A PUBLICATION OF
THE NATIONAL RIFLE ASSOCIATION OF AMERICA

Originally published by Thomas G. Samworth as a
Small Arms Technical Publishing Co. Book
Cover Illustration by Melissa Leith

Published by the National Rifle Association of America
1600 Rhode Island Avenue, NW
Washington, D.C. 20036

ISBN 0-935998-42-X

To

DORO,

Of Course

CONTENTS

BOOK I: GUADALCANAL

I. RIFLE RANGE DAYS

II. THE SAD BEGINNING

III. THE GUADALCANAL FIGHT

IV. THE TOOLS USED

BOOK II. BURMA

PUBLISHER'S NOTE

The National Rifle Association promotes marksmanship for recreation, competition and defense of our country. You will find this book to be most eloquent testimony to the efficiency and value of the trained rifleman in combat. The author's adventures in World War II prove without question the necessity of promoting marksmanship among our citizens. The trained rifleman knows he can kill the enemy with his weapon and his performance in battle reflects that confidence.

You will also find this to be an enthralling story of high adventure in two of the toughest jungle campaigns fought in World War II. Modestly but movingly told, it is a story of suffering, death and eventual triumph. The enemies were many, the allies few, but the American soldier with ingenuity, valor and perseverance carried the day.

The original edition was long out of print when Byron Engle, a crack shot and family friend, brought it to my attention. After reading it through, in one long night, I knew it must be given to the new generation of shooters that had come along since the war. Happily I discovered the author had only told half of his story in the first edition and he has, with a bit of cajoling, contributed an account of the campaign in Burma to this revised, expanded edition. The book is much larger, there are many new illustrations and insights, but the message is the same. Riflemen, trained riflemen, win battles.

Bill Askins

APOLOGY

To the men of our Navy, who shot the Japanese out of the water, and who escorted our transports safely through the Islands, I humbly kneel. To the flyers who contributed so much to victory in Europe, and who forced the surrender of Japan before a single Doughboy set foot on Honshu, I do the same. To the supply troops who kept us from starving, I offer my sincere thanks. To the Ordnance Department, who sent us into the field better armed than our enemy, I owe my very life.

The men who served in all of the above-enumerated agencies deserve an explanation of some of the quotations and views expressed in this text; without such an explanation, I am afraid much of what I have written would seem unreasonable. And, as a brother gun-nut, I would like to qualify my writings to other members of the clan who, fortunately or otherwise, had to fight the war in organizations other than Infantry Combat Units.

This book is a partial account of the early overseas experiences of a rifleman-soldier in World War II. It is intended to present the viewpoint of the Doughboy or Doughboy Officer who has just finished his first period of combat. I have made no attempt, in the writing, to modify or change this narrow angle of approach. The Infantryman in combat looks at the rest of the world with hypercritical vision; he is inclined, to a certain extent, towards a universal feeling of contempt for men who fight a less dangerous or more comfortable war than he.

He envies the Artilleryman, a thousand yards to his rear, the additional safety and comforts back there. He growls at the sight of Air Corps installations, where men are usually sure of a cot to sleep on and warm food to eat. He hates the Quartermaster Corps, who always seem to feed and clothe their own troops better than the combat units for whose supplying they are responsible. Every supply shortage, each failure of artillery or air support, the Doughboy takes as a personal affront, seldom considering the force of circumstance which could have made it impossible for the QM or the Air Corps to do their part of the job. The individual Infantry-man is concerned with nothing but results and he will accept no excuses. And because results in war are seldom gratifying, and be-cause supply shortages are frequent, it is not unusual for the front line Infantryman, who himself must atone for all of the mistakes along the line, to despise his service troops, his high command, and his home front only slightly less than the enemy.

This attitude of prejudice and narrow intolerance remains with the Infantryman for a long time. It is only after years of service or after extensive observation of the non-combatant elements, that he finally develops a rationalizing attitude, so that he takes his own hard knocks for granted, and ceases to begrudge the rear-area troops their greater comforts and security. Only through such ob-servation can a Doughboy fully appreciate the importance of the other services, combat and non-combatant.

If the Doughboy in question happens to be an officer, and is later transferred to high-echelon staff jobs, he will obtain an op-portunity to look at the "big picture" and be able to make sense of the confused and chaotic pattern of large-scale military opera-tions. And he will in time come to realize that the trials facing the front line soldier, the heartbreaking disappointments, the priva-tions, the inordinate casualty rates, even the appearances of stu-pidity from above, are generally unavoidable.

So, if I wanted, I could take the sting out of much that you will read in this book. I could look back on the old months of bitter annoyance and apparently pointless tragedy through the rose-tinted glasses of an Army Group or a Theater staff officer, and I could paint for you a precise picture of the overall conduct of the Guadalcanal fight, making it seem to be a well-organized and co-ordinated triphibious invasion.

But this book is written mainly for my rifle-enthusiast and gun-owning friends. Their interest will probably be in the grooved-barrel weapons and the men who used them. The viewpoints and ideas they will want to hear are those of the riflemen—not the staff officers. The Doughboy who fires a rifle and his immediate associates, his non-coms and officers, are, in their own minds, the only people who really *fight* wars. On the battlefield, where emotion often governs, where hysteria replaces contemplation, there is little chance for a soldier to see the non-combatants' side of things. A Doughboy's weapon is broken or worn out—so the Ordnance is no good; he is short of food—so the QM is a bunch of fat-butted, useless deadheads; his head is tight and buzzing with fever, so the Medical Corps—other than his own Infantry medics—is an aggregation of military drones. The soldier sees himself the victim of a huge conspiracy, with the enemy, the elements, and even his own countrymen allied against him. If he lives through his ordeal of combat without becoming a confirmed cynic, he is lucky.

So this book is written as it would have been written in 1943, when I was an Infantry lieutenant. The personal bias and sympathies portrayed were real—my standard attitude at the time. If I had not been "bitter" in 1943, if I had not been hopping mad, ready to take a pot-shot at the Ordnance repair man who botched up my machine guns, or the QM sergeant who failed to deliver our rations, I would not have been an Infantryman. In fact, I would not have been human!

So here is the story of a large part of my rifle-shooting life. It has been fun to relate it to my beer-drinking companions in the Chicago Rifle Club, and it has been fun—albeit laborious—for me to write this story. The writing is not good, but that does not keep me from hoping that the Shooting Fraternity will enjoy the tales I have to tell.

Lt. Col. John B. George
Military Intelligence Section
General Staff, Far East Command
Tokyo, Japan
May, 1947

July 25, 1947

In 1942–43, during the Battle of Guadalcanal, John B. George, now a Lieutenant Colonel, served as a junior officer in the Second Battalion of the 132nd Infantry Regiment. As commanding officer of that battalion I came to know him well.

Johnny George is a fine officer and an able Infantryman. As a leader he was always capable and aggressive; as an individual rifleman he never lost an opportunity to kill or harass the enemy.

COLONEL GEORGE F. FERRY
Commanding Officer
132nd Infantry Regiment

INTRODUCTION TO THE
SECOND EDITION

In the front of the first edition of this book a letter, signed by
Colonel George F. Ferry, says nice things about my capability and
aggressiveness as an officer and speaks of my eagerness as an individual rifleman to harass and kill the enemy. The letter was sent to my
publisher in 1947, and I wasn't about to argue with it.

If that fine old citizen-soldier were alive today, though, I'd feel
urged to come clean, and tell him that whatever hint of these qualities
that he saw in me, whatever appearance of courage or bravery that
met his eye, was a borrowed, artificial thing. And I'd be inclined to
ask my old battalion commander to re-word his letter to make it
praise not me but the skills and drills of the target range and the
hunting field or forest. The target ranges at Camp Perry and so many
other places, the Missouri squirrel woods, the Wisconsin and Michigan deer forests had made passable marksmanship "instinctive" for
me, so that the basics of good aim and trigger let-off kept with me
under the most pants-wetting fear and stress of a jungle fire-fight. In
the end the only hero of my personal war story is this saving skill, for
it made a potential military coward into what Colonel Ferry could
judge to be an effective combat infantryman.

For a time, before too many Japanese close misses and the sight of
too many of my friends dead or badly wounded had taken their toll,
the war itself was something of an Adventure. And later on, when I
was deeply concious that my number could come up in the next
collision of patrols on a trail, the next drop of a Japanese mortar shell,
the war still had its adventurous by-products. It carried me to beautiful wildernesses, where I could take local leave and hunt tiger and
other big game, walking with tribal hunter-companions: to this
extent my infantryman's service through World War II never lost its
romance and adventure.

In the first edition, published these 34 years ago, I extolled the
beauties of these wildernesses where the war had carried my fellow
infantrymen and me, but hardly enough. In each grand vista of palm
groves and mountains, such as we could admire from the top of a hill
just (bloodily) taken on Guadalcanal, or even glance at through a

XV

Navy transport porthole when we would glide past the odd volcanic island with its palm shaded shoreline and only a beached outrigger canoe or two to represent its human population, I fancied I could make my home for another lifetime.

Ernest Hemingway, writing of his part of World War I, made much of places, as opposed to slogans and ideals. He spoke of the emptiness of big ideas such as Freedom and Liberty and Victory for Our Side and said that only the names of places had dignity. I can't do this, because to me the war against Hitler and Mussolini and Tojo was a necessary war, to stop sick little dictators from taking over the earth, and its slogans and ideals still mean a lot to me. But I share in the fullest Hemingway's love of places, with their special names that commemorate human courage in its most intimate form, and their sometime special beauty of mountain, valley, forest and ocean shoreline when a war moves into an Asian or Pacific island wilderness.

In the original edition of this book the names of places — Lunga Beach, Point Cruiz, the Tanamboga River, Savo Island and so on —were mentioned much more casually. In this second edition I mention them with more respect, using them and the name of a ship as titles for chapters: Fiji, the S.S. Lurline, Deolali, Deogarh, Assam, Shingbwiyang, Walawbum and Nhpum Ga. Each of these locales was the setting of infantrymens' camaraderie, all offered views of land or water that could charm the eye and awe one's sense of beauty, and most of them brought romance or adventure. Only the last two saw the ugly portent of violence and bloodshed mar and dim that sense of beauty and romance.

The memories of these places and their violent happenings may be a treasure to me alone. Also they cannot be complete. Most of the time we were forbidden to keep personal journals, and the official records sometimes are sparse. My impressions of the individual characters in my story are strictly wartime, reflecting perhaps nothing of their larger lives. I knew most of them in this one campaign alone, anecdotally, with only sketchy notions of their civilian backgrounds and none of their military or civilian futures, of course. These gaps in the record don't keep me from hoping again that the Shooting Fraternity, to whom this book again is personally addressed, will enjoy this larger story of a young competitive shooter and hunter gone to war.

A special note to any of my buddies or colleagues in the old 132nd Infantry and the Marauders who may flatter me by reading this edition. As you know we were largely forbidden to keep journals or diaries, even when we were able to keep the paper from disintegrating with jungle rot, and my memory is total only for some of the scenes and settings. So please don't hold it against me if I have a battalion or platoon moving off a day or two early, or give a wrong credit for a supporting mortar barrage or for a bombing and strafing sortie by our air support. Above all please forgive me for any seeming inconsistence. The campaigns described were many thousands of miles apart, in different terrain, under different theater commands. Like the rest of you, I've had years to think about these wartime adventures and to change in my attitudes and ways. I like to think that I'm very different today from the young lieutenant and captain who walked the trails on Guadalcanal and in North Burma, and I'm far less inclined to apologize for those young warrior attitudes and ways today than I was in the 40's.

In the second paragraph of this introduction, I said that my personal story would have a hero that I could praise loudly indeed: a hero that was a talent rather than a man. To identify this hero unmistakably I'd like to refer to my current work on a theory of human behavior, with particular reference to man's evolutionary origin as a primitive big game hunter.

My research in this project dates back to the seven years I spent in East Africa during the 1950's and early 60's; in particular to the 18 months I spent walking with primitive hunters who routinely took elephant and cape buffalo with spears. To refresh my mind on this primitive hunting experience I recently re-read an article that I published in the American Rifleman, October, 1954, about the firearms that I used during these walks.

Entitled *THREE LITTLE RIFLES*, the article was mainly about my choice of an ideal battery for hunting all rifle game, from gophers to elephants. But as I read back through it I noticed a point that I tried to make with an emotional intensity. I told of a deep feeling of nervousness when the need to appraise the weight of tusks, or the amount of meat, forced me to move very close to elephant or other dangerous game in thick cover. Then I tried to explain, via an anecdote, how I was able to cope with this particular variety of fear — fear that had been known to paralyze a hunter in this country and cause his injury or death.

The anecdote concerned a wounded rhino, which came out of cover to the left and rear of me and a Dorobo hunter companion. A scream from the Dorobo, who was following close behind me as we moved on after the wounded animal, had sounded the alarm and indicated the direction of the threat. I had turned left-about, seen the huge bulk coming at us, and realized at once the need for a center, raking hit beneath its snout — as the only way of stopping it in time.

What happened next took seconds, perhaps even minutes, for me to fully recall. At the time I had only a slow-motion, dreamy sense of the fine-fit Shelhamer stock coming up to my cheek, the reticle of the Lyman Alaskan scope aligning itself, and the tinkling sound of ejected cases following the successive jolts of recoil from the featherweight M-70. 375 Magnum. The first thing that registered clearly was the voice of the senior Dorobo hunter, who had run from the rear to join us and who was crying "BAS! BAS! BAS! ENOUGH! ENOUGH!" as the last of four shots patterned close in the center of the rhino's brisket.

These unthought, unfelt movements of mine didn't end there, either. Even as I lowered the rifle in response to the old Dorobo's cry I kept watching the now supine trophy and grabbed at my belt for cartridges, so when I laid the rifle against the carcass and posed for the photograph printed in the article, the little .375 was ready again, with four in the magazine and one up the spout, as the British say.

As strongly as any of my memories of combat, this big game hunting memory identifies the hero of this book, this saving skill that had seen me alive and well through more Banzai charges and jungle patrol actions than any sane man would bargain for.

This skill had been built up through many years of owning and using guns, in particular with the years of competitive rifle shooting that included bolt manipulation exercises that taught me to flip the bolt rapidly without removing the gun from my shoulder between shots. As I re-read this *RIFLEMAN* article I realized more than ever that it was this degree of marksmanship habit, which a timid soul like me had been so lucky to acquire, that had saved me from the paralyzing fear that made three out of four American soldiers, according to the famed military historian S.L.A. Marshall, fail to fire their weapons in combat at all. The hobby of shooting that I loved so much in peacetime had insured against my becoming a practicing wartime coward, and had made me instead into a passable soldier who had struck down his share of the enemy and enjoyed camaraderie with some of the finest warriors that his big Western Tribe could produce.

So there's the hero of this book, and the gift to me of my lifetime hobby which gives me pleasure still today. Readers who are enthusiastic shooters who enjoy firearms and marksmanship and who work hard to retain this right to pursue happiness in this way will understand. Any non-shooter readers, of the sort who might stand quietly by while gun ownership and use are imperiled by Prohibition - type laws, may not. I humbly beg the latter to consider the more detailed military history that is now being refined, which among other things has revealed that the majority of effective casualties in war are created by bullets from small arms, and then to consider where Western civilization would be today had the Germans and the Japanese held a monopoly on small-arms marksmanship and its conception, by the more gun-wise of its soldiers, as a hero to be thanked if not revered.

This foreign monopoly on marksmanship skill is made many times more possible by the existence of yet another and more special group of non-shooters here in America. I have been listening to these people for most of my life, and I encounter them regularly now here in Washington, mostly at Georgetown cocktail parties. Claiming usually to be liberals, and imbued often with that particular kind of liberal mush that accords equal sympathy to the rapist and the raped, they are hesitant to blame individual human beings for any vileness or crime. And for a large range of man's more vicious sins they blame an artifact, The Gun. Every week I listen to their litanies against firearms ownership and to their proposals that would take firearms away from every law abiding citizen (and have little or no effect on criminals, disarming the homeowner and leaving the burglars and rapists untouched by these unenforceable and therefore redundant bits of paper).

To me today, this makes me very grateful to my father and my other boyhood mentors, back in the Missouri farmlands, who did not bar my choice of guns and shooting as a hobby. Had I listened instead to these self-styled liberals then, and turned from my chosen hobby and recreation to handball or pottery, I might never have fulfilled the military duties my country later required of me. Without that degree of instilled and automatic marksmanship that I would pick up on the rifle and pistol ranges to serve me as an antidote to fear, I might have joined what we used to call in Merrill's Marauders *THE SILENT MAJORITY,* a term that has nothing in common with its usage today. The Silent Majority I refer to now, described in detail by the military historian S.L.A. Marshall, was the unbelievable three-fourths of American combat infantrymen who did not fire their weapons, even when they were in great danger for not firing back at a better trained enemy. With the typical love of life that our affluent standard of living had given me, I'm probably much more afraid of death than the enemies I opposed. I might have cringed trembling and helpless under enemy fire, like the anti-hero which the American actor James Garner played so well in the film THE AMERICANIZATION OF EMILY. When I recently watched his image on the screen, lying in the sands of Normandy beach paralyzed by fear and awaiting death or capture at the enemy's convenience, my thought was "There but for the grace of God . . ." That supine figure in the sands, listening to the frightening noises of battle, and bearing out every argument of Hitler and Stalin that Americans are bound to prove militarily soft and ineffectual, could have been mine.

Reflecting the Camp Perry backgrounds of their officers, the soldiers that I served with in World War II were largely immune to this failing: they had the rudiments and the example, at least, of passable combat marksmanship close by. But we'll never know just how many American soldiers, who did listen to the "peace loving" and "liberal" voices against firearms ownership and use, have been condemned to cowardice and to death on our unwanted but recurrent battlefields. In my estimate this number is in the thousands, and I thank God that it didn't include me. Had I listened to my many acquaintances who cried PEACE AT ALL COSTS! right up to Pearl Harbor Day, and who were capable of calling big game hunting "brutal" and "barbaric" while they forked away at a nice cut of baby beef, they might have got me too. They might have sentenced me to a humiliating and disgraceful coward's death before I'd lived out a third of my alotted years.

So I'm sorry. If fine marksmanship becomes the hero of my book, plain logic makes the villain a second human abstraction: this facile, cliche, superficial notion that The Gun is to blame for a wide range of human vileness and excesses.

The men who know what I've just said is true are numerous but not very vocal. Men who have been riflemen and machine-gunners in prolonged front line combat are not much good at explaining their experiences to homefront liberals. The ones I know don't often acquire writing or propaganda skills, and none of them has bothered to conceive that their marksmanship skills, acquired in peacetime through the shooting sports and hobbies, could become the hero of any story. Confronting my cocktail-party acquaintances and hearing their facile but uninformed attacks on firearms ownership and use, they'd be most likely to shrug and turn away. Or, if drunk enough, to face these self-styled liberals (I say "self-styled" because they talk Freedom all the time but would take away one of our most fundamental American liberties), and say what I've so often wanted to but never have: "WOULD YOU PLEASE TAKE TWO RUNNING JUMPS AND GO TO HELL?"

John B. George
Washington, D.C.
1 July 1981

BOOK I
GUADALCANAL

I. RIFLE RANGE DAYS

". . . *As the possession of this last village was important to our future operations . . . I directed that it might be occupied by a detachment consisting of four companies of* riflemen. . . ."

THE DUKE OF WELLINGTON
August 16, 1808

A HOBBY

My fondness for rifle shooting began at the age of seven, when I was first allowed to borrow my brother's rifles and go out from our house, on the outskirts of a small midwestern town, to shoot squirrels. Squirrel shooting, I know, is a sport that rates very highly with me to this day, because I have at this writing just returned from a squirrel hunt on the reservation here at Camp Blanding, Florida. It was a great pleasure to find that the sniping and rifle shooting experiences of a war, and the killing of many head of big game, had in no way dimmed my appreciation of that delightful woodland pastime. My pulse quickened in the same old way each time I cracked down on one of the seven fat grays I bagged; and my mouth waters now as I anticipate a supper of fried young gray squirrel.

Competitive rifle shooting began for me on the 50-foot gallery in the basement of the Lake View High School, in Chicago, Illinois. My family had moved to the city while I was still of grammar school age, taking me away from my cherished Missouri hills and woodlands. From that time on, my hunting in the States was held to short trips and visits to relatives in the country. But I found the sport of punching holes in paper targets almost made up for the loss. I became involved in all sorts of small-bore rifle competitions, shooting on both indoor and outdoor club and state teams before my eighteenth birthday. The big-bore bug also took hold about that time, and I had obtained a National Match rifle when I was fifteen, and had dryfired and practiced with the enthusiasm only a school boy can enjoy.

In due time, I enlisted in the Illinois National Guard, shooting my way onto the State Rifle Team each year that I was able to attend the National Rifle Matches at Camp Perry, Ohio. The Chicago Rifle Club—affectionately and otherwise known as "The S.O.B's" by neighboring organizations, afforded an excellent medium for competitive rifle shooting in and around Chicago, and it was a pleasure to be able to fire on their .30 caliber team. This Chicago Rifle Club had a decided aversion to small-bore shooting. So I also became a member of the Winnetka Rifle Club, in order to participate in .22 caliber shooting too. It kept me very busy getting around to all the necessary shoots—but it paid great dividends in pleasure. By the time I was inducted as a second lieutenant in the newly federalized 132nd Infantry in March, 1941, I had become thoroughly wrapped up in rifle shooting.

At odd times during our rifle matches, the inevitable conversations concerning the possible military application of our markmanship schooling would come up among the small groups of club members formed behind the firing line. As a patriotic youngster, I was incapable of seeing eye to eye with some of my fellow competitors, who failed to connect civilian rifle competition in any way with national defense or preparedness. I seemed to see, in what we were doing, a sport made more enjoyable because it did have a definite end and purpose.

To me it seems that there is something a little noble about the use of modern weapons in sport—a quality not found today in any hobby not associated with the handling of firearms. The tiltyard and the archery ranges traditional in British history are gone as a recreational adjunct to military training and a means of making a people able to defend their nation and their ideals. However, our modern writers still give these sites of ancient competitive sports more color and glamour than is ever accredited to the rifle and pistol ranges which have replaced them. When rifle shooting as a national defense measure is discussed in writing by a layman, it is nearly always in reference to the exploits of Daniel Boone or David Crockett—as though the days of rifle shooting had become a thing of the past.

Actually, more men carried rifles in this war just past than in any war before. Their experiences in the primitive jungles of the Pacific—and in many other areas—have surpassed anything which has been honestly recorded in the early history of our continent's settlement. These men knew the same great dangers that faced our early settlers: savage enemies, disease, starvation, isolation, and death by torture; and, in addition, the soldiers of our recent war have had to suffer the nerve-racking and maiming blast of weapons which men fighting during the 18th Century were never called upon to endure.

Before the war, I had an idea that we did not have adequate appreciation of our chosen sport and hobby, and I often voiced that belief to other "gun-nuts" during friendly readyline conversations. In the light of my experiences in the war I have become certain that our sport suffers that moral defect, and that our country's national defense potential is lessened incalculably thereby.

As riflemen, should we look only into the past for the thrill of warlike achievement? Why can't we make ourselves see its existence in the present—before our very eyes? To enjoy his sport to the fullest, the rifleman should know—as he stands with sling tight on his arm, waiting for the targets to rise from the pit—that his own sport has the same glamour that is conceded by history to the medieval archer drawing his long bow, or to Daniel Boone taking aim with his groove-barrelled flintlock at a painted savage. If an attractive presentation of the spirit of military rifle shooting could be given to the public through newspaper, radio and screen publicity, with particular emphasis on the element of national defense —it could make rifle shooting a national pastime. At the same time it would do patriotism a great service, gain for our sport the recognition it truly deserves and would get a lot more people out-of-doors in the pursuit of the most enjoyable hobby in the world. I have been at this hobby for more than fifteen years, and I hope to keep up this enthusiastic pursuit until the day I die.

For many months I was to utilize the knowledge and skill acquired during pleasant days spent in rifle practice and competition, in the direct and terrible business of killing people. I hope now that I shall never again be forced to apply this deadly knowledge; but, should my freedom and my life ever again be placed in jeopardy by aggressors, my rifle is hanging ready on the wall.

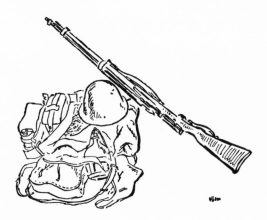

FORT SHERIDAN, JULY '38

It was a typical July Sunday on the range at Fort Sheridan, Illinois. It was one of those sun-boiling days when onlooking laymen come to regard the rifle enthusiast as a damn, stupid fool. Some 200 big-bore riflemen were shooting out the final day for the Illinois State Championships and a berth on the State Civilian Team. Remarks along the line indicated that if the competition itself wasn't hot, the damn weather more than made up for it.

I felt uncomfortably happy that day. I was uncomfortable because I could never get into a bearable prone position without wearing a sweatshirt beneath my shooting jacket to pad my poorly-fleshed ribs. On this account I was faced with a choice of either roasting alive or suffering another torture of the damned—that of having my spare midriff and pectoral surfaces lacerated by the tough northern sod. Because the laceration would adversely affect my score as well as my health, I chose to wear the sweatshirt (certainly an appropriately-named garment) and endure the roasting, which, I believed would affect only my health.

I was happy because through the early stages I had been getting reasonably good scores—nothing phenomenal, but the long run of not-too-bad performances which leads toward a good total in the grand aggregate.

The matches were being fired on two Sundays in July and all of the separate stages comprised the equivalent of twice across the National Match service rifle course, less 10 shots at 1,000. The first Sunday's firing had found me far down on the list. At the end of that day the championship had looked like a cinch for a National Guard team mate of mine, Captain Aurand E. Linker. But the Captain had suffered bad luck early in the second day's firing at the short ranges, and he was now well out of the running. The match was now nip and tuck among several members of the famous (and infamous) Chicago Rifle Club. Ralph Izard, veteran .30 caliber shot and 1929 winner of the Wimbledon Cup, was in the

6

lead when we wearily picked up our kits at the 600-yard line and trudged back through the heat to the 1,000-yard point. As we made this walk, carrying our heavy loads of shooting kit and weapons, we were stared at in open-mouthed amazement by people sitting in parked convertibles on the sidelines. They were waiting for us to get the match finished to permit them the use of the range, which was also the polo field. On observing their somewhat under-standable consternation, I thought of the cliche concerning a rifle shooter's mental qualifications—"You don't have to be crazy, but it sure as hell helps!"

We got back to the 1,000-yard mark and regained our breath while the range sergeant spent the usual amount of breath directing stentorian profanity at the field telephone and Alexander Graham Bell. After much cranking and some splicing of wire he managed to get through to the pits so that the first relay, already on the line, could be permitted to commence firing. In about twenty minutes I heard the catastrophic news of a 94 by Ralph Izard, which gave him an aggregate score to be reckoned with—to say the least. In-wardly, I conceded my small chances of winning to him.

When I moved up on the line in the third relay, I was lucky enough to get a target with a good, fast operator. (Being a nervous character, I have always been prone to die a separate death after each thousand-yard shot I fire until I see the spotter or paddle.) It is a great help to have an operator who is not apparently suf-fering from sleeping sickness. I fired the first shot after carefully checking my sight setting and muttered the familiar 1,000-yard first-shot-prayer: "Please, Lord, let it be on the target—and let the damn man in the pits find it soon, before the suspense kills me."

My prayer was moderately answered and it was just above the butts - on for a sad four at six o'clock. I yanked out the old O'Hare micrometer and put on a minute—not trusting my hold enough to make a full correction. The second shot gave me another four which hit the very spotter of the first. My scorer tried his best to keep a straight face as I cursingly reapplied the mike and added a healthy two minutes. What the hell had happened to the zero of that weapon? As I aimed the second shot, I mumbled about the advis-ability of wrapping my pet National Match rifle around a nearby tree if the third shot should be wide at twelve. The setting was a full minute higher than I had ever used on that rifle—my pet silk-smooth National Match.

The third shot was in the groove—and the next and the next. It was great stuff. The group got to "swimming" in the V ring and I stopped scribbling my scorebook to get into the rhythm of the thing. Without giving myself time for a thought of the enormity of the accomplishment, I blazed away the remaining cartridges,

running up a ranking 98 to win the Grand Aggregate, which was
the state .30 caliber championship (Carlos E. Black Trophy).
Along with it went the Tribune Trophy Match, which was the long
range championship of Illinois—and sundry lesser trophies and
medals.

At this moment, nine years later, I can still feel the keen joy I
experienced and my boyish thrill at becoming the youngest .30
caliber state champ that Illinois had ever had. It was a feeling
which subsequent shooting experiences never did more than equal.

The Chicago Rifle Club convened that evening at Bob Lovell's
and Pat Fahrney's place for small talk, beer, and hamburgers—
and the gang all made much of referring to me as the "Champ."
The only words Ken Smith uttered that evening, so far as I can
remember, formed themselves—perhaps with no intent on Ken's
part—into another one of his "two-cents-worths"which so often
seem to deserve a place in the records.

"George," he said, looking musingly at me over a glass of ale,
"you held nearly everything out there awfully tight, today—kept
your bullets hitting within two minutes of angle on those paper
targets. Think you could do as well on targets that shoot back?"
Before I could answer, he shifted his gaze to the wall and added in
a half jocular, half serious tone, "I sure as hell hope that you and
about a million other guys can shoot good in the next few years to
come. A lot may depend on just that."

CAMP PERRY, SEPTEMBER '39

A group of spectators had gathered on the assembly line behind the Marine Corps Herrick Trophy team which had "gone clean" with but one pair left to fire—20 shots per man at 1,000 yards with no sighters. A new record was in the offing.

The conversation within the group was hushed, to avoid possible disturbance of the two anchor men who had taken over the bull guns and assumed the characteristically low prone position of the Marine team. If my memory serves me well, the members of the last pair were Sergeant Kravatz and Private First Class Wolters —the latter the holder of the new Wimbledon record, established a few days before.

In the Illinois contingent of assembly-line observers, Bill Otis, the one-man bull gun team from Moline; Ken Smith, the dry-humored president of the Chicago Rifle Club, and I sat on our canvas folding seats. Our conversation ran something like this:

"Bill," said I, "You're going to be a doctor by this time next war—and the damn Medics don't use anything but scalpels and fountain pens. You won't have the least bit of use for those gilt-edged sporters and magnums you now keep to decorate your den. They'll just gather dust in the rack waiting for you to come home. Why don't you agree to lend them to me? I'll be able to put 'em to good use when they send me across in this coming war."

"Okay," said Bill, without shifting his eyes from the scoreboard, which was having another "V" marked up to add to a run of some eight or nine, "I'll get 'em packed and ready to ship to you when you get your overseas orders. Hope those good guns don't rust away on the bottom of some sub-infested ocean."

While the two of us were laughing at the intended silliness of our talk the last two shots of the Marine team were fired. Kravatz held his with considerable effort, resting several times before getting it off. He was forced once to remove a round that had been in the chamber too long and replace it with a fresh one. Obviously

9

considering his chances of getting off a bad one to spoil the perfect team run, he was doing his best to make sure of the hold. Instead of calling the shot, he shook his head grimly toward the coach. Everyone waited anxiously for the target to rise from the pit. After an interminable length of time the target appeared with a white spotter showing a plain five, not well centered—but good. Before anyone could find time to worry about the last shot, to be fired by the other member of the pair on the line, it rang out. All of the onlookers sprang to their feet, fearing that the score of the team had been ruined by an accidental discharge; but such was not the case. Wolters had aimed quickly as the target rose and had gotten off his shot with the easy confidence which had characterized his 27 V run in the Wimbledon. The target was drawn quickly and it soon reappeared with a pinwheel spotter. A wild cheer arose from the crowd and the pair returned to the coaching line for a royal back-slapping.

As a big figure "800" was chalked on the board and we turned away from the crowd, the taciturn Kenneth Smith stopped chewing on a blade of grass long enough to speak another one of his quotables: "You know," he said, "they ought to roll that damn target up and send it to Hitler."

II. THE SAD BEGINNING

"No military unit in the history of warfare has ever been adequately trained, nor the individual soldiers and officers who comprised it. Fighting teams and their members can never be properly graded in degrees of sufficiency for the tasks they must perform; but rather in the nearness they achieve toward the utterly impossible goal of military perfection."

MAJOR GENERAL ORDE C. WINGATE
In an address to the assembled officers
of Merrills Marauders, Deogahr, India,
1943

TRAINING DAYS

When the 132nd Infantry of the Illinois National Guard was inducted into the Army of the United States I was privileged to serve with it in the initial capacity of a second lieutenant. The induction took place in March of 1941 and the unit moved to its training location, Camp Forrest, Tennessee, in April. There we took up the job of bringing the organization into good shape. We faced many problems, in that we were short of both equipment and know-how in the lower ranks, if not along the entire chain of command. We had to simulate and improvise constantly. My service at Camp Forrest was to me, from beginning to end, a constant revelation of our nation's pathetic state of unpreparedness. But under the supervision of a few veteran civilian soldiers who had gained experience in the other war and our small allotment of Regular Army personnel, we made headway and became a workable organization in time for the Louisiana maneuvers.

Being assigned as a machine gun platoon leader in a heavy weapons company, I had little chance to keep up my rifle shooting. There was no civilian competition within driving distance of Forrest and I often went for months at a stretch without firing a shot. I did, however, have an opportunity to test the M1 Rifle to my satisfaction and I gained a good bit of respect for it, an alteration of opinion for me. At the beginning, I had decided that a semi-auto was not the thing. It seemed to me that, with the adoption of a semi-automatic, accuracy would have to be sacrificed. Most men would be inclined to blow away their ammunition too fast, and good fire discipline would become more difficult of attainment. This original opinion of mine had received its first setback at Perry in 1939, where I shot one of the weapons in the M1 School and got a 79 out of 80 at 200 yards rapid fire on the 10" "bullseye." Next, the limited firing I did at Forrest sold me on the weapon as far as its range performance was concerned. The conclusion I harbored then was that *if* using this new gun did not seriously increase the ammunition supply problem, there could be no real reason why it should not be a grand performer in combat. The latest improved M1 model with the gas port instead of the older muzzle sleeve, was actually superior in *practical* accuracy to the M1903. Its better sights, stock fit, and lightened recoil made it easier for recruits to shoot. The semi-auto feature eliminated the need for long hours of bolt-manipulation exercises. But with all of this, it still seemed to me a little early to think of discarding the good old '03.

Well—a normal need for building the trimmings of Camp Forrest faced us, and we laid down our rifles to "fancy up" the place. It seemed to me that there was an unnecessary amount of emphasis placed on housekeeping while we were there. All of the time used in landscaping and beautifying had to be deducted in one way or another from training. But that was in peacetime and no one could blame an officer for building duck-walks and finishing them with mahogany stain if he knew that it would set him well with high authority—even if he had to yank the men off the ranges to do the work.

The thought of that incident—one particularly annoying memory of Camp Forrest days—brings me to mention a few things about that camp and the circumstances of our stay there.

I suppose that it was much like any other National Guard post of the period, but even in rationalizing retrospect, I cannot forgive the responsible parties for some of the serious sins of omission and error which were committed, and some of the damage which was done to the really good raw material which we got in the first levy of recruits under selective service.

These first selectees were largely volunteers, with a very high order of intelligence and physique, and they were deserving of the best possible training under fully qualified instructors. Most of them were fresh from schools or businesses, thoroughly indoctrinated with the spirit of efficiency and organization, which are inherently part of American industry. Coming into the Army, they had every reason (if not every right) to be trained as efficiently by the Army for their function in it as they had been trained for industry and business by the various branches of the American educational system.

Most of them were at least a little fired with a feeling of patriotism, and many were of a thinking sort—men who had carefully adjudged the seriousness of the international situation, and wisely decided to get into the Army early. The greater part had relatively high educational qualifications, sometimes well above those of the National Guard enlisted cadremen who were to be their instructors.

The cadre of our division was made up of men of various backgrounds and from various walks of life—but they were men who had kept an interest in the military during the years of peace. By spending a night or two out of each week at an armory where they would learn drill and weapons training, and by going to a two .weeks summer camp, they had managed to pick up a smattering of military knowledge which later proved to be worth its weight in gold. Some few, like myself, were weapons enthusiasts, and our interest in the peacetime military had been primarily one of competitive shooting with the rifle, pistol, and occasionally with the Browning Auto Rifle or machine gun. Many of us were moved to remain members of National Guard units for years, mainly for the pleasure we obtained from rifle and pistol competition, (though often we would gain an interest in tactics and weapons employment as well).

Throughout the ranks of the 33rd, as in other National Guard divisions, there were all sorts of men and officers, ranging in type from the keenly interested non-professional soldier to the yokel who had joined up for the sake of the uniform. However, the most valuable asset each division had, as far as training was concerned, was its small group of Regular Army personnel.

Those few regular soldiers and officers also varied individually, but most of them had received lengthy training and were accordingly possessed of some military knowledge. The great trouble was that they were too few in number, and almost entirely unschooled in the better methods of instructing civilian soldiers. Few of the enlisted Regular Army personnel had educational (or I.Q.) qualifications to match those of the better selectees. And few of them possessed truly specialized military knowledge.

This "specialized knowledge" was the most important non-physical shortage encountered in the early days. War may be a very wide scoped and general business, but Infantry training and tactics are not at all general in character. They are specialized, and, to a degree, highly scientific. No amount of common sense on the part of an officer can be substituted for the minimum requirements of technical knowledge concerning the operation of weapons and the handling of Infantry units in combat. Military rifle shooting, despite its simplicity, is one of these subjects which requires specialized knowledge; in some ways rifle know-how is just as specialized as the knowledge and experience required for the operation of complicated signal equipment.

Rifle shooting instruction in the 33rd Division at Camp Forrest was generally poor. No amount of rationalizing can alter that truth, and there are few excuses. True, we were short of equipment. We did not have M1 rifles, of course, but we had perfectly good Springfields, and an inadequate but worthwhile allowance of ball ammunition. We were also short of good instructors but no alibi is provided there, for there was always a small number of skilled rifle shots and rifle instructors who were kept busy at "more important work."

This was largely a matter of improper placement of training priorities, and over-emphasis upon "appearances"—a term which, in military parlance, is known as "eyewash," and means exactly the same thing as the Oriental term "face" (and which to my mind makes about the same amount of sense). The old Infantry concept which demanded that an outfit be taught, "to shoot and to walk" ahead of everything else, had apparently been forgotten by important people somewhere at the top of our command echelons. That pragmatic, age-old, prerequisite of good, fighting, foot soldier units seemed to have few advocates at Forrest. It seemed that instead those two subjects had been deemed unimportant and had been set aside, for we were taught most everything else first. Shooting and the employment of weapons in the field were intangibles as far as many of the post inspectors were concerned; such qualities did not show up for all to see at a glance—at least not so importantly as a nicely painted mess hall or a well-appointed enlisted men's club!

We seemed to spend endless hours on things which were obviously silly—especially the more spectacular and "showy" subjects. Hours were devoted to hand-to-hand combat instruction and drill —how to fight *without* weapons—long before we had even begun to learn to use the guns we had. It made me wonder if our higher training authorities had lost all confidence in firearms, and had decided to fight the war under slightly modified Marquis of Queensbury rules. Mass calisthenics were taken up in minute detail, with officers staying up all night sometimes to rehearse a complicated routine of commands they would have to give on the following day to a battalion of soldiers who would spend an hour or so emulating the antics of a group of chorus girls—flexing their muscles in unison. Sometimes they would be accompanied by the regimental band playing "The Band Played On." Military courtesy and customs of the service were subjects which also kept constantly appearing on the schedules of Infantry battalions *whose men had not yet learned to shoot or to march.*

All of these other training subjects, which I have mentioned with doubtless bitterness, were not necessarily useless. All of them had definite purposes, though some must be lauded only on indirect points of value such as "hand-to-hand" combat, which, realistically, has practically no combat value. Its apologists say that it is "good for morale." To an extent, I suppose that is true.

Military courtesy and precise close order drill were also beneficial, and their value in the interests of discipline was great. The bitterness I bear toward such training subjects does not come from any belief that they should not be taught to soldiers, for I feel that they are all fairly important. My rancor stems from the fact that commanding officers who were supposed to have some idea of what they were doing went ahead and spent time schooling their men in such finer points of garrison life and duty before these men had learned to shoot well enough to definitely hit a standing man at 100 yards with a rifle, or to march so that their battalion could move twenty miles on a hot day without losing entirely too many of its personnel. We never got around to any properly organized rifle instruction during the whole of our stay at Forrest, except in the case of a few units which were lucky enough to have skilled instructors for their immediate officers. At Forrest, there was no spreading out or mass utilization of specialized instructional talents as far as rifle shooting was concerned, and in most battalions the same story was true of marching.

We blundered through our training period with all units struggling their utmost to look better than the next outfit. This resulted in thousands of man-training-hours being shot to hell in the execution of especially refined housekeeping activities, such as landscaping and beautifying the barracks areas, and neatly whitewashing little picket fences (often built by a company carpenter who sometimes had no time left to make training aids or range equipment). Officers kept trying to comply with training directives, to do the impossible, teaching everything listed in the book, but no one on hand had been empowered to take a look at the whole mess, scrap the entire training program for a necessary length of time, and teach the men to shoot and to walk. So when final checks were made, we were found to be much wanting in both of those abilities.

When we finally did begin to shoot, there was a more than ample measure of stupidity in our range programs. Weapons schools were organized by division and subordinate headquarters in accord with the "book"—which procedure in itself was all right. But the instructors selected were often unqualified in their respective subjects—the operations office sometimes having the weird idea that it was good practice to select an instructor uninformed on the particular subject—so that the instructor himself would "learn by instructing!" (I actually heard a division staff officer express himself along such lines.)

And there was always an element of "eyewash" shoved into each class—a thing or two in the way of decoration or show which wasted everybody's time and benefited only the company or battalion commander who had managed thereby to dazzle the eyes of his senior. This "eyewash" might be in the form of flashy instructional props, or a high instructor's platform, or even some radical departure from regulation training procedure.

In the matter of rifle shooting, the policy was reminiscent of some critical histories I have read of the conscription and training of Civil War soldiery. Reliance on subordinate units seemed to be the rule, and the admittedly keen-minded operations and training officer (G–3) of the division apparently did not know who could instruct in rifle shooting and who could not. In any event, several rifle instructors, who almost literally did not know one end of a rifle from the other, were chosen and charged with organizing and conducting rifle qualifications. The advice of a distinguished rifleman assistant instructor was, on one occasion, disregarded by a battalion commander who had ordered his companies to remove all of their rifle bolts when the weapons were locked up. His orders further prescribed the stowing of the removed bolts in a locker, but made no provision at all for returning the bolts to the proper rifles. Fantastic as it may seem, it is true. That battalion commander—the leader of 900 soldiers—had to learn by experience that Springfield bolts are not always interchangeable!

A good look at our qualification firing would have made a civilian rifle club member laugh. On the date of record firing, officers galore were detailed into the pits to keep supplemental scores, and every shot on the targets was recorded carefully in the pits and on the line, but the identification of firers was not closely checked and in at least a few cases men succeeded in firing for each other. After these score-cards were turned in, they sometimes seemed to be changed. The shooting was on a competitive basis in only one sense—an organizational one. Each of the units wanted to score better than the others. With possession and control of the records in their own hands, there was plenty of pencil-pushing on the part of certain outfits.

This was ignorantly encouraged from above. On more than one occasion, senior officers demanded high qualifications standards from their subordinate commands, refusing to accept anything below a certain level. When a Colonel made such demands from behind his desk, without taking the time to go out and check the ranges and scoring procedures carefully, he usually got his high qualification records promptly indeed—*on paper.*

One brilliant officer (whom many of us later had the pleasure of seeing sent home from overseas before his battalion ever got into combat) organized a rifle school at Forrest as one would organize a circus. He built the highest chief range officers' platform that I have ever seen, made up numerous giant-scale training devices for demonstration purposes, huge washtub-sized markers, sighting bars ten feet long, and numerous other gaudy props. He qualified very few men in that school—even on paper, and he thoroughly insulted the intelligence of the men who had to endure the course.

I served in a heavy weapons company, as could reasonably be expected. I had played around a good deal with heavy machine guns, was a qualified expert over the old and tough "E" course, and was very fond of Browning M–1917s. At that time, most of the men in heavy weapons companies had rifles for personal weapons. (Carbines were still in the process of design or manufacture, and pistols were issued only to a few squad members.)

Regardless of the obvious silliness of arming an already overloaded gunner or number two man with a rifle, it seemed to me that it would have one advantage. At least it would give the men an opportunity to learn how to operate and perhaps to shoot properly a shoulder weapon of some sort. I began to use every available bit of spare time to teach a few men in the company the rudiments of rifle instruction, and we made up a few training aids and selected suitable dryfiring areas close to the barracks.

In due time, our machine gun qualifications were finished. We managed pretty well at it because the company commander stole sufficient time from other subjects, and wrangled someone out of enough old 1918 ammunition to allow us to fire an extra time across the course, (after sorting out all the rounds with cracked necks). A few weeks later, we received an authorization to actually fire with the rifle 15 rounds per man for familiarization purposes—*but we had to do so within two days.*

Our heavy weapons personnel had not been officially available for rifle marksmanship training at any time previously, and their only grounding for using the rifle at all had been a little mechanical and care-and-cleaning training given in spare time. But all protests were in vain, and I was forced on this two-days notice to take the company out to the thousand-inch range and use up the ammunition; otherwise we would not get to fire at all. We had only one morning to get the job done.

It rained that day—a sort of chilly drizzle. I had selected assistant instructors the night before and "crammed" them as best I was able. On the range, I gave up the thought of teaching any positions in the very few minutes we had to spare for the purpose. We simply tried to get across the basic idea of sight picture and trigger squeeze and let each man fire his shots from prone or sitting position, using the sling if he felt like it. The shooting was at inch pasters on big expanses of target background, and the groups were generally pathetic. All of the company officers were distressed, if not thoroughly disgusted, but we all felt that it would be better than no shooting at all, and did our best to coach and encourage men who were flinching with each shot and not taking the recoil properly. It was lucky that we took this trouble, because it turned out that *those fifteen shots were the only rifle practice the men were to be allowed before overseas shipment.*

That experience was a good one for me—a grand lesson in making the most of poor training circumstances. As I continued in the next years to serve in the Army and saw training as it went on in many overseas stations, I was to become more and more certain that the key to good soldiery is not the ability to use well the proper tools of training and war, but is instead the developed knack of getting along with tools and devices at hand, or being able to make substitute tools if normal issues are not available. And when I began to work with the soldiery of other nations—Colonial French, Melanesian Islanders, Burmese, and Chinese, I began to really appreciate the need for a new set of standards to apply to the training of people of much more primitive background than the average American or Britisher. It is an unbelievable truth that it would take months of intensive training and hundreds of rounds of ammunition to teach the average Chinese peasant soldier to shoot even as well as most of the men in my company did with their first 15 rounds from a military rifle.

That fact, however, afforded no excuse for allowing only a few hours' rifle training to heavy weapons company personnel, individually armed with the rifle, and who were later to use that weapon in combat. Arguments that this training deficiency was circumstantial and no one's fault were pure hog wash. We took much time to teach hand-to-hand combat and we took more time to teach indirect fire methods with our machine guns. (The latter technique may possibly have been used to some extent in Europe, but had damn little application in the Islands and in Burma.) Nearly everyone used rifles, carbines, or submachine guns in the jungle, no one knew when he was safe without such a weapon, any place forward of a regimental command post. Pistols were never plentiful, and were used mostly at night for close in "foxhole" protection. We should have been trained better with shoulder weapons.

All of this was to come out later, and all infantrymen were later trained (or were supposed to have been trained) to shoot both the rifle and carbine. These training measures apparently were delayed —or at least were not enforced—until long after early policy had been disproved by actual combat and resultant numbers of casualties. The memories of the last war were not sufficiently poignant in 1941—and someone high up in command had run out of imagination. Every junior officer I knew at Forrest would openly deplore our lack of attention to vital training in the use of important basic weapons. Everyone but the "wheels" saw the mistakes.

We learned enough about grenades, using the methods then prescribed in the manuals. However, most all of the throwing techniques we were taught were never put to use. The formal grenade throwing positions were artificial as could be—even the prone position, which, as it was taught, called for momentary exposure of the whole upper half of the body. Grenade throwing is an easy subject for the average baseball-grounded American, and grenade throwing technique should not attempt to reteach a man how to throw, but rather to simply give a good course in grenade safety (a lot of our men were killed with their own grenades), then give him a large amount of practice throwing at realistic targets. As large a percentage of this practice as possible should be conducted with live grenades. This was another obviously advisable type of training which was discarded in favor of more precise and formal methods. On the whole, however, grenade training in the division was more adequate than rifle training. Some of it, in fact, could have been diverted to marksmanship training.

The most wicked of all our sins at Camp Forrest was concerned with the true occupational speciality of the doughboy—walking. We left real honest-to-God marching almost entirely out of the picture, and confined the marches we did make to roads and good trails. None of the large tracts of Tennessee woods and hills were cut through and marched over by whole companies, properly loaded down with their complete equipage. Quite the other way around: in all marches, we kept ourselves continually road bound, often moving enough afoot, but traversing only the areas trafficable to motor vehicles. On that account we gained no conception of normal Infantry movement across ordinary terrain, and the rigors of such movement were later to come to us as a shock when we got overseas. Roads, we should have realized at the time, are only man-made seams of civilization, and many less civilized areas have none. Our regiment, which a few months later would be especially thankful to find a few hundred yards of cut footpath in the jungle spaces, was conducting all of its marches and movements along paved roads, with heavy weapons and ammunition going along in carriers instead of on the backs of the men. The "book" had made a statement to the effect that distances for hand-carrying heavy weapons should not *ordinarily* exceed a few hundred yards, and that motor transportation would be the *favored* means of moving machine guns. This statement was seized upon and misinterpreted by many officers who seemed unable to even think in terms of large areas without roadnets of concrete or macadam highways.

As our training program went on, we saw each day more evidence of our own military incapabilities; and also terrible shortages of equipment and weapons. How little we actually had to work with!

We were short of everything except a limited measure of willingness. We had no weapons, no equipment, and even worse—no knowledge.

Silly things were done in those days, because we didn't know even the right methods to use. Officers without experience in handling large numbers of troops made errors which adversly and unreasonably affected the comfort and morale of thousands. An over emphasis of safety precautions—always a bone of contention in peacetime—tended to give each tactical exercise, each firing problem, and each small unit maneuver, an unreasonable appearance of morale-sapping artificiality.

As I recall, the classic expression SNAFU (Situation Normal, All Fouled Up) came into being at that time and many of us will always associate it with Camp Forrest, where so many things seemed to go wrong.

Memories of my stay at that place put it in the definite category of an organized bore, worse even than any equivalent length combat period I have since been through. Camp Forrest to me was a chigger-infested land of petulant senior officers, who, never satisfied, were always moaning about some trivial detail. It was a place where gray-haired field officers stood on platforms and lectured in the hot sun to three hundred rifle students, telling them to squeeze the stock of a rifle with all fingers, gripping it like a lemon, to get the trigger off. It was a place where companies were busy building decorative little picket fences and whitewashing them; a place where attempts to devise true and realistic combat training methods as often as not resulted in discredit to the man who went to the trouble.

Worst of all, it was a place in which a thousand conscientious junior officers and non-coms expended months of heartbreaking effort, knowing all the while that too much of it was in the interest of "eyewash"—being totally misdirected.

Camp Forrest—our training period there—served to give proof to every thinking man in the division that we were indeed poorly prepared for war, that our country was militarily a second rate power, that the great mass of American manhood would require much physical and moral alteration before it could successfully fight against foreign armies.

SHOVING OFF FOR THE PACIFIC

At long last, the grind of training was finished, and we were able to call a small amount of time our own. Inspectors checked us and observed our numerous mistakes as they put us through the paces, cracking down every now and then with ridiculous fury on some poor soldier or officer who might be caught eating watermelons on a hike—or some equally vile crime.

General Ben Lear delivered a scathing speech at the inspection critique, yelling through the dust of a camp theater at the assembled officers of the whole division. Then he told us that we were well along in training, and our progress toward combat effectiveness had been great. Privately, he expressed himself very differently; but he sent us off to the Big War Games in Louisiana, where we were to find more chiggers and copperheads than dwelt even in Tennessee.

I served out the Louisiana maneuvers, in the summer of 1941, on detached service with Second Army Headquarters, and did not rejoin the regiment until after it had returned to Forrest. On my return I was assigned to the Anti-Tank company, an organization commanded by an old friend and rifle team mate of mine, Capt. F. R. Brickles. Before I could physically join my new unit I received orders sending me to the Infantry School at Fort Benning, Georgia, to attend a course in motor maintenance. The trip to Benning was enjoyable in that it gave me a chance to do a little bird shooting and to fire a few shots with my little scope sighted M–70, which along with my shotgun, had accompanied me since I had left Chicago.

A minor disaster overtook me at this time. I loaned this Alaskan sighted M–70 .06 to a well-meaning friend who did not know that the use of service ammunition required that the barrel be water-cleaned. After he had the rifle for a week in the Georgia swamps the barrel was completely ruined and I had to ship the weapon to Winchester for repair. This happening was to later be responsible for my going overseas without a satisfactory sniping weapon.

23

Each weekend at Benning I went quail hunting, often spending Saturday night with a friend near Albany, Georgia. After one particularly enjoyable day afield during the latter part of my course at the school I threw my coat full of birds and my gun into the rear of my car and started along the familiar drive back to the reservation. When I casually turned on the car radio I seemed to hear a lot of excited jabbering. When I dialed another station I got the same sort of noise. It took me a full ten minutes to realize that there might be some serious cause for all the apparent excitement. It was twenty minutes later that I finally got the story straight. The Japs had bombed Pearl Harbor, and we were at war.

All other activities on the post were cancelled that night and we all gathered in the barracks to hear the President's speech. On the next morning student officers who belonged to certain organizations were told to pack up and prepare to leave the post. The Hawaiian Department, the 34th Division, the 41st Division, and the 32nd Division officers were all called up. Those from the 33rd Division remained on to finish the course. It looked even at that early date as though it would be our luck to guard the Smoky Mountains for the duration of hostilities.

When the graduation exercises were over early in January I packed and drove up to Camp Forrest, resigned (for no reason at all) to the likelihood that I would be stuck in the states while the war went on. On the way to camp I stopped in Tullahoma, the town nearest Forrest, to pick up some furnishings for my room in the barracks. I met Kolofer, a lieutenant in Second Battalion Headquarters, and asked him what he was doing at the time. He told me that he was closing out a few accounts—which rang rather strangely but did not provoke further inquiry on my part.

On driving into the camp proper I saw many peculiar things. A large number of cars were lined up at the railhead and a sizeable operation of vehicle loading was under way. I drove on into our regimental area where all sorts of unusual-looking things were going on in the way of truck movements and supply transactions.

My first question when I got to the company area, which must have sounded rather naive, was answered by an impatient outburst from Captain Brickles. "Where in the Hell have you been?" he asked, "Didn't those saps down there at Benning give you the dope? We're packing to ship overseas! Go over and help Halsey with the supply job for a while. Then go over to the 130th and pick up a bunch of replacements from their Anti-Tank company. We're being filled out to full strength in officers and men. Another thing, George. Grab a couple of good '03 rifles out of that batch we're turning in and hang onto 'em for yourself and me. Find two with star-gage stampings if you can. Otherwise just pick a couple with good barrels and nice, crisp triggers. Looks like you and I may have use for some sniping equipment, doesn't it?" He grinned cheerfully as he said the last bit. Me? I felt great!

And so we began the task of preparing the outfit for shipment. We were still operating under peacetime property accountability and the administrative aspects of the job were monumental. Finally we threw paper work, records and formality the hell out the window as far as property accountability was concerned, decided to risk jail if necessary in order to get things organized in the time we had available.

How we did it we'll never know, but at least we got loaded on the trains and departed for Indiantown Gap, Pennsylvania, our final processing point in the United States where even the most skeptical of us were finally convinced that we were really going overseas.

At this time I wired Bill Otis, in Moline, Illinois, asking him to ship me some of his sniping rifles at once, addressing them to me at the nearest express office to Indiantown Gap. I also managed to get the folks on the phone and had a last word with my mother and father—went through the old routine (new at that time)— telling them that it would be a long time before I could write, but not to worry, everything would be okay. I also told them to ship my rifle as soon as it was returned from the factory, and to hurriedly send me a Lyman Alaskan scope with a G. & H. mount for a Springfield to my new A.P.O. number.

We sailed before Bill could get his guns to me. I remember well the annoyance I felt at going up the gangplank without a good scope sighted sniper rifle, and I also remember the mental kicking I gave the seat of my pants for being so careless with my model 70. Actually, the only shooting items I had in my baggage were a few rounds of .30–06 hunting ammunition which I packed at the last minute. I had left my shotgun behind also—and I was destined to later regret that action very much, for several fine opportunities to shoot birds were missed on that account.

Each member of the 132nd regiment looked at the green water with a great question mark in his mind. Few in the regiment knew where we were going, and there were certainly not many clues to be gathered from our departure arrangements. We were taking along both temperate and tropical clothing and equipment—mosquito bars and fur caps, khaki cottons and wool overcoats. Some said we were going to Dakar, but the ships were not tactically loaded, so I felt that such certainly could not be the case.

We had a lot of fun guessing—and of course we gradually received indications of our ultimate destination from the course the ship was taking. We passed the lights of the Florida Keys one night and knew that we were headed for the Panama Canal. This would have likely meant the Philippines had we been combat loaded, but we were not. It seemed that it would be Australia—at least for the first stop. But when we were out a few days on the Pacific side of the Canal there was a distribution of maps of a remote tropical island. New Caledonia, it was, and our interesting little guessing games were ended. Soon afterward we were sailing past odd volcanic islands and short time later we pulled in at Melbourne, Australia, docking on the 26th of February, 1942.

After a wild week of wine, women and song in Southeastern Australia the regiment reluctantly re-embarked from Melbourne, for the announced purpose of occupying New Caledonia before the Japs got there. This was one of the United Nation's first moves to "stem the southward tide" of Japanese conquest—part of a plan to occupy a small number of islands overlooking their latest-gained Pacific holdings.

After a voyage which seemed rather short, after the big trip just finished, we arrived at Noumea Harbor, New Caledonia, to take part in an unloading operation, which was plenty fouled up by lack of suitable beaching craft. For some time Noumea Harbor was the scene of a world-beating JANFU (Joint Army-Navy Foul Up,) but thanks to the considerate non-intervention of the Japanese, it finally worked out all right. If the Japs had attacked at that time, even with a strength of ten men armed with firecrackers, the damage and confusion would have been too much!

We sat on New Caledonia for what seemed like centuries to everyone but me. For me the time passed quickly because I received my M–70 soon after my arrival and had begun to capitalize on the islands' natural resources. The place was bountifully infested with deer. The many hunts I enjoyed there for meat and sport would themselves be a book in the telling.

For a long time I camped in a place (Mueo) where it was child's play to kill 1,000 pounds of deer in half a day. I never lost my fondness for the sport and I spent many happy days shooting and observing the large herds of animals in a beautiful natural sanctuary of forest and meadow. The boar hunting was also excellent and our mess never lacked freshly killed wild pig and venison during the whole of our stay.

The place never became tiresome—until offensive operations in the islands began to get under way. It did, then. We continued to sit while the First Marine Raiders came through and began the Solomon Operations. We sat on, now beginning to squirm a little with impatience, while the First Marine Division landed on Guadalcanal. It looked more and more as though the war was going to pass us by. Finally the 164th Infantry went over, in October.

At long last, early in November, we received orders to pack up and concentrate for shipment. The regiment assembled at St. Vincent after turning over our defense sectors to the "Kiwi" Division of the New Zealand Army. I went for one last deer hunt and said goodbye to the several good friends I had made among the French residents, knowing that I would later look back to my stay on that island with fond memory.

We finally boarded the transports and, after a few days delay caused by a glutting of the unloading facilities at Guadalcanal, we left Noumea Harbor on the 5th day of December, 1942, arriving at Guadalcanal on the 8th—a year and a day after the Pearl Harbor attack.

I remember that morning well. It was the first time the transports carrying us had not been bombed during their several shuttles between the Solomons and rear zones. I was on duty on the bridge and the Naval officers who were standing around me were all tautly set, almost shaking with nervous tension as they looked around over the ominously still waters of Lunga Point. Several of them had assured us that there would certainly be fireworks during the landing operation, and we were set for them—but the unloading period was absolutely uneventful, so far as enemy action was concerned.

The Navy, however, made it evident that they were very anxious to get us the hell off their ships so they could get the hell out. And they were not the least bit bashful about throwing our equipment ashore in any way they could, so long as the action saved time for them. It took us quite a few days to clear up the mess they had created with such wasteful haste, but there are two sides to everything, and we could appreciate the fact that an anchored transport made an excellent cold turkey target for submarines and planes alike.

I guess we all had a funny feeling as we loaded into the Higgins boats after climbing down the net. There was no danger involved in the landing operation, we knew—but that island was the place where we would all see our very first fighting. As we roared toward shore, our little craft making one of the many pretty white swallow tail wakes for the planes circling above us to see, I gained a good bit of comfort from the Springfield in my hands. I had fitted a Lyman Alaskan to it and had liked the combination so well that I had acceded to a tearful request from my good friend and boon hunting companion, Major Jim Collins, and left him my M-70 for boar hunting on Espirito Santos. My Springfield was encased to protect it from the salt spray and was beautifully waterproofed by a spar varnish-linseed oil finish inside and out on the stock. The attention I had devoted to it on the ship had given the company commander occasion to tell me to remember that I had a platoon to command and to not let myself be caught popping away with a rifle on my own unless circumstances permitted.

Our landing craft rides were short and uneventful. It was only a few minutes after we climbed down the net that the coxswain cut the motors and we felt our crafts' nose grindingly cut into the sands of combat zone ground. Immediately we became busy unscrambling the mess the Navy had caused with the hasty unloading of our supplies. I only took time off to check the zero of my rifle, using a few rounds of my carefully husbanded M1 boat-tail stuff. My weapon was right in the groove. It gave me a three inch ten-shot group, perfectly centered on a five inch bull at 100 yards.

We bedded down in the coconut groves near the beach and waited during the first night. High flying Jap planes came over in the moonlight to brave a considerable amount of our flak and bomb the unloading and dispersal areas. It was a new sight but not particularly frightening to most of us. We were more interested in the frequent roar of batteries of artillery sited near us, and the distant patter of small arms fire, coming in sound-muffled, from the not-so-far-off front lines. The threat of a counter invasion still loomed strongly, and we were therefore set up to defend the beach from a surprise landing. But nothing materialized.

I managed to see Capt. Henry (Hank) Adams while he remained on Guadalcanal and we were able between us to locate quite a few shooting buddies. The First Marine Division had many familiar Camp Perry names within its ranks. The Fifth, Hank's regiment, debarked on the ships we arrived in. He informed me of the vagueness of the G–2 situation, saying that there were from 3,000 to 14,000 Japanese on the island. They had heavily reinforced the original group in personnel, but were currently believed to be suffering for lack of supplies. They were using destroyers and light craft for supply and reinforcement at the time, not daring to risk any more sizeable transports while Henderson Field remained operational in our hands. I got my first orientation on the front line situation from him and began to think about doing some sniping at a select part of the line, should the 132nd not soon be committed.

I had but recently been promoted to First Lieutenant and transferred to "H" company, there resuming my old duties as a heavy machine gun platoon leader. Strangely enough, my new company commander was also an old rifle team mate. He had been coach of the Illinois National Guard rifle team for two of the three years I fired on it. Captain Earl Cosby (later major) was a fine officer, and it was a pleasure to serve under him.

III. THE GUADALCANAL FIGHT

"... *Here is the backbone of your armed forces, the boiled down essence of combat, the guy who slugs it out personally with the rifle and bayonet. Here is the man who is always too hot, too cold, too wet, too dry, too exhausted, too hungry, too scared, but who still plugs ahead toward his unknown destination. Where this unassuming individual stops, there is the front line of battle. If he gets ahead, we win; if they run over him, we lose ....*"

GENERAL JOSEPH W. STILWELL

BEACHHEAD EXISTENCE

It soon became evident that Colonel George Ferry's battalion was going to be stuck with another period of waiting, this time only a mile from the enemy. We were ordered to outpost and defend the Lunga Point supply dispersal area and to furnish labor for unloading and handling the hundreds of tons of supplies that were coming ashore by the day and hour. This would mean guard duty at night; digging in and preparing defenses against possible attack from the sea; and the continued sweating labor of unloading ammunition, rations, supplies, and drums of gasoline all through the daylight hours.

The boys mumbled about "such a damned base-section commando job" but generally managed to keep such mumblings in their beards. From the battalion commander on down the line we disliked the assignment, and we received little consolation from the thought that *someone* had to do the unloading so that the Seabees would be free to perhaps build themselves a Rec Hall and a canteen to dispense some of the beer that the Navy was unloading even at that early date.

So we settled into an environment entirely different from anything we had previously known, finding our place in the colorful, noisy, humming beehive activity of an island beachhead. It was a change of scenery—and a welcome one—from the monotony of the static defensive positions we had manned on New Caledonia. With all its objectionable features, the switchover from lassitude to vigorous activity did manage to shake the outfit out of its old feeling of boredom. Our new environment was an interesting one.

Under a protective umbrella of fighter and patrol planes, the beach and the water in the vicinity of Lunga Point had become a site of intense human and machine endeavor. Hundreds of watercraft dotted the bright blue waters for a distance of several thousand yards offshore. Most prominent were the huge transports anchored a mile or so out, but still well inside the protective arc continually being retraced by patrolling tin-cans and sub chasers.

31

The transports were disgorging thousands of tons from their holds each day. On their decks hundreds of stripped-to-the-waist members of work details swarmed around the wide, gaping hatch openings, guiding bulging cargo nets hung on taut cables up from the depths of the holds. Below, others struggled and grunted in the utterly stifling heat, manhandling boxed and crated supplies toward the pick-up-spots on the hold's bottom. Out over the side the nets would swing, packed roundly with crates, boxes, bags, and sides of beef, to be lowered down into a tank lighter or Higgins boat cavorting on the choppy waves alongside the relatively steady hull of the transport. Then, when the load weighed down the bottom of the landing craft, the cable would go limp, lifting the empty block up and away. Back over the hatch again the squealing pulley-block was again dropped downward with accompanying cries of: "Look out you dumb bastard!" "Want your brains—the little you have—all over the goddamn deck?" And talk would come up from the holds, often shouts for relief—men could not stay down there and work for more than an hour or so at a stretch: "Send somebody down here to bring up the sick, lame and lazy!" "Send down another sweat crew or we'll all pass out!" "Krist in the foot-hills, but it is hot!" And always mixed in with the unpleasantness, there would be a bit of humor, oftimes manifest in community singing: "Infantry works on de Andrew Jackson; Infantry works while de Navy plays"—to the tune of Ole Man River—with the rest of it too obscene to quote. Any parody to any song was welcome, especially if it were sufficiently profane and anti-Navy.

The Navy did not do too much of their own unloading. Maybe they were not supposed to, and likely they had too few men. Their explanation always was that the crews had to be kept fresh so they could man guns and stations if there was an "alert," which would always force them to weigh anchor hurriedly and take off for the security of Tulagi Harbor. Sailors not in their bunks always seemed to be doing some sort of non-sweating duty. Most of them operated cranes and other ship's machinery.

The metal decks of the ships were sizzling. You could feel them literally burning through the soles of your shoes. The hovering tropical sun, the blazing source of that oppressive heat, was blinding in its reflections converging upon us from the water's surface. Only an occasional breeze had a suggestion of coolness, and that was entirely relative.

Doughboys did not need to keep alert like the sailors, so they were detailed, fifty, a hundred, or a whole company at a time, to go out to the unloading transports as labor parties. And they were generally glad of the chance because it meant that they would receive a meal or two on the Navy, prepared in a ship's galley—not

Here is a pretty accurate sketch of a Japanese officer—far more typical than the slant-eyed caricatures on our war posters. Average Jap officers, discounting a few peasant types, were good looking men; many of them would pass at a glance for Italians or Frenchmen. Their small size, rather than any distinctly mongoloid features, was the chief means of identification. Many of these people were alert-looking, keen-minded, with intellect far beyond the low cunning we gave them credit for possessing. The few starved prisoners we captured on Guadalcanal did not present much of an appearance, but neither did many other people who surrendered earlier in the war.

The Japanese officer was waited on hand and foot, with an orderly to clean his leather and clothing. Uniforms were much better fit than those of enlisted men and polished boots were often worn, even in the jungle. The least presentable piece of clothing was the peaked cap, made to be worn underneath the helmet.

Military mustaches were often worn, with the remainder of the face clean shaven. This particular Jap, not far from the average, could have donned an American uniform and come over to our lines. The only thing that would have roused our visual suspicion would have been his very trim appearance, and perhaps his overly-military bearing.

"B" or "C" rations out of the can. Once in a while they would get some ice cream—something that came to mean a lot to many, after they had gone for a year without it.

Out on deck one would look at the surrounding waters in awe. The sight was entirely too much to be grasped by a mere doughboy. We saw there a display of shipping and Naval craft of unbelievable numbers and variety. Indeed, our faith in the productive ability of our nation was restored. This faith had waned a bit during our stay on New Caledonia where we saw only a few planes and ships at a time.

Besides the Navy transports, there were converted merchant-men, liners, destroyers, motor torpedo boats, landing craft of all sorts, and even coupled metal rafts powered by gigantic outboard motors.

A Sears-Roebuck catalog would not begin to list the thousands of non-combat items we unloaded from those ships. Engineer equipment: bulldozers, generators, dump trucks; Signal equipment: generators, radio sets, watches, and clocks; Quartermaster impedimenta: cots, bedding, tents, and clothing by the ton. All of it had to be handled so many times! Had to be wrestled around in the hold and carried over to the spot where it was to be dumped onto the cargo net. Then the net would be folded diaper-wise around a cluster of articles piled in its center and the big pulley-hook would be stuck through the corner meshes. Nets were usually knotted from $1\frac{1}{4}''$ rope.

When that was done, the hold crew got clear of the net and someone yelled, "Hoist away!" or, "Take her up!" or, "She's pregnant!" A sailor topside pulled a lever causing the two or three tons to rise out of the hold, swinging back and forth to scrape against the hatch sides. The men below had to dodge and scamper for their lives when heavy articles fell from the net. Everyone on deck ducked too, when the load swung overhead as the crane pivoted outward. A few times, men forgot to duck and we could all remember one or more of the nauseating sights which followed.

Over and over the cranes went through their unloading cycles, gradually relieving the transports of their heavy cargos. As each net load was shifted to a landing craft, each hull would rise with maddening slowness in the water, revealing a rusty under-water line. Hooks going down into the well-like holds with empty nets, tugging them up full, going down again, coming up full. Over and over again until it seemed that the entire effort of the war was wrapped up in the stinking-hot and backbreaking labor of unloading ships.

Sailors were working levers a few yards away from their bunks. Soldiers who were guests from the crowded, rotten, mosquito-infested Lunga Point beaches, were grunting, heaving, carrying, lifting, mopping off sweat with forearms already beginning to turn yellow from the atabrine. Officers were always hurrying about, poking their noses into the dark corners of the holds where men were sometimes found hidden in the stifling darkness, drinking warm, stolen Navy beer. But what the hell. Officers were in the same war with the men—felt the same way about the goddamn Navy anyway. . . . Damn Navy sleeps between sheets and has ice cream. . . . Make allowances unless the Joe happens to be a known goldbrick. No crime to steal beer from the Navy. Not a soldierly feeling, that, and not a very officer-like thing to sanction it. . . . But the damn Navy has too much gravy in this war. Next war it is the Navy for me—the Navy or the Seabees.

Always we were hurried in our tasks by urgings from the overly nervous Navy officers pacing the bridge. They were vociferously anxious to get their ships unloaded and the hell away from "Torpedo Junction." These boys kept casting worried glances shoreward toward the beached hull of the *El Capitan*, a cargo ship upon which some slant-eyed sub commander had scored a pinwheel; also toward the *Alcheba*, another supply ship in like condition, though not so squarely hit. Even after the poor *Alcheba* had been beached with a gaping hole in her side, the Japs persisted in pumping more torpedoes into her while she lay helpless. Soon she was stinking to high heaven because the meat which had filled her holds was rotting and crawling in the heat.

The sight of those two ships seemed to make nervous wrecks out of many of the ships' officers. This nervousness manifested itself in an understandable but not entirely laudable goading of the Army unloading details. "Hurry! Hurry! Hurry!" was the theme. "Get that damned junk ashore! I don't give a damn if it is in order or not!" "Don't sort that goddamned stuff out on this deck, Lieutenant! Throw it the hell in the boats and straighten it out on the beach! Do you think we want this ship stuck in this hell-hole for a month?"

Economy, orderliness, and in many cases, common sense were sacrificed for the sake of insane, frantic, haste. "Get it off as quickly as you can!" said the Ships. "Get it ashore in some semblance of order so we can make some use of it!" screamed back the Beach. Arguments between ship and Army officers sometimes became hysterical, but the sailors kept right on turning valves and pulling levers, and the captains kept yelling through megaphones from the bridge; and through it all, the doughboys in the hold kept on sweating. In the end, the ships were unloaded.

Occasionally a soldier, pausing between net loadings in the hold, would philosophize: "Well, I wonder how far they expect us to carry our own personal part of the war effort? I thought we, the Infantry, were intended to close with the enemy and kill him with our weapons. But apparently that idea is all wet. First we load the boat back in New Caledonia, put the Artillery's ammo on for 'em, the Engineer's bulldozers, the Ordnance's trucks. Then over here we unload the boats—take off all of the latrine screens for the Seabees, unload the guns for the Ordnance, the food for the QM, and the electric lights and generators for the Navy shore people. They call us an 'Arm' and the QM a 'Service.' Well, thank krist there are not any more services than there are! It 'ud kill us having to wet nurse any more of the bastards!"

After the mass of matériel got off the ships it had much farther to go, and, apparently, it was another responsibility of the dough-boy to get it there—or at least to help a lot. The Higgins boats and other landing craft traveled in nervous circles or ovals, with the ship and shore at diametric extremes. Their job, too, was a constant repeating of the same monotonous cycle. Lowered into Guadalcanal or Tulagi waters from a week to a month before, these boats had shuttled piles of cargo ashore ever since. They were orphans, in many cases, for ships often left the area in such a hurry that there was no time to pick up their own boats, in which case the Navy beach authorities took them over. We found out about this circumstance chiefly from the coxswains, who were not happy with shore life on Guadalcanal. For them it meant Army chow and Army beds, and they (being sailors) did not take to such a life.

The doughboys detailed to the Higgins boats counted themselves much luckier than the ones who had to work in the holds and on the decks of the transports. They were in the fresh air, and the work was not so hard as on the ships. Loads would come right down into the boat while it was at the ship; and when it got ashore it was easy—just pick up the stuff and heave it over the side to doughboys of the beach detail, who would be waiting knee-deep in the water alongside the nosed-in craft. If the packages could be handled by a single man the shore details would usually form a line, à la bucket brigade, and hand-to-hand it out of the boat by the piece—heavy flour sacks, ammo boxes, nail kegs—until the boat was empty. In that practice it was always fun to get an officer in the line and watch his face get red and his knees buckle as you sped up the laborious unloading. Fifty pound sacks—hand 'em out of the boat, over the side, throw 'em, catch 'em, pivot and pass it into the arms of the man next in the line. Don't lose your balance and fall, but if by chance you should, be sure to remember to come up smiling. Horseplay was always in order in this game, and it was good fun to see, now and then, if you would be able to add a little push to the man to whom you were passing a flour bag and knock

Hideo

Don't try to tell me that the Japanese soldiers were always hog-filthy, either. Sure—we found them dirty and grimy in the pillboxes we took after long sieges, but that's no proof. In other places, where we were stinking to high heaven ourselves and wearing crusted fatigues, we killed Japanese with carefully combed hair, clean skin, shaved faces, neat uniforms. Just as in his homeland, the Japanese soldier is fond of a long soak in a tub full of water so hot that it would turn an American's toenails.

Improvised tubs like the one shown here, complete with a wooden falsebottom to prevent burning the feet, were found in several places on the island. These 55-gallon oil drums were about the number one utility item in the islands —used for a million and one things. We used 'em too, but not so often for tub baths, although now and then we would rig showers from them.

But we weren't a darn bit cleaner than the Japanese when our chances for bathing were equally poor. In fact, they seemed a little more willing to take extra trouble to create bathing facilities, even in their hidden jungle camps, screened from our superior air power. If the Japs on Guadalcanal dared to swim in the streams or ocean, they often got a good machine-gunning for their trouble. One of the favorite targets of 69th Fighter Squadron pilots was swimming and bathing Japs.

him flat on his back, with the sack on top. No harm to get wet—fatigues were dirty as hell anyway. It would not take too damned much time to empty all the Higgins boats in the world, if twenty good men could go strong at it and have a little comedy. The lieutenant or first sergeant falling in the briny with a sack of flour on his head, for instance.

When the boats came into shore the coxswains would race the motors, churning up a huge fan of swell behind the boat in an effort to nose-in hard. The boat would beach itself and hold fast throughout the unloading if she rammed in hard enough, and once lightened by unloading she could easily be backed away. If she stuck to the beach, even with repeated gunning of the motor, the sailor could always call on the doughboys who took the five tons off to wade out and shove her free. If need be, enough soldiers could be assembled to lift the boat up and carry her right off any coral shelf or bit of unyielding sand.

From a thousand feet in the air it looked funny—this scene on the beach. Big transports anchored beachward inside the guard line of destroyers. Little toy scows stirring up white wakes in moving from ship to shore, shore to ship. Men swarming on shipboard and on the beach like ants, dotting the scene all the way back to the coconut groves. Trucks loading in a rough line, with tailgates facing the lowered bowgates of the nosed-in and beached line of Higgins boats. From the air they seemed like coarse stitches connecting a patch of blue cloth—the water—to a strip of burlap —the beach. Often a truck would back too far and mire its rear wheels in the surf. Here and there a boat would get stuck with broken parts and would be left grounded on the beach or anchored in the shallows.

In places on the beach there were huge piles of equipment sticking up at waters edge where the trucks had been unable to keep pace with the boats. That pile-up was getting worse in many areas. In such localities a whole sandy stretch would be stacked high with acres of gear. This made the unloading and the beaching task appear gigantic even from the air.

But, given enough time, ants can undermine a house and make it totter on its foundation. The same rule applies in a beachhead unloading operation. Enough men working hard and long enough can build a mountain of supplies on a beach in a month or a week, and then they can shoot, eat, and burn every bit of it up in a week or a day.

All of this went on under constant threat of Japanese air or sub attack. Planes kept patrolling above, and on the ships, the crews lounged close around their guns with the "talkers" wearing their earphones and mike rigs. Ships bristled with anti-aircraft weapons—even the transports had lots of them. Three inch, 20mm, twin 20mm, Bofors 40mm, and 37mm on deck, bow, and stern mounts. Officers and lookouts on the bridges and in crows nests kept constant watch with fieldglasses over all of the surrounding ocean and sky. Guess it was a little hard on the Navy at that— keeping wide awake in the drowsy weather. Then too, they had a sizeable responsibility in the supervision of the doughboy unloading crews on their ships!

On the beach the great number of gasoline drums became more and more noticeable. Huge piles of them. There were more of those 55-gallon drums than anything else. Didn't notice 'em so much on the ship, where the cranes would lift 'em and they could be rolled across the flat surface of the steel decks, but ashore things were different. There they had to be lifted by hand and dragged over the gunwales of the boats or rolled out of the mouths of the landing crafts. They were brutes to roll in the sand. In handling them you were always smashing fingers on the rims, straining your back lifting 'em up on end or pushing 'em over. There was not much to do to make things easier other than to improvise a ramp with planks and roll 'em up instead of lifting them to the level of the trucks. We managed to find some metal matting to place in the sand so the drums would roll and so that the trucks could keep maneuvering without going up to their hubs. No men in any American factory have ever worked so hard under such poor conditions; but then these men had one thought moving through their minds, pulsating in their temples—keep on with the gas. Keep it coming. Don't let Henderson Field run dry. This heavy drum of gas we're moving now will draw a hundred times its own volume in Jap blood if it gets to the right dive bomber pilot. Catch 'em on the water, get 'em by the thousands where killing is easy. Blow 'em up and drown 'em packed tight on transports, before they get ashore and have to be rooted out one at a time by us, trading a life for a life. Yeah, much harder to kill 'em ashore. . . . One good pilot out there can do a lot with a plane and gas and a 500 or 1,000 pounder.

So we heaped the drums high, crowding more of them on the beach than the trucks could carry away.

While we were working the gas and other supplies, we noticed with a sort of helpless wonder that the drums, in part, were still painted a *brilliant red*—though just recently shipped from the states. A bright glaring red at that! Some of us wondered if there had been formal announcement of the war's beginning back there. Couldn't someone realize that we might come under spasmodic aerial bombardment—and that red was a color hard to conceal from enemy observation? Our bitter reflections against the home front were many in those days, and were surely stimulated by things of this sort. We had acres of those drums around us, and we kept guessing what would happen if a bomb should drop into the middle of them.

Once loaded, the trucks pulled on back to their dumps in the coconut groves. The volume of supplies going ashore to the dumps was so great that it would not allow proper dispersal for security from air attack. As things stood, we had to crowd the stuff or else get a larger space on the island. They kept different items in separate piles in the groves, hacked down thousands of Levers Brothers' coconut trees to make roads into the dispersal areas, and threw metal matting on the roads after they became rivers of churned mud. They kept pushing the dumps farther inward as more stuff came ashore. Soon the beach area became congested and various factions of the "rear area boys" began fighting over space. We Infantrymen were chased from one campsite to another, for the convenience of the Ordnance and the QM, and each time we had to repitch our tents and dig new sets of foxholes at night after our days on the ships and the beach. Most of us were too tired by dark to even think. It became increasingly difficult to enforce air raid safety measures. Men remained on their blankets asleep while the raids were on, taking a choice between sleeplessness and danger.

The weather, as well as the work program was also operating against us. The effect of the climate of Guadalcanal was very pronounced on all metal items which were not absolutely corrosion proof. Radios and other signal equipment quickly built up thick layers of green on their connections, coils, and condenser plates. Everything of ferrous metal turned red with rust if it was not oiled daily. Trucks had their underpinnings shot out from immersion in salt water. The humidity was often so bad that clothing mildewed, grew mould, and would not dry in 90-degree heat unless hung far above the ground.

Our camps were well concealed in the groves. The spreading palm fronds above were good cover, and the heavy undergrowth, ten feet high in places, completed the camouflage of our bivouac areas. Excitement and comedy were never missing in our little Guadalcanal home, despite the very few mediums of entertainment available. Most of our fun was occasioned by the constantly falling coconuts that in the Lunga groves bopped men on the heads with fair regularity, (fortunately the trees were not high) and also by the tree lizards—great three foot monsters—which we heard and saw so often in the undergrowth and trees, sometimes mistaking them for infiltrating Japs. Sometimes we would find ourselves much entertained by a species of dark, long-tailed, light-breasted bird that always pivoted its tail around in perfectly outlined circles as it perched on the fallen coconut logs. Seemed that these birds were trying to imitate some of the girls in the line of a chorus I had seen in a Black and Tan joint in Chicago.

We had a system of prepared defense positions on the beach which was occupied by a skeleton force during the night, and we had a plan for alerting the entire battalion into these positions on a few minutes notice. This plan received many practical tests, as we had innumerable false alarms. "Condition Black" (meaning an attack from the sea) was false alarmed over the telephone several times. The aid stations on mornings after such alerts were usually packed with men begging materials to bandage stubbed toes and scratches incurred in half-naked dashes to air raid shelters or perimeter foxholes.

An expecially strong rumor got around on the 15th of December that the Navy had taken a shellacking, which destroyed our protective screen to the north, and that a night invasion attempt might be made. We heard this with alarm, partly because we knew that a fight on that beach, with so many trigger-happy service units and so much shore-Navy camped near us, would be ghastly indeed.

The fact that our Navy had suffered a setback was later confirmed, but the invasion threat never materialized. We kept on at the same old grind of unloading ships, cursing constantly the waiting and the uncertainty which has always seemed to be the lot of the Infantryman.

The Ordnance had set up fairly close to us. Some of their installations were within the boundaries of our bivouac area. Their dumps of artillery ammunition were near us in the groves—mostly big piles of 105mm shells painted a brilliant yellow. These also stood out to aerial observers like sore thumbs, especially while the sun was directly overhead at noon. Between us and Henderson Field, other Ordnance agencies were busy setting up shops for repair and maintenance work. Their task too, was mainly one of improvising. Lacking tents, they built frames and stretched tarpaulins for shacks and garages; lacking tarpaulins, they worked in the rain repairing unsheltered vehicles. Their area was also in the bomb-target zone, even more than ours, because of their proximity to the airstrip, and they had to dig shelters too.

Everyone thought well of the Ordnance on that island. Theirs was the enormous responsibility of keeping guns in shooting order and supplying ammunition and transport for the Army. To deal with the weapons repair, ammunition, and transport problems that arose each day on Guadalcanal must have been trying, but even so the boys at Ordnance always found time to give a hand to anyone that needed it. I picked up a good Springfield '03 there and enough

parts to make it shoot so that Lt. Don Hogan, a friend of mine in
the 3rd Battalion, could have a good sniper weapon. Another day
later on I managed to sight it in for him—at no little personal risk,
incidentally, since the Marine Corps guards always seemed to become frantically annoyed each time a weapon was fired in the rear
areas. One of their Colonels, in particular, seemed to delight in
riding up and down the beach road arresting every doughboy he
saw shooting at sharks.

Our regiments had little trouble in getting what they wanted
from the Ordnance if the Ordnance had it. To maintain any sort
of a standard of service in that place was an accomplishment;
many of the service detachments failed, but the Ordnance did its
job. Supply of ammunition from the rear was a sure and steady
thing, from all that I was able to see.

However, in the Ordnance shops and in their dump areas overwhelming evidence of the utter waste and costliness of even a small
island campaign could be seen in abundance. High piles of rusted
scrap were everywhere. Disabled tanks and trucks were parked
alongside the roads—burnt or perforated and left to rust away.
Tons of ammunition had been rendered useless by the elements
after it had been opened and left uncovered. Rifles and other
weapons were left untended on the beach, and some of them were
ruined by the effects of salt water and moist sand—rusted beyond
repair, sometimes beyond recognition. Trucks often ran over cases
of mortar shells and boxes of ammunition misplaced in the gooey
mud, mutilating them and driving them into the ground. Pouring
tropical rains melted the cardboard containers in which mortar
ammunition was packed, soaking the increments. Men later paid
with their lives for that circumstance when hundreds of rounds of
those mortar shells were to land short because propellants had
failed to fully ignite. Baggage of all sorts rotted and mildewed
away where it was stored for the units at the front, and the all-
pervading dampness seemed to render everything soggy and
clammy to touch and sour to smell.

It was a picture to remember—the mile-wide strip of beach and
grove on north Guadalcanal. The blue waters, warm as urine, the
beach shallows afloat with debris and rotting human and animal
flesh, the shady, but not very cool groves acrawl with land crabs,
lizards, and scorpions. The beach—heaped up with the tons of
materiél which was ultimately to enable us to crush the Japs; and
above all, the fantastic bustling business of the whole scene—
roaring and rumbling airplanes and trucks and boats, sweating
laborers putting forth an effort as monumental as it was geograph-
ically out of place in the languid tropics.

HENDERSON FIELD

It is a peculiar thing that a man can see so much of a place and yet not be able to give a good description of it only a few years later. Yet that is the way I feel about the fields of kunai grass and chopped down palm groves that made up Henderson Field. It would be impossible for me to draw from memory an accurate outline of the runways and installations, but other impressions left in my mind are vivid.

The field was a huge place and in some ways, it had many of the features of the beachhead. It was, even more literally than the beach and the unloading areas, a beehive of activity.

Of course the field was highly inadequate from the air operational viewpoint, its runways and its dispersal areas were very small compared to some I have seen since. But, strategically speaking, it stood supreme above all other factors, and even to the doughboy its existence was paramount. Every Allied soldier on the island knew that his very life was wrapped up in our ability to hold that little bit of kunai grass, coral dust, and metal matting and keep it operational for our planes. We all knew that there were enough Japs to overwhelm us, concentrated and waiting at points within easy shipping distance of Guadalcanal. Enough to take that island back in a short time if they could only get to it. But as long as that airfield remained in our hands, and in usable condition, we knew that large reserves of Japs on Bougainville would never land on Guadalcanal in numbers large enough to really endanger our hold on that useless piece of miserable jungle and mountains.

Each morning we looked skyward as we heard the roaring motors and saw the Hellcats, dive bombers, and torpedo planes takeoff. The sight was heart-warming. In those days we never tired of it. They streaked out in flights of threes and fives, headed in varied directions. In those days they did not have to search far to find things to shoot at. It was more a question of making the bombs they had available do the most good. If the pilots did not spot a

43

cruiser or a destroyer they could always find a landing craft or a barge of some sort to bomb and strafe. There were Jap camps on the island itself—in the groves south of Point Cruiz—which always made good targets. Jap trucks and artillery were dispersed through the coconut trees along the old beach trail,˙as far southward as Verahue and Visale. And for diversion, pilots could always get in a burst at a group of Japs swimming off the south beaches.

Of course, they paid for their fun. I know little of the statistics of accidents on Henderson Field in the early days, but I do know what I personally saw. Nearly every day there would be three or more crashes—sometimes on takeoff because of a failing motor, but more often on landing due to shot up gears or controls.

We had plenty of admiration for the plucky Army, Navy, and Marine pilots. They would takeoff unhesitatingly, sometimes flying directly over the flaming wreck of one of their buddie's planes, crashed in the harrow-tooth pattern formed by sheared coconut stumps at the runway ends. We watched anxiously each time a fighter would come in and buzz the field to indicate his intention to crash-land. It was the same thing when we saw a chute blossom out behind a disabled plane, though we were most often never able to find out if the pilot survived or not.

It was plain to see at the time that the Air Corps and the Navy were learning some new things about flying, things that perhaps were not to be found in training manuals. How to land a P-38 on one wheel when the other is dangling; how to nurse a plane in with two feet shot off the wing tip; how to parachute out of a ship that suddenly puffs into flame, inside and out; how to come in close to a gun-bristling destroyer, so close that you could not miss with your bomb, taking a ten-to-one chance with your life in order to sink a thousand Japs and save the lives of a thousand dough-boys; and above all, how to live in the intolerable climate, listening to the shooting and bombing in the surrounding jungle all night and still be able to fly for an unreasonable number of hours the next day.

It may have seemed a thankless task at the time, and to an extent I suppose it was, for the flyers to keep on battling against odds which often sent a paltry thirty planes into the air to face a hundred Japs. But the doughboys who were fighting to keep their airfield secure, and who were unloading airplane parts and gas from the ships, knew the extent of their doings. We all held a deep feeling of gratitude for the accomplishments of the pilots and crews on Henderson Field. If one soldier doubted for a moment the extent of the flyers' sacrifice, he had but to walk beyond the south edge of the Lunga dispersal area where he could see the rows of blanket-covered bodies awaiting burial. Most of the feet sticking from

Here is the reason the Japanese Army didn't require as much tentage as we. Their doughboys learned to make use of palm fronds and broad-leaf boughs to build shelters, leanto style. When they had more time, they sometimes peaked the roof or made the shelter larger and tighter.

We may have regarded this as a sort of boy-scout technique, unworthy of our well equipped infantry, but there were many times when a little jungle-craft of this sort would have come in very handy. Later on, we learned it— picked it up from the natives and from observation of the Japanese. Quite often we lost or damaged our shelter halves; more often we left them behind as adding too much weight to our packs.

Most of the Japs had done a good bit of outdoor living in China, and many of them had never had very good roofs to sleep under, even at home. Generally speaking, they got along well in the jungle and on the island beaches. It took us quite a long time to catch up with them in this respect.

under the blankets were clad in heavy Infantry or Marine shoes, crusted with mud, but here and there in the line would be sticking out a pair of Navy blacks or Air Corps oxfords with brass side buckles. The oxfords were always less muddy than the heavy Infantry shoes, but they looked much the same on a dead man, unnaturally askew on a pair of stiffened ankles, and sometimes charred with the flames of a final crash.

The field itself was quite a picture. The strips were paved mostly with coral, which was the only material available for the purpose. The strip surfaces were matted, for the most part, with wire or perforated steel airstrip matting, which slowed but did not stop the erosion of rain. When dry, the coral tended to bake into a fine powder which, when caught up by slipstream blasts, would shroud the field in great billowing clouds, making a landmark for the blindest Jap pilot and rendering all landings and takeoffs doubly hazardous. The insecure coral base frequently gave way beneath the perforated plates, and they would rock and rattle under the landing wheel. Jeeps and other vehicles cruised back and forth on the strip bringing in returned pilots and crews; often the jeeps drove slowly to avoid jarring a badly wounded passenger.

Around the strip, in the immediate area of the too-few plane revetments, were the various tents that were serving as operations and administrative headquarters for some of the tactical units. Slit trenches were dug all around this area, and most of the men on the field were constantly armed. There was no telling when the strip might be subject to attack from either land or air.

The protective line of doughboys was not very far inland from Henderson, and because of the lack of enemy action in that quarter, the inland perimeter was rather lightly defended. The heavy Infantry action was southward from the strip, and even there our lines did not extend far enough in from the coast to ensure against their being outflanked by a sizeable force of Japanese. It would not take many Japs, infiltrated into the cover around the strip, to keep the planes grounded for a day or so.

That the Japs *were* well able to infiltrate back into our rear area was well established by the doings of a group who got through and created, in the execution of their little adventure, what was probably the greatest single example of individual lost opportunity during the whole course of the war. Their feat was as bold and brilliant and as rugged in its demands for bravery as it was stupid in execution and mediocre in results. The story of the "great Japanese Infiltrating Party," pieced together from pretty good evidence, (footprints in the mud, discarded equipment,) is roughly as follows:

In the latter half of December of 1942 a party of Japs, estimated at four, got through or outflanked our lines, which at that time extended not too far inward from Point Cruz, and continued on through our secondary security lines (the Artillery perimeter) and finally through the protective perimeter of Henderson Field itself. The party then walked through the dispersal area, passing a dump of several hundred thousand gallons of hundred octane gasoline, and continued walking through a bomb body storage area where several hundred tons of bombs were stacked in large clusters.

Still carrying their detonators and blocks of picric acid (the Jap counterpart of TNT) our visitors crept carefully on through the tented area and past the shelters where the high-priced pilots of the 69th Fighter Squadron were sleeping peacefully. Finally they got to the strip, and there, laid out before them, was the entire effective strength of single motor airplanes in the South Pacific area at the time! Without hesitation they tied all their blocks of explosive to the propeller end of a single P-39 and blew this *one airplane* all to hell!

Naturally there was an immediate and highpowered investigation: A great ringing call to arms when the explosion occurred, and various Americans in the vicinity of the explosion came nigh to shooting each other in the ensuing confusion. The little brown brethren had played it wise, using a time fuse to help them get away Scot free. No doubt they were decorated for their little job —a marvelous feat of destroying a few thousands of dollars worth of enemy property.

It would be interesting to know how they would react if they only knew what they could have accomplished with just a little more effort and no more risk. They could have utilized our own bombs as explosives, detonating them with their smaller explosives and a match or two. They could have killed all of the pilots in one of the fighter squadrons. Or they could have done all four of these things. With the use of only a little intelligence, they could have certainly blown a helluva big hole in the north end of the island, and made our job there longer and harder. I have had cause more than once since then to thank Jap stupidity for saving my life, but I have never seen such a concrete example of our past enemy's thorough goofyness. Sometimes I almost stop wondering why they lost.

Around the far edges of the strips, batteries of anti-aircraft guns were set up. They were well dug-in and sandbagged, and apparently well sited because they kept any and all Jap planes, (other than an occasional low-flying fool) high in the sky. These guns put on a show for us each moonlit night when "Washing Machine Charlie" came over. Waiting until the high-flying Japs would get almost directly above, they would cut loose, putting round after round of exploding shells so close to the approaching enemy planes that with the naked eye it could not be told whether each blast was behind, in front, above, or below the target.

Such close bursts would invariably make the Japs cavort about a bit but they steadfastly maintained their general course, coming right on in to drop their bombs. These usually hit somewhere on the north end of the island—sometimes landing in the ocean, occasionally ringing the bell and hurting someone.

Outside of the immediate airfield compound was a close-in defensive perimeter manned by resting Infantry units. Such units were envied for their assignments because there were more conveniences close by the strip. Showers were available there and dunnage could be found to hoist the cots in the pyramidal tents up out of the mud. Though the place buzzed with mosquitos, there was thought to be less likelihood of contracting malaria there because the handy toilet and shower facilities made precautionary measures easy to enforce. (Actually, everyone got malaria anyway; areas didn't differ much.)

So Henderson Field remained secure—strategically dubbed an "unsinkable aircraft carrier in the South Pacific," though certainly not resembling a ship from the residents or "inmates" viewpoint. No aircraft carrier was ever so disease ridden and so devoid of basic comforts as Guadalcanal. But the power of that little island reached out several hundred miles into the surrounding Pacific, forming an impregnable barrier through which no substantial amount of enemy soldiers or supplies could be forced or sneaked. The man with the rifle on Guadalcanal was, throughout the campaign, as dependent on that mud-ridden field as he was on his own gun and his own cunning to keep himself alive and able to fight.

SNIPING IN THE POINT CRUIZ GROVES

Things were not long in regulating themselves as far as our duties at the beach were concerned, and I soon felt free to take a little look at the front part of the war, and maybe get a shot at a Japanese or two. So on the morning of the 11th of December, Lt. Art Hantel and I borrowed a jeep and went up to Point Cruiz with a spotting scope, a pair of borrowed Navy 7 x 50 binoculars, and my rifle. We were going to get our feet wet for the first time!

We loaded our gear in the jeep and left the battalion headquarters area under a shower of sarcastic remarks: "Don't get shot!" and "Don't kill all the Japs—leave some for us and the Marines!" Those and sundry other bits were directed at us by the officers on hand. It was seven o'clock when we drove away—just an hour after dawn on Guadalcanal.

Even at that early hour the contrast between the New Caledonia and Guadalcanal climates was very noticeable. The heat was oppressive, but the palm fronds reached across above us to effectually shade the road in most places. We bumped slowly along, looking with interest at the rear area installations as we passed them—truck park, an Ordnance repair shop, and a cemetery with neat rows of crosses and not-so-neat rows of grimly laden litters.

After a while our road left the coconut groves and entered the incredibly dense and verdant jungle of Guadalcanal Island. Huge, broadleaf trees with buttressing roots blocked all direct passage and the road necessarily became twisting and irregular. Evaporation there was slow because of the intense shade and high humidity so the low places in the road became a series of sour-smelling puddles of churned mud. The floor of the jungle was entirely different from the coral shelf of Lunga Point beach, a place we were to remember later as having been very pleasant.

We soon passed our emplaced batteries and began to hear the "chu-chu-ch-" of our own Artillery firing over our heads—answered occasionally by the whirr-whirr burst of a Jap 75mm landing along the axis of the road. Many graves, both American and Jap, were strung along our jeep trail. Jap bodies in various states of decomposition were everywhere. They seemed to be in bunches, indicating that they had been killed in groups rather than individually. This scene along the road comprised a strange series of impressions for Hantel and me. It was our first observation of such things.

Nearing the Point Cruiz front, we emerged from the jungle and came out into coconut groves again—but coconut groves which were different from anything we had seen before. The palms we were used to seeing at Lunga Point had been badly scarred and perforated by repeated flushing with small arms and naval gunfire, but they had suffered nothing to compare with the devastation of the groves at Point Cruiz!

All of the trees were dead. Many of them had been blasted to mere stumps—some even completely uprooted by repeated artillery and mortar barrages. All of the fronds were either entirely torn off, leaving the crests bald, or else they were hanging dead-brown from their anchorings.

The stench of death was all-pervading. Men had done what they could to bury the dead around them, but there were still many lying in the thick undergrowth. The beach was relittered after each tide with more bloated Jap bodies washed ashore from transports sunk days before by planes from Henderson Field. It was my first look at a scene which I was afterward forced to see again and again, and I knew then that I should never be able to adequately describe it.

A guard halted our vehicle in the next few hundred yards and told us we could not bring it beyond his post. He directed us to a place where we could park the jeep, told us that the front lines were but 300 yards ahead, and explained that we could obtain further directions from anyone "up front." We shouldered our equipment and went forward on foot, paying close attention to the few crudely lettered little wood signs which warned of mines and booby traps offside the road. Everyone was alert. A telephone wire repair detail was working with rifles within easy reach—ammunition carrying parties were walking with rifles slung, and with their loads of ammunition boxes and mortar shell containers on their backs. The men were uniformly dirtier and more bearded than we had expected them to be; it was almost as though they had lost all interest in appearance or personal cleanliness.

I found a tired and bearded mortar platoon leader—a lieutenant —and told him that we were merely curious and had no official business in his area, but that we would appreciate anything he might do to get us to a part of the line from which we might be

able to fire a few shots. I marked him as a cooperative sort as soon
as he began to speak. "Well," he said, glancing at the watch which
was threaded through the lapel of his fatigue jacket, "guess I can
take you up to my OP. It is a little late in the day to see anything
—the Nips usually sit pretty tight in their holes after dawn, but
we can most always find something through the BC scope. How
far can you hit 'em with that gun?" He said the last with an interested look at my Alaskan-sighted Springfield, and he became
more interested when I told him that I could likely get hits at
400 yards.

In later experiences I have noticed this interest front line doughboys always have in items of non-issue sniping equipment. A good
sniping rifle is usually a sort of a ticket of admission when you are
away from your own outfit. The boys will usually show you around
and carefully watch the performance of your weapon.

"Come on," said the Lieutenant, "this way to the OP." He
turned to lead the way through the desolate coconut grove toward
a shell-pocked, coral surfaced hill, the reverse slope of which was
one mass of irregular diggings—foxholes and connecting trenches.
The diggings were for the most part shallow because of the resistant character of the coral. We threaded our way along a narrow,
slightly defiladed foot path, being challenged and passed at several
points by hidden sentries. We climbed up the hillside, passing
scattered soldiers performing various housekeeping chores. Some
were washing clothes, using helmets as washtubs. Others were turning their shelter-halves and ponchos in the sun to dry off the night's
accumulation of moisture. Many were cleaning their weapons
which, we observed, were in excellent shape. It looked as though
the men had gotten but little rest during the night and were planning for the most part to doze a little through the daylight hours.

The clean, new appearance of the fatigue uniforms on Art Hantel
and me was somewhat of a source of embarrassment as we walked
up the hill, carrying our unusual loads of equipment. He had the
glasses and the scope with its tripod and I had the rifle, which
was loaded, with the scope in position. We knew we must have
looked a little on the "green" side, something on the order of the
fancy-garbed big city deer hunter during his first trip into the
woods.

There were no marks of undue suffering on the part of the men
we saw; just an unhealthy sort of tiredness, and in some cases signs
of excessive nervousness. Few were clean shaven. Most of them
were tanned to what would have been a deep brown but for the
stained yellow tint from their atabrine dosage. Their web equipment was frayed and their green fatigues were worn and dirt-
crusted. But with all of these unmilitary appearances, there was

a definite air of competence, outstanding in the clean and well-oiled readiness of their weapons, and in the alert expression of their eyes. This latter was unmistakable even behind a general mask of indifference and lassitude.

It was a panting climb up the hill. We were aided somewhat by steps, cut into the coral to give a decent foothold for the heavily laden members of the carrying parties, which were sent down daily for water, ammunition, and rations. "C" type canned rations were being used. The unit had given up the idea of serving hot meals, although the cooks continued to bring up occasional coffee and doughnuts. We received these odd bits of information from the Lieutenant as we ascended the hill.

In due time we arrived at a point a little below the hill top. Just around to our front on the forward crest was the mortar observation post, commanding an extensive view of the coastal strip of beach and coconut groves and overlooking several miles of the Japanese-held portion of the island. The OP was dug in and sand bagged with only the lenses of the BC scope showing above. The immediate area was surrounded by a circle of rifle pits to insure the security of the OP at night against infiltrating enemy. Several of these pits were left vacant during the daylight hours.

At the suggestion of the Lieutenant, Art and I crept forward into one of them and set up our equipment. The pit we chose was about sixty yards forward of the OP. It gave us a good view of enemy-held terrain to the front and our own lines off to the right flank.

The pit was large and well dug—wide enough for comfort and deep enough for security. It had a shelf-like ledge forward which furnished a good support for the scope tripod, and a good forearm rest for the rifleman. Art set up the big scope and I adjusted the sandbags on my left side to make as comfortable a brace as possible for my arms in order to help steady the field glasses. In a short time the two of us were scanning the broad stretch of battlefield before us—he with the B. and L. 19.5x spotting scope and I with 7 x 50 Navy binoculars.

Definite Jap entrenchments were easy to make out from where we were, even with the naked eye, but whether or not they were occupied was another question. The Lieutenant had told us that he believed the Japs were holding the Point Cruiz sector with a small strength of troops, and were depending upon an intricate system of pillboxes, connecting tunnels, and trenches to enable them to concentrate effectively against any local thrust. We searched this far ground with extreme care, looking carefully through the glasses at every bit of digging and examining each shadow. But we saw nothing that was alive during the next hour.

Here a Jap pauses on the march to take a drink. He can raise his canteen (more properly called water-bottle) to his lips without unsnapping latches or unhitching his belt. And the container holds more water than ours.

The pack he is carrying on this thirty mile trek is a more practical one than either our old haversack or the new jungle pack. The horse shoe blanket roll he makes up is a good, practical scheme, and the havelock protecting his neck from insects is also a fine idea.

The rations he carries, mostly rice, and his mess kit are also practical. Quite likely he has with him a couple of tins of canned heat, which will bring his evening rice to boil in a very few minutes after the final halt.

His shoes are hobnailed, and he has an extra pair of sneakers to wear while they dry, or when he goes on a scouting or night patrolling operation.

Discounting his rifle, nearly every item of equipment he has is as serviceable, or more so, than the equivalent American article.

It was this first trip that taught me that it was not wise for an individual to search with binoculars or scope for more than thirty minutes at a time, especially if the ranges are long and the targets obscure. Even then, the eyes should be turned away and rested for a bit every few minutes. This is especially true under conditions of heat where mirage distorts objects and makes focusing uncertain. The mirage on this day was very bothersome, even when looking downward from a considerable height. Its upward boil distorted things so badly that actual discernment was probably limited to objects subtending one or more minutes of angle, making the seven power glasses as efficient, in effect, as the 19½ power scope.

There is no substitute measure for resting the eyes. Careful focusing of the scope does no good. The only thing to do is to find something green and shadowy and look toward it without trying to concentrate vision on any particular part of it. This procedure might draw a few laughs from the sniper's buddies up front but it is none the less necessary. In searching for sniping targets one needs the last fine edge of normal (or abnormal) vision, augmented by the best field glasses and telescopes available.

After we had searched the likely areas within range for a solid hour we looked at each other bleary-eyed, and Hantel gave voice to his disgust. "I don't believe there's a damned thing down there!" This was meant more to signify disapproval of things in general than to state fact. Actually, both of us knew that there were at least a few Japs in front of us. Occasional rifle shots were snapping over our heads—unmistakably coming from the locality we had been observing. But our hurried looks for muzzle blast disturbances were to no avail. The fine sand and dry, decayed leaves should have jumped a little down there, puffing wherever a weapon was fired, but apparently the Japs had found some means of preventing such giveaways.

After a brief rest we resumed our watch—trading off at 15 minute intervals with the field glasses. It began to seem tiresome. At about 11 o'clock a sergeant came crawling down to our position with word from the mortar officer. He slipped into our hole to give us this message:

"See those two coconut trees leaning toward each other down there to your right front?" he asked, panting as he removed his helmet and wiped his forehead on the crusted sleeve of his fatigue jacket. We nodded in assent and he went on, speaking with the nervous mannerisms of a jockey giving a hot tip on a race. "Well, there's some sort of bunker or pillbox or something down there. The Lieutenant just saw a Jap go inside. We're gonna lay about a dozen or so delayed actions on it, and the Lieutenant thinks the

Japs might show themselves making a break for it—trying to get the hell out while we let 'em have it. He just wanted me to tell you to be sure and keep your heads up and watch during the explosions —none of the fragments will get up here. And you be ready with the rifle. We'll begin dropping 'em in as soon as I get back to the OP. They'll come heavy and fast when they start. We don't need to bracket. Got frog hair readings on that place."

We thanked the sergeant for his trouble, and he hurriedly climbed from the hole and ran in a crouch to the OP. I got myself into a steady position with the rifle ready and resting in a groove between two sandbags. There I could remain relaxed and yet be able to get off a quick shot. Art set the scope on the target locality and focused it. He then left it and picked up the glasses for more extensive vision, bracing his elbows on the ledge and turning the eyepiece to correct focus. Then our anxious vigil began—waiting for the initial pop of the mortars which were mounted some 250 yards to our right rear, just off the path used to get up the hill.

Soon we heard the pop of a mortar, followed by another after about a half-second delay. The reports sounded in the distance like champagne bottles being opened. Apparently they were using two mortars in battery—taking a look at one round from each to correct. We relaxed for several seconds while we knew the metal-finned teardrops were inscribing the first half of their graceful, high-curved trajectories; and then we looked at the target with much more intentness than before. I checked the rifle and peered through the scope, ready to shoot. Art bent himself to use the glasses.

An explosion blossomed violently on the precise spot which had been pointed out to us by the sergeant, and another one merged into it an instant later. The first two shells had been perfectly placed. The sound of the explosions—a shaking "slam-salamm"—arrived at our position a moment later, whipping the slackness of our clothing against our bodies. "Krist!" said Art, still looking through the scope, "Just think how they must feel down there!"

Just as this first noise died away, we heard the successive pop, pop, pop of more shells emerging from the tubes behind us to begin their ascendancy. Apparently the strike had been adjudged perfect and the observer had phoned back, "Fire for effect" at the instant he had seen the first strike. This show turned out to be as brilliant a bit of point-target mortar work as I have ever seen.

A small cloud of dust, smoke, and debris was still spreading and rising from the first shells as the other plunked into its center, one after the other. Art later described his telescope view of the explosions as being the most impressive thing he had witnessed up to that time. I did not get such a magnified view through the low-power rifle scope, but to me the successive flashing blasts, hammering into each other on the same tortured target, appeared thoroughly devastating. It seemed certain that they would tear their way through the roof of the heaviest bunker and bring sure death to anything inside.

The last shells landed and the roaring ceased. We had seen nothing recognizable as human beings during the firing—or immediately afterward—but as the debris settled and the dust drifted away we noticed a change in the scene below.

There was no doubt about the target having been a shelter. It had been roughly torn open from the top with roof timbers tossed pell mell to either side. The scorched, yellow sand and coral surface of the target area was spattered with great dark streaks of wet sand radiating from the center of impact, which was the bunker itself. Because of this change, we had to research and reidentify the new objects. Art handed me the glasses and took over the scope. It was not long before I saw a Jap body. It was a dead Jap—but one who had been killed within the previous few seconds. Half of his shirt front was a bright crimson and while I looked, the other half also became red. He was spread-eagled in an unnatural sprawl instantly recognizable, even to one who had never before seen it. Art and I gazed on for a second or so in morbid fascination.

In a moment, I saw something a few yards away from the body that made me drop the glasses and grab for the rifle. A live Jap had just risen from beside the corpse. Stunned and deafened by the blast that had thrown him from the bunker, he was holding his head with both hands in what could well have been a comical expression of exasperation. He remained exposed, probably in great pain—perhaps with bursted ear drums.

With Art giving me frantic directions in a nervous stage whisper, I held the shot. The scope had a tapered, flat top post reticule, with a lateral cross hair, sighted in to strike center on a 10″ bull with a six o'clock hold at 200 yards. As I took up the slack and aimed, the Jap was on his knees in a prayer-like attitude which was far more appropriate than he realized. There was no wind to speak of—just a mild zephyr from the ocean side.

I nudged his chin with the broad post—a measure calculated to plant the bullet somewhere on his chest at the 350 yard range. Then I gave the last pound or so of the three pound trigger pull a "gentle snatch."

The scope settled back in time for me to see the bullet strike the Jap and splash sand behind him. It must have hit in the chest or high in the stomach from the way he looked and the way he fell. As he toppled forward on his face I let him have two more for good measure.

"Look around for some more, Art! See any?" I muttered as I put my nervous fingers to the task of singling rounds into the magazine under the scope tube. (A properly designed swing-over hinged type scope mount would be a great thing, in as much as it would permit clip loading.) After Art said that he had been unable to see any more Japs, I reluctantly laid down the rifle and picked up the glasses to do some more looking on my own. I cannot recall the least bit of thinking about having just killed a man for the first time. All I remember is a feeling of intense excitement—the same as that experienced when one downs a hard sought big game trophy.

I held the glasses to my eyes again—but not for long. This time Hantel called my attention to a target. It was another survivor of the mortaring, who was crawling away from the scene on his hands and knees; most likely he also had been stunned and somewhat deafened by the blast. I could not imagine anything close to the bunker that would not have been so affected.

My first shot went too high, at least a foot over his back, according to Art, who was enjoying his role as the combat counterpart of a rapid fire coach. The Jap apparently was not completely deafened, for he fell flat on his belly the instant my shot went past. Had Art not been there with the big scope, I would have given myself credit for a hit. But he saw the bullet hit the sand in the wrong place. It was luckily one of those rare instances where a sniper is afforded a second shot after he has muffed the first one. The Jap, because of numbed senses or because of basic Japanese stupidity, remained motionless on his belly, possibly thinking that he was being fired upon from our lines below, which were mostly defiladed from him. From my position above, he remained an excellent target, I could see nearly the whole of his body. I fired the four shots remaining in the rifle, getting at least two hits. Art saw that he jerked convulsively while I was firing. By the time I had got my eye over to the spotting scope, he was lying still and bleeding badly.

Art then took over the rifle for a while and we waited around for somewhat less than an hour in the hopes of getting another shot. We did see some more bodies, the mortars and our rifle together had accounted for at least five, but everything we saw was dead.

We left the position by the same path we used coming in, pausing at the OP to give our congratulations to the mortar platoon and receive some of our own from the sergeant. As we walked on down the footpath leading to the road Art spoke his mind to me. In passing by, we had been looking again at men whose current lot was one with which we were later to become intimately acquainted. We too were to remain for weeks in that environment of evil stench, filth, heat, and death. "This place is a damn good place to leave!" he said. I was inclined to agree.

In an hour we were back at our camp at Lunga Point, which by then looked comfortable and secure beyond words. In another fifteen minutes we were bathing in the cool, fresh, fast-flowing waters of the Lunga River.

So ended our first sniping venture. It was not spectacular in any sense of the word and it could by no means be regarded as a feat requiring courage. From a rifleman's standpoint, it was not an independent affair. It was a jackalish exploitation of another weapon's skillful employment. But two Japs were dead who would otherwise have been likely to survive!

Hideo

NIGHT ON GUADALCANAL

On Guadalcanal, dawn and sunset always came about the same time each day, regardless of the season. At six o'clock it would begin to get dark inside the jungle and the groves, and almost immediately afterward the entire island, beaches, grassfields and mountains, would be veiled in moon-mellowed purple. Being close to the equator, the sun rose and sank below the horizon much faster than in the latitudes we had come from. To those in rear areas, the darkness meant respite, because normally, with the approach of night, the work on the beaches would be halted, details would return to their units, and all activity would cease until day break.

If the planes or subs had that day reported any suspicious ship movements north of the island, we would move into our beach defense positions out near the water and stand watch. If there were no such reported movements, however, we would sleep in our tents, leaving small details at the guns to stand watch and alert us in case of trouble.

Our tent area was in the palm groves near the water, close by our prepared beach defense positions. And at night each gun position became a site of much friendly gossip.

The men not entirely exhausted by the day's labor would gather in little groups around the guns and talk in hushed tones of days gone by and of days to come. The present seemed to be left entirely out of every discussion, as though there was nothing worth noting in the days that were passing by. Only memories of the past and the prospects of better days to come were discussable topics to most infantry soldiers on Guadalcanal.

Conversation centered mostly around the familiar soldier subjects of women, drinking, and city life. Only rarely was there any reference to the beautiful natural scenery surrounding us on all sides. As one of the "boys," I was halfway afraid to call anyone's attention to the unspeakably beautiful skies, the brilliantly blue ocean, and the complementing effects wrought both by blinding sunlight and gorgeously mellow moonlight. The whole little world we were living in was, in one way of thinking, no less than a fairyland of natural beauty, with its charm regrettably lost to the greater portion of us. This was so because of the entirely understandable limitations imposed on all sense of appreciation by the absence of the comforts of home and the pleasures of family life.

These little chats were usually conducted in or near the several shelters built close to the gun positions. The defense positions had originally been built by the Marines, and each unit taking them over had effected some improvement, so that by the time we moved in they were safe and comfortable indeed. They had all been dug as deep as the water level in the groves would permit, and then sandbagged up and revetted for almost complete protection. Ammunition in both open and unopened cases was stored conveniently, and shelves were arranged within the gun positions so that hand grenades, spare parts, and accessories could be handily located. The separate pillboxes, strong points of the defenses, had been connected by communication trenches, deep enough to permit crawling between pillboxes on all fours.

Most of the gun positions were logged-over with coconut trees and floored with box board dunnage to give the crew solid footing. The use of canvas ceiling in the construction of the positions eliminated the nuisance caused by dribbling sand, which would normally constitute quite a problem to gun crews in beach defense. Sand was always sifting down, getting into the working parts of the guns. It would be jarred continually by shell bursts, near and far, and if the covering of the logs was not made of canvas or some other sand-proof substance, the entire layer of sand on the roof would gradually sift through the logs and onto the gun and its crew.

These defenses looked out to the waters of Lunga Point, over an inadequate tangle of barbed wire strung immediately in front in the tidewater. On the far side of the channel could be seen the island of Tulagi, and to the right the little thumblike upward projection of Savo Island. The intervening waters comprised the burial ground of untold numbers of ships. With the moon fully out, the beauty of the scene was indescribable. The waters were nearly always stilled at night to a glass-like smoothness, with no surf whatever, just a gentle lapping against the farthest-in shelf of coral. The air was warm and usually laden with tropical fragrances. Only when the winds were active was the horrible odor of decomposing flesh brought to our present campsite. When that happened, all of the beauties of the night were blurred by a terrific stench of death itself, which I still remember as one of the most distasteful of all the sensations of war.

But we were never able to enjoy the moonlight for long in silence. The local stillness after sunset was more than compensated
for by the increased sound transmitting quality of the night air.
The heavy roar of artillery, both primary and secondary explosions,
seemed to double in loudness during the night. This was not all
illusion, for the guns actually were firing twice as much as through
the day.

The enemy preferred to do most of his offensive fighting during
the hours of darkness, and this preference was as strange and frightening to our people as it proved to be foolish and costly to the Japs.
In between the artillery salvos, the sound of scattered small arms
fire was also clearly audible at night from our positions on the
beach. It came from different inland directions. All through the
night there would be shooting at some point of the compass in
the groves or jungle.

We were entertained from the waterside also. Our own and the
Japanese ships gave us a nice performance in sound and fireworks
each night. Depth charges would often be exploded close enough
to us to rock our gun positions noticeably, the shock always occurring before we were able to hear the actual sound of the muffled
explosion. All sorts of patrol craft were out in the channel indulg-
ing in that sort of activity, many of them shooting off a long
string of tracers now and then, presumably at some small Jap boat.
Sometimes the sky would be lit up to noonday brilliancy by repeated flashes of gunfire, and there would come booming across
the water to us the sounds of what seemed to be a knockdown,
dragout naval fight, although it was probably only a couple of destroyers. We always gazed awestruck at such exhibitions, speculating upon the magnitude of the fight going on and the possible
effect of the outcome on ourselves. The men of my platoon, and
thousands of other doughboys like them, were greatly concerned
about our Navy. It was their only means of ever getting off that
damned island.

But of all the annoyances we had to put up with and of all the
interesting displays we were privileged to watch, the most aggra-
vating, and, at the same time, the most entertaining were the almost nightly raids of the "Washing Machine Charlie" bombers.
These bombers, large two-motored heavy jobs, came over almost
every moonlit night. Many stories about them and their pilots
were circulated about the Island. Several Marine signalmen told
me that they had monitored in on the Jap frequency and listened
to a Jap pilot speak in English, telling of his attendance at a San
Francisco high school, and joking about it as he announced the
dropping of each bomb. Others confirmed the story, claiming to
have heard and recognized the same voice night after night saying:

"Well boys, here I am again, get into your holes, now; I'm going to lay an egg or two. Don't worry, boys, this raid shouldn't be hard to take. Wait until we start coming over with a hundred planes at a time instead of only three." Then, they claimed, after he had dropped his bombs, he would speak a cheery goodbye before he turned to go back towards his base: "So long boys, take good care of the island down there and build us a nice landing field on it. We'll be around in about a week to take it back. Sweet dreams!" I never heard any such voice over the radio, but it is possible that the story had some foundation.

The threats, of course, were mainly bluff. The raids did little substantial damage. To our advantage, they had the effect of keeping the rear area people on their toes, and they gave everyone on the island something to talk about. After the first few we found them far more entertaining than frightening.

These night raiders were liable to come over any time after darkness, but usually we had ample warning. Radar would pick them up an hour or so ahead of time. Then the "Condition Red" would be sounded throughout the rear area and all over the airstrip, and everyone would know what was going to happen. At that time we had no night fighters, so the only active measures taken were by the anti-aircraft artillery batteries.

We would always remain in our bunks when the alarm was given, and for a few minutes afterward. No use to go out and be eaten up by the mosquitos until you knew that the planes were going to make their runs in your direction. A lot of the time they would go on across the channel to bomb the harbor and installations at Tulagi, leaving us alone for an hour or so. And when they came back we would always be able to hear their motors long enough before they got overhead to give us plenty of time to get into our shelters.

First the sound would come to us from an indefinite spot way up in the moonlit skies. And almost immediately the scissors-blade shafts of the searchlight beams would commence slicing through the darkness—groping for the least touch of a silvery wing tip or fuselage.

The sound made by the Jap planes was for all the world like that of several old, worn out washing machines grinding away in some basement. It apparently was operational procedure for the Japs to throw their motors out of syncronization—some said it was intended to confuse our sound detectors, and render us unable to make an accurate estimate of the number of planes approaching. But whatever the intent, it held a definite advantage for us, because we were nearly always able to identify the planes as Japanese by the sound of their motors alone. Once in a while, a close forma-

Hideo

The Japanese always were quick to try any method, new or old, if it would enable them to get a little closer in. Barbed wire was one of our best means of preventing them from creeping up unnoticed. Pretty hard for a man to get through a good tangle of barbed wire without making himself heard.

Watanabe here is using wire clippers, apparently to clear a way for himself and his buddies to get in and close. Not much of this sort of thing was done during the day, but some was in moonlight bright enough to permit observation and shooting. (Had we had those infra-red aiming devices on Guadalcanal we could have killed nearly all of these people.)

If you shoot this man from a very short distance be sure and hit him away from the pouch he is carrying on his midriff. You might set off the detonators and the picric acid it probably contains. And if you only wound him he might pull a ready lanyard and do the same thing, blowing away the wire he would not have time to cut. Many Japanese sappers who crawled up to our positions kept suicide charges tied to their bodies with this idea in mind.

tion of our Hellcats would sound much like a single Jap plane, if the Hellcats were very high up, but this would not happen often. If we heard an even and regular drone, we could always be reasonably certain that it was an American ship.

When the Jap night bombers came, they nearly always remained well up in the sky—usually between 20,000 and 30,000 feet. Our guns kept them up there so high that their bombing was mainly guess work, and their antics in the face of our accurate anti-aircraft fire were sometimes amusing.

It was the same sort of a show each night. They would come over and make their several runs on the field and the searchlights would promptly begin to seek them out. This searchlight activity would often be preceded by a blind barrage thrown up over the airstrip, intended to discourage any ambitious attempts to come in and lay one on our parked airplanes. The pencils of light would knife back and forth across the sky, bouncing now and then off a cloud, until one of them struck a bit of metal up there. Then, like a pack of wolves on a downed deer, all of the beams would converge, catching the hapless pilot and concentrating their altitude-waned candlepower to make him clearly visible at 25,000 feet.

Then there would be a brief pause while things got under way at the 90mm batteries. During this time the planes, tracked precisely by the searchlight beams, would hold steadily on their run. Then there would be repeated gun blasts from the ground close around us, a breathless period of suspense while the shells followed their long paths upward, and then the sky around the plane or flight of planes would be spotted with blossoming explosions. We would observe the silent puffing of the shell bursts around the target, thinking it amazing that we must wait so long to hear the sound of the explosion. We were in most cases unable to tell which sound was which, muzzle blast or explosions, because as burst after burst was sent up around the ships, and round after another was being fired by the batteries on the ground, the sounds began to confusingly blend into each other.

The planes would continue, running a gauntlet of flying fragments, usually swerving only slightly to avoid the shells; but sometimes rolling almost completely over from very close blasts. They generally stuck to their course. Hanging onto a direct course as the Japs did was a true test of courage because it enabled our batteries to plot the exact position of the plane in advance and place their bursts right on the button. It also enabled the Japs to occasionally ring the bell with their bombs. Some of them came very close to our positions at different times, missing the airstrip only a few hundred yards. And some of them made lucky hits on tents and shelters, killing and injuring a few men. But most of the bombing, perhaps due to the high altitude from which the bombs were released, was highly ineffectual.

When a bomb did come down close to you, you had a good warning. The bomb itself would make a sho-sho-sho sound, not entirely unlike the sound of a crow's wings beating the air in a struggle to gain initial altitude after jumping off a limb. You would be able to know that the bomb was coming your way several seconds in advance if the night were silent enough to permit listening for such a sound. Because of that noise-making characteristic of the Jap bombs, it became more or less standard procedure for us to sit on the edges of our shelters and watch the fireworks, waiting to duck into the holes until the last second. Air alerts had become so commonplace after our first ten days on the island that we accepted them as a standard and necessary interruption of our normal night's sleep and made the best of it. The worst loss of all was the sleep they caused us to skip and the exposure at night to the bite of Anopheles mosquitos. Some of us might have been spared malarial infection if we had not been forced out of our mosquito bars by the persistent "Condition Red" alarms.

Night on Guadalcanal and the varied and numerous impressions it held will likely make it the most outstanding and enduring single memory in the minds of all men there during the fighting. It was full of many sensations so foreign to the things we had been used to: there were the vast differences in climate, the many natural jungle sounds, the crawling land crabs, the lizards rattling in the undergrowth. More than any natural phenomena though, we will remember the sounds of man's own war in the jungle, the rattle of small arms fire, the roar of artillery, the drone of bombers overhead, and the blast of bombs striking the ground near us. There is no need now to separately evaluate the natural and the man-made effects. We know that the two types of disturbances—fear-creators, natural and artificial—combined effectively to make the place absolutely unforgettable. Night was the darker tint of green that made up our "green hell."

FIGHTING BEYOND THE BEACHHEAD

On the 16th of December our regiment (132nd Inf.) was attached tactically to the Second Provisional Marine Brigade and we were ordered to occupy Mount Austen (Hill 27) with a reinforced company, and to later move the entire Third Battalion into the position. As this change was made, the First Battalion was ordered to move into the "switch position" as the Third moved out.

On the same day the Regimental Intelligence Officer, Capt. Marty Kynett, led a patrol through the jungle to the foot of Mount Austen and bivouacked there for the night. He returned on the morning of the 17th with all reports negative.

"L" Company was selected for the initial occupation of Mount Austen and was reinforced and moved up on the 17th. It got as far as the Kynett patrol had gone without difficulty, but just beyond that point it ran into heavy enemy resistance and was placed under hot rifle and machine gun fire. The balance of the battalion moved forward to reinforce Company "L" as planned, arriving late the same day. The trail leading to the foot of Mount Austen was extremely rugged and cut through dense jungle, and the troops were too exhausted to attack when they arrived. Therefore, Lt. Col. Bill Wright, the battalion commander, completed a personal reconnaissance and planned to attack at dawn. Because of the dense jungle and the Jap skill at camouflage, it was impossible to make an accurate estimate of enemy strength or even of their precise locations. But Wright went ahead, marked his flanks with smoke and called for a fighter bombing attack, which he hoped would have a softening effect on his objective.

Wright's attack got started on schedule but bogged down early in the day. The dive bombing, so frightening in sound and sight, actually had little effect. In those early days, with the development of air-ground liaison techniques still in the early stages and with the small knowledge we had of the effectiveness of different types of bombs in jungle terrain, we were all inclined to overesti-

66

mate at first the value of aerial bombardment. So it was with considerable disappointment that Wright's battalion learned of the small results the air attack had had on the Japs. Actually, in the light of later experience, (which was to reveal the true values of the employment of tactical aircraft), such air support would probably never have been used. Its most telling result was alerting the enemy and warning them of the front which was later to be attacked by ground troops.

Like the stout soldier he was, Bill Wright became understandably impatient at the initial delay of the attack, and at the first holdup, he ran forward to get the "squad picture" of the resistance. In so doing he was caught in the fire lane of a concealed Nambu and was raked across the short ribs with a burst of .25 caliber bullets. The wounds were fatal but death was not instantaneous. Several attempts were made to get him out of the fire-swept spot where he had fallen, but to no avail. Lieutenant Edward Dunne was seriously wounded in the same action, shot through the face. It was not until the afternoon that Marty Kynett led a patrol out front and managed to bring back Colonel Wright's body. His death was a serious blow to the battalion, for Bill Wright was as well liked as any of our field officers. He had two brothers in the regiment, one commanding a company and one a staff sergeant in Second Battalion Headquarters.

When news of his death reached us in the rear areas, the war, for many of us, began to take on a more serious outlook. Bill, like the other officers who were killed in the early action on the island, was a chap that no one seemed to be able to associate with the thought of death.

Maj. Hoyne Sheldon, my old company commander of Camp Forrest days, took command of the battalion and ordered it to dig in at its foremost point of advance. He was replaced in a few hours by Major Lou Franco, former executive officer of the First.

The setup remained static for the next few days, during which time the First Battalion was moved forward and placed in reserve. Franco had decided to reconnoiter to his front in force, rather than order a general attack. All of his patrols which were sent to conduct this reconnaissance determined by contact with the enemy the location of the Jap flanks. In the light of that intelligence, the First Battalion was detailed to hold on the left and the Third was moved to the right, strengthening the grip on the line along which the regiment was disposed.

The operation had been steadily hampered by the primitive supply system forced on the unit by the terrain. Some improvement over hand-carrying methods was necessary if any measure of the battalions' strength was to be employed in the assault. Carrying parties were absorbing too many men from the already under-strength companies.

The needed relief was soon provided through the efforts of a company of the 57th Engineers, who had been working desperately to build a jeep road along the axis of Edson's Ridge. By the 20th this road had been pushed forward to the top of "Burnt Knob" (Hill 35). All of the Engineers' work had been rendered much more difficult by persistent infiltrating and sniping around our left flank.

There followed a several day period of semi-static fighting, with our First and Third Battalions holding and probing and the Japs doing the same thing. News of all this leaked back through official sources and the grapevine to the beach-bivouacking Second Battalion, now contemptuously referring to itself as the "unloading detail." Our position on the beach became less and less enviable as time went on. Finally two of our boys accosted no less a personage than Major General Patch, and asked him—in almost as few words —"When in the hell are we going to fight?" The general told them not to worry, that they would get their chance very soon. But no change in orders was forthcoming for the next few days.

There must have been a bit of uncertainty in all levels of command on Guadalcanal at that time. There were no decent estimates of enemy strength available, and it seemed that the only thing to do was to move forward and find out. Actually that is what most likely *had* to be done, for I have never been able to find out what worthwhile intelligence was made available to the division or higher commanders. As far as the regiment was concerned, the enemy situation, other than that of contacted front line units, was highly vague throughout the entire campaign.

So the commander was pretty nearly held to the procedure of basing his decisions on the estimates given by the units who were actually in contact with the enemy. This forced him to *guess* the strength and dispositions in enemy rear areas, and it naturally caused delay in the issuance of orders to tactical units. No commander likes to make up his mind without some enemy information. Consequently, troops were left sitting in the jungle in semi-defensive positions for long periods, trading fire with enemy patrols and front line pillboxes—getting nowhere fast.

These key hills we were attempting to take, overlooking the tenable north tip of the island, were of the utmost importance to ourselves and to the enemy. As long as they remained in Japanese hands, the Japs would enjoy excellent observation of all of our unloading activities, and more importantly, they would also be able to see every plane take off the main fighter strip of Henderson Field. This observation would of course be all-important for them in the conduct of any counter offensive, especially should it involve

Hidee

"Now Applejack, I'm a reasonable man, and I've never expected too much of my subordinates, but I must say I find it hard to understand why your outfit remains dug in at the same place for more than a week. I know you have had a hard time with casualties; maybe I was a little hasty last week in ordering you to assault those pillboxes with bayonets. But I've been operating under a strain back here, too. Half of the Division Staff has been breathing down my neck for the last four days—the General wants to know what in hell is causing the delay. . . . Scuttlebutt has it that I'll be relieved in a week if something up your way doesn't move forward.

"This leaves me no alternative but to. . . . What's that you say? Thirty litter cases—twelve more dead—more stuff coming over—building up in front? What do you mean, stone wall?

"Now listen, Kid! Pull yourself together and pay attention to the Old Man. I've looked that hill over from one end to the next from my OP, and I'm convinced that you're overestimating the resistance. Things aren't as bad as you think.

"Another thing to consider is that you're a professional soldier, and I'm your superior officer. I'm giving you a simple order to take that damn hill and then dig in and hold there at all costs! And you do that within the next four hours; understand?

"Yeah? Well, if you don't feel equal to the job just turn the outfit over to your second in command and report back here to me. I'll package you up and send you back to the General—with a very neat letter of transmittal!

"Over and out!"

the employment of artillery or tactical aircraft. It is almost impossible to fight intelligently when you cannot see.

So again it was the Infantryman who suffered from the unusual circumstances. He had to wait and hold his ground in those highly untenable jungle wastes while some sort of a plan was devised. And the waiting was far from pleasant. All of the jungle in which our unit was deployed during those days was made up of huge trees of tropical rain forest varieties, mostly of the buttress rooted type, which reached their straight trunks up to great heights before spreading their branches to form the absolutely sun proof roof. The ground spaces in between the trunks were crowded with a dense undergrowth of huge ferns, thorny growth, and all sorts of vines and palmetto-like plants. The jungle floor was made up of centuries of accumulated debris, rotted and decaying logs and leaves, all lying on top of yellowish clay which would hold moisture like a sponge. Visibility from the ground was almost nil. You could not see ten feet in front of yourself except when looking down a trail.

In such country the advantage was overwhelmingly in favor of the defender. Silent movement was a virtual impossibility, and while the poor visibility, of course, worked two ways, it was nevertheless much easier to lurk in such cover and see your enemy approach than to go out and look for him. If you were defensively hidden by the side of a trail, you had but to remain quiet, with your weapon ready, and wait for your enemy to expose himself. When he did it was easy to kill him because the range would seldom be more than thirty yards—often much less than ten. (It was this that accounted for the extremely high ratio of killed and wounded in some jungle battles; you were nearly always so close that you could not miss the vital body areas with a rifle, pistol, or submachine gun.)

During this period of what seemed to be command indecision, the mission given to the committed portion of the regiment was that of cutting the "East-West" supply trail, upon which it was assumed the local enemy forces were dependent for supply and evacuation. Patrols that were sent out into suspect areas, however, failed to locate such a trail, though they did run into scattered enemy resistance.

The only decisive achievement of the units so far had been the gaining of a foothold on the slopes of Hill 31, which permitted serious planning for the capture and consolidation of the entire hill. Such a gain would facilitate the ultimate attack against Hill 27, final objective of the regiment in the first phase of its Guadalcanal fighting.

The persistent efforts of the two battalions met with the first large measure of success when the Third Battalion took the crest of Hill 31 late in the afternoon of the 22nd of December. Holdings were successfully consolidated in the new and advantageous position, and engineers had managed to push their road through Burnt Knob, shortening hand-carrying trail distance considerably and greatly increasing the volume of supplies transported forward.

Major Franco attacked again on the morning of the 24th driving the enemy southward to a point about 250 yards from his starting point, Hill 31. After this substantial gain he was counterattacked in force and subjected to heavy machine gun and rifle fire. This forced his leading elements first to halt and then to sacrifice a certain amount of their gain to adjust and dig in a defensive line.

After that, the situation stagnated again. An attack on the following day gained little ground although the entire three rifle company strength of the unit was cooperatively employed at one time, leaving only the heavy weapons company in reserve. In their first series of actions, the regiment was tasting the very worst sort of fighting in the Japanese repertoire—defense in the jungle. Our organization and equipment allotments at that time were not properly based on concepts of jungle fighting, and no one had advised us to make those alterations and allotments of weapons and men, as should have been done. For instance, our heavy weapons companies were just in the process of learning the jungle limitations of their weapons, and many valuable hours and much effort were wasted in moving weapons and ammunition into areas of jungle where they could not possibly be used. Also, we had not developed methods of observation that were later to come into being, and were therefore unable to employ our mortars. Officers were uninformed as to the uses to which water-cooled machine guns could be put to in the jungle simply because there was no one present who had sufficient experience. So for the most part, the use of that splendid weapon was lost to units in the offence, though it was properly revered for its value in defense fighting.

Many of us realized at the time that the days we were passing through constituted a period of blind groping similar to that which had been the lot of our early fighters in the last war. Here was something forced upon us by the shortsightedness of our national leaders and our whole pacifist people, who had insisted on drawing the purse-strings on national defense in peace to save dollars which would later be paid for in lives. Half of the lives that were lost on Guadalcanal were lost solely because of a greenness that could have easily been overcome with proper training, and because of a shortage of equipage which had been designed years previously, but for which mass-production methods had not been devised—because of this same shortsighted economy. No wonder our fighting progress was slow.

A brief probing with small patrols soon revealed that the Third Battalion was facing a veritable stone wall of Japanese defensive positions. Large numbers of tenacious little brown soldiers were dug in on the forward slope of a low ridge in a line which extended nearly the full length of the Third Battalion's front. Heavily logged and sodded pillboxes were the key points. They were spaced close together with openings so arranged and with lanes so cut that fire would be mutually protecting.

In approaching one pillbox to silence its gun, our people would invariably run into the fire of another. In the words of Lt. Don Hogan: "It would cost us one or two men to find the direction the fire was coming from, then it would cost us two more men to get up to the back door. When we finally got on the dome it was easy to kill the crew, just like rats in a trap, but getting ourselves out was likely to cost us more. Not very good trading—one for one, or even worse, all the time."

It was the strongest point in the makeup of the Jap Infantryman—his ability to carry on a stubborn, do-and-die, sacrificial defense. For although the Jap directives of that period belittled the wisdom of any defense—and emphasized, above everything else, the marvelous capabilities of the Japanese Infantryman in the attack—it soon became very apparent to us that the Jap was as stubborn and cunning in the defense as he was stupid and suicidal in the assault. Japanese self appraisal was in this case 100% wrong.

On Christmas Day the Second Battalion, still back in the beachhead area, enjoyed a turkey dinner. All of the trimmings were there, including cranberry sauce. A special supply ship from Australia had been sent over for the purpose of supplying all of the kitchens with frozen birds and fresh vegetables. We ate to our hearts content, but nevertheless put in a full day's work. It had naturally never been expected that we would take even an hour off. The fight was going on stronger than ever on Christmas Day for our Third and First Battalions.

The Third had attacked again on Christmas Day, jumping off at daylight with the previously made allotment of strength, all three rifle companies in the assault, only the heavy weapons company in reserve. All forward elements were pinned down by intense fire during the first minutes of the advance. Because of this, the ground gained was negligible. Desperate, Franco attempted to out-flank the Jap positions, and, in so doing, over-extended his frontage. It was realized then that frontal attack was out of the question, and that the one battalion could not hold and flank at the same time. The only solution would be to have another force go

Hideo

Japanese were not all either skinny and scrawny or chubby and bow-legged. Some of them were magnificent examples of what a Spartan existence can do for the body beautiful. Starved prisoners were usually emaciated, but many of the freshly killed were muscled and framed like the soldier depicted.

The Japanese are nearly all athletic enthusiasts. Some of the finest acrobats and tumblers in the world come from Honshu. Despite the size handicap they have done well in certain branches of international athletic competition.

Aside from athletic accomplishment, the little brown brothers are able to do long hours of hard work. If someone else is there to furnish the brains a corps of Jap laborers could move a mountain. Any American who has seen the prodigious diggings in the hills of Guadalcanal or Burma or Okinawa can verify that.

This man swinging the pick is digging a gun emplacement. Maybe he has first marched thirty miles with a full pack to warm himself up. . . .

around—widely around—Franco's front, and outflank or envelop the enemy force.

With that idea in mind, the First Battalion was ordered to move generally south and attack the enemy's right flank. The movement of the First Battalion, commanded by Lieutenant Colonel Ripstra, took more than a day. It got into its assembly area in the evening and jumped off the following morning. It immediately ran into resistance and during the ensuing confusion it was discovered that because of an error in jungle navigation, the assault elements had not gone far enough inland (east). As a result, they were unable to properly debouch for an attack; they were too close to the Third Battalion.

In an attempt to make the best of an unfortunate situation, Major Franco withdrew his forward elements a short distance and laid down a heavy concentration of artillery fire on the Japs to his front, attacking as soon as the fire was halted. But it was no use. The Japs had either remained steadfastly in their positions, or else had withdrawn for the duration of the barrage and reoccupied while Franco's attack was getting under way.

A stalemate continued through the remainder of December, with activities confined to artillery and patrol operations with the exception of a single small-scale fiasco. This incident involved a hurried withdrawal of Blank Company elements, who failed to wait for the members of an anti-tank gun crew to carry back the parts of a weapon which they had laboriously manhandled up to the front lines to use in blasting pillboxes. Stories leaked back to us, telling of a hot-headed anti-tank sergeant standing up during the "withdrawal" and calling the fleeing men bitter and picturesque names. According to the story he remained there frothing at the mouth while the group wilted away, and left the scene only after he had been completely deserted. When the lost ground was retaken it was found that the most important part of the gun, the barrel, had been appropriated by the Japs. The sergeant has never forgiven the men of Company Blank for leaving him in that embarrassing position.

The regimental commander had for weeks past been steadily requesting the use of the Second Battalion, which was still cooling its heels while unloading supplies back on the beachhead. But the unloading was a highly necessary task and the unit could not be spared. Those of us in the unit were discontent with our role of a provisional port QM battalion, as I have previously stated, but that did not change the situation. It was not until the last day of the year 1942 that it was felt that we could be spared, at which time we were told to get the hell ready and be quick about it. With the realization that "This is really it?" we set about the task of clearing out of our areas on the beach and turning them over to some combat weary Marines, who were damned glad, by their own admission, to get the well deserved rest.

I went with Captain Cosby, my company commander, to attend the meeting in which we were informed of the plans the regimental staff had made for committing the Second Battalion. We learned that there was going to be a change in regimental commanders, another sample of things that troops must put up with from time to time. Most of us were enormously fond of the old man, and it was with great regret that we saw him leave the regiment. Colonel Nelson had been my regimental commander for many months through our training period in the states and overseas. All of us had more or less of a lump in our throats when he said goodbye. But our feeling of loss was alleviated somewhat by the realization that we, the "Non-Fighting Second Battalion," were going to be committed at last. And we found that our mission was to be a thrilling one indeed. We were to make the proposed wide sweep around to the left—wider than any yet attempted—and attack the enemy's extreme right flank or rear and the long contested, hard sought for Hill 27 was to be our battalion objective. It gave us an inflated feeling. The pivot point of the current Guadalcanal operation, Mount Austen itself! We ran back to our companies like a group of recessed school boys, anxious to break the news.

HURRY UP AND WAIT

The regimental plan, like nearly all workable combat schemes, was simplicity itself. It called for a three pronged thrust against the Japanese position, two of the prongs being holding or diversionary attacks directed from rather predictable frontal points. The third effort was planned to strike a heavier blow, with the advantage of surprise, against a possibly unalerted flank or rear. And the Second Battalion was selected for this vital role because of its relative freshness. Of course, any of the three units might be called upon, by circumstances, to put forth an effort greater than the other two, but it had seemed most likely to Colonel Nelson and the cagey Major Luther Adams, Regimental Operations Officer, that the flanking show would offer the best chances. So Colonel Ferry's Second Battalion was selected to swing out the long, looping left hook which, it was desperately hoped, would administer the final knockout blow to the Jap garrison defending Hill 27.

The simplicity of the plan by no means indicated that its execution would be easy. The terrain itself would present plenty of obstacles. We knew, for instance, that one of the greatest single problems of the operation would be that of getting the three attack forces into the proper assembly areas and to have them jump off in proper timing when the attack began. Aside from the obvious danger of encountering enemy outposts while still en route to the assembly areas, the initial difficulties boiled down to a problem in jungle navigation—an art which was certainly not well developed in our unit at that time. To cope with that problem the battalion possessed two definite assets. One was the perseverance and never-be-discouraged attitude of its commander, Lieutenant Colonel Ferry, and the other was the uncanny sense of direction and general terrain-wisdom of its executive officer, Major Wirt Butler. Added to that, of course, was the accepted competence of the unit's officers and non-coms who were to lead the patrols and locate the trails to be used.

76

The value of this ability to find one's way in the jungle is often belittled by beginners who put forth the idea that any officer or platoon leading non-com must have it as a prerequisite to leadership. Actually, I know of no single leadership deficiency which has caused so much confusion in jungle operations as in that one simple matter. And I know of few other phases of training which I would consider as important as that of teaching the individual to find his way around. The only possible way to learn is by experience, unless the trainee happens to have been born and bred in jungle country. General Orde C. Wingate, whom many adjudge to be one of the great all-time masters of jungle warfare, made a definite point, during his early Burma operations, of holding the *senior* officer in each of his columns personally responsible for the navigation of the unit. The job of getting our unit to the right place was properly given to Wirt Butler.

That assignment and others were meted out by Colonel Ferry at the meeting of battalion officers, held immediately following the receipt of instructions from the regimental commander.

On hearing the description of the jungle we were going to have to move through it was decided to split up the heavy weapons company, and to form two lightly equipped and armed platoons to move with the assault echelon, and one larger unit to later bring up the 81mm mortars and water-cooled Brownings. The colonel saw no use for the heavies, in that particular engagement, and decided to have them brought up later. He also knew the wisdom of using maximum fire power wherever possible, but to attempt to bring heavy machine guns over the tortuous approach to our objective would have only resulted in a hopeless overloading of personnel. It would have also made the column more vulnerable to ambush. If we had had animal transport and some assurance of continued air-drop supply (such as I was later to see so beautifully demonstrated during service with Merrill's Marauders in Burma) it would have been an entirely different story. As it was, we were unable to carry more than four minutes of fire per gun with the understrength squads we had. Besides, in the event of a reversion from the offensive to the defensive it would be lifesaving to have the heavies held fresh in reserve.

The same story held for heavy mortars. We left them back also. Their ammunition transport problem would have been even greater than the machine guns, and their weight made it even more necessary to temporarily leave them behind. Only about half of the heavy weapons company's strength had moved out with the assault echelon; the two components of it were commanded by Art Hantel and "Cowboy" Simmons, another Lieutenant in "H" Company, leaving me behind. I was to remain back with the reserve

.30s and my active role in the operation would not begin until those weapons were called for.

It did not look as though I was going to get in any sniping for a while. I did, however, obtain permission to visit the assault echelon as I saw fit during its advance to the assembly area and beyond, in order to keep myself abreast of the situation.

The battalion was shortly relieved in its beach defense position by a Marine unit, the regimental designation of which I do not remember. Besides the dug-in positions, we passed on to the Marines several permanently installed dual-purpose 37mm guns which were mounted in beach defense sites overlooking the waters of Lunga Point.

In walking around the area where we had installations placed in extensive palm groves, I first became fully aware of the vast amount of weapons and equipment which falls into the hands of a battalion that receives a static beach defense mission. We had large numbers of .50 caliber MGs mounted all over the beach, with tons of ammunition heaped nearby. The Marine officers who accompanied me throughout the tour of these defenses had a few laughing remarks to make about the great increase in the number of weapons gained with each successive occupation.

It had definitely become a tendency for the unit assigned to the defense of the Lunga Beach area to steal every possible metal-throwing big weapon it could lay its hands on, because guns in that kind of a setup need not be carried. Once installed, each new weapon became another bit of fire power, which we all knew might sometime become precious. When the first unit had started to organize the beach defenses, they were suffering an extreme shortage of guns, but as more and more ships came in, that situation continued to remedy itself nicely.

As soon as we had managed to turn over our assorted collection of guns to the Marines, we also began to get rid of a lot of extra impedimenta, both personal and organizational, that we had gathered in the year we had been overseas. Some of it we stored, mostly the personal items for which we would perhaps later have some use. The extra bits of organizational equipment we managed to give away to others who might need them. These items were extra rifles, pistols, Reising guns, ammunition of assorted calibers, and various other things. The Marines, who were especially hungry for M1 rifles, got the lot.

After disposing of the excess property, we moved down to the junction of Wright road and the beach trail, where we set up a comfortable camp for the part of the company that was to remain behind. It was in another segment of the coconut grove, which, with minor breaks, extended all of the way around the island. It

Hideo

The Chinese have for a long time referred to the Japanese as "Monkey People." There are a few justifications for this: some few of the Japanese have receding chins and other monkeylike features, and many of them can climb trees with the greatest of ease.

The soldier shown is walking up a slightly slanting coconut palm, where he will post himself as a "sniper." If he were going up to observe or to pick coconuts he would have left his rifle and ammunition on the ground.

To me it seems fantastic that snipers actually were posted in the tops of nut palms. I've climbed them myself and found them very poor places to stay. Their tops are infested with a large red ant, which will literally eat you alive if you remain for any length of time. I guess the Japs must have had some sort of effective insect repellant to keep them off their bodies.

The split-toed sneakers worn on this Jap's feet make this sort of climbing very easy for him. The soles are treaded to grip anything, and the separated big-toe feature permits him to grip and feel his footing much better than he could with regular shoes.

was high-floored in comparison with previously occupied areas, and it was less inclined to become muddy because of the very shallow top soil. The coral was only two inches from the top sod, showing clean white at the first stroke of an entrenching shovel. Within our area there was a huge pit, from which a preferred type of coral was being quarried—machine-gouged for paving purposes, to use on both roads and air runways.

We had barely begun to get organized in our new area when our first two platoons jumped off, moving with the assault echelon of the battalion. They were now armed with BARs and rifles, and organized into BAR teams instead of MG squads, as they finally faced their long-delayed commitment to combat. A last (and somewhat laughable) touch of grimness was noticeable in face and hand smearings of grease paint, a greenish and intolerably messy substance which was meant to camouflage your face in the jungle. Later we got wise and abandoned its use, but at first all of the men were wearing it. If it had no other effect it certainly did manage to make an outfit look weird—a bunch of green uniforms with green hands and heads sticking out of them. I said goodbye to them all as they left, feeling as they did, that it all was a sort of anti-climax. It had come rather late for the company and it had not come to me at all. I did not find much consolation in the thought that the war would be a long one, with plenty of opportunities to get killed. Memories of my impatient attitude then have since provided me with numerous laughs, especially on many occasions when I was able to think back on it from a hot spot in the middle of a raging fire fight.

It had bothered me a bit to see Hantel leave. He had been my closest friend since I had been in "H" Company, and I knew him well enough to be sure that he would be constantly taking risks. But somehow I felt sure that he would come out alive. I guess I automatically included him in my own, personal illusion of immortality. He was too entirely full of fun to get killed, it seemed.

We completed our rear-area camp in a day, not attempting to make ourselves too comfortable, because of likelihood of being called up at any moment. I saw to it that the guns were in good shooting shape and ready to go, and I made a thorough check on the organization to see that I was properly set to move on ten minutes notice, night or day. After that, I constantly visited the regimental command post in order to keep myself up to date on the Second Battalion's progress and the overall regimental picture. And as soon as I found time, I went forward to see Colonel Ferry and get a picture of things on the ground. At the time I went, the battalion had been out one day and had completed the first third of their semi-circular route toward the enemy's purportedly unsuspecting right rear. This was a distance of less than four miles, but it was over some of the most nearly impassable terrain and "impenetrable" jungle that I have seen during my life.

I took time out, before I started on a second trip, in order to check my rifle, and see if there had been any change in the sight adjustments or any warpage of the stock. To do this I simply climbed down into the coral-quarry near the tents of our camp, and shot from one wall to the other, after warning the bulldozer operators who might have gotten into my line of fire. For a target I used a cardboard box with a four inch bull smeared on with red China-chalk.

For the first time, the weapon had changed its zero and I had to do a rebed job on the stock in order to get the group back to small size and keep it centered in the bull. This took the better part of an afternoon and the resighting took an hour or so, so I missed my second day's visit to the battalion, though news came in through the regimental command post that it was still proceeding on its route, still without enemy contact.

The next day I filled my belt with some of an especially good lot of Denver Ordnance M–2 ammunition, which I found to shoot with consistency and accuracy, (unusual for 150-grain cartridges) and got ready for the receipt of orders to join the battalion. The unit, because of the expired time, could not possibly be more than a few hundred yards from Hill 27. In other words, all hell was liable to break loose at any minute.

I left word behind for Sergeant Prunckle to be ready to move the unit up to the regimental command post on my call, assuming that it would undoubtedly be routed from that point to join the battalion when Colonel Ferry began yelling for his machine guns. Then I went up to the regimental command post to get the latest hot dope.

It was on this trip that I first saw our new regimental commander, Colonel George, and the impression was a lasting one. I had, of course, heard of the colonel previously, for his reputation as a skilled leader and a capable officer had gotten well around on the island. Back on New Caledonia, too, his reputation as a fine pistol shot and enthusiastic deer hunter had been legend. He had gathered together on New Caledonia a selected group of officers and men and made them into a fine outfit—the Mobile Combat Reconnaissance Squadron. The squadron did a grand job on "Canal" prior to his being transferred to the command of the 132nd Infantry.

From a distance the colonel was not impressive in appearance. He was a small man, very short in stature, but his knotted figure possessed a wiriness and a muscularity which would have been a source of pride to a distance runner. His weather-beaten, sun-tanned face, Indian-like in profile, was equally impressive. It could freeze into an impassive and merciless mask—or it could break into a flashy, warming smile. He was richly gifted with every natural quality of leadership, possessing a spark of personal magnetism that gained friendship, instant respect, and devotion from all his military subordinates. It is not difficult to describe him, for the picture he created is a bright and enduring one.

Until ordered not to do so by higher authority, Colonel George wore shorts made out of fatigue trousers, exposing a pair of muscular, knotted calves, scrawny, and devoid of all surface flesh. They were pure muscle, with the veins standing out directly beneath the dead-oak-leaf colored skin. He often went about stripped to the waist, his weapons carried on a heavy web belt. These weapons were only two, a handmade knife with a beautiful handle of selected New Caledonian staghorn, and a National Match .45 Colt, which he could shoot with rifle accuracy. The belt of weapons complimented his appearance—he seemed to wear them as though they were part of him, and so they nearly were. For headgear he wore a green fatigue hat, brim usually turned up all around and cocked sidewise to accentuate a bantam-rooster walk and generally aggressive mein, making a fighting cock the best non-human counterpart of our regimental commander. He seldom wore insignia, not for any fear of Japs—just one of his eccentricities, like his ordering the personnel in the unit to curb their profanity, while he in no way modified or altered the use of his own indescribably picturesque vocabulary. He could chin himself with either arm in his fortyish youth, and he could run 100 yards in close to ten seconds.

More than any other of his tributes from junior officers, I remember one given by a captain named Zimmerman. He said of Colonel George, when he first heard that he was coming over the regiment: "The first time you see him you like him; the first order he gives you you joyfully obey. After he has commanded an outfit for a week he invariably has the absolute loyalty and devotion of every man in his unit." Time made evident the truth of the captain's statement.

The circumstances of my first seeing this fireball regimental commander were dramatic. Capt. Clyde Joy and myself were trying to hunt down a "sniper" who had been reportedly harassing the supply trail to the Third Battalion. Joy and I went up to the suspect spot in a hurry. (I had arrived for my visit to the Regimental S–3 to get the dope on the progress of my battalion.) A frightened man had come running down the trail, yelling hysterically that he had been shot by a sniper who "just missed me a few

Hideo

The peasant background of the average Japanese soldier was not completely a disadvantage. With Pvts. Yamamoto and Ito so used to carrying two hundred pound loads of rice seedlings on their backs, it became a small problem to teach them to lug heavy equipment over long jungle trails. Here we see a dismantled artillery piece—several mule loads in our army—being manhandled into position.

We found these guns in the darndest places; some of them were deep in the jungle where there was no ceiling clearance to allow firing, but others were on high ground where they could be effectively laid. Lots of the artillery fire we received came from very unexpected directions—inland, from the heavily jungled mountains.

And here the Jap Officer deserves much credit, too. He had carefully appraised the staying power of his men on such long, heavily loaded marches, and he didn't make the mistake of underestimating. Japanese Infantry were, I think, the first doughboys in the world to learn that there is no such thing as an impenetrable jungle. . . .

inches." I was skeptical from the beginning, but Joy and I never-theless decided to investigate the matter. We proceeded up the trail to a point near the "sniping" incident. With all of my mis-trust of the man's judgment of bullet sound, I still did not feel like walking upright down the middle of the trail and neither did Joy. So we sat off to the edge and strained our eyes, trying to find a sign of the sniper at ground level or in one of the many big, shadowy-leaved, knotted and vine-tangled trunks of the many trees around us. With a fair-sized fire fight less than 1,000 yards away, I felt certain that it was the snap of some deflected Amer-ican or high aimed Jap bullet that had scared the soldier.

As we intensified our search of the foliage for our possible enemy I began to wish that I had brought my field glasses along. There were so many suspicious shadows which I could better examine with the aid of binoculars. When I shortly saw a man come up from the regimental end of the trail with a pair of glasses in his hand, I naturally decided to make use of him. "Hey soldier!" said I in a stage whisper, "Look up in that big tree at the bend in the trail, fourth limb up, and tell me if that is a man hidden in the ferns." The soldier with the glasses looked but said nothing, seem-ing to take much too long a time to focus the eyepieces. I became impatient. "C'mon," I yelled, "Tell me what the hell's up there!" The soldier then complied, speaking back with a crispness of tone alarmingly out of keeping with his buck-private-rear-rank appear-ance. "Nothing up there but a bunch of damned leaves," he grunted, and the *Colonel* whom I had been calling "soldier" then turned and walked back to the CP, having satisfied himself that the sniper report had been a false alarm. Joy immediately came over and informed me of my mistake, which was needless, for I had recognized an unmistakable ring of authority in the man's voice.

Captain Cosby introduced us back at the CP a few minutes later. The colonel waved aside my attempted apologies, grabbed my hand with tempered steel fingers, and turned me to face the crowd at the CP. "Look here," he exclaimed heartily to the staff, "It is an occasion of a sort when blood brothers meet. Here's another officer named George, and he flattered the hell out of me a minute ago by calling me 'soldier.' Get him a drink, someone!" The last few words were in jest—there was no liquor to be had, as far as the colonel or I knew—(though I was to learn that there was—that very night).

The Second Battalion was still feeling out its route, trying to locate itself exactly before it jumped off in the attack. Without maps or adequate aerial photos, the job of navigating through the jungle and swamps was proving to be a nightmare. Learning just that much, which was almost nothing, I returned to my camp.

The battalion had not yet fired a single shot, and in alerting my gang in the groves, telling them to be ready to leave on a moment's notice, I had done something unnecessary and harmful. As I sauntered back along the crest of Bloody Knoll, my unfired rifle slung on a peculiarly tired shoulder, I felt a little disgusted with myself and the world. It was beginning to get dark when I arrived at my tent and told the men the news. I told them to all turn in, except the minimum number of guards, and get some rest. The damned waiting was becoming a war of nerves. I went to sleep thinking about the effects of keeping an outfit which was eager for combat waiting nine months on New Caledonia, and then moving them forward to fight at such a continuous snail's pace.

This last bit of waiting might prove to be especially demoralizing. We were camped just below the aid station, where each day numbers of wounded, sick, and dead were brought back past our area—some of them close friends of mine and my men.

We would all like something to take our minds off it for a while —something besides an air raid, which, on that moonlit night, was all that we could reasonably expect.

RAISIN JACK

That night we were bombed again. I had hardly gone to sleep when the "Condition Red" was called out from a nearby Marine Command Post, and shortly we were listening to the irregular droning of Jap motors way up above the thin clouds. Loath to endure the discomforts of our slit trench shelters, the most of us continued to lay in our bunks, waiting until the last minute to climb out into our holes.

The "last minute" was not long in coming this time, for almost immediately after we first detected sound of the motors we heard the familiar "Sho-Sho-Sho" sound directly above. Jumping out of our nets, we scampered like rats for our foxholes, tripping, cursing, and being eaten alive in our half nakedness by swarming Anopheles mosquitos.

"Turn out that light, Goddamn it!" "For Krist's sake, why don't you get in your own damn hole?" "What the hell is the matter with that damn air force of ours?" "Why don't they get one of our planes up there and shoot the bastards down?"—"Why did we have to camp on a Goddamn bomb target when we had the whole Goddamn beach to pick from?"

Those and a thousand other cries filled the grove for a while, then, when everyone was secure in his shelter—concentrating on listening to the drone from above, a stillness gradually spread through the grove.

I had crawled into my hole along with the rest because it was evident, from the general direction in which the mass of tentatively weaving searchlight beams were pointing, that the planes were more or less directly above our area. And I got underground just in time to hear the first bomb explode about 400 yards south of us. The first one in the stick, that is.

The next hit about 300 yards away only a second later, and another followed in line, striking terrifyingly close. We all crouched deeper in our shelters, knowing that the next of the string would

86

explode within our area, and waited with our hearts in our mouths. If we got away unscathed by the next bomb we would be able to stop worrying for a while because the remainder of the stick would go beyond us. Lifetimes seemed to tick away during the ten seconds we waited, though the actual period of suspense was so minute that it could hardly have been measured on a stop watch. The "Sho-Sho-Sho" grew louder and louder, indicating for sure that the bomb would hit our camp dead center. And that is exactly what it did—but it fortunately detonated in the top of a palm tree, exploding with a blinding flash and an earth-shaking roar. Particles of fronds and smashed coconuts were driven into the ground by the blast, and bits of pulverized palm rained down for a matter of minutes. There was a period following the blast while the men speculated individually on the number killed and while the remaining bombs in the stick went boom-boom-booming away from us that also seemed at least a century in duration.

Beyond us, the planes were now paying for their fun. The search-light beams had caught them and the first rounds of AA fire were already on the way up. The initial flak explosions were very close, but did not knock planes down. Additional batteries quickly opened up, and in a moment the formation of three planes was cavorting madly about in highly disturbed and fragment-filled air. As I made my check to see who of my own were hurt I hoped that the damn crew members of those planes would all be hit.

My check was miraculously negative. Not a man was hit, and only two men were complaining of temporary deafness and ringing in the ears. A check by the medics would reveal if their eardrums were broken. (I correctly assumed that they would not be, as neither of the men was in great pain.) The damned planes got away; none was shot down. All we could do was to hope that they had been fragment riddled so that they would not make it back.

Before going back to bed after the raid I decided to visit the kitchen and see if there might be a cup of coffee handy. As I walked beneath the fly I heard a peculiar sounding "pop." It came from the stove side of the kitchen layout, where a bunch of men were gathered. This "pop" was followed by a gurgle as some sort of liquid was poured into a canteen cup. Then slurred words were heard in the darkness. "Drink it pretty quick, buddy," said a voice which I recognized as belonging to the mess sergeant, "if you leave it in that cup very long the inside'll turn black. Probably turns your own insides black the same way. And don't let the lieutenant find out that you've got it. He don't drink himself, and he thinks that anyone who does is a damn fool."

It was obvious that I had not made enough noise in approaching the kitchen.

I was just about to leave and return with more fanfare, kicking and humming on the way, when the sergeant turned suddenly and looked directly my way, recognizing me at once in the moonlight. He looked hurriedly from side to side, and finding no hole to jump into, looked back at me, saying the only thing he could think of: "How about a drink o' raisin jack, Lootenant?" He handed me a cup.

It tasted good. Any resolve I may have had to spoil the party left as that lovely stuff went down. I had it refilled. The other members of the group, noticing this, began to return to the kitchen from the surrounding shadows. There were only about five of us to start, the mess sergeant and four of his friends. We all had a drink out of a bottle while the cups were going into a washpan. A cook wiped the cups and passed them around. We all sat down in a circle around a packing box and began to sing like a bunch of vodka-primed Cossacks.

Between verses of the bawdy songs the sergeant waxed lucidly proud of his little moonshine project. He had gathered a few glass jars—"liberated them from the Marines," he said—and he had perforated the tops slightly, to somewhat control the fermentation. He had then misappropriated a few raisins and some corn meal. Water, sugar, time, and the fermenting capabilities of the Guadalcanal climate had done the rest. It was a brilliant achievement, a splendid morale building effort, and the sergeant was unable to see why he should not be decorated on the spot for its doing— "What other non-commishined officer could have don anyshing half sho shmart? Where, indeed, could anyone of such fine cababilishties be found to sherve in a common ordinary, shtinking Infantry outfit. . . ."

The next song was "The Road to Mandalay," and the coconut groves echoed its robust resonance. It sounded pretty good, for a fact, and it brought forth a burst of applause (or comment) from the tents nearby. I noticed at the time that our little singing circle was being strengthened in number by infiltrating reinforcements. These late comers, attracted by the noise and frustrated in their efforts to get some sleep, had decided to rise and find out what it was all about. Finding it to be genuine merriment with official approval, indicated by the lieutenant's presence, they remained and joined in the song (after returning to their respective tents for their canteen cups). Another and another jar of that terriffic joy-juice was drawn from hiding, and the tropical night became increasingly filled with exultant song.

I made a contribution to the evening myself. I sang "Boots" in a way that must have caused Kipling to turn over in his grave, finishing the last note just as the OD of some adjoining Marine outfit walked into the area. He came stumbling over our way flashlight in hand, with the hope of obtaining an answer to his Colonel's petulant question of: "Who in the hell is castrating those 5,000 cats over there?"

Someone promptly shoved a canteen cup into the hand of this unknown Marine officer, and he stayed with us. I have always regretted that I failed to secure his name, because he had an excellent bass voice (the hardest kind of a drunk to find, as many say) also because he was not always trying to steal the lead from the baritone, who was me. If all Marine-Army relations could have been as *figuratively* harmonious as ours were that night, the Pacific campaigns, I know, would have proceeded with far greater smoothness.

Recollections of the closing hours of that evening are dim, but it seems, (and I have verified since) that another plane came over and straddled us with another stick of bombs. I remember the whole group scurrying for their holes, with the first sergeant's voice roaring all-important orders above the roar of the motors and the bomb explosions. "Holt them canteen cups steady, you bastards! Don't spill that stuff! Drink it in your holes!"

APPROACH TO BATTLE

In a dream the next morning a huge spider was moving closer and closer to me—a spider about twice my own size—and I seemed to be hopelessly tangled in a net of adhesive coated half-inch rope, woven high in the tops of huge jungle trees. How I got there I did not know, but I was silently screaming for help and writhing like the damned as I woke at dawn to find myself in my own cot, but fully clothed and tangled and rolled in my mosquito bar so that I could hardly breathe. I felt cotton-mouthed and dehydrated, trying to collect scattered thoughts into a dried up brain which seemed to be rattling back and forth in my skull.

My first waking thought was that I was back in my deer hunting camp in New Caledonia, getting up after a rugged night with Butch and Frank, brother subalterns (and disciples of the flagon) in the old AT company. I staggered to my feet, walked out of my tent and straightaway forgot my hangover in admiration of a beautiful ocean scene.

Dawn was just breaking and the waters of Point Cruiz were barely rippled. The groves were cool and green, and the waters were beautifully blue. Then a plane—a Grumman Torpedo job—roared over my head, its motor straining in takeoff. I walked out onto the strip of sandy beach, took off my clothes, and waded out into the warm but refreshing water, breaststroking back and forth where it was little more than knee-deep. I gargled a few mouthfuls of salt water to remove a dark, muddy taste; then I went back to loll in the sands. No one else in the area was awake.

I pulled a well-worn and faded pair of fatigues out of my bag and put them on directly over my atabrine-stained skin. Underwear, we had found, was more of a nuisance than a help in the equatorial tropics. It quickly sweated into a sodden mass, and then "crawled up and packed." Very few men wore it for that reason; also, it was almost impossible to keep laundered. Simplicity, we learned, was the keynote of jungle warfare and jungle living.

Simple weapons, simple clothing and equipment, simple tactics were to prove themselves time and time again in the Pacific war.

I relaxed and let the light breeze dry me off. By the time I got back to the company area the cooks had been up and about for some minutes and a steaming GI can of hot coffee had become the center of all organizational and individual activity.

The kitchen area, I noted, was spic and span and except for a few red eyes, there was no indication of revelry the night before. The gang was generally observing an amused sort of silence. I was ready to take good care of anyone who would refer in any way to events of the previous night, but no one made that mistake. We all sat down and leaned our backs against coconut trees, looking dreamily out to sea as we sipped that delicious black stuff.

We had a formation after breakfast and I inspected the guns and ammunition, finding them to be in perfect shape. Packs were checked for the amount of rations required by the alert orders, (two days of Type "C"—we had no "K" at that time) and I then went back to my cot for a luxurious nap, telling the men to do the same if they felt like it. They stared round-eyed at this generosity, and not without evidencing a certain amount of suspicion. As they walked away I heard a phrase or two delivered with lifted eyebrow: "We who are about to die—what's all this leisure for?"

The flaps of my tent were rolled; looking up, I found a beautifully patterned screen of palm fronds between me and the cool, white clouds. The zephyr had grown into a healthy breeze and was adding the last finishing touch to a perfect Guadalcanal morning. The booming of artillery from the south and the bursts of machine gun fire seemed natural now, but somehow the scene on that beach seemed more removed from the thought of war than any environment we had known since leaving home. Warm sun, cool shade, blue waters and sky, the embracing tenderness of a tropical paradise on all sides of us.

Pretty soon the traffic on the beach road in front of our area began to hum to and fro; each passing vehicle raised a small wake of coral dust. Men got up and went about their housekeeping chores, washing the clothes they had taken off and hanging them in the sun to dry, oiling a personal weapon—rifle, pistol or trench knife.

I sewed a few holes in my mosquito net and then sat down to take apart and clean the bolt of my rifle—just to pass the time away, for I knew that it was in perfect shape. It was kept so by the thin poplin case. The finely woven cloth protected the weapon from the effects of moisture and yet would not cause condensation during rapid tropical changes in temperature, as leather and heavy canvas cases always seem to do. I went through the old ritual of wiping off the cocking piece and the firing pin rod, the firing pin spring, the striker, the sleeve, the insides of the bolt and bolt sleeve. Then I did the same to the friction surfaces inside the receiver, the lug races and recesses, the magazine walls. An oily patch through the barrel finished the job and I carefully put the weapon back into the case and tied it, muzzle down, to the front pole of my tent. I withdrew the little Lyman Alaskan scope and checked it over, working the scope mount levers to see if there had been any dirt lodged within their bearings. A soft handkerchief served to clean the lenses on the outside surfaces. Assured that it was in perfect order, I carefully restored the scope to its leather case and looked about for something else to do.

Finding nothing at first glance, I gave up the search and dozed off on my cot, resting my eyes in the cool shadow of my tent top.

Later on that morning artillery, emplaced uncomfortably close to us, began to blaze away, apparently in support of our people up forward. It seemed funny, being where we were. It was well nigh impossible for us to visualize (from where we rested at the moment) the fact that men were fighting and dying only a few thousand yards away. That feeling is one of the amazing impressions of warfare which is so evident to the newcomer and which is taken completely for granted—and hardly noticed—by the old timer.

The long awaited word came that morning. Russel Hill, my platoon sergeant, called me at ten o'clock to answer the company phone. I heard Captain Cosby's voice, "Pick up and move to Burnt Knob as soon as you can, George . . . bring the .30s only —leave the .50s behind. Ferry is on top of his objective now and he needs you to help hold it." We were ready in ten minutes, and in another five we were loaded on a group of the Company's three-quarter ton trucks. Within half an hour, the two reserve platoons of "H" Company were assembled at Burnt Knob to receive final orders from regimental.

We had left all excess property in the area to be guarded by the kitchen force and had gone forward light, with a view to carrying a maximum amount of weapons and ammunition with our column. But at Burnt Knob we found that Ferry had sent back an urgent request for even more ammunition and more food. He wanted it brought up by native bearers with my column so that it would be protected on the unguarded trail.

The native bearers, who were more than reasonably courageous chaps, were none the less cognizant of the dangers to be encountered along the trail and were understandably concerned about their hides. When they were fired on they would habitually break and run, and if they had no escort at the time they would most likely fail to reassemble. In considering that they owed no particular loyalty to us it is not at all surprising that they behaved with this little regard toward the protection—much less the safe delivery—of loads of food and ammunition they were carrying. Early after our arrival at Burnt Knob we learned that a group of these native carriers was to accompany us, and a few armed natives were to go along as auxiliary guards. This made us feel better for at that time we were inclined to overestimate the value of jungle natives' services. This feeling of increased security was not entirely justified. It was true that natives were of great value for some purposes, but at that time we tended to give them credit for much more common sense than they later proved to have.

Lieutenant Stan, Assistant Regimental Supply Officer, told me that we would have these natives with us as we passed his outfit on the first subcrest below the top of Burnt Knob, where he was supervising supply operations and dealing with the native carrying parties. He had a small supply dump there—piles of boxes on improvised dunnage with strips of Jap canvas hung over to protect it from rain. And he was continually on the move.

He had had little respite from the continuous grind of complying with desperately urgent requests for food and ammunition from the three committed battalions, and he resultantly had little opportunity to properly organize his supply depot. It was necessary for him to keep running around to personally supervise things. Stan was a hard worker and a respected officer. "You're going to have a hell of a time with these people," he said as we marched past. "Don't know how many you are going to take along with you, most likely it will depend on how many we will be able to scrape up. Ferry has asked for a lot of stuff." I thanked Stan for the info and went on by telling him that I would be back to see him as soon as I got the dope from regimental.

We had detrucked below Stan's dump, at the only turnaround point for the vehicles. The empty trucks were soon grinding their way back over the roller-coaster-washboard of Edson's Ridge. I rested the men on the trail and then walked on up to the Regimental command post where Captain Cosby and Colonel George were waiting.

When he saw me approaching Cosby looked up from the situation map he was holding. "All set, George?" he asked. When I answered in the affirmative he turned around and spoke to Colonel George, who, seated cross-legged on the ground, was enjoying a canteen-cup of tea. "Your namesake is here, Colonel. I've got the map and plan here at hand and can orient him right now. Do you want to talk to him first?"

While Cosby spoke, Colonel George had eased up from the

ground with athletic grace, setting his canteen cup down. "Go ahead and give him the dope, Cosby, but I want to talk to his gang before they jump off. Can't let a bunch of men go out to get shot at without saying goodbye, can I?" With that the colonel went by us towards the resting platoon. In the meantime, Cosby gave me final instructions and answered the questions I asked. The regimental and battalion plans were already clear in my mind, and all we had to do was to join the main body of the battalion, moving along the same trail they had used and overcoming on the way any infiltrated enemy that might be blocking it. Satisfied that I had been completely informed, I turned and trotted down the ridge to catch up with Colonel George.

George, always undesirous of speaking *up* from his five feet plus to a crowd, began looking around for a platform to stand on. He usually relied on nearby jeeps and large supply boxes for this purpose, but there were none around. But there was a tree with a gnarl and a short limb projecting at heights of four and eight feet respectively from the trunk.

The colonel took a quick look at the tree, and then ran and bounded up its trunk, catching the gnarl under his left foot and grasping above his head to get a grip with his left hand on the limb. Braced thus, with one leg dangling and his right arm free to gesticulate, he delivered an excellent pep talk, peppering his speech throughout with a picturesque brand of profanity. Sans the profanity it went something like this:

"Well, Gang, you've waited a long time for this. Colonel Ferry has gone ahead and cracked this damned sector wide open. He is sitting right now on a hot spot, the most important damned hill in the war today, and I'll bet my last Bank of Indo-China franc he will stay there with the help you're going to give him.

"The slant eyes are trying like hell to knock him off, and the battalion is piling 'em up three and four deep on the ground in front. All he needs up there right now are some good machine guns and mortars and some good men to shoot em, and you have both. Now get the hell up there and make that hill safe as my back yard in Louisiana, so I can come up for a visit! You know how nervous it makes me when I am shot at. If you run into anything on that trail, shoot your way through it. Tap it on the wire and tell me about it if you should be held for any length of time. Should take you about five hours hard walking to get there. So long!"

Stan led a group of the natives up to join our column. They were a funny, fuzzy-haired lot of chaps, all toothy grins and black as the ace of spades. They were of smaller-than-average stature— the standard type of inhabitant usually found in malarial South Pacific areas. They were not the more nearly ideal physical speci-

Hideo

This is something we didn't encounter so often, but still had to keep the possibility in mind. The Japs seemed to use trees more for observation purposes than for sniping, but every now and then there would be proven instances of shooting from trees.

Naturally, we'd never get a view like this of a Jap in a tree. They were far too camouflage-conscious for that. Most of the time we would spray the suspect trees with BAR fire and hope for something to fall. Sometimes Japs tied themselves into position so that they remained in place even if killed.

Notice the manner in which this rifleman (he's no sniper) holds his weapon. Because of the great length and weight of the Jap service rifles, they learned to fire them in ways that the forearm would be artificially supported. This was true on the ground as well as in trees. They liked to take rest on sandbags, log parapets, or anything else. This chap is making good use of a limb. Holding the butt to the shoulder with the fingers of the non-trigger hand was another common Jap practice. It was the standard method of firing the bipod supported Nambu light machine guns, frequently carried over in shooting the rifles. If you didn't care how long it would take you to operate the bolt this method was all right.

mens which we had seen in New Caledonia and were to see later in the Fiji Islands. In those places the natives were unharassed by constantly recurring malaria, consequently they grew up heavy-framed and well developed.

But, scrawny as our carriers were, they were hardened and toughened to a state of physical ruggedness far beyond that which any ordinary American has been forced to attain since our pioneer days. They were almost entirely indifferent to the things which we regarded as "hardships." Sleeping on the ground and eating food which they foraged from the jungle enroute were parts of their everyday lives and their ability to carry heavy loads long distances in mountainous jungle country was amazing. I do not believe that the ones who worked for us would have averaged more than a 130 pounds in weight, yet they could carry more than half of that poundage and still outmarch a tough, lightly armed American Infantryman.

They were dressed in varied sorts of clothes. Many of them wore the traditional sarongs of the islands, but most had khaki shorts and ragged upper garments. None of their clothing gave protection from thorns—so necessary to a white man's continued existence in the jungle. Their knees and arms were bare to the pricking of thorns and nettles; they wore no footgear. A few of them carried knives, but most of them went entirely unarmed.

Of the natives Stan brought over, four were armed guards. These men were bare'footed like the others, but they were uniformed in light khaki shirts and shorts, and were armed with Short Model Lee-Enfields, carrying their .303 ammunition in improvised bandoleers. They did not look particularly effective to me, and this initial sizing up that I gave them—completely at variance with the opinions of my men—proved later to be accurate. They were good scouts, junglewise, but they were not good men to stand and fight when subjected to heavy fire from automatic weapons, artillery or mortars.

It took only a few minutes to place the natives in my column, which had been organized with myself, First Sergeant Prunckle, and twenty rifle and Browning Auto Rifle men in front, followed by the natives and the men carrying the guns and by the remainder of the riflemen in a rear guard formation. All of the riflemen were carrying boxes of ammunition which they could quickly drop to wield their weapons if the column should be fired on. As the column was finally made up and we took off on the well trampled trail leading down and north from Edson's Ridge, Colonel George walked alongside me and passed a joke or two about "Ferry and his gang of rowdy Chicago hoodlums." When we had covered the first mile he turned to walk back up the trail alone, waving aside my offer of an escort. I could not help but admire the courage of any man who would voluntarily walk alone on that trail where every huge rooted tree and every bit of green jungle undergrowth might conceal a Jap infiltrator.

We continued along the wellworn trail, which was tracked solidly in most places and was sidelined with several strands of combat telephone wire (double strand wire small in diameter, which once laid is considered expended—no recovery contemplated).

The trail led us over and through a variety of footing and cover for the next few minutes march. First we wound along a grassy hillside, skirting close to the top fringe of a heavy jungle which filled the valley below. Then suddenly the path dipped down into the jungle and became more or less of a tunnel cut through the almost solid undergrowth. The ground now was spongy underfoot and in the center of the trail where the bulk of the battalion had walked, the yellowish, oozing mud was ankle deep. The path was laced with slippery, tripping roots and the going accordingly became slow. Progress was often blocked at chest level by large vines, their knotted thickness having withstood the slashes of many machetes, and men had to shift their heavy loads from their backs and crawl under them. Many men fell because of the poor footing, pushing themselves back up from the mud with violent curses framed on their lips, and their fatigues sodden-yellowed with island clay. Fortunately the trail did not traverse any of the tortuous swamps which fill the lower areas of Guadalcanal. That was a blessing; things were rough enough as they were.

The route over which we were travelling was different, but not vastly so, from many we had walked before on other islands. Doubtless a little more densely enclosed on sides and top by heavier vegetation, perhaps a little more dampaired, but there was something else—a sort of difference in atmosphere which we could all feel, but not explain. It may have been the knowledge of danger which we knew waited at the end. I choose to believe that it was a spiced combination of many physical and psychological factors —something that a hunted animal might feel. It was a stimulating sensation.

Things that we saw then we would remember forever—each frightened bird disturbing the cover on the side of the trail, each small twig springing back up from a hobnailed footprint in the mud, the unmetered sequence of rifle shots up front. It was a strange, unaccountable sort of feeling, peculiar to that battlefield and no other. I was to later discover that each new engagement, each fresh intimacy with death carried an equivalent impression all its own—an individual taste-thrill produced by a special combination of ingredients. And that, I think is the only lure which seduces the veteran of past battles into voluntarily facing death over and over again.

There was Jap sign galore on the trail—numerous footprints mixed in with our own, and bits of Jap clothing and equipment. But none of the signs was fresh and there was nothing to be alarmed over. The column, however, was now moving with an increasing tenseness, in spite of the dulling fatigue, felt by many even at that early stage in the march. Too many of the men were burdened with heavy loads of equipment—guns and ammunition.

We were deeper than ever in dark jungle and the path was constantly varying, leading steeply up and then down so that most of the time we were busy clawing with both hands at roots and vines. And our movement was leading us closer and closer to the source of the rifle, automatic weapons, and mortar fire going on up ahead —leading us closer to the moment when we would all face the acid test of closein Infantry combat as part of a rifle battalion.

Packstraps were cutting painfully into shoulders and the backsides of our fatigues sagged, dripping with sweat, as we climbed one little hill after another. But as we drew nearer the fight we noticed these annoyances less and less. After we had climbed a particularly steep rise I called a halt. I sat down for a breather myself after checking and being reassured by finding a reasonable state of "vigilance" up front in the formation.

Sergeant Prunckle sat down close by and mopped the accumulated sweat from his forehead with a swipe of his herculean forearm. A particularly rugged product of several good Chicago boxing gymnasiums, he was well respected by both the soldiers and the ruffians of the outfit. I accepted his attitude as strong evidence that the march was a hard one. If *he* was feeling it, the other men must be well nigh exhausted. My own particular state of fatigue was not at all indicative of that of the average man in the column because I had not been carrying a gun or a tripod—only a rifle and my own pack.

I had slipped off my pack and was enjoying the ecstacy of relief which always accompanies the removal of the tight, welt-raising bands, which on lightweights like myself always seem to grind unmercifully because the only insulation between them and the collar bone is a thin layer of skin and a well worn fatigue jacket.

Seated with my back against a fallen log, I had just begun to enjoy the brief rest when I was startled into a hammer-pulsed lather of excitement. The leaves on the brush some twenty yards down the trail had been moved suddenly and noisily by something heavy and close to the ground. I threw my rifle over and covered the spot, searching for the form of a crouching Jap in the field of the scope. I could see nothing for the next few breathless moments.

Hideo

Here we see a battalion of Japanese Infantry getting across a stream with dry feet and clean rifles. An American unit in a similar situation would probably have splashed through, soaking themselves and their gear, and taking about 15 minutes longer to get to the far side. If Engineers were attached we might have erected some sort of a foot bridge.

Building a bridge such as this is the work of only a few minutes for a Japanese pioneer detachment. A few axe and machete blows provide the necessary number of bamboo trunks, and bamboo peelings furnish the lashings if rope is unavailable. The pilings are quickly placed and the leading platoon supplies the men to stand and support the bridge while the battalion is trotting across. Naturally, if the far bank is suspect, the reconnaissance elements will have thrown out a perimeter defense to protect the crossing.

Despite the fact that we had seen demonstrations of this sort by our own Philippine Scouts before the war, most American officers failed to learn this trick. It took us two years of fighting—often with cold, wet posteriors—before we learned to make such good use of available bamboo and common sense.

Then he slowly appeared, with myself, Prunckle, and a scout looking on. I kept observing him through the bright field of the scope.

"He" was a huge, scimitar-tusked boar, who pushed his head out through a solid sheaf of leaves, and stared at us with apparent distaste, something like Milady with her face between the shower curtains. He blinked his eyes three times, snorted, then twisted and ran viciously through the brush alongside the trail, snapping small vines and rattling along like ten charging Japs. He alerted the whole sprawled column into a palsied sort of readiness. It pleased me that the men did not fire at him and I am of course glad that I also abstained, but it is with some irony that I realize at this moment that of the score or so wild boar which have fallen to my rifle since then, none could match his tusks in size. There are few trophies in my collection that I would value half as highly as that wicked looking head-—or just the tusks.

The boar incident provided me a convenient reason to get the column moving again. The frightening portion of it occurred at exactly ten minutes after we had sat down—the break had been of exactly ten minutes duration. So with our tenseness broken by a hearty laugh, we struggled to our feet, slung our packs and rifles and moved off, following our trail which was now leading deeper into the jungle. A guess I made at that point, that we would not see daylight until we finally reached the heights of Mount Austen (Hill 27) itself, proved later to be correct. Our current route was well inside the rim of dense vegetation which I had so often seen indicated on the aerial photographs by a darkened mottling, deceptively similar in appearance to the texture of a cotton bath mat.

We passed some piles of Japanese fired shell cases, neatly stacked offside the trail, also a box of assorted Jap machine gun parts which had been dumped into the mud in a hurried effort at destruction. The trail was well marked by discarded bits of paper—food and candy wrappers of our own for the most part.

If it were possible, the march became even more difficult as we went on. Men were no longer walking and climbing by themselves. The condition of the "trail" had now become such that we had to pass equipment from hand to hand in order to negotiate the almost perpendicular slopes. We were grateful for the presence of vines and brush to hang onto because without them we would have needed alpinist equipment in order to complete the march. There were frightening instances in that trek where trail windings and other terrain conditions absolutely precluded the observance of normal march security, laying the column wide open to ambush while its men fought with the natural obstacles of the jungle. At such times, all our hands were occupied and only a few men could have quickly brought weapons to bear had we been fired on.

The battalion before us had taken three days to make the trip which we were trying to make in a single afternoon. It was impossible for me to accurately estimate the distance we had covered, and at that time it was highly doubtful if anyone, even Colonel Ferry himself, knew just what mileage had been made by the battalion over that route. So as the march continued, my hopes of getting my column to Hill 27 by dark dwindled to nothing, and I began to turn over in my mind the thought of getting someone forward to Ferry to inform him of our inability to deliver his guns as soon as he would want them.

About that time we saw some of our own men coming toward us on the trail. After we got close we identified them as two walking wounded, returning down the trail without escort. One was a sergeant who had been shot through the biceps, the bullet passing through the bone making a nasty hole in exit. I asked him how far it was to the battalion and he replied that it was four miles.

"Four miles!" If that were true we would never get there by dusk. Not on a bet! The trail was a climb and a crawl in its present length, and afternoon had already set in. Ferry was up there, desperate for those guns and ammunition. What a hell of a thing to not be able to get them to him! I decided to nurse the outfit along as well as I could, getting them as far as possible, and then I would leave Prunckle in charge and go on ahead with one or two men and contact the battalion before dark to give Ferry the unwelcome news—no guns for the night.

In the next mile's climb—the most tortuous I saw during the entire Pacific war—three of my men collapsed—not from mere exhaustion, but from the killing type of lung-bursting overexhaustion that strikes a soldier whose will to keep on going is greater than his bodily endurance and strength. I talked it over with Prunckle, and after another few hundred yards I halted the column, oriented the men on the security plan for the night, and left Prunckle to bring them forward the next morning. Many were so tired that I feared for their alertness that night, though it seemed that Japs would be highly unlikely to get around that far to the battalion's rear. The jungle was just too dense, even for them.

One of the toughest walkers in the regiment asked to accompany me forward. I was glad of that because I could not with fairness expect any of the men to be able to walk on with me. They had been taking turns lugging the heavier mortar and machine gun equipment all through the march. We took off at once, feeling rather alone as we left the outfit with three miles of unpatrolled and rugged trail ahead, where the possibility of enemy infiltration would increase as we got closer and closer to the fighting.

We were to make those remaining three miles in an hour and a

half, not letting our breathing subside for a moment below a gasp-
ing rate. The trip seemed like the last hundred yards of a quarter-
mile run. But we were no longer held back by the platoon or burdened with heavy baggage. Over one ridge after another, through
the ever-lasting jungle, we stumbled and fell, wishing now and then
that we had elected to remain with the outfit back on the trail!
But we kept going at an even pace so that the athlete's second
wind, which both of us could call upon at that time, broke through
the feeling of fatigue and kept us going. When we did fall, we
helped each other up, and went on without a break. At times I
mulled over the possible silliness of taking myself forward with
but one other man along that trail—just for the sake of bringing
some negative information to a harassed battalion commander.

Soon we passed a stretcher with a dead doughboy lying in it.
We did not even need to stop to see what the story was. That man
had been gutshot sometime early in the fight and four of his buddies
had started to carry him back out over that unforgettable bit of
trail. In spite of large compress bandages, his bullet-riddled body
had emptied the greater part of its blood, pooling it in the canvas
of the stretcher until it actually overflowed. Death there had not
taken very long. The carriers, knowing that they were badly needed
back at the fight, had not taken time to bury him, but had left him
offside the trail where he had died. Then they hastened back to
risk a similar fate on the fire-swept slopes of that terrible hill.

Possibly intense fatigue had dulled my imagination because I
was strangely unaffected at the sight. Something inside had given
me surcease from the familiar pain that I remembered so well from
previous observations of freshly killed men.

The mild snapping of the bullets passing overhead had by now
changed into sharp, whiplike cracks, and the primary sound of
small arms fire had suddenly grown loud. The tearing of leaves
above and the whine and rattle of ricochets through the air and
off limbs went on as before, but now in tremendously increased
volume. The fire we heard so loudly (though the jungle muffles
sound) was not sporadic. It was a constant, hot exchange of bursts
and individual shots, blending into each other so as to make an
almost steady rippling sound, like strings of firecrackers going off
close by your ear. And as I listened, a sinister conclusion was
reached in my mind. *The Japs were returning ten shots to our one!*
The isolated, greatly outnumbered, and unsupplied garrison on
Hill 27 was undergoing a severe counter attack.

As we topped a final rise we met on the path a young-looking
medical officer and two aid men coming back towards us. The men
were bearded, haggard, dog-tired. The doc looked awfully pale
and underweight.

"How much farther?" I asked. I had never seen either of these men or the doc before. They were apparently from an attached field hospital unit. "A tough 200 yards," answered the doc, and as we went past he added a further word, visibly shuddering as he spoke, "You'll see another dead man on ahead. Started to carry him back but he died right away. Didn't seem to be hit so bad, but it would kill a healthy man to be carried over this Goddamn trail."

With a cold feeling in the pit of my stomach, I realized the truth of his statement. Evacuation of seriously wounded under present circumstances was an utter impossibility. God pity those who had been hit in the lung and intestinal cavities. There was no way of getting them out, and with torn intestines, internal bleeding, and the infectious nature of the Guadalcanal climate, death would quickly follow.

It was very late afternoon and darkness was not far off as we contacted the first outposts in the battalion's rear. I simply found myself staring into the muzzle of an M1 as I rounded a bend in the trail, and the alert sentry told me to come forward and be examined. As I approached I noticed with pride that another rifleman in the adjacent cover had also drawn a bead on me.

The rifle was lowered and the sentry smiled at me in recognition, his teeth gleaming out through a tangle of black beard. "Howdy, lieutenant," he whispered; "Looks as though you got here just in time for the fireworks. Gonna have a reg'lar Fourth of July up there on that hill tonight. Mebbe down here too." His eyeballs rolled suggestively towards his partner as he said the last words. I walked on, wondering just what he meant by saying that there was "gonna be fireworks." What in the hell did he think was going on now? When he talked, I could hardly hear him for the firing. A bit further on we were challenged and passed by a sergeant in charge of a few men who were guarding a water hole. He pointed out a path leading toward Ferry's command post, which was located on a 45° slope. In a few moments I saw light through the trees ahead—pale light from the evening sky, and in the foreground a broad expanse of comparatively clear jungle floor, scene of a life and death struggle, or rather a scene close by life and death struggle. The real fight was raging on ahead some fifty yards, on the high bare top of Mount Austen—one of a thousand peaks in the Solomons, but one with a name that would be long remembered by a small group of Americans—and the few Japanese that survived.

THE FIGHT FOR MOUNT AUSTEN

Enemy fire was being directed at the battalion from two sides, for the maneuvering element of the Jap counterattacking force had gotten a foothold on a knoll overlooking "F" Company on the battalion's right flank. This fact had a strong bearing on the behavior of the men on the reverse slope of the hill (mostly battalion headquarters people). They were pinned down in their holes by machine gun fire and mortar explosions. Those who did not have holes (there had been no time to dig—the only ones available had been dug by the Japs) were making the best of a few defiladed areas and the protection afforded by the always-handy roots of large jungle trees. Individual movement from point to point within the perimeter was accomplished by dashing from cover to cover. The only safe place was a dry stream bed which was used as a route for the men who were carrying water. Each water carrier was loaded down with ten or more canteens, held clustered together by the cap-chains.

The perimeter was egg shaped and lay around the hill top like a crown of thorns, the larger curve to the front. That bigger side of the egg shape was the portion which was withstanding the main Jap effort—the only part being attacked by movement, though the entire perimeter was under fire. The sharp end of the "egg" was trailing down the reverse slope, and within it were the headquarters installations of the unit. Our path led us into this area, to Ferry's command post.

Men were disposed along the path, crowded somewhat, and digging in as well as they could while under fire. The Japs had left an improvised handrail along the steeper sections of the path which was a great aid in climbing. Footing was extremely poor and, with the necessity for taking cover from time to time, the going was very slow indeed. Cover alongside the path was cut away in swaths in many places. These "swaths" were Japanese fire lanes which they had evidently planned to use in the defense of the feature but for some reason had not. We could thank the diversionary efforts of our other two battalions for that. Their fight on the other side was what had enabled us to take the Japs by surprise. Had those fire lanes been covered, the Second Battalion would have never gotten to the top of that hill in one piece.

There were other proofs that the enemy's initial surprise had been almost complete—that they had been entirely fooled by the pressure from the Third and First Battalions, attacking inward from the coast. The Japs had shifted many of their weapons to counter the first-felt threats, and had come to realize their mistake entirely too late. An American battalion, moving in from the inland stretch of "impenetrable" jungle, had squatted on the hill behind them.

It was just another outflanking maneuver—the old tactical cliche—"the long left hook"—as ancient as the hills in warfare, but always practical.

The Jap mortars were mounted close to us, for as I walked along, crouching low in the open areas, I could clearly hear the champagne-bottle "pops" on the other side of the crest. Each time we would all duck and wait for the knee-mortar shell to come rattling down through the leaves and branches. Most of the "shells" were really grenades fitted for launching from knee-mortars (more properly called grenade launchers). They were a feeble sort of an affair, loud in explosion but dangerous only when they scored a direct hit on a foxhole or made a lucky strike with a fragment. They would usually sputter before they went off and give ample warning of their presence, and though they did kill a few men they were far less effective than our own grenades. The regular knee-mortar shells were entirely different. They carried a much larger charge of explosive and were many times more destructive. Built smooth-sided and bottle-shaped, with an expanding flange to fill the rifled grooves in the mortar tube, they did not tumble in flight, but nosed over naturally and detonated with real authority the instant they struck the earth.

Less than half way up to the CP we got a dose of knee-mortar fire. I hit the ground as a grenade exploded on the path in front of me, so close that the concussion slapped my clothing against me with stinging force. I thought fragments had struck my shoulders and back, and it took a few second's examination to convince me that I was still unhit. Those hurried examinations later became a routine procedure. We got used to doing it several times each day. Rise up from the dirt, shake your head, curse, and feel all over for blood.

Just before I got to the CP—or rather as I walked into it, I took in at a glance one of the most vivid memories I now retain from the entire war. It was the battalion aid station—or rather an excuse for an aid station. All of the equipment being used there had been carried forward on the backs of the medical officer and his aid men. There were two stretchers, half a dozen blankets, and a small kit of medicine and bandages. For aid station personnel there were two aid men and the battalion surgeon, Captain Phillip Cecala. For patients there were some dozen hopelessly wounded men whom everyone knew would die; about ten seriously wounded whose chances were obviously small; and another thirty or so shot badly through the limbs. Many of the latter had splintered bits of bones sticking out of raw wounds. Doc was doing what he could for all of them, and that was plenty. He was saving many of their lives, enabling others to die in peace, working hard—with a pitiless sort of priority dictated by merciless circumstance. I have never since discussed that situation with Phil, but I believe that he was faced many times with the need for adjudging a man's condition too serious to be worth his time. The dying were attended to *after* treatment had been given those who had a chance of survival.

Shock was a factor to consider, too, with such a shortage of blankets. Many of the men lent ponchos and raincoats for the wounded and everyone would have fought stripped to the waist if necessary. There was no shortage of sweat-soaked clothing for the aid station, but there were not enough blankets and not enough stretchers. Wounded and dying lay on palm fronds or the damp ground. . . . I was not horrified or appalled at the time, I remember. Still, that scene in the Guadalcanal jungle is unforgettable.

The CP was just beyond the aid station, set up around an old entrenchment. Colonel Ferry and Major Wirt Butler were sitting side by side on the dome of the pillbox. Ferry was talking to the artillery liaison officer, a Marine captain named Hitt, organizing a fire plan for the night. Captain Casey, the artillery officer who was to take Hitt's place and conduct the remaining artillery support of the fight, was sitting on the ground close by. Hitt had been shot through the shoulder and was carrying his arm in a sling, but aside from a small paleness he was not badly sickened or shocked. Fortunately, he had been struck by an ordinary .25 caliber bullet and since that little needle had failed to strike a bone, it made a neat and clean hole. This was Hitt's second cluster for his Purple Heart and yet he was cheerful and bright, smiling continually as he spoke. The battalion admired him.

Major Butler was patiently cranking the field phone to get through to regimental, in order to see how they were making out toward the delivery of some urgently requested supplies. He had been cranking for some time, and he gave up the attempt just as I approached. He looked up at me, his face showing that lack of

The Japs, like all good soldiers, were very comradely. I have known several to be killed in an attempt to recover a body under fire. Probably their extreme inhumanity with prisoners stemmed partially from this feeling, augmented by the fact that they themselves would not surrender, considering the act to be the very epitome of cowardice.

Often enough their cannon-fodder was recruited from given areas and allotted directly to selected units, so that many members had been neighbors. Most of the Japanese regiments, by our own recent standards, were veteran outfits, with integrity maintained through years of the China War. Men who have endured long campaigns together become close friends. . . . That, I guess, is the reason why Watanabe here looks so annoyed over the expiring of his buddy Yamamoto, who seems to have received the attention of someone's Garand.

expression common to all tired doughboy officers. "Glad to see you, George, got some guns for us? Bring any ammunition along?" Those were his first words.

With a horrible desire to be far away, hidden in some bottomless hole, I acquainted him with the facts. . . . The balance of "H" Company was three miles back on the trail. They would not be able to get up until some time after dawn the next morning. Ferry was listening by this time, and it was he who answered, shrugging fatalistically, "Well, if we don't have the guns we will have to hold the damn hill without them. Tell the companies to allocate their ammunition carefully—don't let them fire at *anything* except well defined targets."

As Butler went to relay those instructions, Colonel Ferry brought me up to the hour on the situation of the outfit. "We took this hill with little trouble, George, everything seemed to be pointed the other way, when we walked up on it. Fell heir to this pillbox and a 75mm gun, without firing many shots. Just scared an outpost group off the place. I expected a reaction soon, figured that there would be some sort of a counterattack as soon as they had time to get it planned. But the coral underneath the sod didn't make good digging, and we were not set for it when they finally let drive at us. Swept the whole damned hill with fire and banzaied us three times. We piled 'em for that, but we paid for it. Too God-damn much!" He growled the last words as he looked over at the grisly mess in the aid station. "As I see it though, tonight is the big show. We'll keep our toe hold on this place till daylight and from then on it should be easy. The yellow bellies already have a lesson under their belts. I think we killed a hundred or so in the first few minutes of the shooting. You bed down some place here for the night—find yourself a hole—and we'll send you back at dawn to meet your outfit and hurry it up here. We could use that ammunition right now!"

Major Butler returned to the CP. The popping small arms fire which was passing over our heads after it had raked across our positions forward on the crest of the hill seemed to lull a bit in the next few moments. During this lull I heard the distinct pop of a knee-mortar somewhere on the other side of the hill. I shouted a warning and ducked just before the grenade fell and exploded between Butler and myself. I hurriedly rose and went through the old routine, feeling all over myself for wounds and looking up sheepishly when I found none. Butler had ignored the blast completely, calmly puffing a cigaret while the fragments sang past his ears. "Y'know," he drawled, "those damned things have to go off in your lap before you can feel 'em, don't they, George?" I lyingly agreed, and left the CP without delay. I had just seen Art Hantel about 30 yards up on the hill, and he had motioned with his arm, inviting me to share his foxhole. He was a grand guy. I'll never forget his hospitality that night.

It was beginning to get dark, so I successfully throttled any curious urge I may have had to go up on the very top of that hill and wander back and forth amid the foxholes, which were filled with trigger happy doughboys. Art and I took turns sleeping from early evening on. The march had made me so tired that keeping awake was almost an impossibility, even while our shells whirred overhead and exploded just beyond the crest, and while a thousand or so Americans and Japs were shooting, screaming, and throwing grenades with wild abandon.

During the periods that I stood watch I saw a fulfilment of our expectations that there would be increased Japanese activity as soon as night began to set in. A group of Japs crawled up on "F" Company's part of the line, a short distance to our right front, and attempted to break through by outright assault. Sergeant Humply, a tall, brawny platoon leader of Company "F," cautioned his men to hold to their holes—to sit tight and shoot anything that moved in front. Three times that night he had to jump out of his hole and wait while a Jap grenade inside continued to sputter and finally exploded. Each time he would jump back in as soon as the explosion occurred, to avoid—as much as possible—the hot replying rifle and MG fire. The Japs had his hole located perfectly, but his luck held and it did not do them any good.

All along the front of the hill, where "E" Company's line held fast, the Japs attacked, using grenades and employing infiltration tactics. Moving up the slope, the Jap had the advantage of being able to see our movements against the sky, while his were effectually hidden by the shadowy background of the valley. Lieutenant Geisel remained on the very top of the hill and gave directions to the artillery for part of the line, and it was partly through these efforts that the Jap attacks were badly chopped up by artillery fire before they reached the crest. He would hear the yelling and the movements far down on the hill, denoting the start of another rush which would culminate near the lines in a banzai charge, and he would give the dope to Captain Casey, who would phone directions back to the guns. The shells ordered by Casey usually got over in time to tear up and thin the attacking ranks considerably, and sometimes to completely destroy them.

All around the front of the hill, throughout the length of that staggered line of riflemen, it was a do-or-die effort to hold for the night at all cost. The men of that line had been there hard at it since noon of that day, holding on tightly while the fire of assorted Jap flat-trajectory weapons poured steadily upon their positions, bullets crackling and snapping around their ears as they made desperate attempts to entrench themselves in the unyielding coral. They had heard the enemy fire build up in frightful crescendo, as more and more weapons were brought to bear on their exposed position. It was a sore thumb—that hill—a mound of grass, sod with coral beneath, with jungle all around. And the enemy was making full use of that jungle—enjoying to the fullest the advantage of firing upon a helplessly exposed target from good cover. Regardless of the overall strategic importance of the top of Mount Austen, its little garrison was locally held at a tactical disadvantage.

Knee-mortars, of course, had been banging away from the start, but along toward evening a new and louder series of blasts were heard and felt. The Japs were now able to place the hill under the fire of *heavy* mortars. Men clung tighter and tighter to the bottoms of their overly-shallow emplacements as one after another of the larger 90mm shells burst on the hilltop. Their blasts continued and grew more frequent as night came on, and their explosions glared brilliantly when it became dark, lighting the entire hilltop with each burst.

After dark, Art and I experienced some trouble. Japs moving around "F" Company's flank got on the ground above us and set up a machine gun—a Nambu light—and sighted the thing right across the top of our hole, which was deep enough to leave a safety margin of about two inches when we crouched as low as possible. And to add insult to injury, the Japanese fired half-tracers in each clip. They poured them directly over our heads, making us feel like the upper edge of the lower four ring while a rapid fire group is forming in the bull at six o'clock. Occasionally the lower half of that cone of fire would spatter into the rear lip of our foxhole and sting our faces and hands with flying bits of mud and coral. The worst of it was that we were absolutely helpless through it all. We were inside the ring of the perimeter and were therefore forbidden to fire at anything not actually coming into our holes with us—a necessary precaution, taken to prevent us from shooting each other.

Each time either Art or I attempted to rise, that gun would cut loose and send another clip over, streaking the air around our ears with tracers. Finally I had to get up, when Sergeant Humply came down to get some more grenades for his platoon. His men had thrown all they had at Japs who were trying to crawl up in the darkness, and resupply was a matter of life and death. We finally located an unopened box and had to break it open and peel each grenade out of its individual taped cardboard tube. The effort took some fifteen minutes of wild scrambling around in the darkness with both of us answering innumerable challenges from nervous boys with loaded rifles. We finally got Humply's jacket filled full of unwrapped grenades, and he was able to crawl back to his position with them. Fortunately the Jap machine gunner did not open up on us while we were so long above ground. I began to have some hope that he had been killed or forced to fall back by some of the grenades that Humply had exhausted just before he crawled down. He had certainly been within grenade distance of the outer perimeter, because I could hear the snap of the bullets and the muzzle blasts as a single sound, indicating a range of less than 100 yards. If only daylight would come! We would undoubtedly see and kill that Jap with only a little light. But we did not have the ammunition to shoot aimlessly in the dark, even if we had been foolish enough to do so.

As the night went on, the Jap machine gunner resumed firing and Art and I made feeble jokes about the ease with which either of us could acquire a Purple Heart. Just to raise a hand a few inches and hope for a round of ball ammunition instead of a tracer to hit it. We jokingly decided that it would be just our luck to get a tracer.

Through the night, as we exchanged sentry responsibilities between ourselves, we passed my .45 back and forth. I would put a round into the chamber and let the hammer down to half-cock, holding the weapon in my hands so that my left thumb was ready on the hammer spur. It was comforting to have that gun with us —as it is *always* comforting at night to have a handgun around. In the confinement of a foxhole even a carbine would be difficult to manipulate against a target which might be jumping right into the hole with you. Something very short—a powerful handgun— was the only answer. We didn't have to use it that night, however.

I awoke at daylight with a guilty thought that I had gone to sleep on watch, but no—Hantel had the pistol in his hands and was sound asleep against the far wall of the hole. I woke him and cussed him roundly for having so little regard for my life. But I felt so good to be alive that morning—the dawn was such a lovely, welcome sight—that I found it impossible to be riled at anyone except the Japs. And looking back, I guess I was not as mad at *them* as I was supposed to be. It took a few minutes for the situation to dawn upon me. Good news! The men on the outer ring had held fast for the night. The Jap fire was still going on, but now greatly slackened! The battalion had held the hill for the night!

I was not the least bit tired or hungry, in spite of the fact that sleep had been spasmodic and I had not eaten since noon the day before. I looked around me and saw for the first time in full light the scene inside the perimeter. It was still the same desolate, corpse-strewn place, but there was a cheering note of hope in the sunlight.

And there was a thrill of a sort in the realization that we would have twelve hours of daylight to deal with the nocturnal animals we were fighting.

I went over to the CP, reported to Colonel Ferry, and then learned what had happened to our Jap machine gunner. While Art and I were asleep he had fired another burst off at an angle from the usual line of fire, so that it did not pour across our foxhole, but a few yards to the left. While those tracers were ripping across in an even stream, a salvo of 105mm shells came over from our artillery and landed where the Jap was. The remainder of the machine gun burst trailed off skyward, like a Roman candle swung in the hands of a youngster, and we heard no more from that chap. I was pleased. Sometimes the things these artillerymen did made you want to kiss 'em—or get 'em twice as drunk as they had ever been before!

There was more cheering news which had come by phone from regimental. A supply column was on the way up and the supply trail was being shortened and made passable for jeeps to a point farther forward. If they got through okay, we would have plenty of ammo and chow before that evening.

I said goodbye to the boys at the command post and took off on the trail to meet my column, which had been moving for an hour or so by that time. Captain Hitt, the Marine artilleryman who had been shot through the shoulder, decided to walk along with me. He was pale and still felt a little weak, but he refused to let me carry his musette bag. He tried to exchange his full canteen for the empty one of a doughboy on the hill, because "he was going back to a comfortable hospital and would not need a drink till he got there."

Before we got to the rear foot of the hill we saw some evidence of the night's fight. A fair number of dead Japs, residue of a bayonet charge, were scattered along our right flank. The survivors had withdrawn to positions from which they could fire without exposure. Fighting towards the rear of the perimeter had been moderate; it had been "hotter" on top of the hill and forward.

Hitt and myself eventually got to the trail proper. We walked along it with the cultivated fatalism of men who know that danger lurks on both sides, but that nothing can be done about it until the shooting starts. You can not creep up to each and every bit of cover and examine it before passing. The only practical solution is to walk casually along and not consider the possibilities of ambush at all. Pretty hard for a man who has a good imagination.

The first men we ran into were Hitt's relief from the Marine artillery. They had been travelling fast and light, trailing my party. As I remember there were several noncoms and a lieutenant

Hideo

This is the way the Japanese won the war in China, Indo-China, Sumatra, Borneo, and then lost it nearly everywhere else. The old Banzai Charge, which proved so effective against colonial troops and poorly armed Chinese was the outstanding feature of Japanese tactics. Based on the nineteenth century concept that cold steel could stand up against fire power, it became the very symbol of Japanese stupidity.

The soldier sketched above has probably just sprung from a covered position, where he whipped himself into a fever with a spasm of insane yelling. Maybe he remembers times in China when such behavior paralyzed with fear his poorly armed and starved opponents. He feels that death under these heroic circumstances he has created will give him a sure ticket to heaven.

He makes a big target in this sort of charge, and usually announces his exact location during the rush with a lot of loud yelling. The poorest shot can mow him down with ease, even with a bolt action rifle. With a semi or full automatic weapon you can stop a Banzai Charge with usually negligible casualties on your own side. A hundred Japs to one Yank was not an infrequent ratio.

in the group, and their hearty exchange of pleasantries with Hitt was testimony of their respect for him. From them I learned that my own people were not far behind. We ran into a group of aid men in a few minutes and Hitt rested with them while I went on, impatient to see my outfit and find out how things had gone with them during the night. I found my guns and crews within the next half mile of trail. They had started early and made good time. For them the night had passed uneventfully.

The trail was evidently clear of infiltrators for its entire length and it was going to be kept so by guards from the anti-tank company. That was all we needed to know. If we could get supplies and get our wounded back to safety, nothing more would be necessary. We were sure that we would be able to hang on to Hill 27 under these improved conditions. It was wonderful what a change in outlook one could undergo within a few hours' time.

In an hour we had made it back to the battalion with all of the machine guns and one of the 81mm mortars. Five minutes after we got there one of the guns was in action, spraying Japs in the cover on the right flank. Another was soon busy pouring fire into the mouth of a pillbox which the Japs had constructed during the night. In another hour all four of the guns were emplaced along the line, more than doubling the battalion's fire power. The ammunition was pulled from the belts in some of the boxes and loaded by hand into M1 clips. Riflemen who were nearly out were overjoyed to get it. The battalion now had a new lease on life with some ammunition, machine guns, a mortar, and knowledge that more of everything was on the way! There was also a cheering rumor that stoves on which to make hot coffee were coming up, also that several thousand doughnuts were en route. When the doughnut rumor was confirmed a few moments later by the mess sergeant, who had walked ahead of the bearers, a resounding cheer went up from the entire perimeter. The Japs answered the cheer with a few bursts (fire had been slack for the last half hour) and the men who had left the line went scurrying for their foxholes.

A minor counterattack developed with the sudden resumption of enemy fire. It consisted of a suicide rush against the center of our line by a platoon of Japanese. The charge, led by an officer whose sword was dangling at his side in its sheath while he flourished a pistol from the front of his flying wedge, wilted and faded to nothing before the fire of two platoons of "E" Company. With full ammunition belts the boys were no longer so inclined to spare the lead, so when they let drive it sounded almost like a rapid fire relay on the "A" range at Camp Perry. The officer and two of his men got closer to us than the others. Their bodies formed the high-water mark of Japanese movement on the slope of the hill.

I did not see this, nor up to that time had I seen any of the forward outer perimeter action at the time that it was actually going on. The shooting was only fifty yards away, yet I had been isolated from the action and comparatively safe. Jungle warfare is like that, especially in mountainous country. I have many times seen an entire battalion sitting casually on a trail, nibbling away at "K" rations, while one of its platoons, only 100 yards away, was fighting a hell of a battle.

I was faced with a period of relative inactivity after the next few hours. My guns were all quickly emplaced and I had turned over the last mortar to Captain Peterson, who was personally attending to their disposition. With responsibilities fulfilled as far as my command was concerned, I began to think about taking my rifle up to the forward line of foxholes and seeing if there was anything to shoot.

The Colonel had been outspoken in his feeling that unit commanders should not "go popping away or playing Boy Scout" unless it was "necessary in the leadership of their commands." But with the situation turned defensive and with the employment of my guns left pretty much up to the squad leaders, I felt free. Besides, I wanted to take my rifle and binoculars up over the hill top and break the nervous monotony I felt. Battalion command posts are nerve-racking places where one has to sit and sweat out every bit of shooting that is heard along the front with absolutely no opportunity to do anything about it.

Before going up I decided to have something to eat. I was disturbed at the thought of having gone without food for so long so I crawled into a hole with Lieutenant Lochbihler and shared a can of fish (tuna, as I remember) with him. That can had been in my pack for several weeks, but it was good. After the first taste I realized that I had been plenty hungry—whether I'd been aware of it or not. We contented ourselves with the one can, though, saving the rest of my food for another time. We were not yet certain that all of our supplies would get through and we knew that ammunition would have priority over food for sometime.

In between bites I talked over my plans of going up topside. The Colonel came by on an inspection of the inner perimeter and I secured his permission to leave the command post. Captain Frank Raymond came over and told me to see Sergeant Fornelli before I went up. Staff Sergeant James O. Fornelli had been carrying on a one-man sniping and countersniping campaign during the first day and his feats were the talk of the battalion. But according to the stories, he had nudged his luck rather far and had gotten a few bad scares. Several bullets had creased his skin and once a Jap had sprung at him from cover several yards away. Fornelli had come out of it unscathed, but with a sort of a shaky feeling which was very understandable to me.

Fornelli's efforts, as I heard of them, had been chiefly directed against an aggressive group of Japs. They had been trying to gain a foothold and build up a base of fire on a bit of high ground on his company's right flank, but he had been entirely successful in repelling them. Moving forward, he had been able to fire on the group from a flank while they had been frontally engaged with his own line. He had killed the greater part of the group before they located his position and forced him to crawl to cover. After that he had continued in less spectacular exploits, shooting at Japs as they moved in the jungle on the edge of the hill.

I met him as I walked up the hillside through the now-secure center of the rear perimeter and he was a sight that would amaze anyone unacquainted with front line jungle Infantry combat. Though in so doing I am likely boring some readers with a none-too-good description of things you have seen many times and want to forget, I would like to describe Fornelli as he looked at that moment. He was typical of thousands of good Infantrymen who fought the Japs.

He was naked from the waist up, having torn his shirt off early in the fight, and his tanned skin was smeared yellowish with mud and coral dust which was kept pasty by a constant ooze of sweat. His elbows and the powerful, bulging forearms below them were so badly scratched that the red smear there was composed partly of sweat, partly of coral dust, and partly of semi-dry blood and scabs of untended cuts. He was a moderately tall and very huskily built man, his chest and shoulders swelling out over a relatively thin waist and hips, and he carried his M1 in his hand as though it were of feather lightness. His shoulder was swollen and scratched raw from the continued recoil of a gritty buttplate. (Memories of this have made me laugh inwardly several times since when I have seen a competitor in a service rifle match sitting in his tent and diligently sewing another pad of sheepskin on the inside of his shooting coat.)

Besides his rifle, Fornelli had no equipment other than his helmet and cartridge belt, both of which were also caked with mud. His face was a mask of strength—not fatigue as one would expect. He was tired—as attested by red rimmed eyes and his relaxed, careless stride. But any tiredness evident in his expression was more than neutralized by the firm set of his jaw, the fierce glow of his eyes in the shadow of the helmet's rim, and a general attitude of aggressiveness. That difference—the mark of a man whose physical stamina enables him to carry his ideals and patriotism into the demoralizing and exhausting atmosphere of the front lines—is a

quality that makes for winning combat leadership. Fornelli was
a throwback to one of the better of his ancient Roman ancestors.

He took off his helmet as we sat down to talk things over, exposing a head of curly hair so clotted with coral that its true color
could not be seen. We leaned our rifles on a stump nearby so they
could be grasped and brought into action in a split second and
braced our backs against a shelf cut in the bank. There were frequent interruptions caused by a Jap knee-mortar which was laying
one or two rounds a minute on the hill.

"I feel a little unsteady after last night and this morning," said
Fornelli, "and I'm not quite up to crawling around that place
without my shirt. They've been shooting at me more often since I
lost it. Must be that I show up better. So if you want to get some
of them you'll have to go after them yourself, but I think I can
tell you where to find them."

He smoothed out a flat space on some heaped-up soil beside us
and drew with his finger a rough sketch of the perimeter. Outside
of that he drew a large circle to represent the edge of the surrounding jungle. He then punched a series of dots with his finger to
indicate the known enemy positions. Some of these were inside the
edge of the jungle and some were in the fringe of small cover closer
to our lines. It was apparent at once that I would likely find good
shooting all along the forward half of the perimeter if I looked hard
enough for it. So I reasoned at the time that it would be better to
go to a more quiet side where I could move around with greater
safety. The only sniping experience I had behind me was the long
range variety of hill-to-beach shooting at Point Cruiz and I felt
no special desire to become involved in a close-in grenade battle
while on my first jungle sniping jaunt. So, with Fornelli's concur-
rence, I chose to move up to the left flank positions, which were
not under heavy fire. I would do my observing into the jungle,
the skirting brush, and across a small dip to the front of the foremost center positions of the battalion.

I left Fornelli and walked on up out of the jungle and on to the
bare exposed top of the hill, where I ran from cover to cover to
the part of the line I was interested in. I crept past several holes
before I found a vacant one reasonably large enough to crawl into.
It was near a light machine gun position and would be occupied
during the night, but was left unmanned during daylight hours. It
was close enough to allow my conversing with the light machine
gunner, whose gun commanded parts of the area I was interested
in. I was pleased with the height of the position; it provided as good
a view of the whole left front and flank as was obtainable from
anywhere along the line. After receiving the gunner's assurance
that he did not mind the intrusion, I slid my rifle across the lip

of my hole and asked him about the presence of Japs in the cover in front of us. The suspect area was a fan-shaped strip of irregular ground and brush, no longer than 200 yards at most, and bounded on the far side by jungle.

"Haven't seen any since those," he said, nodding his helmet toward the sun-puffed bodies of eight Japs who had charged his position on the previous afternoon. They were lying where they had been shot, scattered on the ground some thirty feet from us. "Some nice souvenirs out there for anybody damn fool enough to go out after 'em. That first one must be an officer or sumthin'. He's layin' on a sword; had it in his hand when I shot him. Hope it don't rust all to hell before I get a chance to get out and get it." As he rambled on I started to examine the ground far out in front, where I felt that there might be a target.

It was hot on top of that hill. No wonder so many men were brought down half out of their heads from heat exhaustion. The shallow foxholes were like ovens. Vision across the hill was blurred by thick smears of heat waves, rippling above the grass and bare spots where mortar shells had scraped off the sod. With that kind of heat there was no use for binoculars. The images would be so distorted by mirage that you couldn't see a thing. I had given the whole area the once-over without seeing a target and had just begun to divide it up into sections and search again with greater care, when an unusual and unaccountable thing happened. A man near the crest of the hill was behaving in a suicidal manner.

My attention was first attracted by a series of yells from the whole center of the positions. "Tell that dumb yokel to get down!" "Get down, you crazy bastard!"

I rolled halfway over and twisted my neck around to see a man standing upright on the highest point of the hill. The cries continued, "Somebody grab him! He's nuts!" All within sight joined in frenzied yelling, but no one was close enough to yank him down into a hole. Before anyone could get to him, a single shot was fired. It came from the jungle to my left flank—the plainly identifiable crack of an Arisaka .25. The exposed man crumpled to the ground, his helmet rattling loudly against the coral clods in the momentary hush that followed the shot. The Jap rifleman fired a second and a third shot at the still-exposed body, now lying face down on the hill crest, and his bullets cracked across my front on their way. Both of these shots missed, but it did not matter. The first shot had hit the man's chest and he hardly twitched where he lay. Then two men ran uselessly up to carry him away, luckily without being fired at. This I did not see, for I was looking at the cover where that shot came from, hoping for a crack at the Jap. But there were no more shots from that quarter, and I never saw him.

Hideo

Looks at first glance as though the local Bull o' th' Woods has just come forward to show one of his juniors how things are to be done. Captain Applejack is getting a good lecture on platoon tactics, as evolved by the mental giants in regimental headquarters. Outstanding features of this harangue will be particular emphasis on Aggressiveness, Drive and Guts in the assault, and Stubborn Tenacity in the defense.

The captain will listen politely while the colonel talks. He knows that the Old Man will move back to the regimental command post before the interesting and exciting Pacific night approaches. And when it does the captain will most likely forget the conversation with his senior—and the quoted axioms of Napoleon and Jeb Stuart—and use his good common sense.

Most likely a sketch, drawn on the pages of a field message book, is serving as a lecture-poster. Notice that both officers are wearing the same uniforms and equipment that might be seen on any private, and that the painted eagle is no longer on the colonel's helmet. Maybe he smeared it with clay or borrowed an unadorned soup-bowl from one of his command post people.

It was surprising the number of front line visitors who were hit during this last war. In most cases they tended to show less respect for enemy fire than did the men who were exposed to it 24 hours a day, seven days a week. Such visiting firemen, wallowing around the forward line of foxholes, frequently gave away to the enemy the exact locations of men who had gone to great trouble keeping themselves concealed.

Generally these visitors from higher echelon were about as popular with front liners as an epidemic of dysentery.

This episode seemed as fantastic then as now: no one was look-ing at the man at the exact moment he arose—everyone became aware of his foolishness only after he was up and out of his hole. His reasons, if any, for committing that suicidal gesture, are to this day unexplained.

With a sort of amazed feeling I continued my inspection of the terrain in front of me, giving very close attention to the area from which the shots were fired. Sporadic fire from the other side of the perimeter was snapping, but on the whole there was little noise. I had crouched somewhat lower because I felt that though I was probably well defiladed from the ace Jap sniper's view, there could well be another one around. It was easy to imagine him drawing a bead on my helmet from a camouflaged position in cover only 80 yards away. The drama of the situation was mocked at that time by the words of the machine gunner next to me. I felt like rebuking him for what I heard him say so shortly after a man had been killed, but I let it pass. "Hey, next door. . . . No use both of us stayin' awake . . . I'm gonna get some shuteye . . ." With that he curled up behind the rear legs of the tripod and dozed off, in the baking heat!

As the very front of the battalion was clearly visible from where I stayed, I had naturally not concerned myself with a close scrutiny of the narrow strip of ground immediately in front of and down grade from that portion of the line. Nor had it entered my head that a Jap infiltration attempt might be made in broad daylight. The notion seemed too fantastic. But a movement in the low brush, not more than thirty yards from the foremost positions, caught my eye. I looked more closely and I clearly saw a man crawl across the front of a small boulder just down hill from our foremost diggings. It gave me a terrific start and I instinctly jerked the barrel of my rifle around to take aim at this surprise target.

Then I checked myself, cursing inwardly that I could think of shooting at a target so obviously one of our own men. It was just a silly error of my own—a failure to properly locate our own lines. I should have had sense enough to have inquired about men work-ing in front of the line before going up there to blaze away at any old target. Likely it was someone out planting booby traps or re-covering dead. Another shape moved by the boulder and I shifted the rifle over on the parapet so that I could look through the scope. Mere curiosity prompted me to do this. When I looked through the scope again I got another start. "It's a Jap!" I almost yelled out loud. But again I checked myself, thinking of the appalling number of our men killed by careless shooting. I actually refused to believe what I was seeing. Only half of the man who had moved past the boulder remained visible. It was the rear half of his body that I could now see, and I suppose that I continued to look at it for a minute before the truth finally dawned.

Despite the proximity to our lines, despite the broad daylight, there was one all-powerful proof that the man in the field of my telescopic sight was not an American. *He was wearing wrapped leggings!* The short stocky body, the suspicious cut of trousers, the strange looking color of the uniform—all of those I might mistake. But no American wore wrapped leggings in this war.

Now I damned myself for having held fire so long. The Jap squirmed backwards while I took aim and, in so doing, he turned his face my way. He slipped down until all that I could see of him was his face and his helmeted head (the helmet did not have the usual Jap camouflage net). But at 80 yards that face was enough target. I must have been pretty steady at the moment of the shot because I remember being able to set his chin precisely on the flat-topped post in the Alaskan reticule. Also, I was able to hold it there while I squeezed the trigger. It was the sort of a squeeze you use on the last shot of a rapid-fire string when you see the target start to move! My bullet struck him squarely in the teeth and he pitched on his face, giving a single convulsive jerk. I found myself aiming for another shot without memory of having operated the bolt. I uselessly fired a second shot into his chest.

Breathless with dumb, unreasoning excitement, I continued to watch the dead Jap through the scope, common sense and hysteria battling in my mind over whether or not I should wildly continue to fire into the dead body. Common sense, I am glad to say, won out and in a few minutes I was examining the ground through the rifle scope with relative calm. But calm, on a battlefield, is a highly interruptible thing.

An explosion blossomed in the center of the scope field, only a few feet from the body. At the same time I noted a related disturbance over in the four o'clock side. A grenade had gone off down there. Looking up momentarily from the scope I saw movement in our positions above the dead Jap. The boys had rolled a grenade down to make sure. . . . Well, what the hell—Uncle Sam has plenty of 'em. But No! There was another yellow belly down there! Sure as hell there was!

Flushed from cover, perhaps wounded by the grenade, the second Jap ran a short distance, getting in partial defilade from those on the hill. He was soon safe from the men above him, well below their line of vision. But he remained exposed to me all the while. He began to crawl in foot-deep grass on all fours, apparently unconcerned with my part of the perimeter, looking back over his shoulder at the spot from where the grenade had come. Perhaps the sounds of my two shots had been altered by local acoustics, perhaps he was stunned and wounded. Whatever the cause, he was certainly unaware of any danger from my quarter. He continued crawling down a shallow cut, at right angles to my line of vision. It was as easy a shot as the other. I tracked him for a moment with the scope, keeping the post on the thick, upper part of his body as he crawled, then I moved the post well up in front of him and let him crawl toward it. When his armpit was right above the top of the reticule post, I gave the trigger a last ounce of pressure.

When the scope settled after the recoil I saw that he was dead. I put another in him for good measure and then I shakingly crouched back to get my breath. The machine gunner sang out congratulations to me—he having awakened to witness the shooting. Like myself, he had first feared that I was shooting at our own men. He had definitely recognized them as Japs when I shot, however.

I had forgotten about the heat of the day. There was a cold clammy sweat all over my face then, and my knees felt weak even without my being on my feet. It seemed wise to sit there for a while, talking with the machine gunner before I returned to the battalion CP. The aimless chatting with the doughboy next to me was calming. I felt able to leave in a few moments, but my pulse took a long time to return to normal. Shooting Japs at less than a hundred yards, I had found, was a lot different from sniping them at long range.

As I dashed from cover to cover on my way back, I felt a rather logical fear that has assailed me many times since. After killing one or more enemy, I have always sensed a proportionate increase in danger to myself. That fear was renewed in my mind after each exploit—on through the war. Another enemy killed—an increased likelihood of being killed myself. It is strange the way a man manufactures his own mental handicaps.

The rear side of the hill around the command post had been cleaned up during my brief absence. The dead had been removed from around the aid station and a burial detail was busy down on the slope digging graves. Shovels and entrenching tools could now be spared from the more important task of digging shelters for the living. The necessary areas had been cleared of enemy, and the command post was no longer subject to rifle fire. Mortars and knee-mortars were still banging in as before, but their effectiveness had not increased and they produced fewer and fewer casualties as shelters were improved.

All of this I saw as I got out of the fire zone on the top of the hill, moving that short distance to relative safety which takes a battalion officer away from what he would call The Front. I was to find out later that there was no term in the war which was to be so variously defined by different authorities. The Front, sometimes incorrectly confused by laymen with the combat zone, has meant entirely different things to different people. Sometimes anywhere within range of enemy attack aviation or buzz bombs. But to men in Infantry battalions it has meant the outer row of foxholes in a defense, or the advance-guard squad in a patrol. The Infantryman's front was where close and hot contact with the enemy was assured, where a soldier might at any moment find an enemy springing into his shelter to knife it out, or maybe where a grenade could roll sputtering into a foxhole with fuse burned too short to allow for throwing it outside. The Front, as the doughboy thinks of it, is a place of grime, horror and heart-breaking effort, often rewarded by semi-starvation and lingering death.

Existence at this Front, especially if prolonged, leads any human to the realization of a new set of values. There the soldier prays to his God (or his luck) for his life—or for a quick or pleasant death. His great fear is that he will be horribly wounded and live a cripple—blinded, castrated, deafened, or without limbs. His greatest wants are for a little time to sleep every 48 hours or so, and for ammunition and food. His companions are his buddies and his officers—and he seems to notice a marked shortage of officers from where he happens to be huddling in a hail of enemy fire.

I rolled a tongue around the outside of scummy teeth and began to think about the toothbrush in my pack, as I got down to "Harry's New Yorker" (the name Art and I had given our foxhole). Art was not there, and most of the nearby diggings were also empty. I asked a lone occupant of a "three-manner" close by where the hell everyone had gone. "Lieutenant Hantel went down to get a cup of coffee; they got plenty coffee and doughnuts down there."

I could have kissed the grimy face of that soldier, beard and all, for saying that. While I was getting out my canteen cup I found that the troops on the top of the hill were being relieved by relays, so that everyone could get down and have as much hot coffee as he wanted. Four big doughnuts, fried as only "H" Company's mess sergeant could cook 'em were handed to each man. As I walked down where the ranges were set up I saw by the cheeriness of a hundred faces along the way that it does not take long for a man's appetite to be summoned back into existence by the smell of hot coffee, and the taste of good old doughnuts.

There were other sniping adventures for me during the next few days. I was placed in charge of the garrisoning of a hill on our flank as the threat of counterenvelopment increased. But all of these shooting parties were of similar stamp, all at rather short range—nothing to place any demands on true marksmanship ability. One of these affairs, because it was depicted in the original cover illustration of this book, is perhaps worth relating. It happened one morning while there was still considerable shooting on Hill 27. This little minute-thriller concerned several members of "E" Company, defending the left-hand curve of the perimeter on the morning of January 7th.

All through the night there had been weird sounds and sights along the outside of the line; yells, exploding grenades and intermittent flashes of automatic fire. One man, looking at the skyline in front of his hole, had seen the unmistakable outline of a crouching enemy. He let fly a few rounds from a Reising gun and saw his target fall. After that, for a while, there had been silence, broken occasionally by a gurgling moan from the spot where the Japanese was lying. The men knew that the moans would not long continue, because each one of them trailed off with a hissing sound, clearly indicating that some of the slugs had found the Jap's lungs or windpipe. But the noise bothered the men. They were waiting for dawn, when all of the uncertainty could be cleared up. The men would be able to see the ground to their front and tell what other things had happened. Necks began to be craned a little as it got lighter; eyes began to be lifted higher above the parapets.

The situation outside of "E" Company's perimeter had been described to us over sound-powered telephone, and I had left my foxhole near the battalion command post to investigate. I got to a point about twenty-five yards from the concerned platoon CP —fifty yards from the outer line—when a single rifle shot, passed close over my head, caused me to lie down and get ready with my rifle. From my prone position I stared fruitlessly at the wall of jungle off to my right. It could have contained a hundred camouflaged enemy. For the moment I had lost interest in the dying Jap in front of the line.

I set my eye to my rifle scope and began looking for a giveaway movement of foliage where the shot had come from. The direction was off to my right, a full ninety degrees from line of vision to the scene of original interest. Just before the shot had scared me into lying down I had noticed two foxholes, dug closely together, just a little below the very crest of Mount Austen. They belonged to two of "E" Company's riflemen, rather apart from the rest of their platoon. Just as I took cover, I noticed that one of the occupants had raised his head and shoulders above ground level, pointing his rifle nervously towards his left front. Apparently he was trying to draw a bead on a fleeting target.

In searching the green tangle of leaves, vines, and trunks, during the next few seconds I examined and eliminated many suspicious looking objects. I saw a definite movement about fifteen feet up on the trunk of a large tree which I decided might be my target of the moment (might be a lizard, too). Anyway I figured that three shots or so through the foliage immediately around the spot would do no harm, and might do a lot of good. I held the first one in the center, and fired all three as fast as I could operate the bolt, so that the suspected tree-sniper would be unable to take cover if the first one missed. I planned to hold the scope on the area, after getting a fourth live round ready in the chamber, and look for more suspicious movements, hoping that I would be able to watch the death-flounderings of the man who had shot at me.

But I had no such opportunity to survey the results of my three searching shots. The last shot I fired blotted out in my ears the first syllable of a shouted Japanese battle cry, coming from in front of the two closely-dug fox holes. But the trailing last half of the word was enough.

. . . "ZAI"! it croaked out loudly and terrifyingly, shouted through a wide-opened Oriental mouth, and with every ounce of strength in a Japanese officer's lungs. And then it was followed by a chorus-yell of the same word: "BANZAI! BANZAI!" High pitched; blood-curdling; croaking with fanaticism, savagery, hate. And so keen is my memory that I can remember the exact sounding, the rheumy hoarseness of the voices, as though each of the attacking Japanese were suffering from a bronchial ailment!

I wrenched the forward half of my prone body around, to bring my rifle to bear in the direction of the yells. As I did so I obtained a lasting mental picture of the two riflemen, weapons to their shoulders, twisting to the left and listening with breathless tenseness to the attack party coming up directly at them. The Japs were then out of view and below the riflemen's field of fire. These riflemen had not more than thirty yards in which to halt the attack with fire. They would have to kill or seriously maim every member of the Japanese party during that short rush. Thirty yards space, and about five seconds time—for a charging Jap covers ground like a sprinter.

I reasoned these things out before the five Japanese came over the rise; a dynamic picture of gleaming whites of eyes, bare teeth and steel of sword and bayonets. These steel blades, it seemed, did not merely reflect the dull light of morning, but radiated light of their own, flashing, infernal. At the sight all controlled thought fled from the minds of all involved in our little drama; only instinct, and wild, pointless emotion remained. Sequence and the pattern of events were lost. I saw what happened—clearly, through eyes and senses amplified by obsessive fear. I remember it all. But to place each event in proper turn would require a later piecing together of the story by participants, if we lived. History, if it were interested, could wait. This, as best as I have been able to learn, is the story of those very few seconds.

As the first three Japanese loomed over the rise, bounding toward the two foxholes, the left of the two riflemen fired, as did I along with him. The leading and farthest left of the three Japs was an officer, brandishing at shoulder height a gleaming Samurai blade, wearing their peaked, star-emblemed cap. The rifleman's bullet caught him just above the belt buckle, missing his spine by an inch on the way out. He halted, straightened upright from the crouched position in which he had been charging, staggered backward for a pace or two. Then he fell over on his back, raising his arms above his head and casting the gleaming blade from his right hand as he fell.

My own first shot was fired in great haste, aimed frantically at the leading Japanese rifleman, just to the ill-fated officer's left. A bound he had taken just as I fired had carried him as much to the left as forward. My bullet sped through, missed, but killed the last of the party, some twelve yards behind. My second shot, timed perfectly with the first of the rifleman on the right, shared credit for slowing down, but not stopping, the charge of the third member of the party. The right hand rifleman's first shot hit the Jap I had missed squarely in the chest at a distance of about eight yards. It took a second shot to finish the job.

With only two cartridges in my weapon when the action began, I was now reduced to mere helpless watching (and fumbling to awkwardly load the magazine of my Springfield, occluded for clip loading by the damn bracket type mount of the scope). The two remaining enemy, now practically atop the two riflemen, were dealt with before I could manage to tear from my belt and cram into the chamber a single round.

The first of these two to go down was the most distant—the extreme left flank member of the attacking force. A third shot from the rifleman on the right did the work. This Jap threw his rifle forward as he fell.

His killing had taken perhaps a half second—precious time to the remaining Jap. Being almost abreast of the officer at the time the rush began, this second fellow was now nearly upon his objective, close enough to use his bayonet. Some part of my mind, working subconsciously during this crisis, caused me to remember and to later marvel at the infinite bravery and courage of this stout hearted little Oriental. He was charging the two men, his arms and body cocked back to deliver a piston thrust to his bayonetted rifle—a thrust which would surely have killed the rifleman on the left.

Both of the riflemen saw him now as their last remaining (and greatest) danger. They pointed their Garands, still holding more than half-magazine capacity, at his chest. Then they pumped the triggers until both clips were ringingly ejected from the receivers. They lowered aim to keep the stream of metal pouring through him as he fell to his knees, then to his haunches, then on his face, clutching his rifle tightly to the last. This continued fire was not hysterical—not a waste of ammunition. That Jap was alive and dangerous until perhaps the last two rounds were fired.

What I saw during those few seconds made me glow with pride at my belonging in the same outfit with the two men out in front. They had killed twice their number of Japs with only minor assistance; they had not lost nerve in the face of the most savage and terrifying weapon in the Japanese repertory. Other men before, in Burma, in Indo-China, in other lost territories still under unchallenged Japanese control, had permitted themselves to be paralyzed with fear and slaughtered under similar circumstances.

Now those two men were ready again, with rifles loaded, scanning the ground to their front. One of them turned his head my way for a moment, and I saw under the shadowed brim of his helmet that though his face was ash-gray above his beard, his teeth were partly bared in a grin, of self-confidence—even of triumph. As I loaded up my rifle, filling the magazine as well as the chamber now that I had time, I too enjoyed another feeling of bolstered faith.

On the 9th of January we were visited by a few of the staff officers of the 35th Infantry, a regiment of the 25th Division, and we made arrangements to be relieved. Late on the 10th the physical relief of the battalion was finished. I remained over through that night with the turnover detail and left the next day.

As we walked out over the shortened and improved trail, panting from the exertion of mounting the hills it covered, we all became aware of how weak and exhausted we really were. We had all been in the sun, but the tan we had gotten from that exposure had not given our skins a healthy glow. Everyone had lost weight, and inches had been added to the curves of stooped shoulders. Clothing was ragged beyond belief and mud was crusted over all of it. With several halts—no need to hurry now—we soon arrived at the junction of the main trail on Edson's Ridge. The trail had been cut much further in than when we had left. It was when we got to that jeep path, up on a ridge and out of the stinking jungle, that the full realization of our luck in coming out of the Valley of the Shadow was to dawn upon all of us.

The battalion had 27 killed in the operation, and we all knew that it was a small fight in the big scheme of things. No one can ever say that any particular gain was worth such a loss. But 500 Japanese had been killed, and prisoners which we were to take a month later in our operation against the rear of the Japanese forces on Guadalcanal would be heard referring in tones of dread to what they had named, "The Battle of the Mountain of Blood."

To them, much more than to us, the fight for Hill 27 had been no small thing.

The day we marched out was a bright and sunny one. The sky, the ocean, and the green land were vying with each other for first honors in a great concerted effort of all nature to tell us that the world was a wonderful, magnificent place, and that life was grand.

A SHORE TO SHORE OPERATION

The day I am about to relate started with a bang—several of them, in fact. The empty "C" ration cans, hanging like Christmas tree ornaments on the barbed wire outside the inner perimeter, rattled loudly, rousing one of the company platoon sergeants from an especially sound slumber. He opened his eyes to see a sight which sent various kinds of chills up and down his spine and out to his trigger finger. The sergeant had little thought for the peaceful rest the battalion was enjoying at the time. He raised his tommy gun and took none-too-careful aim at a pair of evil looking eyes glowing down at him over the lip of his foxhole. Then he let fly about half a drum of .45 slugs.

The whole drowsy command sprang into immediate action. Officers rolled cursing from their bunks. Half naked crews ran out to man their weapons, stumbling over the cut vegetation and slipping in the soft mud. The trails and paths leading through the jungle to prepared positions were crowded with scurrying doughboys. All through the brush surrounding my tent could be heard the hurried sounds of preparation for a last ditch fight. M1 rifles were being charged—I could hear the distinctive sounds as clips were shoved home and bolts went forward, driving first rounds into the chambers. Forward, on the line which was crowded with heavy machine guns, each bolt was clangingly pulled and released to bring the weapon to full-load. The rattle of machine gun bolts was the last sound heard. I counted them and knew that all six crews were on the job—waiting for the attack to develop. The attack would have to cross a 100-yard cleared field of fire out in front of the entrenchments. With that last rattle the noise subsided and the battalion settled into absolute silence—watching its front—waiting.

It was a satisfying thought to know that the Japs had not achieved surprise. We were ready. It would take a lot of them to get through the stuff we had out there. Three double aprons of barbed wire . . . Interlaced fire from three times our complement of heavy machine guns . . . Dug in 37mm anti-tank guns with piled up cases of cannister shot . . . Fifty-caliber ground-mounted jobs ready to take care of any Japs who came in low. (The fifties would penetrate the spreading roots of any large trees within the cleared field of fire.) All of that—plus a substantial line of riflemen out in front, gave all of us a good feeling of fitness in the matter. We were almost certain of our ability—as an entrenched battalion of American Infantry—to hold off all the Japs in the Solomon Islands, attacking in a column of regiments one behind the other. And, with Henderson Field behind us but a few hundred yards, we did not doubt that the Japs might try that very thing. The 164th Infantry's Third Battalion had killed hundreds of them on that very same spot. That was a month earlier when a Jap regiment made a very desperate bid for the Field.

We waited with bird-dog tenseness for the fire fight to begin. We knew how it would come—a few scattered shots, then a chorus of wild yells and screams followed by a furious charge with bayonets and grenades. The silence continued for a full ten minutes. Then a murmur passed up and down the line.

"Check on those damned shots—where did that firing come from?" To me, ignorant as the others of the exact source of the firing, the sound had been definitely recognizable as one of two things—a Nambu light machine gun being fired *toward* us or a tommy gun being fired *away* from us. Either would indicate some sort of Japanese action—and that to me could mean but one thing —an attack directed toward the air strip. And, at that very moment, Henderson Field was making its exact location known with the sound of many motors. Morning fighter sweeps were getting warmed-up.

The scene continued to be one of tense alertness. Helmeted heads projected above the shelters only enough to clear eyes for observation. Everything was lined up and ready to go—and it remained so, waiting anxiously—almost eagerly—for the first sign of the coming attack.

The sergeant remained quietly in his hole, raising his head occasionally. He did this to check the defiladed spot into which his target had fallen when the slugs tore squarely into it. He could no longer see the target—the eyes he had fired at—but he could hear convulsive threshing in the declivity where the body had fallen. He kept the spot covered and shouted a warning (when at last his voice returned) telling his friends on either side to watch the spot and to "not let the bastard get away." Perhaps he thought the hail of .45 slugs had merely wounded.

A doughboy on the sergeant's right climbed from his shelter and moved forward. He did not even go to the trouble of crouching to lessen the six foot target he was offering. The sergeant told him to get the hell back in his hole at once but the man disregarded the order. Along the line all the men within view kept their eyes to the front, ready to cover this man with fire if anything should happen. Obviously he was going out to investigate the body of the Jap that Hill had killed.

He got down into the declivity where it was and went to work on it with a trench knife—apparently cutting off the collar tabs to get the insignia of rank, or perhaps cutting a shirt front to get to the diary and flags so often kept inside there. In a moment he arose, lifting the bullet ridden corpse for all to see. A great ringing chorus of laughter broke out and spread along a whole company front, causing the doughboys in flanking outfits to look at each other curiously and tilt their helmets forward and to scratch their heads.

The sergeant's victim, held up for all to see, was a huge long-tailed reptile—the giant tree lizard of Guadalcanal.

So began the day on which we were to get things underway for the big shore-to-shore operation, calculated to trap the remaining Jap forces on the island in the jaws of a vise and then to squeeze them into the inland mountains or the sea. (We held no fancied hopes that they would surrender.)

The Second Battalion, 132nd Infantry had been chosen to do the job. General Sebree told us our success in the Mount Austen (Hill 27) battle had been taken into account in the selection. The plans had been communicated to us early and we had made the necessary administrative arrangements for the move. We were to concentrate at Lunga Point for loading the next morning. We were to be moved in destroyers and LCTs (Landing Craft, Tank) in a sweep around the enemy's left flank, landing in the vicinity of Visale, a small village in the extreme rear of the main Japanese forces. This would give the Japanese a second front. We had the whole of the day to make ready—embarkation was to be at an early hour the following morning.

So, after the comical happenings brought about by the lizard and the unsteady nerves of the half-asleep platoon sergeant were terminated, we set ourselves to the business at hand and moved from the perimeter to the beach, where we began the actual ammunition and supply loading at about noon. The LCTs were nosed in to the beach and the regimental supply officer was with the regimental ammunition officer busy supervising the loading. For a while things went along smoothly but soon the customary unpleasantnesses began to occur. First of all we were told that the number of LCTs was to be reduced for some reason or another. When we received this news a great cry of pain went up from the slide rule boys from division headquarters. Their loading tables were all messed up by the change. We set to making adjustments of our own while they went into a highly technical huddle to devise new loading tables. (I believe that by the time this was accomplished the convoy must have been underway for some hours.) Anyway the job was done; we were loaded before darkness overtook us.

After the loading we went back to the beach for a night's rest. But there was no rest. Some one of the gang had gotten hold of some torpedo juice from some closeby Navy people. There were many sounds of discordant singing from around the dispersal area. I know that it is not good for me, as an officer, to mention this and at the same time admit that I did nothing about it. But I considered my sleep that night especially valuable, as I was not feeling well at the time.

My arm and shoulder had turned to raw beef with a recurrent allergy rash which I had picked up on New Caledonia a year before. It had been necessary for me to talk fast in order to avoid being hospitalized. So I lay still, enjoying the anonymity given by the darkness and the confused situation. I failed to hear the yells of high brass which were ringing through the night, threatening things dire and disastrous if responsible officers did not take immediate action to stop the drunken racket. It turned out later that my abstaining from action was a good thing, because most of the merriment came from certain naval officers and a few army guests—all of whom were of much higher rank than myself. Finally I drifted off to troubled, nightmarish sleep.

At midnight part of the unit struggled up from sleep and climbed aboard the boats. The indefatigable adjutant of the battalion had slept so soundly that it took several yells from the leather voiced battalion commander to rouse him. After he was properly roused he managed to get on the wrong boat or something. The darkness became blue with profanity as Colonel Ferry summoned him to his proper place.

There was a strange mosaic of sounds filling the night air. Back of everything else, of course, was the roar of the Higgins boats as they shuttled the troops out to the destroyer. The roar of landing craft motors was a standard sound each day at Lunga Beach but it sounded strange during the night.

Something more than a thousand men were gathering their equipment and getting aboard the LCTs, which are miniature LSTs—nothing more than ocean-going Higgins boats. They had a conventional trap-door bow to permit unloading personnel and equipment, including tanks and trucks, directly on a beach. The thousand men were not happy with their task—as no soldier ever is with anything which gets him up so damned early. Inasmuch as

Hideo

Peekin' and Snoopin'—not a Japanese speciality; at least not in the day-time. They were great for scouting and observation, all right, but generally they didn't use daytime unit infiltration tactics. If they crept up on us they did it by ones and twos. When they moved in bunches they most often rushed.

Notice the cheese knives fixed on the rifles. If the Japs ever took their bayonets off, they had to have a good reason. Guess they figured that the mile-long barrel and the heavy wooden forearm didn't provide enough balance.

These two boys are stalking something, probably some American machine gun position spotted earlier. Usually such a stalk would be conducted in a wide half-circle, around a flank, with the objective of getting within easy grenade distance. Sometimes this method worked against us; more often we got the Japs.

the beach was secure and there was no need for silence the men took full advantage of the situation. There were many discontented grumblings among those who were throwing on board the last of the task force's equipment. They were working in complete darkness—darkness which was particularly treacherous within the landing craft. Inside the craft there were a million and one sharp articles for a man to bang his ribs against. And there was nothing comfortable for him to lie on once he was loaded and his work finally at an end. Some of the more lucid were heard to insinuate that all of these difficulties and irritations were in reality parts of a cleverly conceived plan, meant to enrage the soldier just prior to combat, so that by the time he met the enemy he would be conveniently obsessed with an insane desire to kill and tear apart everything in sight.

The destroyer "Stringham" left Lunga at 0100 with the task force staff and "George" Company—which at that old-fashioned time was known simply as "G" Company. This unit had the mission of establishing the initial beachhead at a place named Verahue. The rest of the force would arrive in the afternoon—if all went well. The remainder of the force got under way somewhat later than the scheduled 0400. Dawn found the landing craft out on the open sea, taking the water route around to the rear of an estimated 4,000 to 7,000 Japs.

In those early days of the war we had none of the present day conveniences such as vomit bags or seasickness prevention pills. We went along our sad way, with a man at the helm of our overgrown mudscow who gloried in breasting—head on—each and every ground swell. Men would crawl up the sides of the ship to lean over the edge and vomit while the ship went right on heaving. I was back near the two sets of twin 20mm guns near the stern, and so did not get the worst of the undulations. An LCT in rough weather seems to pivot from the stern—the bow does the worst jumping.

I placed my Springfield in a little green poplin case which I have always carried along, took off my pack and looked for a place to lie down. There was nothing I could do for the men. They were sitting around their machine guns—the sick ones being unmercifully kidded by those unaffected. The voyage continued without incident—which was surprising. We would have been a most remunerative target for the light bombers the Japs had been sending over lately. We had for water escort, as far as I could tell, a single Australian vessel which looked like a cross between a destroyer and a mine layer; nothing else. Overhead, however, we had a good umbrella of fighters. There have been several times in my military career when I have prayed with especial fervor that the situation would remain non-tactical as far as the enemy was concerned. This was one of them. Our LCTs' only defenses from air attack were two 20mm guns. These small weapons did not inspire much confidence. Neither did their drowsy crews.

Along about 3:30 in the afternoon we began to nose in eastward towards shore, which at the time was several miles distant. We could make out some craft on the beach and there were a few huts there to indicate that it was most likely our destination, the village of Verahue. Such it proved to be and we clambered onto the sand as soon as the clumsy barge-like boats had made their way in. They raced their motors for a last spurt of speed in order to jam the heavily-laden bows upon the sand. This allowed the drawbridge of a front gate to span the last bit of water and permit the guns and vehicles to get ashore dry.

We came in nicely, encountering no coral shelves and immediately began to unload. Apparently someone had seen fit to take steps to prevent the poetically snafued occurrence of the ramp becoming stuck. We all had heard stories of ramps failing to open, leaving 200 men and their equipment penned up in a craft under enemy fire.

It was evident that there were no Japs on hand to receive us— only our own advance parties who had effected the landing without resistance and had sent out security in all directions. We all felt that a reaction was coming soon though, and there was no slowness in unloading the supplies and getting things organized. We fully expected to have to fight in order to hold and enlarge the beachhead. There was a ludicrous occurrence (which could have been tragic) which took place a few minutes after our landing, while the craft were still unloading.

The coconut groves came right down to the water's edge on the shore of the narrow little cover. I think we owed a lot to those tall palms, huddled in a ring around the noses of the ships, for, after a two seconds' warning roar, two bombers came in directly over us at treetop height. We had not seen any enemy planes while we had been relatively helpless out there on the water so our worries had more or less left us when we hit shore. But we were still concentrated—a lot of men and matériel in a small area— and therefore a good air target. Hearing the sound of the motors, I hoped against hope that they were our own planes. But as they roared over I saw big red "meat balls" on the wings and knew otherwise. I watched them carefully, expecting to see the bombs leave their racks and start downward in their curved path. But no bombs came.

The only explanation that I can find is that the Japs did not see us until they were directly above us. We were as much a surprise to them as they were to us. This explanation received further credence from the planes' subsequent actions. They flew on, directly away from us, streaking straight for the destroyer. It was a golden opportunity for anyone who had a weapon ready but we were all asleep.

I stood by with my rifle in my hands.

The equally stupefied 20mm gunners on the landing craft stared open-mouthed until the planes were more than a mile away. Then they scrambled frantically to get their guns into operation. One jammed—even at that uselessly late moment.

The destroyer, however, had its own best interests strongly at heart. It met the incoming planes with a stream of tracers and Bofors explosions. Both bombs struck close on the first run, but only one plane remained to make a second. The leading two-motored light bomber was fatally hit and crashed into the water a mile beyond the destroyer.

The surviving plane made a courageous second trip, circling and coming back in for another try—braving again the fire of the little ship, which by that time was fully alerted. This bomb went wide again and the Jap made the classic decision about discretion and valor and streaked back towards where he came from as fast as his two motors would carry him. The saucy little destroyer nosed around, signaled "Good Luck" to us and went back towards Tulagi.

We stopped watching the interesting small-scale naval and air battle and returned to our serious work which we knew could become a hell of a lot more serious in a matter of hours. The Japs, unless they were utterly blind, would know now that a sizeable American force was behind their lines. Our G–2 reports had indicated coldly that the Japs would be there in strength. They would be able to liquidate our little group if they concentrated against us or reinforced their rear with that in mind.

We organized a perimeter and bedded down with the entirely natural apprehension of people who know that their enemy is most likely to become active during the night. We were awakened at 10 o'clock that evening by the flashes and sounds of a naval battle in the vicinity of the Russel Islands, off to the west.

It was a strange feeling to lie on the quiet beach and see the sky light up over the water with flares and star shells. We could feel the very earth quiver and vibrate with the air as sounds of exploding torpedoes and depth charges reached us. The feeling became doubly poignant when each of us realized that his very life might be wrapped up in the vast war of machines out there in the distance.

We were all aware of the close tie-in of ground, air and naval cooperation in that island struggle. There was no need for orienting our men on the overall picture. It was always there before our eyes—the complete cycle of island war. The ground forces rooted out the Japs, killed them and defended the air fields. This allowed the planes to get into the air and kill Japs in larger bunches— at less cost in human life.

The Navy got us there in the first place, landed the heavy equipment for the air bases, kept the Japs from sneaking in and reinforcing at night or in bad flying weather, and kept our supplies coming in by the hundreds of tons, piling up on the beach. Back at Lunga we sometimes saw all this going on in the same place at the same time. Transports were in the harbor unloading with planes overhead fighting off the Jap air force, while marines and doughboys kept their link in the chain solid by fighting the Japs off more ground and keeping the air field secure.

So we all had an interest in this naval battle which would probably not have been felt by troops in continental warfare; we observed the flashings and listened to the uninformative rumblings with great wonder as to what could be the outcome of the fight. We were all well aware of what the consequences of a major naval defeat would have been to our own little group.

The next morning came, breaking through night with poetic impatience. Our patrols of native scouts reported negatively from their reconnaissance northward to Bahi and Titi. The entire unit made ready to move. The absence of a decent coastal road, perhaps overlooked in the planning of the expedition, compelled our transport to remain at Verahue and forced the first part of the move to be conducted without assurance of artillery support.

Our battery of Marine 75mm howitzers would be unable to move forward until our engineer detachment managed to bulldoze a road for them and our trucks.

We began our northward march over native trails of tropical beauty at 8 o'clock that morning after a breakfast of pancakes and syrup—the last hot meal we were to receive for sometime. Our trip, made carrying our heavy weapons by hand, took us into the foothills of the mountains—which were not far from the coast on that side of Guadalcanal. The jungle we passed through was not quite as dense as that near the air field but it was just as interesting and of equal beauty. We often crossed banana groves and other cultivated fields. Many of the men picked papayas at the halts and munched them en route. A lucky few found a patch of ripe watermelons in a deserted village. I laughed a little as I watched them eating, remembering that an officer of my acquaintance had been crucified for permitting his men to buy melons during a practice march of the regiment at Camp Forrest, Tennessee, some two years before.

During this march I was being kidded for putting up with the weight of my rifle and scope. Other officers were carrying lighter weapons—pistols or Reising or Tommy guns. Most of them had no idea that a scope-sighted rifle had an application in the jungle— and they regarded my carrying one as the height of eccentricity. Art Hantel was there though, and between us we were well aware of the capabilities of the weapon which he was by then speaking of as "our rifle." I had cut a piece of bamboo and shaved it into a good cleaning rod, cutting the tip in the manner of a Parker jag. The rod was tied to the rifle so that no matter what inconvenience the strain of combat might impose, I would always be able to clean my weapon after I had used it. I kept the scope on the rifle during the march—not wanting to miss any opportunity to use it. It was not especially likely that fighting would take place back in the heavy weapons section of a column, but I knew from past experience that it was possible. Besides it was nice to have something to worry about besides the present ticklish situation. In concerning myself with the care of my cherished sniping weapon I kept my mind off greater worries.

We arrived at Titi without incident in the afternoon and set up a hasty defense around the village area, taking advantage of available commanding ground. It was a pleasant, comfortable place— a large, grassy clearing with many shade trees and a pretty beach. Things now looked as though we *might* have an absolute pushover on our hands. The Japs had been in that village and had left it several days before. But the indications, as usual, were not correct; we were soon to find out that the Japs were very close and that our fighting was about to begin.

A patrol from "F" Company ran into a Jap patrol and engaged in a head-on fight which was indeed a sour deal. Five of our men were killed or missing and one of our native scouts was lost. The Japs had a heavy machine gun up front, in a four-man carry. They dropped it the minute they saw our people and it hit the ground popping. It was several minutes before our patrol could pin down the Japs and withdraw and the damage was mostly caused by several lucky bursts from the Jap strip-fed gun while that was being accomplished.

I only know what I heard of the fight—but it was an exceptional performance for the little brown brothers. It has been my experience that they almost always misbehave in that sort of fight, trying to close with the bayonet or some such foolishness. In this instance though, they sat tight and shot it out, completing an unusually good transaction for the Japs. (They only lost eleven men in getting five of ours.) We found one of our men days later, 12 miles north into their territory, where the Japanese had apparently left him to

Hidee

Japanese had to rest on the march, too. The one in the foreground who has assumed the universal "position of the soldier" is employing his headnet to keep off gnats and flies. With his sleeves rolled up we know he isn't greatly worried about mosquitos. He has pushed his rear cartridge box around to his side and unslung his pack, for complete comfort.

That was one Japanese failing, and a much worse one than we had—alertness during halts, I mean. These two Nips are about as alert as a hibernating bear. The intensity of Japanese march efforts made them able to cover a lot of ground, but with considerable sacrifice in security. Notice here how the near Jap's rifle is lying—where it would be hard to grab quickly; chances are that there is no round in the chamber.

This sketch does not show their tendency to bunch up on halts, making an easy target for automatic-weapons fire. They committed that error also; killing them was child's play if you could lay an ambush at a likely halting spot along the line of march.

die with a shot through the body. Another was never found. The bodies of the rest were later found, stripped naked and knifed in the legs, close to the scene of action. It is a sure thing that this all worked to the later disadvantage of the Japs.

After the patrol pulled back into the perimeter and gave us this information we got set for a night's stay. While we were so doing two other tough events happened. First of all one of our men was killed by our own artillery, registering in. This man had made a show of violating an order to take cover and had paid for it with his life—another tragically useless casualty, foolishly leaning against a tree, disregarding a shouted order to take cover. He taunted his buddies for worrying about "those little pop-gun 75s" while the shells "shooshed" over his head. The next moment he was a palpitating, unrecognizable mass of flesh and bone.

The second happening had comical aspects—after it was over. Colonel Ferry had just moved his command post outside a metal roofed shack for the evening when one of our noble little naval craft came by steaming about 1,000 yards off shore. It took one look at the activity in our little seaside village behind the Jap lines and without further ado began to shell the merry hell out of us. The first salvo struck the Colonel's erstwhile command post and turned it into rubble. The second screamed over with the distinctive sound of "light" naval artillery and exploded spitefully in the treetops, showering the area with fragments from which there was little cover. A third and a fourth followed but by the Grace of God, no one was killed.

A man sharing a ditch with me during the shelling looked to the sky and muttered a deeply intoned "Jesus Christ!" The way he said it lead me to believe that it was not meant to be profanity. It sounded more like an earnest appeal to some one up there who should have been keeping a closer watch, and not allowing such embarrassing things to happen to us. In undue time the destroyer ran up a "so sorry" signal, realizing the mistake. The battalion commander was by this time almost dead with rage. The lack of casualities did not lessen the dressing-down the commander of the destroyer got from Colonel Ferry—or at least that is the story I heard, and did not doubt.

I was scheduled to command the first force to head north the next evening with Capt. Danny Prewitt due to leap frog over me on the following day. I went to sleep that night with the myriad wonders and doubts of if, when, what, whirling in my mind. I had a feeling that it would not be long before my sniping rifle would be fired again. It was a beautifully clear and pleasantly cool, starry night. Its warm charm seemed wonderfully appealing to me, perhaps because af a fancied fear that I might not live to see another.

MOP UP ON THE TANAMBOGA RIVER

I took off north the next afternoon with a section of my own machine gun platoon and a rifle platoon formed into a combat patrol. We were to "point" the forward movement of the force. Our orders were to advance approximately 1,000 yards into the area where our last patrol had been shot up and to dig in and hold for the night. The whole of "G" Company was to leap frog over us if the resistance we encountered was not adjudged too heavy. Otherwise "G" Company would be reinforced and would take over. We proceeded quietly through our lines and took to the same trail used by the unfortunate patrol.

The terrain was very open compared with the ordinary coconut groves we had traversed; there was very little underbrush, barely enough to cover prone or kneeling men in most places. Our trip was a scary but uneventful one. We passed a scattering of cartridge cases left there by the Jap heavy machine gun and went on beyond, walking along with extreme alertness. We kept eyeing available cover and outlining ahead our individual courses of action should we be fired on. But the Japs had withdrawn and our passing was not contested in any way. We arrived at our halting point, which I adjusted farther northward for best use of automatic weapons fire. There we put up barbed wire and dug in.

Our artillery delivered harassing fire on the village of Morovovo, several thousand yards to our front, throughout the greater part of the night. When dawn came one of my men expressed his hopes that the harassment of the Japs had been commensurate with the harassing we had received. Intermittent salvos had passed directly over our heads, making sleep well nigh impossible despite the unusually comfortable holes we had dug.

Captain Prewitt arrived at dawn, walking at the head of his column with a Colt .45 held swinging in his right hand. He was a little annoyed at the orders he had gotten from force headquarters: First, he had been told to move as far as he could; then he had been told to go only as far as Morovovo. While we were organizing our columns the battalion commander arrived on the scene and cleared up the confused orders. He told Danny to move on to Morovovo, a few miles north, and hold there for the night. I was to follow along with my previously organized group and serve as reserve for "G" Company. A Marine lieutenant from the 75mm battery was accompanying Danny's point. Along with them was a detail of signalmen who carried a radio, and uncoiled telephone wire behind them, as double check means of communication.

I allowed the tailend of the new advance guard to clear me by about ten minutes before pulling out. My group had a 511 radio set for communication while moving and a field phone handy to tap onto the wire when we halted on the trail.

We moved along with a feeling of suspense building up constantly within us—things had to happen pretty soon. After all, we had moved several miles into territory which was alive with Jap sign—footprints, discarded cigaret packages, odd bits of equipment, diggings—all very fresh. As hours passed this feeling grew. Surely the Japs were not going to let us walk right into their back door!

We heard the column ahead of us splashing into the water of some sort of a stream. I paused to check my map and found that it had to be the stream upon which our objective—the village of Morovovo—was sited; there were no other streams around. We walked on, 100 yards or so behind "G" Company, and began to ford the stream, glad that it was near the end of the march so that we would not have to walk far with wet feet.

We were half way across the stream's 30 yard width when the long-expected shooting began up at the head of the column. The noises were uncertain, rapid bursts, indicating one of two things: A Jap Nambu light machine gun was being fired toward us, or a Tommy gun was being fired by one of our own people. The bursts were followed by more firing, then a babel of Jap yells interspersed with American profanity.

I took a very dim view of my little group's situation at that moment. I was standing in the middle of the stream, thigh deep in the water when the shooting began. The rest of my outfit was behind me in the water and on the bank, entirely too exposed. I pulled the whole unit back on the far bank and ordered them to take up positions to cover a possible withdrawal of "G" Company across the stream. Then I tapped my field phone in on the wire. I heard several familiar voices in excited conversation. The shooting was still going on and its sound had not decreased appreciably in volume. Lieutenant Quast was giving a shot-by-shot description of the fight over his phone from a spot right in the middle of it.

"Got five of 'em—laying right here in the village when we

walked up! We're shooting up another batch on the far side now! Krist! Watch 'em run!"

Colonel Ferry's voice broke in jubilantly, coming from group headquarters, back near Titi. "Good Work! Six slanteyes done for!" Captain Prewitt had his bit after that. His voice sounded calm: "Nothing has happened back here, Quast; need some help?" Quast's answer was drowned out in a burst of Jap bullets that popped too close to his phone. Then I got in on the party line. "Weren't hit, were you, Quast?" I asked. When I found out that he was okeh I sought a word with Captain Prewitt. I asked him what he wanted me to do, telling him that I was behind him and on the other side of the river. Danny told me to get around to his left flank, to cross the river at the beach and to out-flank the Japs.

This seemed like a very sound idea indeed, and it took only a few seconds to issue the order. In a few minutes we had doubled back to the beach and started back north. We performed this maneuver at a dead run, maintaining a workable tactical formation the while. However, when we got to the point where the trail crossed the river we paused in dismay. There was no cover for the next 200 yards. Some sort of diggings were on the other side, probably for automatic weapons covering the sandy delta in front of us. There was nothing else for me to do but cross on the spot as best I could. I crossed the outfit a squad at a time, with the remainder of the force covering their movement, ready to open up on anything that started to shoot from the far bank.

Luck was with us in the extreme. We were inside the Jap diggings in a few moments. There was still some hot rice and several lighted cigarets left by the Jap gun crews. They had picked up their weapons and fled just before we arrived. The imprint of the tripods and butts of two "lights" were fresh in the sand in front of their deserted positions. Had they stood fast they could have killed half of my outfit.

I reorganized hurriedly on the far bank and got my 511 operator to working on his set, trying to get in touch with "G" Company. Firing was going on as hot as ever in the village which was now directly inland from my command. In a few minutes we established radio contact and the breath-taking word from "G" was: "Hold fast if you are on the north side of the river. We are driving the Japs towards you."

In frantic haste we set up a firing line, using the narrow strip of the sand from the roots of the coconut trees to the ocean as the axis of the line. This gave the men some cover, but it gave them no organization in depth. They were stuck with their backs literally against the sea, with absolutely no choice but to hold where they were. We were much concerned over the danger of shooting our own people and took the best measures we could to prevent it. I cautioned all of the men to be sure of their target—no shooting at anything not clearly recognizable as Japanese. I then began to site all of my automatic weapons to shoot across our front—another measure to lessen our chances of firing into "G" Company.

While I was finishing this task I was shot at by a Jap rifleman. The bullet passed so close to my left ear that I felt a sharp pain and the snap of the bullet was louder than any such sound I had ever heard in combat or on the range. While I was down on the ground, wincing and holding my ear, a group of Japs blundered into our left flank and more firing began. I had a rough idea of where the Japanese who shot at me was lurking, and as soon as my ear stopped killing me I started looking for him with the thought of shooting him in the belly so that he would die slowly.

The report of the Jap's rifle had merged into the pain-producing snap of the bullet so I knew he was close by. The rows of palms were so arranged that all aimed fire was confined to the alleys in between the rows of trunks and the ocean eliminated half of my directional guess work; he couldn't be out there. By a process of hasty deduction I located his approximate position. He was at the base of a palm about sixty yards down one of the two available fire lanes, crouching low, and observing from the left (my right) side of the tree. Unless he happened to be a southpaw I could see no reason for this; anyone in his right mind would have been peering around from the right, body hidden by the lower trunk of the cocoanut palm.

Since the even rows of trees obstructed fire from all but two directions, there had been but two truly suspect spots. And these had been limited in depth by my knowledge that the shot had been fired from very short range. Actually I had but two narrow strips of ground—perhaps four by fifty yards apiece—to inspect. I had selected the most likely to search first and, luckily, had found him there.

The fight was going on hot then, over to my left, but somehow I managed to keep my mind on the individual who had come so close to killing me. I got into a huddle with myself behind the roots of a tree. The Jap had apparently assumed a kill, for he was now not even looking in my direction. My relatively long stay in the dirt had perhaps fooled him, though it is doubtful he would have seen the small portion of helmet that I *now* exposed. He was glancing around, scanning the area where the main body of my platoon was disposed—craning his neck like a buried gobbler at a country turkey shoot.

He towered in the field of the scope, visible to the third shirt button, the sweat of excitement and exertion showing on his face and khaki shirt. His lower body was screened by the thick weeds—which might have caused me to forget my animal resolve to shoot him through the middle. I set the picket post on his chest, fired, and saw him lurch forward as though struck from behind with a sledge hammer.

The main body of the crestfallen Nips staggered our way, fleeing "G" Company's attack. The confusion reached a new high. These Japs had Americans behind and in front of them, with common sense dictating that they turn right to escape annihilation. With typical Jap intelligence they chose to turn to the left, which brought them bang against the river—where some of them had started from! Having gotten over there they blundered into us again.

Results of this move were largely fatal. Four of them ran down an alley between the rows of coconut trees in obvious terror, without weapons. I shot one of them on the way and I suspect that the rest were killed by riflemen on the right flank of "G." The last shots of the engagement were fired by myself and several other men at two armed Japs who were attempting to drag one of their wounded comrades to safety. All three were killed.

The firing died away suddenly. Immediately I became terribly worried about the likelihood of our firing at "G" Company as it would come into view. I got the operator busy again trying to make contact with Prewitt or Quast—both of them had been involved more than we in the shooting spree. As radios often do, this one failed us utterly. Nothing to do but sit tight and wait. I could not outrightly tell the men to cease fire. The next people they saw might be Japs. However, I decided to risk a yell or two and I called out in my loudest voice: "Lollypop! Lollypop!" which was a universal password on Guadalcanal. No answer came but in a short time there was a movement in the bush in front of us. One of Prewitt's native scouts emerged. I have never been happier to see anyone.

I secured a quick nosecount from my platoon sergeant and was pleased to find that we had only a few scratches—no one badly hit.

I went on with the native to find Quast, walking along a path on the bank of the river. Even this venture turned out to be risky. After we had taken our first few steps along the high bank in some manner a grenade fell from the native's belt and began to sputter at my feet. I immediately dived headlong into the river, completely immersing rifle, scope, pack and myself in the water, which was quite briny so near the ocean. Forgetting the rifle and scope I remained submerged to the neck until the damned grenade went off, whirring its fragments merrily past my ears. Drenched to the skin I crawled back up the bank, feeling the while a fiendish hope that the careless native would be dead. He was quite alive, though, having stepped behind a palm. The narrow trunk gave ample protection to his pencil-like body, while the fuse burned and the grenade harmlessly detonated.

The native enjoyed a big laugh. He did not even stop laughing when I angrily took his other grenades away from him. He had bent the pins straight, so that they would come out easily; he had not substituted tape but had merely hung them by the levers on his Japanese leather belt. How he had lived as long as he had with such habits was beyond me, especially after he told me in pidgin that he had had several grenades go off on him before. His hand, he said, was too weak to pull the unstraightened pins. I told him to shut up and to go to hell.

After this disturbing delay we continued our walk toward "G" Company and in a few minutes Lieutenant Quast and I were slapping each other on the back and congratulating each other on still being alive. We had many things to do—and quickly. We were not set up for the night and it seemed quite likely that the Japs might counterattack in strength. Captain Prewitt, Quast and myself went into a huddle to decide on a plan of defense for the night.

With the policies of the regimental commander in mind, I held out against Danny's idea to draw back across the river. It seemed to me to be foolish to give up ground that we would have to retake, but Danny prevailed. At the moment I held it against him, but events of the night were to prove how very right he was and how absolutely wrong my idea would have been. We organized again —Danny had not lost a man either—and we withdrew to the other side. As we waded back to the south side I wondered how many lives it would cost us to get back across on the following morning.

We sat up a triangular perimeter with one edge against the sea, strongest side facing the north. Lieutenant Wojek, the Marine artillery observer, set up his phone close by the command post and he and I shared an enlarged foxhole that night. He gave me an account of the experiences he had during the day while we were digging in. His day had been an unusual one for an Artilleryman. Twice he had been involved in fighting at near-bayonet distances while walking with Prewitt's point. One of the Japs that Quast had announced killed while speaking over the phone had fallen to his .45 automatic.

Just as we were crawling in our holes for the night a Nambu on the far side of the bay cut loose and fired a clip at us. Its bullets streaked across the water, splashing and kicking up sand on the beach, finally ricochetting into our positions. I grabbed my rifle and ran out to a little vantage point, hoping to locate the gun. But the shadows on the far shore of the bay were dark beneath the palms—so dark that the additional luminosity of my scope would not bring out the hidden palm-trunks. The gun did not reopen fire.

While we were still looking Wojek handed his field glasses to Captain Prewitt, asking him to identify a certain group of objects on the far beach. "Two camouflaged Jap barges!" said Danny after peering briefly through the glasses. "You're wrong, Skipper," said Wojek, "there are *three* barges over there; I'm gonna try to get some hits on them while I've still got enough light to observe by."

He phoned back a fire order and promptly got two rounds over. The rounds struck, exploding short, in the water. He then rolled into the boats and hammered them as much as the limited ammunition supply would permit. (A day later we were able to examine the effect of those few rounds. They had destroyed the barges and a large batch of Jap equipment stored inside with apparent intent to get it off the island.)

The night passed pleasantly but not quietly in our perimeter. No Japs, no lizards. Only hundreds of land crabs, crawling every which way, across the bellies of sleeping men, dropping down now and then on a poor soldier asleep in the bottom of his hole.

But across the river, in the village we had assaulted and then left deserted for the night, things were different—vastly so. Several 90mm and quite a number of knee-mortars gave it a heavy pounding through the early part of the night. While the mortaring was still underway the Japs machine gunned the deserted huts to a fare-thee-well, adding a heavy volume of rifle fire, which was delivered in volleys, apparently by command.

Then the little brown men filled the night with weird screams, clearly audible from our position a mile from the village and subjected the vacant huts to a terrifying banzai charge, followed by scattered rifle fire. The shooting and yelling continued for an hour, indicating that some of our friends were meeting a glorious death —fighting amongst themselves in the darkness.

Laughable as all of that was, it was nevertheless an exhibition of considerable Jap strength in our locality and many of us cut our laughter short on that account. For myself, I now felt that Captain Prewitt had certainly been correct in his decision to return to the south bank of the river. Without barbed wire we would have had great difficulty withstanding the attack had we set ourselves up in the village. And we would have set up there had we remained on the north side; it was the only tenable position in the vicinity.

Had my recommendations been complied with I might well not be writing this story. It was our good fortune that Captain Prewitt's better judgment was available. I told him so the next morning. Had I not mentioned it though, Danny would never have directed an "I told you so" at me. He wasn't that kind of soldier.

The next morning my platoon was consolidated by the arrival of my other squads and I reverted to the control of force headquarters. My MG platoon was then assigned to reinforce "E" Company, (commanded by Lieutenant Geisel) and we marched inland on a wide enveloping movement. Our route looped into the lower hills east of the coconut groves, along a series of trails that would have been impassable in most places for animal transport.

After a long march through jungle which had been vacated some hours before by withdrawing enemy we came to a high, commanding spur. It was a fine commanding position, reaching from the mountains across the coastal plain, all the way down to the sea. Just as darkness overtook us we organized a defense line. We dug as long as we had light, clearing short fields of fire in front of our positions by cutting the deep grass with bayonets. When it became dark we passed along the word to stop all digging. This was necessary to prevent giving away our position to possible Jap infiltration parties and to enable our outposts to listen more effectively.

It was the most interesting and eerie night that I spent on Guadalcanal—that night on a ridge top overlooking Beaufort Bay. It was also one of the most memorable examples of lost opportunity I have ever seen. A Japanese destroyer or submarine pulled into the bay just after dusk and took on a number of evacuees. All sorts of craft: boats powered by outboard motors, row boats, life rafts, landing barges—all were used that night in effecting the escape of several hundreds of Japs. One of the principal embarkation points for the operation was within spitting distance of us—less than 300 yards below and to our front.

Yet we could do nothing. We did not have ammunition to fire blindly—we had only a few rounds of 6omm mortar stuff. No machine gun or rifle ammunition to blaze away with at area targets. But we were sitting and watching hundreds of Japs leaving an island that rightly should have become their last resting place!

The most tantalizing factor involved was that we had our artillery in position, in readiness to bring deadly fire to bear on a closely observed enemy. We could have engineered a wonderful slaughter with a few rounds of high-explosive. But it was the ancient and honorable military problem of communication. The damned radio always weakened as night set in. Just a characteristic of that particular set—the M511. Geisel struggled heroically all night in an effort to make contact with Force, but luck was not with him. He climbed a tree to gain height for the antenna; he yelled into the mouthpiece at intervals all through the night; but to no avail! The guns of our Marine battery, which had displaced forward during the day in order to keep fire ahead of us, remained silent. The Japs loaded and escaped under our noses. That is, all that the vessel could carry escaped. Many wounded and sick were left behind. Many able bodied Japs were left behind while officers pulled their rank and lived to fight another day. That we learned later on when we killed or captured those who remained.

I moved over with Geisel and together we watched the activity below. Geisel was beside himself, angry beyond words that the Nips were making their escape. When one of our Navy patrol planes came over and dropped a flare on the scene we took up hope that perhaps some action would be taken. We anxiously waited for a cloud of bombers to come over from Henderson Field—even made plans to pull our people back on the south side of the hill during the bombing, but nothing came of it.

I went to sleep shortly after the plane came over. The last thing I remembered were the few words that Geisel uttered, expressing measureless disgust: "Isn't this the Goddamnest foul up you ever saw?" With that pathetic question he threw down the useless radio and lay down on the ground, pulling his poncho over his head. I did the same except that I had no poncho. I used a Jap ground cloth.

The next day had its brimfullness of action, excitement and triumph. Prewitt's column, which had been held up at dusk the day before by machine gun fire, enjoyed an early breakfast of "K" ration (we were getting it for the first time on this show) and shot its way through the Jap block, moving quickly to join us. We then waded down through the wet grass of the ridge and into the coconut groves. The whole grove was strewn with discarded equipment and abandoned Jap guns of all sorts left by those fleeing the island. Heavy machine guns in perfect condition, 90mm mortars, dozens of rifles, tons of supplies.

We halted and waited for the newly formed column to go on so we could take our proper place in it. Our halting place was the middle of a large leanto camp which had been used for some days by the Japs. It had the foul smell characteristic of all places where Japanese soldiers live. It was filthy; flies buzzed around in millions, feasting on bodies and offal.

I selected a coconut stump and sat down. Subconsciously I began to fumble with my rifle which had remained loaded and locked through the night. I had cleaned the barrel, of course, but I had been unable to disassemble the weapon after its immersion some 48 hours before. The salt water had nibbled a bit on the scope tube and mount—that was the first thing I had noticed. But in a moment I examined the weapon and found that corrosion had set in on the action to a dangerous extent. I could no longer depend on the little piece and there would be no immediate opportunity to get it back into shape. I regretfully turned it over to an officer from rear echelon and transferred my pistol from holster to hand until I located a good M38 Arisaka .25 carbine and some ammunition for it. I fired a few shots at some floating bottles to check the sighting and the results were pleasing. The points of appeal which made me decide to give the little gun a try were its compactness and its light weight. I loaded it with some of the long-nosed .25 caliber Jap cartridges, after discarding the useless receiver cover. I felt quite happy with the little barleycorn front-sighted job. It was a bit of a novelty. Then too, in the back of my mind was the thought, I guess, of shooting a Jap with a Jap weapon.

When we were falling into the column and getting ready to move, a broad-shouldered, squatly built officer approached me. He had a Tommy gun held aggressively in his hand and a stub of a cigar in one corner of his mouth. This gave him such a striking resemblance to the Hollywood version of a Chicago gangland character that I almost chuckled. When he came closer, however, I recognized him as Lt. Col. Paul Gavin, the dynamic G–3 of the American Division. He paused not for a second but went on by at a slow gallop, yelling as he went, "You're in pursuit; the Japs are giving in; get going!" The column moved faster; Gavin broke into a trot to get up to the front. The trail we were then on ran alongside the water, with only a few yards of coconut grove between it and the beach. In compliance with the Colonel's order we were ignoring flank security and plodding straight ahead. At this point our march was interrupted.

Two shots were fired over our heads from the rear. A Jap was lurking in the narrow band of trees to the left of the beach road. All took cover for a minute while we hunted him down. I saw him in the brush some yards from a side path, so close that I killed him with my pistol. Sergeant Hill and myself walked cautiously up to the Jap who was then in his death struggles. Hill reached down into the death-retching Jap's inside pockets and with a callous remark of "pardon me buddy, but you won't be needing this anymore—" removed the dying Jap's billfold and a battle flag. We needed the information in the billfold and we did not have time to be too polite about getting it.

The column went on its way, shooting itself through very weak Jap resistance. Up at the front, Colonel Gavin was having the time of his life. He ran forward and applied his Tommy gun on more than one occasion—and once he shot dead a stubborn Jap in the center of the trail. After the point was moving to his satisfaction he came back and joined the headquarters of the assault echelon, walking along and kidding the group in a heartening way.

Even at the rapid pace we were making, some of the natural phenomena of the island drew our interest. I became fascinated by a large cloud of black and purple butterflies milling above a group of Jap bodies beneath the palms. The accordion action of the column had caused us to halt in the spot for a moment. I had never before seen so many butterflies in such a small space—in fact, I had never counted that many butterflies in all my life—and each butterfly bigger and more beautiful than any previously observed.

While I was looking at the butterflies the U. S. Navy again entered into our little show. Another destroyer hove to and immediately—to our consternation—gave us a broadside. The shells screamed over our heads and exploded inland from us. A second salvo hit lower.

Colonel Gavin began roaring above the sound of the shells: "*GODDAMN THE GODDAMN NAVY; GODDAMN 'EM! GODDAMN 'EM!*" Furious, he called for a telephone. Lying beside him I helped strip the insulation and tap it in. "Krist almighty!" he yelled into the mouthpiece after giving the instrument the hardest and fastest cranking it had ever received. "Answer me, Goddamn you!" He continued in tones that should have made the metal and plastic instrument come to life and speak on its own—but the phone was dead.

A signalman down the line suggested that the phone might be on ground-return circuit, so the Colonel yelled for a bayonet while the Navy kept pouring in the shells, which, thank God, were still going high. I drove the bayonet into the ground and reversed the phone while the Colonel continued his energetic cranking. My job became more entertaining at this time because the Colonel's voice had become loosened with his initial burst of profanity. He set out upon a new succession of oaths which were more varied in vocabulary, more explosively delivered, and far more descriptively vivid. He spoke of the admirals in the Navy and the officers of lesser rank, discussing their ancestry, moral standards and intelligence. He dwelt at length on the value of the Navy as a means of National Defense, comparing its ships unfavorably with the teats of the male swine. As if in answer to the Colonel another, and a closer, salvo came over. Some of us wondered if they could hear him out there.

The phone just would not work. He rose to his feet and heaved the phone, box and all, into the dirt. "As usual!" he roared. "No Goddamn communication."

With that the ship ceased fire and steamed off—perhaps having been informed of its error by force headquarters. Our march continued without further incident other than the shooting of another Jap. In two hours we were halted on the trail for a long time, wondering what had happened and waiting for word from up front.

Our artillery had been ordered to cease firing; contact with our own main forces pushing south was imminent. Perhaps that was the case. We all hoped so and our hopes were fulfilled. The word was not long in getting back. It was the best news we could expect. Contact had been made with friendly forces!

That night we heard it announced by radio that the end of organized Japanese resistance had been officially declared by General Patch, the popular commander of the Americal Division and the XIV Corps. It was the best news anyone on the island could hear.

We knew of course that there were still a lot of Japs running around loose on Guadalcanal—but the big job was done. The rest would be nothing in comparison to the task completed. We had little trouble with the last ones we had killed. Knowing that more were left was not discouraging when we believed that their last remnants of organization had been shattered. It was a great thing to be able to get a good night's sleep with the prospect of a good bath the next day. It was a good thing to have the last veils of fear lifted in respect to the Jap's competence as a foeman. We knew now that the Jap was in many ways a definite bush-leaguer.

That was what the final capture of Guadalcanal meant to us. We wondered what it meant to the folks back home and to the rest of the world. After all it was the first bit of territory which the Axis Powers had been forced to give up in the war.

REST FOR THE WEARY

The assault echelon of the force halted on the south bank of the Tanamboga River—a spot that had been beautiful before it was visited by the influence of war. We camped there to take a first breath after the fight had ended and to execute a new mission. We were to mop up the nearby hills of the scattered enemy parties which had been cut off from rescue by our march down the coast.

The scene that surrounded us was one of intense human suffering and death. Japanese dead—dead from all causes, wounds, disease and starvation—were everywhere; their maggotty bodies breeding clouds of flies. The insects swarmed onto our food during meals and prevented any rest during daylight hours. We were camped in the coconut groves where the stench and the flies were worst. For a few days we went to work burying the dead and burning the filth left by the Japs. We had lived like animals for a long time, and it became a pleasure to set about housekeeping tasks again.

There were few supplies shipped out to us other than food and essential clothing. We had to improvise shelters from the materials at hand—materials left by the Japs, for the most part. Little hardship was involved there, however, because there were plenty of canvas rice bags and serviceable mosquito nets. After cleaning or boiling they were utilized for shelter and bedding. Our stoves were brought down to us by the supply boats and we were fed cooked "B" rations while we conducted the mop up. All of us had tremendous post-combat appetites; we ate ravenously, making up for missed meals and regaining weight lost during the operation.

We built frame shacks and covered them with canvas salvaged from Jap tarps and rice bags. In a few days we had the makings of a well-policed jungle village. The clouds of flies had been greatly reduced by the burial of hundreds of dead Japs and our kitchens had been screened with the captured mosquito bars. The trimmings of an American camp were not entirely left out either, for here and there among the rows of shanties could be seen little plots of

flowers and palms, and the usual mock street signs were not long
in making an appearance. When they did appear they were all
Chicago names. My shack was situated on State and Madison—
so attested by a painted marker in front of my ever-open door.

With all of the new feeling of security we continued to maintain
a thin perimeter outside the village. There were many Japs around
—a fact that we were not long in verifying as we sent our first
patrols.

Major Wirt ("War-Horse") Butler took over the battalion
from Colonel Ferry when the Colonel became force commander.
He conducted the mop up operations, which were highly successful
in that the area was practically clear of all enemy before we left.
Fifty-two prisoners were taken and hundreds of Japs were killed
during our stay at Tanamboga. Our casualities were negligible.

It was a period worthy of memory to me—those days in our
little camp there on the shores of Camp Esperance. It was crowded
with comic anti-climaxes—happenings that could be viewed with
humor again, once we knew that the great dangers were gone. The
Navy was still fighting in the waters near us and each night we
could hear and see their activities. But we settled comfortably.

I secured my rifle and got it into good shape again. The scope
had not been damaged; all the corroded parts were found to be
all right. After a good boiling and a light going over with some
emery cloth it was as good as ever. Indications were that there
would be more Jap hunting so I hurried to sight the weapon in.
Accuracy was good—unaffected by the submersion in salt water.

Art Hantel and myself had a chance to get together again during
our easy time at Esperance and do a little everything from going
on patrols with each other to shark fishing off Savo Island. Our
excursions, plus a few fantastically high-stake poker games, permitted the time to pass fairly well, even when we were not busy
with patrols or housekeeping tasks.

For our sporting pleasure we had many things at our disposal.
There were plenty of Jap plywood folding boats with outboard
motors. We were able to improvise fishing tackle and even some
athletic equipment. Art and myself were anxious that our lost
weight would not come back on in the form of fat. To insure
against this we climbed a thirty foot rope six times each day, going
up hand over hand without using our legs. Each morning we took
a good swim in the none-too-safe waters of the bay.

After things were fixed up in our camp we really had little to
complain about, other than the obvious shortages of women and
entertainment. All in all, Cape Esperance was not a bad place. We
all fattened and got brown as coconut husks. I've had many worse
times since.

The battalion headquarters continued camping at Cape Esperance, functioning as a clearing station and a coordinating agency for patrols. The patrols fanned out into the hills each day on missions to hunt down and capture or kill Jap stragglers. They did not have far to go to run into the enemy for there were plenty around close by; nearly every patrol brought back prisoners or souvenirs. Collections of swords, battle flags and handguns showed a steady increase. Rifles were no longer regarded as worth while. I even gave away several Type 14 pistols to visitors. Later on in rear areas I was to see soldiers selling similar weapons for $100.00 or more.

The Jap survivors, now reduced to cringing animals by starvation and complete disorganization, became little more than ordinary quarries of the hunt. They were no longer thought of as dangerous. Those of our men who remained in the camp became more or less accustomed to the firing which would usually commence a few minutes after the patrols left the area. They knew what was happening. The patrols would come upon a group of the enemy and call upon them to surrender. Almost invariably the Japs would resist and end up dead. Standard Japanese behavior had given us little urge to take undue chances to capture them alive. But later on as their collapse became more and more apparent, we began to take more prisoners. As I remember, the total number of prisoners we took was 52; which at that time in the war against the Japs must have been some sort of record for a unit the size of a battalion.

We gathered the prisoners into a little bull pen enclosure in our camp and placed them under heavy guard. Having no interpreters we were forced to conduct our conversations by means of phrase books—(supplied by the Japanese propaganda or intelligence service). All of the Japs carried excellent little pulp-printed pocketsize books with phrases and sentences in Japanese characters, Japanese phonetics and English. There were chapters to cover every form of military conversation. A section on personel inquiry included the questions: "What is your name?" and "What is your age?" and "Where is your home?" and such. It was this part of the book which we used most often, questioning each Jap as he arrived.

Prisoners behaved in various ways. They were meek for the most part; only a few were sullen and slow to speak. Our men crowded curiously around them, giving them "D" bars (chocolate field ration), cigarets and candy, listening to their talk and watching their improvised sign language with great interest.

Most of them were ill with one disease or another. Many had symptoms of beri-beri, swollen ankles and lower calves from dietary deficiencies. Half of them had dysentery. To a man they were stinking filthy.

Their uniforms were the standard ill-fitting khaki or green cotton trousers with wrap leggings and coarse, poor-fitted leather shoes. The shoes had hobs set in a radial pattern around the edges of the soles. Some few had short-sleeved cotton shirts; most used the cotton blouse with turtle collar. Leather belts with matching ammunition pouches had been largely replaced by reinforced rubber or composition substitutes. The soup-bowl Jap helmet and peaked cap with star insignia were standard.

Inside their uniforms they wore flannel belly bands, thousand stitch belts, and money belts containing all sorts of Asiatic and island currencies. There were sums of American money on some.

The Japs, too, we found out, were also souvenir hunters. They had collected trinkets like greedy pack rats. Kits and map cases were filled with all sorts of loot—cameras, fountain pens and pencils, cheap jewelry; many photograph collections—a few albums, in fact, which displayed real photographic talent—were found in packs.

Much of their equipment was found more practical than ours. Their rifle cleaning kits were better than anything we had. They came in a little canvas roll not much larger than our oil and thong case, with a short-jointed cleaning rod cleverly enlarged at the joints to prevent buckling. (Ours had that on the old Krag-Jorgensen.) The tip supplied was of jag type and could be fitted to either the kit rod or the one carried on the rifle. The Japanese also had neat and well-made little oil cans, nestled in special compartments in the cartridge pouches. Included in the pocket-type cleaning kit was a wood or plastic guide for the rod. It replaced the bolt and insured against getting dirt and sludge in the action when withdrawing the rod from the breech.

Their oval bottomed kettle-type mess gear was very practical for field use. It was excellent for cooking rice and other foods, and the enclosed nestling trays were good to eat from. They would not have been satisfactory for our company mess system but were perfect for individual or small group cooking and eating in the field. A Japanese variety of canned heat was sometimes furnished for cooking. Two cans of flaming jellied alcohol fitted neatly beneath the kettle. Water would boil in a very short time if the cover were left lightly on. Most of the men supplied themselves with Jap mess kits and shovels, discarding their own.

We found the shovels to be better than anything we had at the time. Our own shovel of that date was a ridiculous toy by comparison. The handle of the Japanese instrument was beautifully shaped for easy handling; its tempered steel blade would hold a sharp edge to cut through roots. The last degree of practicability was in the perforations in the center of the blade. These prevented moist soil

Two Japanese soldiers, seeking to supplant their rations with a few pan fish. This method of fishing with very light bamboo poles and tiny baited hooks has always been popular in Japan, where many varieties of fish which we would call "minnies" are considered legitimate game fish. Tiny gut leaders and very thin silk lines were also standard, making tackle in Japan more delicate than anywhere else in the world. I have always laughed thinking of it—the incongruity of a squat, heavy muscled Samurai warrior seated on the edge of the Emperor's moat, fishing for shiners!

But the Japs learned, even before we, that a hand grenade or a block of picric acid detonated under water was a much better method of filling the griddle. Best bet was to station one man at a good looking fish hole to drop the charge, with the remaining sportsmen lining the banks downstream, ready to pick the stunned fish out as they would float past.

Reminds me of an incident:—

An American battalion commander once came in and reported the results of a Guadalcanal fishing trip to me, just after beaching his captured Jap outboard. "Georgie," he said with great enthusiasm, "Look at that boatload of fish! Best fishing trip I've ever had! Caught better than forty pounds of those little shiny ones, and more than two hundred pounds of the big brown scaled ones! Wonderful Sport!"

As an afterthought "And I only used twenty blocks of TNT!"

"Anything that works," I sez.

from clinging by suction. There was a larger hole near the handle for tying the shovel to the pack—a great convenience.

All of the Japs had handy little iodine dispensing bottles—little glass affairs with a small opening and a cork-gasketed bakelite-threaded top. These had our iodine swabs of that period beat all hollow. (Our later-manufactured jungle medical kit wisely imitated the Japanese bottle.)

Jap clothing, bedding and all cloth articles, other than those made of canvas, were vastly inferior to ours. Their blankets were of cotton, almost useless in the Guadalcanal climate because they absorbed moisture and became clammy during the night.

The weapons we found—an assortment of all types of foreign guns as well as those of Jap manufacture—were not as good as ours. I will discuss them later in detail but a mention of their names now will give an idea of what museum-collector propensities must exist in Jap ordnance circles.

There were different models of Mannlichers, Steyrs, Enfields (M1917 and British), Mausers, and of course their own rifles as well. Hundreds of pieces rusted on the ground or were buried in filled-in pillboxes and shelters. We found several anti-tank 20mm ground rifles (semi-auto ground mount jobs that fired from the shoulder) and an assortment of heavy and light mortars and grenade throwers. I, being the accepted battalion authority on firearms identification, was embarrassed several times by my inability to identify guns brought to me.

Picric acid, the Jap explosive used in place of TNT, was piled all over the place. Stretches of the surf along the beach were stained a bright yellow from the tons of it dissolving in the waves. Also in the water on the beaches were several Jap planes, trim little Zeros, unpainted except for the big red spots on the wings and fuselage. We put the ships under guard to prevent dismantlement by our own souvenir hunters.

The collection of pistols at battalion headquarters reminded me of a pawn shop window. There were Colts (Frontier models and others) and there was every conceivable make and type from Belgium, Spain, China and England, good stuff and junk. So the place was a natural spot for a firearms enthusiast as well as a fisherman or beachcomber.

Our hideout in the coconut groves became more pleasant as time went on. The area was steadily improved and we enjoyed more leisure. Soon everyone had an opportunity to clean his clothes. We had a bathing and washing point at the mouth of the river with a guard posted to shoot at sharks.

Feeling lazy, I tried to save myself the trouble of laundering. I staked my only pair of fatigues out in the surf, using a short length of rope and a rusty Jap rifle barrel. Then I draped a piece of parachute silk about my hips and waited. After I picked the garment up and emptied the accumulated sand out of the pockets I felt rather proud of my labor-saving ingenuity. The clothes were perfectly clean. A rinse in fresh water and a half hour in the sun finished the job. They seemed perfect but it was too good to be true. Something happened. After a deceptive two days, during which I advised everyone else to follow the same procedure in cleaning their clothes, all of the seams gave way. It took tedious work with a Jap sewing kit to undo the damage and release myself from an involuntary nudist status. I was not alone in my unhappiness though; several others had followed my ill-given advice and their clothes also fell apart. Naturally they blamed me for everything.

We often fired our weapons at sharks and birds right in the area. One day a lizard got up in a tree and we all witnessed a neat exhibition of pistol marksmanship by Major Butler. His Frontier .45 knocked the reptile out of the very top of the high palm. The major was mighty handy with that weapon; it was all he had carried in combat.

Esperance was happily apart from the details, the bombing and the noise of the Henderson Field end of the island. Lunga Point we knew would be much more uncomfortable—glutted with the huge supply unloading operation.

So our stay at Esperance (on the Tanamboga) proved to be of interest. Much of it was by no means dull. Many things humorous, many things serious, many things thrilling, occurred there.

BUSHWACKIN'

A heavy machine gun, sited about 80 yards from my sleeping place, fired a long, frightening burst at 4 o'clock in the morning. It was the first firing that had occurred during the night; all of us were startled. I sat up in my bed, grabbed my pistol and operated the slide to get a round into the chamber. After waiting a moment I let the hammer down to half-cock and relaxed somewhat. The darkness offered no explanation—no further sounds were heard. I could not understand why anyone would open up with a heavy machine gun at a target in the dark. Why couldn't they have done the job with a rifle or a grenade? I guessed that some gunner must have gotten a little too excited.

I pulled a pair of socks from beneath the small of my back and put them on. I was sleeping with my fatigues on—the only way I could keep warm without blankets and the only way I could keep my clothes from becoming clammy wet during the night. In the intense humidity after darkness it took body warmth to keep clothes dry.

I lifted my mosquito bar, stepped out of my hut and walked, pistol in hand, toward the machine gun position. I muttered the password over and over as I threaded my way between the huts. In a minute or two I arrived at the gun position and noticed that the gunner and the number two man were stretching their necks nervously watching the beach where the weapon was pointed. I got into the digging and asked them to give me the story.

The corporal spoke to me in a nervous whisper. An outboard-powered folding boat was out in front of the gun. It was a Jap boat that Art and I had been using. Something had approached in the night, lifted and placed the oars inside and started to pull it into the water. The gunner had aligned his weapon on the shadowy figure by loosening the elevating and traversing clamps and swinging the gun free. He had flushed the rear end of the boat with a long scattering burst.

We sat in the entrenchment and waited for dawn. I could see no point in going out to investigate the shotup area in the darkness. I sent one of the men back to give the story to battalion headquarters and remained there to wait for daylight.

The shadows of the palms took on a familiarly ghastly appearance in the dim starlight. The water was lapping audibly. This night, like the previous few, had not been brightly moonlit. One could always visualize the heads of swimming Japs out in the water among the bits of wreckage, or the forms of Japs creeping through the black shadows in the palm groves. The three of us strained our eyes together for a half hour; then we came to our senses and established fifteen minute watches at the gun.

Everyone felt nervous because of the firing. The gun's position had been given away by the burst; a Jap might sneak through the thin line of riflemen in front and grenade the emplacement. Or he might accurately throw a grenade from beyond the protecting ring of riflemen. We strained our ears as well as our eyes—trying to detect the sputtering of any grenades before their explosion. But for a long time we saw nothing but shadows; heard nothing but jungle sounds and water lapping on the sands.

But the first peep of light did the trick. Dawn came up over the mountains and the direct rays of the sun were glancing high for a while. But the sky reflected enough grey light to expose a distinctly unbeautiful scene below on the beach.

An emaciated Jap, cut almost in two by the machine gun burst, was lying in the sand. He had apparently been pushing at the boat when the burst struck him in the middle. Apparently he had been alone. I hurriedly organized a patrol and searched the adjacent groves for signs of more Japs but there were no others around.

To one without our hatred for the Japs it would have been a pathetic scene. Killing a starving, helpless Jap as he made his feeble attempt to get off that island was no feat to boast of. The Jap was obviously young and some photographs on his person told us of his former health. He would have weighed a well-muscled 160 pounds when the pictures were taken; now he would go 85 or 90 pounds. There were also snapshots of his family in his billfold —his mother, father, brothers, along with some trinklets—his "chop" or signature-stamp, and some Chinese money.

We dug a hole in the earth and coral of the coconut grove and buried him. To us, dropping him in his grave, he was merely another enemy with whom we would not need to deal further.

After he was buried we turned our thoughts to breakfast. I'm afraid we may have neglected somewhat the job of burial, hurrying things up. We were hungry; we went over to the kitchen. Hash and canned tomatoes with "C" ration biscuits—a whole messkit full.

The few flies and comparatively mild stink that remained in the area did nothing to lessen our appetite. Even with the excitement of the night we were all ready for a meal. Our mess was still operating on a semi-tactical basis with the platoons messing one at the time. But it was a pleasure to be eating hot food away from actual combat. I fancied, looking at the stripped-to-the-waist men in the mess line, that some of their surface flesh was being restored. None of them had been emaciated—but many were down to almost bare muscle which knotted itself against their skin, displaying abnormally cordlike veins. There were no hidden ribs in our outfit; no one was overweight.

I was still sitting at the officers' table, enjoying a third helping of our sumptuous repast when one of the guards on duty at the hut where we kept the Jap prisoners came up to the table and asked the adjutant to visit the stockade; one of the prisoners wanted to talk.

Much enthused of getting a complete story from a Japanese, the officer concerned arose and slipped out through the mess-shack mosquito bar. He started to thumb through his Jap phrase book as he walked away. The others at the table—Lieutenant Hantel, Captain Peterson and myself got back to some serious eating.

There was everything there, I thought, that we had been missing for a long time. Around the kitchen the cooks had made the place as neat as possible. The aluminum field ranges were spic and span, though there were only two to feed 300 men. The captured mess gear with which the kitchen staff had supplemented the inadequate issue was equally clean—probably much cleaner than when in the care of its original owners.

The prize objects of the captured mess gear were two large, heavy stainless steel pans, very shallow, shaped like huge soup bowls and they were apparently made to be braced from the edges. They had no hooks, eyelets or legs. (I was later to find out in Burma that the Japs habitually built clay furnace-type foundations for this sort of utensil.) It was a very clever cooking arrangement. The captured pans were being used for heating hash and canned tomatoes. A further addition to the kitchen equipment were a few fine aluminum pots and pans that the Japs had taken from a shotup and beached American PT boat. Our cooks had salvaged it from one of the deserted Jap camps.

It was also apparent on looking at the kitchen area that a certain amount of landscaping had been done after a few carelessly buried Japs had been exhumed and reburied elsewhere. Small palm sprouts had been planted to outline a path and regulate the mess line traffic past the serving board. The "serving board" was an inverted Jap folding boat—a nice, easily scrubbed piece of plywood.

Hideo

Isn't there an army in the world whose Infantrymen are free from the fetters of Ordnance-convention? The Japs as well as ourselves were sent into the field with ammunition which would corrode a barrel overnight. Here they are, laboriously cleaning a barrel with water—the same as we had to do until belated shipments of bore cleaner got to us.

These boys are not in great danger at the moment, or they certainly wouldn't be fooling around with this complicated rig, just for the sake of keeping a rifle barrel bright. We sure as hell didn't, and accordingly our rifles rusted. It's asking too much of any man to keep a rifle bore clean when each shot fired deposits salt in the barrel. And the time consuming effort involved in water cleaning didn't increase our love for the people who provided our rifle and machine gun ammunition.

Finally, we did get bore cleaner; it was a good artifice to help nullify the fault of improperly compounded primers. It did away with the need for water cleaning. When carbine ammunition came out, with non-corrosive primers, at a much later date, we began to scratch our heads. If the Ordnance crowd could do it with the carbine, why couldn't they do it with the rifle ammunition?

We're still wondering about that. But it's a consolation to know that the Japs were up against the same thing. . . .

In the center of everything was a nicely lettered sign which gave the heavy weapons company of the battalion a neat sort of crest. "Snaky H" was the inscription—below a comic, coiled viper on a suspended shingle. The kitchen area was raked and policed twice a day with improvised bamboo brooms.

All of this, along with the lately-unfamiliar sound of the rattling mess gear and milling soldiery, comforted us and made us feel almost at home. In the afterglow of our good meal we were all inclined to be a bit cheery.

When the meal was finished we all leaned back around the table, the others looking at me with some envy. I was a non-smoker, the only one in the crowd, and the only one that at that moment was not acutely suffering from the pangs of after-meal cigaret hunger. Conversation waxed rabid around the table over the cigaret shortage on the island.

That talk about cigarets, however, amounted to nothing more than a beating about the bush. Soon the inevitable subject of sex was broached and energetically plunged into by the young bloods of the group. It seems that all chatter in an overseas army has to do only with topics concerning scarce commodities—women, of course, leading the list of shortages. I leaned back and listened, as I have a thousand times before, to the accounts of numerous conquests (and surprisingly few rebuffs) loudly described, with gestures and everything. Having heard most of them previously I found my pleasure in listening to the color these tales gathered with each retelling. It was amusing to note the changes in names and facts. I would let the little errors slip by, but I would always call the narrator if he changed the name of a city, or a blond to a brunette. It was more or less excusable to switch the names of hotels or even girls, but it stands to reason that a man won't forget the color of their hair and still vividly remember the other minute physical details.

A lieutenant across the table from me was glowingly relating the story of an affair with a preacher's daughter in Tennessee when our after breakfast bull session was interrupted by the returning adjutant. The adjutant came back with a handful of papers and a puzzled look on his face. We all pretended not to notice him.

The "adj" was a serious-minded, competent officer—but a deliberate clown. He had some entertainment at hand. He was about to issue one of his hilarious interpretations of the Colonel's orders —and with maps and stuff. He fumbled and fussed with the papers while the table was being cleared by a couple of tired-looking KPs and all leaned back and got ready for a good joke. We could always get the adj's goat when he was trying to be serious. We winked at each other as he fidgeted about the table, hurrying the KPs in their task. After the mess gear had been removed and the table top wiped off he spread his sketches, maps and aerial photos and cleared his throat. He had our undivided attention.

His opening remark was illuminating. "Boys," he said, "there are some Japs around here in these hills." He paused for a moment to give us time to digest that complex bit of intelligence, then went on. "And I have just found where some are hiding." More winks were exchanged, more looks across the table, and Captain Pete nudged me in the ribs with his elbow. The group was on the verge of a spontaneous guffaw. "One of those Goddamn prisoners decided to talk," the adj continued, "and he gave me a pretty good idea of the hideout location. It is right about here." As he said this last he laid a heavy thumb on the high altitude aerial photo indicating an area large enough to bivouac a division. Everyone laughed; Hantel spoke through his mirth. "Old Socko, did you ever hunt a needle in 14 haystacks?" Old Socko conceded that he had not. "Well, if you didn't you're going to have one hell of a time locating those Japs. I'm for sitting here and letting them come to us. We all know damned well that they are short of food. We'll lose a hell of a lot more men going after them than we will the other way. Let the bastards starve to death. It'll save ammunition and maybe a life or two. Maybe *my* life!" We all began filing out through the slit in the mosquito bar, leaving the adjutant to address coconut trees.

The adj then said something to me that destroyed my feeling of well being. "Wait a minute, George; the old man wants you to lead a patrol up to that place and capture those Japs." I stopped laughing at once. That damned place was a three-hour—maybe more—climb into the mountains. I asked the adjutant if he gave the old man the idea of sending me. There was no doubt about it —the joke was on me—I learned that as soon as I looked at the other officers.

Then the adj had his revenge. "Yah, Georgie," he said in his most irritating Irish tones, "the old man decided that you are getting too much lard on that skinny butt of yours. A little walk will do you good. Sure I put the bug in the old man's ear; I'm your friend. I have your best interests at heart. We can't afford to let your health deteriorate, can we?"

The adjutant added insult to injury. He told me that I would have to draw the men from "H" Company. I wondered how those tired boys would like to climb up the mountains and through the tangled forest to that damned spot he had indicated on his photograph.

The sun was almost directly above our heads as we began to gather and organize the 20-man patrol. I had pulled most of the men off their improvised but comfortable bunks (at that period in the war the term "sack" was unknown). They came willingly enough but it galled me to lead those men on what might well turn into a dangerous sort of wild goose chase.

The formation of the patrol was a strange scene for civilized eyes. A lineup of tattered uniformed men, falling in with an air of competent unconcern—an extreme casualness, welling, I guess, from self confidence. One glance down the line of tan faces would have informed any layman that the men were not worried. Most of them were merely annoyed.

About the only point of uniformity in the unit was the men's facial cast. They were all clean shaven. Their green fatigue clothes were so ragged, so worn out, and washed to such a variety of shades, that there was almost no similarity of attire. Shoes were frayed and unoiled. Most of the men wore the old style leather field shoe; only a few of the new Marine shoes had been stolen or bartered from the Navy. One of the group had a pair of black Navy oxfords which he had found on a beached PT boat. Three men, fortunate enough to have short but wide feet, had equipped themselves with Jap hob-nailed field shoes. For the country we were in they were by far the most practical of any footgear available.

Men were largely armed with weapons of individual choice. We had no carbines at that time; we had only heard of them, read statistics of how they were being manufactured by the millions back home. About half of the patrol had M1 rifles; the rest had Tommy guns or BARs. The Tommy gunners were carrying clips in preference to drums on this patrol. Drums were bulky as hell in the belt pouches; when attached to the weapon they were absolute rib breakers. We usually kept the drum magazines in the company baggage for use in defense situations only.

Many of the soldiers did not wear ammunition belts. All of them carried Jap water bottles—an item of equipment definitely superior to our own canteen. Also, many were wearing Jap haversacks. One man was carrying a short-barrelled Arisaka, a weapon of particular appeal in those pre-carbine days. It was light and handy; as I had determined it was not a bad rifle, once you removed and threw away the receiver cover.

In our little village street we were enacting a scene not unlike some I had seen in the movies. It might have been a posse being lined up and sworn in for a manhunt. The scene was like some western boom town with dusty streets and cheap board-built huts. There at Esperance we had everything but the horses. The lineup of the shacks in our little village was not unlike the false fronted buildings along the main street of a frontier town. The sand was much the same as dust in the wagon wheel ruts. The generally raw and disorderly appearance was appropriate for almost any Hollywood horse opera. The weather was hot and for the moment dry —another bit of American frontier atmosphere.

I walked the length of the file, shifting men from spot to spot, planting steady-nerved NCOs at critical points. I distributed my firepower through the column, avoiding clusters of automatic weapons. And in so doing I could not help feeling somewhat removed from the regimentation and uniformity of modern military craft. Because of the intensely personal aspects of jungle fighting, the thought of leading a small patrol was exciting. Every man would hold his life in his own hands with his chances for survival and his effectiveness against the foe depending upon his own skill and cunning. Huge scale, combined-arm teamwork would not be our task. These impressions made me feel more like a bandit chief or a guerilla leader than an officer in a modern Infantry division. It seemed a romantic, storybook sort of venture.

After we had organized the tactical formation of the column I called a huddle for final briefing. I then related all that I knew of the suspected Jap party—strength, suspected location, and probable state of alertness. This took less than five minutes. There was little that needed to be said. It was only a variation of an old, old story; the men had been on many similar missions.

There was small variety of expression on the faces of the men. As we organized in column and moved off only a few showed the least glow of expectancy. These were the men who were sick of the monotony of beachcomber existence. Also there were a few who were souvenir happy. But a great majority had the dull and disinterested look of men who were merely doing something which they would rather not be doing. This dull look can be described as a simple sagging of expression. The muscles of the cheeks apparently relax, the flesh hangs heavily from cheek bones. Only eyes remain alert.

A few faces were set with a sort of aggressive firmness. Most of those belonged to noncommissioned officers. These few men, regardless of peacetime backgrounds, had attained a sort of athletic bearing since landing on Guadalcanal. The strain and punishment that had bent the average soldier had seemingly added inches to their stature. Such men stood out in the group. No force could ever be victorious without a few of them. Our patrol of twenty was lucky to have three. I placed them carefully in the formation. They were the patrol life insurance.

I consulted a little checklist which I kept in my pocket to be sure that I covered all of the elements of a field order before we moved off. We did not synchronize watches because I had the only one in the group.

Quite a few of the men who were not going on the patrol gathered to see us off. These onlookers had maintained a grudgingly respectful silence during the organization of the patrol but as the column began to move out they contributed an amusing lot of chatter. All of the hackneyed remarks were heard:

"Gee! look at that bunch of sojers; ain't they purty?"; "Boy, what a rugged looking crew—bet you could scare hell outta the whole bunch with a handful of firecrackers!"; "Where's the brass band?"; "C'mon, get in step you guys! Lookit the Sarge! Clean uniform; ain't he the dude though!" and so on. I was glad when we cleared the village and walked through the main perimeter— still on the wide trail along the coast.

As we passed through the outguards, the column extended and staggered itself without command. I sent two scouts out front. A look backward at the march formation satisfied me that the men would be able to gain cover quickly if the trail should be enfiladed by a surprise burst.

That was the big worry—that first burst. If the Japs did any damage it was usually in that first blazing away. We would more than likely get off easy if we could get out of the exposed part of the trail before the second burst. Still you must be able to maintain some contact between patrol members. We struck a reasonable compromise between "dispersal" and "control" by keeping a staggered file with about eight paces between men. As the patrol leader I was constantly afraid of finding myself pinned down and too far away from my base of fire to exert control—unable to issue orders to influence the course of a fire fight.

I seemed to notice a tendency in the patrol for the men to spread out too much and I passed word along the line to not increase the distance. It was a fault which was very uncommon in the regiment several months previously. *Then* there had been a persistent tendency to bunch up. An organization will benefit quickly from the lessons of actual battle—lessons that demonstrate their worth in the conservation of human life.

My whispered orders were repeated back along the file and the march continued at a lessened pace. The scouts were threading their way cautiously; keeping a nervous lookout. The men behind kept up a steady searching of the vegetation on their flanks. These men had developed in a few months the keen eyes of the experienced outdoorsman or big game hunter. They had learned to instantly detect the least change in color in the jungle foliage; the slightest movement; they could also tell the difference between the mottled appearance of a fern and the netted surface of a Jap helmet. Terror is a great educational incentive.

Nothing had happened so far. Most of us were hoping that noth-

This is a typical Japanese stunt. In Burma and Indo-China Japanese doughboys added much to their mobility by utilizing every bit of civilian transport they could steal. The moderately decent road-nets there made bicycles and automobiles rather useful. The same was true in the Philippines and on some of the islands.

In places where there were no roads at all the Japs continued to place a high value on "transport." Most of them had never before so much as owned a bike so they were strong to keep the ones they had looted. A few bikes with Singapore tags on them were found on Guadalcanal, carried into remote jungle areas.

This drawing also shows the religious Japanese observance of camouflage discipline, from which our own Infantry could gain a lesson or two. Japs always used leaves and branches to break up the outlines of their bodies and their weapons. Most of them wore nets on their helmets, too.

Personally, I have always been able to see eye to eye with them on the camouflage, and sometimes on the idea of employing captured transport. On Guadalcanal, however, I think I would have chucked that damned bicycle into the woods.

ing would happen. We all felt that we would not encounter any Jap parties of equal strength but we were not eager to get into any kind of a fight.

We had reason to feel confident. The Japs who remained on the island (after General Patch had declared organized resistance to be terminated) were indeed disorganized, demoralized and starved. No soldiers of any army could be expected to endure such hardships and yet retain the will to fight or even to live. Malnutrition —a diet of straight coconuts—had weakened the average Jap to the point of death. Many had died in their shelters. Bodies without visible wounds were found by the hundreds.

When approached by our men, many of the surviving Japs could be counted on to make a feeble grab at a weapon. Some offered no resistance at all—they simply remained sitting or lying, looking up glassy-eyed at us. The latter were captured; the former usually were not.

The Jap soldier was now seen in his true light. We still respected his ability as a specialized jungle inhabitant, skilled at junglecraft. We knew he was capable of making himself very comfortable in island terrain. But the faults of the Jap individual Infantryman, as well as the recklessness of Jap Infantry tactics, were now evident to us all. Men of the Americal Division were no longer awed by anything Japanese. Our doughboys had met the Jap in the terrorizing closeness and intimacy of jungle warfare—and they had felt him give way before them.

Soon the scouts in front of me halted and took up rest positions; they wanted to scan the vicinity of a trail junction ahead. We had arrived at the place in the coconut grove trail where we were to turn eastward into the mountains, away from the sea.

I passed an order along the line for a ten minute break and went up to join the scouts. They had turned up the side trail and were looking without eagerness toward the jungle clad range of foothills which we would have to traverse. This trail was a very short one, petering out within a few hundred yards of the junction. We would quite likely have to cut our way along a good part of the route—a risky way to travel in enemy country because the noise will alert the entire jungle around you; and the men who wield the machetes are momentarily helpless if fired upon.

After the ten minute break we moved on with redoubled caution. The trail narrowed into a footpath and the column closed up, leaving a scant three paces between men. As we reached the edge of the groves and began to climb the slopes of the first hill the path became a mere hog trail. Then it disappeared altogether in a tangle of roots, vines and decayed leaves. Soon, in order to maintain visibility, the interval between men was cut to two paces.

We noted that the cover was not impenetrable. We could thread our way through without getting out the machetes and without stooping and bending backwards under branches and vines. Everything in this jungle was moist; dampness was in the air and every leaf was wet to the touch. The atmosphere was faintly reminiscent of the first trip I made to a tropical plant conservatory and the smells too, were similar.

But the dampness did not make silent movement possible. Our rubber-soled shoes would slip on the roots and we would fall to the jungle floor, cushioned on impact by the decayed and spongy mass of roots and leaves. But rifles would thud against trees and vines and other items of equipment would unavoidably rattle.

We used our hands constantly, gripping vines for support as we swung beneath lateral obstructions. But only one hand was free for such support. Our weapons were never slung on a shoulder; they were always at the ready.

The men helped each other. They lent a hand to a man behind, lifting him over an obstacle, held branches bent away from the path while comrades passed. A book could be written about march etiquette in the jungle, stressing points of always warning the man behind of pitfalls, thorns and nettles; always helping a fallen man to his feet; trying to avoid pointing your weapon at a man in front of you; and innumerable other small politenesses.

After an hour's walk we saw light ahead through treetops and I went forward to the scouts to investigate, calling a fifteen minute rest to give them time to return and report their findings.

As I expected, we were nearing the bald spot on the first crest. Obviously it was inadvisable to emerge from the jungle and avail ourselves of the better going on the grassy top of the hill but temptation to do so was great. We had to turn to the right and remain in the cover. More than likely any party of Japs in the hills above would have an OP overlooking any of the lower crests and had we emerged from cover our chances of catching prisoners would be greatly lessened.

Sergeant Hill suggested that we might take a look at things from a handy tree but I shelved the idea until we should arrive at the next crest. I had previously scanned the area we were in from the beaches carefully, through a pair of Jap observation binoculars, but I had seen nothing. Then too, our airplanes were constantly patrolling above these hills and no sign of enemy activity had been reported. With such measureless areas of jungle to hide in, I figured that our chances of seeing anything from a tree OP would be just about nil.

On starting to reorganize the column to move on after the break, I found a man huddled against a tree, shaking like a leaf, with

teeth chattering to beat the band. He was pale and a little nauseated, but he was listening with some humor to the remarks of a
few men around him. His skin was a greenish yellow, attesting that
he had been religiously taking his atabrine. But no doubt about
it—the man was suffering an acute malarial relapse.

It was considered proper (on Guadalcanal) to laugh at a man
in such a state. The poor soldier (an 18-year-old) had buttoned up
his fatigue jacket and was still shivering in the 90-degree heat.
Back in the states he would have excited a good bit of sympathy
from any crowd. We kidded him, gave him some quinine tablets,
and told him to go back to camp and lie down. We sent no one
back with him. I chuckled to myself. Had the boy been back home
his mother would have put him to bed and frantically summoned a
doctor.

We moved on again in a generally southeastern direction. For a
while the light showed increasingly through the treetops to our
left to indicate the bald crest's location. Then we moved into the
deep jungle low on the next hillside. We didn't use the brush
knives, though there were many places we could have saved time
by so doing. We wished to move as quietly as possible.

Up to this point we had seen no sign of the enemy and had all
begun to relax somewhat. I think that a few of us must have begun
to devote a small part of our minds to things unconnected with
danger and death. Certain of the men were undoubtedly thinking
of girls back home and ports visited. Others were thinking of other
things they had not seen for a long time. I found myself taking an
interest in the botanical aspects of my jungle surroundings. I had
never been able to get thoroughly used to the marvels of the Guadalcanal jungle. The huge, shadow casting, columnar tree trunks
with great buttressing roots, spreading outwards from the trunk
for three and four yards, were constantly awing to me. The exotic
shaped, huge leafed plants on all sides kept my eyes fascinated.
It took effort to get myself out of a wandering state of absent-
mindedness. To me the jungle never became commonplace; in the
early days of the war it seemed an especially interesting environment, constantly revealing fresh wonders.

I forced my attention toward the front—the space through
which the two nervous riflemen-scouts were gingerly stepping
along. I looked back behind where the main body of the patrol was
worming its way through the undergrowth, noting the close formation with apprehension.

The going had been rough for a while. The incline we were
travelling up was becoming more and more steep; the fast breathing of a few of the heavier men in the group could be heard above
all other sounds. As the trail eased over toward litup treetops to

the left I began to think about calling another break. It looked as though we were approaching some sort of rise in the ground, and I decided to wait until we got there before calling the halt. Just as I made that decision the lead scout halted—froze in his tracks in the attitude of a dog on point. Without shifting his feet or twisting his body he showed me the palm of his hand. Its message was plain to understand:

"Stop where you are!—Fade into cover!"

The second scout had already slipped from sight. I turned and relayed the signal to the rear, noticing as I did so that more than half the men had already complied. The crookedness of the path would render the patrol unable to lay down any fire in the area of the scouts. I therefore signalled back for a Browning Auto rifleman to join me. (No, I did not use the conventional arm and hand signal. I simply motioned with my fingers.) He came forward at once, and when I had him placed to cover the length of path in front toward the scouts I moved cautiously forward to see what was up. On the way I saw Jap tracks in the trail—the old cloven hoof sneaker, zig-zag tread, all over the place. Funny, I had not seen any farther back on the trail. I could blame my day-dreaming habits for that.

I looked back once or twice at the BAR man to make sure he was on the alert. In retrospect it seems foolish to think that the man would be anything other than "on the alert" but my life was in the balance then and it made a real "double checker" of me. It was good to see the BAR man behind me with his shoulder to the weapon, bipod on the ground, ready to send a stream of bullets popping past me either side, on a tenth of a second's notice. I was ready to *clear out* with less warning than that! (The expression "haul ass," unknown at that time in the war, would have been very apropos.)

I got to the lead scout and found him looking at a sheet of paper, hung impaled on a twig of a rubber tree. The characters on it were Japanese, inscribed in red pencil with an arrow-like mark below the writing. The arrow pointed southwest—the direction from which we had come.

The scout's attitude was pretty cool—he did not seem to be worrying much. I felt annoyed. I had been steadily expecting things to start popping at any moment during my approach. Now I wanted to call the scout down for not passing back word that there was no great danger. As usual, I thought the better of it.

After I sent the second scout back with the word we got up cautiously and continued on. Soon we came to a fork where our path ran into a larger one. There were Jap tracks and other signs galore, but all at least five days old. We began to scent the rancid

rice smell of an old Jap hideout soon, as we passed odd pieces of
Jap equipment—a pair of shoes, an old haversack, an oil can and
an improvised bamboo crutch.

The path was broadening into a trail. There were connecting
paths with vine handrails rigged on them, apparently for feeling
the way at night. We were nearing a bivouac area—one which
must have housed plenty of Japs. Still no fresh sign though.

Well, this was good. We might get shot up as we continued on
the trail, but it was better than rattling slam bang out of the brush
and into a big bunch of enemy. With good luck we might now get
the drop on any Japs we might see. We passed a Jap latrine—a
little slit in the ground with two footrests for squatting. The odor
was old. More discarded trash. Gaudy cigaret wrappers with silly
drawings of Japanese women. The trail was now on level ground
and wide enough for a jeep.

The path soon became solid with Japanese footprints, not absolutely fresh. The lead scout froze and gave the take cover signal. I
ducked at first but noticed that he had crouched and was looking
at some footprints or something on the ground. When I got to him
I saw what he was concerned about. The marks in the soft dirt
were the unmistakable impression of bipod and butt of a Nambu
light machine gun—and they were only hours old! Trouble ahead!

Simultaneously with the sight of the machine gun markings I
became aware of the familiar stench of decaying bodies. Something
nearby was dead, undoubtedly Japs who died in the bivouac area
we were approaching.

With great circumspection we moved on, each man in turn looking knowingly at the gunmark in the path. Soon we saw fresh
tracks. Then the path led out of the jungle into a cultivated banana
grove. Feet were lifted and lowered with the greatest of care.
Everyone now had the posture of a bird dog on point. This period
of silent tenseness would not be terminated by the whirr of quail
wings—that exciting sound that used to thrill me to the bone on
crisp autumn mornings on my sister's farm.

This silence would likely be shattered by the ripping sound of
automatic weapons, the blast of grenades; maybe close to my ear,
there would sound the gurgle of blood and fluid running out of
gaping wounds. Yet we wanted the suspense ended. We felt that
it would be a relief to be able to make a noise—to wildly fire a
weapon.

It seemed the largest banana grove I had ever seen, though only
50 yards across. What was on the other side? What was happening
to the scout who had turned from my sight where the trail bent?

I found him waiting with the other scout, crouched in a listening
attitude. I crept up and listened with them. I signalled the man

behind me to halt the column, indicating that silence was to be absolute. We heard talking through the cover to the front—barely perceptible but unmistakable. Human voices, maybe natives but most likely Japs.

Our present location was in a little pocket of shade-stunted kunai grass between clumps of banana trees. We could see nothing beyond the end of the banana grove—evidence of a clearing ahead. We had not run into the Jap bivouac area, which would surely be in the jungle—certainly not out in a native clearing.

I called three more of the men forward and held a little pow-wow in sign language and silent lip movement. The plan I tried to get across was old. It was the only one I had ever been able to dope out for this frequently occurring jungle warfare situation; we had located the enemy by sound and knew his approximate position and strength, but were unable to see him because of intervening cover. We could not approach through that cover without alerting him—we had to use the trail, which might well be under observation.

It sounded like only two or three men talking, though of course there might be more. But we were willing to gamble with that possibility. I knew that it would be very unlikely to find more than 10 in a single party. Larger groups would starve in trying to live off the land.

The plan was simple. Its elements were automatically understood by the men so that it needed no outlining, but if I had been able to issue a formal order it would have sounded something like this:

"They are up there in front of us. I don't know how many but I don't think there are more than five. We only hear two talking. If we keep the drop on them we ought to be able to take care of them with no damage to ourselves.

"We better not risk trying to scout them out and determine their exact strength. If we do that we'll give ourselves away. I do not think that anyone can get close enough to see them in this damned cover without being seen or heard himself.

"So I'll take the two scouts and a BAR *up the trail*. We'll look 'em over if we can. But we will start shooting the minute they see us.

"Give us a little start and then follow us. Be sure not to bunch up there as we are now. If they do not see us we won't shoot until more of you come up. Then we can throw the book at them. If we run into a hornet's nest we will peel off *one at a time* and run back. In that case men who are not running will cover with fire. We *will not all take off* until we are no longer in contact. If we contract any litter cases we will remain and shoot it out."

That is the order I gave—and I did not have to say more than a score of words. Much of it was standard operating procedure. Some of it I conveyed with gestures. But for the sake of the record that was the text. (It would at least be that formal in the movies.)

While my heart beat like a hammer against my Adam's apple we moved ahead. First a scout, armed with a Tommy gun, then a second scout carrying an M1 (I had traded a minute before) and then the BAR man. We were no more than two paces apart—that was part of the plan. I wanted all of us to be able to shoot at once so had sacrificed dispersal entirely.

The path bent again, this time to the right, and we saw the smoke of a small fire no more than 50 yards from us.

The talking began again, and it sounded as though it were from only 10 feet away. We were now sure that it was Japanese. It had a different sound from the island natives' gibberish.

Inch by inch we crept forward. The continued talking was a good sign. While it went on we could know that they had not heard us. When it stopped we would stop and hold our breath with a prayer.

The hammer doubled the strength and frequency of its blows on the inside of my Adam's apple. The scout ahead of me looked pale as a ghost. We were nearing the smoke which was rising straight up from above the high grass where the talk originated. "Krist Almighty!" I thought, "wasn't there some sort of clearing?" Were we going to encounter those yellow bellies hand to hand in the kunai grass? "Please God let there be a clearing—only a small one!"

There was a clearing and we saw it in a moment. We crept out to the place where the six foot grass ended and the cover was only two feet high.

I saw the first scout crouch, ooze forward an inch at a time and then freeze so suddenly that he gave the impression of having been moving much faster than a few feet a minute. He raised his Tommy gun to the firing position and then gradually half-lowered it. I fervently thanked God for that. The talking had stopped; in another second I would have broke and run to a point where I could see to shoot. As things worked out, we were all three able to move up to the lead scout and join him in looking at four live and healthy Japs, no more than 50 feet from us.

They were squatting around the fire, completely unaware of our presence. The Nambu machine gun was not with them. None had weapons in their hands and there were no grounded weapons visible. I "felt" the muzzle of the BAR slide past my ear, saw it steady as the man took aim.

I did something then which was probably wrong. I signalled

with my hand for the auto rifleman to hold his fire. He stood looking at the Japs, ready to kill them all at the least move. In our
paralyzed situation there was nothing that could be done to plan
further. We would just have to let the first part of our scheme
work itself out.

The Japs were all facing away from us, looking off to our left
front as they lolled about the fire. One of them was apparently
cleaning his toenails with a bamboo sliver. The others were simply
squatting and looking at the fire which had a single Jap messkit
hanging above it with the lid off. It was not boiling at the time.
It would have been better for us if it had been boiling; at least it
would not have been so breathlessly quiet.

Something had to break pretty soon and it did. The lead scout,
a corporal named Bleimfor, sprang upright with Tommy gun at his
shoulder, aimed at their bellies and shouted at the top of his lungs:
"NOW STICK 'EM UP, YOU GODDAMN SONSOF-
BITCHES!"

That did it. From that instant things happened fast. The four
Japs looked up stupefied for a split second and then jumped to
their feet, one of them reaching for a sword that we had not
noticed before. We all opened fire at once but made the mistake of
aiming at the same man. The one who had been cleaning his toenails went down with a dozen holes in him. The other three scattered like chickens before a fox. We four ran into the clearing,
joined by two more who had run up at the sound of Bleimfor's
shout.

The BAR man was practically on top of a Jap who had floun-
dered at the edge of the little pocket in the kunai grass. He aimed
the Browning at the Jap's face and jerked his head to indicate
that the Jap should rise and walk to the center of the clearing.
The Jap answered by making a wild grab for the muzzle.

That left two. I looked around and saw at a glance that things
were not well under control. The sequence of events then became
vague. The next thing I remember is the other scout standing all
bloody in front of me.

He had grabbed one of the Japs in his arms, evidently eager to
make a capture or else crazy with excitement and I had taken a
second or two to get him out of the ensuing mess. The Jap proved
stronger than expected; the grappling pair rolled over and over in
the grass, making it necessary for me to intervene. I dispatched the
Jap by placing the muzzle of my rifle against his ribs and firing
it once, probably hoping that the bullet would not be deflected by
bone from its side to side path. It was not, but it was a while
before I was sure who I had killed. The American had more blood
on his uniform than the Jap.

That left the last Jap running for his life from three men, none of whom had sufficient presence of mind to stop and fire an aimed shot. The Nip had dropped his sword, apparently considering it too heavy to carry.

As they threshed through the cover I listened to hear them shooting him and was pleasantly surprised. A subdued Jap came back in a minute, walking meekly and tremblingly, with arms stretched overhead and a rifle muzzle pressing the base of his spine.

A brief check through the area gave us all the information we needed. The rest of the bivouac area was deserted—just another old Jap camp, and we had little appetite for further patrolling.

"Let's get the hell outta here," I said.

"Second the motion," said someone else.

With little loss of time we did so. We were back at headquarters with all hands and a prisoner in an hour and a half. (The kid with malaria had gotten back okay and was being doped with quinine by Doc Cecala.)

BACK TO THE BEACHHEAD

Our mop up operations—many patrols inland and to the south —were completed early in March and as soon as there were landing craft for the purpose of returning to the Lunga area we were ordered to break camp.

This order was not relished by many of us, though the great body of men in the battalion welcomed it as a portent of a trip back to a rest area on some other island—perhaps even home. Even at that early date the Army had its wishful thinkers—and hadn't we been overseas for eleven months? (Many, many months later, in Burma, I was to remember these Guadalcanal hopes and look with amusement at my fatigue sleeve where the six overseas stripes would have been sewed had it been a blouse.)

Taking us away from Esperance would not improve our lot, I felt. In the first place, it would get us back together as a regiment, so that centralized training programs could be gotten underway too easily by the Regimental S-3 (Operations and Training Officer); also it would locate our battalion, with all of its manpower, within very easy distance of the damned unloading beaches. We had all had enough of unloading Higgins boats. And the dangers of getting bombed in the Lunga area were now just as great as ever, with planes still coming over on every moonlit night. These disadvantages would more than counterbalance the very slight danger of being bushwhacked which we risked back at Esperance.

But such ideas of our own were merely stock for conversation; Corps headquarters was in charge of troops on the island. So we packed, swept clean the little gardens of our canvas frame houses and boarded the battered landing craft which were to carry us back to the busy beaches of Lunga Point.

Our kit for this trip was fantastically light and simple. The packs and gear which we had taken with us on the mission had been reduced to a minimum—a selected few items of the long list of "necessities" of earlier days. Cartridge belts and other web

179

equipment had been worn out and rotted away in the dampness; mess gear, the lid and spoon we each carried, had been lost. Only of weapons was there a full issue.

My rifle, newly bedded and zeroed in, rested well oiled in my arms, and comprised more than half the weight of my entire kit. My improvised knapsack—my original officers' QM bag, with Infantry pack straps sewed on to replace the useless suspender arrangement—was all else that I carried onto the boat with me. It contained a half-blanket; a few souvenirs light enough to carry; and a few rounds of that good lot of Denver Ordnance Depot ball ammunition which I had selected back in New Caledonia. By allowing myself only a few rounds of the special stuff for each trip away from our baggage, I had managed to never run out. (I was to fire the last three rounds of that store months later in India, bringing down three fine head of game—but that's another story.)

The coxswain invited me to climb up onto the rear deck of the craft, where the crisp sea breeze would buffet me about, giving a sensation of coolness to the skin—particularly enjoyable to one long left in the still heat of the groves. I was wearing no insignia at the time, and, as always, was enjoying the resulting anonymity. The coxswain didn't know if I were a Marine private—or an Army captain; perhaps he didn't care. There had been no need for me to give my rank away by shouting orders while my men loaded onto the boat. An outfit gets that way after a while—each man does his job and no one needs to tell him what to do or to hurry him and as a result all situations are handled by the unit through a quiet, efficient, united effort. (The end of the war, incidentally, seemed to destroy that cooperative bond between men of the platoons and companies and regiments of the Army.)

Before stepping up onto the wheel deck I paused and began to pull the stocking-like poplin case over my rifle to protect it from the spray. The coxswain reached down and tapped my shoulder, motioning for me to leave the weapon outside the case. I couldn't get a reason from him because the motor of the Higgins boat was roaring at the time, pulling the front end of the boat off the beach. In a few minutes, after we had pulled out and gotten under way toward Kokumbona, he told me the reason he had asked me to keep my rifle ready by pointing down to the water, and shouting above the now lessened sound of the motor, "May see sharks—fun to shoot 'em!"

He chatted with me for the next half hour of the trip, asking the usual layman's questions about my telescope sighted rifle. "Nope," I said, "You don't use the front sight at all—just look through the scope tube; everything's inside. You just set the spot you want to hit on top of the post and then blaze away."

I was enjoying the ride very much because it had been weeks since wind had brushed over my skin at more than the very few miles an hour we had dared to push the captured Japanese plywood hulls with their outboard motors. The bay was smooth as glass and the foaming wake of our craft stood out harshly behind us upon its surface.

Savo Island was gradually moving behind us, a great mountain peak sticking sheerly out of the water, and many of us looked dreamily back at it, envying, in a way, the peaceful lives of its inhabitants. Savo had been close to a lot of the war. Thousands of tons of shipping had been sunk within gun range of her narrow beaches where Japanese torpedoes had driven themselves high and dry on the sands; Savo's night skies had been lit brilliantly for hours at a time by burnings and explosions; but her people and her villages remained virtually unharmed. I saw them myself, for we had gone over one day on a wild goose search for a parachuted pilot, using a Japanese barge to carry the patrol of twelve members. The clutch on the boat's drive-shaft system had broken, marooning us there for three days.

It had been a pleasant marooning, for we were able to trade our rations for fresh bananas and to gorge ourselves on fresh fruit for the first time in months. A Sergeant Anderson from the 164th Infantry was there with a few men on outpost duty and he played the good host. He and his crew were even more sun tanned than we and they were properly pleased with being "stuck" on Savo.

The natives, less spoiled than any we had seen, fitted well into a teamship of paganism with the average of my men. I recall the laughing pidgin English of a village headman, who was joking with one of my sergeants while a dance was being staged at his village in our honor. "Tonight," the chief said to the sergeant, "You no get one lak dis!"—he held his hands high against his chest, cupping them upward to indicate the contours of a young, attractive girl's breast. "You get one lak dis!"—he lowered his hands almost to his waist, cupping and moving them to indicate the long, pendulous breasts of a less desirable woman of the tribe.

The women and girls of Savo wore only the shortest of "grass" skirts, made from a single half banana leaf, split many times up to the stem, which part became the drawstring of the skirt. This was poor coverage below and there was none whatsoever above— breasts bared to the sun. The missionaries had not taught the native women on Savo to wear mother hubbards as they had on other islands. The people of Savo had been spared the curse of modesty, condemned as such by medical men when it was learned that continued wetness of the skin, caused by wearing clothing while wading, bathing or fishing, had fostered tuberculosis and pneumonia in these islands. Our short holiday on Savo was a memorable one, though I believe that some of my men worried for months for fear of an aftermath to a last nights' celebration there. We were finally picked up by a boat from a Navy salvage ship.

I was musing on the memories of the voyage, looking back at the little pinpoint of an island growing smaller, when the coxswain called my attention to a big shark some 20 yards away from our craft. He was a large, boxnosed creature and he rolled over just as I looked, showing us his fine white teeth, set in a pair of jaws wide enough to be passed untouching over my shoulders. I put three bullets into him—wondering as I fired if he had tasted any of the thousands of human bodies which had been buried in the waters nearby. Sharks were especially bad around Savo and the natives there refused to wade even knee deep in the ocean.

We didn't take time to chase down the wounded shark, for we were then nearing Kokumbona Beach and soon we turned in shore, once again experiencing the thrill of tropic landfall. We saw a distant yellow line enlarge gradually into a broad beach and a thin layer of green and neutral color above reveal itself gradually as a grove of coconut trees. Still closer in we were able to distinguish a strata of graceful fronds weaving in the breeze, above the bleached, rough surfaced trunks.

We remained a night at Kokumbona and it wasn't nice. No American troops had camped near our landing area; the Jap bodies, dead for some weeks or maybe a month, had not been disposed of. The place stank to high heaven, with corpses strewn all over, each one of them seeming to be in the very worst stages of putrification. There were very few carrion birds on Guadalcanal, certainly not enough to meet requirements, and so the bodies just continued to lay and stink where our people had been unable to bury them. Flies, of course, had flourished, so that by day there was a constant buzzing annoyance added to the almost intolerable odor.

Our trucks arrived the morning after and we were all glad to leave. The grove at Kokumbona was nothing like our camp at Esperance had been, though in the beginning at Esperance there had been even more bodies. We went hungry at Kokumbona during the day, waiting until the flies went away so that we could eat our food. You had to pick the ravenous insects right out of your mess gear; waving a hand above did not faze 'em.

The trail continued through ungarrisoned grove areas for some distance, so that I felt inclined to keep a few weapons ready in each of our three trucks but it was not long before we were able to dispense even with that measure, for the road became lined with pyramidal tents. The troop areas had been extended and units

Hideo

More Japanese cleanliness here. Japanese were pretty good launderers, considering that they had little soap, and no washing machines. Often their uniforms were clean, and I doubt if they ever made my mistake of washing them in the surf. Where they had permanent camps they would always rig drying lines. The first Marine landings on Guadalcanal disclosed this commendable domestic trait. Clothes were left hanging in front of some hastily-evacuated officers quarters which, by the way, were pretty comfortable huts. Just another point in the makeup of the Japanese soldier that tended to make him live comfortably though far from home. Even there he hadn't been used to commercial laundry service or Maytag machines.

were being camped farther and farther out into areas held by Japs not many days earlier.

Returning after only a short absence, we were seeing big changes in the old areas. More troops had moved in; Guadalcanal, with many Japs still alive and free in its hills, was fast becoming another "rear base" for supply and staging purposes.

Later elements of the 25th Division had arrived and along with them had come mountains of stores. Docking facilities were now under construction and gasoline was being pumped ashore via pipeline, as well as by the older barrel-handling method. Some pattern of organization was being given to the supply installations in the groves. Red drums of gasoline—at least the top layers— were being painted over in OD, an overdue but still needed measure of safety. Everyone was bedding down and making themselves comfortable too. "Houses" were built in some places—nice frame shacks for headquarters and mess halls. The Air Corps and the Sea Bees had not neglected the matters of housing and comfort, and the dispersal area around the field had been well improved from every standpoint. Especially was there improvement in the various air raid shelters, attesting well to the continued Japanese air ac- tivity. Many *live* people were now sleeping—cot, mosquito bar and all—three or four feet beneath the ground.

We noticed all these changes within a few days after we were camped in our new area, again in the eternal coconut groves, not far from the campsite we had been given just prior to the Hill 27 show. Henderson Field was bombed the first night we were back but once we had located the direction of the planes' flight we went back to bed. We were tired and reasonably secure in the knowledge that the flames at the field would draw the rest of the Jap bombs. I wondered, lying in my cot and listening to the distant crackling of ammunition in the big fire, if anyone had been hurt on the strip. As a rule the damage there was to materiél, rather than men. But the airstrip got it on the chin many a moonlit night so that some of the men must have been hurt. Now, however, we were no longer fired with morbid curiosity. We didn't even ask each other about casualties.

We were, of course, immediately given a training program to carry out. We got word of it on the second day, while I was suf- fering a fit of extreme annoyance over the loss of all my spare clothing. Another bedroll had been left behind, in charge of our rear echelon, and the storage area had become flooded. All of my clothing, a spare watch, a couple of fountain pens, nearly all of my films and a camera had been thoroughly soaked. Later the waters had receded and the rear echelon people had satisfied their con- science by restacking the bedrolls and wiping off the outside mud, without emptying them and drying their contents. When I opened mine, my beaver shortcoat came apart in my fingers, my extra fatigues were eaten through with rot, and my fountain pens and watch were, of course, ruined. I had left only the clothes on my back and my rifle, which items, thank God, never have to be entrusted to rear echelon people.

I was lying disgustedly on my bunk in the mood brought on by the bedroll incident, still attired in the same tattered, reseamed and patched fatigues which I had worn back from Esperance, when a clerk from battalion headquarters brought and waved under my nose a copy of our training schedule. It called for hours of calisthenics, close order drill and other subjects which there is no need to enumerate here.

I resolved, regardless of consequences, to do everything possible towards shirking every bit of spirit and letter that training schedule contained, utilizing in my evasion every trick, every blind, every ruse which I had for years seen so well demonstrated by old soldiers in my command.

I suddenly discovered friends and relatives in the camps of other units, far over on the island, who in all decency *had* to be visited. I trumped up obscure reasons for visiting Tulagi Island, and once there I trumped up better reasons why I should not return on time. Each hour's errand, on which I was sent away from the area, turned out to last the better part of a day.

After my imagination had run dry and I had no stock of pretenses left, I simply absented myself from the area, muttering something unintelligible to the charge of quarters as I left and not even making a decent sham at truth when I later would explain the absence to higher authority.

Actually, most of the time I was away during the day was spent hunting boar in the kunai grass fields inland from Henderson Field and the nights were spent not far away on a hill dubbed "Concentration 101" where the pigs were roasted and eaten native style —washed down with "bamboo juice" and raisin-jack to the accompaniment of much drunken, boisterous song. All of this activity was in company with some of my Air Corps friends with whom I had hunted deer on New Caledonia.

I further dissociated myself with the battalion and its training program by renewing contacts with my old friends in Anti-Tank Company, spending days at this camp when the weather was no good for pig hunting. They too were game for a few nights of poker and torpedo juice guzzling.

In this organized evasion of duty I enjoyed almost complete success, being hooked only once to instruct calisthenics for half an hour. Lieutenant Singer snapped a picture of me leading the class in arm and shoulder exercises so he would have proof that I had failed in my resolution to participate in none of the training outlined in that damned schedule. Other than that one bit of drilling, however, I did nothing and even today I recall the fact with a sense of morbid pride.

In these activities I had risked courting the ill favor of the battalion commander and executive officer, but I limited my worries on that score because I felt that Lieutenant Colonel Ferry and Major Butler must have entertained feelings similar to mine toward that typewritten sheet from regimental headquarters. After quite a few days, however, I began to sense a certain coolness around both the regimental and battalion command posts, but I went stubbornly on with my program of inactivity, counting it interesting to see from which direction the axe would fall. I have since heard stories of torn up citations, recommendations, and the usual krap; things which bother me now even less than then.

The axe fell soon and in a strange way—as much due to the Japs, perhaps, as to offended people up the line. A mastermind at some headquarters had seen or heard of some lights up in the direction of "Gold Ridge." He had immediately connected the incident with the most annoying and urgent factor of current Guadalcanal existence—the nightly air raids. The chap in question suspected that the planes were being talked-in by radio or guided by lights, so that they could bomb Henderson Field more accurately.

It was decided (perhaps by this same person) to send a patrol out to the suspect ridge, through miles of intervening jungle, to investigate the matter. The original decision was made in some headquarters above regimental—probably corps, perhaps division. Our regiment was ordered to make the investigation; division kicked it down to regiment, Colonel Andrew Casper, regimental executive officer, or someone told the S–2 to take care of it, and Captain Cosby came down to battalion, caught me during one of my twenty minute stays in the area and gave me orders to organize a ten-man, heavily armed patrol and to take it up into the mountains to destroy or capture a Japanese outpost. This was just a week before we were to have left that effing island for good.

PATROL TO THE BOONDOCKS

Cosby jeeped me up to an OP situated somewhere beyond Burnt Knob on Edson's Ridge and let me look through a BC scope at the point which was to be my objective. It was marked by a small tin roofed shack, where lights had allegedly been seen burning for the last three nights—visible during and shortly before each air raid. The "lights" were said to have resembled flares, or some form of pyrotechnics, rather than any ordinary campfire or electrically created signals.

The shack was built on the side of a huge ridge, a rather prominent spur leading up to the main central range of peaks, high above the lower hills and coastal flats where the greater part of the fighting had raged. Only the merest bit of a clearing surrounded the shack and the large trees of the hillside jungle were clustered close on three sides, so that even the roof was hid from view from all other directions. Practically the only elevated point on the island which shared intervisibility with this shack was the very spot on which we stood.

This lack of intervisibility afforded me with a ready argument against my trekking to that out-of-the-way cabin—an argument against any likelihood of its being the scene of any Japanese aircraft directing agency. "How," I asked, "can any Jap pilots even see the damn place, when it is obviously blocked off by trees on three sides?"

I got nowhere with that point. The lights, I was told, had been *near* the shack—not necessarily burning upon its very roof. The Japs would more likely burn their flares in the top of one of the large trees, making no use at all of the shack proper; or perhaps they used it merely as a shelter at night. To support that contention, a "charred" spot on the side of one of the nearby trees was pointed out to me. The men at the OP had better eyes than I had, to be able to identify a dark spot on a large half-dead tree as having been "burnt" there—at several miles range!

187

I depressed the BC scope and looked without relish across the tangle of jungle intervening between my nearest jumpoff point and the distant objective. The damn trip, come hell or high water, was going to have to be made.

I returned to the battalion command post and briefed the men whom I was to lead on the patrol—they had been ordered to assemble in front of the message center tent. They seemed to share my own lack of enthusiasm, so I wasted little time in issuing instructions. I told them where we would assemble the next morning and when, and announced what they were to carry in the way of rations and weapons.

All reported on time early the next morning, walking from their scattered areas. They had been requisitioned from all the companies of the battalion, and I did not know by name even one of the noncommissioned officers. I had to allot responsibility in direct conformation with rank—a method which is at best a poor expedient, definitely second choice to the selective procedure possible when a leader knows personally each one of his men. Perhaps I should have asked the battalion for at least one noncom with whom I had worked before, but I didn't. I knew nothing against any of these men and they had probably been selected to go with me because it was now their turn. If I asked for someone I knew well, I would be yanking a good man out of a well deserved period of bunk fatigue, and I just didn't have the heart to pull such a trick in the interests of "military necessity."

With my lukewarm attitude toward the job, I had failed to check in advance on the matter of native guides, depending upon the word of authority, which had given me to understand that the guides—two natives who could speak understandable pidgin— would be waiting for me, on time, at the jumpoff, which was to be the observation post. As often happened with those people, they failed to show up. We waited for thirty minutes, I vainly calling the native camp on the phone all the while. Finally we took off without them, the men of the patrol cursing the laziness of Guadalcanal natives.

Navigating jungle areas is always much easier if the services of native guides are available, and not having such service is always a serious handicap—often spelling the difference between knowing where you are and being completely lost. On Guadalcanal, where few worthwhile maps were ever given to us, this was doubly true. As the trail on which we had walked from the OP gradually dwindled into a path and then finally faded out altogether I, too, pondered bitterly—in between machete whacks—on the inadequacy of the Guadalcanal guide service.

Two capable officers were running that "guide service," and a labor pool along with it, keeping many natives housed in a compound near the airstrip, and performing invaluable service thereby. Major Clemens and Captain (later Major) Trench were their names, if I remember correctly, both Britishers. The "sad control" of the guide service was no fault of theirs, as both of these men were hard working officers, kept steadily busy at a thousand and one tasks involving the services of natives all over the island. The guide service was only a small part of their total headache. We knew this—and it was one reason why I did not run down to the camp for assistance.

But early in the trip I began to wish that I had done that very thing, for it looked as though we would never find a trail—never get through cutting. We chopped on for two hours, trading off on the machetes, and halting now and then to take a hone to a blade nicked on some of the resin bearing vines. Blade edges were often chipped on particles of hardened minerals, which had solidified into tiny stalactites on vines or saplings. We kept hoping, as always, to find a ready trail which would make our trip easier, but until we should see one we would have to continue cutting our way, navigating through the densely undergrown rain forest by the only sure method—that of following a compass azimuth.

Following an azimuth in the jungle is like many other things the Infantry has to do, it is as simple as can be, but difficult as hell. Having no view ahead, the leader cannot practicably sight an azimuth from tree to tree and cut straight along the established line. Trees are usually too close together in the jungle, and undergrowth closes in front like pea-soup fog, so that the route must be laid out by pointing the compass as a finger—after offsetting the dial for proper allowance—and then trying to cut in the proper direction. If the proper direction happens to be blocked off by trees or other insurmountables, the cutting must "tack" around them; if a larger barrier, should intervene, such as a dropoff or a swamp, a correspondingly wider detour must be made. Such expedients in jungle navigation are the rule, rather than the exception; and they result in the cutting of a crooked path, thereby destroying the patrol leader's one sure means of easily checking the direction of his planned course, for only by sighting back along a section of straight-cut trail can he know that he is proceeding in exactly the right direction.

Practically, then, in the jungle the compass becomes an instrument of estimation, only roughly accurate. For purposes of navigation it can no longer be considered a precision instrument, providing easily followed directions for the bewildered jungle traveller. Men who would bet their lives on a compass reading in open country often lost all such confidence during its employment in tangles of tropical rain forest. But even so, we all knew that any compass would be far, far more accurate than any mans' alleged sense of direction.

There are a few methods by which jungle navigation can be accomplished with fair precision. With knotted twine or engineer tape staked out behind on the cut path, one can accurately plot direction and progress. This method, within its limitations, worked well. Obviously, it has little application on Infantry patrols. I mention it only because it was used by the Engineers for laying out trails, and because it was used once in a blue moon by us— when extreme accuracy in routing was of prime importance, or when every less complicated means had been tried without success.

Because he could not practicably use this staked out cord and tape, and because he was hardly ever able to cut his route as a straight path, the patrol leader, in order to find his way in the jungle had to fall back upon two important qualities of leadership: common horse sense and patience.

The former quality is one that many of us had been forced to acquire in at least small measure, but few Americans possessed enough patience to feel at home in the Solomon Islands. Delays of all sorts ground against my nerves on Guadalcanal, and of those encountered by a patrol, cutting through the jungle was more annoying than all the others put together.

As soon as our path petered out we ran into a swamp, around which we obviously would need to detour. Before we had cut fully around to its other side, we ran into a floodfill of rotted wood which gave way under foot like quicksand so that we had to detour again. Then we ran into a tangle of bamboo, too heavy for our machetes. Before we had cut for twenty minutes I found myself reduced to almost complete reliance on my limited amount of common horse sense, and I began to use the compass only as a rou . indicator of direction.

This threw an element of gamble—larger than any gambler would desire—into the march-routing of my little command. I knew that when I was up on the observation post I had not been able to count all of the ridges intervening between our jumpoff and the spur upon which the tin shack was sited. I had seen six ridges in between, but the actual number might be anything up to twenty. Many, I knew, had been defiladed behind higher ones. So I could not tell when I was about to reach or pass over the final rise, merely by the number of ridges already crossed. I could only guess. That—come to think of it—was all that jungle navigation seemed to be made of: guess, guess, guess. Guess how far right you traveled on that last tack. Guess an hour later on whether or not you had traveled a compensating distance in the opposite

Here a few coconut logs are being cut by a pioneer detachment, probably for bridge supports. A few green coconuts and some heart-of-palm salad will be the culinary by-products. The man with the axe is doing the usually awkward job; the Japs are expert at using their draw-type wood saws, but poor at chopping. They don't know how to cut and their blades are poorly shaped, often dull.

Coconut logs were one of the standard engineer building materials in the Pacific, like bamboo. Our own engineers made great use of them for many different forms of construction. Most of the conventional varieties of timber were too far inland for lumbering, and we had to cut many palms anyway, in order to clear the necessary roads. May as well make use of the fallen trunks.

I hear rumors that Lever Brothers collected some sort of settlement for the trees we cut down. Must have been somewhat of a job to count em. . . . Must have been quite a chore to tell which ones we cut and which the Japs cut.

direction. Guess the total airline distance you have covered . . .
Then *halve* that last figure, to be anywhere near correct.

Along towards early noon we had crossed three ridges with less
than an hour and a half's break in the cutting. No paths at all.
Most of the way we could have wormed through the undergrowth
without cutting, but it would have taken longer to do so. Along
part of the route not even a panther could have gotten through
without biting away the fine toothed tangle of vines and thorns
as he went. We had hoped to get on higher ground soon, above the
dense valley forest and into the hillside growths, which had a thinner floor-growth and were well lined with pig paths. But after
topping each rise we had always seemed to dip back to the same
level on the other side.

I hadn't yet called a halt. Usually you don't have to on a ten-
man patrol cutting through thick stuff with only two active blades.
Halts come naturally for men who are not cutting, because the
cutting speed varies in different types of cover, sometimes slowing
to a near halt. Men just relieved from the blades can sit for a
minute or so, allowing the column to pass slowly while they regain
their wind.

The cutting was the hardest kind of work and the jungle heat
was not helpful. The cutting reliefs, except for those manned by a
few unusually strong members, were of short duration, for men
tire quickly after a few yards of hacking. Successively, the men
behind stepped up each time without a word to take over the two
blades—the leading one breaking way, hacking through principal
barriers, the second one trimming ends and widening the path a
bit. We were a small body, so we did not employ an extra pair of
followup blades to widen and improve. In the heat the use of four
machetes at a time would have overtaxed the strength of the
patrol. Shade or no shade, it was plenty hot.

Sweat lay unevaporated upon skin, welled up in plenty to drench
clothing, and dropped onto the ground after clothes became soaked
to the limit and were plastered to bodies as though each man had
just climbed out of deep water. Sweat lay unevaporated because
the air, like our clothing, was already holding its limit of moisture.
The morning coolness had left the jungle and the dew, as fast as
the atmosphere would allow, was turning to steam. This dew was
heavier than ordinary rain, and it splashed heavily from leaves as
they were shaken by hacking machetes.

The machetes were being wielded with skill, now. Most of the
men had already learned how to swing them, hacking diagonally
through vines and stalks, with just the right amount of force behind each blow. There is a wide difference in the resistance of
various plants and vines to such cutting. On Guadalcanal we had

learned quickly that mere diameter—thickness of stalk or stem—
meant nothing; it was hardness and resiliency that counted. A huge
banana stalk, a foot through, can be cut easily at a stroke, while
a bamboo shaft of a third that diameter might require as much as
ten strokes to sever, depending upon its greenness and the length
of arm swing allowed by surrounding vegetation. Only by learning
to judge the force required for each stroke, by recognizing the type
of material being cut, can the machete wielder properly conserve
his energy and make himself last for more than a few feet of trail
making.

Blades must be kept sharp, and the honing must be done so
often that deftness in this specialty becomes another prerequisite
of the good jungle soldier. Good hackers stone their blades often,
usually carrying the stone in a free hand and swiping the blade
every few strokes so that the edge is constantly of almost shaving
keenness. Good hackers swing their blades with a regular rhythm,
varying the angle and force of individual swipes, to keep the blade
cutting at a constant speed. And if they are good soldiers, they do
not hand the blade to their relief until they become tired. Until
they become *tired*.

American civilian workmen and the laborers of Europe have
come to recognize as symptoms of "tiredness" such indications as
heavy heartbeat, labored breathing, noticeable perspiration, ach-
ing and early numbness of muscles and joints.

Good jungle Infantrymen have another definition for the word
and the only symptoms to which they pay attention are those of
acute dizziness, disturbance of the sense of balance, complete
numbness of limbs, the appearance of dancing spots before the
eyes, involuntary buckling of the knees or hip joints and vomiting
or fainting. Heavy pounding in the temples, panting breath, and
clothes soaked with perspiration are normal and expected—part
and parcel of every jungle trek.

We rattled on rather loudly, hacking incautiously through the
first of the bamboo grove, so that we failed completely to detect
in advance a stream which ran across our front only 150 yards
away. Light, coming in through the high leaves above us, gave
away the stream's location before we heard the sound of its fast
waters. We would know soon that we had made some little gain
in elevation and were now approaching the lower foothills, because
the small river, when we got to it, was found to be very fast
running. It had a series of rapids coming down from our right
front, the water foaming slightly yellow in a strange manner as
it surged and eddied like a mountain trout stream. Not that it
much resembled a trout stream, however, since its color and bank
vegetation made it look much different from anything in the

States, though much like some trout waters I have since seen on lower Honshu.

The stream was using only a portion of its floodtime bed and its wide gravel floored expanse of sunlight was affording us a pleasant relief from the jungle darkness. Such relief would hardly have been welcome a few weeks before on Guadalcanal when we were constantly worried about being seen by the enemy, but on this occasion we had no great concern. I did not suspect a danger of ambush at the moment, but I felt that special care should be taken. Casualties incurred just before we were ready to leave the island would be ironical. The stream we were now crossing was hardly in a danger area. Any enemy there would have been reported and likely dealt with by Major Clemens' natives.

I took the lead and we began to walk along the stream, moving inland against its current. We were able to walk on the gravel most of the time without wading—an improvement only in footing, because our feet were already wet by the dew-drenched jungle growth and the swamp areas we had come through. Keeping feet dry in the jungle is an impossibility.

Dubbin-coating or waterproofing leather shoes is not the good practice generally thought. True, it waterproofs the foot gear to an extent, but in tropic climates that merely serves to increase the dampness of the feet, holding the perspiration right in the shoes and giving encouragement to athlete's foot and jungle rot. Perhaps it does increase the life of shoes a little, but other than that there is little to be gained from the use of dubbin or from the excessive use of oils on any footgear in the jungle. Leather of all sorts will rot there, no matter what you do; and if oil is used it takes twice as long to dry the insides of shoes once they get wet. The best bet is to leave the leather untreated, and merely remember to dry footgear as often as possible.

Under such conditions of constant wetness, the feet can be kept in best shape by very frequent changing of socks, and by persistent use of foot powder. Every man, we learned, should carry two changes of socks on every trip, and if the trip is to be a long one, he should bring foot powder also. There are only a few exceptions to this rule—lucky individuals who are fairly immune to tropical skin diseases and are able to go for long periods without taking any of these precautions. Any man can get along in a pinch without the powder or extra socks if he will now and then go barefoot about camp, so that his feet will get some sunlight. Two days of barefootedness on the hot sands on an ocean beach will temporarily cure an ordinary case of athlete's foot.

I was wearing better footgear than any of my men—the last of two pairs of hobnailed, old style field shoes, which I had broken in and stored for the purpose while still in New Caledonia. Hobnails are the only solution for travel over varied tropical terrain. They are much better than any of the rubber or rubber cleated soles which were later issued, though the rubber ones were far longer-wearing. From the supply officer's standpoint, the rubber soled shoes were better and, as Infantrymen were to rediscover many times over, front line preferences throughout the war were often subordinated to the convenience of ranking staff sections, whose officers always had a louder voice in things than the doughboy or doughboy officer.

Despite my own good footgear, my feet were bothering me when I first began to wade in the water. My recurrent jungle rash had blossomed out again—this time on my ankles—and a gathering of gravel in my socks just at the shoe tops caused me to call a halt at the next bend.

We spotted lookouts up and down stream and broke out our "K" ration, which, early in 1943, was yet quite a novelty to us on Guadalcanal. It was nice to sit in the sunlight and nibble on a cheese luncheon, drinking a citric acid solution called lemonade, made by dissolving a powder contained in the "K" ration packet in a canteen cup full of water. But for a hungry man the "K" ration was not enough—especially the meal unit marked "dinner."

It took us about fifteen minutes to eat and while the patrol rested during an additional fifteen, I climbed a tree to see if I could get a hint of where we were. Luck was with me and I was able to roughly orient our position by intersection—taking a compass shot at a recognizable point on Edson's ridge, and another of the far edge of Henderson Field. I could not, however, see either our starting point or our objective. We had made up for lost time by walking up the easier stream route, and I felt that we must be almost halfway to the shack. We would take the first good looking trail or stream bed to branch off to the left.

The sun was boiling straight down when we resumed march, and its light made the wax surfaced leaves glitter like bits of green glass. The heat bore against our fatigue hats with almost real weight. Now and then we would scoop up hands full of water to splash in our faces. Our shoulders and upper parts of our clothing, so dampened, quickly dried again, as did the socks which we would hang on pack straps after rinsing them in the stream. The air in the stream bed had become a little dry itself, the sun there in the open dehydrating it faster than the jungle on either side could seep in more dampness. The yellow stain had now left the water, it was perfectly clear and very cold. With good footing and no cutting other than an occasional hack at a trip-vine, we were now making very good time.

All along the stream there had been old Jap signs, as we had learned to expect of all of the streams on the north end of the island, but no recent marks were present, either in the form of discarded equipment or of tracks in the stream bed.

We knew, of course, that many Japanese were still alive on the island—possibly moving about in small bands, undoubtedly armed. This small danger—the only one left, now that the Japanese organization had been thoroughly broken—seemed greater and greater each day, as our date of departure from the islands came nearer. No one wanted to risk being hurt or killed after the fight had been officially finished, and everyone felt that he had already done his share and deserved a little rest before the next big risk. Inland patrolling was going on as a matter of course with many units required to send people out into the hills, but there were generally very few who wanted to go for the fun of it. Mostly the patrol missions were *assigned*. I don't think the volunteer system would have worked.

Knowing that some armed Japs were left alive was enough in itself to make inland trekking unpopular as a sporting diversion. At earlier times, while we remained highly uncertain as to whether we would ever get off the island, there was less objection, on the part of men and officers, to normally dangerous duties. Lately, however, life had taken on a new value. We all pondered upon these ideas as we walked on, heat and fatigue making us grow more lax. The scouts, particularly, were causing me much apprehension with their lackadaisical state of "alertness." Seldom, I noticed, was there a moment of marching when less than four of us would be lined up at a time, so that we would all be clearly visible to any Jap gunner lurking around the next bend.

I increased my pace and got within conversing distance of the lead scout, so that I might caution him to be on the qui vive. We were "laid wide open" I informed both scouts, and while it would be entirely okeh with me for them to walk along half asleep if only their own individual lives were at stake, it was no part of my intention to let their carelessness get all of us shot. A moment later I felt sorry for this petulance, but I did notice that the scouts were paying more attention to business.

Then a peculiar thing happened, one of the many surprises of which jungle warfare has such a great store. The column was hairpinned around a bend in the river when a copious burst of rifle fire was heard deafeningly in the narrowness of the stream bed.

And the firing had broken out at the *rear* of the column!

Nothing could have been more confusing. Everyone's first thought was to get under cover, get out of the open river bed and down behind a log or into some of the nearby jungle. There were a few seconds of scurrying, with men slipping and falling on the mossy stone river bottom—some making it to the bank on all fours, fighting the current, others getting to safety with comparative ease, wetting themselves only to the calves in the effort.

I was one of the fortunate latter group, and it was a matter of short seconds for me to get myself laid away, crouching low with a large upturned stump between my body and the resounding rifle shots. Mentally I began to act, noting the locations of the men who had been near me in the column when the firing had started. Having marked them down, I began to concern myself with preparations to shoot anything showing up where my buddies weren't. The cracking and reverberating rifle fire, coming from somewhere back towards the tail of the column, continued.

As we listened to the shooting I gradually began to get back a measure of calmness. No thought but ambush had entered my head when the first shots had been heard, but this second bit of listening seemed to reveal another important fact—a comforting one, too.

The fire all sounded like that of American arms—and nothing else. It could have been 7.7mm Jap rifles, from the character of individual reports, but the spacing of the shots was too regular for bolt action guns of any sort. It had to be Garands, I reasoned. In a moment I heard eight go off in an even string and knew for sure.

Another good indication that the shots were not fired by the enemy had been the absence of secondary bullet cracks over our heads. The stuff was apparently going away from us, with nothing much coming back. I listened in particular for the familiar, whip-like cracks for two full seconds before I made up my mind to go back and see what was causing all of the racket around the bend, less than a hundred yards away. I motioned for the two men nearest to cover me as I made my way. It was but a matter of seconds for me to get to the tail of the column, where I found two of my men firing away. The frequency of the reports had decreased, perhaps by then the shots were being more carefully aimed. I got back in time to verify that; got back, as a matter of fact, in time to do some shooting myself.

The fusillade, I discovered, was being directed at a small party of enemy stragglers who—for some strange reason—had seen fit to let us pass where they had been hidden in the brush of the banks. Then they foolishly ran out and exposed themselves while we were still within range. Their poorly-selected route of escape took them down the stream bed, straight away and in full view.

The bed was very straight for a long stretch where the Japs had flushed, and the banks there were too high to allow quick ascent. To gain cover that way, each Jap had to expose himself for a moment as a stationary target. On that account the two men in the rear had been able to shoot at the fleeing Japs a fairly long while. When I first saw them, two Japs were still visible and under fire—but running like hell. I, of course, immediately joined in the shooting, taking rest on a slanted bit of bright yellow clay (so bright-colored that it khaki-dyed the chest of my jacket). We still got to fire a few more shots while the two Japs scrambled on across the rocks and river bottom in a way that made them appear to be badly hit. They both slumped, tripped, and fell awkwardly several times while our numerous bullets kept speeding their way from about 400 yards.

The water all around the two Japs was being splashed by the fire of the M1s before I rested elbow and forearm to draw a bead. I fired a whole clip at them—and never actually learned the results. Certainly I cannot claim a hit.

Why?—

Well, the Japs were a long way off, and we were not shooting very well. I was holding the shots while trying to regain my breath, and the Japs—because the rocks near the edges of the stream were very irregular—were forced to stumble in a way that made it impossible for us to accurately calculate leads. Furthermore, all of us had lately been used to shooting at very short ranges so perhaps our holdingover was a little careless. Still, with so many shots fired, there was no excuse for our not dropping both targets.

We didn't though; we may have winged or even fatally hit the two. The way they fell and stumbled would have led a beginner to so claim, but not us. Neither went down for good, and my own guess is that a good scaring was all we dished out. Maybe they would each have several holes in the loose thighs of their breeches, for there was a lot of lead thrown very close. But when a man's number isn't up he just can't be killed, not even by the law of averages. I hope personally, if they lived through the nightmare experience we gave them, that the two Nips are now alive and doing well. They deserve it.

We were all shaking a bit after the shooting, especially the men whom I had passed coming back to the rear. Several had stayed in the covered positions they had taken at the first sounds of shooting, and they had consequently remained uncertain of the situation during the fireworks. It would have been easier on their nerves for them to have been in the middle of it.

We turned from the direction of the shooting and walked back upstream, the patrol assembling around the bend where its front end had been at the start. A quick nosecount and check revealed a single casualty: one man had gone completely under water in the first rush for cover, stepping into a six foot hole and getting

Japanese march columns never presented a very military appearance. These doughboys had a tendency to walk, rather than to march, getting to their objective in the quickest and least troublesome way. And they made themselves as comfortable as possible on halts. It was not at all out of order for them to pick up items of camp-making equipment along the route; apparently there were no inspectors present to condemn this noncom for carrying a nice dry piece of firewood on the last mile.

Years of active fighting and realistic training had drilled into the Japanese Infantry organization a healthy respect for results rather than appearances. In the Jap Army, parade ground spit-and-polish was left for the parade grounds. In the field, emphasis was on marching and tactical training.

Somehow I cannot ever appraise this good quality of the Japanese Infantry without thinking of the faults of our own. One of our better officers was crucified for eating a piece of watermelon during a practice march in Tennessee. An added feature of this crime, of course, was that it was committed in the presence of enlisted men!

The Japanese Army made a lot of mistakes, but it certainly did not have a monopoly on stupidity.

a lung full. Aside from that the patrol was just as good as new. There was no discussion of pursuing the two Japanese. You just don't do that sort of thing. If you pursue the alerted enemy, they lie in wait and hear you coming—before you see them. Pursuit in the jungle is not sound tactics—even for small units—unless there is some important objective to be gained which would make worth while the sacrifice of a few men. In our case there was no such important objective.

In spite of ourselves, we were all apprehensive over leaving live enemy astride what might prove to be our only practical route of return. I felt a peculiar sort of fear myself, thinking once more that it would be a very hell of a thing to get killed NOW! I was tempted—especially when I felt certain in my own mind that our primary mission was nothing more than a wild goose chase—to go back and report on the two Japanese we had seen, putting forth a front of naivete when I should be asked why I did not proceed to my assigned objective. Somehow I felt sure that the whole show would turn out to be either a complete fizzle (a satisfactory outcome), or else a big, slam-bang affair, with shooting, casualties, and a rough time on the way back carrying litters.

Our prayers were against the latter.

After we had rested long enough to settle our jangled nerves, we resumed the arduous, wading march upstream. I got my compass in hand again and was pleased to find the general course of the stream now leaning toward the desired azimuth, so that we could keep following it for a while longer, before taking a side path.

The water was becoming more and more swift and clear as we went on, and the stream itself was leading us noticeably uphill so there were occasional cascades and increased unevenness of footing on the bank. We were stumbling more often now, each one of us sitting inadvertently down in the water several times. The sensation was a pleasant one; the wetting did not hurt us, and the water was nicely cool.

Hillside jungles began to crowd the sides of the stream as we moved on, and underbrush began to grow right down to the water's edge. For more than a mile we did nothing but wade while the stream became more and more narrow, and the jungle got so closedin that we soon had a solidly-leafed ceiling overhead, which blocked out the sun. This was all right; it was the atmosphere we were used to. We felt at home in the solid, danky shade.

We had come to regard the deep shadow of the jungle as a sort of a protective covering, like the concealment one might obtain through the use of skillful camouflage, for we knew that in shadow only very bright objects reflect the light and are easily seen. Certainly we had on many occasions strained our own eyes, for hours at a time, vainly trying to see an enemy whom we knew to be only a few yards in front of us. But the jungle, always the friend of the static defender, hid the camouflage-wise Japanese, protecting them effectively with its vines, shadows, leaves. Always we had had to pay a price for locating these Japanese, trading casualties while we listened and watched for little giveaway sounds and sights—the shaking of leaves from the muzzle-blast of a weapon, or the deceptive sounds of individual rifle shots in the cover.

Now we knew that any movement of our own in the stream bed would not be seen from any great distance, or heard from even a short one. The sound-deadening and vision-blocking leaves, and the noise of the running stream were comforting. There would be no sunlight to glint from our rifles—from parts unavoidably worn bare of parkerized finish.

The Garand was a particular offender in the matter of shiny reflecting surfaces. Its gas chamber and front sight base, necessarily made of corrosion-proof metal, would not blue or parkerize, so it was finished with a sort of stove blackening which would not even wear for one week in combat usage. It always came off after a few days, presenting a bright nickel surface, rounded to catch and reflect each gleam of sunlight. When a man carried the weapon in his hands at a high port, this damned gas chamber would always show bright on some part of its surface. And when he got into firing position, it became a brightly polished ornament, far more visible to the enemy than any other part of the firer or the weapon. We got into the habit of carrying a few small cans of flat black paint in the company baggage for the purpose of restoring the black finish. In combat, however, there were so many other details to worry about that this one was often forgotten, and those men armed with an M1 would each end up with a Christmas tree decoration on the front end of his weapon. I am certain that several of our men were killed on Guadalcanal because of this one ordnance defect.

I had time to think about such things as we walked up the shady stream—I with two shadowy shapes, the scouts, out in front of me and the rest of the unit behind. Each man was another shadow and the noise of our wading was drowned by the gurgling of the stream.

Birds of various kinds flew around in front of us, frightened from their perches. A few of the more stolid types sat in the undergrowth and watched us pass. One bird in particular was noticeable in the deep jungle—as much so as the little "twirl-tail" which I discussed earlier.

The bird I refer to now had no particular shape to remember—it was something like a crow in appearance, but it made a very distinctive sound with its wings when in flight. This sound was absolutely indistinguishable from that made by a Japanese shell in flight—especially the type fired from the 75mm battalion gun. On this trip the familiar "whirr-whirr-whirr" shouldn't have bothered us. We knew we would not be potted at with Jap artillery while going up the stream bed. On previous occasions, however, we had been bothered plenty. Each time we had heard the sound we were frightened and often jumped for cover because no one could tell whether it was a projectile or a bird coming over our heads. When we were entrenched we always ducked down and cursed. Strangely enough, we would complain with equal violence whether there was an explosion or not.

We saw several of these "artillery fowl" along with other kinds of birds as we continued up the stream. We were now beginning to look anxiously for a path leading off to the left. The shack we were going to visit had been located in what had been a mining area before the war, and I felt that there should be a recognizable path leading to it. The path would logically cross or join the very stream we were walking in. But for a while there was nothing in the stream bed other than the inevitable pig rootings. Even the old Japanese sign and tracks had petered out in the last mile.

Several bends were negotiated and we had all become a good bit more fatigued before I found the trail I was looking for. But when I did locate it, I was sure of the find. There was a rough log bridge across the stream, two heavy trunks in width, with a well-worn path leading across.

We nosed the column up the left bank, and the scouts and I began to examine the ground for recent Jap sign. We saw nothing which could be regarded as recent, other than a few bare foot prints which seemed too wide, even for Japanese. Most likely native.

The trail was wide enough to allow two men to walk comfortably abreast, and it had been kept clear so that we could walk upright most of the time. Some of it led through clumps of heavy saplings which would certainly have been circumvented, had the original cutters intended the trail to be a temporary one. It had been cut with intent to provide a good path for relatively heavy jungle traffic, most likely native carriers loaded with supplies or produce. After reasoning things out on those lines, I began to feel reasonably sure that we were on the right trail, the one leading up to the shack. Compass readings tended to substantiate this conviction.

Up we went, over several small rises, and then over a large one. After that we began a steady climb which promised, by its very steepness, to take us soon onto a high observation point, from which we would surely be able to get our bearings. It was only a quarter till four, and it looked as though we were nearing our objective—an achievement which I calculated would take much longer than our then elapsed march time. We had been very lucky to find the stream and the paths so that we did not have to cut trail for the entire distance.

Now we had only to locate the shack and, as things worked out, we did so much sooner than we had dared to hope. We were able to see it—less than a hundred yards away—in a few moments, after climbing up onto the partially bare top of the ridge. I had feared that we would approach the shack blindly, unable to see it until we had actually hit it, because it had appeared so guarded by forest on three sides.

The ridge had a bend in it though, or else a spur leading up to it, for we could see the house top easily. I climbed a tree to get a more complete view of it, and studied it intently with binoculars, trying to determine the direction of approach which our path would take in its last few yards to the building.

Around the shack, the trees were more distant from it than had seemed to be the case when I observed it through the scope at our OP back on Burnt Knob. There was a fair sized clearing around, with a few planted trees growing amongst the weeds and short bladed grass.

We kept the house under surveillance for fifteen minutes, saw nothing. Then I took one of the scouts and walked cautiously up the trail, which had turned to follow the ridge leading upward.

Naturally, we carefully examined the ground as we walked forward, stopping now and then to listen for any human sounds up ahead. It was not until we had covered about 200 yards that we saw anything exciting. These were imprints in a soft part of the trail, fresh, and definitive enough, to make our hair stand on end.

There in the dirt at our feet were many of the familiar, unmistakable marks of Japanese field shoes. We froze for a moment, and then eased back into cover. The prints were not identifiable as to the time of impression—they may have been made an hour, a day, or three days previously. But they were not old. I wished sorely, now, that I had heeded the advice of one of the men at the OP, who had told me to take more than ten men on the mission.

I motioned the scout to lean an ear my way and gave him orders to go back and get the rest of the patrol, lead them up to where we were. I would remain under cover in my present position and cook up some sort of a scheme for closing in on the place, or at least for probing and determining how many enemy were there. It would not be long until dusk, and I wanted to get this chore over with, if possible, before we should be halted by darkness and have to wait out the night short of our objective.

When the scout left I felt very much alone and out on a limb. During his absence the seconds ticked slowly away, their little sights and sounds impressing themselves on my memory so much so that I can now recall each little part of the scene. There was a long string of red ants coming down the trunk of a small tree close to me, each ant following in the same serpentine path taken by his predecessors. This seemed silly because the trunk was smooth and the ants could travel as they saw fit anyplace on its bark. At least they could straighten out their line. As it was, though, the lead ant had chosen a rather drunken downward course on the trunk and the other ants had followed, snake-dancing behind. That much I remember very well, despite the fact that I saw it only through the corner of an eye.

My visual powers were primarily being strained in an attempt to see anything which might come along the path up ahead, and my ears, too, were straining—to hear the least human-made sound from the shack. I was painfully aware then of the slight loss of hearing in my left ear which was caused by the work of the Jap rifleman who almost got me near Morovovo. My hearing hadn't been the same since his bullet had cracked so close to my ear.

I heard and saw no man, however, for quite a few moments, and then I detected a friendly sound—the sound of the rest of the patrol coming cautiously up the trail behind. Nothing in the way of unnatural sounds came from the other direction; in fact, the stillness had become very intense and ominous.

We were all quiet ourselves, experiencing again an old feeling which we had all expected to be spared, after Esperance. The air was charged with a peculiar variety of electric tension which only the jungle soldier can know. This is a spicy mixture of fear, anticipation, anxiety and exhilaration set in the exotic jungle atmosphere of shadows and dank, sweet smells.

Ahead we had an objective, a point on the map to be visited and acted against solely to satisfy the eternal curiosity of higher echelon staff officers. Always in every army there are many questions being asked about the enemy situation, and it has always been the duty of the intelligence officer (G–2 or S–2) in each outfit to be able to answer whatever questions the commander may see fit to ask about the enemy or the terrain he occupies.

"What is the enemy troop strength in forward areas? In rear areas? Where are the various enemy units located?" These are the general questions asked by commanders who may be engaged in tactical or strategic planning or shifting their divisions and regiments and battalions to attack or organizing them for a defense. Their "curiosity," to the men who had to actually secure the information, seemed utterly insatiable.

Against the Japanese in the jungle—at least in the early days
—intelligence generally bogged down. There were no sources of
information other than a few natives and a very few prisoners,
neither generally able to give accurate information—even had they
wanted to; and to other agencies, such as observation aircraft and
ground observation posts, the jungle was an almost solid blanket,
hiding everything from view. Whole regiments could bivouac under
a solid green ceiling without danger of detection by aerial observation, and they could move at will with no enemy the wiser.
Wide paths—sometimes even roads—could be cut through tropical
rain forest and yet not break the solid overhead cover.

Our own intelligence organization was rather inadequate at the
beginning of the war, and our people possessed very little specific
knowledge of the practical field methods of determining enemy
strengths, whereabouts, or dispositions. This made it impossible
for a commander to judge enemy effectiveness with any degree of
sureness. It took time for this situation to improve, and eventually
it did, because it *had* to.

But on Guadalcanal it was never improved enough, and reliance
for the securing of dependable enemy information had to be placed
principally upon our own agencies that would get into actual contact with the enemy: front line elements, forward observers, patrols.

We were one of these patrols out risking our necks in order to
satisfy what often seemed to us to be rather whimsical curiosity
of local Intelligence Officers. If we should all be killed during our
little closein on that shack, a little mark would go up on a piece
of acetate transparent sheeting stretched across the situation map
at headquarters. A small measure of this boundless curiosity would
be satisfied, and another patrol would be sent out to find out
more. Military Intelligence (information about the enemy) is a
priceless, hard-to-get item, and many men who have toiled at the
worst of it—that of going on patrol into enemy territory—are
the only ones who know how really priceless it can be.

In a few moments we would move from our present position up
to the suspect spot and, by some means or other, get a good look
at the place so that we could later paint a word-picture for some
desk man back at headquarters. In getting one good look at our
objective, we would have finished our task had we been only an
intelligence patrol, but we had another mission—we were also a
combat patrol.

That meant that we had to do our utmost to destroy or capture
all that we should see in the way of the enemy or enemy property.
So we were to move up to this little shack, look it over, count the
enemy there and then kill or capture them all.

All these things I thought of as my men assembled behind me on the path and as the last man drew near I ceased cudgeling my brain for a shortcut solution and decided to use an old simple method of doing the job—one that would get it over quickly. The group, in the meantime, had crowded around me where I had edged off the trail into a little declivity, and I whispered out an order which went something like this:

"I believe that the trail approaches the house from below, and comes up into some sort of a small front yard. I don't know whether the sides of the shack are solid. If they are we'll have to get inside before we learn what's there. If not, we will be able to take care of it from the outside unless the place is dug in. Anyway, we'll have to get up there right soon and get the thing over with. It'll be dark in another hour or so.

"I'll move up ahead with our scouts and a BAR man. The rest follow at about twenty-five paces, but keep fairly well together back from there. I don't want the outfit too scattered if we have to do something in a hurry.

"We'll do one of two things; either we'll walk in and take the place—no use staging a battle if there aren't any enemy around, or else we'll rush the house and get inside before any of the Japs can get the drop on us. If the walls of the shack are intact, so that we can't see inside, we'll have to assume that there *are* enemy inside—and we'll have to rush the place.

"I'll plant the two BAR men to cover us, and they are not to shoot unless they see Japs, or unless we should be fired on and pinned down before we get to the shack. If that happens, though, I want that shack riddled all across its bottom.

"By the time you join me, I'll have my mind made up as to whether we rush or walk in, and I'll signal you. If I am fired on before hand, hold tight back there and cover me if I have to haul out. Any questions?"

We moved along the trail, cautious, ready to spring to cover at any time, but also possessed of an impatience—a dangerous desire, like a patient in a dentist's chair—to speed up the proceedings and get the damn thing over with. Our walk up the trail was cautious, carefully trodden, with always a little bend kept in our knees to give us leg-spring so that we might quickly jump to cover, or fall into firing positions. The undergrowth remained thick so that we could not see ahead more than the only occasional straightness of the trail would allow. Because the trail was very winding, we came upon the clearing suddenly, almost stepping out into its brightness before we knew we were there.

The house, viewed obliquely from its front as we faced it, could now be clearly seen. No one was in sight in the clearing. The house

Two Jap doughboys halt for a noonday snack. The rice which nearly fills the mess kit of the man in the foreground was probably cooked in the morning, to be eaten cold on the march. The chop sticks being used are carried in a little pocket box, or are cut from bamboo along the march. The fancier ones are carved of ivory or bone.

Japanese soldiers always fed individually, or in small tactical groups. There were no field kitchens in the Nip Army, and no designated cooks for units in the fight. Every man was a combat effective—no deadwood or overhead. Each man was responsible for the preparation of his own food.

Rice was a compact, easily carried ration. Usually it was carried in a sort of stocking, opened at one end for pouring. The mess gear usually had one or two trays, not shown here, which nestled under the lid. These and the lid would serve as extra "plates." Our own mess gear, for field purposes and for cooking, could not even be compared with the Japanese.

walls were solid. The distance was short from the edge of the clearing to the door, and it looked to me as though the only solution would be to rush the place. I spotted the one BAR man so that he would be able to rake the house with fire, and than we waited for the rest of the patrol to come into view on the trail behind.

I motioned with my arm to the other BAR man, indicating a position for him to fire from, and a central direction for them *not* to fire in should the maneuvering element of my little attack force rush the building.

Then I looked down at my rifle and read the word READY on the lock lever, took off my pack and laid it under some fern stems, and watched for a second while the other men who had arrived behind me on the final stretch of the trail took off their own packs. Then I waved my arm forward.

All of us broke into a wild bounding run, disregarding all caution as to whether we were bunched or scattered or lined up one behind the other. We were only interested in getting into that shack—visible and open doored—before any of the occupants could recover from their surprise and grab weapons. We had good reason to believe that they were not on the alert—maybe cooking or resting. Well, with luck with us, they would all be dead before they learned what was going on.

The lead scout beat me to the door. I followed him inside, cursing because it was dark and I had not thought of pre-accommodating my eyes by holding them closed before the rush. Unable to see in the darkness, we prodded with our weapons, trampled about with our feet, ready to shoot any living thing we might feel or step upon. Four of us were inside the hut by now, and our eyes gradually began to adapt themselves to the darkness.

The earth and board floor, we saw, was scattered over with objects of various sorts, but there were no human forms there, alive or dead.

Nothing was there.

Somewhere in the back of my head during the planning of the assault was an idea which kept soaking through to the foreground of my thoughts, through the furious seconds of the rush and its anti-climax. It was a marked fear of some sort—a little voice which had kept repeating "no, no, no" against my plan of rushing the shack. This thought struck both me and the senior noncom at the same time, but it did not mature in either of our minds until it looked as though it was entirely too late.

The whole reason for this fear dawned suddenly upon me while we were still prodding the dark corners of the shack. As I saw that the place was empty, I suffered a great, rising pang of fright which nearly numbed my knees—an impulse to which I reacted instantaneously. I turned and yelled to the six or so men who were inside the hut with me: "Get out of here! . . . Back to the trail and take cover!"

The men obeyed at once, and as we scrambled back out I had the sensation of having droplets of cold sweat come out on my forehead to join the hot, grimy film already there. Elbows, rifle butts, and equipment of various sorts banged against the doorway and we all struggled out while I was still overcome with a dread of what I felt sure would happen—that I would be responsible for the deaths of my men and myself.

The sides of the shack were galvanized iron and woven bamboo, and the packed floor was above the outside earth surface. There was no shelter from rifle fire within twenty yards of the damn shack, and only one open way of getting out. Three men with rifles or one man with a Nambu hidden in part of the surrounding cover, which we had not checked—could kill us all, while we remained helpless to fire back.

That was the fear. In walking up to the clearing and then in rushing the house I had led my men into what could well be a baited and set trap; as we frantically got out and back down toward the trail I fully expected the air to become filled with crackling fire. We would all be swept off our feet and then riddled —while we lay on the high, exposed ground in the shack's immediate yard.

What would I have done had I been a Japanese officer or noncom in charge of a crew living in that house? There could be only one answer—one solution: Camp—not in the house, but around it— or move in only at night. Keep some men in position at all times so that they could sweep the house with fire and perhaps set off booby traps placed inside on a moment's notice. Then allow any enemy parties to proceed unmolested up the trail and wait until they get into the house—let the suckers walk right inside or rush it as we did. After they all got inside the work could start: riddle the damn place, leaving one or two guns aimed at the door, free to crack down on any survivors who might pop out of the door, one at a time—like clay pigeons. As a double check measure, a trail block could be thrown also—just to make sure that no one got away.

That was what any smart Jap would have done—what I was certain of for a few moments; I *knew* that we were being ambushed —the clues had all been there. Our approach had met with no enemy on the last mile of trail. We had seen the fresh, clearly identifiable Jap shoe tracks, though, and everything had been too damn quiet in the moments before we rushed the house, strongly hinting that something was fishy. The hint had become an idea and then had turned into an absolute conviction when I learned that no Japanese were in the house. My immediate reaction was a feeling of stark terror—a fear that my sands, and those of the incompetently led patrol, had run out. Death has certainly been nearer to me many times than on that occasion, but I have never worried so much about it.

We were back on the trail now and we soon got down into cover, without being fired at—me thanking God for that bit of luck. I had taken cover near one of the BAR men, who had remained outside and I asked him if he had seen anything suspicious in the cover or edges of the clearing. He had not.

Then we scouted around the house, two men going out with the rest of us covering, and we found the area to be clear, all around, with no path leading away from the house to the rear or sides— only the trail we had used ourselves. The Japs had pulled out, left several days before, apparently.

My fears had all been for nothing—just a case of combat jitters, I told myself.

There was a Japanese mess kit on the floor, all blackened from use, with a bit of mouldy rice crusted on its bottom. Odd bits of Japanese equipment lay about—a pack, two pairs of worn out Japanese field shoes, a big mosquito net, large enough to cover a good sized tent, and a few knee-mortar shells and grenades. The latter were handled very gingerly in brief inspection, and then we buried them.

The place had been completely vacated.

We made no use of the shack that night, but cut our inspection of the premises short in order to dispose ourselves comfortably before darkness. We bedded down on one side of the trail, with two foxholes dug in block positions, so that their inmates could fire at anything coming up the trail. We trip-wired the trail in two places, using long-cane stalks hooked to special grenade pins which would furnish us with both protection and extra measure of vigilance—they would go off with a very loud noise and serve as warning devices.

Naturally the trip wires do not differentiate between large animals and men, so, of course, with time spacing perfect for disrupting an entire nights sleep, two of the booby traps were set off by the damn wild pigs. The first one wasn't so bad, because the hog identified himself after the explosion with a succession of agonized cries, not unlike those I remember from farm days, when one of the more sadistic rites of hog raising was being performed on the boar shoats. In this case, however, I am afraid that my annoyance at the noise swept completely away any pity I should have felt for the wounded pig, whose injuries were obviously akin to those we caused back on the farm. Actually, I have since forgiven the squalling animal, and I hope that he is recovered and now enjoying the life of a prime boar, with a big family.

The second pig didn't even murmur, was probably unhit, and we didn't even know that it was a pig that exploded the trap until we saw the tracks in the morning. For that reason we enjoyed little sleep through the last hours of darkness.

Dawn, always a welcome thing in the Pacific war, came at the usual time, six o'clock. We were up before it, at first dim light, our faces bearing the least bit of refreshed appearance laid unconvincingly over the sagging masks of fatigue and ill-health which all doughboys would wear after so many months of work and fear.

We waited on the ridge at the house until the morning mists lifted and we could see Edson's Ridge well enough to identify our OP near Burnt Knob, proving that we were truly atop our objective. Then we started the return trip.

No need to stay at the shack, we had done our job: got there, inspected the place, and checked it around for enemy. There had been a time when I would have gone beyond my orders and checked ⁺he whole length of the ridge, but several days would have been required for such a task and I did not have enough rations along. Furthermore, I didn't want to stay up there and get left on the island if surprise shipping should become available to the regiment within the next few days. It would be just like the rest of the outfit to go off and leave us flat. I had assembled the patrol and asked if anyone thought we should stay longer. *No one did.*

We would take a little different route on the way out, I decided, just to make things a little more interesting. We took the trail down only as far as it held to the ridge top, and then we struck due north, trying to connect up with one of the several trails which I had heard about in that area, some leading to Koli Point, others to Lunga. Either destination would be satisfactory to the patrol.

The cutting seemed easier going back to the beach (funny how much more heart a man can put into a march that leads him toward home). Our spirits, compared to their recent state, had been lifted to a level of near exhilaration. Jokes were frequently heard behind the hacking machete blades, and not a few comic speculations were voiced concerning the anatomical injuries sustained by the poor pig we had booby trapped. I had brought the subject up at the start of the return trip, and an ex-farmer member of the patrol had strongly concurred in my exact diagnosis of the pig's injury. Then the subject was exploited from every angle. "How would the grenade incident affect the pig population on Guadalcanal? Would the injured animal's voice become high and shrill, changing his grunts to squeals and his squeals to squeaks? What would the sows in the local herds think?" (More laughter.)

We walked on behind the cutting blades for a while, and finally got into a patch of lovely tropical rain forest which was strangely devoid of heavy undergrowth, allowing us to stow the machetes for a while. For a few paces the men argued good naturedly over who was to carry the machetes and then the blades were strapped on the losers packs, between the haversack flap and the meat can cover, if the man had an American pack—on the outside if it was a captured one.

The machetes we were carrying were of the issue variety— heavy and long and wide of blade, with a composition handle riveted on. They were almost perfect for cutting, but were very poor for carrying. A later date would see many such blades cut off at the tip to reduce them more than a third in length and make them much easier to carry.

It is hard for the jungle soldier to settle on a single ideal shape and weight of brush knife. Largely I think it is a matter of local preference, with men in different areas using blades of different types. And to a great degree, is a matter of terrain—the particular type of stuff which has to be cut.

A long slender bush blade, such as was sold in the shops of New Caledonia—actually nothing but a lightweight and elongated butcher knife—was not worth a damn for cutting heavy bamboo, but it proved perfect for soft vines and brush. The short machete bolo, in its various forms—our own army design, the Philippine bolo, or its curved bladed cousin which the Ghurkas call the *kukri* —is very good for bamboo and sapling chopping, but poor for trail cutting. Even in a given jungle area there is no all-round blade. Each ones does some particular tasks better than the others.

The way I see it, there should be a variety of knives in each Infantry jungle squad, and perhaps a small axe as well, if the squad is operating in tropical rain forest or coconut grove islands. This variety should include at least two of the machete type trail cutting blades.

Sharpening the blades is a constant problem, however, it is more easily solved if the lightweight, long, and only slightly curved blades are used because it is an easy matter to sweep a hone across their edges. The heavier blades of bolos and kukris become nicked rather often, and the thicker metal demands a file or a heavier stone.

The Army carborundum hones (which were issued to us in later campaigns) were well designed, of palm size, and were furnished with two cutting faces; one coarse grained, for sharpening, and one fine, for finishing. Those stones which we had on Guadalcanal were individually purchased on New Caledonia—the QM apparently assumed, when they issued machetes, that the original edges would hold sharp forever.

As the patrol walked on I could see demonstrated the technique of good jungle cutting. The cutters were not using work gloves to protect them from thorns and nettles because we had none, but they were none the less cutting as they should—free swinging most of the time, occasionally gathering a handful of vines to hold stiff against the sweep of the blade, stopping now and then to scrape with a hone.

We kept getting lower and lower on the ridge, losing height fast, and I wondered what the straightaway would hold for us when we got down to it. I hoped that we would not be plunged into a swamp, to struggle around for hours knee-deep in mud.

No swamp awaited us below, but rather a majestic stand of jungle which would require, for adequate portrayal, the use of descriptive abilities far beyond mine. Undergrowth continued to be somewhat stunted by the very deep shade, and the principal impression of this forest was given by the large amount of parasitic growths on the big-trunked broadleafs. These parasitic growths were huge and imposing, big clusters on the pillar-like giants. The shade was as intense as I had ever seen, and there was moisture and resultant rot. Nothing would ever dry there.

We were still getting along without cutting, and the blades remained stowed on the packs, which was good. Also we were no longer in much danger of encountering Japanese, for our route was taking us farther to the north, away from areas into which enemy stragglers would tend to drift. As we stepped on through the patches of huge ferns, which comprised the greater portion of undergrowth, I lapsed again into a dreamy state of awed admiration at the eternal vastness of the primeval rain forest all around —incidentally, a good way to get your mind off march fatigue.

Some peculiarity of the local soil had made the surface of the decayed wood and leaf mass firm enough for good footing, and this condition improved as we went on our way, apparently moving down toward some valley floor. In other places there had been pit-falls—soft spots in the rotten jungle floor—where a man could fall in over his head if he failed to test the path ahead with tentative toe pressure. Elsewhere on Guadalcanal the jungle had been strewn with fallen logs in various states of decay, often obstructing our way with six foot thick trunks and forcing us to cut around their supine length as much as forty yards. Here, strangely enough, the trees all seemed to die standing up, rotting away from the top, with roots clawing the soil firmly to the very last.

Visibility was improving, too, as we moved in this northwesterly direction. The vegetation seemed more and more to deserve the name of "rain forest" rather than "jungle." The fern undergrowth was not becoming sparse, by any means, but in many places the principal leaf strata of the undergrowth was above eye level so that only the upright stems, trunks, and vines were blocking our vision. Occasionally we ran into narrow alleys which allowed us to see for as much as a hundred and fifty yards.

Part of our solid footing was provided by a heavy growth of root vegetables of different sorts. These plants were of various shapes, some looking like tulip bulbs, some like horse radish, some like turnips. I suppose that they really were turnips of a sort and the place was a regular pig feeding ground because the soil had been rooted up and the exposed vegetables eaten on the spot.

Twice we heard pigs snort and take off in front of us and I walked for some time at the head of the column with the safety on my rifle thrown, but the pigs were too clever on that island, as a rule, to let one get an easy shot. Generally the jungle was not the ideal pig shooting grounds. The edges of grass fields and the coconut groves were preferred. Natives were the only successful pig hunters where the cover was so heavy, and nearly all of the pigs I have shot in such cover—I am ashamed to admit—have been shot when a native guide was along.

We met a party of natives moving in the opposite direction on a river trail which we came upon a little later. They were loaded down with their own household goods—pots, pans, lanterns, and the like, strapped and tumplined onto their backs. The meeting was a welcome one, even if we did go through the usual nervous preliminaries of taking cover and scouting them out with a lot of trigger fingers holding ready while our advance members peeked and snooped.

The natives were coastal villagers who had holed up in the hills at the time of the first big fighting, leaving their comfortable but unfortunately exposed homes near the beaches. A questioning in pidgin revealed that these people were still afraid to move back into the groves where so much shooting and bombing had recently taken place. Their hideout in the hills was good enough, they said, and there was plenty of jungle *kiki* (food) to keep body and soul together. This jungle *kiki* consisted primarily of wild yams, several varieties of fruit, and game—pigs and birds. No one looked starved in the party so the supply must have been adequate.

There were six males in the bunch, varying in age from perhaps eight to thirty years. They were the usual unattractive type of Solomon Islander with the deathly masks of malaria and other diseases showing noticeably on all but the youngest. Enlarged

spleens gave each one a slightly pot-bellied appearance and an unnatural bend in the lower spine exaggerated this effect. Their feet
were bare, of course, with the forward portion so widely splayed
that toes were completely separated and their legs were badly
scarred below the knees as the result of unattended wounds from
sharp coral reefs and thorny jungle underbrush.

Native women were seldom seen on Guadalcanal, for good reason. The Japanese had misbehaved for one thing and another was
the natural aboriginal suspicion that all wars are fought over property or women and that both sides would behave accordingly.
So the Solomon Islanders were quick to take protective measures.
They lost no time in hiding their property, food stores, and their
women in the hilly interior where they knew yellow or white men
would not often trespass. Once they had succeeded in stowing
these commodities away, they would return to the beaches and
wander around, making friends with the strangers and perhaps
working for payment in food or trinkets. The party we met had
apparently been on such a venture to the beaches, and now they
were returning to their women in the hills, loaded down with gifts
of bully beef, Japanese clothing, rice sacks, canvas, and empty tins.
The last would be made into cooking utensils.

While we were halted on the trail talking with and looking over
the natives, another pig was heard snorting offside the trail and
running through the cover. The two older men, armed with metal
pointed bamboo spears, jerked around and peered intently into
the underbrush, craning their necks trying to follow the animal's
movement as it ran. This gave me the idea of seeing if we could
organize a little pig hunt on the way back, perhaps get one of
the natives to turn around and accompany us to Koli Point, guiding us through some good pig jungle and walking up front with
me to help me get a shot.

It turned out that it wasn't a difficult bit of salesmanship. The
second eldest of the crowd volunteered unconditionally, very willing after he had made a very good swap of gear with one of the
men, getting a good Remington hunting knife for a rusty Nambu
pistol. He knew we would fix him up well when we got back to
the beach. Turning his load over to another one of the party, he
aboutfaced and started back with us. His presence at the head of
the column relieved our minds somewhat for the whole remainder
of the walk. With a junglewise native at the front of a patrol,
there is much less danger of walking blindly into trouble.

I had taken some minutes to explain to our new scout that we
did not simply want to go on a pig hunt, but that we wanted to
shoot a pig on the way back to the beach, and were willing to
make a slight detour enroute in order to go through better pig

country. I couldn't imagine better pig country than we were in at the moment, however, since obviously there were thousands of hogs around and only the thick cover made it hard to bag one. I also tried my best to let him know that rifle hunting was much different from hunting pigs with a spear. With a rifle, I explained, you did not need to be close to the pig—only within sight. I made it clear that I did not want to go crawling and squirming through the heaviest type of cover, where a spear would be just as good as my weapon.

Apparently he understood, for he did not lead us off on a side trail until he found one going through undergrowth of the less dense variety. He and I moved out thirty yards ahead of the rest and we all moved along as quietly as possible, individually thinking of how nice it would be to have a pork dinner that night.

To say that pig sign was plentiful would have been an understatement. Pigs on Guadalcanal were like deer on New Caledonia —just as plentiful only less visible because of the heavy cover. The jungle floor was literally turned over with rootings, and all the trails and side paths were marked solidly with hoof prints. Droppings—not so euphemistically referred to when they were inadvertently sat in by a tired doughboy—were all over the trails. But the same tropical climate and soil that provided an abundance of roots for the pigs to eat had also given them an abundance of cover to hide in. After only a few tries, I had learned that jungle hunting without a native along was a chance business, and I had shot my independently-bagged pigs in the kunai grass fields rather than put up with the continual disappointment caused by hearing many of the animals each trip—and yet seeing not a single one.

I would like to tell a long story of this particular pig hunt-hike, but I cannot. It was too short and lacked enough drama to make any kind of a tale. We had been off on a side trail for only a few minutes when the native froze, looking intently into the brush to his left front at something which would not even have drawn my attention had I been alone. To me it would have been passed as just another shadow, but to him it was a marked irregularity in the hang of fern fronds—something undoubtedly caused by an animal, not just another plant.

If my eyes served me poorly in the task of locating game, however, they served me very well indeed at recognizing it once it had been pointed out. The brief piloting of the native's trained vision was all the assistance my own eyes needed, and I instantly recognized the pig—a young boar—looking squarely at us with his body in three-quarters view, only twenty-five yards away.

Only a few fern leaves intervened, but I was still afraid to throw my weapon suddenly to my shoulder because such a movement would cause the pig, now standing perfectly still, to bolt. Instead I began the age-old trick of inching my weapon slowly from the carry into the firing position, a very difficult task because the native was in my way, only two feet in front, and the rifle was in my right hand. I would have to draw my arm back and lower the muzzle of the weapon, then point it across and grip with left arm, and *then* bring the damn thing gradually into shooting position. All of this in very slow motion. While I started at this nervous procedure, the native and the men behind were helpful. They stood perfectly immobile.

Like many good and proven plans, it didn't work.

The pig, I guess, heard my own breathing or heartbeats and bolted, pivoting around to run away. I naturally threw caution to the winds and sprang around in front of the native, trying to follow the animal's progress through the brush, going by the sound and the shaking vegetation.

Instinct, lately developed by shooting the fast running pigs on the narrow path in the kunai grass fields, served me well. I calculated the pig's direction and assumed that he was headed for the trail we were on and decided to gamble on a shot as he crossed or turned down the trail. I held the weapon half cheeked at my shoulder, with both eyes barely clear of the barrel in order to have a clear view ahead. When a movement in the undergrowth indicated the pig's point of emergence onto the trail, I brought the weapon into complete firing position and peered through the scope, maintaining a wide field of vision at the same time by keeping my left eye open.

The pig came out onto the trail and remained on it for some twenty yards, running like hell until he disappeared into the cover on its right side, crashing pell-mell through the small stuff growing low down.

By the time he regained cover, however, I knew that he was a very sick pig because somewhere during the split second of his exposure on the trail my rifle had gone off with a bang that sounded dull in my intense concentration on the task of keeping the post of the reticule on the darting black target. The post had been squarely at twelve o'clock on the pig's back when the rifle recoiled. The slight smoke and flash had blotted out the target in the scope, but a fleeting glimpse with my left eye attested that the pig had run into cover. The call, however, was such that it permitted no argument—it was one of those rare times in the shooting game when no doubt remains in the rifleman's mind. As I ran forward toward the spot where the pig had disappeared, I knew that the hit was a good one and close to the spine.

On through the thorns I ran, trotting recklessly into the area where I thought the legs of a pig who didn't know he was dead might carry him. After a few yards, though, I drew up, realizing that by this boyish show of excitement I might lose face with the guide. I told the guide that the pig was hit, probably dead. When he displayed doubt, I went further in explaining, pointing to the small of my back and then to my face to show him where I thought the animal was raked by my bullet. "Pig, him fella dead!" I pidgined, "Damn dead, very dead. *Beaucoup* dead!"

We combed the cover for a while before I found the pig, as dead as I had announced; it had butted against a root and expired. The hit was just about where I had said it would be, although the bullet had emerged lower down on the animal, coming out at the belly instead of the chest. Either the hog had jumped when I shot, or else the M2 bullet had curved or glanced sharply downward from the spine. The last was the more feasible explanation of the bullet's course, because the animal would have had to be almost upon his hind legs in order to let the bullet exit at the belly as was the case.

Extensive damage had been done by the service bullet—as much as could reasonably be expected by an expanding type. The pig had dragged its entrails for the last five yards at least, and the slit in its belly was six or so inches in length. I had located the carcass, in fact, by an almost solid blood trail, four inches wide, which had commenced about five yards from where he lay.

I handed my knife to the native and asked him to gut the animal. For some reason, perhaps because he thought it was so pretty, the native didn't want to use his own newly acquired Remington, but kept it in the sheath. (No doubt that knife will become an heirloom in a Solomon Islander family, witness to much adventure in the next century.)

Because he had relieved himself of his pack when he left his other party, the native was now free to carry the whole pig for us, saving the bother of quartering the carcass. The weight was about sixty pounds—a nice eating hog—much better than a bigger one. After dressing the pig, Joe (we were now calling him by that name) adapted it to back-packing exactly as we do a deer in the states. (The origin of the term "piggy back" maybe?) I told him that we would like to go to one of the coastal villages near Koli Point, where the hog could be roasted native style.

The village proved to be too much out of the way for our purpose, too far to the north, and visiting it would entail too much delay. I was not being pricked too strongly by my sense of duty, but I did want to get a prompt report in to Captain Cosby. I first became aware of the width of the detour our guide was taking us on when I noticed him ever turning in a northward direction.

Hideo

The Japs knew how to live off the land—to make the best of any surroundings. Their supply service wasn't used to sending out large quantities of foodstuffs from the homeland. Expeditionary forces in Burma and China got their food by procurement demand, from the local populace.

In more remote areas the Japs did a bit of hunting and fishing for the pot. They potted game with their rifles, they fished a bit in honest fashion and, like us, they learned what a grenade would do if thrown into a likely pool in a jungle stream. The fish in this sketch was probably obtained in the latter manner.

Once they killed the game or fish they cooked it well. Rice was just about all they really needed, and a little salt. The Jap shown seems about to cut up the fish and boil it in the four mess kits tandemed on the fire pole. If he didn't have the mess gear handy he would be able to do an even better job of cooking with a bamboo joint.

Japs learned to make their camps comfortable, even if they were to remain but a day. This man's squad might have spent two hours in preparing this fire and catching the fish—but they'll have a good meal for their trouble. Something better than cold "C" or "K" rations, anyway.

Since we might soon be going directly out of the way, I had to change the plan.

The native obviously wanted to get the patrol to the village, perhaps for the trading and bartering of rations which he thought would take place. We wanted to go too, but sense of duty, augmented by a fear of disciplinary measures, triumphed after a brief tussle with our hedonistic impulses. I told Joe to turn westward and lead us toward the beach roads. We would have to take pot-luck in finding a pig roasting site to camp at for that night. I also told him that we would have to do the cooking and eating after darkness, in order to lose no time on the march.

At this time we were travelling on a jungle trail which wound through the edge of a rain forest bordering a large grass field. After a mile or so, during which we put up another pig, we began to make occasional cuts out into the grass field to find a good bit of dry ground, so that we could bed down and build a fire. It was getting towards dusk—about five-thirty.

The first few cuts out into the field had revealed only soggy, swamp-like ground—a bedding surface much less desirable than even the insect crawling jungle, and so water-soaked that a bar-becue pit could not be dug. It was not until the fourth or fifth try that we found a suitable bivouac site—a mound-like knoll, strangely overgrown with kunai grass, just as the flat land that surrounded it on three sides. Its east slope butted into the jungle edge.

We found a path leading up its north side, cut through the very heavy growth of cane-like grass winding over the very crest. About half way up there was a sort of shelf, large enough to bed down the entire patrol, organized for sleeping and for night defense.

This defense setup, or harboring arrangement, would be a sort of hedge-hog perimeter, with listening areas and fields of fire allotted radially to the individuals on the edge. The trails could be covered by BARs, and reading right into the tactical plan, we located a good, covered spot, away from the perimeter, where the pig could be roasted. This spot was connected with the bivouac site by a good path, so that the cooked pig could be carried from the fire and eaten in the harboring area—a further avoidance of the danger of ambush, very remote now, anyway.

We got into the harboring area rapidly, spreading the thick grass to make little paths offside the main path, and beating it down in places to give a few limited fields of fire. Our miscellaneous ponchos, raincoats, and groundcloths were laid in a short time and the positions were all located to eliminate any danger of our shooting one another. This, because we were to be above ground that night, was most important. I had decided against digging in anything other than the two trail blocking positions so we could be free to rest and enjoy the pork dinner.

In the meantime, the native had gone down into the jungle, found a clump of bamboo, and cut several large joints of the green stuff. He had also picked a few onion-like plants and dug some edible roots to be cooked with the dinner. By the time I was through checking our bivouac area so that I could go down to the pig roasting site, Joe had assembled the green bamboo joints, the bamboo kindling, some fairly dry firewood, and had a fire blazing in the small pit which he had dug for that purpose.

After heaping the pit fire high with deadwood, he built another fire a short distance away and rigged two green forked sticks with a cross member offside the blaze so that the long joints of bamboo could be filled with water like deep buckets and then propped up with their sides across the flames to serve as boilers. As soon as he had stoked a second fire to boil the water, Joe returned to the pig carcass and went to work in earnest, quartering it with knife and machete, chopping lengthwise down the center of the spine. This was good, I reflected, for we would not have time to barbecue the pig whole, and I did not want the pork undercooked. The danger of trichinosis, contracted by eating pork not thoroughly cooked, was something all of us had learned to keep in mind. While Joe finished with the quartering and began skillfully to prepare the individual pieces for initial cooking in the pot (which would be the several green bamboo joints), I continued to watch the exhibition of jungle craft with interest.

Joe had lost no time in getting started, and he was tackling his various tasks in the proper sequence; both fires were set and going early, which would allow them to burn down into the ideal state for cooking during his other preparations. After the hog was quartered, Joe picked up his bamboo joints and walked to a trickle of a jungle stream some hundreds of yards away to fill them, taking along half of our canteens at the same time. We were not entirely out of water because there had been opportunity to refill during our afternoon's walk. Without the halizone tablets (which we did not have on Guadalcanal), our only method of purifying water was the awkward improvisation of carrying one extra American canteen in each patrol. This extra canteen was kept full of a concentrated chlorine solution, a single portion measured in the tiny canteen cap being sufficient for purifying a full canteen of water. This gave us protection against everything except amoebic dysentery, which, thank God, was not epidemic on Guadalcanal.

Joe soon got back, walking with confident step in near-darkness that would have caused the rest of us to feel our way along. He immediately put water to boil in all four of the tubes, propping them across the flames, leaving the top ends uncovered. He then moved over to his little outdoor butcher shop and carried the parts over into the firelight, where he removed the skin from all parts but the hindquarters. Those he left unskinned and with the hair on, while he got some scalding water out of the quickest heating tube of bamboo. A gradual pouring of the boiling water over the two hindquarters scalded the skin and prepared the bristles for scraping, which he accomplished with a knife edge. (This was the only bit of inefficiency in the whole procedure. It would have been better for him to have scalded the whole pig before quartering it.)

After this last task of scraping, which was made very tedious by the looseness of the skin on the disjointed parts, the pieces were all cut to size—some of them deboned—and stuffed into the bamboo tubes to boil. As Joe walked back to the pit and rigged a roasting rack, the air became rife with a very pleasing odor.

I had wished for a large quantity of salt so that it could have been used to season the meat during boiling, but all we had with us would barely suffice for use in a final basting, or to sprinkle on the meat as we ate. We had to powder some of our small supply of salt tablets in order to have even that little bit. Salt, much taken for granted in our own homes, is an all important commodity in primitive areas, often being used as legal tender by natives to trade for a cow or a wife.

I returned to the harboring area and detailed three men to go back to the fire and carry the cooked meat for the entire patrol. Actually, there seemed no need for this precaution and it would have been nice to move down and have a good community feast around the fire, but somehow I couldn't bring myself to throw caution to the winds as I had on several private pig-eats.

Warmth, of course, was not important, for the night was balmy, but there is something about a fire at night that appeals to every man in the woods. One of the worst complaints I have against the war in general was that Infantrymen were so seldom able to build or enjoy fires. A fire, we came to know after long months of doing without, was ofttimes the greatest comfort a man could have. When weeks would go by without warmth or heated food, sometimes even without heated drink, you could almost see added sagging in a man's face, a tiredness over and above that caused by danger and ordinary combat hardship. Man may have been able to divorce himself from many of his more recently acquired habits, but I believe he would normally die in a matter of months —in anything but a perfect tropical environment—if he were denied the comfort of his basic weapon and ally.

The minutes crept by while we bedded down on the hillside

shelf, piling some of the dew-soaked kunai grass into a sort of pallet with my groundcloth placed over it. Mosquitos were present now in their usual numbers, biting and droning around our ears, defying our best efforts to repel them. Some of us had little bottles of fly dope which we passed around to sprinkle on palms and rub onto other exposed parts, but it gave only temporary relief. Guadalcanal mosquitos were large and equipped with stout probes, fully capable of penetrating at least one thickness of new herringbone twill, the material from which our combat fatigues were made. The frayed and worn state of our own uniforms greatly aggravated the mosquito problem by enabling the damn insects to get at us in all places, stabbing through the cloth wherever it lay along the surface of flesh. And if they were too lazy to probe through the cloth, it was easy for them to search a bit and find a hole or frayed spot in the material. They went on biting us unmercifully, raising itchy welts, sometimes causing septic sores, and giving each of us a concentrated dose of malaria which would have us burning, shivering, and vomiting through one relapse after another for the next two years.

Looking downward from my bedding-down spot on the hillside, I could see the firelight shimmering upward against the wet leaves of the undergrowth, and I knew that the cooking was going well. From previous observations I knew how it would be done. The boiling pieces would be removed from the bamboo casings and grilled while the tender roots and onions were left to simmer in the tubes. The meat would be either spitted or supported on improvised grills over the fire, which was by now burnt down into a glowing mass of coals. It would be done to a near crisp on the outside, retaining juicy tenderness within.

I lay back on my groundcloth, resting an arm on my rifle which lay propped on a forked stick alongside, and looked up at the stars, no longer trying to remove my mind from the gnawing hunger which I had felt for more than an hour. I knew that the sensation was only "belly hunger," a feeling caused by an empty stomach—not the weakness or faintness of true hunger—early starvation. But I gave it free reign, enjoying anticipation of the coming meal to the fullest. I kept thinking of the slow turning, juicily laden spits on the fire down the hillside.

I had told the men who were to carry back the meat to make certain it was cooked through—to test the center section on each spit for the least trace of redness. I wanted no one to contract that gut-gnawing disease trichinosis. Also, they were to choose only solid pieces of meat—to let the native dispose of the bony section, which would probably be slower to cook. Pork well done is the best anyway.

The stars had become brighter and a little of the balminess had left the night air by the time the men returned with the cooked meat and passed it around. My portion was delivered wrapped in a leaf, still burning hot, attesting to the thorough roasting it had received by falling apart in my fingers. We all ate sitting on the ground, most of us handling the meat with our fingers, rubbing a little salt into it as we munched away. The noises of our eating could be heard above the night sounds; mosquitos, for the time being, had been forgotten.

Thoughts wandered for me, as they always do during and after a pleasant meal, and I found myself thinking of other meals I had eaten and enjoyed—fine steaks aboard the ship coming over, dinners in some of the choice little basement restaurants in New York, but I couldn't then, and I can't now, recall a better dish than that tender native-cooked pork.

Pork the world over seems to me to be a rather uniform meat. Wild or domestic, if properly cooked, it always seems tender and tasty. The only variation I have noticed between the domestic pork and the flesh of wild pigs has been in the amount of fat— always greater on the domestics, of course. The leaner and thinner cuts of wild pig have to me always seemed more succulent than any market-purchased meat could ever be.

We all ate to our hearts' content. I gorged myself to such an extent that keeping awake during my two hour turn at watch was a mighty chore. We were all overcome with the luxurious drowsiness which comes from a hard day's work, followed by an evening feast. When I was finally relieved at watch, I simply returned to my groundcloth and collapsed, not even noticing the continued attack of the mosquitos. I slept soundly until first light.

Then we broke camp, saddled up, and prepared to leave. A quick look in this light oriented me, and the roar of the planes from Henderson Field gave us a constant direction indicator so that we would have no trouble finding our way back. The trail ahead was leading in the right direction, and it seemed wider and better as we went on. We gave Joe the rest of the pig, loaded him down with other gifts, and sent him to rejoin his friends on their way to their hideout in the hills. He had been away from his woman for several weeks and was eager to get back. I can still remember him walking fast away from us, burdened down with a great load of pig meat and "C" rations, headed for his grass shack in the interior. I never saw Joe again, and neither did the others who had enjoyed his cooking, but I doubt that any of us will forget him.

The mists lifted suddenly from the hills, just as the sun's rays leveled downward, and the air above the grassfield became at once clear. No fog or mist could stand for long against the weighty pressure of the equatorial sun. Moisture could lay unseen and heavy upon the air, but visible mist would be scattered into small pockets within ten minutes after sunrise proper. Only when heavy clouds blocked the way or during predawn while the sun was not visible, could any of Guadalcanal's lower hills and coastal flats remain blanketed by fog or mist.

Night stiffness soon worked itself from our limbs as we walked along the trail, winding in and out of the jungle's edge which lay against the kunai grass field. We forded a small stream, skirted more jungle, and continued on in more kunai grass, soon finding ourselves walking upon an old familiar trail—one leading directly west from another moundlike hill (the one upon which my earlier pig feasts had been conducted).

Being close to camp, most of us stopped gnawing upon candy and "C" ration cookies—we would arrive at our own kitchens in time to throw ourselves upon the mercy of our respective mess sergeants. All of us were hoping that nothing would be going on back in our areas to keep us from getting a good freshwater bath and a scrubbing for our clothes. We all needed a shave too. The rear area looked like home to us.

The airfield was crowded with new planes, visible as we walked around its southern end; and it seemed to be busier than ever. And the cemetery beyond was still doing a landoffice business. Part of the effort there was one of reorganization and beautification, with the ground being raked and the mounds being covered with fresh palm fronds; but down at the south corner there were more graves being dug—with the grimly supine line of blanket-covered forms still there. The friendly chatter of the patrol quieted as we passed that place.

An empty two and a half ton truck pulled up on the road beyond the cemetery and one of our own drivers offered us a ride, saving us a last mile's walk. After collecting some sketches drawn by two of the men, I dismissed the patrol directly from the truck, letting the men get off as we passed close by their areas. Only a few yards to the right of the road was a swimming beach where they could enjoy a swim before returning to their units.

I rode past the battalion to regimental, waited briefly outside the S–2 office, and then was admitted to give my report to Captain Cosby. A lieutenant colonel from some higher headquarters was present through the interview, and I derived some satisfaction from being able to offend his sense of nicety. It was clear, from his manner, that he didn't think much of lieutenants who would dare to come into their regimental staff offices so dirty and unshaven. The Colonel, clad in well-starched khakis, could not have been on the island more than a few days, and he looked as though a good smell of a soldier's dirty fatigue jacket would have knocked him over. I hope mine bothered him.

Cosby listened to my story without comment, asked only two or three questions, and appeared completely satisfied with the information I gave. He also concurred in the action I had taken. In the interests of military decorum, I did not report the pig hunting incident, though I knew Cosby would have been interested. I didn't think the visiting colonel would have been pleased.

The waiting and the interview at headquarters had taken the better part of an hour, so I begged a ride back to battalion so that I might get there in time to enjoy a bath and a meal before dark. On the way back in the chauffeured jeep I dosed off twice, nearly falling out once. My tired and sweaty body was crying for a bath and I was hungry. I wanted to wash, eat, and sleep—sleep the damn clock around once and a half.

But back at battalion, a man had injured himself in tinkering with a captured Jap M14 pistol, getting a badly grazed calf and ankle. In doing the necessary telephoning and in getting a jeep to carry the injured man to the hospital, I used up another hour— thereby losing my chance at a good bath. When the company formed for chow, I hurriedly washed my hands and part of my face and ate as only a hungry man can. It was dark by that time.

In order to be able to sleep with myself, I had to substitute some sort of washing for the good soap and fresh water bath I had failed to get, so I dragged my weary bones out into the ocean and scrubbed myself with sand, swimming back and forth to soak and loosen the thick grime. Then I shaved, hung my dirty fatigues on a tent rope, and crawled into my cot naked—so exhausted that I did not properly tuck my mosquito bar edge under my blanket, allowing the mosquitos to nibble away freely—as some of the men put it, giving them a chance to read the blood type marked on my dog tags. Only I had no dog tags, and my blood had never been typed!

"T'Hell with everything. . . . Be off the damn island in another few days. . . ."

One hour later the telephone at the orderly tent sounded off, and an orderly came over to my cot, shook me into wakefulness, and told me the call was for me personally.

"This is Cosby, George. The old man read your report and is more suspicious than ever about that damn shack. He wants to send out a stronger patrol and garrison the place— You'll have to go back there tomorrow."

"Yes, sir. . . ."

AGAIN?

The next morning I borrowed a jeep and went over to Major Brite's ordnance setup where a kindhearted sergeant loaned me a pair of coveralls—a garment which I have never thought to be ideal for jungle wear, but one which would be a hell of a lot better than my own wornout two piece fatigues. With the one piece "zoot" suit rolled up and laid safely on the seat beside me, I drove to the Lunga River and finally enjoyed a freshwater bath, using plenty of laundry soap on myself and the remains of my dirty uniform. Afterwards I lolled in the sun for a while, comfortably stretched atop a big fallen log.

Having played hooky this hour and a half I dutifully climbed back into the jeep and returned to regimental headquarters, wondering about the details of this second trip I was to make up to that damned ridge. "Why on earth does the Brass want to keep sending our people up into those hills?" (All I had to do was to turn my head and I could see the rugged jungle clad mountains I had reference to.)

"And if someone must go up there, why in the name of Hannah does it always have to be me?" As I drove on, knowing what would be in store for me in the way of responsibility and work, the day seemed less and less cheery. Organize a larger patrol, arrange for a five day level of rations, lead a bunch of tired, unenthusiastic men back over a route which I already knew to be a torturous one—and with twice the pack loads we had carried before.

Soon I turned left and commenced driving up the ridge road toward the OP where I was to again meet Cosby. I was half consciously toying with the thought of suddenly wrenching the wheel of the jeep and rolling it over sideways, crashing down the steep slope into the heavy trees a hundred feet below. I obtained satisfaction from a mental vision of the jeep hurtling end over end, tearing itself to pieces on the way down, throwing off a part here and there.

227

Before the idea matured, however, I got to the OP and began to chat with Cosby. That, at least, was one pleasant aspect for the whole damned mess; Cosby was an old friend, a good man to talk to; and I knew that he would, if he could, give me every break possible.

Cosby introduced me to an Artillery lieutenant who was using the BC scope, looking again at the damn shack on the ridge and then Cosby gave me the second set of orders, telling me what I was to do this second trip.

"From your report, George, it has been gathered that Japs are making some use of the place you visited—at least that's what Corps seems to think. You saw some sign of Japs up there and the lights were seen out that way again last night. Maybe they just moved out when you got there and then right back in when you left. It may be just a group of stragglers, or it may be the bomber-directing station that Corps is worried over.

"You are to take this patrol back to that point again, camp in the locality, and set up a good radio. Maintain a schedule for a few days with the regimental set. Meantime you are to patrol in all directions from that shack and run down those Japs. Savvy?"

I nodded and stated my few requests.

"I'll want guides this time and some more natives to carry that radio. We had better not try to cut through the way I went last time if we go so heavy—had a hard enough time before with the little bit we took then. We'll have to find a better route. I'll go down to the native labor pool and talk about guides and carriers if you'll see to it that the men are all assembled down at the foot of Wright Road, so that I can check them over and get out early this afternoon. Please try to get the radio operators down early—we'll have to break the set down into handcarry loads."

Before leaving I noticed that the Artillery lieutenant was plotting on a map, drawing a line from the point of the distant shack back to a spot near Point Cruiz. He showed the map to Cosby, shaking his head and speaking in a discouraged voice, "Nope, we can't do it; not a gun on the island could reach that target from where we could set it up. Only way we could reach her would be to bring a 155mm rifle up here on the OP—and that's damn near impossible."

Cosby grinned. "Well, Georgie, there goes our last possible argument against this thing; might as well go get your guides and carriers." Both of us walked over to our jeeps and started down the roller coaster undulations of Wright Road, Cosby peeling off at regimental and I continuing down through the groves to the native compound.

When I got to the compound—a comfortably situated tent camp

When you include the time spent in fencing drill and the effort of keeping these cheese knives maintained in the field, you have to concede that the Japs went to more trouble over their swords and bayonets than we did with hand-to-hand combat and kitchen inspections. Every Jap who carried a sword also carried a silk cloth and a puff of very fine abrasive to polish and clean his blade, and he whiled away his idle hours by keeping a mirror surface on the steel.

Most of the better Japanese blades were hundreds of years old, handed down from early generations. They were treasured accordingly.

This officer is wiping his blade, but not in the formal manner. (There is a regular ritual for handling swords, a right and wrong way to draw, grasp, and re-insert them in the scabbard.) Most likely he is eager to use this weapon, and maybe he'll be foolish enough to try to close with it in the next assault he leads. He's pretty confident in its ability to kill, because he has cut the heads off several Chinese prisoners. One stroke to a head.

near the fighter strip—I asked at the headquarters tent for Major Clemens or Captain Trench, but found that both were out. Instead I dealt with a character named Smyth, an oldish sort of Aussie or New Zealander, I guess. I laid my problem before him, telling where I was going to go, what I was going to do and what I wanted in the way of native guides and coolies.

Smyth produced a map and asked me to pinpoint the objective. When I complied his interest seemed to increase greatly and he asked me to tell him about the trip up, the approach, and what I had seen there. When I told him that I had been at the shack only two nights before he began to subject me to a detailed and highly annoying questioning, asking how many men I had taken along; what the shack looked like; and exactly what I had seen on the way.

As the interrogation continued I began to get impatient with the old boy. After all, was it any of his business how many men I had taken up there and what route of approach I used? I felt I had important orders to carry out, and so without showing disrespect toward an Ally and a man of considerable years, I tried to get Smyth back on the business of furnishing me with guides.

"Sir," I said, "I came here at the direction of Captain Cosby, staff officer to Colonel George. He told me you could arrange for me to take some natives along on my patrol—some to carry and some to guide. Can you do that much for me? If you cannot I will have to make other arrangements. It would help a lot if you could let me know what you can do right away because I'm supposed to leave on the trip early in the afternoon. Can you give me an answer now?"

Smyth's ruddy face grew ruddier. He was a slender, well coupled man, unstooped by his years, but his cheeks had a "fat" color. He looked at me threateningly, as though about to reach for his Webley, and shouted at me in Cockney—the pitch of his voice was high and sounded like a sick bagpipe—:

"Ye little whelp! D'ye know ye skeered the divvle outta one ov our outposts? You and yer bloomin' patrol goin up inta the hills and chasin my blacks all over, skeerin 'em so bad they won't ivver come back! It's bad enough to havta keep yer blasted headquarters satisfied, with all the stoopid reports it's always asking fer, without havin ta always put up with a bunch ov wild Yanks running through the blasted weeds!"

I was shocked; I was amazed.

"Do you mean to say that you had an outpost up there in that shack?"

"Dommed right we did! A white and six blacks with a bloomin radio! They saw ye comin and ran; said ye were Nips!"

That was right; one of our scouts had been a small, dark Italian boy.

"And that radio was in contact with you back here?"

"No! Not with us, Yankee Doodle, but with that brainless Island headquarters o' yers! It's a wonder we haint all been kilt, the way ye bloody blokes behave!"

I was inclined to agree one hundred percent with Smyth on the score of his last remark, but I wasted no time in telling him so. Instead I took out a notebook and jotted down the facts of the case and got Smyth's signature.

I returned to regimental and told an equally amazed Cosby how I had come within an ace of killing some of our British and native Allies due to a headquarters foulup. Then I promptly sat down, devil may care, and wrote a two page report on my findings, ending it with a set of conclusions which included an Infantry lieutenant's studied opinion of any Corps or Division Headquarters which could manage to send out a patrol on the express mission of shooting up one of its own intelligence outposts. I never got a reply.

The second patrol, of course, was called off.

OUT OF IT

It was the 7th of April 1943, one day less than four months after the Second Battalion had arrived at Guadalcanal aboard the Navy transport *Andrew Jackson* and we were now loaded on the *Penn* and leaving. Over the waters of Lunga, not far behind us, a first-class air battle was raging. The Japanese were making up for the quiet reception they had given us when we arrived by seeing us off in grand style. They had sent over a hundred planes for the purpose.

We had gotten under way early on that account, the ships weighing anchor and leaving with their hatches open, sans many of their small craft; and the departure had been none too early. The sky a thousand yards astern was alive with flak bursts and the sound of heavy gunfire was so loud that we had to shout to talk to each other. Our engines on the *Penn* were under full draft to get us away from that hornet's nest.

A huge column of black smoke rose up behind us as a tanker anchored near Lunga Beach took a direct torpedo hit. All of us could remember that beach now as a good place to be from.

Our gun crews were standing nervously by their pieces; "talkers" with earphones and mikes fitted; while the ships's master paced the bridge, halting often to sweep the surrounding horizon for lowflying torpedo planes. Out around us plied two little destroyers, also on the lookout for planes and submarines. Air coverage we did not have, for every operational fighter on the island was tied up in the unequal battle with the Jap Air Force—there wasn't a plane to spare for us. But they were protecting us best that way, keeping the Japs more than busy back there at a distance. While we had been watching the first part of the air battle, we had seen both American and Jap ships go down in flames, but most of them were Japanese. We had seen one Japanese plane streak across the water in the distance and launch its torpedo at a group of transports. The tin fish had gone wide, however, and the plane itself crashed into the water a few hundred yards beyond.

232

We were wearing life jackets, alert at general quarters, ready on a moment's notice to abandon ship as well as we could. We knew that if the boat we were on should take two good hits, a lot of us would go down with her before we could get clear. Navy transports were better in this respect than the Army ships, but they still did not seem to be compartmented well enough to suit us landlubbers.

But we were beginning to feel better as the island we had come to know so well and to associate in memory with so much intense feeling, gradually diminished into a low, cloud-like object on the horizon. We all began to breathe easier again. The old term "a new lease on life" had a very literal meaning for us, just as it had had four months previously for the Fifth Marine Regiment we had relieved.

The newer members of the ship's crew looked upon us with great curiosity, asking many questions regarding our experiences on the island and causing a slight feeling of importance to dawn on the organization. It came with the realization that we were "veterans" now, a part of the first few thousand the war would produce and the first Army troops to be employed aggressively in any theater against the Axis Powers. When the Americal Division had started to land on Guadalcanal, the Japs had been there in great strength, confident of their ability to take back the small area of land taken by the Marines—and numerically capable of doing just that.

Now we were leaving; the Japanese force had been completely destroyed, their headquarters had seen fit to try to get its last remnants off the island and there was now little Japanese hope of ever recapturing the territory lost.

Very soon after its first elements had landed, a part of the division got its first combat experience, with the Third Battalion of the 164th Regiment saving Henderson Field from probable capture during the month of October. Thereafter the relief of the Marines was continued until the beginning of the Army phase. The XIV Corps, under General Patch, took over the responsibility and only a small minority of Marines was left. Most Marines are honest enough to refute the claims of their news correspondents, who led the public to believe that all of the Japanese killed on the islands were killed by Marines. The cold truth of the matter is that of the thousands of Japanese killed there by men on the ground, the Army killed much more than half—and that is a conservative figure, I think.

On the island the doughboys got along well with the Marines. We were all in the same fight and glad to see each other to the right or left. The trouble was mostly caused by newspaper people who were often inclined to sacrifice veracity for color, and this helps to account for the popular conception that the Guadalcanal operation was a one hundred percent Marine-Navy show. The Army didn't go in for great hordes of those people the way the Navy did—at least not at that stage of the war.

Neither of the services on the island actually cared too much what the people might think back home. We all felt rather isolated from the home front by the very nature of our recent experience. Three thousand of us had gotten through with a loss of 118 killed and 270 wounded—not heavy casualties as wars go but not negligible by any means. Find thirty young men sometime and ask them how much they would want in cold cash for drawing a ticket from a hat containing twenty-nine "win" tickets and one "no win"—the "no win" one bringing the reward of a painful death to the drawer. Oh yes, include about two tickets for "nasty cuts" and "splintered bones." I wouldn't do it for a million dollars!

The physical wounds were only a part of the show; there were other kinds. The sights we had seen had not been the best for a young man who would like to keep his illusions—educational as hell but not so palatable to the eyes or mind. Many of us had grown old on Guadalcanal, and a few, lacking the all important sense of humor with which tragedy must always be watered in order to make it endurable, had left their experiences there with beaten and permanently damaged minds. A few of these men would take their own lives in the months following. Others would go on living but would never recover. To men lacking a balanced sense of humor or to those who think too seriously and profoundly, a first taste of war is sometimes more than enough proof that life is a fruitless waste of time, carrying insufficient rewards.

Leaning against the rail and looking back at my erstwhile home, my own thoughts held little of such cynicism. I had been through a Great Adventure, torturing at times, but well worth the while. My rewards had been many, making the involved risk of life seem a small price to pay. No one, I was convinced, can live fully until he has felt the nearness of death—not the calm death of a hospital ward or a sick bed, but the violent, noisy, self-proclaimed presence of a terrible battle death—or else a gnawing fear of being blinded, maimed, killed lingeringly.

I have heard men say as much during a lull in a fight. The true worth of life can only be known to one who has lived in the shadow of this new, different kind of death; death so obviously real that its very person is painted in crackling tracer streaks in the air above a foxhole or is rattling through the jungle leaves in the form of fast flying steel or is blasting close by with flesh and bone rending concussion.

An American, transplanted onto a Pacific isle, walks down a lane in the rain forest. Except for the canteen, pack, and bayonet, this man might be a Tennessee squirrel hunter on his way home.

Probably he's a little tired, not picking his feet out of the mud anymore, but dragging them, slouching along with an easy gait. He'd be safer carrying his rifle at a high port with the safety unlocked. Japs might be hidden offside the trail, and since he's walking all alone they would be doubly inclined to pot him. But the trail is miles too long for that sort of alertness to be maintained; the pack and rifle are very heavy in the humid heat.

There's no great evidence of eagerness or ambition in this man's bearing, either. After two weeks of it he lost interest in the war and wishes it were over with.

But we had believed in the importance of our war; we knew how important Guadalcanal was to the Allied cause, in its moral rather than material gain. This minor victory had been a great stride in many ways; we knew now that we could meet and defeat the Japanese and that campaign had been the all-important first inch in the miles we would have to gain. At last we now had solid proof that we *could* win!

And, if there is any satisfaction in pure revenge, we were already well on our way to evening up a score with the Japanese. Some 40,000 of them had paid with their lives in an unsuccessful attempt to hold that miserable bit of jungle and coral, dying from every possible sort of combat injury and hardship; starvation; wounds; disease. That we knew. However great an impression Guadalcanal made upon us it had made an even greater one upon the Japs. They had come down to the Solomons full of hope, flushed by years of continuous victory in Asia, and fired with that aggressive spirit which betrayed itself over and over again in reckless and irrational tactics. Against us these tactics had failed for the first time. And they failed time after time.

Their bayonet rushes, usually successful in Asia, had crumpled and melted away before the deadly blast of a fire power more intense than they had ever seen. Their individual efforts in hand-to-hand combat had nearly always resulted in the destruction of an entire command; and on the water it had been the same. Their ships had been sunk by a more powerful air arm than they had ever imagined—the same air force which had strafed and bombed their troops on land, harassing their every daylight movement.

Up forward, Japanese Infantry had been chopped to bits by a new type of Artillery fire, much different from the scattered rounds occasionally fired at them by the Chinese. Our shells fairly rained down upon them—thousands in a single barrage.

Finally, after months of hammering, the Japanese doughboy was faced with his first really big defeat. He took it like a man— like a hero. No surrender for him; instead he died by the thousands —starvation, wounds, disease, suicide. From Point Cruiz to Esperance the coastal area was crowded with his dying-plots—old bivouac areas stinking with rotting bodies. In some of the groves all of the coconuts were gone—grim proof that after all other stores had been used, starvation and malnutrition had followed. Supplies of rice and other staple foods had been consumed or hoarded in scattered dumps months before the big fighting ended. For a long time, the Japanese rank and file on Guadalcanal had operated effectively without food and with acute shortages of all supplies.

We were leaving it all behind now. Our ship was tracing a zig-zag wake across the waters, headed for Esperito Santos, then Fiji, where we would rest, train, be treated en masse for malaria and then, when we were fit, go north to fight again.

Several of us had drawn deck duty during the early part of the trip and we were frequently above the stuffy troop quarters, where we could enjoy the view of the convoy around us. This view included the little escort vessels, always very active on either side of the convoy and an occasional Army or Navy aircraft which was always watched closely, even tracked suspiciously, by our guns until its friendliness was clearly established.

Finally that day we were clear of the greatest dangers. Even the smoke column above the torpedoed tanker had waned on the horizon. I was relieved at about that time by another officer and I went below to the wardroom to engage in a game or two of acey deucy and have some small talk. The atmosphere, strange as it was, was pleasant. Coffee was passed around, the chairs were comfortable, the lights were bright enough for easy reading. The faces of the Navy people looked strange until I realized that it was due to their clean and healthy looking complexions. Most of them had not been taking atabrine.

A rather friendly, middle-aged Naval lieutenant offered me a chair and we began a conversation which hinged around the fighting on the island. The lieutenant, a veteran of World War I, was keen on the subject of ground warfare and intensely interested in the jungle fighting ramifications of it—how it might differ from his 1917 experiences in France. I got a kick out of answering his questions and the afternoon passed pleasantly. Nothing provides a garrulous young man with more stock for enjoyable storytelling than his first combat experiences.

Dinner, our second meal on the ship, was served early. With real fresh meat and vegetables on the menu, it amounted to a feast for us. Afterward I went downstairs, enjoyed a good hot, freshwater shower, scrubbed my coveralls to a thorough state of cleanliness and hung them to dry. Then I crawled into the clean whiteness of my bunk and slept for twelve hours, aware only now and then of the throb of the ship's machinery.

There were six men in our room and not a one snored. This was especially remarkable in that three of the inmates were Artillerymen, a service which always seems to produce the greatest number of loud snorers. We all awoke with the hesitant sort of wonder one would feel in awakening from a sound sleep in heaven itself. We pried ourselves out of bed, two getting up at a time so that the limited toilet facilities would not be overtaxed, shaved, dressed and went up to breakfast.

The gentle roll of the ship indicated that we were out of the glass-smooth waters around the island, but no one, not even the chronic sufferers, were showing the least signs of seasickness. A natural reaction of appetite stimulation, following our long period of eating unappetizing food, demanded that we all eat heavily. And nature would not allow us to lose time in this necessary recovery by becoming nauseated. We all felt well and ate hearty. Even the pets, one of them a dog with a decided tendency toward violent seasickness, seemed to get along well.

This dog's name was "Atabrine," which was an inevitable monicker for him since he was a bright yellow color with few markings. Atabrine was a cur with terrier blood, about the size of a stunted rabbit, and was mischievous as a monkey. Some of the staterooms referred to him as "Puddles" because of his adamant refusal to be housebroken. Personally I despised Atabrine.

Little Atabrine had a bark that was absolutely piercing—shrill and loud at the same time, and he had a habit of yapping repeatedly at anyone who might trespass upon what he regarded as his own domain. This "domain" was gradually enlarged until it came to include the whole of "B" deck, and any person who crossed Atabrine's path in that area would always be subjected to an interval of yelping. As the trip went on he became more and more overbearing, capping the climax by hiding in an Artillery captain's bed and biting him sharply in the face as he climbed in after dark. One of the captain's nostrils was completely pierced by one of the pup's sharp fangs, and the injured man's cursing filled the forward end of the ship while he climbed from his bed and grabbed at the dog.

Atabrine was not seen on board the next morning. All of us missed him except the injured captain who was appearing at meals with a heavily bandaged nose and was heard speculating on the sharpness of shark's teeth.

We cruised for a while past Esperito, once again seeing the huge groves of neatly planted trees all over the hills and beaches near the water. We noticed many changes since our last visit, mostly in the unloading beaches and the dock area. The place had been neatly laid out in streets and the tents were framed and had board floors. There was plenty of Navy on hand too, with several cruisers and destroyers riding at anchor.

Colonel Ferry was always on deck to watch such things, commenting every now and then upon the easy life the rear area boys were having now. He was always the same jovial officer with a sense of humor which never seemed to desert him for one moment. He had the right idea—always tending to take the war not too seriously, a view not entirely appreciated by some of his equals in military rank. He made great light of our troubles during the trip

to Fiji, telling us jokingly that we "had all been on a delightful
tropical tour at government expense," that we were now going to
"another beautiful, fragrant, tropical island, alive with beautiful
women and well supplied with liquor of all sorts; what the hell
were we complaining about?"

The cruise went on with everyone enjoying the fine weather,
the good food, and a certain new freedom from worry. We were
still in submarine waters, of course, but that was the Navy's concern—not ours. Boat trips for Infantrymen are not always enjoyable but this one was.

Before we arrived at Latoka, Vita Livu Island, Fiji, we were
carefully coached on "white man's manners"—rules of conduct
in dealing with the native population of that island. The natives,
we were told, were to do all of the physical work of unloading—
we were merely to supervise. The most menial task allotable to a
soldier would be driving a truck or similar mechanical control.
Natives were to do all of the hand labor.

We all listened to this drivel with tongue in cheek, for the story
to us was an old one. We had gotten the same sort of misinforma-
tion about the colonial setup on New Caledonia—how all of our
work would be done by indentured Javanese and native labor.

Perhaps the colonials of the French Empire *could* stand around
and watch a bunch of awkward native labor do the work—but not
us. We would watch for a while with growing impatience, seeing
the unskilled natives go about everything "bass ackwards," and
then we would brush them aside and take over. We knew damned
well how things would actually work out on Fiji; and that's the
way it did work out.

We drew into a small, sheltered bit of water and docked at a
sugar mill pier near Latoka, where hundreds of heavily muscled
(and fat-bellied) natives, very black skinned and with the usual
fuzzy tops, were waiting to help us unload (sorry, I forgot; I mean
to do our unloading for us). Despite their fine physical appearance
and their large numbers, these natives were of limited value.

They did not even know how to handle baggage and our men
lacked the patience to teach them. Soon we were doing the greater
part of the work ourselves, with the natives looking idly on or
perhaps trying to trade some of the men out of their souvenirs.
One particularly obese native, apparently a strawboss of sorts,
had brass enough to ask me to give him the Japanese officer's
sword which I was carrying attached to my pack.

The British officials who were in charge of the native "labor
corps" were rather confounded by our handling of the situation
and in considering the matter of face, I suppose they were justified in resenting such an unsightly exhibition of white men doing

"menial" labor in the presence of natives. But we wanted to get our ships unloaded in a hurry. We did not care to keep those precious "bottoms" occupied too long. Especially was this true when our men found that the crews of the ships *wanted* a delay in Fiji, where there were apparently plenty of entertainment facilities.

This gave our boys a chance to crack back at the Navy. They had rushed the hell out of us when they were in dangerous waters, throwing our stuff into the Higgins boats in any old confused manner so they could pull away at once. And now they wanted us to deliberately slow down so they could spend a few easy days. We unloaded the damn ships as fast as we could, sweating mightily in the effort; we didn't have much gear with us anyway.

We piled our rather negligible baggage in a railyard near the dock close by the refinery. The railroad was a narrow gauge type with toy-sized locomotives and cars, primarily constructed for hauling the lightweight but bulky cut sugar cane. After we had set up a guard at the railyard dump, Colonel Ferry and a few officers went forward to look over our new area and to take over the property which the 148th Infantry Regiment was not moving out with them. We were to relieve the 148th as part of the island garrison, guarding a sector of Vita Livu.

The 148th had been garrisoning the broad, beautiful Sambeto Valley, which lay between Nandi and Latoka, with their headquarters centrally located. During their long stay on Fiji they had gathered a good bit of information which we would need to secure. This information would save us much bother in scouting out the beaches and likely routes of approach an invading enemy might use. At this stage it was still feasible for the Japanese to attempt to take Fiji. Like ourselves on New Caledonia, the 148th Infantry, 37th Division, had long been in a position of static defense. They were looking forward to their trip north with the same impatience which we had felt a few months before and most of them had an accurate impression of where they were headed—New Georgia.

We found our new home to be a lovely one, getting a first good look at it as we jeeped up the coastal road toward Nandi where the Second Battalion would be stationed. It was the same old story again—a beautiful tropical island, much more settled and civilized than New Caledonia, with some differences in vegetation, but still the same sort of a tropical isle.

The main crop on Fiji was sugar cane and we could see it everywhere along the coast; huge fields of it growing tall and thick of stalk. Temporary layings of narrow gauge railway were put down during the harvest season and the stalks were cut and heaped high upon the little rail wagons which would then be coupled into trains and towed to the refinery by toy engines.

Here is a Japanese officer doing a little front line observation. Anyone would think that he could have left his cutlery and dispatch case back at the command post. A water bottle, pistol and binoculars should have been enough, especially if he had to do much walking or climbing in the hot sun.

But wherever Jap officers went they took their swords. Pilots carried them in planes, visiting staff officers were never photographed without them, and nearly all doughboy lieutenants and captains had them buckled on at all times. Many of the noncommissioned officers carried swords too. I guess that the sword and leather dispatch case became a sort of caste emblem, in the army as well as in the Nip cities. The white-collar worker in Tokyo is usually identified on the street by his polished leather dispatch case, identical with the ones carried by army personnel.

Maybe that accounted for the craze to carry these useless items in the front lines. Certainly, toward the latter months of the battle of Guadalcanal, the Japs came to realize the uselessness of the sword as a weapon. But still they carried it; often enough the blades found on freshly-killed would be so wrapped with protective cloth or chamois hide that they could not possibly have been drawn for use. Sometimes, in assaults, officers were killed with pistol in hand and sword sheathed—even at close quarters. Swords, dispatch cases, polished boots seemed to serve more as marks of rank and distinction than anything else. Our own souvenir hounds were the chief beneficiaries of these Japanese vanities.

We were driving on a road which paralleled this little railroad and even shared bridges with it, the rails and road converging at each bridge approach. This was an economy measure which was perhaps practical in Fiji, but it would have caused trouble in the States. Just picture driving over a bridge on railway tracks each time you had to cross a river, stream or ditch, while driving in the United States!

The scenery was beautiful along the way. We had the mountains on our left, rising out of the cane fields and foothills near the road and off to our right was the coastal area, more fields, mud flats and mangroves.

Soon we passed the Nandi airport, a huge air staging area not unlike Tontuta or Plaines des Guyacs on New Caledonia. Aircraft of all sorts took off and landed in the moments we spent in view of the place. Once again it was apparent that we were to be stuck close to a noisy field where our sleep would always be interrupted by roaring motors.

A short distance beyond the airport we ran into Nandi itself—a small mainstreet of a town with Indian-run shops and stores. A little beyond we found the headquarters of the battalion we were to relieve. We noted, with our first pleased glance at the new campsite that we were to have floored tents, well founded on crushed rock, with waterproof paths and very fine looking prefabricated huts for messhalls. Captain Petersen, Art Handel and I got in contact with the heavy weapons officers and began to learn about "H" company's billeting area.

Tents were plentiful—no need to crowd men in and each officer could have a 9 x 9 of his own, with the fly rigged out front to give him a bit of veranda, and a nice solid frame and floor boards. The 148th had been in place there long enough to make itself quite comfortable.

We moved in during the next day and spent but little time getting settled. There was a P-X in Nandi run by a lieutenant from Louisiana with the unforgettable name of Antoine F. J. Hotard; so we were able to buy khaki uniforms, watches, fountain pens and other badly needed items.

A ration of liquor followed closely after our arrival and an officers' bar was set up at battalion headquarters. Speaking of "bars" my old friends back at Anti-Tank Company (now commanded by Frank Halsey) had fallen into a very nice deal in taking over the site of an old officers' candidate school for company billets. Everyone in the whole damned outfit lived in a house of some kind. These buddies of mine also seemed to have more liquor on hand than did the entire remainder of the regiment. We had many good times there at Frank's headquarters.

Captain Brickles had taken over the regimental intelligence officer's job (S–2), portending a well deserved promotion in line with new tables of organization which had elevated the S–2 to the authorized rank of major. The whole regiment was being reorganized to conform with these new tables, allowing more generous staffs for battalions, and I soon found myself relieved of duties with "H" Company and placed on the battalion staff as intelligence and scout officer. Later, when we got around to training, this change was to give me a lot of headaches inasmuch as I had to conduct an intelligence school for scouts and observers.

From that point forward Fiji became another colorful chapter in our service overseas. It was a place that later became monotonous with the grind of training; with various inspectors paying close attention to administrative minutae; with laborious organization of defense positions; with long maneuver periods in the hills; and with days that finally dragged beyond imagination.

Training, which we badly needed, continued. The only trouble was that a certain brigadier general was identified with so many of the exercises and demonstrations. We began to despise the training program because of this unpleasant association. Our stay on Fiji was bearable, not because of, but in spite of, the demoralizing influence of this officer, who—whether those in high authority were ever aware of it or not—did much to disgust the men of the division with the otherwise pleasant surroundings on that island.

The next few months went by bringing an occasion upon which date this story can properly end. It was in September, 1943, that a large group of men and officers left the Americal Division and the Fiji Islands, with Major General Hodge, the division commander, shaking each one by the hand as he boarded the transport. We were headed initially for New Caledonia on the first leg of a journey which would see us all through a long trip down under Australia and on to India and incredible adventures in Burma later on.

A Brigadier Wingate had conducted successful operations behind the enemy lines in Burma in 1943, employing a new type of Infantry organization which he called a "Long Range Penetration Group." After his return he had accompanied the British Prime Minister to the Quebec Conference, where it was decided on the highest allied level that there should also be an American Long Range Penetration Group to fight in Asia. This group would be made up of some 3,300 volunteers, a third of that number to be men with jungle combat experience in World War II.

The first inkling of this had come to us in the form of a wire asking for volunteers for a hazardous mission in another theater and adding that the unit would be trained in receiving supplies from the air and living off the land.

Petito, Farley, Zimmerman, Brown, Hogan, Coeburn and I were the officers that were among the Americal Division volunteers— all of us jumping at the opportunity to find more adventure, to see new lands and to leave the monotonous life we had been leading on Fiji.

The ship got underway and the hills of Fiji—forest and grass covered—faded in the distance. Again we were leaning on a ship's rail, wondering what the future would hold.

My rifles were with me—this time I had a spare, fitted with a scope—and I still had a few rounds of my selected ammunition. We were all refitted with clothing and I had made up another pack and kit so I felt ready for anything. We had supposed that we might be trained for coast-watching purposes and sneaked into Jap occupied areas for intelligence or guerilla work.

Actually, we were headed for India where we would train for a while before walking into Burma as a part of the original 5307 Composite Unit—the outfit which was to become famous as one of the fightingest, hardest marching units in the world, under the name of "Merrill's Marauders."

IV. THE TOOLS USED

"The Rifle is Brother of Allah."
—Iranian Nomad Tribal Proverb.

JAPANESE USE OF RIFLES

Because there were many outstanding faults in the employment of Japanese rifles and riflemen against us, and it was therefore unlikely that we could learn much from them, most of us were not inclined to make any great study of Japanese rifle technique and methods. We all, however, made a few objective studies in order to devise protective measures and successful counter tactics; and in so doing many of us learned things we did not know before.

We had no Japanese training manuals available, and had to go entirely by what we observed or had described to us. On several occasions we were able to interview prisoners taken. By far the greatest source of information, as far as the writer was concerned, was gained from personal observation.

The Japanese use of rifles was different from our own; first of all in the matter of accuracy. The sights on their weapons, and the weapons themselves, were not as accurate as our own, and their standards of marksmanship were not on a par with ours. Most of their rifles had a base setting of 400 meters, which would allow only rough holding at the shorter ranges. The absence of peep sights and drift compensating devices precluded them from any fine shooting at longer ranges. In spite of all this though, it would not be fair to say that the Japanese could not shoot. They killed too many of us to permit that assertion.

Their field marksmanship methods were practical. As far as I made out, they did their firing from the principal body positions; prone, squatting and standing; and like us, they naturally preferred the prone position with its advantages of greater steadiness, protection from enemy fire, and concealment. When in defense, of course, they always dug in, and fired their rifles by resting the forearms on heaped-up and camouflaged spoil (dirt from which the trench was made) or other materials placed there for the purpose.

The Japs were skilled at using natural forearm rests in the field and, given a choice, they would always take position behind a

247

Hideo

Not so hot. I've never really felt that there was the slightest need to spread the legs as directed in our manuals, but the prone position depicted here reveals other faults. Both elbows badly out of place, left one nine inches from where it should be. Japs are poor belly shooters.

Japanese seemed rather dependent upon improvised rests when shooting prone. Hardly ever were they seen without some sort of sandbag or fork to steady the rifle.

This sketch has the firer's body a little more out of line with the axis of the rifle than was usual with most Japanese. They ordinarily got a little more directly behind the weapon, probably for the purpose of reaching the bolt. Short armed as they were, Japs always removed the butt from the shoulder to operate the action in rapid fire. Even had the stock been sufficiently shortened, the straight bolt handle would have precluded keeping the rifle at shoulder.

Notice how, for prone position firing, the leather cartridge boxes can be pushed around to the soldier's sides so that he has nothing bulging beneath him. This is another point of advantage which makes me believe that our own Infantry should give this cartridge carrying system a trial. We might like it better than the present web belt.

log or stump which would provide such a rest. Then they would slide the long barrel of their rifle out, and fire with both hands held in almost the same place on the weapon—left hand back against the trigger guard with the weight of the rifle lying upon the log or stump top or heap of dirt and supported at any point along the length of the forearm. On a few occasions I have seen evidence of the Japanese using a short, forked stick which they would cut and carry with them to provide a firing rest for the forearm of the stocks on their long Arisakas.

This enthusiasm for the use of forearm rests to increase the steadiness of holding for prone or dug-in riflemen was emphasized by the inclusion of a light steel wire bipod on the 7.7mm M99 rifle—the official Jap rifle during the latter years of the war. This wire bipod—really a monopod, because the ends of the two legs were only an inch or so apart—should not be laughed at. It could do a lot to help steady a nervous Infantryman's hold in battle, and it weighed no more than the extra length of sling strap which we carry around for the sake of steadier holding—but which we never use in battle.

It seems pretty evident that the preferred system of firing, as far as the Japanese were concerned, was from the prone position with rest, and it is certain that every Japanese soldier was properly discouraged from firing from the less steady positions, except where necessary. Even Jap "tree snipers" (from indications given by a very few examples) were inclined to improvise a rest for their rifle, if they could.

We can take a lesson from this. While it may seem ridiculous for the rifleman who will have to shoot his target at less than fifty yards to utilize a forearm or muzzle rest, any combat veteran knows well that such a measure is not silly. When you are going about the business of killing a man you want to be sure of every little detail. With a good rest to aim from, a man can have an awfully bad case of buck fever and still do relatively good shooting. That the Japanese realized as much, and apparently taught their riflemen accordingly, is entirely to their credit.

I have seen all sorts of artificial and natural rifle rests which were designed and used by Japanese Infantrymen, many of them displaying great individual ingenuity. Everything from heaped-up coconut logs or husks to little slabs of spike-based armor plate, about nine or ten inches high by a foot in width, with "U" shaped notches in the top for the rifle forend. Our Pacific enemy used a rifle rest whenever possible.

Often it was not possible though, the Japs met that situation in their own way; they used their version of the prone position, without rest or sling. A tough proposition for short limbed Orientals.

Hideo

Squatting position à la Nipponese.

This would be very awkward indeed to an American, less flexible of muscle and tendon than his little brown brother. It does have the advantage of being somewhat higher than the conventional squatting position, which gives knee-rest for the right as well as the left elbow.

The strange thing about it all is that this squatting position was never formally taught in the German-guided school of Japanese marksmanship. Troops picked it up in the field, apparently. I have seen it used several times, and I think it is a more or less natural adaptation of the Japanese civilian "squat." (Peasants squat down to talk to each other in rural Japan—and use the position as a standard attitude of rest.)

This and kneeling served to replace sitting entirely—at least as far as I have been able to learn. Little use was made by the Japs of the sitting position which we know. This might have been because the sitting takes a little more time to assume and arise from than the kneeling or squatting.

Our own prone position, which calls for the left arm being well out forward and the hand just behind the upper sling swivel, works pretty well in the field; but I am inclined to believe that it has been somewhat influenced by our almost universal use of the gunsling during range practice. When a sling is no longer used—and it is seldom used in combat—there comes an immediate tendency for the rifleman to move his left hand farther to the rear, bringing his lower arm into a position a little nearer vertical. For men who habitually fire without the sling, this tendency is even stronger, and many of the better shots will so shoot with the left lower arm held almost straight up and down and with the left hand grasping (yes, *grasping*—you have to do that without a sling) the stock at the magazine. This measure has the effect of removing another set of muscles from the task of supporting the weapon, so that its weight in front will rest directly upon the grounded left elbow instead of being held up by the quivering tension of the biceps.

For that reason and also for others the Japs have adopted this far-back forearm grip as standard for prone shooting. I found that out by handing an unloaded rifle to several of the first Jap prisoners we took, and making them assume the various positions. All of them used the prone position I have described, with the hand far back and the body line around behind the rifle rather than at "45° from the line of sight." The adoption of this position by the Japanese was undoubtedly influenced by the shortness of reach of the average Japanese soldier, which was so short in most cases that it could not be compensated for by merely shortening the buttstock. Also, the distance from shoulder to cheek is very short on Jap bodies, which further increases the need for short buttstocks. But the high, far-back-hand-grip prone position which the Japanese used was adopted principally because it made for better shooting. The rifle stocks could have been shortened enough more to permit a lower position with extended left hand, if they had thought it advisable.

The prisoners I was interviewing then went ahead and demonstrated the squatting position for me. I was conducting my "interview" in our camp at Cape Esperance at the little stockade we had improvised by tying ropes from one coconut tree to another. I had undertaken the task with due precautions, selecting several of the less sullen prisoners to do the demonstrating with boltless rifles (their own long Arisaka 38). Two guards with loaded Tommy guns were on hand to prevent any monkeyshines while I spoke to the Japs by means of sign language and one of their captured phrase books (we had none of our own at that time). I would take the rifle from them from time to time to illustrate the position I wanted them to take. When I demonstrated the sitting position the par-

Hideo

Kneeling, a great favorite with the Japanese because it finds advantageous application in the assault. Most Japs could assume it with greater ease than even the youngest and most supple American doughboys. The characteristically loose-tendoned Nips felt very little pain in sitting on the heel, or in front of it, or even behind it as in the case of the amateur contortionist in the sketch. Our NRA slide-rule boys might question the legality of the "kneeling" position shown.

Inasmuch as most Jap fighting was in wooded or grassy areas, the height of rifle above ground was usually important. There was little application of prone shooting in anything other than prepared defensive positions. But on the move you can't aim through the grass—you've got to shoot above it. And a lot of grass in the Pacific area is three or more feet in height.

Notice again how the cartridge boxes on this soldier's belt automatically shift around his middle so that they do not block the movement of limbs or cramp his body. This holds true even if the belt is hung low, around the hips, rather than tightened about the waist.

The rifle this chap seems to be using is one of the medium length Arisakas. The standard model would stick out quite a few inches farther. Sight leaf, as nearly always with the Japanese, is down. This might also be okeh; most Jap rifles did not have apertures even on the rear sight slides, so no great advantage was to be gained by lifting the damn thing.

ticular Jap who was next given the rifle immediately assumed the *squatting* position. I was to discover that the Japs seldom used the sitting position.

I was greatly impressed with the apparent ease and speed with which all of the Japs could assume the squatting position and return to their feet. They could all get down and up in nothing flat, though three of the four men I was examining were in bad physical shape. The explanation is of course simple, though it caused me some puzzlement at the time.

The Japanese are Orientals, and all of the Orientals become adept early in life at squatting. In fact, it is bred into them. They squat on their upper heels, buttocks resting against the Achilles tendon region of their rear ankles, with feet flat on the ground. In their homes, in the streets, and everywhere else. Most of the toilets in the Orient are made with two places for the feet to be positioned on both sides of a trough about six inches wide (this goes for their modern water closets too, not just privies in the back country). The squat is the natural Oriental position of rest, and from what I have seen, it has played hell with the furniture business in the Orient. In most Japanese homes there aren't any chairs, and the same can be said of the more primitive places in India and Burma.

Being more comfortable flat on their feet, their balance is better than our own in that position, and they can lean forward from the ankles to counterbalance the recoil; which all but the more freak-ishly flexible Americans cannot.

The squat corresponds to our sitting position with them, in that it comes next to prone in steadiness; and it has a great advantage over our sitting position because it can be assumed and recovered from in half the time. For some types of fighting I believe it would be the most practical of all combat firing positions. In a moving fight in high grass or sparse bush, it would be the answer. All of this goes without its other advantage of keeping the rifleman's posterior—so subject to rheumatism from sleeping on the cold ground—from an occasional dampening in cold mud, wet grass, or swamp ooze. From the standpoint of positions, the Jap has a slight edge upon us in his greater flexibility of body. We would be better off if we could squat with equal ease.

The sitting position used by my prisoner-demonstrators was awkward, and one of them grinned sheepishly as he fumbled around with it. All of them would have assumed the squat instead, by choice. They could all fire from the standard army kneeling position, though one of them indicated that he could stretch his squatting position upward to attain the same high line of sight he got by kneeling. Naturally, if he could do that there would be small point in his using the kneeling position at all. The only

Perfectly normal; a better standing position than the average American learns in his basic training. And he's not wasting time fooling with any hasty sling position. Maybe his feet are a little too far apart, and perhaps the left hand is a bit farther out than the average Camp Perry veteran would approve, but the stance is still a good one.

Left elbow seems to be under the weapon, where it should be, and the rifle seems to have the right position in relation to the face and shoulders.

He has the sight leaf down, and is probably using the battle sight for some rough shooting at a short range. This was a great fault of the Jap rifles, matching ours with the Springfield. The battle sight was normally leveled for too great a range. Now and then, firing at a small part of a face or body in the jungle, one can overshoot with a 300 yard or higher setting.

Note that this chap is not wearing a shooting jacket of any kind, but rather his full combat kit, less pack. Canteen and cartridges are slung.

Note the handy position of the leather cartridge boxes. Believe I'd think twice before turning down this clever (originally German) method of carrying ammunition. Given a fair trial, it might prove better for Garand clips than our present web cartridge belt.

advantage it possesses over squatting (for fire at ground targets) is the higher line of sight it provides for the purpose of clearing cover intervening between firer and target. It is much less steady, and it is no easier than "squatting" for the Jap to assume. That one prisoner was a bright Japanese boy.

When I got these Japanese up into the standing position they began to reveal a lot of faults. Either they had had no training in shooting from their hind legs or else they had paid no attention to the instructors when it had been given. It was a cinch that they had done little firing from it. They were awkward, with every tendency to misplace the left elbow, to lean forward, to spread the legs entirely too far—in short to make every possible mistake.

Two of the Japs had become quite interested and they were being very cooperative by this time. Perhaps, for all I know, they themselves were the nearest thing to rifle shooting enthusiasts that there could be in a country where few individuals could own firearms. I was just about to get a bolt for the rifle and try to get an idea across to them that I would like to see them manipulate the bolt as in rapid fire. I figured that by removing the follower and spring I could have one of them operate it and perhaps confirm my suspicions that Japs always removed the rifle from the shoulder before manipulating the bolt. I was also interested in trying out that test on a Jap we had who was a southpaw, to see what advantages the straight Arisaka bolt would hold for the left-handed shooter.

I had gotten quite an audience by this time; quite a few men were assembled around outside the "stockade" to watch the proceedings. They were all entertained considerably by the antics of their late enemies, and I felt inwardly that it was all to the good. A close look at these Jap prisoners would convince the men, once and for all, of their own superiority. I wanted to get along with my inquiries, but I was interrupted.

A jeep came putting up the beach trail from the North, with a visiting fireman in it. Some major from Corps Headquarters. He stared in wide eyed disbelief at the scene of an American lieutenant who was apparently conducting a class of Japanese prisoners in the subject of rifle marksmanship!

I hastened to report to him and explain, dismissing the "class" as I did so. We didn't have many visitors at that time, but I knew how to treat them—knew what they wanted. Show 'em around the old Jap bivouac areas—let 'em see all of the bodies and skeletons, tell 'em a few stories, give 'em a sabre and a pistol. Then they'll go away happy and likely write you up favorably if their visit happened to be of the usual staff snooping variety.

These staff officers were a pain—but then I had just about finished with the prisoners anyway, and didn't mind the interruption so much. Besides, it was almost time to have evening mess.

At my invitation, the Major accompanied me over toward the mess area, where the usual canned foods had been heated—only for this one meal we had got several bunches of ripe bananas over from Savo by dugout canoe and hence were going to have an unusually tasty dessert.

It was getting on toward dusk; the sun was going down over Savo way across the channel, and the heat of the day had partly gone from the shade of the grove. While some of the men wrestled with the Major's bed roll the two of us walked along the grassy trail, each of us in one of the ruts which had been worn by Jap trucks traveling there only a few days earlier. Me in my only pair of green fatigue trousers, stripped to the waist and armed with an empty Jap rifle—walking in worn-out shoes with Jap socks. The GHQ Major in a brand new pair of coveralls, helmet, belt with canteen, compass, field glasses, wire clippers, sheath knife— and carrying a Tommy gun with a loaded clip.

JAPANESE RIFLES

Japanese rifles used in World War II were all copied from the basic Mauser pattern, and as in the case of other nation's modifications of Paul Mauser's good rifle, most of the changes proved to be steps backward. They retained to the last the straight bolt of the old 98 Mauser, made quite a few minor changes in the ignition assembly, adopted a different floor plate latch, and extended the tang portions of both receiver and guard to facilitate the use of a laminated buttstock. It would have been a more practical procedure to have simply tooled up for the Model 98, as was. The Japs simply joined what might well be called an international association of fumblers, who, faced with a near-perfect model to work from which they were absolutely unable to improve, went ahead nevertheless and worked a few of their own ideas, producing their so-called "version" of the good old German man and game killer; and like our own Ordnance Department, they produced a bastard rifle.

For one thing, they made their rifles entirely too long. The standard Model 38 6.5mm, for instance, had a ridiculous thirty-one and a quarter inches of barrel screwed into it, which gave the weapon an overall length of fifty and a quarter inches. The only worth-while purpose served by making the barrels that long was a great reduction of muzzle blast and flash—which furnished the American uninformed (including one high ranking general) with reasons for stating erroneously that the Japs had developed an absolutely smokeless powder, much better for jungle fighting than any of ours.

There were, of course, numerous disadvantages to the longer rifles. They were unwieldy and awkward, especially in the jungle. They were too heavy for their caliber. And this excess of weight and length, unlike certain other features built into Jap rifles, was certainly not demanded by any of the peculiarities of the Jap soldier. The Jap doughboy was an awfully little man, on the average, for such a big gun.

Another fixed idiocy of the Japs was manifest in the adoption of the receiver cover for all rifles. Its utilization necessitated the cutting of two deep grooves for almost the full length of the receiver, which certainly did nothing to strengthen the action. The protection which that foolish contrivance could give to the working parts of the rifle was negligible, and if it was kept on during temperature changes—such as those incurred in transferring the weapon from the shade into the sunlight—it worked to facilitate the condensation of moisture and the resultant formation of big gobs of rust on the bolt surface and ignition parts. Whenever the action was operated with the receiver cover on the weapon rattled like all of the proverbial tin pots and pans in hell. I know of at least two Japs who were located by our people because of that rattling sound as they operated their bolts, and who were killed before they fired a second shot.

The Jap-instigated alterations of the ignition mechanism tended to increase the weight of the moving parts over those of the Mauser. A hollow firing pin and upper sear engagement such as the Japs developed must have been rather difficult to manufacture— even if it did eliminate the need of the Mauser-type locking arrangement of upper sear engagement and firing rod. It is nice to aim this criticism from an entrenched position. Standing in my own shoes I can criticize the Japs for the changes they wrought in the Mauser firing pin mechanism, but if I happened to be one of the "experts" who developed the action of our own M1903 modification of the Mauser, I would keep awfully quiet about the whole thing. Because compared to the ill-conceived ignition system of our own bolt action, which was designed with no regard whatsoever for the basic principle of firearms design which demands a firm, crisp blow on the primer, the Japanese modification is a dream of perfection. When our own experts chopped the sturdy one-piece Mauser firing pin in two, and then coupled the two poor dismembered parts together for operation with an inherently ill-functioning joint, they succeeded in accomplishing at one stroke of the drawing pen a point of extreme unreliability for the Springfield rifle, and they also made certain that there was at least one part of their rifle that would break with great regularity, causing the target shot to have to fire many alibi runs on the rifle range— and making the soldier do God knows what on the battlefield. The United States and the Japs alike, in my opinion, would have done well to have adopted the Mauser ignition system as it was.

The Japanese extended their dirty work farther back on the bolt and produced a safety and lock that, though mechanically sound, was vastly inferior to the one on the Mauser, being equally difficult to manipulate with cold fingers, and generally more noisy in operation. Its flaring rear, mushrooming outward on the end of the bolt, did provide some protection from the escaping gases which naturally accompanied the use of poorly loaded Japanese ammunition, and its secureness against allowing bolt parts to be blown rearward into the firer's face was likely greater than the Springfield.

The Japs, like many of our experts, were still living in the dark ages when it came to weapons-sense, and were similarly overly bayonet conscious, going to great lengths to make their rifles into good bayonet handles. They built massive upper bands and hooked good strong studs onto them and kept the front sights and the muzzle ends well adapted to the fitting of these long-obsolete toad stabbers. And they accordingly increased the weight of all of their rifles. The folding bayonet on their Model 1911 6.5 Cavalry carbine with its massive hinge and latch provided the high mark of this foolish and barbaric influence in modern weapons design.

In case the foregoing paragraph has not made my stand in this matter clear, let me give you my own opinion on the bayonet and hand-to-hand combat in general. It is my belief that the bayonet is about as useless a bit of equipment in this present day and age as the cavalry saber. We should have dispensed years ago with both the weapon itself *and* the hours of wasted effort which went into bayonet instruction. The present-day apologists for the retention of that obsolete item will argue for the first few minutes of a discussion and claim an actual combat value for the weapon; then, when loudly called down and corrected by all of the men in the room who happen to be wearing Combat Infantry Badges, they will lapse into a lot of drivel about "stimulating morale" and "improving the physical condition of the soldier."

Such arguments are as stupid as they are dangerous. There are plenty of the useful phases of training which will serve to teach a useful subject to a man and harden him physically at the same time. And if you want to give a man calisthenics—well, give him calisthenics. Don't try to sell an intelligent American on the idea of killing his enemy the way Sir Galahad did. Let the foreign nations retain their ideas about bayonet fighting. After our experience in this war, we can rely on our own judgment—at least in the evaluation of foreign methods.

For all practical purposes, there hasn't been any bayonet fighting in this war of ours—and it is time we admitted our past foolishness in hanging on to the bayonet all of these years. It will be even more foolish for us to continue to weigh down the front end of our weapons with a lot of extraneous wood and metal in front of the lower band.

(We are not *now* making that mistake, for the bayonet has been

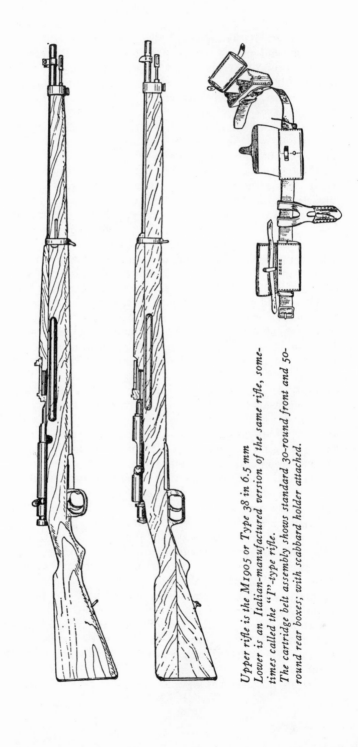

Upper rifle is the M1905 or Type 38 in 6.5 mm
Lower is an Italian-manufactured version of the same rifle, some-
times called the "I"-type rifle.
The cartridge belt assembly shows standard 30-round front and 50-
round rear boxes; with scabbard holder attached.

cut to knife length—and is mainly being used as a knife. It was to our advantage that the Japs wasted much more time and effort than we did with pig-stickers. It is to the great discredit of our intelligence that we waited so long to change our bayonet into a sheath knife that would be put on the end of a rifle for morale and other purposes.)

In addition to the features of the Jap weapons which were more or less arbitrarily decided upon by Japanese ordnance authorities, there were a number of points which were more or less demanded by the fact that the Jap soldiers were, on the whole, mechanically stupid. Jap weapons design had to be influenced by the faults of the Jap soldier.

I refer in particular to the barleycorn front sight and the open V rear, which are the simplest, the most rugged, and the most practical sights for the use of men of peasant background and I.Q. After a great amount of personal experience gained in instructing the Chinese, that fact has at last become obvious to me. The great problem faced by the Jap marksmanship instructors was more mechanical than visual. They had to get across the idea of trigger squeeze, so that the canny Jap would not tend to buck his shot two paddy fields to the right of his target. Those people weren't worried about making their man able to put all of his shots into a ten-inch bull at two hundred yards—they were worried about enabling him to stand some chance of hitting a man standing up at a hundred. (We could have done well at some of our IRTC's to have reoriented our own training program in that same direction.) The barleycorn sight, age old, familiar, simple as hell, made just as good a sight as any for the mine-run Jap doughboy. Anyone who has faced the abysmal ignorance of the common Oriental soldiers, as I have, will readily back me up in this.

The Japs were more or less *forced* to use open sights because there were no good military peep sights for them to copy at the time they designed their rifles. The first peep sight which was *optically* worth a damn was put on the Enfield and the Browning Auto rifles in 1917, and it was a *mechanical* abortion of the first water. The first practical aperture rear sight which has gotten into popular military use can presently be seen on our own MI. Before its advent, there just wasn't a good all around peep sight. So, with the exception of a few peep type drift slides seen on an occasional Arisaka, the Japs stuck to the V-notch.

Now, before all of the snipers of World War I jump up and cry for my blood because of my inference that the '03 Springfield sight is no damned good, let me do a little explaining. It took a highly skilled marksman to use the too-far-forward and entirely-too-small aperture that was on the '03. The common soldier didn't fool with it in combat, any more than he did with the sling. And there weren't enough good shots in either one of our recent wars to cut any ice at all. If, at the outset of this war, we had not had available the excellent MI rear sight and the properly positioned aperture rear sights which were built into some of the wartime versions of the '03, I, for my part, would have preferred to see barleycorn-type sights in use on our rifles in preference to the old '03 sight. Not for my own personal use, mind you, but for the use of the great mass of men who had to be taught to use their weapons in precious few hours time, with a definite limit set upon the amount of marksmanship training of all sorts to be given them. The Japs, at least, recognized one or two of their limitations. If our Garand had been out in time for them to copy it (by 1900 or thereabouts), it might have been a different story—not the war, for it would have taken more than a good rear sight to have changed that— but the Jap that missed my ear a few inches at Morovovo might have hit me in the bean, and that, I think, would have made a big difference, to George at least.

The great mass of rifles which I have so far seen in the hands of Japs has been almost entirely made up of the types commonly referred to as the Arisaka rifles. These are all of the various models officially adopted, which are normally issued to the Japanese Infantry. The great variety of rifles that were seen on every Jap front was present because of the Jap's great hesitancy to discard anything he had captured, regardless of its uselessness or the unavailability of ammunition. Then too, the Japs frequently captured certain models of rifles and machine guns in such quantities that they thought it wise to load ammunition in their own factories to fit the captured weapons. So, we found large numbers of British Enfields, Dutch Steyrs, American M1917 Enfields, Mausers and Krags in the possession of the Japs on Guadalcanal, with ample evidence that their use was not the idea of individuals, but rather the carrying out of a directive from higher authority. The M1917 Enfields I saw had been modified a bit to take the Jap bayonet, and quantities of Japanese-loaded ammunition were on hand in .303 British caliber for use in the captured British weapons.

There were, of course, far more Japanese than captured weapon around, the long-barrelled Arisaka .25 being seen most often.

The Japanese Model 38 6.5mm Rifle (which is the official name for the standard length .25 Arisaka) is not a bad gun, in spite of the things you have read elsewhere and the derogatory remarks I have just finished making about it. With the exception of the innovation of a hollow firing pin with an inside mainspring, a combination bolt head and safety lock, and the addition of a third lug, the bolt itself is rigidly held to Mauser pattern.

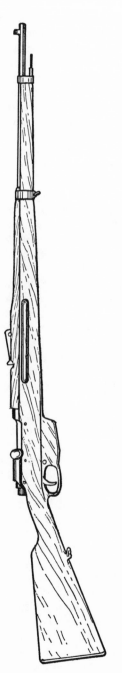
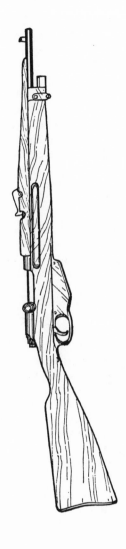

Weapons captured and used by the Japs
The M1895 Netherlands 6.5 mm rifle and carbine.

This additional duo-functional lug on the forward part of the bolt which follows the left lug race, is slightly to the rear of the left lug proper, and acts as a bolt stop, thereby saving the important rear surface of the lug itself from being battered, during manipulation, by the bolt stop. This feature, combined with a rearward lengthening of the receiver, acts to prevent the cramping of the bolt in rearmost position. This benefit is secured through firm support of the bolt in its rearmost position where it retains more than two full inches of its length within the receiver barrel. This is an improvement over the Mauser, but it is gained at some cost, for it tends to increase the overall length of the receiver for a particular cartridge.

The extractor is of conventional Mauser design, attached to the bolt by means of the usual collar, and riding in the right lug race. The bolt handle is projected straight outward from the bolt in a direction at right angles to the axis of the locking lugs and is positioned three-quarters to the rear on the length of the bolt. It is some two-and-a-quarter inches in length; and its knob is elliptical in cross section, and its base is square, forming a substantial safety lug. The rifle I have present at hand has a single, large gasport cut through the left side (closed position) of the bolt just forward of the extractor collar. But there were varied types of gasports in other Arisaka bolts which I have seen.

The Arisaka bolt can be disassembled faster than any others of the Mauser type; a rank amateur can jerk it into its five basic units in four seconds and keep a hand free to toy with his gal's ear all the while, if she happens to be close by.

There is nothing wrong with this bolt except the rather glaring fault of a straight bolt handle. Except for that major shortcoming it would seem to me that the Japs actually committed less non-constructive butchery on the Mauser than did the designers of the '03 rifle. The guts of the bolt are certainly more foolproof than the unnecessarily complex '03 arrangement of striker, collar, firing pin rod, and spring; and I don't think there would have been as much field breakage with the Arisaka if the Japs had used metals equal to ours in their weapons.

The receiver itself follows the old Mauser design with the most apparent alteration being an extension of the tang strip to the rear, for an inch or so. This is mainly for the purpose of facilitating the joining of the two pieces of wood which make up the buttstock of the Arisaka and to provide bedding necessary with the usage of such soft gunstock woods. I doubt if there are any other reasons of importance. The guard, of course, is similarly extended on the under side of the grip and the two are joined at the rear by an extra guard screw set into the rear of the receiver tang through both pieces of steel so that the wood joint is gripped tightly between the guard rear and the receiver tang. The bottom cut for the sear is positioned much farther forward in the receiver than on the Mauser, and the engagement is forward, within the rear receiver ring. This position is necessary because of the deeply (forward) cut stroke-space in the rear of the bolt, which allows the use of a relatively short firing pin with its full length retained, at cock or relaxed, within the actual body of the bolt proper. The action does not have a bolt sleeve, its functions being taken over by the rear of the bolt and the safety lock assembly.

The bolt stop and ejector assembly is a clever gadget. It is similar to the Mauser in appearance but a little different in function. The bolt stop acts as does the stop of the Mauser, though it butts against the third lug on the bolt instead of the usual left locking lug. The cleverness of the assembly shows up when we examine the ejector. It is of the pivoting type, similar in principle but not in appearance to the Springfield, and much stronger and more certain. It does not depend upon the continuously maintained pressure of an ejector spring as does the Mauser; nor upon the short radiused and critically timed pivoting action which is used in the Springfield. The Arisaka has instead a long-radius pivoting type ejector which is actuated by the third lug ("bolt stop lug") as the bolt approaches its rearmost position during the back stroke. There can be no failure due to a clogged or tired spring, which frequently causes trouble in the Mauser, and it is not unduly delicate of construction or critical of fit as is the ejector of ye good old Springfield. The size of the ejector and bolt stop assembly was increased over the copied Mauser in order to gain the advantage described above and, it would seem, the advantage was sufficient to warrant the additional weight and bulk.

The trigger mechanism is roughly similar to that of the Mauser, producing the orthodox military type trigger pull, with a preliminary take up before the full resistance of the engaged sear is felt by the trigger. The trigger looks to be positioned in a much more forward position than the Mauser—an appearance created by the increased length of the Arisaka receiver and the forward position of the Arisaka sear.

The receiver ring is not enlarged to exceed the diameter of the receiver proper and it has two holes in its top, drilled concentrically through the ring. These are presumably gasports; I have seen a few rifles that did not have any, and some which had one such hole.

Throughout my description of the receiver, I have been unconsciously avoiding mention of the useless metal cover which I spoke of earlier in the text. Its stupidity of design is too obvious to merit more than a mere speaking of, and the two unsightly grooves which are cut lengthwise along the receiver to guide the contraption back and forth and keep it in place as the bolt is operated are even worse. The guy that thought that abortion up did dirt to the Jap soldier. Most of the Japs on Guadalcanal were smart enough to throw away this bolt cover and use the rifle with the unblued bolt flashing boldly forth in the sunlight.

The barrels are—in wise retention of the Mauser design—fitted and cut for the extractor in such a way as to give the greatest possible support to the cartridge case. The entire cartridge, head of case and all, enters into the chamber of the rifle, as does the head of the bolt, and the breech closure is the most complete of any modern bolt action rifle in existence today.

The follower is a metal stamped adaptation of the Mauser and the follower spring is a wire substitute for the flat strip equivalent in the Mauser and Springfield. The floorplate is essentially the same as the Springfield, as is the entire guard, though the latch is a modified one of simple lever design to replace the hidden Mauser type. Also, the guard is extended rearward to match the metal of the receiver tang above and to furnish a rearward location for a third guard screw—an artifice meant to hold together the two-piece buttstock. There is ample room in the trigger guard for a heavily gloved finger, though it is not as large as the standard military Mauser's. The possibility of releasing the floorplate latch with the trigger finger during firing is only theoretical, the latch spring being powerful enough to insure against such mishap.

The profile of the Arisaka's 31.4 inch barrel is not shaped for accuracy, being bottlenecked abruptly from a point about 1½ inches in front of the receiver. The barrel from that point forward is rather small in diameter, tapering only slightly outward to the muzzle. The rear sight, of the long, folding leaf design, is mounted on a base fixed to the barrel, after the manner of the Springfield, but a little farther forward, with the rear end of its fixed base jutting against a shoulder in the bottleneck of the barrel instead of the receiver itself. The tall, roughly graduated leaf swings upward from the front from a folded-down carry position, pivoting on a pin-type hinge similar to the one on the '03. It is graduated up to 2,400 meters in increments of 100 meters each, starting with 500, and is scored on the side with a notch for each graduation. The battle leaf is presumably set at 500 and the bottom of the leaf has a notch cut in it to provide a 400 meter setting. These sights are obviously crude and unscientific, but nevertheless highly suitable for the Oriental soldiers to use. The open V notch, which is the only rear sight profile used (there are three separate Vs cut into the rear sight leaf and slide assembly) is matched up with a

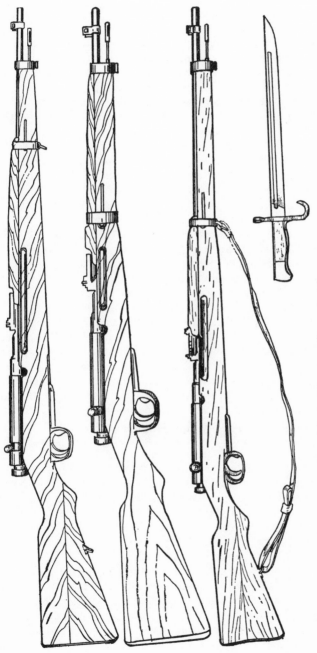

Upper is the M1905 or Type 38 rifle.
Middle is the M1905 or Type 38 carbine
Lower is the M1905 or Type 38 rifle with M1897 bayonet.
All are in 6.5 mm caliber

barleycorn-type, sharp-pointed front sight. The forward position of the rear sight, several inches in front of the Springfield's, is less critical of focus and has the desirable effect of sharpening up the definition of the rear sight for older eyes—a feature that becomes more desirable when barleycorn and open V sights are used.

Adjustments (for elevation only) are made in the rear sight by pressing a latch on the right side of the elevating slide and moving the slide freely to the desired elevation, where the latch, when released, will take hold in the proper notch on the right side of the rear sight leaf. There is no ready provision for lateral adjustment or windage, although the front sight blade can be driven over to obtain a mean zero. An allowance for bullet drift is not provided for in the design of the rear sight, and in view of the myriad inexactitudes inherent in the barleycorn-type of sights and Japanese marksmanship alike, we can certainly excuse the Jap ordnance experts for skipping over the relatively unimportant factor of drift allowances. This neglect, however, provides proof that in spite of the 2,400 meter rear sight leaf, there was no intent to build a weapon suitable for ultra long range fire at individual targets.

The sling swivels are widely separated on the rifle to make it easy for the rifleman to carry the weapon diagonally across his back and yet keep both hands free for climbing or carrying. The sturdy lower band, which carries the upper sling swivel, is set far out on the forearm of the stock, much too far to permit any use of the sling for shooting purposes, unless the sling might possibly be used in connection with the legs in the Continental back position. The lower sling swivel was almost identical with that of the Springfield, but situated much closer to the grip. In some rifles I saw the lower band was cleverly bedded-down upon a steel fixture neatly fitted into the forearm; this prevented bending the long barrel. The handguard was "packed" against the barrel here with a pad of thin greased cloth.

The stock and handguard, along with the excessively massive buttplate and sling swivels, were obviously constructed with the constant thought of bayonet employment in mind, and they were much stronger than would have ordinarily been necessary for such a light calibered rifle. However, some of that appearance of undue thickness was brought about by the required usage of third-rate wood of which the stocks were made.

The upper band was also heavily built and rather tightly fit about the barrel. The bayonet stud was an integral part of it, cut out of the same piece of metal and placed in the same position as the Springfield or Mauser. A good, steel cleaning rod projected outward from a hole in the forend inside the upper band and was held securely in place by a spring loaded latch inletted into the forend at six o'clock, just to the rear of the upper band. The slings furnished with the rifle, as seen on Guadalcanal, were mostly of good leather, though a few rubberized canvas ones had begun to come through by that time. Later on, in Burma, the Japs seemed to have run entirely out of leather.

The accepted Jap method of firing this long rifle from the prone position seemed to call for gripping the forearm just in front of the trigger guard and lying at the usual twenty-five degree angle from the line of fire while aiming. This put the left forearm nearly vertical, which has its advantages (when not using the sling) with a hell of a lot of long barrel quivering out in front. It could not have been an especially steady position. The more deadly Jap shots, of whom I have encountered a few, were past masters at the improvisation of different forearm rests, which enabled them to fire with greatly increased accuracy. There were not so many Dead-Eye-Dicks to be found, thank God. It doesn't take very many to be *too* many and much of the respect which I now have for the deadly effectiveness of rifle sniping is based upon later experiences which, though few in number, drove home in my mind a first hand knowledge of the terror-instilling damage to individual and unit morale which can be meted out by a few accurately aimed rifle shots.

The Arisaka rifle I have just described is a pretty good gun. It is clumsier than any of ours, but in slow fire it is easier to shoot. It has practically no recoil, what with its lengthy barrel, its moderately loaded cartridge, and its weight of ten pounds with sling. It has fair accuracy up to about 500 yards and a muzzle velocity of 2,400 foot seconds, which puts it up in the high power military class and gives it a maximum range of some 2,600 yards. It loads and operates in the same manner as any Mauser type rifle, and although it would not show up as well as the '03 (or, of course, the Garand) on the rifle range, especially in rapid fire, it would not be much slower to operate and reload under combat conditions.

All of the other rifles I will describe in following chapters have evolved themselves from, or were forerunners of, this basic rifle of the Japanese Army. It was, I believe, the most extensively used Jap weapon in World War II and although it was superseded by later models of different caliber it remained popular with the troops. All of the Japs I have talked to expressed a marked preference for the old reliable Arisaka 6.5 over any of the later Jap guns and all of the foreign guns—except for the Garand. In spite of all of its shortcomings, some of which were so stupid that they defied belief (almost as much as certain of our own ordnance inanities concerned with the adoption of our Springfield) it proved to be a good, reliable combat rifle. And it killed many thousand Americans who were armed with the best weapons in the world.

THE MODEL 1939—7.7mm RIFLES

After a few weeks in battle in jungle areas most any Infantryman will admit that he cannot possibly tell the exact caliber or
type of rifle from its report alone. He will generally say that any
bullet coming over at short range will crack like a whip as it
passes, and that the crack will become less sharp and less loud as
the range increases. But he will also tell you that the primary
sound of the rifle (the actual muzzle blast) can seldom be considered a giveaway as to the caliber of an enemy weapon. Terrain
surroundings do much to alter the sounds of weapons; acoustics
in the jungle and coconut groves are treacherous.

When different calibered weapons are being fired, side by side,
on the range, the difference in sound, even though the calibers and
charges are nearly the same, will be noticeable. And on the range
the same is true of various Japanese weapons. We all knew that
the 6.5mm cartridge always made a sharp crack in the rifle; thin
and piping, compared to the deeper roar of an M1 or an '03,
whether it was fired from a carbine or rifle. But this difference
was distinguishable only in the open, or in areas where the fighting had been fixed for a while and the sounds of certain weapons
had been heard over and over again in that area so that they were
cataloged clearly, each in the soldier's mind. After several day's
fighting in the same set of holes it would generally be possible to
determine the caliber and distance of a weapon from its report
alone.

On the third day after the Second Battalion had taken Mount
Austen, it was reported by many men along the outer line that
they were being fired at with our own M1 rifles, and a few '03s too.
I was almost certain that the Japs had not gotten more than four
of our rifles during the previous fighting; the men we had lost
during the early hours had been covered pretty well by artillery
fire during the first night and the Japs did not get to their bodies.
But in the shooting going on all along the line, we had recognized

a louder and deeper series of reports, which indicated that at least thirty enemy rifles of caliber larger than 6.5mm were being used.

The new weapons were heard first at about nine o'clock, and as I gradually became aware of the meaning of those different sounds, I began to suffer from a gnawing fear that the unit we were pitted against had been reinforced during the night by other troops—armed with a different weapon. It was not the greatest fear I was feeling at the time, because there were other things to worry about, and I didn't tell anyone of it; though the new firing sounds were being discussed all along the perimeter.

While I was nibbling away at a can of meat and beans, and cursing the QM for accepting rations in a style of can which could absolutely not be opened without a third of its contents being spilled over the poor soldier's lap, a Japanese rifleman, who had infiltrated around our right flank, started potting away. Not with any great effect—but he scared some men down at the water hole into taking cover, and he also got a part of the CP on the slope pinned down. I got my rifle and went stalking him, getting a somewhat better idea of his location after each of his shots.

I had sited myself on that part of the slope which he had under fire, and I was kneeling behind a big fallen log which did not give any too much protection because it was rotten and pithy inside. I knew it wouldn't stop a bullet, and that concern tended to hamper my concentration upon the difficult problem of locating the infiltrator's position. But I had to make the most of it, and get underway as quickly as possible, as one good rifleman in such a position can raise merry hell with the people he is shooting at. There was no safe place to conduct the search from which would give me the good view of my present position. So I continued the search, hoping with sincere earnestness that I would find the Nip before he located me.

My efforts were forestalled—fortunately not by the Nip. I had just begun to get my bearings when a bunch of people over in "F" Company, to my left flank and above me on top of the hill, began to open up on the base of a large buttress-rooted tree. I instantly aimed with my rifle at a spot on one of the great flattened roots, where the burst of their Browning Automatic rifle had centered itself, tearing away at the bark and splattering the green moss crust. Something fell from the top of that root, where it joined the trunk, and then the slumped form of a Jap, with a tightly strapped helmet still hanging on his head, slid down along the upper edge of the root. His shoulders, head, arms and hands were hanging down on my side. As he slid on downward someone in "F" Company continued to let him have it with the BAR, so that when he came to rest at the bottom of the root he was churned up into a reddish mess—but that helmet, shot through several times, remained on his head. He had evidently followed the creed of the ancient Samurai warrior and "tightened his helmet strings for the battle."

The object which first fell from the higher part of the root had been the soldier's rifle—one of the new ones which had just been heard for a few hours, a Model 99 (1939) 7.7mm job, official successor to the Arisaka 6.5mm. I got hold of it a day later, in rather good shape, with only a few flakes of rust on the outside. The Jap's body had fallen clear of the rifle and the rust was of the ordinary type, not the deep, pitted corrosion which is caused when a weapon is wetted with salty blood.

From first glance it looked to me as though the decision to adopt this new Japanese rifle as the standard Infantry weapon must have been made on a level above Infantry command circles, for except in the interests of caliber standardization, the weapon had little to offer in the way of advantages over the older 6.5mm caliber weapons.

The older guns were easier to shoot, having much less recoil; their ammunition was light to carry; and the carbine model of the Arisaka 6.5mm was much lighter and handier in the jungle. And the ballistic qualities of the old 6.5 were entirely adequate for mankilling.

The Japanese knew all of this, and while they had decided to adopt the heavier calibered weapon they did not do it in whole-hog fashion. They simply began to manufacture it along with their other weapons, and to gradually increase its quantities in the field. I was to learn of this later on in the war, though the trend was indicated pretty well by what we were to see on Guadalcanal itself.

This first 7.7 rifle I looked at was nearly new, and the varnish finish and light color of wood used in the stock were considerable handicaps to camouflage in the jungle. This complaint held true for all Japanese weapons, though—all of them used the same sort of light colored and unduly porous wood, which would not take an oil finish at all. Like other Japanese rifles, the new 7.7mm job was blued in finish; that was the only finish I saw on enemy weapons on Guadalcanal. The Japs apparently did not use the parkerizing finish at all, and with the glossy blue and varnished stock they used this weapon tended to reflect lots of light—entirely too much for a military rifle.

The M99 can be described as a rather ordinary military rifle, weighing 9 pounds, with an overall length of 44½ inches and a barrel length of 25½ inches. It has a monopod (which could be called a bipod, as it has two prongs) front support which folds forward from the lower band; this is about 12 inches long. It retains the same type bolt and receiver, and nearly the same type of action as the M38 Arisaka. Differences in these parts are very minor, such as the adoption of a "cocking piece" of slightly different shape from the Arisaka, although its function as safety lock remained the same. The rear end of the receiver bearing against the rear of the bolt handle base was altered, apparently in the interest of manufacturers short-cuts. It was lighter and thinner than the M38s. The length of the receiver extension piece on top was increased so that its rearmost tip was nearly back to the point of comb—a full three-and-a-half inches from the rear of the receiver proper. This permitted the rear guard screw to actually be placed

The M1939 or Type 99 rifle in 7.7 mm caliber

through the stock *behind* the pistolgrip, and enabled the weak wood of the grip to be reinforced by inletting steel straps on top and below. It would seem that the rigorous program for bayonet practice must have broken quite a few stocks to cause this precautionary measure.

Backward steps were taken in the design of a plain spring-loaded ejector, and the employment of a hole drilled at twelve o'clock in the receiver ring for a gas vent. The bolt itself had the usual large oval gas vent cut just in front of the extractor collar cut. The ubiquitous Jap action cover was stubbornly retained, God knows why.

Viewing the action from the underside, other changes in the old Arisaka design could be seen. A hinged floorplate had been adopted with the hinge forward; and a new type latch was employed at the rear, with its operating portion mostly inside the trigger guard; a rearward pull on a small up-bent protrusion being necessary to unlock the floorplate. The guard was extended far rearward to match the increased length of the receiver extension above, giving the entire guard and floorplate assembly an overall length of 11 inches. The extended rear part was bent to fit the outline of the slightly curved pistolgrip into which it inletted. All three guard screws were inserted from the under side.

The sling swivels were fitted on the left side of the rifle, possibly a compromise measure, as it was planned to use the one length of weapon for both Infantry and Cavalry. The buttplate was of the shallow, stamped metal-cap variety, extended forward at the top so that its upper screw could be inserted downward at right angles to the one in the heel.

The lower band was more massive than any yet seen, and was held in place by a through bolt, which did away with the excessive weight of the two spring retainers used on the Arisaka. The band's under portion swelled into a solid block which provided a base and hinge for the heavy wire monopod. Its left side held the upper sling swivel, the loop of which was lopsided to assume a comfortable position, or "bearing angle" of the sling on the carrying shoulder.

Some slight economy of weight was evident in the construction of the upper band. It was still amply strong, but lacked the heaviness of the one on the Cavalry carbine. A full-length cleaning rod was set in the forend and retained by means of a push button latch; this latch was built lighter in weight than the one used on the Arisaka and the Thirty Year Model. The visible parts of it were small, just an inletted guide with a square push button about an inch-and-a-quarter behind the band.

A handguard was employed to cover the top of the barrel from rear sight base to the upper band, different from those on the Arisaka rifles, which went forward only to the lower band leaving the barrel beyond that point bare on top. This new procedure permitted the upper band to be placed in the normal position, to hold the sling swivel, instead of in the far forward position to bind the far end of the handguard. (The far-out position of lower band, so used on the Arisaka, made carrying very awkward, causing the far dangling lower part of the rifle to bang uncomfortably against the thigh and hip of the carrier.)

The front sight was on exactly the same pattern as the Arisaka, a barleycorn blade dovetailed into a base with side guards. The base had a good flat front to give a surface for the bayonet guard to rest against—a practical field sight, but not built for good all-round accuracy.

In the rear sight of the M99 rifle, though, the Japanese did themselves proud, trying out several new (to them) ideas at the same time. The sight was mounted in the same place as on previous weapons, an inch-and-a-half forward of the receiver, but its construction was different from any other Japanese rifle. The only retained feature was the basic folding-leaf design; practically every other concept followed in the case of the Arisaka was discarded.

They adopted the peep sight, and went for it wholehog. Even the battle sight was a peep. At the same time, they left off the earlier ideas of short range zero; where all previous rifles had

A Japanese soldier puts an edge on his bayonet.

It wasn't often that Jap bayonets were found sharpened for more than a very few inches down from the point. All the blades I saw were dulled along the rest of the edge.

Japs were great for using the bayonet off, as well as attached to, the rifle. Sometimes they conducted very minor shore-to-shore operations, a squad or so swimming in the ocean around our flank at night, carrying bayonets in their teeth. Such doings were generally disastrous—to the Japs.

Notice that this soldier is wearing a cloth to keep the flies off the back of his neck. This wasn't such a bad idea in a lot of areas. The simple cotton uniform used by the Japanese was nearly as practical as our own, except for the feature of wrap leggins and tight fit trousers, which most of them were silly enough to keep wearing, even in the jungle.

minimum settings of 400 meters, the M99 had provision for zero-ing at 100 meters; and the battle peep, which came into position when the main sight leaf was laid, was apparently zeroed for point blank firing. Both regular and battle apertures were made large enough, each measuring roughly 3/32″, but like our own '03, they were positioned too far from the eye for optical correctness. The leaf was of the conventional type, and no windage adjustment was provided in its base. Ranges were laid off by scored lines from 100 to 1,500 meters, odd numbers on the left standard, even numbers on the right. Designating numerals were provided from "3" on up, the lower lines being too close together to allow room for the figures "1" and "2."

The elevation slide was moved by depressing two spring-loaded levers located at opposite sides on the top of the slide. When so depressed, the bottom inward edge of each lever would disengage itself from its side of the leaf and the slide could be raised or lowered to change the elevation. A notch was provided on one or the other side for each hundred yards of range. There was no provision for adjustment to intermediate ranges, nor was there any provision for shifting the position of the aperture within the body of the slide, either laterally or vertically.

The rear sight contained a fantastic innovation in the form of a pair of horizontally jutting scaled markers which were part of the rear sight assembly, attached to the slide. Each one, when folded down from the upraised leaf, projected outward an inch-and-a-half, making the overall width of the rear sight measure some four-and-seven-eighths inches. Apparently these devices were for anti-aircraft fire, to calculate very long leads. Each one was scored at center and end with the numbers "2" and "3," each numbered from the inside out (i.e., the "2s" closest to the sight leaf proper).

With all the gadgets in operating position—the monopod down, the sight leaf up, and the right and left anti-aircraft lead scales folded outward—the weapon had a truly weird appearance; the sight looking like a cross with a low lateral member. Add a bayonet and it looked like some highly complicated hari kari machine.

But with all the fun we can poke at it, the weapon did indicate a trend toward improvement in Japanese ordnance design. It retained a lot of the good features of the Mauser-fathered Arisaka, such as the neat bolt disassembly system and the improved bolt stop arrangement. The adaptation of aperture sights was also an improvement. There was some proof that the Japanese had profited from their early jungle experience—given by the provisions for precise short range zero in the new rifle, the first one of a long line that did not require holding under at short range.

The weapon had been evolved from the Arisaka .25 with the simultaneous purposes of standardizing calibers and providing a larger bore diameter to permit the use of properly-designed and effective tracer and armor-piercing bullets. As a gun it compared favorably with the better military rifles of Europe, being better than some models. It was, of course, a very crude item when compared to our Springfield. When compared to our Garand it was utterly obsolete, and its use against that weapon placed the Japs at an enormous combat disadvantage.

But the 7.7mm Model 99 rifle is numbered among the weapons which killed a lot of Americans in World War II and therefore it deserves a certain amount of respect.

THE "THIRTY YEAR" CARBINE

One of the most interesting weapons of the obsolete group which were found on Guadalcanal was the Thirty Year Carbine (and rifle). We ran into limited numbers of them in the early days of the Mount Austen operation, and a few more when we arrived at Cape Esperance. At first glance they were easily distinguishable from other Japanese shoulder weapons, and a quick examination of one gave me the opinion that they had likely been the immediate predecessors of the Arisaka series.

As carbines they were welcome to us, and several men in our column who had lost weapons during a river crossing incident armed themselves with the short and handy little weapons.

It would have embarrassed some of our American weapons and equipment designers if they had been able to see my column during the latter days on Guadalcanal. Half of my men had Japanese haversacks; all of them had Jap shovels and water bottles. It seemed a little strange to me to see our men armed and equipped in such varied fashion—to see one of my men go on guard or sentry duty and stand post with a Jap carbine, wearing a Jap leather belt with a set of cartridge boxes attached.

In some way, one of the corporals in my platoon had got hold of a Thirty Year Carbine in perfect shape—and had used it with good effect during the last few days of patrol activity on the Tanamboga River. When he was off duty, I borrowed the weapon and looked it over carefully, firing a few shots with it at sharks swimming in the shallow water out in front of my little seaside leanto.

Superficially, it was a beautiful little gun. It was of .256 caliber, of course, and weighed about seven pounds. The barrel length was nineteen inches, and the whole gun measured thirty eight inches. The front sight was of barleycorn variety with sideguards provided and a dovetailed semimovable base which could be driven to and fro to obtain a basic lateral zero. This sight, as far as I could tell, was exactly the same as the one on the Arisaka. The folding leaf rear sight was graduated from five hundred to fifteen hundred meters, and when it was lowered, a battle sight notch came into position and supplied a 400 meter setting. (Apparently the Japanese of that period gave little thought to the advantages of being able to obtain an absolute zero at shorter ranges; as in the case of sights on other Japanese shoulder weapons, the leaf of the rear sight failed to provide any allowance for bullet drift.)

The operation of the rear sight was the same as the Arisaka. The open notched "drift" slide had a spring loaded lever lock on the right side which was scored on the surface for easy finger-grip; its lower tip was forced inward by the action of the spring where it would engage in the appropriate notch of a series (one for each hundred meters of range) which had been cut at intervals into the right side of the leaf. The lowering and raising of the leaf was accomplished by the standard hinge-and-flat spring system. When lowered, the leaf was engaged at its forward end by a stud which fit the forward (upper) inside cut of the leaf to brace it against shock or strain. The fixed rear sightbase was fitted around the barrel about one and three-quarter inches forward of the receiver. As with the Arisaka, this was a measure taken to sharpen up definition of the open notch rear sight by placing it at a greater distance from the firer's eye.

The upper band, which held the characteristically heavy duty Jap bayonet stud was stoutly made and fitted around the barrel with very little clearance, once again attesting to the high regard given to bayonet tactics by the Japanese. The forend tip, which in the case of the Springfield is left sticking out bare with the end-grain of the walnut free to pick up moisture, was neatly capped with a metal plate, drilled for the cleaning rod.

The rifle cleaning rod, which the Japs have the good sense to put on all of their standard rifles and carbines, was held in place by a spring loaded lever which was positioned at six o'clock on the forend tip, extending about three inches back from the upper band. The rod was of conventional Japanese design, and threaded for the excellent Japanese jag-type tip. On the particular weapon examined, the rod handletip was of brass, and enlarged to form a bore filling slug with a hole drilled in the very end, which was also used as a tool for the disassembly of the bolt.

The lower band was massively constructed, with the sling loop fitted on the right side to permit the rifle to be handily carried. It could be slung diagonally across the back by mounted cavalry and by Infantrymen who need both hands free for carrying or climbing. One unsolvable mystery, as far as I am concerned, is provided by the fact that the sling was swivelled to the *right* side of the weapon. This meant that the bolt would have to be raised while the weapon was slung to keep it from grinding into the soldier's short ribs. This lower band was held in place against the forward shoulder of the enlarged rear portion of the forearm by an inletted spring-and-pin arrangement similar to that used on the Springfield; only it was much heavier in construction, and of twin design (i.e. there was a spring inletted on each side—one at 3 and one at 9 o'clock). Some small excuse for this extra weight and work may have been provided by the fact that the band, unlike the Springfield's, was of solid and fixed construction, with no constricting takeup afforded by the use of a tightening screw; and it therefore needed this double support to prevent its rocking

A Model 1897 or Type 30 rifle in 6.5mm caliber which is a longer version of the "30 year" carbine.

forward while the full weight of the weapon would be dangling on that "swivel" as the concerned soldier took his horse over some rough country.

Both upper and lower bands differed slightly from those on the Arisaka carbine in the fact that neither of them were adapted to fit over a handguard—because the Thirty Year Carbine had no handguard. The rear sling swivel was of the same design used on the Springfield and other rifles, but it was screwed into the right side of the buttstock, centered about four inches upward (forward) from the buttplate and about two and one-quarter inches below the top of the comb.

The buttplate was a heavy, well-finished cast steel affair with the top extended forward and inletted into the stock so that one screw could be placed pointing downward, making it almost impossible to wrench the buttplate off to the rear in any sort of a field accident. The other screw was placed in the toe, about an inch from the bottom tip. The plate was smooth finished, very slightly concave, and rather larger than is generally thought necessary for a military carbine of light caliber. It had no trap arrangement, and actually needed none—what with the cleaning rod on the weapon and the Japanese procedure of carrying cleaning equipment in the compartments and outside loops of their cartridge pouches.

The stock of this particular carbine was made of wood with a **texture** very similar to the poorer grades of American walnut and it was of rather thick, one-third pistolgrip construction. As in the case of a few Arisakas I have seen, the entire stock proper was *of a single piece of wood*, without the usual Japanese artifice of fitting an extra piece to fill out the lower third of the buttstock. The metal of the upper and lower tang surfaces was extended to the rear, however, just as in the case of weapons with the two piece stock. This instance would tend to nullify the concept that the rearward extension of metal was a feature incorporated solely for the purpose of binding together the forward part of the two piece stock; especially when it is realized that the Thirty Year Model was designed prior to the Arisaka. It is rather more likely that the rearward extension of metal was for the combined purposes of strengthening the stock at its inherently weak grip portion and at the same time increasing the area of rearend wood and metal contact to help take up the recoil. With the soft woods available to the Japanese, it is doubtful if the recoil shoulder system of recoil absorption—as used in the Springfield and the original M–98 Mauser—would have proven satisfactory for their weapons. Most likely the metal parts would have set back if this system were used.

The fit and finish of the particular stock which I examined were tighter and finer than those normally seen on Japanese ordnance products, and the same compliment can be paid its fittings, which were carefully polished and blued. The short forearm space betwixt receiver and lower band was inevitably graced with a short pair of finger grooves, which have been classically designated "hog wallows" by the late E. C. Crossman; and this is the only weapon I have seen on which their existence might have been justified. The carbine was a military weapon which might have to be fired at rapid fire rates for sustained periods, heating the barrel considerably—and there was no handguard; therefore the finger grooves might serve the purpose of reminding a man to grip the lower stock rather than let his fingers curl naturally around the barrel and fry on the tips.

More than likely, though, the Japanese just overlooked the importance of a handguard, and failed to provide one. The finger grooves also appear on their rifles which do have guards, (and all of their later weapons *were* equipped with guards). After a sufficient number of years' experience, it seems, all ordnance departments come to realize the importance of keeping parts of the soldier from coming into contact with bare metal parts which are liable to be heated by friction and combustion.

The trigger guard and floorplate assembly, including the joined rear grip extension piece are almost exactly the same pattern as on the Arisaka. The floorplate latch is similar, too. All are heavily built, and they are rigidly held in place by three screws, the two forward ones being inserted from the underside, of course; and the rear one going through from the top, having its head seated in the upper tang piece (upper receiver extension piece).

The magazine, follower, and follower spring are all slight modifications of the Mauser, and are therefore similar to the Springfield, Enfield, and others. As far as I could make out, those on the Thirty Year Carbine were exactly the same as on the later Arisaka. The width of the magazine well, of course, was designed to stagger the cartridges. The receiver bridge has the conventional positioning cuts for holding the "charger" properly while the cartridges are thumbed down into the magazine.

The receiver is inordinately long for a weapon of its cartridge length. Parts of the "lengthening" occurred in front, where the receiver ring is actually more than two full inches in length and even exceeds that of the Arisaka by three-eighths. Part of it occurred in the rear—equalling the equivalent "stretching" of the Arisaka. Overall, the receiver exceeds the length of the 8mm Mauser by about seven-eighths of an inch. The forward lengthening of the receiver ring is—in a way—a necessity with this weapon, because of the peculiar ejector and bolt face system used. The rearward extension of the receiver tube serves a purpose too. It eliminates the cramping fault of the Mauser.

The carbine does not have a buildup of ejector and bolt stop mechanism on the left rear of the receiver; the only thing showing outside is a simple spring loaded lever, which when not depressed by the firer to allow removal of the bolt, always remains with a heavy forward surface pointing inward and blocking the left lug race, to firmly halt the bolt's rearward travel. But strangely, it does not come directly to bear against the left locking lug. It is struck instead by the rear shoulder of a uniquely designed ejector, which rides forward with the bolt, remaining constantly in the left lug race. This ejector in turn strikes the rear surface of the left locking lug, after slight further travel of bolt to the rear— (about three thirty-seconds of an inch). The peculiar construction of the ejector, which, viewed from above, shows a cut in its right side as deep as the outward projection of the left lug, and about three thirty-seconds of an inch greater in length. This discrepancy provides the leeway to permit a good hard ejector thrust (or "blow"), and it constitutes the slack space which has to be closed up by the rearward movement of the left lug before the bolt reaches its final rearmost position.

The trigger and sear mechanism offer nothing new to change the regular Mauser military mechanism. They provide the double pull; however, the takeup portion of the pull is very short, with the trigger moving only a sixteenth or so before the harder portion of the squeeze begins.

In function the weapon differs considerably from the M–98 Mauser. The magazine loading is the same, and the initial ramping of the cartridge into the chamber is very little different, but there is no camming action on the final closing motion (downward movement of the bolt handle). The round is finally seated in the chamber by hand pressure on the bolt alone, which pressure is resisted not only by any tight fitting, oversize or dirty cartridges, but also by the tension of the rather powerful firing pin spring—for the cocking action is also accomplished during the forward stroke of the bolt. This, of course, is not good.

The firing of the cartridge is the same as with the Mauser and the lock against backthrust is almost identical. Two forward lugs, which rotate 90° from travel to lock positions, do all of the work. The left lug of these two is smaller, protruding only half as far as the right. This is a measure to allow space for the unusual ejector, previously mentioned, which fits over the lug during the forward and backward bolt travel.

At first glance, the bolt itself appears approximately the same as the Arisaka—nearly the same as the Mauser M–98. Its overall length, completely assembled, matches that of the M–98 8mm Mauser (as withdrawn from the rifle, with firing pin back); its bolt handle, the square base of which serves as a safety lug, is the same distance to the rear; and its diameter is roughly the same.

A second look, however, discloses great differences in both appearance and function from the Mauser, Springfield or Arisaka. At the rear, the firing mechanism includes a hook which serves as safety and cocking piece, projecting upward and blocking the line of sight when locked, and pointing to the left when otherwise. The "safety" position or "locked" position of this device is in reality an uncocked position, for in locking the weapon on "safe" this "safety-lever cocking-piece" is eased nearly all of the way forward. There it is held slightly to the rear by an arrangement in the rear of the bolt, so that the firing pin will not rest against the cartridge primer. Another difference in appearance is provided by the absence of the usual Mauser extractor along the right side of the bolt. The Thirty Year-type extractor is fitted into the bolt facepiece, with its inch-long spring completely concealed within the bolt thereby dispensing with the need for an extractor collar. With no camming action at all in the extraction operation, but only direct handpull instead, the Thirty Year extractor would not need to be so strong. If a cartridge should become badly stuck in this weapon, the firer would most likely have to knock it out with a cleaning rod anyway (he could, of course, set the butt on the ground and apply a heel to the bolt handle—in order to make "something" give). This feature of design is a definite disadvantage, and it makes the weapon highly critical of ammunition.

The bolt has no guide rib, but with the long-radiused support given by the lengthy receiver, none is needed. The very rear of the bolt proper (a complete circle) is enlarged considerably in diameter over the rest, apparently to provide the firer with protection from gases escaping back along the lug races. Protection from ruptured or perforated primer gases, which would otherwise course back through the inside of the bolt, is fairly well provided for by a hole drilled at two o'clock (closed position) some three-quarters of an inch to the rear of the locking lugs. Further protection is given by a tightly fitted Mauser type shoulder on the firing pin rod and an enlargement of the upper sear engagement which would help prevent the firing pin from being driven, Springfield-wise, back into the firer's face.

Back near the handle there are two cuts on the body of the bolt which serve to perform an important safety function. One of them will not permit the weapon to be fired until the bolt is fully locked at which time the cut provides leeway for upward movement of the stud which when forced down acts to prevent accidental discharge. The other cut provides the stud with leeway at non-critical times—when the weapon would not fire on other accounts. Without these, this carbine would be very dangerous to use, for with no camming action at all on the closing stroke it could easily be fired when the bolt would be only partially locked forward; in which case the firer would certainly suffer serious, if not fatal, injury.

The receiver ring is perforated by two gas vents, both visible on the top of the ring, which completed the gas precautions taken throughout the weapon. The Japanese have treated this problem with great care in the case of nearly every rifle they designed, probably because of rather low standards of ammunition uniformity which now and then cause excessively high breech pressures.

The most radical difference from the Mauser action in the whole rifle is the false, nonrotating bolt face—a device which possesses a few theoretical advantages, but which does much to complicate an otherwise simple and rugged action. The foremost three-eighths of an inch of bolt length on the Thirty Year Model is not an integral part of the bolt. It is a "false face," attached by means of a metal projection to the rear which fits into the forward end of the bolt body proper and is held in place by a lug. The extractor and ejector (already described) are attached to this separate bolt face, and ride along with it in the right and left lug races, respectively.

Unlike the Mauser, Springfield, Enfield and Arisaka, this face, (or extreme forward portion of the bolt) which contains the firing pin port, does not turn with the bolt. Instead it remains in the same stance during the locking and unlocking motion of the bolt handle. It is kept so aligned during these operations by the action of the extractor and ejector, both of which remain in the lug races.

The advantages of this system are created by the small amount of friction encountered between the two polished steel surfaces of the bolt and bolt face assembly—as compared to that existing with the regular Mauser bolt face which twists against the head of a cartridge. Also this feature eliminates the need for an extractor collar and cut on the outside of the bolt, and for an ejector assembly in the receiver (the latter being theoretically less reliable than the type used in the Thirty Year Model).

But the faults of the system are obvious. It is unduly complicated and it has many small parts, difficult of manufacture. It increases the length of the bolt, which is a trend directly against important present day concepts of rifle design. And though some small advantage is gained by opening up the front end of the bolt in normal disassembly for cleaning; it is more than outweighed by the necessary use of two separate pieces in the bolt body, with small parts placed in the critical forward position where they are continually subject to heavy shock.

The bolt, after being removed from the rifle by depressing the bolt stop, is disassembled by first removing the "false face group" by rotating and pulling to the front. This group includes what I would call the bolt face, the extractor, and the ejector. These three parts are easily separated from each other—in fact they will fall apart when separated from the bolt. Next a tiny latch is depressed, a coin is inserted in the slot of the cocking piece screw (in same position as cocking piece head on Springfield) and it is turned counter clockwise about eight complete turns, which frees the threads on its forward end from engagement with the upper sear body inside the bolt's rear half. After these eight turns the screw continues to rotate, clicking each time, but it will emerge no further. This is where the brass slug on the end of the cleaning rod comes into use.

Grasp the bolt in the left hand, handle end upward. Place the brass end of the rod against the tip of the firing pin in the forward end of the bolt. Then, holding the cleaning rod and bolt as a single rod (the firing pin will fit into a hole in the end of the brass slug), place the steel end of the rod on a hard surface and press downward on the bolt holding firmly onto the cocking piece hook the while. As this is done the firing pin spring will be compressed and the cocking piece screw will be gradually forced upward, at which time it will be discovered that the cocking piece screw is really in two pieces—being split down its center into two equal halves. These halves will fall apart, releasing their engagement with the grooved end of the firing pin rod, after which the firing pin rod and spring can be removed from the front end of the bolt and the upper sear body from the sear cut by merely lifting the bolt a bit farther and letting them fall out.

The entire bolt, disassembled, can be laid out in ten pieces, not including the small latch inletted and pinned permanently into one of the halves of the cocking piece screw. Assembly is accomplished by repeating the process inversely.

It can be seen at once that the Thirty Year Model is by no means as simple and rugged as a good military bolt action should be, and the principal objectionable complications seem to be in the design of the bolt—and nearly all of them in its front end. The lack of a camming action on down stroke of the bolt is another serious objection; and of course the difficulty of large manufacture attendant with utilization of such small parts—all machined and critical of fit—would be strongly felt by the factories.

The other objections are minor. If the weapon were equipped with an Arisaka bolt and ejector, and if it cammed on closing stroke it would be a good gun—a very good gun.

But then, if the weapon were so fitted, it *would be an Arisaka,* for those were the only modifications made when the Arisaka was adapted from this model.

All in all, the Thirty Year Carbine didn't seem a bad weapon to me when I was sitting on the Guadalcanal beach, stripped to the waist, back resting against a coconut log, feeling the warm sun and breeze. I was lazily shooting at shark fins and floating coconuts; all the while looking out over the blue channel between Guadalcanal and Savo and reflecting happily that the dangerous part of the Guadalcanal fight was over. I felt so lazy that when I got through firing I handed the weapon to a native boy to clean, crawled into the shade, and stretched out on a blanket until dinner time.

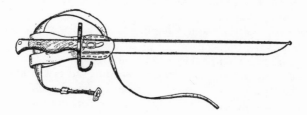

THE MODEL 44 6.5mm CARBINE

We had to wait until near the ending of the Guadalcanal operation before we were to come upon the most outstanding evidence
of Japanese enthusiasm for cold steel. The astounding fact that
bayonet fittings were used on light machine guns was discovered
in the beginning, when we saw the first captured weapons on Lunga
Beach, but it was not until the Cape Esperance show that we were
to come across the Model 44 (1911) cavalry carbine, which had a
bayonet permanently attached to the barrel, like a jack-knife
blade, making the carbine muzzle-heavy and clumsy beyond belief.

This gun was meant to be used by mounted troops, and by a
few Infantrymen who were in jungle areas. It had a feature of
handiness for jungle work in that it was not necessary for the
soldier to have a long bayonet scabbard attached to his belt.
(American doughboys moving in jungle country often fastened
their bayonets to the underside of the forends on their Garands—
to dispense with the need for carrying that unhandy item.) But
with all of its other faults, and from the viewpoint of military
common sense, the adaptation was unthinkable.

It was a carbine almost exactly the same as the M38, (1905)
carbine—from the buttplate to the lower band, that is. Between
those areas the differences between it and the regular carbine were
small, consisting of a trap in the buttplate, unnecessarily complex
in design, which permitted a cleaning rod to be carried within the
buttstock; and a groove cut four-and-a-half inches back from the
upper band into the bottom of the forend, which provided a
nestling-place for the last few inches of bayonet when it was
folded back.

Yes, the bayonet folds back under the stock like the blade of a
pocket knife.

The front end of this weapon, five inches back from the muzzle,
was much modified in order to accommodate this weird looking
device. The front sight was moved back to a position 3″ from the

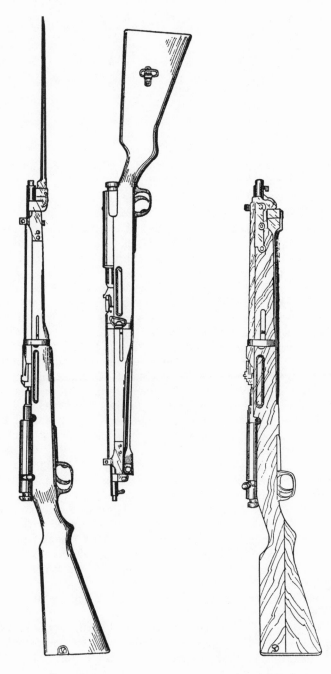

Three views of the M1911 or Type 44 Cavalry Carbine in 6.5mm caliber.

muzzle, and a massive forend tip was installed, made of solid steel, and containing a female hinge-half and two lock studs; one of them forward of the hinge under the muzzle, another an equal distance to the rear. These lock studs' function was to hold the bayonet in the fixed, folded position—about one inch to the rear of the hinge. All of these devices, hinge and studs alike, were centered on the underside of the forend piece, which must have weighed at least a pound.

A poinard type bayonet, triangular in cross section with a deep blood-run on the upper side, was fitted to the rifle by means of a male hinge-half at its base, which fit into the massive female hinge-half located two inches back from the muzzle on the underside of the special forend. It was secured there by a large rivet which was extended on the right side to form a hook of the type found on nearly all Japanese bayonets; which hook is used for stacking the weapons and also in bayonet fighting, to wrench a weapon out of an opponent's hands. On this carbine the hook stuck out to the right and forward at all times. On other rifles the hook is with the bayonet, pointing downward and forward.

The bayonet of the M44 measures sixteen inches overall, with a blade length of fourteen inches. The two inch section at the rear was enlarged and contained a heavy latch mechanism which was unlocked by means of a knurled-top push button sticking out from the right side. This locking action was automatic when the bayonet was swung forward or backward into either the ready or the retracted positions and pressed strongly upward. As far as the qualities of ruggedness and dependability are concerned, the device could be called a masterpiece. But its overall weight seems excessive, and it throws the little carbine completely out of balance, making it muzzle heavy and slow-pointing, even for a man used to the weight of match rifles, which the Japanese certainly were not.

Another outstanding disadvantage also accrues from the fact that the bayonet on the carbine is not removable and can not serve its owner as a knife or bolo apart from the weapon. The edges of the bayonet are of necessity dulled, because part of it will rest in the palm of the hand when it is not extended. A certain amount of effectiveness is thereby lost.

The lower band is creased inward at 6 o'clock to admit the bayonet into its inletted groove when folded back, otherwise there is no change from the M38. Its really just a hashedup version of the same gun.

The particular carbine of this type which I first examined was hanging, oiled and well-cared for, in a banana leaf leanto where the floor space was filled by three bodies lying side-by-side in three

different stages of decomposition. One had been dead a month,
another a week, and the third no more than three days. It took
many day's exposure to the air and sunlight before the smell left
the wood of the stock and I could get my face down on it to aim.
This carbine shot pretty good—the ponderous weight forward was
somewhat steadying.

But this weapon was about the poorest example of ordnance
design that I had ever seen. Perhaps it should be called "ordnance
butchery" because without the M44 modification of a permanently
fitted bayonet, the M38 carbine was a pretty nice little gun. But
I wouldn't give hell-room to the Official Cavalry Weapon of the
Japanese Imperial Armies.

THE M38 6.5mm SNIPER RIFLE

Though we had all heard a lot of talk about Japanese snipers who were reportedly using telescopic sights in other sectors, we did not capture any such weapons during the Mt. Austen fight. I was actually skeptical of their existence by the time we loaded up for Cape Esperance, though I knew that the Japanese were adept at the manufacture of good optical equipment from the few looks I had gotten at Japanese binoculars and mortar sights.

We all felt a marked tendency toward skepticism on that island because if there ever was a place rife with rumor, hokum and downright lies, it was Guadalcanal. All of us had heard lengthy stories of women snipers; about whole platoons of Japanese who spoke perfect English; and even one especially wild tale that Amelia Earhart and her navigator had been found alive in the island's interior. Most of us even got to the point where we would believe what we could see and nothing else.

It had become a sort of religion with me to conduct a private crusade for truth—to challenge every abnormal account I might hear with the classic old Missouri quotation. I had stretched out on the ground alongside a score of Jap corpses, for instance, to prove that there were not any six foot Japs on the whole island and to abash a large number of men who claimed that they had just seen a six-feet-four body just down the road. So, whenever anyone came up with that old one I would always jump up, go down to the site which they had mentioned and go through the old ritual of lying down alongside the carcass. I knew that a man looked awfully big when he lay dead on the ground, especially if he were lying face up, but I had still become thoroughly annoyed with the constant repeated exaggerations by men around me and I had vowed to listen to them no longer with politeness. In the first three months I had never found a Jap measuring more than five-feet-eight; I had never seen a sniper rifle; and I had announced on several occasions a firm disbelief in the presence of either on Guadalcanal.

One day after the big fighting was all over, I had the double embarrassment of being proven dead wrong on both counts. Within two hours I saw a Jap that was over six feet tall and a brand new M38 sniper rifle, complete with telescopic sight!

It was shortly after dawn one morning when some of the guards on the perimeter of our Tanamboga River camp saw a figure approaching down the trail. They didn't shoot as he came in and I rather think that it might have been his height that saved him—he was so tall that he didn't look like a Jap. When he got close he raised his hands and they saw from his uniform and belted-on equipment that he was an Oriental. With due precaution they led him to headquarters—one man in front with a Tommy gun pointing back and one man following behind. We were at breakfast when he was brought by the mess tent, and Art Hantel pointed at him across the table and motioned for me to turn and look.

"George," he said, "I sure wish I had taken that $50.00 bet you wanted to make the other day; there's a Jap that's taller than I am!" Art was six-two; I turned around and looked in amazement but I still was slow to believe. "Betcha he's a Korean or a northern Chinese!" I grunted back at Art but I didn't answer when he reached into his pocket and asked "how much?"

I walked over to my tent-shack and got out the little Japanese-English phrase book and then ambled over to the stockade. When I got there I was flustered further to find myself having to *look up* into the face of a Japanese soldier and I motioned for him to sit down on the ground. He hastened to obey, squatting low on his heels at once—not at all sullen, like some of the prisoners had been. I sat on a felled coconut log and began to communicate with him by means of the phrase book.

First I pointed to the set of characters which inquired of his age. He indicated that he was 23 years old by counting on his fingers. Next, I pointed to a line in which the English characters read "Where are you from?" Without hesitating he answered "Kobe."

The questioning went on and on. "Where were you born?" "Kobe." "Where is your home?" "Kobe." "Where does your family live?" "Kobe." "Where were you before you came here?" "Singapore."

Well, that was definite enough. I went back to the mess tent and admitted to the other officers that my ideas on the height of Japanese were wrong—and I also told myself that the day had gotten off to a helluva start! It should have been some consolation to me to know that at least one person was really happy that day; and one was. When I left the stockade the Jap prisoner was noisily at work on a messkit full of spaghetti, fumbling awkwardly but cramming effectively with a fork. There was no doubt about the last few hours having wrought great improvement in his lot; and this didn't make me feel a bit better.

Things got brighter, though, after I had finished my coffee; they always do. I had a nice sunny day to look forward to and there had been good luck fishing out in the bay for the past week so we had planned to go fishing again today. We had picked up several outboard motors (Evinrudes) and a couple of collapsible boats that the Japs had left and with a few emergency fishing kits obtained from the Navy we were pretty well set. But our troubles were not all ended, we discovered, when we tried to start the two outboard motors; each of them balked in turn.

Under these conditions back in the States, a man would probably have to make the damn motors work—but not so on Guadalcanal. We simply left the defective putt-putts where they were and went looking along the beach for another. We found one about half a mile down the beach hidden in the bushes with some other equipment. One of the officers with me got impatient with my taking time to rig a rope to pull the motor off its dunnage from a safe distance and walked right in, lifted it up and carried it out into the trail for examination; luckily it was not booby-trapped.

While he was examining the motor I became interested in three boxes which had served to keep it out of the sand. They were as large as burial caskets and very well built. I fastened a rope to the latch of one and dragged it out into the open, checking it well for evidence of booby-trapping before reattaching the rope to it. The same officer (far braver than I) got tired of seeing me fool with the rope and walked up to the box with a slice bar. I held my breath and closed my eyes while he tore it open. It didn't explode and it proved to be a case of rifles, all in grease. One of them had a leather case attached to it and the breech appeared to be a bit modified. One glance told me that it was a sniper rifle.

I immediately lost all interest in fishing and begged off the trip, then took the rifle and telescope back to camp to examine more closely, carrying with me the bolts of the other six rifles which the case contained. There were still lots of Japs alive and free on the island so I sent a detail back to pick up the rest of the rifles, most of which appeared to be brand new M38 standard jobs, and bring them in to camp.

I was chided a second time when I got back into camp and it was discovered that my statement about Jap sniper rifles had been disproved by my own find, but I was so pleased with having the weapon that it didn't bother me at all. I borrowed a can of gasoline from the kitchen and went off to my shack to remove the storage grease. The rust-proofing compound used on that particular rifle was stiffer and gummier than any I have seen on

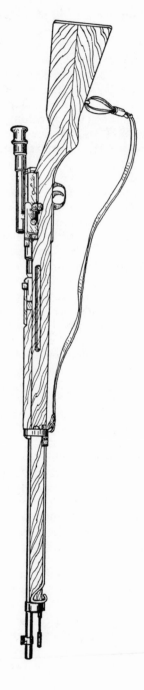
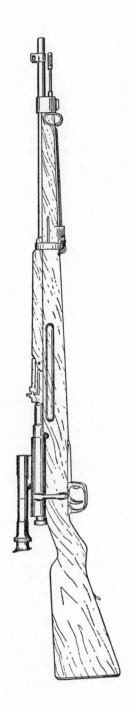

Two examples of the M1905 or Type 38 Sniper Rifle in 6.5mm caliber with telescopic sight and monopod attached.

freshly stored American weapons. It was like old cosmoline which had set for twenty years.

The gasoline cut it, however, and it took me less than an hour to get the weapon ready to shoot, including washing each small part in a can and flushing and brushing out the inside of the receiver and magazine. The bore was like a mirror and the outside of the weapon had a new appearance.

As I proceeded with the disassembly and cleaning it became apparent to me that there were few modifications in this weapon from the Standard M38. The bolt handle had been bent down into the position Americans would consider about normal and a small rugged scope was fitted to the receiver by means of a dovetail arrangement which would permit ready removal.

The chief difference was, of course, the telescopic sight. It was very short, having an overall length of six-and-seven-eighths inches, excluding the rubber eyepiece. With the rubber eyepiece (reminiscent of the old Warner-Swasey type scope of World War I) it measured an inch and a quarter more.

It was mounted far back—a measure made doubly necessary by the Japanese shortness of neck and the very short eye relief of the glass, which measured something less than an inch and three quarters. It was mounted off center—to the left—in order to permit easier loading and passage of the bolt without too great modification of either the bolt or the receiver. With a 12 o'clock cut in the receiver, offside mounting was the only solution. This offset feature facilitated low mounting of the scope which, though it appeared at first glance to be hung way up above the receiver, was really mounted fairly close down, giving a clearance of only one-quarter inch (vertically measured) between tube and receiver cover. The receiver cover was retained on the sniper weapon.

The mechanics of the scope mount were good. It employed a massive dovetail joint, with the female section on the receiver end, surface vertical, and the male section an integral part of the telescope tube. The scope was fitted in the field by sliding it forward into the female joint until the rear shoulders of the movable base came to rest against the rear of the female joint. Then a rather awkward protruding handle on the outside of the movable base could be cranked from its forward position (open) to a rearward position (locked), thereby securing the scope firmly in mount. The crank was held in place at the two extremes of position by means of two outward plunging poppets, which could be disengaged by pulling outward on the handle of the crank. At each extreme beyond the poppets there was a stud projecting to block the path of the locking crank, serving to prevent the lock being strained beyond its limit of normal tightness.

This crank turned an eccentric which caused the whole center third of the male dovetail (attached to the scope) to move upward and out of line with the front and rear portions, thereby creating a perfect triangular bearing within the dovetail. There was no ready means for taking up wear, but the bearing surfaces were so large that it was perhaps unnecessary.

The scope was nothing to marvel at but it was rugged and probably practical for the Jap soldier to use. It was certainly more weather-and-foolproof than the first ones which we were to be issued some eight months later. It was of two-and-one-half power magnification with a field of ten degrees and was so labeled in white letters on the scope tube. The objective was very small, not more than half an inch of glass, and the ocular lens was only a little larger. From the standpoint of appearance and function, based upon concepts of American hunting equipment, the scope was certainly not good. The only good point which was evident at first glance was its reticule. It was a simple three lines, graduated vertically in range settings for holdover and graduated horizontally for windage holdoff or lead.

This reticule left the entire upper half of the field clear of obstructions and the lower half of the lens was not even completely crossed by the vertical crosshair line. The lateral line went all the way across and had a few graduations marked near the center only. The vertical line was nearly all below the lateral one, with only a very slight protrusion of the tip above center.

The weapon was set dead on at 300 meters and all other ranges had to be held over or under. This would add even more strength to the idea that the Japs were coming more and more to realize the importance of accurate zero at short range. Fifteen hundred meters was the longest range marked on the vertical line and there was no provision established for correcting for drift at the longer ranges, other than the markings on the horizontal line, which were entirely too coarse for such purposes. The reticule of that weapon was the best military reticule I have ever seen in any telescope; and the telescope—with all its faults—was the best issued sighting device I was to see during the entire war.

Especially good were the weatherproofing measures which had been taken by the manufacturers of the scope. The lenses were firmly sealed, heavily protected from both moisture and shock by the stiff, closefitting tube assembly. The outfit would obviously stand up very well under the trying conditions of humidity and changing temperatures encountered in the jungles. Once again, the Japs gave evidence by the design of their weapons that they were interested in practical results, rather than theoretical advantages. It is difficult for the average American "gun nut" to stomach the way the Japanese sniper rifle and scope flaunted the long-respected principles of design, which call for zero adjustment and ready means of allowing for drift, but it is a fact—whether we like it or not—that the Japanese sniper rifle was actually better than the ones we got for combat use later on.

The proof of the pudding, however, is always in the eating, so I decided to take the weapon down to the water's edge and test it for accuracy by shooting at various-ranged targets.

To do this I got some boxes from the kitchen and smeared large charcoal bullseyes on them. Spotted at various points along the far curve of the beach they provided me with the ideal lazy man's target range. I could shoot at various ranges without going to the trouble of walking back from the butts after each stage. Two men who had nothing to do volunteered to act as target markers.

I opened a fresh case of 6.5mm ammunition which we had in the dump we had captured at Esperance and selected several hundred rounds to use with this weapon. I have always had a great fear of firing a "booby-trapped" enemy cartridge, loaded with grenade explosive, so I carefully checked the neck of each cartridge to see that the bullet had not been tampered with after the round had left the factory. Fortunately, the Japanese crimping system does not lend itself to bullet pulling. You can generally tell by looking if a round has been disassembled. With that in mind, I went through the case, discarding any rounds which I thought were the least bit suspicious looking. I also tore several rounds apart and checked to see if the flakes of the powder appeared normal; they all did. Actually, I have never come across a proven instance of the planting of exploding ammunition by the Nips, but at that time I was still following the doctrine that a soldier should always give his enemy credit for as much intelligence as he himself possesses. It took sometime for us to learn that this doctrine did not hold true for the Japs; they missed a lot of good bets.

In a half hour the whole thing was set—the gun, the range, and the targets. There was no rest handy at my selected firing position and I looked about for some time until I remembered that I had a monopod on the rifle and might as well use it. It opened out from the rifle easily and I stuck it into the sand to the right depth and took aim. By cradling the stock in my arms and laying on it while the long front end of the rifle was held up by the monopod, I could secure a very comfortable and steady hold. I dry fired a couple of shots from that position and then loaded up and yelled a warning to the pair of men who were to mark. They got into defilade before I fired the first shot. By arrangement they were to come out after each shot was fired and mark; I would fire only one shot at a time.

I fired at the short ranges first, taking the initial five shots at a five-inch bull on the target closest to me—as near 100 meters as I could estimate. All of these shots were bulls. The sixth was a bad hold and went out at three o'clock—just where I called it. A walk to the target and a look at that first group convinced me that the rifle I had was a good shooting weapon. The entire six shots had an extreme of less than four inches—enlarged by an inch and a half by the single wild hold. I went back to the firing point while the two men who were marking, impressed like myself by the rifle's performance, moved away to the next target.

At 200 meters the weapon kept almost everything inside eight inches, even with some bad holding involved and I found that the reticule holdover mark for that distance was perfectly placed. I fired shot after shot at that range because I wanted to be especially sure of that setting.

To make a long story short, the gun continued to behave beautifully, not missing any of the settings for ranges up to 400 meters. Beyond that I didn't bother to test the weapon. By firing 100 rounds I had adequately tested the worth of the scope and rifle and I was satisfied that it was a surprisingly good outfit.

To check the zero-return qualities of the scope mount, I took the scope off the rifle several times during the firing, with no noticeable change in the point of impact. There were no ready adjustments on the scope, which I naturally recognized as a fault, but at least the Jap soldier would not be able to ball up what zero his rifle had been given at the arsenal. That was more than could be said for our Weaver-Springfield.

The 6.5mm cartridge was not new to me at that time, as I had fired it in both the carbine and rifle versions of the M38, so I was not as much impressed with its qualities as the Infantryman who had not done extensive shooting would be. These qualities made for extreme ease in shooting—a marked characteristic of the long 6.5mm weapons.

Compared with our own Springfield it can be said that this Jap sniping gun had practically no recoil or muzzle blast. They didn't even jump badly when fired from the hip. And the great giveaway of the Springfield or Garand—the great kickup of dirt and leaves by the muzzle blast in front of the firer's position— was comparatively nil in the Arisaka. To the ordinary rifleman this would be a great advantage and to the sniper striving for concealment it would be a Godsend.

This exhibition of accuracy had stimulated my interest in the gun and as I took it back to camp and began to clean it, I looked it over with increased care. On this closer examination it was clear that the weapon was much better fitted and finished than the

minerun Arisaka 38. The inletting of the stock was to closer fit
and the firing mechanism and bolt were tighter. The trigger pull,
while by no means up to American match standards, was smooth
and broke, as I remember, at about five pounds. For a Jap weapon
that is marvelous, as all who have fooled with them will know.
The bent bolt tended to put the gun on better terms with me, as
did the smooth fitting, jag-tipped cleaning rod with which it was
so very easy to keep the bore clean and free from rust. I used
American bore cleaner on the gun, and it worked beautifully (the
Japs apparently used a chlorate primer, too, as I have seen some
of their barrels rusted overnight).

It was a slick little weapon, that rifle, although in its present
condition it was long, heavy and ungainly beyond all practical
use. But if I had not possessed a sniper weapon of my own, I would
most certainly have cut that rifle down to a decent size and used
it in preference to any gun—American or Japanese—with iron
sights. With the receiver of the sniper rifle removed and fitted to
the rest of a M38 carbine, I would have had a good substitute
sniper rifle, much better, in my opinion, than the Weaver-sighted
Springfield which we eventually got.

As it was, though, we didn't get back into the fight for some
time, so I turned the weapon in at headquarters rather than to
have to nurse it all the way back to Fiji with my baggage (which
consisted of the greens on my back, my rifle, and a small rucksack, improvised by sewing Infantry pack straps on a Jap bag).

My experience with this rifle was of no particular consequence
but it did provide me with another beef against old "Colonel
Whoever-Was-Responsible." It drove home the fact that at the
beginning of the war the Japs had a sniping rifle which was as
good and maybe a little better than anything we issued in worthwhile quantities at a much later date.

THE NAMBU PISTOL

We noticed from the first on Guadalcanal that the Japanese Army seemed to possess a great fondness for good leatherware. The first troops which we contacted on Hill 27 wore very neat dispatch cases of well cared for cow hide; some of them had packs made of well tanned skin throughout, many of them had leather straps and fittings on their canvas packs and of course all of them had leather cartridge belts and pouches which were both neat and practical. But the most outstanding of all the leatherwork I saw were the excellent holsters in which officers and noncommissioned officers carried their handguns.

Many of these holsters were of nondescript patterns, made to fit the wide variety of handguns which (by God knows what diverse means) the Japanese had gotten hold of. All kinds and calibers of foreign handguns were carried by members of the Japanese forces on Guadalcanal, the most popular being the .32 Colt Automatic, the .30 and 9mm Luger, and the 7.65mm Browning. Others were there in smaller quantities—everything from Frontier model Colts to .25 caliber Walthers. And each of them had a special holster, carefully sewn and fitted with belt loops and a set of clip or ammunition pouches. Found in madeup units, complete with holster, these guns all made pretty good souvenirs. The .32 Colt was an especially nice outfit in that respect, very neat to wear, and I can recall with a laugh how many of the men were swaggering around with belts slanted around their hips, making our little camp look even more like some Hollywood set, tropical boomtown full of cowboys and "rough customers."

But the Japs were not solely armed with foreign handguns. They had their own weapons, too, and in greater numbers than any single foreign model. There were three different designs of Japanese pistols which I saw on that island—the M–1925, the M–1934, and the Nambu—all of 8mm caliber. Of these the Nambu was by far the best weapon and the most interesting from the standpoint of firearms design. It was always found inside one of those pretty, weathertight, leather holsters, provided with a belt loop and a shoulder strap—thereby becoming the nicest souvenir of all the handguns we knew of on Guadalcanal.

I got my first look at one early in January up on Mount Austen, at the battalion command post. It got back to the CP in the usual way. Sgt. Russel Hill picked it up under ordinary but interesting circumstances.

He was on the line one night after the moon had come up and things had begun to pop around a good deal. The usual number of hand grenades were being flung about, and the usual number of trigger happy Japanese and Americans were blazing away at one another with wild abandon. Hill was doing his damndest to accomplish the impossible feat of getting his head low enough in his hole so that he wouldn't stand much chance of being hit and yet remain able to look around in front, guarding against the likelihood of suddenly finding a live healthy Jap in the same hole with him. Relatively silent during the day, the Japs were now pulling their usual stunts and behaving like a bunch of hop happy idiots. They started things out by scoring three near misses on Hill's position with grenades—two of which exploded in the heaped coral spoil on his right side, their fragments whizzing across his body, which was pancake-flattened in the muddy bottom of his hole when they went off. Hill yanked his Tommy gun bolt to the rear, threw the safety and discarded his ideas about sleeping that night.

He sat on, in the way many thousand doughboys have since, trying to filter out the confusing natural noises of the jungle night so that he could hear and distinguish the sounds made by men out in the cover, thirty yards away, who were at the moment trying to kill him. As his ears struggled trying to make something out of the confused mosaic pattern of bird and insect calls, wing whirrs, falling leaves and twigs, his eyes also strained at the narrow bit of bare ground in front before the shadows farther down the slope. He knew that the Japs were playing it wise—keeping down below in the deep shadows, while they could look up and see every move of his helmet outlined against the moonlit sky.

Another Jap grenade plunked into the mud four feet from his hole, its fuse sputtering as it hit. He ducked and it exploded brightly—lighting his position up for the blindest enemy to see. "Thank God those grenades sputtered and sparkled! Man! Oh Man! Hell ain't got nothin' on this place!" Hill gritting his teeth, fought back a wild impulse to raise his Tommy gun and fire wildly into the shadows—to run cursing down the slope and close with those little yellow fiends who were driving him crazy, even to stop his cramped, baited breathing, and yell—yell at the top of

Hideo

It was surprising, the number of pistols in the ranks of the Japanese Army. I don't know whether or not they were officially issued in such quantity, but many units seemed to be solidly armed with pistols—one for each soldier in addition to his rifle. In many cases these "issues" were nondescript, with the men of a single unit having at least a dozen different types of handgun. We found all sorts of American, Spanish, Belgian, German and other handguns in the deserted Jap bivouac areas on Guadalcanal.

Generally, these pistols were in a condition indicating that they had been well cared for. Japanese were pretty good at taking care of the simpler weapons, and long experience with the use of guns in humid, corrosion-aiding climates had taught the Jap to be constantly concerned that his gun was well oiled. Such careful maintenance is a tribute to the Jap, because his pistols generally were not as readily broken down for cleaning as ours.

The soldier shown here has removed his Model 14 from the rubberized holster and is giving it a going over. The rubberized holsters, worn during the day, tended to cause moisture to condense on the metal inside; for the jungle, however, they were better than leather. Incidentally, the diagonal strap method of slinging this holster is superior to our own belt method.

his lungs. "Come and get me, you cowardly yellow bellies! Come and get me!"

But he did none of these things. He kept his eyes focused on the grassy places between the shadows where he stood some chance of seeing any human movement; sitting there with the rim of his helmet just above the dirt line, the compensator of his Tommy gun just nosing over the edge of his foxhole.

His friend out in front hadn't thrown a grenade at him for a few minutes. The dangerous screen of jungle noises still jammed the jungle night. Were the damned little savages maneuvering into a better position out there? A cloud was dimming the moonlight now, and they would be taking advantage of it. There weren't many out there, maybe only two or three. But this one hole was the most prominent one of the whole line. They had spotted it during the day—maybe seen him get into it at five o'clock and now they were trying their damndest to get a grenade inside. Hill tensed up even more and the muscles of his eyes pulled trying to see what was down there in the shadows. . . .

He heard a scraping sound—very faint; the kind that any tree lizard could make with his belly—not especially different from a hundred such noises which he had heard in the past half hour during this nightmare he was living in—but it seemed to be connected with some kind of an unnatural change in one of the shadows. He looked carefully at the suspected spot, and detected nothing at first—not even a rapid lizard movement. Then he saw a round stone which seemed curious because it was smooth surfaced, not rough and mottled like the surface of coral. With his pulse turned into *two* trip hammers he kept looking carefully at that smooth round stone, with the merest amount of moonlight being reflected from it.

Then the stone moved. A little short raise upward, and then it settled back into place. Hill blinked his eyes and looked again, gripping his Tommy gun tighter. Once again the stone, which he could now make out as being only twenty-five feet from his foxhole, moved upward for about an inch and settled back down— only this time it rocked a little bit and the highlight of moonbeams danced the least little bit on its surface. Again it repeated the process.

Hill slowly inched his Tommy gun over, ready so that he could take aim and fire in a fraction of a second. For the hundredth time he re-examined the stone and the shadows around it—and he noticed at last that the stone *was wet*—glistening in the moonlight.

But it hadn't rained! And that moving up and down—that was breathing! And by God, that "stone" was a piece of equipment on some soldier's back or side—a messkit or something moving up and down with the swelling of his lungs. Again Hill fought down a wild hysterical impulse to raise and fire his whole fifty-shot drum at that rounded surface.

But he waited—and the procedure paid dividends. A little increase in the moonlight, coming with the passing of the cloud, permitted him to make out the outline of a Japanese soldier, practically under his nose. The "stone"—the "messkit"—had become a shiny leather holster, riding above the Jap's short ribs in the upper small of his back, as he lay quietly in place. The merest silhouette was all Hill could see, but the holster with moonlight on it, was a sure thing. He glanced down the white streak on his Tommy gun barrel and held a foot front of, and six inches below, the holster top; then he pressed the trigger and ran out twenty rounds, holding the gun down as best he could, while the successive flashes blotted the target and all around it from view.

Then he ducked low at once, to avoid the grenades he felt sure would come at him after he had exposed himself by firing such a long burst; but none came.

As he crouched there the jungle itself had become silent—his firing had quieted the birds and insects around him. But from twenty feet to his front was heard the unmistakable groaning, snore-like, horribly labored breathing of a man who had several big holes through his lungs each one obstructed with flowing blood—and who no longer has cause to remain quiet. And in a moment that sound died away.

No more grenades came over Hill's way that night. He had killed his only stalker; and at 10 o'clock the next morning I was looking over a beautifully finished little pistol, in a handsomely made leather holster with a bloody but uncut shoulder strap on it. I recognized the gun as a Nambu.

It was a nice little souvenir, and for Hill it was certainly a well earned one.

This first look didn't give me much of a picture of what the weapon was really like. While I was examining it three Jap 90mm mortar shells landed within the perimeter, not doing much more than to give a cheap purple heart to Lieutenant Conley, but they scared everyone a good bit. I did see that the weapon was a well finished little gun patterned roughly after the Luger in appearance, with the same slant to the grip and a similarly shaped trigger guard and magazine. It obviously was not at all like the Luger as far as functioning would be concerned, and it didn't seem to be the good all around pistol that the Luger was known to be. But I was greatly interested, none the less, and like Hill, I would have put up with the weight of it rather than to have thrown it away.

Later on, at Cape Esperance I was able to conduct a more leisurely examination of the weapon, and I am now referring to some of the notes made then as I do this writing. In that malarial but otherwise pleasant spot I had ample opportunity to examine all kinds of Japanese weapons—piles of them.

There were two types of Nambus which I saw on Guadalcanal, one with a groove in the butt to take a wooden shoulder stock-holster (a la Mauser and Luger), and one without any such adaptation which was used exclusively as a hand gun. I have never actually seen the shoulder-stock holster itself, only pictures of it in the manuals. On Guadalcanal, it was a pretty scarce item. Without it, however, the pistol remains a neat and well finished little weapon; the only difference in the two types being a cut in the lower rear butt of the model adapted for shoulder firing to engage a male fitting on the holster shoulder-stock. Both types of Nambu pistols—designed incidentally by the famous Lt. General Kijiro Nambu—were well finished guns, nice to handle and shoot.

The little weapon is very presentable. Coming as it does in a neat leather holster, trimly designed, which contains all things necessary for maintenance and care, the outfit would sell fast on the counter of any gun store in the U. S. A. A cleaning rod, two extra clips, and extra loose cartridges can all be carried in the holster—a compact and handy little bit of kit. Next to the sword, it was the preferred weapon for wear by the ranking Japanese officers. In battle, for actual use, it was of course preferred to the sword (and so were all other Japanese made pistols). Several Jap officers I saw were killed with their swords sheathed, but a pistol —often a Nambu—in their hand. It's not a bad looking gun.

The Nambu is nine inches in overall length, and because of the Luger-like protrusion of the rearward receiver, the greatest over-all length is measured straight from front to rear on the barrel and receiver assembly. The heel of the grip does not reach as far rearward as the very rear portion of the cocking piece, even in closed position. Vertically, the gun measures five and seven-eighths inches, the two extremes being the upper parts of the leaf rear sight and the aluminum butt of the magazine. With the magazine removed the measurement is five and one-quarter.

The barrel length, measured from the face of the bolt in closed position, is four and five-eighths inches, four and one-sixteenth of which protrudes from the receiver. The barrel is thin walled and tapered, lighter in weight than the Luger, and tapped in front with a permanent dovetailed base, into which a barleycorn front sight is driven.

The rear sight is of the variable slant leaf variety pivoting up-ward from the front, with the height of the rear end controlled by the position of a movable leaf slide base which rests on a ramp sloping rearward. The more forward the slide, the higher the rear sight notch. This notch is cut into the very rear end of the slanting leaf. The top of the variable slant leaf is graduated in increments of fifty meters with the even hundred lines on the right side, numbered from one to five with a line below each number; and the odd ranges of 150, 250, 350, and 450 meters indicated by plain lines on the left side of the leaf without stamped numerals. A very

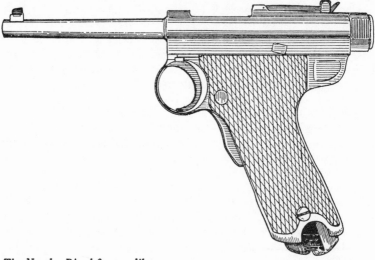

The Nambu Pistol 8mm caliber.

simple arrangement, probably patterned after German ideas, in accordance with the sight graduations. Adjustment is obtained by positioning the sliding base.

The trigger guard was circular in appearance and, of course, a part of the receiver, looking much the same as that of the Luger. The trigger itself was broad and very sharply curved, leaving too little space forward of it within the guard to permit a gloved finger to safely rest—in fact, there was hardly room for a large Caucasian finger to enter it—even without glove.

Right below the trigger guard a grip safety had been inletted into the guard and forward strap, so that it could be squeezed inward by the second and third fingers. When so squeezed it pivoted from the top against the action of its spring and lowered a stud which was otherwise engaged at rest with the bottom of the trigger, locking same against rearward (firing) movement. There were strong reasons why this safety would not be fool proof; in the first place its only engagement was with the trigger—it did not act directly against the final firing mechanism; secondly, because of its forward position, it would nearly always be depressed by the firer's first casual grasp of the weapon, so that the first fumbling reach of finger inside the trigger guard would likely find the weapon ready to fire. The upper-rear position of grip safety, which is used in the case of the Colt (and for a few American Export Lugers), is much better, because it is not normally depressed except by the final hand grip which the firer employs when advertently aiming.

On the lower rear of the receiver, just below the cocking piece assembly, there is a lanyard loop which would be convenient for mounted troops to use.

By far the most unique point of appearance in the Nambu pistol is its peculiarly positioned recoil spring housing, which is located along the full length of the receiver's left side. When viewed from the top it gives the pistol a lopsided appearance— creating an impression that the barrel emerges from the receiver in an offcenter position.

The conventional magazine catch is used on the Nambu, with the push button release located immediately to the rear of the guard in approximately the same position as that of the Government 45.

Field disassembly of the Nambu, as with all good automatic pistols, is simple. The only tool required is a screwdriver or a substitute which will fit the grip screws. (These screw slots are too narrow to permit the use of a cartridge rim—an obvious fault of design.) To completely disassemble the weapon a single small drift and hammer would be needed, and the operation would require only a few more moments time. Only four pins and rivets would need to be removed from the magazine and trigger group.

The first step of disassembly is the removal of the Luger type magazine, which is made fairly long in order to hold eight of the special bottlenecked 8mm cartridges. This removal is commenced by depressing the magazine catch and withdrawing the magazine body from the grip.

Next the knurled rear protrusion of the cocking piece, which can properly be referred to as the firing pin spring base, is pressed inward with the thumb and turned gradually counter clockwise for ninety degrees. This will disengage its two holding lugs from their hold against a rear shoulder inside the cocking piece. Then the firing pin spring guide can be removed with the firing pin spring hanging onto its forward end. Next, the cocking piece itself is removed, by pulling it to the rear against the tension of the recoil spring and unscrewing it from the threaded rearend of the recoil spring guide. Then the recoil spring guide can be removed from the front (unless it has already "removed" itself by flying out when the recoil spring guide came free from the cocking piece).

Then the firing pin assembly (and spring too, if it did not come out with its guide) can be removed by squeezing the trigger and safety together and shaking the weapon with the muzzle elevated so the parts can fall out from the rear. The magazine catch is removed by means of its left side (magazine catch lock) which is depressed and rotated 90 degrees counter clockwise and then released outward. This permits the catch proper to be easily jockeyed out with a finger tip.

The left grip is next taken off, by means of the exposed left grip screw. Then by pushing the barrel about one-eighth of an inch to the rear, the trigger and safety group become free to move downward in the groove in the forward strap. If it is stuck with gummed oil—as often seems to be the case—some little pressure or a slight jarring of the butt against a wood surface might be required. On some Nambus the trigger group will merely fall down about three-quarters of an inch, remaining engaged in the grooves in the forward strap; in other models it can be removed completely by pulling outward on the safety and sliding it down further. With a drift and hammer, though, either model can be ordnance disassembled in a few minutes by removing the trigger and safety pins.

With the trigger and safety group in the low position or removed entirely, the barrel, barrel extension, bolt and bolt lock can be withdrawn to the front from the receiver and their components then disassembled from each other with ease. A pointed instrument (or a small finger) can afterward be inserted into the receiver to pull the bolt lock spring out of its position in the upper rear corner of the magazine housing.

The rather long and complicated sear and sear lever, which fits beneath the recoil spring housing, is removed by means of the knurl-headed sear pin which is turned by thumb pressure to unlock position and then withdrawn by the fingernails, thereby freeing the sear and sear lever along with the sear spring, sear lever extending plunger, and sear lever extending plunger spring, (all in one unit).

That would complete the field stripping; and, for all practical purposes this breakdown is fine enough. It would serve the purposes of field repair and parts replacement adequately. And, as previously stated, further complete ordnance disassembly would also be simple.

In operating the weapon, the general instructions for automatic pistols would hold. The magazine is loaded like the Luger, and a thumb piece is provided to permit the magazine follower to be depressed as the cartridges are inserted, which makes the task of clip loading much easier. The magazine is inserted—pressed into final position—the same way as that of the Colt 45. The first round is loaded by drawing the cocking piece to rearmost position and releasing it, whereupon the bolt goes forward, ramping the first cartridge into the chamber. The weapon then stands cocked and ready to fire.

When the safety is squeezed it frees the trigger. Firing pressure on the trigger transmits itself to free the firing pin from rearward hold through the following force-train: it (the trigger) pivots on the trigger pin, causing an integral extension to press upward against the forward end of the sear lever assembly; this causes the rear end of the sear lever to move downward as the entire lever pivots on the sear pin, thereby disengaging the rear sear projection from its small and rather precarious engagement with the tiny firing pin shoulder, located on the extreme rear of the firing pin body. This frees the firing pin and it goes forward by action of the not overlystrong firing pin spring. Semi-automatic fire is assured by the sear lever extension plunger, located forward on the sear lever (as part of its actual length), which permits the sear lever to be compressed to shorter overall length during recoil, thereby disengaging the forward contact with the trigger and avoiding full automatic operation. This contact is reassumed automatically when the trigger is released.

This entire ignition system is rather haywire of design, having many of the faults of the Luger, with a few more of its own thrown in for good measure. Springs are not strong enough, sear engagement surface is not great enough and the whole works makes for a springy and cushioned trigger letoff, which nearly all American shooters would despise.

In operation, the weapon does not compare with the Colt 45 in functioning reliability, or, as far as I am concerned in accuracy. (Which latter comparison constitutes a crowning insult.) It is more sensitive to grit and dirt, and its maintenance is more of a problem than that of our own handgun.

Its chief advantages are not military ones at all. They are neat in appearance, nice "feel," good finish and fit, all of which make it an attractive and desirable souvenir. The leather holster furnished with it also adds much to its eye-appeal.

(Just think of what might have happened to Sgt. Russel Hill if it hadn't been for that "eye appeal"!)

As a souvenir or a collection piece it's nice to have. Even its little bottlenecked cartridges—with the crimp secured by three little punch marks—look very pretty. For military use, though, I wouldn't give it hell room either.

THE "BABY NAMBU"

My impression that the Nambu 8mm pistol was the best hand-gun which the Japanese had to offer our souvenir hunters held until after the Cape Esperance venture was well under way. By the time we were relieved at Hill 27 there were several such pistols in the hands of members of the battalion and I had had ample opportunity to look them over. Smooth-finished and trim in appearance they seemed the nicest of all items of enemy equipment we had seen. Every man in the outfit wanted one for himself and there were always great expressions of disappointment each time a soldier opened up a leather or rubberized canvas holster lying in one of the battlefield areas and found it to contain a Model 94—rough-finished and loose fit.

But when we got to Cape Esperance proper (on the day we were shelled by our own Navy) I saw the neatest souvenir of all. It was the Japanese 7mm Nambu—usually spoken of as the "Baby Nambu." A sergeant of Company "H" found the first one any of us had seen, on a Jap he killed that morning.

We had started moving down the beach trail in pursuit of the defeated Japs, the assault echelon driving straight ahead with no flank security whatsoever. Colonel Gavin had told us to trot down the trail as fast as we could and not to worry about our right flank which faced the jungle and hills. We naturally had no worries over our left, which, from our feet to the ocean, was no more than a thin band of coconut trees, seldom wider than twenty yards. We slowed down only once when Danny Prewitt was halted for a few moments during the early morning on that trail but soon he got through with a little shooting and on we went.

| Near the rear of the column the men had more time to look around to right and left, checking their flanks for safety's sake. The sergeant was doing that very thing when he came upon the Jap with the Baby Nambu pistol. This Jap had huddled behind a tree not more than fifteen feet from the trail, concealing himself in the low undergrowth.

All that the sergeant could see of the Jap was his peaked cap sticking above the weeds, but it was enough to allow him to aim his Tommy gun and let fly a few rounds—which took good care of things.

The sergeant had assumed that the Jap had just moved into his position at the side of the trail a few seconds before he had been detected, but an examination of the Jap's weapon—a neat little pistol of a type which was instantly recognizable as a smaller version of the Nambu—proved otherwise. The pistol had been in the Jap's hand at the time he was killed, *and the eight cartridges which were found on the person of the Jap, in the pistol, and on the ground near the tree, were each dented deeply in the primer by several blows of the firing pin.*

This Jap had taken up a "sniper's" position on the trail, sitting there and ineffectually snapping his weapon while the whole front of the column had gone by. All of the cartridges had been loaded into the chamber several times—their cases were badly scored and their rims were nicked by the ejector. Undoubtedly the sniper had aimed at everyone in the column who looked like an officer and snapped away bravely, but his ammunition had let him down. The cartridges had been handled in such a way as to remind me of those in the revolver of an old Chicago police friend of mine. They had evidently been left in a weapon which had been drenched with thin machine oil and the primers had been completely deadened by oil penetration. That the fault did not lie with the weapon was attested by good, deep firing pin impressions.

I never did get the story of whether or not the Japanese were generally ignorant of the effect of oil on small arms ammunition, but I have since come across several other instances which would tend to prove that they were. But whether ignorance or a shortage of good ammunition was responsible, it is almost a certainty that the deficiency saved someone's life. At a maximum of twenty feet it would be difficult for a Jap to miss a standing man.

The body of this Jap yielded other things of importance—a good battle flag, a diary, a photo album, and twenty perfectly good American dollars. I looked them all over that evening, in the comfortable and secure surroundings of our camp at the mouth of the Tanamboga River, where we soon effected a junction with the main forces pushing south, thereby terminating organized resistance on Guadalcanal. We had bedded down for the night and I had bathed in the fresh water of the river while we still had a little bit of daylight left. I sat on my poncho and tinkered with the little gun until it became dark and the land crabs began to seethe all through the sand floor of the grove, making it difficult indeed to get badly needed rest.

I liked this little weapon at first glance; it was hardly more than a handful for a big man yet it retained the lines of the Luger, lacking the boxlike appearance of the small American automatic pistols. Mechanically it was only a smaller version of the Nambu, having all of the Nambu's faults—especially did it have the fault of a small trigger guard which did not allow enough room for a large finger to rest with any degree of safety.

In overall length it was much shorter than the Nambu, taking up only six and three-quarters inches in extreme measurement along the barrel and receiver groups. It had a barleycorn front

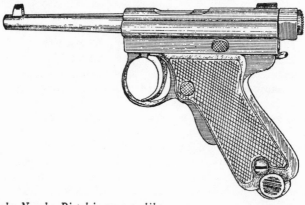

The Baby Nambu Pistol in 7mm caliber.

sight, the same as the Nambu, but the rear sight was different, being of the plain "V" type notch with no adjustment. It weighed less than one and one-half pounds and had a barrel length of about three and one-eighth inches.

Six rounds were all that could be crammed into the magazine of the little weapon and the ammunition, as in the case of the weapon itself, was a similar appearing cartridge, made smaller than the 8mm stuff used in the Nambu.

Ordnance friends have since told me that the cartridge gives a muzzle velocity of some 950 foot seconds, and that it has considerable penetrating power. Regrettably, the first weapon of this sort that I saw was the only one which I was ever permitted to examine at close range, and I was never able to shoot it because we never found good ammunition. It would have been fun to plink around Tanamboga at lizards and coconuts with that little gun.

Before we moved out of our beach camp we were visited by a group of souvenir-hunting officers from the Navy, and rumor had it that the sergeant sold the little gun, complete with its natty little belt holster, for $200. According to the story, he didn't really

want the $200—he had merely asked for two bottles of whiskey
or $200. The Navy chap apparently felt that he could do better
elsewhere with the booze, because he shelled out the $200 and let
the sergeant go thirsty.

THE TYPE 94, OR MODEL 1934 PISTOL

It is difficult to believe that the Baby Nambu and the better
finished regular Nambus could have been turned out by the same
people who later on manufactured so much junk. In 1934 the
Japanese brought forth a handgun to disgrace their crudest black-
smith. They called this pistol the Type 94, and wisely issued it to

The M1934 or Type 94 Pistol.

people who did not have great use for a weapon, such as pilots and
crew members of aircraft. Some few of them got into the hands of
Infantrymen later on; I saw a few in Burma in 1944–5.

The weapon was of awkward appearance, with a profile made
ugly by a thick breech and a small, outwardly tapered grip. The
guns I saw were very roughly finished, with deep tool marks showing on all surfaces, inside and out. I would not have fired one of
them for a price—some of the parts appeared to have been cast
from pot-metal. Elements of the trigger mechanism projected from
the left hand side of the receiver so that a blow against the receiver
wall could cause accidental discharge.

The magazine held six rounds, and it took the standard Japanese
8mm pistol cartridge. The sights were of crude fixed type, seldom
having more than a very rough degree of relationship to the axis
of the bore. Some of my braver friends who fired the monstrosity
told me that it would not hit the side of a barn.

For anyone who might doubt the inability of the Japanese to turn out both good and bad guns, a look at the Baby Nambu and the M–1934 alongside each other is more than enough. One has the polished smoothness of a first class handgun; the other looked like a second rate pipe wrench. Most of the doughboys who recovered M–1934 pistols were bright enough to barter them with some of the souvenir-hungry visitors. A lot of M–1934 pistols have gotten back to this country where, I hope, they will serve as horrible examples of what a handgun should never be.

The Baby Nambu—as far as workmanship is concerned—can continue to serve as a model for our best gunmakers.

THE NAMBU LIGHTS

In the tangled jungle surrounding Hill 27 and Hill 31, the Japanese had made good use of their engineer tools. They had dug and hacked extensively all along the forward slope of Hill 31, probably wearing out the blades of many brush knives and dulling many axe blades on the soft but resistant wood of tropical broad-leaf trees and tangled vines which were sometimes two feet thick.

They had burrowed under and around the roots of forest giants in a manner that would have done credit to a New England wood-chuck. Sharp-edged entrenching shovels, far better than those used by the Americans swarming on the beaches five miles away, had been plied day after day, night after night, providing for the comfort and security of an old and traditional type reception com-mittee, which would wait attentively for the arrival of the first wave of green clad, light skinned, blond haired visitors.

These reception committee shelters were sighted with care so that there would be little or no chance of any visitor approaching unseen or unheard. The visitors would have to make their way through particularly inhospitable stretches of foliage before they approached their "hosts," clawing often at plant stems and turn-ing now and then to remove the sticky, holding whip of a wait-a-minute vine from the cloth of a jacket or the flesh of a cheek or hand. The last few steps toward the waiting hosts would be in clearer, more open, spots in the jungle—not completely clear, but open as though these spots of ground had perhaps offered less appeal to roots of jungle weeds than had the surrounding area. And the first guests these hosts would receive in time-honored style would, at the moment of reception, be breathing thanks for a few feet of clear space in front of them.

But while the hosts were taking every step to prevent the guests from arriving unseen or unannounced, it was none the less their desire that the reception was to be in the nature of a surprise party. Along with the committee housing project there was also heavy effort under way to prevent the excavations from becoming an eyesore and smearing the pretty green landscape with unsightly mounds of yellow clay, framing the entrances to the committee chambers in a highly unartistic way—all out of keeping with the natural tropical garden atmosphere.

So, while some of the hosts dug with shovels and picks, others were busy with baskets woven from vines in which they carried away load after load of yellow dirt to a hidden place to the rear of the line of diggings. There the dirt was scattered around the roots of heavy brush where it would not change the garden picture of the "back yards," or else it was thrown into a little stream where it was washed away, yellowing the clean spring water. So thorough was this operation that scarcely one clod of yellow dirt was left to mar the perfect scene of green and dark shadow which surrounded the picturesque area.

After the rough line of shelters was finished, the sturdy, well muscled little builders got to work industriously upon a series of connecting tunnels, just large enough for the small and wiry bodies of the hosts to move through with comfort. These were artistically done, with the little bites of the shovels showing on their inside walls like adze marks on hewn logs. Roots were sharply and cleanly cut, cross-sections showing and oozing sap, mostly milk white and latex-bearing. And after the tunnels had been dug —a regular network of them to connect all of the individual larger shelters with each other—another project was begun. The chambers were enlarged and made more comfortable, and their roofs were built up solidly against the elements, with layer after layer of logs and pounded earth, which was now needed in such quantity at the building site that there was no need to carry it away. But the unsightly yellow of it was still not allowed to show. It was carefully covered over with sod, carefully matched to the local landscape. The hosts were still much concerned about the outside appearance of their dwellings.

Each of the chambers had a small window, left open permanently, facing to the front. This was to serve the combined purposes of ventilator and living room window, permitting the host to breathe comfortably, see his front yard, and greet his guests. And the chambers were as near stormproof as structures could be. Any one of them would have made an absolutely safe hurricane shelter. The areas in front of the windows were sodded over carefully so that no dry leaves or other substance could be blown up into the chamber by a sudden gust of wind, and then the square outline of the window was artistically broken up by the bending and sometimes actual transplanting of pretty leaved plants, making the whole dome of the chamber-structure blend perfectly into the shadowy undergrowth.

Remaining improvements were in the way of gouging little shelves along the chamber walls. These would contain bits of bric-a-brac to be presented to the visitors!

When they began to build these shelves the hosts were able to sigh with relief and know that they had finished their greater preparations before the visitors arrived. It is always embarrassing for visitors to arrive before one is ready to receive! The small finishing touches were still being completed when the visitors finally got there.

It happened on a bright morning in December, and there was really no need to look carefully for the visitors, for they proclaimed their coming five hours in advance with a vast and imposing display of fireworks. There were repeated blinding flashes and deafening sounds all around the hosts' chambers through the last darkness and early dawn. The hosts waited and gave no reply because they still wanted it to be a surprise party.

Soon after dawn the fireworks let up and there was silence. Each host stood ready in place for the greeting ceremony. Naturally there were various grades of hosts. There were little hosts who waited in smaller chambers with small gifts to give the visitors, and there were large hosts who waited in larger chambers, prepared to give gifts in much larger quantities. These larger hosts were the most important, and the whole scheme of the reception had been planned with great consideration for the part they were to play in the ceremony.

The smaller hosts were situated in smaller chambers with smaller front yards, and in locations where they would be less likely to receive large numbers of visitors. They were not so well supplied with gifts, and they lacked the means to distribute the presents as fast as their more important colleagues. Their chief concern was not so much the distribution of gifts as it was the saving of the larger hosts from embarrassment if several visitors were to arrive at the rear entrance. In such cases, they had been told to greet the visitors themselves so that the larger hosts could devote their attention to visitors approaching the front doors.

Despite all of these beautiful preparations, the reception on Hill 31 was not too much of a surprise. A large group of visitors were proceeding through the undergrowth. When their leader saw the front yards of the reception committee shelters, he halted the main body of guests and went forward to look. He passed through the front yard of one of the lesser greeters, who either did not see him or else left him to be greeted by one of the larger hosts. After all, the whole ceremony had been planned around the larger hosts since they were the ones who were really prepared to greet guests.

A dark-haired little man, whose brown skin had gone white

from continued life underground and in jungle shadows, finally saw the first visitor through his small window. The visitor had walked to the edge of the host's little front yard and hesitated for a moment, then he had walked into the center and looked back toward the rest of the guests, ready to call them forward, or perhaps ready to tell them to wait—it will never be known which. The host became over-anxious, perhaps fearing that the other guests would be lost to his hospitality, perhaps not knowing of their presence. Anyway, he put his whole heart and soul into the matter of greeting this one guest before him, throwing a full twenty gifts his way.

A young officer, nameless here, was the greeted one. Trained in the States, gifted with little knowledge of the wilds—certainly none of junglecraft—he had none-the-less sensed danger and saved the lives of his command. His own fate was of a quick sort, by no means the type of death a soldier prays for, for most of us would prefer to die with enemy blood on our hands, but there was no suffering for him—not more than a few seconds.

A Japanese automatic weapon, one of several models which were to earn our unqualified respect through the Islands and in Burma, had been sighted at the calves of his legs at a range of less than thirty feet.

The first few rounds of the clip, ripping out at the cyclic rate of 500 per minute, had made jelly out of his legs and swept them from under him, causing his body to fall into the stream of fire still sizzling past. The last few rounds of the clip were clustered in one area, raking his heart and lung cavity from upper left shoulder to lower right ribs.

The gun that killed him was a Nambu Light, always the base weapon of the Japanese fire plan in defense, the deadly automatic gun which some of us believe killed more men than all other Japanese weapons combined—an efficient, well-designed, and practical weapon. Had it not been for the gunner's impatience, or had this platoon leader been less alert, it might have killed a dozen men instead, as was the case in many later instances.

This incident was the first experience of that particular American unit with the Nambu Light, but it was by no means the first contact known with it on the Island. The Marines had developed a healthy respect for it in the very first battles they had had on Tulagi and Guadalcanal. The first Army troops who saw action on the Island had seen it employed first in the attack, fired from the assault position with great carelessness, spraying bullets wildly. But later they had encountered this weapon as we encountered it—in the defense—and it had proved to be as dangerous and consistently fatal as any of them had dreamed. And its most dangerous role was in this sort of defense—holding ground in the jungle.

The Japanese seemed to lack imagination when they were moving into us. They attacked with matchless savagery and courage, but the effort always seemed to lack the important element of common sense—which has a more important place in Infantry tactics and weapons employment than any place else I know. The fire of Japanese attack forces was usually frontal, giving away the direction and positions of the attackers. At the same time, it was greatly limited in accuracy because it was "assault fire"—fire delivered by men who were moving forward, firing a shot or burst now and then from the standing or kneeling position.

Perhaps it would have been excusable for the Japanese to follow the Banzai attack procedure with the riflemen only, allowing the automatic weapons to provide a covering fire. This fire could be from a position selected as a "base of fire"—off to the side, or on higher ground. But the Japs didn't even do that much. They usually went whole hog for the advancing elements. The result was that no one was shooting during the very moments which logically required the greatest volume of fire to be delivered. With the entire attacking force in on a big bayonet rush, there was usually a lull—if not a complete break—in the delivery of accurate fire.

The adverse effect of such poor use of firepower is too obvious to even describe. The members of such an attacking force would move into a deadly hail of fire delivered by men who were not forced to keep their heads down. They could crane their necks about and carefully aim at oncoming cold turkey targets—Japanese soldiers at point blank range. In such cases the slaughter was unbelievable, even if the attack was delivered during bad conditions of visibility or at night. And I have personally been involved in enough of these affairs to know that they occurred frequently. If the defenders had enough ammunition and kept their heads, these attacks always ended by being terrible fiascos for the Japanese. And they received a name, often repeated by a million doughboys and Marines, which became familiar to everyone throughout the Island—the "Banzai" charge.

The Jap high command itself, at least in the beginning of the war, continued to think that they really had something in that Banzai charge, for they whooped it up in all of their books on tactics. They maintained that the attack was the only honorable form of fighting, and that a good, aggressive commander need never rely upon defensive tactics; and they greatly neglected defense in their training publications, at least through the early Pacific war. However, they conceded in some of their later publications that Japanese soldiers were not especially skilled in defensive warfare—that perhaps there were European armies that knew more about it and were better fitted for it. Japanese Infantry was strongest, they said, in offensive fighting. The attack —especially the night attack—was, by their own appraisal, a specialty of Japanese Infantry.

Actually, this conception was one hundred percent wrong. Japanese Infantry was clownish and stupid beyond belief in the attack—the phase of war which involves fire, movement, and which demands the taking of ground from a defending force. But in the defense, entrenched or in the cover of the jungle, the Japanese were *absolute past-masters, far more capable than they imagined themselves to be.* Their rugged physical condition and peasant background made them skillful and untiring at digging, and their unlimited tenacity and guts permitted them to hold bravely in the face of superior numbers.

Some of the Infantry training manuals of all Armies carry a hackneyed paragraph or two which says outrightly or infers: ". . . in the defense, unless ordered otherwise, our forces will always hold and fight to the last man. . . ." The Italians made a joke of that sentence; in many cases the Germans did too; we certainly did. Only scattered American units can claim that they fought to the last man, except in the later days of the Pacific War, after we had learned that surrender to the Japanese was useless.

But the Japanese I have been up against, with negligible individual exceptions, carried out that pledge to the letter. How often did we hear the familiar communique, "Blank Island was taken today, the Japanese garrison of fifteen thousand having been destroyed. Eighty prisoners were taken. . . ."

Eighty out of fifteen thousand! Figure it out. . . .

The Japanese Infantrymen and fighter and kamikaze pilots were, as a class, the bravest men who fought in this last war. Rationalizing individuals have called it fanaticism and ignorance instead of bravery, and have sold a lot of people upon the story that Japanese Infantrymen would have surrendered freely if they had known they would not be tortured after capture. For my part, I don't care what is said about the Japanese. They have a lot of moral and spiritual defects, the greatest of which would seem to be a sort of malignant racial inferiority complex. But most of us who have fought in the Pacific are ready to admit here and now, away from all the convincing first hand evidence we have seen—mass starvation, untold suffering, shell shock, cannibalism, mass suicide—that for sheer, bloody, hardened-steel guts, the stocky and hard muscled little Jap doughboy has it all over any of us.

And I admire him for it. He fits—far better than the Sudanese for whom the lines were written—the familiar words of Kipling's tribute to good soldiers in Africa, part of which are perfectly apropros to his combat behavior:

> "'e rushes at the smoke when we let drive,
> An' before we know 'es 'ackin' at our 'ead;
> 'es all hot sand and ginger when alive,
> An' 'es generally shammin' when 'es dead." . . .

Our rifles don't "smoke" much now, and it didn't do him much good to rush as "we let drive," but he did it all the same! To do everything the Japs did in this war, American Infantrymen would be required to be a lot more stupid and foolhardy than they were, but generally speaking, they would also have to be far, far more brave.

It is beginning to seem (even from my viewpoint) that I have been driving at the subject of this writing in a very round-about way—after all, this chapter was to deal with Nambu Light machine guns. The point I have been trying to make, though, is that the Japanese were the most skilled fighters in the world as far as the Infantry aspects of sacrificial defense in jungle country are concerned. There are no other soldiers who would give them a run for their money in that type of fighting.

Their excellence in that field was only part guts. A lot of it was due to their remarkable entrenching ability. The way they could build pillboxes and covered foxholes and organize them into clever, mutually-supporting positions is perhaps their greatest defense asset. And their skill at camouflage was part of this remarkable entrenching skill.

Once Japs complete their diggings, there are no ready ways for an enemy force to outflank or to move in from the front. And there are few types of artillery projectile which will have worthwhile effect upon such positions in heavy jungle, even if the shells are lobbed over in terrific quantity. Only the heaviest delayed-action shells, penetrating directly into the shelters and exploding inside, can be relied upon to do sure damage. And by digging shelters behind and under huge jungle trees to be occupied during barrages, the Japs have shown themselves able to evade even that one point of vulnerability.

In the long run, the only thing that can be done against a prepared Japanese jungle defense is for the Infantry to move in with maximum artillery preparation (not concurrent support, which is not often possible in heavy jungle) and take the bull by the horns, going at the pillboxes with grenade, pole charge, and flame thrower —potting heads with rifles and carbines as they show above the ground—doing the best that can be done in the most hair-raising situation that war can furnish.

Such fighting is the old problem of storming a defense which has proved itself to be impregnable to attack by fire alone. And it *is* a tribute to the men and the plan of any defense to say that it is "characteristically impregnable" to mere weapons attack. Japanese jungle defensive diggings were generally entitled to that classification. On many occasions they remained virtually unaffected by fire—artillery and mortar—for great lengths of siege.

They achieved that impregnability through intelligent use of their weapons, more than by any other means, and by selecting certain guns as the key units to spot at certain points along the line. After selecting these key points and emplacing automatic weapons there, they built up other weapons around, to attain a mantight fire plan. This last requirement demanded that each enemy must be forced to walk visibly through the fire lane of at least one weapon (usually three or more) before he could get into close quarters with any of the defenders.

So the fire lanes of the Japanese key weapons were usually sighted to crisscross at an angle of ninety degrees or more, and they were usually established along a rough line, staggered irregularly according to the terrain-lay. The less important weapons were distributed in such a manner as to support and protect the key weapons.

The key weapons in any Japanese plan of jungle defense were invariably automatics—light and heavy machine guns—*and the lights always predominated.*

There were always plenty of Nambu Light machine guns, one or more to every Jap squad. They were at least as thick—in the Japanese units I have seen—as Browning Auto Rifles were in our own platoons and companies. And there is not the slightest question in my mind that they killed more of us on Guadalcanal than any other weapon—perhaps more than all others put together.

Normally, when we encountered these guns in defensive positions, we would find them inside pillboxes which were logged and earthedin overhead and thick on the sides, with only a small firing port in front. Sometimes these ports were as much as two or two and a half feet wide, permitting considerable traverse, but that was rare. Most of the time the port was little wider than it was high—no more than twelve inches at the most—in which case the gun would have no traverse at all, being able to fire only straight ahead. Always the machine gun pillbox dome was carefully camouflaged, and the front of the site was sodded or dampened to prevent giveaway muzzle blast, stirring dirt or leaves when the gun opened up.

When the fixed gun position was used, the direction of fire was always carefully sighted along or across some natural approach, with every possibility of outflanking routes and defiladed approaches well considered. Then the flanks and front were carefully spotted with covered riflemen's pits, indistinguishable from the larger pillboxes in outward appearance. The adjacent trees and high ground points were usually manned, at least in the early phase of a fight, by riflemen spotters. To a certain extent, this made up for the greatest fault of the Japanese roofed entrenchments, their extreme blindness. This blindness was further made up for by the interlaced and mutually protecting lanes of fire, which would work effectively against enemy infiltrators.

The problems which faced our Infantry platoons assaulting such positions were vast. First the pillboxes had to be located and distinguished from dummies, which were frequently present in annoying quantity. Then they had to be approached from a route outside their fire lanes. More often than not, both of these tasks were utter impossibilities and the ground had to be gained by blind assault, which would depend upon good luck, good, fast shooting, and the intelligent application of pole charges and flame throwers.

In such an attack, or even in an attack where the boxes had been carefully located by a skilled platoon leader, there were many, many ways for a man to become a casualty. He could be picked off by a rifleman, struck by a grenade fragment, or be blasted by an electrically detonated charge planted in front of the shelter which the Japs could operate from within the pillbox. More likely than all of these, however, he could be shot with a machine gun.

Ranges in true jungle country are always short, seldom over a hundred yards, with the average being nearer twenty-five yards. In the jungle assault, the ranges are at bayonet distance in many cases, with thirty yards being the extreme if cover is of average density. You don't even look for targets farther away than that. Should a man be shot with a rifle at such range—especially the highly humane and clean-killing ball 6.5—he will stand a chance of living through it. Usually though, he will be shot through the body or face, for the ranges are conducive to center holds, even for the flinching and trigger-jerking Japanese. If he is hit with only a few grenade fragments, his chances will be even better. Japanese grenades were unusual performers in the manner of noise, but they didn't seem nearly as effective away from the immediate blasts as our own. A mine explosion will usually either knock a man cold or kill him, depending on how far he is from the center of its explosion.

But with a machine gun, especially the high cyclic rate light machine guns, a man hit at such close range is a dead cookie forty-nine times out of fifty. Always sighted to shoot low, such weapons will hit a crawling man in the helmet or the body, and a standing man in the legs, in which case they usually get him in the body when he falls. The Japs normally didn't open up until the enemy was well in the sights, probably feeling that there was little point in giving away their location for a mere leg or arm shot. Most often they got a big piece of you.

Model 1936 or Type 96 Light Machine Gun. 6.5mm caliber.

One reason a machine gun nearly always kills outright or wounds fatally is because of its rate of fire—the fact that a man is never hit with a single bullet at that range, but rather by a cluster of them, coming so rapidly that they might have as well been fired simultaneously from a multi-barrelled weapon. The average number of such hits is usually around four or five—that many going in before the stricken man writhes or falls out of the way.

That number is enough. If they strike a man in the body, they kill him. If they strike him in the bones of the arms or legs, they lacerate terribly and give fatal shock effect or else they bleed a man to death through a leg or arm artery. It doesn't take long for a man to pump out the critical two and a half quarts through the half-inch tube of a leg artery that squirts like a half-open water faucet; and it's quite a chore to stanch such bleeding with tools on hand while the shooting goes on. It takes a good aid man, and he has to *be there!*

That terrible thought often chills the mind of the soldier in the period of waiting before he goes into an attack against Japanese jungle defenses. This terror is born of the memory of horrible sights which he has seen before—visions of splintered, jagged ends of bone, with bloody flesh and marrow; of gaping wounds with intestinal juices and bits of semi-digested food gurgling out of a man who is still alive and feeling it all. . . .

"And if it wasn't for *those Goddamn Nambu Lights*, there wouldn't be half as many. . . ."

Those light machine guns (more properly called machine rifles) were good weapons, either the hopper fed M–11 (1922) or the clip fed, Bren-profiled M–96 (1936) job. They had many points of superiority over our equivalent weapon, which continued to be the BAR throughout the entire war. Most of these points arose from the fact that the BAR was a weapon which had been adapted to do a machine rifle job, while both of the Nambus were designed for machine rifle purposes in the first place. I have shot both weapons rather extensively, and I am sure of myself when I say that I would rather be armed with a M–1936 Nambu than with any of our BAR types. I believe it to be a better gun, though slightly less reliable in function. And if I had had an equal amount of experience with the older M–1922, hopper feed and all, I might even prefer it to the BAR as a machine rifle.

The Browning Auto Rifle, stripped of all of its machine rifle adaptations, has a role of its own in jungle warfare that is entirely different from the ordinary mission of the machine rifle. In that capacity, the Browning is a good gun, and I would not put any other brush-sprayer we have in the more vital section of a moving column on a jungle trail. Criticism here is directed against the weapon as a machine rifle, not as an assault weapon to be fired during movement. For that type of work, the Nambu would be no better.

Our own respect for the Nambus was apparently shared by the Japs, for there were firm indications that when they had had to discard weapons because of casualties or sickness, they would nearly always throw away other guns and keep their light machine guns. That procedure was often carried on to a point where every Jap along a given line would be armed with one of those damn weapons—a situation not to be desired by the opposing unit, especially if the Japs were on the defensive in the jungle and the opposing unit was ordered to root them out.

We saw both of the older 6.5mm Nambus, the M–11 (1922) (which is often not considered to be one of the true "Nambu Lights") and the M–96 (1936), and we also saw the newer 7.7mm M–99 (1939) during the Guadalcanal show. All three models were found by our battalion and the tendency was for the weapons in a given area to be of the same type. The M–1936 was seen most often and the hopper-fed M–1922 was the most scarce of the three, as far as I was able to tell.

Of the three types, the M–1936 was most preferred by the Japanese, as evidenced by their leaving the other models behind after heavy fighting had lessened the number of operators, and hanging onto their later-designed 6.5mm weapon. This measure may have been forced by a shortage of 7.7mm ammunition, but more than likely it was an unqualified preference on the part of the troops. Anyway, we used to now and then run across discarded M–1922s and M–1939s as we moved forward through contested areas. Sometimes these weapons had been properly ruined by disassembly and scattering the parts, or by smashing the operating mechanism, but just as often, they were found whole and in perfect shape. The Japanese were always rather slipshod in the destruction of equipment left behind in the areas where I have had contact with them. In the final phase of the Guadalcanal fight, they seemed to discard all caution in that matter and nearly all of the weapons we found at Cape Esperance were in workable shape.

In that area, I had ample opportunity to give time to the study and testing of many Japanese guns. And because I rated the Nambu Lights as the most effective weapon the Japs had used against us, I lost no time in picking several of them up and looking them over. The first one I concerned myself with was the M–1936.

The M–1936 had had my sincere respect from the start. I had seen what it and the other Jap lights could do to us when we tried to move into its territory, and my first noncombatant contact with that neat little job was somewhat in the nature of the first personal meeting of two friends who had known each other for years through correspondence only. And like many such unions, this bit of personal contact served to greatly increase my respect for my old friend, confirming the good opinion I already had.

On first picking the weapon up, one is inclined to like it. It has a good "feel"—that indescribable something that our bipod-and-buttrest-fitted Browning Auto Rifle lacked completely. You could grasp the gun by its handle and run with it much better than with the BAR; it fitted to the shoulder in a much more comfortable hold than the BAR afforded; and it handled and fired better, in spite of the poorer quality of the Japanese ammunition.

The M–1936 was gas-operated, of course, and could be fired full automatic only. It was not great in length, measuring 42 inches overall on the average, with individual models varying more than an inch in extreme measurement because of variations in the length of the upper buttplate portion, which was curved back to retain the butt on the shoulder during firing.

The total weight of the weapon was 20 pounds, unloaded and with the carrying strap attached. The barrel was 21¾ inches long, apparently kept short on account of the long length of the receiver, which stretched out for some thirteen inches or so to house a bolt which travelled rather far for a shoulder fired weapon. A replacement barrel was nearly always carried along with the weapon (by one of the riflemen of the same squad) for alternating to prevent overheating during periods of sustained firing. This barrel, complete with front sight, gas port cup, and permanently attached carrying handle, weighed five and a half pounds.

The sights were offset an inch from the center of the barrel, and were of conventional Japanese pattern—the front one being a barleycorn type, properly enlarged and protected by a very heavy and strong set of side guards. It could be driven laterally in its dovetail in the fixed base, in the interests of making the gun shoot where it looked, and it enjoyed—on the models I have seen—one unique distinction which made it different from other Japanese front sights: It had a vertical cut in its face which had been filled with a luminous backed substance, which may have given it some value for night sighting or for shooting in the jungle.

The rear sight was a peep, securing elevation from a drum mounted on the left side of the receiver, which operated in conjunction with an attached eccentric, lifting the spring loaded rear sight lever to various heights as the conveniently knurled drum was rotated counter clockwise. The inner portion of the drum was graduated in hundreds of meters from two to sixteen, inclusive, and there was a port drilled into the rear part of the housing through which the appropriate number would come into view. A poppet arrangement served to retain the setting against jarring, and it also provided a click, which could be easily heard and felt when the setting was made at any hundred meter point. There was no provision for intermediate settings, nor was there any provision for firmly locking the sight at a given setting. A good but coarsely graduated windage adjustment was provided for by a micrometer screw in the rear of the rear sight lever.

The peep itself was of practical field type, with a small rim and a fairly large aperture. A luminous dot was set into the face of the peep disc, which would presumably be used in connection with the luminous line on the front sight. How it could be used for this purpose with any effect, though, is beyond me, because it is located below the peep, which would not allow it to be lined up with the front sight—unless the firer happened to have X-ray vision to see through the metal of the rear sight assembly. Possibly these luminous markings had other uses—I haven't been able to figure them out.

The weapon had the rough profile of the British Bren, but with marked differences in appearance showing up at a second glance. Notable among these would be the prominent spiral cut on the barrel which replaced the conventional cooling flanges, and also the appearance of the buttstock and grip, which possessed marked differences in contour from the Bren. The handle, of course, was the greatest point of similarity.

This Bren type carrying handle, which in the case of the Nambu is placed a little too far forward of the loaded balance-point, is a great convenience on any military weapon of excessive weight, providing an easy grasping point which is not too large in circumference for even a small hand. If I carried an M1 rifle all of the time I would be strongly influenced to try some such sort of a handle on it, because like most weapons of the semi-auto and automatic type, it is entirely too thick at the balance for easy grip—even if the user has a large hand. The advantages of such a handle show up when a weapon is used in combat. Our BARs certainly should have had one attached on the side. The twelve o'clock position of the handle on the Bren gun or Nambu is excusable from the visual standpoint, because the weapon already has a large half-moon magazine blocking off the view up there and another obstruction in the line doesn't matter. The offset sights, of course, are a necessary outgrowth of this magazine arrangement.

The position of the thirty-round, half-moon magazine on the M–1936 Nambu brings up a debatable point of firearms design, and reveals (to the doughboy who has had to use the damn things) a great fault of the Bren and Nambu alike.

This position of magazine atop the receiver is highly undesirable, first, because it dangerously obstructs the view, and second, because it still more dangerously sticks up out of the grass or cover like a flag, wiggling when the weapon is fired to betray the position of the firer to any observer who happens to be to the right or left front or flanks of the gunner.

The position of any staggered-round magazine on an automatic shoulder weapon is a matter which calls for careful consideration.

The six o'clock position is out, of course, if the magazine is to hold thirty rounds. And a magazine should hold thirty rounds, the twenty we use in the BAR is not enough. To my mind, one of the chief points of the Johnson Machine Rifle which helps to make it look so much better than any of the weapons I have seen or fired, is its horizontal magazine position. It would have a few disadvantages, would probably impede movement through brush and cover somewhat, but it would get away from the primary fault of the topside jobs, which are almost suicide to use in low grass or on bare ground. Throughout the war, we generally needed to see a Jap in order to kill him with the rifle and know that we got him. Not so with the Nambu gunners—all we had to do there was to use the prominent reference point, shoot, and watch it fall down as the Jap's shoulder gave way behind it. This fault existed, of course, with the Bren guns too, and the Britishers whom I later came to know in the Fourteenth Army were well aware of that fact. Most of them repainted their clips in appropriate colors each time they were fighting in different cover, and some of them even devised little camouflage nettings to break the clean cut outline of the tops. The Japanese I saw were not that smart.

In their infinite present wisdom, two residents of the Nipponese section of Valhalla should now be aware that I removed both of them from this world with great ease, by aiming low and to the clearly indicated rear of prominent, upsticking magazines which danced in a very eye-catching manner as they fired each burst. And I have heard of so many similar instances that I would not attempt to calculate the total number of Japanese killed by that same method.

The M–1936 buttstock utilizes only a small piece of wood, heavily reinforced in front by a sort of sleeve piece and in rear by a cupped buttplate, with screws at twelve and six o'clock. A heavy but narrow looped swivel is attached to the right side of the buttstock, about two inches forward from the rear, by means of a sturdy through-bolt. The separate grip is a solid piece of wood, held in place by a screw and sleeve arrangement going up through its center.

On top of the receiver, when the clip is removed, the large and convenient thumb-piece which is used to release the clips for removal sticks upright for about two inches. It is located just to the rear of the magazine port, which is covered when the clips are detached for long periods of time by a thin metal door, closing by means of a hinge on the right side. The hinge is sprung to hold fast in either of two positions: —fully open or fully closed. This feature allows the weapon to be loaded quickly with one free hand. The edges of the clip port are funnelled from front and rear only, but that fault is somewhat overcome by the clip release thumb-piece, which serves as a guide against the rear surface of the clip. There is also a projection on the trap door cover which sticks out from its under side and helps to guide the clip into place.

Quick and easy clip loading is a feature which cannot be stressed too much in the design of shoulder-fired automatic weapons, and it becomes increasingly paramount as the magazine capacity of a given weapon is decreased. Our BAR can be loaded with greater ease than a Nambu or Bren, and with fewer give away movements on the part of the firer, but that damn gun, with its twenty round magazines, has to be loaded more often than a weapon with the more sensible capacity of thirty rounds. Fifty would even be better!

To operate the Nambu is simplicity itself. The weapon is pri-marily built for firing from the prone position, and the bipod legs are made to give the gun the height which the Japanese seem to think is necessary for that type of firing—this is a little more than Americans generally think necessary. These legs lift 15 inches above any hard, flat surface. The legs are not adjustable for length, and they have only two positions at which they may be locked for use (plus one for stowage, of course). The forward of these rests the bore a slight distance closer to the ground, due to the legs pointing down at something more than the ninety degrees of the rearward position. Both positions are rather high, but in the field the high prone position has more universal use than the good old Camp Perry corn-borer position, beloved by many small bore shooters. (This latter position always seemed to have twin ob-jectives of effecting a firm junction with good old Mother Earth and simultaneously driving the range officer nuts.) But for all its fine points on the range, the extremely low prone position has only limited application in the field. Although the combat rifleman or machine gunner has a far, far stronger incentive than the target shooter to keep very, very low, he usually has to raise his weapon and his head in order to see over the grass, stones, weeds or uneven ground, and to aim at his enemy; so the greater bipod length is not necessarily excessive.

Each of the legs is held in place by a latch near the top, and can be quickly and easily released and swung out into functional position. A clip is inserted from the top and pressed down into the port until it clicks into place. The port trap door must, of course, be opened prior to this operation. The loaded clip can be pressed home with much greater ease if the bolt is pulled to the rear before insertion.

The bolt is withdrawn initially by means of the operating handle on the left side of the receiver. The handle is hook-coupled to the bolt so that it does not fly back and forth during operation, thereby beating hell out of any part of the firer (most likely his left hand) which might get in its path. The handle will seem too large at first trial because the resistance of the driving (or recoil) spring is easy to overcome, but this size shows itself necessary when the first stoppages are encountered in using the low-standard Japanese ammunition. In such emergencies, you need a good hand-hold to operate the weapon. This feature would also be valuable for cold weather firing when hands are likely to be numb.

With a loaded magazine in place and the bolt handle withdrawn and returned forward, leaving the bolt hung up in rear position on the sear, the weapon is ready to fire. It can be put on safe by means of a safety lever located in the forward trigger guard, left side; when the lever points up the gun is on safe—forward, fire. Firing is accomplished by the open breech method—the release of the sear allowing the bolt to move forward, rather than the firing pin.

In the unloading operation, the user will find that the thumbpiece is not really a thumbpiece, but rather a magazine lock, operated by the heel of the hand (either right or left) which grasps the magazine to yank it out. This is a good combat feature because if the firer makes a wild grab for the magazine, even without thinking of the latch, his hand will still release the magazine as it grabs.

The gas piston plug located under and in front of the front sight base portion of the barrel has five opening positions to which it can be turned. Numerals are stamped into the metal for reference, though there is no set rule for adjustment other than selecting the setting which makes for ideal functioning; providing enough force to operate the weapon, but without too much margin to cause excessive shock and damage to parts.

I have almost forgotten to mention that the weapon had as standard equipment a telescopic sight of two and a half power, with a field of view of some ten degrees, roughly the same optically as the one on the sniper M38 rifle. This scope was seldom used against us on the Island, and it was a part of the weapon which was easy to throw away. For that reason, we did not get a chance to test one properly. For a gun which is capable of the close grouping of the Nambu Light, though, a scope would be a definite advantage for long range spot-target shooting. For jungle use on a machine rifle, I would be strongly inclined to set aside my almost universal preference for telescopic sights and do just as the Japs did—leave the scope in the case, and plug away with the lighter and less vulnerable iron sights.

The M–1936 Nambu Light Machine Gun was plenty good,

either with or without the scope, and as I have already said, it may well have killed more of us than all of the other Jap guns put together. It was easy to shoot, easy to carry for a weapon of its great firepower, and it was hellish hard on the people being shot at. Possibly the greatest tribute which can be paid to it is that the weight-hating American Infantryman who got to know the Nambu would sometimes carry it for long distances in order to get to shoot Japanese with the very few rounds of ammunition which he usually captured with it.

A secondary tribute I can give; "secondary" because it has never been any great accomplishment for an enemy to frighten me—most any healthy or sick Jap could do *that*:

It is that my knowledge of the capabilities of the Nambu Light Machine Guns caused me the greatest and most demoralizing fear I have known in all the combat I have seen. It was one thing to be shot; it was another to be shot with a Nambu Light. In the first case, you had a chance of unmaimed survival, but in the second, you had practically none.

Model 1939 or Type 99 Light Machine Gun 7.7mm caliber.

THE ORIGINAL NAMBU

Before the Japs designed their M-1936 light machine gun, they had already equipped themselves with a good lightweight automatic weapon to be used in their rifle squads. With the economy characteristic of the Japanese Army, this weapon was kept and used throughout the war by various units, and it was found in quantities until the very end—at least, in certain zones.

The M-1922 was a true Nambu Light, almost indistinguishable from its more recently designed kin as far as performance in the jungle was concerned. When it was being fired at you, it sounded much the same as the M-1936, and it could group its shorter bursts and hit with nearly the same effect.

In appearance, it was only roughly similar to the newer gun, and the same was true of its handling and feel. It lacked the comfortable hold and natural pointing qualities which the other 6.5mm automatic had, and in operation it was not as positive or reliable.

One of its outstanding faults was that it made necessary the use of reduced charge ammunition, with ballistics slightly inferior to those of the regular cartridge. This complicated the overall supply problem somewhat, for it added another cartridge to the list of troubles already harassing Japanese supply officers. It also brought forth the inevitable danger of getting the standard cartridge into the weaker guns during combat mixups.

Within units which had only the M-1922 for a light machine gun, this problem was not so great. It was standard procedure, in such cases, for Japánese units to issue the reduced charge ammunition to everyone—riflemen and all. And the recoil-sensitive Japanese soldier came to prefer the more gentle cartridge, often going out of his way to get it for use in his rifle and carbine. It made less noise than the standard round (range did not matter in the jungle) and the ordinary Japanese soldier could not have been expected to properly evaluate the advantages of penetration—which was all that could be gained by using regular ammunition in the jungle. At odd times in jungle areas, I have wished for a reduced load myself—though I would have preferred one reduced much more than was the Japanese 6.5mm.

Units using the M–1922 to the exclusion of other light machine guns did not have to worry about special clips, either. The older gun was hopper-fed and didn't need any. To load, the firer had simply to raise the large, rearward projecting trap door handle of the hopper and place six five-round rifle-loading chargers into the space provided. Knocking back the trap door would bring it down into powerfully sprung action against the top charger ("clip") of five rounds, forcing them all downward so that the bottom clip could be tracked into the receiver by the feed assembly on the hopper's bottom. Loading was not as fast as could be on account of the six separate packages needed for a single firing, but the weapon made up for it somewhat by dispensing with the high-projecting, giveaway clip of the later M–1936—an advantage which served the combined purposes of supply and security.

The hopper, however, gave an ungainly bulk to the weapon at its balance point, denying it completely the quality of feel, which was later incorporated so beautifully into the M–1936. Positioned as it was, it blocked the operator's view and made necessary a very unorthodox and awkward mounting of the sights. They had to be offset *to the right* for more than an inch to avoid occlusion of the normal or left side line of sight. This, in turn, caused a need for a radically offset buttstock in order to permit the shooter to get his shooting right eye more than an inch to the *right* of the bore-line. The weapon would be well nigh impossible for a left-eyed shooter to use—even if he were left-handed.

Naturally, these faults gave the weapon a strangeness of hold for anyone who had previously learned to shoot an ordinary shoulder-weapon and undoubtedly it caused a lengthening of training time. It would have been very difficult to train American soldiers to shoot the M–1922 after they had developed holding habits for orthodox weapons, and the Japanese were certainly no more versatile than we.

A debatable effect—chiefly a disadvantage—was caused by the use of the rather broad hopper. It had less height than the half-moon clip of the M–1936, but it was wider, and its top was above the shooter's line of vision, blocking from view the entire area to the left of his immediate target. The firer was further blinded by the bulk of the oil chamber, which extended the blacked-out area of the hopper to the right for the full width of the receiver, leaving less than an inch of clear space to the left of the offset rear sight notch, or line of sight. It might be truthfully said that this fault effectually half-blinded the firer because it cut out almost fifty

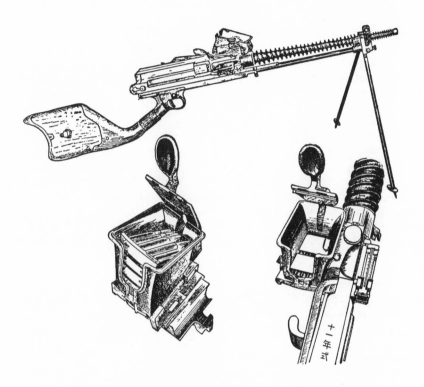

Here is the automatic the Japs developed back in the early days and kept in use throughout this last war, too. In looks and feel it left much to be desired, and the need for using a special reduced-charge ammunition couldn't have made it more effective, either. Most of us were inclined to laugh at it—at first.

Actually it was a very good weapon for the well-disciplined but mechanically inept Japanese doughboy. Since it was capable of firing short bursts only, it tended to conserve ammunition even when the gunner became trigger-happy, and for the ultra-short range bushwacking (a Japanese specialty) the short burst proved sufficient. No point in shooting a man more than five times, as often happened with other Japanese automatics.

Despite its awkwardness and obvious mechanical crudities, this older Jap light machine gun was a highly effective weapon, though not in the same class with the later Nambu or Bren . . .

percent of his field of view while he remained in the firing position. Because of this, he had to raise his head frequently, deserting the line of sight with his right eye in order to check that eternal dead space on the right flank of his target. In so raising his head, he was often killed—a rather serious consequence!

The only advantage the hopper oiled arrangement gave was that it did put a vast amount of metal in front of the gunner while he sighted his weapon. This naturally held true only when he was fired at from the front, but it was effective. I know of one case where a Japanese gunner went through an entire light machine gun squad, with which he was fighting a fifty yard headon duel, before they got him. This occurrence was, of course, no tribute to the marksmanship of the Americans, though an inspection later showed that the Jap would have been killed very early in that hair-raising, ten minute affair if he had not had that heavy, bullet deflecting hopper and oil reservoir in front of him. He had suffered several wounds in the shoulders and legs but still continued shooting until he had killed or wounded four men. The fifth soldier got him, but his gun was still in working order when picked up, though the sights were shot off of it and there were great lateral lead smears through the cooling flanges where bullets had raked along the barrel.

Each time I think of fortitude in a general way, I remember the example of that Japanese gunner who had walked up to within fifty yards of an American outpost, set up his weapon to fire in the middle of an exposed trail, and remained steadfastly there until he died. Death for him had loomed as a certainty from his very first move.

This older Nambu had sharp points on the tips of its bipod legs, with slanting hilts about an inch up. This was the same error of design which we committed in the case of our early machine rifle adaptations for the Browning Auto Rifle. The later Japanese weapon (M–1936) had flat shoes on its bipod tips, with a ridge running the length of each sole to assure against sideward movement. Our later BAR had a set of similarly shaped shoes on its bipod.

The offset buttstock of the M–1922 was styled weirdly. It had a twisted tang and grip portion which was made entirely of metal and was checkered for hand grip at the small stem. This metal part also came into contact with the cheek during firing, so on that account this must have been hell to fire in extremely cold weather.

The sights were of conventional design, with a slanting leaf rear, open notched, and elevatable in 100 meter jumps to a maximum of 1500 meters. The front one was a barleycorn, dovetailed into a side guarded offset base—said dovetail providing the weapon with its only lateral zeroing adjustment. There was no provision for windage. The position of the rear sight was at least eight inches forward of that of the peep on the M–1936, cutting the sighting radius of the weapon the same amount.

It lacked the highly desirable carrying handle of the M–1936 or the Bren, and had nothing to serve in its place. For that reason, there was no getting by without an asbestos mitten for the firer's left hand, which had to be used whenever the weapon was moved during a fight. For some reason, the weapon lacked the bayonet fittings with which the later M–1936 was cursed. This omission constituted a virtue which, from the standpoint of common sense, would almost make up for the loss of the carrying handle.

Because of the weapon's hopper mechanism, it had to be fired in five-round bursts, with a multiple pawl dragging one chargerful at a time into the receiver for firing. This was less of a fault than is first imagined because it helped to assure the conservation of ammunition—so important to the Japanese—and for jungle purposes the five-round burst is almost ideal. Five shots do the trick nicely in the jungle, and the recovery for a second five is so fast that the feature would never give the enemy time to complete even the shortest assault rush while the gunner fumbled.

The methods of stripping both the M–1922 and the M–1936, while not generally as good as those of our own weapons, were nonetheless sufficiently simple. No special tools were needed, other than a drift and a screwdriver, to disassemble the weapon for field purposes. In the matter of maintenance the employment of the M–1922 was somewhat complicated. Gunners had to always have a quantity of oil on hand to lubricate the cartridges, by keeping the reservoir atop the receiver filled. This measure, made necessary by the poor extraction method used, is the real cause of the weapon's failure to handle the regular full charge ammunition. The side-clinging qualities of the expanded brass case were not utilized in the Nambu M–1922 to help brake the backward motion of the moving parts, but were eliminated by the use of chamber lubrication.

The large rear part of the barrel is not really barrel at all, but barrel jacket. The true barrel, which lacks the quick changing feature of other weapons, is smooth on the outside surface for three-quarters of its length, the projecting tip being the only part cut for cooling effect. The heat of firing is chiefly dissipated through conduction and radiation by the spiral cut barrel jacket. The spiral cutting, giving the effect of cooling flanges, is the same in principle on the M–1922 as on the M–1936, but the cuts are deeper. With no quick-barrel-change feature incorporated, it is necessary that the older weapon have more radiation surface to allow cooling for sustained firing. This has caused the use of a thicker profiled barrel assembly, giving the gun a heavier appearance than the M-1936. The larger overall appearance of the weapon is caused by that adaptation.

The appearance is most affected on the M-1922 by a peculiar shape and outline of the buttstock, which appears unique when looked at from any angle. I recall that distinctive appearance with special keenness because a year later in Burma, when we were fighting in an area where there were Chinese armed with Bren guns, I was able to distinguish the exact nationality of a small group of Orientals by recognizing the weapon which one of them was carrying over his shoulder. This group had walked toward us from a direction which would have normally identified them as Chinese. So it was fortunate that I could quickly recognize the difference between those weapons—the Nambu and Bren—because the enemy were no more than a stone's throw away when they first came into view. After I had settled the matter of the nationality of the approaching group, we promptly dealt with them, and in a rather thorough fashion, for about ten men were kneeling near me with rifles leveled, ready to let fly when I gave the word.

After we killed them, I ordered that their weapons be destroyed. Our fight then was behind the Japanese lines in the Hukawng Valley, and we could not afford to encumber ourselves with souvenirs. I did not check carefully on the carrying out of that order, and during another ruckus the following dawn, I was violently frightened to hear the distinctive sound of a Japanese light machine gun firing *from inside our perimeter.* With many a shake and shiver, I set about the task of stalking it in the low kunai grass, with grenade and carbine.

The upshoot of it all was that I came as close to killing an American as I possibly could without actually harming him. I held my sights upon his helmet for a full minute while I pondered the possibility of a Jap wearing an un-netted helmet and shooting toward his own people from within our lines.

After an officer named Kramer had successfully disposed of the platoon of Japs who were causing the trouble, I took our man who was using the Nambu by the arm and led him down to the river where, under my personal supervision, he disassembled the weapon and threw the parts into the stream.

But don't gather from that that I don't have a lot of respect for General Nambu's fine little automatic weapons. They're all good, well within the class of our own.

JAPANESE GRENADES

When a man gets into a hole of sufficient depth he can generally count himself secure from enemy flat-trajectory fire.

There are exceptions to this rule, of course, on occasions when the possession of nearby high ground or tree positions permit enemy riflemen or gunners to direct fire into the open tops of foxholes, but such a circumstance is rare. Infantrymen the world over have usually ceased to worry about rifle and machine gun fire during all periods when they could get their heads a foot or more beneath the surface of solid ground. Then soldiers worry only about descending missiles which can fall down into a shelter through openings in its top (or sides if it is roofed), or which can be rolled freely into an open foxhole.

Curved trajectory missiles are of several varieties and are launched in several different ways. There are mortar shells, fired at very high angle from light-tubed weapons; there are artillery shells, fired from heavier guns at lower angles and with greater velocity; and there are grenades, which can be thrown by hand, fired by rifles, or projected from lightweight, mortar-like launchers.

By far the most commonly used of these projectiles, as far as the Japanese on Guadalcanal were concerned, was the grenade, found in great quantities everywhere in captured territory. Of the methods of delivery listed, more grenades were probably hand-thrown than were projected from mortar launchers or rifle launchers. However, in that matter there is some room for argument, for many grenades were fired from the ground launcher—the standard knee-mortar.

Every Jap who could do so carried grenades, and many of them were of types not fitted for launching except by hand. For that reason, I will cling to a belief, until someone proves otherwise, that most of the grenades which exploded in close to us were thrown, rather than launched or fired from rifles.

Whether the grenades were hand-thrown or projected our way

339

was an important point, because if one would be hand thrown at a given position it became an automatic cinch that a Jap—alive and in good shape—was awfully close, probably within thirty yards or so. Grenades could be launched, however, from more than 200 yards, in which case there would usually be a tell-tale bottle-cork "pop" from the launcher—heard some seconds before the grenade explosion.

Both offensive grenades and fragmentation types were used on the island, though the fragmentation was much more often seen, perhaps because of its more universal application to various targets. The offensive type, which depended for its effect upon explosive shock rather than surgical damage, was generally limited to employment in the assault, where it gave the thrower an advantage of being able to use it safely from a close and exposed position. Its lack of distance-carrying fragments allowed him to throw at a man only a few yards or feet away and then close in quickly to finish the job with a bayonet while the victim remained stunned or dazed.

This was a good trick, throwing a grenade and rushing at the same time, for even if the attacked individual went unhurt by the blast, it would at least have a distracting and shaking effect, which would give the assaultman better chance to get at him safely. The Japanese learned things of this sort by their early Asiatic experience, and it put an ace or two up their sleeves when it came to close fighting.

At most, however, Japanese employment of these blast type grenades was decidedly limited, and the large body of soldiers who were on Guadalcanal will better remember the several types of fragmentation grenades, which were used more often and dealt much nastier wounds. Many of the men with experience on Guadalcanal are also able to report authentically upon the performance of our own grenades because many of our grenades were found along our old trails by Japs. These grenades, discarded by overloaded doughboys, were quick in coming back at us.

The actually disproportionate employment of grenades, as against other weapons in the Pacific war, was influenced by two main factors: First, the jungle cover brought opposed forces close to each other where the ranges were often short, and the grenade is a short range weapon; Second, the Japanese officer placed an emphasis upon night operations, conducting most of their attacking and probing during hours of darkness. Because no weapon which we had at that time could be accurately aimed in the dark, the grenade—an area-covering affair—became the accepted medicine for all close-range night targets, concealed or above ground. There is still another reason for the popularity of the fragmentation grenade as a night weapon—its launching would not give away the firer's position, as would the flash of a rifle, carbine, or buckshot-loaded shotgun. (I mention the shotgun because it would have been a good night weapon. Actually, we never used them in my own units, though I saw some with the 25th Division supplies.)

It was the same old story almost every night along the active fronts on the Island. As dusk came on, the exchange of rifle and automatic weapons fire would gradually slacken and die out. Then, after an interval of half an hour or so, while we would freeze into position, the Japanese, who would normally have stayed immobile during the daylight hours, would organize their "scare parties," sending people crawling towards us, each hoping to drop a grenade into one of our shelters.

They were skilled at such business, and although we all knew well enough that such tactics would in the long run enable us to kill more Japs, we were all scared of these night prowling parties. The knowledge that at any moment a live Japanese soldier might join you in your foxhole is not at all conducive to sound sleep. We were generally kept awake during a good part of the night on that account, listening to the sporadic explosions of grenades, our own and the enemy's, along our front.

Much of the time these attempts at night infiltration would be accompanied by deceptive sounds off to one or both flanks, several yards away from the actual effort. Firecrackers were employed on occasions for this purpose, and I have personally witnessed a Jap attempt to create deceptive sound effects by tapping on dry bamboo in schoolboy imitation of machine gun fire. Once in a while during one of these night "creeps," the Japanese would open up with an automatic weapon, but the mainstay was grenades. Knives and bayonets would also have figured importantly in this fighting had we been foolish enough to play ball with the Japanese —their rules—but we did no such thing. Our men were allowed to fire at will during the night if they were positioned on the outer perimeter of a battalion or company. Normally, men on the inside were forbidden to shoot unless the target was actually looming over their foxholes or was by some other token clearly recognizable as an infiltrated enemy.

This practice put the Japanese at a disadvantage because the ones bent on aggression had to move about in the darkness while we sat tight in our shelters, seeing or hearing them in time to gain the necessary two second's warning or "drop." Also, the shelters we usually had would protect us from grenade fragments unless a direct hit should be scored, while the prowlers, above ground, would be liable to hits by fragments from explosions several yards away. Lurking in holes, carefully watching the shadows around and above, listening for man-made sounds in all directions, the American usually was the one who fired the fatal shot or threw the grenade that killed.

The Japanese were apparently unaware of the really small numbers of casualties they were creating at night with such great cost to themselves, for they kept using night infiltration tactics all through the Guadalcanal show. On the other hand, knowledge on our part that we were never secure at night, that we were likely to find a sputtering grenade in with us at anytime, or that we might have to wrestle and knife it out with an enemy on a moment's notice, was a fear and a mental handicap to be constantly reckoned with. It made sleep a dangerous luxury, peace of mind a nonexistent, forgotten thing.

We knew that our shelters, in daylight hours or while we were digging in at dusk, had been spotted carefully, and some of them had been marked by the enemy as targets for infiltration or grenade attacks during the night. With deceptive sounds or in attempted complete silence, individual Japs or small groups would creep up and attempt to grenade or assault the more vulnerable positions in the outer perimeter.

The assault efforts were nearly always complete failures, with the Japanese killed before any of them got within bayonet distance. Only very, very, seldom would there be an instance of hand-to-hand fighting, and when these rare occurrences did take place, the Japanese generally came out second best.

The small success these attacks enjoyed was nearly always reaped through the use of grenades, much more than any other weapon. So if the Japs in front of us were well supplied with grenades we could always count on a few casualties each night of action. The grenade, more than any other weapon I know, other than the grenade launcher (knee-mortar), was a distinctly Japanese weapon, well adapted to their tactics.

The Japanese were good throwers too. They came by it naturally, through a national enthusiasm for baseball which surpassed even the American zest for that sport. Nearly all of them could throw well, either overhand or sidearm, and all contrary information, given to us by so-called experts on the Japanese, was absolute hokum.

For an Infantry which had a tactical leaning toward night operations and closein assault techniques, it was no more than natural that good grenades would be developed. And the grenades which these soldiers used were good in both design and manufacture, having many points of superiority over ours. We could have learned much about grenade design and type distribution, if we had made a careful, unprejudiced study of the Japanese grenades and launching devices which were developed before the war.

The Japanese had adopted, before the year 1932, a set of fragmentation grenades with almost universal adaptability. They could be thrown by hand, discharged by a light, handy, mortar-like projector, or fired from a spigot type rifle launcher—either directly-aimed for short distances or lobbed afar. We were issued nothing to match these weapons through the entire course of the war, at least not where I was able to see it.

These grenades were of standard size, compact and easy to grip in the palm, with no lever to spring uncomfortably against the heel of the thrower's hand. They were just as safe as our own, as far as design was concerned—the danger from their erratic fuses was due to manufacturing sloppiness. Customarily issued in their lightest form for hand throwing, it would take only a minute for a soldier to fit an attachment for launching from the knee-mortar, or an attachment for firing the same grenade from a discharger-fitted rifle. We had nothing so good in design, not even as a throwing grenade, although our manufacturers did see to it that our grenade was more reliable and sure-fire in every respect than the Japanese pineapples. Our explosive charges and detonators were better performers, too, giving the American grenade a performance edge—with much greater effect secured through more uniform fragmentation. The more harsh explosive used by the Japanese frequently powdered sections of the case, thereby cutting down effective fragmentation.

But all of these faults—from the Infantryman user's standpoint—could be corrected by good manufacturing. If Japanese grenade designs could be mass produced in American factories, along with a modified launcher copied from the knee-mortar, and a rifle-launcher, simply designed by our own ordnance people, we would have something much better than we can boast of at present. And we could still standardize upon one model of fragmentation grenade, just as we do now. But that one design of grenade should be adapted to launching by rifle or by miniature mortars within each Infantry rifle squad, thereby trebling its usefulness. The grenade would then become specifically fitted for several tasks which we presently allot to specialized weapons, which are heavier, less handy, *and seldom there when needed.* Such versatile grenades could be fired accurately into pillbox ports with rifles or could be lobbed over 200 yards to harass or pin down the enemy. This latter feature would prove especially valuable when the fire of heavier mortars or artillery is not available.

Perhaps the most important application a small grenade launcher has in the jungle is in bringing prompt fire against leading enemy elements at the moment of contact. This type of fire

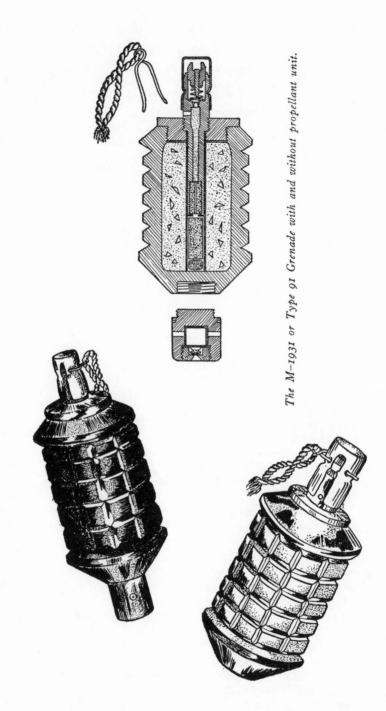

The M–1931 or Type 91 Grenade with and without propellant unit.

is always helpful in case of a meeting-engagement or headon collision of patrols on a trail.

It is always a great morale factor for troops in contact with the enemy to know that the other side is under explosive-projectile fire, and to be able to hear the explosions as they occur. From the other side's standpoint, it constitutes a grave disadvantage, causing casualties and hampering movement on the trail. In some instances knee-mortars can interdict, cutting advance elements off from their support, sometimes pinning everyone in the point (first few scouts and riflemen) flatly to the ground.

And the Japs always threw that sort of stuff at us—usually during the first few seconds of engagement. We would make contact; first a few rifle shots would be fired by the scouts and possibly one or two automatic weapons bursts would be exchanged. Then without delay we would begin to hear the blasts of those damn knee-mortars—grenade explosions, on the trail behind or amongst us. It was annoying as hell.

We tried to counter it, of course, using materials at hand. We had to do something to enable our platoons to fire back at the knee-mortars. Several methods were tried and all of them gave some measure of success but, in the long run, none were as practical or economical as would have been the adoption of an American knee-mortar with matched grenades.

The first and most effective of our improvised counter-measures was to attach an artillery forward observer directly to the point squad—place him with the first eight men in an advancing column. By being *there*, the artillery man (usually an officer) could keep in radio contact with his battery and promptly lay a bunch of 75s or 105s on the necks of any Japs encountered. That, of course, was effective, but it was not often practicable.

In the first place, there weren't many artillerymen who wanted to do that sort of thing—with sound reason. Secondly, the usefulness of such a setup is dependent upon reliable radio communication between the forward observer and his guns. With portable sets in the jungle, steady radio communication is too much to hope for—it just doesn't exist. The forward observer may be in perfect radio contact with his rear at a given point on the trail, and a hundred yards further, around a bend of heavy growth, he may not even be able to hear a faint hum from the set back at the battery. And you can bet your last coconut that such a time is the very moment when twenty Nips will be seen on the trail ahead. Telephone wire, unrolled on the trail by a team of linemen, affords a more reliable means of communication, but it too is subject to interruption. It can be cut, trampled, or broken by any one of a hundred different friendly or enemy agencies.

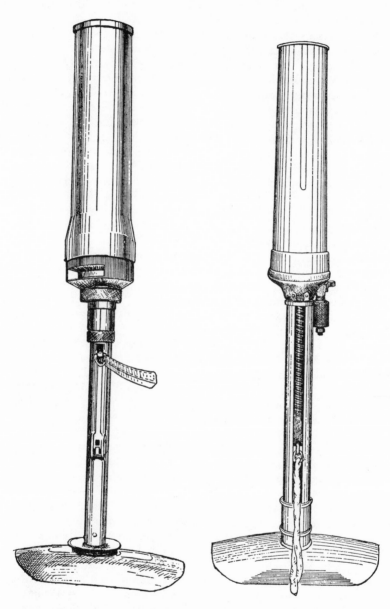

"Knee Mortars"
Left—the Model *1921* or Type *10* smooth-bored grenade launcher.
Right—the Model *1929* or Type *89* grenade launcher with rifled barrel.

The next remedy was to substitute our own 6omm mortar for the grenade dischargers we didn't have. The entire gun was too heavy to carry, too slow to mount up to be used as was, so we streamlined it. We carried only the tube, and distributed loads of light high explosive shells for carrying among the members of the point and men immediately behind. As soon as contact was made and our point opened fire, the mortarmen would commence firing their weapons, using the shells at very short range with minimum increments or none at all—merely the cartridge for a propelling charge. The tube would be aimed "by guess and b'gosh" by a trained man who would simply hold the muzzle end of the tube in his left hand and pivot the butt against a root or the hardest ground he could find. No baseplate would be used, the gunner would vary the angle of the tube to adjust the range.

Although the light 6omm high explosive shells were individually more effective than anything the Japanese could throw with the knee-mortar, their employment still left something to be desired. We had no time-fused shells, for one thing! All of our ammunition went off on contact, or with slight delay thereafter. Nearly always there would be a screen of leaves and twigs above the trail, which the Japs could fire right through with their time-fused grenades. Our shells would detonate above our heads unless we took time out and adjusted the position of our weapons beneath an opening. Sometimes, in desperation, we blasted clearance by firing repeatedly into the jungle ceiling. Such procedure bordered on suicide, of course, but risks not listed in the book are now and then taken in the field.

Another complaint against this method was the fact that elevation had to be secured by varying the slant of the mortar tube. This created a need for a wide swath of clearance through overhead foliage in the jungle, and it made the weapon difficult to fire accurately. The Japanese method was better. It let the tube remain set in one position (for regular ranges), keeping it at 45 degrees above horizontal (or a straight line from gun to target), and allowed the gunner to change the range by means of the variable-volume combustion chamber.

For extremely short range work, the Japanese knee-mortar, trigger fired, could be braced against a root or the ground and a foot, and pointed almost flat along the ground. Our own 6omm mortar, which depended upon the fall of the shell to the tube bottom where the firing pin was fixed, was useless for this last purpose, which proved to be a great disadvantage for firing at less than 200 yards.

We finished the battle of Guadalcanal without having a satisfactory weapon with which to talk back to the Japanese grenade discharger, grenade launcher, or knee-mortar, whichever you want to call it.

From the standpoint of hand-thrown grenades, we were on a more even footing. Our grenades were generally more sure-fire and reliable, storing longer in the wetness of the jungle, and detonating after such storage with greater certainty. They were also more effective in the matter of fragmentation, for their balance of metal-brittleness vs. charge-burning-speed was good and provided for more uniform breakage. In short range shock effect they seemed not quite, but nearly, as good as the enemy's.

The standard complaint we had against everything issued to us with high explosive in it held true against our early allotment of grenades on Guadalcanal. All were painted a bright yellow, so that each Jap they were thrown at could quickly find them on the grass or in the dirt and throw them back. Why in tarnation anything in the way of Infantry equipment is *ever* painted yellow is more than I can understand! It seems to me to be a very short-sighted, perverted idea of safety procedure—even in peacetime. There must be some other way to mark shells and grenades obviously enough to serve our safety purposes without violating the dictates of common horse sense. The Japanese painted their grenades black—not glossy, but dull—as good a color as any in the jungle.

We first saw Japanese grenades back at the beaches, mostly duds left laying where they had been thrown some weeks before. The 5th Marine regiment and our 164th Infantry had fought over that ground, doing a good bit of their battling in fairly open coconut groves. The absence of heavy cover enabled us to see all the marks of the fighting: the rotting remains, the discarded uniforms, the abandoned or captured equipment.

Unfired grenades were scarce there, indicating that the Japanese had cherished them. The only good ones were usually found on bodies, rather than loose on the ground.

Japanese equipment for shipping and carrying grenades was sturdy and practical—though made with insufficient regard for weatherproofing. They had heavy wood cases, twenty grenades to a box, with neat rope handles and cradling-braces inside. For individual packing there were both bandoliers and belt pouches, as well as special back-packs and belly aprons. While we were still on the beaches we learned that nearly all of the Japanese always carried grenades.

Later we were to see evidence of one of the most widely known uses for grenades in the Pacific war—the old individual grenade type of hari-kari. Plenty of Japs had taken that way out, igniting grenades by banging their ends against a helmet, then hugging the sputtering explosives to their chests and waiting for the explosion. Stories were told of Japs being found dead with several duds lying alongside—each one used before the last one was tried and worked. Just picture yourself going through all of the motions of suicide four or five times before you got a grenade which would go off! It seems that *anyone* would deserve a fate better than *that*. Stories heard later from Attu were not lies, for grenade hari-kari was traditional in the Japanese army—and its wide use was a testimonial for the courage and fanaticism of the brave little men we were fighting.

Perhaps a description of grenades should not be given in a book written especially for gun enthusiasts. Compared to any grooved-barrel weapon, the grenade admittedly is a crude and primitive device—not nearly as scientific, not half so precise. Then too, any rifle devotee turned soldier will always possess a certain antipathy towards the use of grenades, thinking of them as unfair instruments—not clean killers, like rifles. In such attitude I concur, for the grenade, whether of fragmentation, offensive, incendiary, or smoke type, is a nasty and brutal weapon.

But like so many other wicked and unreasonable devices, the grenade has become intimately associated with the everyday life of the modern combat Infantryman. In the Pacific war, it became on occasions the only weapon used during night time by opposed thousands of Americans and Japanese.

The closein nature of jungle fighting caused this out-of-proportion popularity of the grenade, and the Japanese flair for night infiltration tactics added to it. With opposed front lines ordinarily within throwing distance of each other, there was always an emphasis on the use of grenades. The Japs knew this would be the case, from past experience, and they supplied their troops with good ones.

On Guadalcanal, as far as I was able to make out, there were only three distinct models of explosive grenades used. Two were of the fragmentation or metal-case bursting type, and one was a potato masher offensive type grenade. Of these three models, the most effective was not only a grenade, but also a mortar shell which could be hand-thrown. Officially it would be called the M-1931 50mm Fragmentation Grenade, I suppose. It seemed more effective than the other grenade though it contained the same amount of explosive in its casing. It was generally more reliable, as we found, because it was normally packed and shipped with greater care than the more common grenades. It came packed in boxes, reasonably wetproofed against the deteriorating effects of moist tropical air. On that account, it usually went off, which could not be said of the other captured Japanese grenades.

In body the M-1931 was cylindrical, with a smaller front end which held the fuse. It looked more like a grenade than a mortar projectile. Its bottom portion contained a screwed-on primer and propelling charge which obviously had no function if the weapon were hand-thrown, but which adapted it for its perhaps secondary purpose of launching from the M-1929 or M-1921 grenade dischargers (knee-mortars). This propellant-containing portion would be unscrewed if the grenade were hand-thrown, making it lighter to throw and less bulky to carry.

On the M-1931 the conventional type Japanese grenade fuse was employed. This fuse was in the shape of a long, upward projecting button which was held at "safe" by a two shafted crosspin, shaped like a strong hairpin with straight sides. The grenade would be armed by withdrawal of this pin, which action was facilitated by a loop of heavy twine tied to the "U" of the hairpin.

Then, when the grenade was to be hand-thrown, the fuse was ignited by striking the front end of the button against a hard object—usually a helmet. This action drove a firing pin into the fuse percussion cap and set the eight second fuse to burning. Small sparks would sizzle around the loose fitting edges of the button.

The firing pin mechanism included a lever arrangement whereby it was possible to unscrew the firing pin inside its little collar so that its point could not possibly strike the cap. We soon got into the habit of screwing the firing pins back into place before we fired the grenades in a launcher or threw them by hand. When fired in the launcher, there was no need to strike the endcap or button to start the fuse burning. An inertia-principle arrangement reliably caused the firing pin to set back against the action of a very weak creep spring, as the projectile left the barrel. The fuse time of eight seconds remained the same, whether the grenade was hand-thrown or launched. I suppose this exceptionally long fuse time was arranged to accommodate the long time-of-flight to more distant targets.

The M-1937 was identical with the M-1931 hand grenade except that it had no provision for launching from a grenade discharger. There was no propellant-container attached to its base, and there was no threaded hole provided to permit the attachment of such a device. But otherwise it was the same, an inexpensively-made version of the more versatile M-1931, usable only as a hand-thrown bomb. It possessed no advantage over the earlier grenade except ease of manufacture. Its compactness could be matched by the M-1931 by simple expedient of unscrewing and discarding the propellant base. Its explosive effect, of course, was identical with that of the M-1931.

In the matter of effectiveness, the manufacturing faults of the Japanese grenades became very obvious. Fragmentation was generally erratic, with individual performance varying greatly from grenade to grenade. One would explode perfectly, cracking its case into neat little pieces, and possibly killing several of us with its single blast. But the very next one might fall squarely into a foxhole on top of a man and yet not kill him.

Both of these grenades gave themselves away with sputtering and sparks at night, so that men usually were able to evade them before they exploded. Their fuses seemed to be set for a count of three or four before throwing; however, I rather think that Japanese soldiers were just a little bit loath to hang onto them so long. We usually had warning and time enough to jump out of our holes and let one go off inside, or to duck low while a close one exploded on the parapet, holding our hands over our ears to avoid bursted drums.

A helmet placed on top of a live Jap grenade was said to be a good neutralizer, though I never saw it used. We learned from the Japanese the trick of keeping a sandbag handy in permanent shelters, so that it could be quickly grabbed to effectively muffle any grenade. In one pillbox we had captured, we found evidence that the three Japanese inside had played a lengthy game of muffle the grenade, getting three sacks of sand blown to tatters during the siege of their surrounded shelter. What a hair-raising half hour that must have been! Just picture the plight of three human beings penned up in a five foot cubicle, frantically muffling grenades which were tossed one after another through a port they could not block because it had a steady stream of Browning Auto Rifle fire pouring through!

From our own viewpoint there were enough grenade incidents to scare us into idiocy. A sputtering grenade in a foxhole with a man gives him an experience he won't easily forget. And should a pineapple fall into his lap during a fight, with the air above his foxhole being laced with fire, the memory of the incident (if the man survives) will provide him stock for nightmares through the remainder of his life. In such instances the trained doughboy's action is to jump from the hole and brave the fire. There is an overwhelming natural compulsion to act only to keep your face away from the grenade. Men who surrendered to that impulse generally paid with their lives.

If the grenade falls in the foot end of your hole, however, you can stomp it into the mud and then withdraw your feet a few inches, holding the soles toward the blast. This will usually prevent severe injury and *sometimes* save a man from anything worse than bruised feet. But if the Japs should throw an American or British

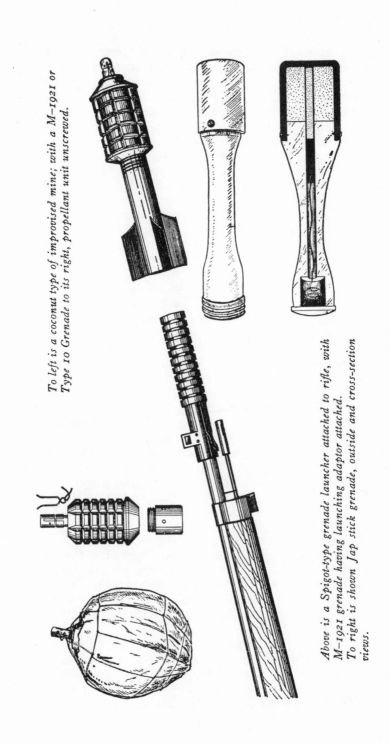

To left is a coconut type of improvised mine; with a M–1921 or Type 10 Grenade to its right, propellant unit unscrewed.

Above is a Spigot-type grenade launcher attached to rifle, with M–1921 grenade having launching adaptor attached. To right is shown Jap stick grenade, outside and cross-section views.

grenade—as they did whenever they could get one—using heavily-shod feet for a shield will not save anyone from severe injury. It takes much more than a well-soled pair of shoes to stop *our* grenade fragments.

In daytime, the Japs sometimes attack in jungle country by using a grenade barrage followed by a sudden rush with the bayonet from nearby cover. The Jap potato masher grenade, which depends largely on blast effect rather than fragmentation, was often used in such tactics. The idea was to stun the defenders with grenades, and then to rush in with the bayonet while they remained unconscious. This method generally failed against us, usually because the grenades left one or two of our men unaffected, and even one man with an M1 rifle or a BAR can take care of a lot of people rushing his way with bayonets. Against an isolated outpost or a single sentry such tactics would possibly be worth while, at least enough so as to justify the retention (in the Japanese Army) of the stick type high explosive grenade.

This weapon had several advantages over conventional pineapples. Its fuse and arming mechanism was housed within a long wooden handle, well protected from moisture—a necessary precaution in the tropics. It was very handy to throw—especially from the prone position. A stick type grenade is much easier to throw from any cramped position because less arm movement is required.

This stick grenade had a pull cord concealed in the handle with a metal ring attached to its end, the ring of finger size. With the length of pull cord providing considerable slack, it looked as though the proper throwing procedure would be to first get at the ring by unscrewing the metal cap on the handle's end, then place the ring on a finger of the throwing hand, and then grasp the handle and throw. This would cause the grenade fuse to be ignited in flight as the motion of the grenade jerked the pull cord free. The friction-type primer would thus ignite and start the rather fast-burning fuse. It would seem better, however, to jerk the ring first and ignite the grenade before throwing. In so doing the thrower would avoid giving his position away by throwing a grenade which might, after starting on its way, prove to be a dud.

The potato masher grenade seemed especially nasty in that it had a short fuse (seemed less than four seconds), and because it was used often in heavy grenade fights, mixed in with frags. Also, it sputtered and sparked less than the others, giving it a special effectiveness against men who had gotten used to the regular kinds.

Speaking of this, brings to mind a story; one of the dirtiest tricks of the war was pulled on us during the Hill 27 affair.

We had an unusual amount of confusion on one of the nights

we were holding that hill, during which I seemed to notice a lot of scrambling and movement in the darkness all along our line.

There were the usual scattered sounds of grenade explosions, with accompanying whir and buzz of fragments, but there were also growls of annoyance mixed in. Once, two of the men jumped out of their holes at once and lay clinging to the ground outside. No explosions occurred. For a minute or so the two men remained breathlessly prone on the edges of their holes and then eased cautiously back inside.

"Duds," I said to myself.

At that moment a grenade rolled into my own shelter, striking me in the arm, scaring me half to death. I didn't take time to feel for it on the bottom of my hole. I hurtled outside, took cover behind the heaped soil, and clung there—so close to the ground that my heart beats were thumping directly against the dirt.

I waited for the explosion, head held down, but none came.

Soon I began to realize that in my present state I would be cold turkey for any Jap; I was helpless in my fear, not even looking around. So I drew my pistol arm around in front of me so that I could shoot quickly. It was possibly ten minutes later that I eased back into my hole, toeing the bottom carefully so that I would not step on the dud grenade. From the sounds I continued to hear the rest of that night, it was evident that my experience was being repeated over and over again all along the line, and I reflected that the Japs were throwing plenty more grenades than usual, but were apparently getting a lot of duds.

That was the best conclusion I could reach until early dawn, when I was able to examine more closely the "dud" grenade lying in a corner of my shelter. It was not a grenade at all, but only a sun-baked clay ball, patted and rolled into the rough shape of a grenade; and it was the same way with a hundred other "duds" tossed into holes along our lines. The Japs had enjoyed a tremendous joke at our expense, scaring the living daylights out of us all through the night—with mud balls! The ingenious little bastards!

It was funny, by God; no gag, no humorous incident since, has made me laugh half so loud or long and the same is true of my bewildered buddies—that gaunt, bearded, rheumy-eyed bunch of jungle rats who crawled out one by one and incredulously picked up the rounded clods, emitting great shouts of laughter when the truth dawned.

We thought we knew about humor—gags, puns, practical jokes. Here was a real joke, a monumental one; no prankster in a peaceful world could ever hope to equal it. Alongside such soldier jokes, such battlefield mirth, civilian humor has ever since the war seemed effeminate, lifeless, synthetic.

JAPANESE MORTARS

Mortars are an absolutely essential tool of jungle warfare—a weapon which any wise commander would hate to do without. Lacking mortars, profitable Infantry operations would be difficult to conduct in the jungle, even against a half-armed foe. In their various types and calibers, these light-barrelled, generally smooth-bored weapons have an application in almost every jungle fight, even those involving only a few men and lasting only a few minutes.

Mortars are versatile; they can often substitute for artillery in the jungle and they are transportable in areas where terrain may be so rugged as to completely preclude the employment of even the lightest sort of pack howitzers. And artillery, fine weapon though it may be, cannot so often take the place of mortars. It cannot give the same closein and intimate sort of support, or be so constantly available to officers who are right there on the ground. In order to get quick help from supporting artillery the frontline doughboy must rely upon telephone or radio communication, both of which are definite uncertainties that become more and more uncertain as the fighting becomes more violent and the local situation becomes more desperate. Usually a loud shout, an arm and hand signal, or a word over a *very* short range phone or radio circuit will enable the doughboy in a forward hole to bring 81mm mortar shells, equivalent to 105mm artillery in destructive effect, smack down on the very enemy he has in sight.

Then too, the mortar is a simple weapon, easier to operate and maintain than the heavier artillery pieces which throw similar weights of high explosive. The only advantages which mortars concede to artillery are those of longer range and superior long range accuracy. Both of these advantages are frequently lessened in importance by the exigencies of jungle warfare; often they are of merely theoretical import. For instance, what good is fine accuracy and long range when the nature of terrain has forced

355

opposing units into very close grips with each other—when ranges are short and support fire must be laid very close in; or when there are no forward observers or no rearward phone or radio communication with supporting forces? To our battalion commanders, mortar support was a "bird in the hand"—a heavy weapon force under immediate control which could be wielded at their own bidding. Artillery and tactical aircraft support, though far harder-hitting, were things which would have to be asked for—obtained from another organization. *This always takes time.*

We always had and used artillery while conditions were more nearly ideal, but mortars were often our mainstay during more critical moments, such as surprise attacks, or during breakdowns in communications. And, as we learned to properly use mortars in combat, we grew more and more fond of them and we wanted to see the ones we possessed improved or modified to better fit them for jungle warfare.

The biggest trouble we had with mortars was that the Japanese had also grown fond of the damn things—years before we did—and they had *already* made their modifications and improvements.

The China Incident provided an excellent opportunity for the Japs to develop good mortars. Within the natural technical limitations of the Japanese ordnance, these weapons were brought quickly to a state of near-perfection, considering the specific tasks they were to perform and the personnel which would man them. The latter factor could not have been a severe limitation, for the Japanese, as I knew them, were good mortarmen.

We encountered skilled mortar crews on Guadalcanal, and we had nothing on them other than our usual quantitative superiority. In practical weapons they had us outgunned—we merely had a lot more mortars and ammunition.

But what the Japanese had they threw at us, teaching a few new tricks to the cleverest weapons-man we had, and causing us to quickly gain respect for several types of their mortars. The first models we were to learn of were the smallest—one of them not even considered a true mortar because of the crude method of laying and the fact that it was used for grenades as well as shells. We called this particular weapon a "knee-mortar" on Guadalcanal although we all knew that it could not be fired from the knee or thigh. It was a ground launcher and would project ordinary grenades beautifully for short distances—not far enough and not with sufficient destructive effect to be technically considered a true mortar, however.

But when they loaded this same gun with shell-type projectiles, longer and more streamlined than the grenades and containing a heavier explosive charge, it would step right out of its class and become a near-equal—in the jungle—to our own little 6omm mortar. For handiness and utility in small unit or patrol operations it was even better than the 6omm.

It was easily carried; its ammunition was light and handy; and it could be put into action on a very few second's notice. It was eminently suited for use against Americans—for, as I have previously mentioned—we had nothing with which to talk back. In the early days we often had to endure this type of Jap mortar shelling without replying, and when we finally did evolve a means of countering this quickly-laid fire, it was through a series of artifices which resulted in the utilization of a good substitute—not in the development of a good, quick action, short range mortar. There is a definite need now for such a weapon to bridge the gap between hand-thrown grenades and the heavier standard type mortars. To this day there has been no satisfactory weapon adopted by our Army to fill this need, just as there has been no standard organization of our hand grenades, rifle grenades and light mortar shells into a few simple and interchangeable patterns. Both of these deficiencies should have been corrected during the war.

The knee-mortar was discussed in the chapter on grenades, with emphasis on its employment as a grenade launcher. The description here will deal mainly with its capabilities as a mortar—or rather with what I myself consider its mortar usage.

This line between the knee-mortar's use as a grenade launcher and a mortar is thinly drawn. Different people have different ideas on the subject. My concept of a grenade launcher has always been that it must be fired directly, with the gunner observing the target and aiming right at it, and that it also must be fired with grenades for ammunition. When so used, the weapon is merely serving to increase the distance of grenade projection beyond the limits of hand-throwing and perhaps to also increase the accuracy of the throw.

A mortar, on the other hand, is used to increase the weight of the missile as well as the range, throwing a heavier charge a greater distance and performing a mission beyond the capabilities of any mere grenade launcher. A mortar is also habitually fired from defilade and aimed indirectly more often than not. So when the Japanese 5omm rifled grenade launcher, knee-mortar, or whatnot is fired with its heavier shells I prefer to call it a mortar. It fills the same job with this heavier shell as our own 6omm weapon which our books refer to as a mortar.

The real benefits of the Japanese knee-mortar are derived from its extreme lightness and portability, which make its support available to the very smallest fighting units. Its employment allows a group of four or five men to actually attack or hold with the ready support of a reliable, curved-trajectory weapon. In Japanese book tactics the platoon was the unit which utilized the weapon in coordinated support with one of its squads firing four such weapons to keep the enemy pinned down while the remainder of the platoon's squads maneuvered in the attack or held in defense. Such employment, under a platoon leader's control, is very similar to the role of our own light mortars.

The official designation of the knee-mortar was the M-1929 50mm Grenade Launcher. (The obsolete M-1921 is not considered here since it was unrifled—purely a grenade launcher—and only a few were found.) The M-1929, fired our way, had a set pattern of behavior and we were damned sorry to have it used on us so often. It could always go into action faster than our 60mm. Always we would feel the shells coming down on us in the very beginning of any kind of a fight, the explosions following immediately after the first few rifle shots, and our ability to reply was only theoretical. We had to go to a lot more trouble to make our 60mm gun do the job of answering these quick shooting knee-mortars. We had taken the bipods off and carried only a few light shells, burdening down the advance guard with the load, and yet the best we could do would be to commence firing a full minute after the first enemy shells had come down. Our gun was simply too heavy, even without the bipod, to permit it to be in the right spot and ready at the time the shooting began. This was because the tube and shells were too heavy and bulky, the latter usually packed or slung in a manner that would cause a period of fumbling before they could be armed and dropped into the tube. Marching is hard in the jungle; you can normally expect lightweight weapons to be in an alert position—perhaps even ready in a man's hand— but guns which are so heavy as to be a problem in manhandling are generally slung by an improvised strap. Often they must be carried on the back of a man who does not know how to use them while the tired gunner is regaining his wind. *Lightweight* is the greatest single advantage an Infantry weapon can have.

The M-1929 Jap knee-mortar was reasonably light in weight, going a little over ten pounds, and its shells weighed a bit less than two pounds each—not too much to be carried by men armed with pistols or carbines. We could have developed an even lighter weapon of the same type, had we tried.

This lightness was a common characteristic of most Jap mortars and artillery, especially as the weight of weapon was related to weight of missile. By designing them to throw the heaviest possible projectile with the lightest possible charge, the Japs got the most out of their weapons. They sacrificed range, and often accuracy, for target effect. For jungle warfare this was the right idea. Range has never been an important consideration in terrain where visibility is cut to almost nothing and where accurate observation of fire is usually impossible, even from elevated points. The M–1929 was a very lightweight job, but it threw a man-sized shell, not far behind our own light 60mm in effectiveness.

Because of its lanyard-firing arrangement, the weapon could be aimed at nearly all angles above horizontal, the curve of the spade base allowing a grip on the ground (or a log) when the lower angles were being used. Our 60mm tube could do nothing like this because it depended for ignition upon the fall of the shell against a fixed firing pin in the breech. However, the Japanese weapon was meant to be fired normally at a fixed angle of 45° with a variable chamber space providing an accurate means of adjusting range while the angle of tube was kept at 45°.

The Nips who used them soon learned that the knee-mortars could be used very effectively for launching grenades at very short distances, for pillbox ports and window targets. They could lay the barrel almost flat along the ground and fire at small openings with far better than hand-throwing accuracy. In this role, of course, the weapon was serving purely as a grenade discharger.

The greatest advantage of the variable volume chamber is one that is seldom mentioned in the books, but which none the less has great value in the jungle where one of the biggest problems of the mortar gunner is to find clearance for his gun to fire through a ceiling of tree limbs and leaves, usually almost solid above his head. With any ordinary mortar it is necessary to have a fair sweep of clear sky above the mortar in order to fire at all—in order for the shell to get through on its way up; and if the mortar is to have leeway for adjustments in range and deflection, this hole needs to be that much larger. This posed a great problem for the designers of jungle-employed mortars and yet the Japs neatly solved the problem by using two methods—one for the heavy type mortars and one for the lighter grenade launchers.

With their heavier mortars (medium mortars) they redesigned the ammunition to include a time delay device to prevent the shell from becoming armed immediately upon leaving the barrel. This assured that the shells would not detonate, regardless of what they hit, until they had gone a good distance above the treetops on their way up. Such shells could be fired through the usual screen of leaves and twigs without danger to the gun crew—a considerable advantage over our own early mortar ammunition which could detonate at any time after leaving the barrel.

In the case of the knee-mortar a different method was used but with the same result. The grenades for knee-mortar launching were time-fused, rather than impact-detonated, which allowed them to be shot through a ceiling of leaves and twigs with the same safety provided by the device used in the 81mm ammunition. Also, the variable chamber of the knee-mortar gave the gunner a whole scale of different ranges, finely adjustable, which could be lengthened or shortened without varying the angle of the barrel or the early path of the projectile. The shells would use the same route upward regardless of the range. This allowed various-ranged shells to all go through the same small hole in the ceiling of leaves, branches and twigs. This, in view of the usual scarcity of such holes, was a great advantage, much more important in the field than can ever be seen on paper. Our own 60mm didn't have it, so we often had to sit and endure the fire of an assortment of Japanese knee-mortar shells without handing anything back.

This assortment of projectiles for the knee-mortar included the high explosive shells, grenades, smoke shells, incendiary shells, and even some signal flares and rockets. Only the first two of these gave us any great trouble. This limitation was fortunate, because the high explosive shells and the grenades alone gave us trouble enough to last for the next hundred years.

THE 50MM MORTAR

The Japanese reached the ultimate in their interpretation of the heavy projectile-light gun concept when they designed their so-called 50mm mortar.

This gun was a small-calibered weapon with a bore diameter of only 50mm, but it threw an explosive charge which was all out of proportion to the mortar itself, both in caliber and weight. This charge was so large that any unit under fire would never dream that it could possibly be from a 50mm weapon, unless they had had previous experience with it. With such experience the weapon could be identified by the distinctive shape of its projectiles, or by the extremely short range from which they were fired, if there should be any means of determining the range to the gun.

In actual practice, the deceptively loud sound of the shell explosions would usually prevent true identification of the weapon until a projectile on the ground or in flight should be seen. When one would be actually seen, however, there would be no doubt of the weapon which fired it, for it was shaped like nothing else on earth—this unique shape providing the means by which such a large charge of explosive could be launched from a relatively small-calibered weapon.

The actual shell body of this weapon did not even fit into the barrel of the gun. It could not do so because it was of more than

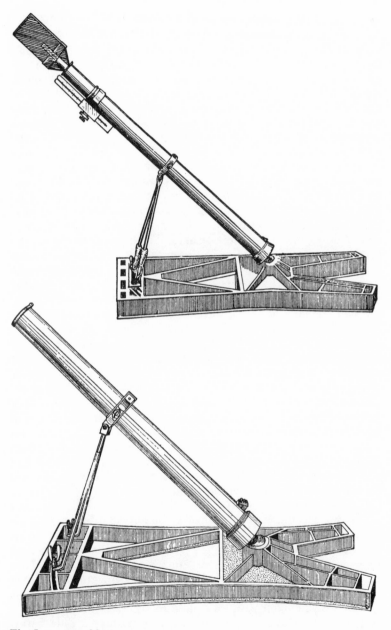

The Jap 50mm Mortar.

The M-1938 or Type 98 mortar; upper view shows gun with a stick bomb in loaded position.

twice-caliber thickness, and cubical in shape, not even roughly rounded off. The bore was filled and sealed instead by a long wooden stick, stoutly attached to the rear of the explosive charge head, which remained, when the weapon was fully loaded *outside* the barrel. The complete round had the appearance of a gigantic potato masher, with the long bore filler stick forming the handle and it soon received the semi-official name of "stick bomb."

When unloaded, the mortar looked rather like many of the conventionally designed European light mortars with an elongated baseplate, and a rather short and light bipod which fitted into the baseplate instead of resting upon the ground. The barrel was not exceptionally strong or thick-walled, and the barrelcap and socketball which fit into the baseplate were not massive either. The only piece of heavy duty construction was the recoil area of the baseplate; there plenty of recoil surface was provided to give a firm bedding in any soil, soft or hard. To obtain this advantage a certain amount of handiness had been sacrificed because the baseplate was of bulky construction. A rather large flat space would have to be cleared by the crew before the weapon could be steadily mounted, inevitably making it slower to get into action.

The baseplate, however, was the only bulky item of the entire assembly. With a barrel length of only two feet and the very light bipod, the weapon tended to be extremely portable—probably the most portable weapon in the world, considering the charge it threw. We had nothing like it in our own mortars. Its crudities were in the main no more than a few simplifications—the elimination of a few gadgets which could be done without.

One of the most obvious of these crudities was the traversing arrangement, which consisted of two arcs cut into the baseplate to permit the bipod legs to be shifted, with wingnuts to lock them in place. A second crudity, more apparent than the bipod arcs, was the lack of an elevating mechanism. The barrel, so long as the baseplate was kept leveled, could only point at a fixed angle—about 45° above horizontal.

On this account, the range had to be adjusted by varying the force of propulsion, a procedure with which the Japs had long been familiar—the same as they had used in their earliest designed knee-mortar. The 50mm mortar utilized the old variable-volume chamber principles which provided for various degrees of propulsion force by altering the powder burning space behind the shell. A simple and reliable gauge was used to accurately adjust the size of the combustion space. By means of a graduated slide fixture which clamped on the muzzle, the depth of the stick's projection into the barrel could be accurately controlled, with adjustments allowing a variation of about six inches in chamber length. By altering adjustments according to the markings on this slide fixture, the gunner could obtain a wide variation of ranges without changing the number of propellant increments. Further adjustment could, of course, be obtained by the latter means.

These propellant increments were furnished as a part of the complete round, which also included a lanyard-operated friction primer for insertion in the primer hole in the base of the barrel, and a set of two friction-type pull ignitors for the explosive charge. The strings of these pull ignitors were secured to the mortar after the ignitors themselves had been affixed to the explosive charge; on firing they would be torn loose, igniting the charge fuse.

In loading the sequence of operation was as follows: (a) Drop the desired number of increments into the muzzle; (b) Insert the stick bomb, fix the detonators and secure the string to the loops provided; (c) Insert the primer. (d) Fire by pulling the lanyard.

The gun would not shoot very far—the maximum range must have been something less than 500 yards—but when the heavy projectile arrived it would create one heluva disturbance. Accuracy could not have been much to brag about, with the poor ballistic shape of the projectile and its resultant sensitivity to wind, but in the jungle country accuracy, like range, is sometimes a secondary consideration. Despite such disadvantages the 50mm was a damn good weapon and we could have made good use of one like it.

However, I don't think that we should have copied, or even followed this weapon in its basic design. It was but one of the many devices for the solving of the weapons problems confronting Infantry in the jungle; there were many others just as good. We could have settled upon a new short mortar, or an adaptation of our current 81mm, to provide us with a weapon of lightness and portability, which will always remain the paramount consideration to the jungle Infantryman. A sawed-off and lightweight version of our 81mm, with a trigger firing mechanism and with simplified accessories, would have done the job neatly. It was evident from the start that we were severely handicapped without such a gun and even making every possible allowance for the difficulties involved, I still cannot see why our ordnance department failed to fulfill this need.

This sort of short 81mm weapon was what we needed—a better gun than the Japanese stick bomb thrower. But we didn't have it and didn't get it. Instead the Japanese got the jump on us a second time and added insult to injury by coming out in 1939 with the very gun *we* needed. They called it the M–1939 81mm Mortar, and it was the most perfect medium mortar for jungle fighting ever built—better than anything we had at the beginning or the end of the war.

THE MODEL 1939 81MM MORTAR

This fine weapon was nothing more than a jungle modification of the world famous (in all Armies) basic Stokes-Brandt design. As far as I know—in its newer, ultra-lightweight version—it was a pure Japanese idea, modified for handy carrying and short range use. Its development was obviously the result of a careful study of field needs. The Japs in the late thirties were fighting in the rugged hills and jungle tangles of Asia, while our own Army was at home getting so motor transport conscious that some of our officers were allowed to think that machine guns and mortars would never again have to be hand-carried beyond the truckheads for more than 500 yards. The Nips were organizing their Armies wisely and equipping them in a way that placed the correct amount of emphasis upon practical, usable weapons for the Infantry, while our own authorities, their butts firmly planted in station wagons or staff cars, kept dreaming of fighting a war on their own terms, in a country networked with concrete highways; at least it would seem this way from the sort of weapons we were given—all of them too heavy and bulky.

The Japs were not making these errors as far as most Infantry weapons were concerned. The lightness and compactness of some of their guns tended to make up for the tremendous blunders they were inclined to make in Infantry tactics. Surely it was not asking too much of the ordnance department to demand the design and production of a lighter version of another weapon already well proven in the field.

All that they had to do to the M–1937, their standard mortar which is very similar to our 81mm, was to reduce its length and weight, and then to modify it as necessary in order to make it function well in the lightened form; then they had the beautiful little M–1939. The modifications necessary—after the weight reductions in the barrel and baseplate—consisted principally of a slight reduction in bore diameter to obtain a better gas seal (more important in the shorter barrel) and in the addition of a trigger firing mechanism to permit the round to be fired *after* it had seated itself against the breech.

This last feature was necessary because the shorter barrels did not permit enough of a drop to provide a forceful blow against a conventional fixed firing pin, and also because the tighter fit of the bore tended to slow down the speed of the fall, reducing the impact of the round against the bottom of the tube (breech). In the longer-tubed mortars, the fixed firing pin was by far the best and simplest means of ignition, and its use served to increase the rate of fire. The trigger (or mallet) method of firing, however, is at least as positive as the fixed firing pin method and a little more safe.

These modifications from the conventional mortar design resulted in a greatly altered appearance for the M–1939, the shortness of the tube and bipod giving the weapon a comically, sawed-off profile—especially so to the eye of an old, range-trained mortarman. Men who were fresh from the States, cared very little for the weapon and all of them objected to its looks; but to the

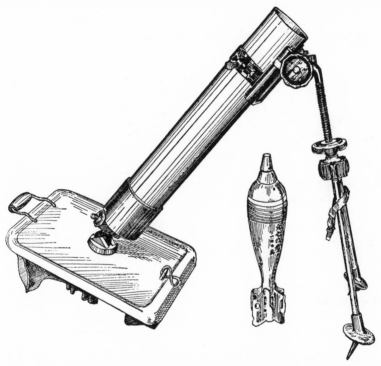

M–1939 or Type 99 Mortar in 81mm caliber with the M–1940 high-explosive shell.

man who had sweated for many weary miles under the load of a mortar tube or baseplate of conventional size and weight, the sight of such a trim and light little job was strictly for sore eyes. Here was a gun that could keep up with the battalion it was supporting; when called for *it would be there!*

With a total weight of 52 pounds, the gun was light enough to be carried almost anywhere a rifleman could go. It would be a much improved pack-animal load, allowing quite an enlarged number of rounds to accompany the weapon on the same mule-load—available and on-the-spot, not back 100 yards on another animal. The gun was very compact, the tube assembly being only twenty-five inches in length, and it could be broken down into loads which any group of men could carry without undue hardship. The barrel and baseplate were about eighteen pounds each in weight and the bipod assembly about sixteen, so squad members need not argue at length as to who would carry which. (This would have been an important consideration in the American Army—probably was in the Japanese too.)

As it always must, the ammunition remained heavy, the rounds weighing approximately seven and fourteen pounds each in the two weights found on Guadalcanal. I presume that the lighter shell was designed to lengthen the range of the weapon, what with the limited propulsion thrust in the short barrel. Of course, the heavier shell was more effective, retaining the punch which an 81mm mortar should possess. You can make the weapons themselves light for jungle use but you cannot lighten their ammunition without severely reducing the effectiveness of the combination.

The book gives this gun, using the light shell, a maximum range of 3200 yards—a rather imposing reach for a mortar. With the heavier (fourteen pound), more effective projectile, the range was reduced to 1300 yards. This is a little on the lean side for all-around mortar work, but entirely ample for any battalion weapon in the jungle. It is very seldom indeed that any part of a battalion's deployed combat echelon will be more than a few hundred yards to the rear of the fight. Sometimes our own battalions have been strung out to great lengths by the very weight of our unnecessarily heavy mortars and machine guns. Generally, maximum range is the very last concern of a mortarman in the jungle. His biggest worries concern the problems of weapons weight, overhead clearance, ammunition supply, and, often enough, *minimum range*.

Minimum range—the shortest distance at which a given weapon can be fired using the lightest possible charge—is something that was seldom considered when we were training in the States. It apparently did not occur to our instructors there that situations would occasionally arise where gunners would be unable to fire because their targets were *too near*. Rather, the problem always seemed to be concerned with long ranges, or complicated indirect fire exercises. Consequently, we went overseas without our gunners ever being warned that they might one day need to fire several shells at 100 yards range against a very important target, such as a grenade or Banzai party lying in defilade, maybe thirty yards from our frontline foxholes.

We performed such tasks with our mortars time and time again, though our early books declared it to be an impossibility. Our own ordnance publications, by listing the minimum ranges of the Jap 81mm, repeats, in spirit, this mistake. It gives a minimum figure of 207 or 545 yards for the seven and fourteen pound shells, a figure which is bound to be wrong in each case.

Actually, the *emergency* range of any Infantry mortar has no inward limitation. By devising various means of shifting the barrel upward, such as raising the bipod legs, or changing the resting angle of the baseplate, and by providing a means of bracing the barrel in an exaggerated, nearly-vertical position, the bursts can be moved inward until their explosions begin to endanger the crew. Ordnance experts would no doubt condemn this practice as unsafe, but on many occasions the poor doughboy longs yearningly for the comparatively slight dangers occasioned by close-hitting shells —especially when at the moment he may be in a much greater danger because of a half-dozen grenade pelting Japs. I have repeatedly called in mortar fire so that the shells were exploding thirty yards from my hole. It was dangerous and I got a big dent in my helmet, but I also got rid of a lot of big worries.

Short range work is done better by a mortar having the modifications of the M–1939. The tube and baseplate lend themselves better to the manipulations which must be accomplished to get the barrel pointing almost straightup, and the trigger firing mechanism is also helpful, though there is a slight reduction of the maximum rate of fire on its account. The M–1939 mortar was rated at fifteen rounds per minute—not exceptionally fast for a mortar.

The accessories and sights were simple, with the latter consisting of a collimator and two-way level unit, operating upon the same principle as our own mortar sights, which allowed the weapon to be easily operated by any of our own mortarmen. Loading and firing differed from our own only in that a stud at the breech must be struck sharply with a mallet after the round was seated instead of the shell firing itself by falling against a fixed firing pin in the base of the tube. This adaptation was necessary because of the shortness and tight fit of the tube and it brought with it at least one advantage—in emergencies the weapon could be braced against a stump or log and fired with the barrel in a nearly horizontal position; something almost impossible with the mortars Americans were using on Guadalcanal.

It has occurred to me that our weapons always seemed to lean too far in design toward technical perfection rather than field practicability. Somewhere in between the poor doughboy who carried, maintained, cleaned and fired the weapons, and the ordnance experts who designed them, there seemed to be a weak or missing link. In talking to the doughboy about his guns you would invariably hear him profanely state that the damn things were too blankety-blank heavy. He would always tell you to go ahead and sacrifice accuracy, range, or anything, but give him a gun he could carry as well as shoot—something reasonably light and compact.

In this the Infantryman is absolutely correct. Ordnance started him off in this war with a lot of guns which couldn't get up front in time because of their pounds of unnecessary weight and a gun that isn't *there* is worse than no gun at all.

Something has been done to correct this but not enough. Nearly every Infantry weapon—other than the carbine—should be further reduced in weight; the present rifle, machine guns and mortars are all entirely too heavy. Ordnance people will (with good reason) moan to high heaven that current weights should be maintained, but where Infantry weapons are concerned, the Infantry should furnish the specifications; and by "Infantry" I mean boards of selected young officers, experienced in combat or realistic exercises —not a group of grey-haired seniors who have been away from a rifle platoon for twenty years.

I wax bitter here for a strong reason. The Jap weapon I have just finished describing was a nearly perfect model of a specialized Infantry weapon, designed for practical field use. It fit the jungle and Infantry jungle tactics like a glove. The fact that we had nothing so good at the beginning of the war is one reason why someone should catch holy hell. The fact that we had nothing so good at the end is proof that the honest-to-God doughboy in our Army had damn little to say about the design of his own guns and what he did manage to say only fell on deaf ears.

The Model 1934 90mm Mortar

When they designed this weapon, the Japanese seemed to be going to the other extreme. They appeared to be building a gun almost as heavy as possible—far too heavy for practical hand-carrying. The gun had a total weight of about 350 pounds, with a heavy baseplate, a ponderously long tube, and a massive shock absorber group. The supporting bipod, of conventional design, was also very weightily constructed.

At first sight of this gun we felt that the Japanese, like ourselves, wanted to see their poor soldiers loaded down with a lot of needless iron. Much of the weight seemed superfluous, especially that of the shock absorber group (which Ordnance had been kind enough to leave off our own mortars).

Actually we were wrong in this criticism of the Japanese because what we were looking at was not a heavy mortar in a functional sense, but rather a lightweight artillery piece. It possessed tremendous range for a mortar (some 4000 yards), threw a fairly heavy charged projectile, and because of its especially stable mount, it tended to give the finest accuracy possible to obtain from an unrifled barrel. By our own standards the gun performed as a field piece, not a mortar, and by the same token it was not a suitable artillery weapon. But it must always be remembered that the Japanese were not as rich as we. They couldn't afford so much artillery or the trucks to do the towing, so they stretched the natural role of the mortar a bit farther than we. This was somewhat to their advantage because, in so doing, they could exploit the natural Japanese knack for employing mortars. Japs were generally good mortarmen and usually very poor artillerymen.

In principle, this heavier mortar was the same as all Stokes-Brandt mortars, but it had one unusual feature—a shock absorber mechanism which added a very heavy fourth member to the customary three-piece mortar breakdown load. In addition to the baseplate, tube, and bipod, the M-99 would employ this yoke, or shock absorber group, which consisted of a U shaped arrangement of two recoil cylinders.

The barrel or tube was also especially heavy, and it had a step about half way up on its outside surface which served to thicken the walls of the barrel at the breach where pressures would be greater. The gun was generally more massive of tube than any of ours, attesting to the Japanese idea of using the weapon as a comparatively long range gun, with heavy propelling charges.

Because the M-1934 was not truly an Infantry weapon, being mostly employed in artillery roles, it does not merit wordy description in this book. It was heavy, ungainly in appearance, with a 52 inch tube, a big rectangular baseplate with three separate socket holes for the single breech knob (which was on the yoke instead of the bottom of the tube). The weapon had a rather heavy bipod which made it look like the conventional type mortar from a distance—which, in principle, it was.

Its method of loading and firing was the same as our own, the gravity or fixed firing pin system. The firer simply dropped the shells, fins first, into the muzzle and they were automatically fired when they struck the fixed firing pin at the bottom. Aiming was also accomplished in roughly the same manner as our own, though an artillery type telescopic sight was employed instead of the usual collimator.

How well the gun filled its role for the Japanese, I do not know. On several occasions, however, its effectiveness was well demonstrated to my own battalion, creating quite a few casualties. It is probable that, for the relatively small use made of it, the weapon was highly effective.

As an Infantry mortar though, the M-1934 was about 150 pounds heavier than it should have been. For support from 3000 yards back, however, we would all rather make use of the weapons

Jap M–1937 or Type 97 Mortar in 81mm caliber.

we had such as the 105mm howitzer, which served us so well. Any mortar would be a second choice to good artillery for that purpose.

For the Japanese, however, there is little doubt but that this technically perfect mortar was a good investment, being the best possible mortar substitute for heavier and more expensive artillery. The Japanese always had a special tendency toward the wide use of mortars, even in units outside the organization of an Infantry regiment, so for them it was probably a good arrangement.

OTHER JAPANESE MORTARS

Of course, the Japanese had dozens of other mortar types on Guadalcanal, some their own, some captured. The ones I have described were those used against us or captured by our own regiment. Notable among these was the popular 81mm M–1937. This gun was the longer weapon which furnished the model—only two years after its own date of design—for the sawed-off, jungle adapted M–1939. So we see that the Japanese took only two years to develop the shorter weapon, proving themselves more alert than we. We took much longer to utilize even the single feature of the shortened tube—and even then we failed to properly pare weight off the other parts.

Other Japanese mortars worthy of mention are the M–1922 70mm rifled mortar, the 70mm Barrage or "Spike" mortar (used with parachute-suspended explosive segments against low-flying aircraft), and various other models ranging from 70 to 120 millimeters in caliber.

Hideo

JAPANESE ARTILLERY

A few words will suffice here; on Guadalcanal, thank God, the Japanese never used a lot of artillery against the units I served in and with, so I didn't learn much about it. Organized employment of Jap artillery, if there was any, occurred during the Marine phase of the operations or perhaps during the very early Army actions, before the 132nd Infantry was committed. Later on, they employed their guns only locally, sniping or pirating at individual targets— often timing their fire with that of our own guns in order to avoid detection and counter-battery fire. They would often fire just as one of our own salvos landed, and if they scored a hit we would nearly always get our own batteries on the phone and raise hell over the "shorts" we thought were being thrown at us. It took us a while to learn the truth. Sometimes we had to actually find the warm shell fragments, clearly recognizable as Japanese, before we would believe that the damage was not done by our own guns.

Generally we would identify the Jap shell fragments as coming from one of two different models of gun, either of which we had seen and could describe, because several of them had been parked back in the ordnance dump at the beach. These were the guns which the Japs were most likely to carry up front and employ because they were not merely in support—they actually *belonged* to the Infantry regiments and battalions.

They were of 70 and 75 millimeter caliber, and were correctly referred to as the "battalion howitzer" and "regimental gun." The 70mm, M–1932 was standard equipment for the Infantry battalion, with an issue of two per battalion being normal (sometimes there seemed to be more—perhaps the additional had been taken over from annihilated units). The 75mm, M–1908 was issued to the larger units, four to each Infantry regiment.

For the most part, we were shot at with the smaller weapon— the battalion howitzer—because this piece was generally more plentiful and easier to transport into difficult terrain areas. Wherever the Japanese went they would take that gun with them. It was designed to be animal-drawn or packed, but it was usually hand-carried—for which purpose it could be broken down into not-impossible loads. We found one such weapon (attesting to this quality of portability) setting smack atop Mount Austen—a very remote and inaccessible point. This gun was complete and

Jap M–1932 Battalion Howitzer caliber 70mm.

intact, with a fair supply of ammunition stacked nearby in pack-strap rigged ammo carrying cases.

We were too busy to pay much attention to the little gun when we first came upon it because we had close to sixty wounded and dying on our hands and a raging fight all around. But later on we fired it under circumstances which gave me the unusual opportunity of seeing a Japanese weapon in action—against the Japanese.

The shooting was done by the Marines who had been with the artillery liaison party under Captain Hitt, before he had been wounded and sent back. They fired the weapon in fine style, loading it up in the most indifferent manner, with the whole crew kneeling nearby, completely unconcerned, while the lanyard was jerked.

We were all looking on interestedly—largely from dispersal

shelters since a fair bit of enemy fire was still crackling through the air. This was during our first long breathing spell—the third day after the assault.

The first round was loaded up with only one increment—the lightest possible propellant charge. The gun went off properly. The tube recoiled, wheels jumped slightly, and the projectile, clearly visible, soared off in a mortar-like trajectory toward Tojo-land. We watched the shell plunge into a bit of Jap occupied cover and waited for the explosion. None came; the Marine had neglected to arm the fuse.

He disassembled another of the semi-fixed rounds, this time arming the fuse and leaving two increments in the case. We were able to both hear and see the explosion after we had watched the shell on its way. The blast threw a big cloud of debris upward and slammed like Billy-be-damned.

The Marines, happy with their new toy, chuckled—the rest of us, looking on, chuckled too. Then the gun crew took a few minutes time out from firing, and prepared all of the remaining ammunition for loading. Then they blazed all of the shells away, loading and firing as fast as they could, shouting formal-sounding commands at each other in mock-Japanese. One of the Marines was even costumed for the show, he had donned a Japanese helmet. He would pivot around after each shot and shout at the onlookers.

BANG! "So sorry!" he would shout, "Wrong Island! Chalkie up one!—BANG! So sorry! Wrong Island! Chalkie up two!"

And so on. By the time the last round was fired the entire hilltop was in stitches. The corny imitation and the silly looking miniature helmet perched atop the big Marine's long-grown mop had been more than we could stand. Some of us were rolling on the ground. The Japanese must have disliked the sound of our belly-laughs for as soon as the gun ran out of ammunition, they sent over a barrage of knee-mortar shells and got us all back to serious thinking again.

A later examination of the captured gun brought forth a certain amount of approving comment from all of the artillerymen on the hill. They all seemed to think it a pretty good little weapon, well constructed on the heavy-projectile, light-gun theory. Its ammunition was strange looking because of the relative largeness of the projectiles. These were almost three times the length of the case, which was tumbler-size and barely large enough to hold a small amount of silk-sacked propellant powder. The gun was in comic miniature, with a barrel length of only 30 inches and with shells not much more than two feet in length. The total weight was 470 pounds, maximum range some 3000 yards. Muzzle velocity varied from 340 to 650 feet per second, depending on the charge used.

The M–1908 or Type 41 Regimental Gun in 75mm caliber.

As a performer, the gun was nothing to stack alongside our own little pack 75mm, but it was still a nice little weapon—even if it did look like a toy.

The Regimental Gun

This 75mm weapon, the M–1908 Infantry gun, was identified by the peculiar tubular construction of its single trail. The piece breaks down into six mule-loads having a total weight of 1200 pounds, and it is ballistically in a class with our own 75. Its ammunition is, of course, heavier than that of the 70mm battalion howitzer in order to attain the 7000 yard maximum range. Higher velocity—some 1200 foot seconds—allows the shells of the 75mm regimental gun to keep up with their own sound and strike without warning. This is a marked advantage over the 70mm, which has slower-moving projectiles, always proclaiming their arrival with a long-drawn-out "whirr-whirr-whirr" long before they land and explode. With the 75mm there can be no comfortable lolling on the foxhole edge. To be safe one must keep below ground level.

The general appearance of the piece is not imposing. It is larger than a battalion gun, but to American eyes it is still cast in miniature with its largest feature—the 12-spoked wheels—being of no more than medium size. In actual use, however, the gun was a good performer, shooting well and ranging far. More than a year later, in Burma, this same weapon was to cause my friends and myself much trouble. Even with the small number of rounds fired at us on Guadalcanal, it succeeded in making a lasting impression. The Japanese Army had some pretty good tools, and this was one of them.

They had other artillery models and calibers, some of which I've had shot at me, but most of which I never knowingly encountered. Many of these were of 75mm caliber—it seemed to be a popular bore with the Japs—and many were 105mm howitzers captured on Guadalcanal, though they were fired very little in the sectors I knew. In Burma I learned how lucky we were to have been spared that bitter cup.

In general, Japanese artillery was seldom employed in the American tradition of massed fire—which made the war a lot less tough for our doughboys. This, of course, was partially due to a shortage of weapons and ammunition. Japanese Infantry seemed often to be limited to its own organically assigned guns, fighting without outside artillery support. This circumstance—doubtless furthered by poor Japanese inter-arm cooperation—was our own good fortune. It saved our artillery from great worries about counter-battery fire in the Pacific war. It made things much easier for the doughboys.

If there were no other unglamorous aspects to frontline fighting at all, one well-laid artillery barrage would still be enough to convince any reasonable man that during the past hundred years war had lost all of its glamorous appeal. Artillery is the most wicked and unfair weapon in modern warfare.

ANTI-TANK GUNS

Having had very little to do with their employment, I can write but briefly of these weapons. The Japanese had a few models on the island and used them very infrequently. Most of their anti-tank and anti-vehicular measures were concerned with the employment of mines and grenades rather than guns. We came across many land mines and hand-thrown mines and learned to respect some of them very much, especially the magnetic hand-thrown type or "turtle" mine, which was as effective as all of the other Japanese anti-tank measures put together. Regular anti-tank guns were very scarce, and I saw only a few. I was able to fire one model, however, and I found it to be a very interesting weapon.

It was the M–1937 20mm AT Gun, a low-profile bipod and butt-rest mounted automatic rifle, chambered for a very heavy-charged 20mm cartridge which was loaded in both armor-piercing and high-explosive types. I got my first good look at this weapon at Cape Esperance where we captured several and played with them until we ran out of ammunition. They were fun to shoot.

They looked like a lot of gun for shoulder firing, so when I first shot one I did so by remote control—by kneeling off to one side and reaching gingerly for the trigger. I couldn't see the idea of placing a shoulder against the small pad at the rear of the weapon when the gun fired such a huge cartridge. I was needlessly afraid, of course. The rear leg of the tripod (or buttrest) had a deep shoe which kept the weapon firm against recoil.

In my shooting of the gun, which must have included the firing of at least fifty rounds, I never learned very much about its characteristics. In fact, I guess I proved myself to be about the most non-observant human alive. After popping away for a half-hour, shooting at sharks and floating objects, one would expect to learn at least whether or not the gun was a semi- or full-automatic, but I didn't. I had to read about it later in a manual. When firing I squeezed off one shot at a time, with no conscious efforts to release

378

the trigger quickly after each shot. Yet—though the gun had a full-auto action—it never once doubled, and I went away thinking it a semi-automatic. All of the present day manuals call it a full-auto and say that it cannot be fired semi-automatically. All I can say is that it must have one hell of a slow cyclic rate.

It was gas-operated, used 7-round top-fitted box-type magazines, and weighed 150 pounds with the carrying handles attached. Though more powerful, it was in roughly the same class as our .50 caliber ground mount machine gun, which we later discarded as ballistically inadequate. For modern armor, a heavier caliber is required.

However, the Second Battalion liked these Jap 20mm guns a lot. They were fine weapons for our beachcombers' club—good for sharks, especially with high explosive shells.

I saw, but did not examine, some of the M-1934 37mm split-trail AT guns. They were all in beach defense positions (in which role they would have proven highly effective), and had all been either rusted or demolished by the time we got to them. They were roughly like our own 37mm gun, but lacked the high speed carriages. Instead, they had regular artillery or metal-stamped wheels, suitable only for slow towing. Their ammunition, as I remember, seemed to have rounds which were lighter and smaller than our 37mm stuff, with less powder space in the case. Like ours, the loadings were in both armor-piercing and high explosive types. In an overall appraisal, the gun looked good, but not quite as good as ours.

The Japanese had another gun of 37mm caliber, a small howitzer, which was similar to our M-1916 of the same caliber. We found these smaller 37mm guns in several places on the island, mostly in spots considerable distances inland where heavier guns could not be carried. With an overall weight of only 200 pounds, four men could carry the gun for very short distances. A few additional men, trading off with the broken down loads, could get it into places completely inaccessible to ordinary artillery.

Employment of this obsolete weapon on Guadalcanal should by no means be criticised. There was, in fact, a crying need in our own organization for such a gun. In those early days, before the development of rocket launchers or rocket guns, a lightweight 37mm gun would have been worth its weight in gold to jungle Infantry. With an explosive shell of some sort, it could have been used as a means of penetrating the log and dirt pillboxes in Japanese defense positions—a task for which we had no satisfactory weapon at that time. Certainly it would have been much more useful to us than was the heavier, standard 37mm of our own anti-tank squads. We took twelve of those guns to Guadalcanal with the regiment and they proved to be wellnigh useless. Except for beach defense missions, there was no proper need on Guadalcanal for any new, high speed carriage anti-tank guns. Our own and those of the Japanese could have been left at home—with mutual benefit.

We often heard of heavier anti-tank weapons, of 47mm and larger caliber, but I never saw any. Except in a few of the operations of the 25th Division, employment of tanks on Guadalcanal was negligible; and such countermeasures were seldom called for. The only specific instance I know of was a short fight in which the Marines quickly knocked out several Jap mediums as they attempted to cross a sandspitted river mouth.

There was some use of AT guns for anti-personnel purposes, either potting from ridge to ridge at targets of opportunity or else firing in last-ditch defense at very short range, using cannister shot ("grape") and high explosive. At best, though, Guadalcanal was no testing ground for AT weapons and tactics. It just wasn't good country for tanks or anti-tank weapons.

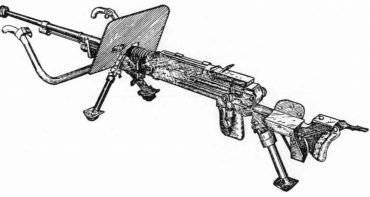

Jap M–1937 or Type 97 Anti-Tank Rifle in 20mm

JAPANESE SMALL ARMS AMMUNITION

One of the Japanese failings was in the poor care they gave to the packaging and storage of their ammunition. None of the thousands of rounds I have seen had been hermetically sealed, even in the climate of Guadalcanal. Most of it was not even well protected with waxed cardboard or waterproof paper—which seemed to me the least that the Nippon home front could have done for her fighting men. It was the height of stupidity to load ammunition carefully and then store it in ordinary boxes with inside containers of lowgrade cardboard.

It was handled in such a careless manner as to cause a good deal of real trouble for the Japanese, too. Much of their ammunition would misfire and otherwise malfunction, and some of it which was not well finished to begin with, soon became so corroded that the cases would not extract from the chambers after firing. In the storage areas the packages of ammunition and supplies were well cared for—stacked on dunnage and covered, but in the Islands that is not enough. The very air is a corroding agent, capable of rusting any poorly protected ferrous-metaled surface in a matter of hours, and brass or copper in a matter of days.

Packing boxes used by the Japanese were generally well constructed, but the boards and lids were not tightly fitted, leaving wide cracks for moisture and white ants to enter. The little cardboard boxes on the inside were usually unwaxed, serving only to subdivide the contents of the case—rather than to protect the contents, and the white ants would quickly tunnel the cardboard containers into tatters. The Japanese cargo parties had an easier time than we did in carrying these wooden cases because their loads had rope handles for lifting, while our cases were bare.

Most Japanese ammunition is unmarked—you have to see the containers or else recognize it by size and shape of round. The only marking on the cartridge heads is generally the primer-crimp stampings, normally made in the form of punch marks. These mutilate the cartridge head badly and cannot help but have a bad

381

effect on headspace, chambering, and loading. In appearance, these punch marks are shortline indentations, usually three in number, radiating out from the primer pocket, with their inner points leaning naturally in to lock the primer in seat—a crude arrangement, by our standards. Lacquer identification colors sometimes appeared on the cartridges with the rule seeming to be red for ball, green for tracer, and black (as with our own ammunition) for armor-piercing.

The caliber most often seen was the 6.5mm standard semi-rimmed rifle cartridge. It was packed in the conventional boxes, some with each clip placed in a separate cardboard fold, others with three clips packed together. This last was for convenience in loading the conventional 30- and 60–round Jap cartridge pouches. Other calibers were packed in wooden boxes, even the 7.7mm stuff, which was in cloth-protected 30-round strips for the heavy machine guns.

Immediate combat loads of rifle ammunition were carried in bandoleers and in the leather (or ersatz rubber) regulation Japanese cartridge pouches, which were worn by all Japanese Infantrymen—three pouches per individual. Two of these pouches were of 30-round capacity and were worn in front of the belt on either side of the buckle. Another with a capacity of 60 rounds was worn in back, attached by loops to the leather (or rubber) belt. The complete cartridge belt was bulkier than ours, and the cartridge boxes protruded farther out than did the filled pockets of our belt, causing some difficulty in crawling or creeping against the ground or through cover. From the standpoint of protecting and keeping ammunition clean, this arrangement was probably superior to our own and it could hold 120 rounds against the American beltload of 80 rounds.

After coming across such large amounts of 6.5mm stuff in every imaginable form (even some in which the bullets had been pulled and reseated backwards in the cases), we began to discover large stores of 7.7mm, both semi-rimmed (for the 1932 HMG only) and rimless (for both rifle and machine gun use). We also saw a lot of 8mm pistol ammunition and a few rounds of 7mm for the Baby Nambu. There were also considerable amounts of Jap-loaded .303 British cartridges lying all around.

As well as I can remember, that just about closes the list of popular calibers of Japanese ammunition which we saw on Guadalcanal. It doesn't touch the scores of foreign calibers, of which only a few rounds were found with weapons the Japs had picked up as souvenirs. To adequately describe *that* list, one would have to make up a catalog of all the modern (and earlier) weapons now used in the entire world.

Probably the larger part of these different foreign guns were not being officially adopted, even by small units. They were mostly picked up by Japanese soldiers who, like our own rank and file, were generally unable to appraise the true worth of a handgun or rifle. The Japanese were souvenir hunters, pack rats like ourselves, only a little less discriminating. They apparently stole everything they could find, whether they could use it or not. Some of their rear areas, which had been hurriedly deserted, looked exactly like junk yards, with every possible type of old European, American, and Asiatic manufactured handgun laying around. Most of them had a few old corroded cartridges alongside marked, often enough, with the trade mark "UMC" or "WRA."

Hideo

OUR OWN GUNS

An appraisal of our own Infantry weapons, made by persons who have used them in combat, will generally result in uniform findings—our guns were good and they did their job well, but they should have been one hell of a lot better! We got along all right with what we had, but we could have gotten along much better. In many ways it was tragic that our weapons at the beginning of the war were not as good as they have become since.

The criticisms which can be directed at our entire Infantry weapons outlay are few in number, but sometimes justifiably bitter when made by men who have suffered because of their deficiencies. Perhaps the greatest of the general criticisms, applicable to nearly all of our Infantry weapons, is that most of our guns were overweight.

Nearly all of our guns were too heavy. Insufficient attention was devoted in their design and manufacture to reduction of weight by skeletonizing, fluting, and otherwise removing excess metal. Too little thought was given to the employment of lightweight metals and alloys in the manufacture of appropriate parts of most hand-carried weapons. With the exception of the carbine and the new rifled rocket guns, our guns were too heavy. A constant effort should be made to lighten them. No matter what the diehards say, the need for such reduction in weight and bulk is vital. Several things were proven by World War II battle instances where our forces, who were in pursuit of a beaten foe, actually discarded and left behind to rust more weapons than they captured. The most important of these proven points is that equipment was wasted because doughboys were too heavily loaded down. His load was perhaps reduced somewhat from that of the soldier of World War I, but it should have been pared down much more. A man cannot fight half so well when he is exhausted by a few excess pounds of equipment which could have been eliminated with only a little more effort from the rear.

384

Next, after the weight criticism, comes the fault of nonstandardization. Our guns are perhaps better standardized than those of any other Army, but there is still room for more effort in that direction, particularly where grenades and grenade projectors or small mortars are concerned. Many of the natural advantages of grenades have never been exploited in our army because of the lack of standardized grenade bodies and an adequate assortment of launchers to fit this standardized grenade. The very design of rifles, for instance, should be engineered with the idea of ready adaptation to grenade throwing devices. Every individual rifleman should have at his disposal means of rifle-launching grenades, as well as throwing them by hand. This would double range and accuracy and enable the rifleman to fire grenades at targets too difficult for hand-throwing.

Grenades too, should be designed with the realization that they may be projected by several different means: hand-thrown, rifle-launched, or even set as boobytraps. And one type of grenade should be interchangeable, or nearly so, in all of these launching devices. By screwing a small tailfin assembly on a regular fragmentation grenade, the rifleman should be able to adapt it to his rifle launcher. And two men in each squad should be able to fire the same grenades from ground launchers, after simply screwing small propelling charges onto the grenade body.

Standardization, however, should not be interpreted to amount to absolute uniformity—that one set of Infantry weapons must be made to do for all types of operations in every variety of terrain. For fighting in flat, open country, with plenty of transport available, our present heavyweight weapons could be used. But it should be remembered that heavy guns, regardless of caliber, are specialized weapons, unemployable on many battlefields.

THE GARAND OR M1 RIFLE

This rifle was probably the very best in the war, and the best military hand weapon ever placed on the battlefield in appreciable numbers. Its employment had the very desirable effect of doubling the strength of our frontline platoons, in either defense or attack. It gave an American squad the ability to slug it out on the trail with a Japanese company, and hold for a long time. The gun was amply accurate, powerful, and it was quite reliable.

I doubt if any of the far-sighted men who recommended, years ago, that we adopt a semi-automatic service rifle really knew what an understatement they had made when they said such an adoption would be "advantageous." Advantageous is no word to even halfway describe the true value of a semi-automatic military weapon!

A soldier is able to shoot faster, to be more alert, to keep his senses glued where they should be—away from the rifle he is shooting and *on* the target. Such a weapon allows the doughboy to fire several shots in rapid succession, trebling the effectiveness of his fire against briefly exposed or fleeting targets—which are the types most often encountered in combat. He does not have to aim at the exact outline of an enemy concealed in the brush, he can blaze away at an approximate location and distribute his fire so that he will be very likely to score a hit. And there is no bolt to be awkwardly fumbled between shots. Thousands of Infantrymen will remember instances in which they fervently thanked God that they were able to "fire that last shot" without the delay of bolt operation. If each of these soldiers had had to fumble in recharging his weapon, *he* would have been killed instead of the Japanese or German.

The reduced recoil of the M1 was another advantage worthy of note, as was the readily adjustable rear sight and the wide and sturdy front. The whole weapon was substantial, practical, and reliable—by all past standards the Infantryman's perfect weapon.

But past standards are not sufficiently critical. They are based upon the guns which have already been made and used, mostly by the Armies of other nations. History can supply only a part of the necessary stimulus for weapons improvement. Our guns should be continually re-examined in the light of testimonials from men who have used them in combat, and every effort should be made to correct revealed faults, to strike a better compromise between field practicability and technical perfection, which is after all the principal goal of weapons design.

Looking at it from that angle, we can find quite a few things wrong with our current service rifle, viz.:

First of all, the weapon has too much wood, metal, and leather or canvas in it and on it. It is too heavy, and it is too thick about the balance. The largest hand has difficulty in obtaining a comfortable carrying grasp around the thick magazine portion of the stock. The sling swivels are unnecessarily massive, the leather sling unduly heavy—a light carrying strap would be better.

It is not really up to the Infantryman to tell Ordnance *how* to lighten the service rifle, all he should have to do is to tell the design and manufacturing agency that it *is* too heavy. It is logical that every effort should be bent to fill the doughboy's stated needs, without requiring him to make the changes or to go into detail in answering the question "How?" But in the case of the M1 many of the errors, as far as weight is concerned, are obvious at first glance. The buttplate, the gas chamber, and sections of the receiver are unnecessarily heavy; weight could be removed from all of these parts.

If a certain amount of performance must be sacrificed to achieve this lighter weight, then let the doughboy in combat decide how much performance can be spared—not the test sergeant on the range or the ordnance engineer. If it is feared that the lighter version will recoil too heavily, let the man who will carry the gun twenty-five miles a day decide how heavy it will be—and it'll be light; better a bruised shoulder than a man out cold on the trail from exhaustion, or a fight lost because badly needed reserves, weighed down with equipment, couldn't march fast enough to arrive in time. For my part, if they leave the Garand at its present weight, I am going to fit a Bren gun type handle to mine so that it can be carried like a machine rifle rather than an individual weapon. (This is truth, not attempted humor; handles of this sort would be a convenience.)

And while fitting this carrying handle, I would be fervently wishing myself able to make a more complicated change, one to rectify the second greatest fault of the Garand—its magazine system.

An eight-round clip is fine—it's nice to be able to fire that many times without reloading. But it is not so good to *have* to fire that many—to be obliged to completely empty the gun before it can be reloaded, which is almost a necessity with the M1. There are times when one wants badly to restore the full magazine capacity of the weapon before the whole eight cartridges have been fired. Picture the plight of the soldier whose unit is in the assault, who has fired four or five very necessary shots, and then finds himself under the last bit of cover, only a few yards from the enemy positions.

What can he do? In a moment he will have to spring up and rush the enemy shelters. It would be awfully nice for him to have a full eight rounds ready to fire then, but he has only three. Or was it two? Hard to remember.

In order to load up he would first have to unload the remaining rounds. Such an operation is simple, but not easy. With nervous fingers he has to pull back the bolt and eject the chambered cartridge, then press the clip release and pick up the clip from the top of the receiver, causing the remaining rounds to fall out loosely on the ground. Then he must fumble with belt or bandoleer, slip in a fresh clip, and close the bolt. He may as well forget about the three cartridges that fell in the mud, dust, or snow—no time to search for them.

For the doughboy, all of this amounts to a nervous ten seconds or more, during which entire period he must fumble with both hands, rise to a semi-exposed position, *and render himself temporarily defenseless, with a weapon which cannot fire. If the loading operation had to be halted suddenly and the weapon put into action, the result would probably be a jam.*

It is a serious fault in design which makes all of this fumbling necessary. No claim of perfection or even of technical adequacy can be justifiably made for any rifle which is as awkwardly loaded as the Garand. A rifle should permit easy loading of any number of rounds at any time, without emptying the chamber or rendering the weapon inoperative while its magazine is being filled. The rifle should *always* be ready to fire.

So far as I know, the Johnson rifle is the only military rifle which meets this specification, and it does so admirably by means of a cleverly designed rotary magazine with a sidegate loading port, independent of the bolt passage. The Johnson can be loaded by a rifleman on the run—one, two, three, or any number of rounds (up to ten) at a time. The individual cartridges are simply thrust through the gate, or five-round chargers (Springfield clips) can be handily stripped into the magazine. In the field, a Johnson type magazine would eliminate two thirds of the present delay and danger of reloading.

The faulty magazine is the last of the major complaints against the M1—the remaining defects are minor, and could be easily corrected. The gas chamber is too bright—a dead give away after the finish wears off. The front end of the weapon should be better adapted for the attachment of a grenade launcher and the ridiculous and outmoded stacking swivel should be left the hell off. And, for my part, so should the bayonet stud. Cold steel is a thing of the past, no matter how dear it may be to the hearts of the grey-bearded diehards.

With all its faults, however, the Garand remains a splendid weapon. No bolt operated rifle merits comparison. Perhaps the best proof of its true combat effectiveness was in the attitude displayed by Marines on Guadalcanal. Nearly all of the Marine personnel had been armed with the Springfield, reportedly because of Corps preference—not because of the unavailability of Garands. So the first "allied aggressive effort" of World War II was made with a World War I rifle.

The mistake was soon realized. From almost the first minutes of combat on Guadalcanal the Marines began wishing for a basic semi-auto rifle. By the time we landed we had to keep ours tied down with wire. Leathernecks were appropriating all they could lay hands on by "moonlight requisition." In daylight, they would come over to our areas to barter souvenirs with the freshly landed doughboy units; any crooked supply sergeant who had an extra M1 rifle could get all the loot he wanted.

When the Marines began to get a few Garands up to the front

the demand proportionately increased. They quickly learned that the M1 did not jam any more often than the Springfield, and that it was equally easy to maintain. The disassembly system, especially, made the M1 much easier to clean and oil.

In the matter of jams and malfunctioning it seemed very doubtful if the Springfield proved as reliable as the Garand, round for round. The old faults of the M–1903—a frequently-broken firing pin assembly and a delicate front and rear sight—seemed to account for as many stoppages in combat as feeding difficulties did with the M1. Springfields, over a long period of time, might show less operational defects than an equivalent number of Garands, but this proves nothing. The Garands would have been fired a lot more and a lot faster, and would most likely have caused the greater number of enemy casualties.

I know of several instances where the firing pin rod tip broke on a Springfield, rendering the weapon useless or very unreliable. I have also learned what a little jar it takes to bend or loosen the front sight blade. The defects alone caused more trouble among those I have seen employed than all of the feeding difficulties encountered with the Garand. *This is despite the fact that I have observed perhaps fifty Garands to each Springfield.* And most of the stoppages encountered in M1 firing are not "stoppages" at all. The greater part of them merely nullify the semi-auto feature, leaving the soldier yet armed with a weapon that can be hand operated almost as fast as a Springfield in perfect condition. Yes, the Marines were justified in their yen for the Garand. Once in combat, no one could see logic in remaining in the same armament class with the Japs. Most of the officers who had been appalled at the Garand's lack of target accuracy were quick to give it due credit in combat.

The behavior of one Marine corporal seemed to epitomize this attitude. It was during the organization of a joint Marine-Infantry patrol, shortly after we had landed. I saw this Marine, a member of the 2nd Marine Raider Battalion, place and keep himself squarely behind one of the army sergeants in the advance platoon. When the march was well under way the sergeant inquired as to why the leatherneck kept treading on his heels.

The answer came quickly: "You'll probably get yours on the first burst, Mac. Before you hit the ground I'll throw this damn Springfield away and grab your rifle!"

THE OLD M–1903 SPRINGFIELD

The old timers in the shooting game may as well face it—this last war, which caused the breaking of so many sentimental attachments, has broken one for them. The good old army rifle that performed so well in World War I and earlier and which, in its National Match version (with an O'Hare micrometer) endeared itself to the hearts of thousands, is slated for the junk-heap. The coming generation of competitive riflemen will spend their sunny and rainy range days shooting and cussing at a new and different military rifle. True, most of the present matches are still being conducted under old rules, with the Springfield still holding its own, but it's only a matter of time. The current (and possibly the last) military rifle is now a semi- or semi-and-full-automatic. Any nation who sends her Infantrymen into battle with a manually operated rifle in the next war will place her soldiery at a clear disadvantage. For no matter how smoothly a bolt action operates, no matter how conveniently it can be recharged, it is a weapon always second best to a properly designed self-loader.

Fire-power, that fetish of modern tactitians, is a factor in battle that cannot be disregarded. Only veteran troops can overcome the natural feeling of fear that assails any doughboy who finds more coming at him than he is capable of throwing back, even if the shots are poorly aimed and physically ineffectual. That's the psychological side of it.

When opposed squads, platoons or companies of soldiers face each other in battle with one side armed merely with bolt operated guns and the other with semi-autos of current design, the outcome will generally be easy to predict. The group with the semi-autos will win. Exceptions to this rule there may be, but of very rare occurrence. That's the physical side of it.

So, those of us who used to seasonably wear callouses on our hands with hours of bolt manipulation exercises, finally glorying in the way we could flip the bolt in rapid fire with a hand motion as sudden as the strike of a rattlesnake, will find things changed on the ranges. We'll fire almost twice as many rounds in the same time during rapid-fire stages, and the chances are that the individual shots will be held just as well as before. The rifles will be a little more awkward at first—the target shooting clan will have its troubles learning how to hash these new guns over, to make them shoot where they look and to keep the zero constant, but in time they will be accepted and do just that. Maybe a National Match version of our current military rifle will be brought out, and some good ammunition loaded for it. In time, this combination will surpass all existing target records.

Well, it's all according to History's pattern, seen many times before. The match lock enthusiasts were skeptical of the wheel lock and flint locks, and the flint lock riflemen were distrustful at first of the percussion cap. Breech loading rifles received a cold reception in the beginning. Many of us, who thought we knew what we were doing, were open in our condemnation of the Garand at first appearance, but it proved its worth to all.

I don't think the Garand the latest-word in rifles, by any means, but it will never be replaced by a manually operated gun. Autoloaders are here until something even more revolutionary comes along. In a few years the M–1903 will take its place alongside the Krag and the Trap Door Springfield, as a museum piece.

As a basic Infantry weapon, the M–1903 rifle had a minor role in our army in this last war. We armed the troops of other nations with it, and it performed for them as well as any good bolt gun could be expected to. Marines, skeptical of the M1, used it in the early part of the war, including, I think, the whole of the Guadalcanal fight, but they were quick to get rid of it afterward. Aside from a few sniper weapons I saw little or no use of the weapon in the hands of good troops. It would be quite unfair to the gun to list its behavior in the hands of our Oriental Allies, the Chinese.

Most of my info concerning it is therefore hearsay, and little is complimentary. Nearly every one I have talked to who used the Springfield in combat—without a scope—would have much rather been using a Garand. Marines begged, borrowed, and "promoted" from us every M1 they could lay their hands on. Those who had to keep the '03 were inclined to complain.

First of all they hated the slow-firing quality of the weapon. Many did mention that its lighter weight was a point of advantage over the Garand. But at the same time they would bitch about the breaking strikers, the ill-fit stocks on the older ones, the excessive recoil, the standard uncheckered buttplate on some models. One big complaint was that they had to move around between shots to operate the bolt, giving away their location to enemy riflemen. And, of course, there were eternal moans about the mere five shot magazine capacity. Five shots aren't as good as eight.

Accuracy—the last edge you could get at long range with the M–1903—was of absolutely no value in 99 per cent of our fights. Most men could shoot the M1 better anyway. All with whom I talked complained bitterly about the poor combat sights on the '03. And in the matter of malfunctioning I am not sure that the M–1903 was not much less reliable than the M1. Strikers and ejectors broke, so did firing pin rods, sears, and even bolt-lugs.

In the climate of Guadalcanal it was a great advantage to be able to *frequently* disassemble and clean all the working parts of the weapons. With the M1 this could be readily accomplished, with the Springfield it was not so easy. The trigger and sear of the Springfield gave occasional trouble on that account. On the basis of cuss-words per gun-hour in combat, I am willing to bet that the Springfield would beat the Garand all hollow. In fact, about the only advantage we can concede to the '03 over the M1 is that of lightness. A half pound makes quite a difference, though not enough to make me think for a moment of using the Springfield for anything but a sniping weapon. The old gun is simply obsolete, that's all.

I'm a little glad to have seen the M1 used in battle, and to have used it myself. I know it's a good gun. And when the groans of disgust echo along the firing line of the next National Rifle Matches I'll try to make sure that mine are for the usual reasons—a trey or a deuce in the wind, and *not* because I am fed up with shooting a damn lead squirter instead of the Precise old Springfield National Match!

THE M–1903 SNIPER RIFLE

We were not issued sniper rifles in any form in time to use them on Guadalcanal. The models sent out later, with Weaver scope and two-groove barrel, could hardly be called more than reasonable excuses for sniper arms. The most that can be said for these outfits is that perhaps they did give a few men the advantage of a telescopic sight (of very limited optical value, however), and perhaps they may have accounted for a few Germans and Japanese who might otherwise not have become casualties.

It was obvious from the outset that little was being done (on proper staff levels) to develop a good sniper weapon or to even train snipers. The M–1903 Sniper Rifle, World War II version, was a substitute measure—and a poor one at that. It placed a delicate and optically inadequate weapon of only moderate accuracy in the hands of troops untrained in its use—and even that at a very late date. What we needed was a good, sturdy scope on the M1, and we didn't get it until the war was over.

Specific complaints against the M–1903 Sniper Rifle are as follows: (1) Scope insufficiently rugged and shock proof; (2) Scope optically inadequate—not enough luminosity; (3) Scope adjustments insufficiently foolproof and rugged; (4) Location and design of mount precluded clip loading—a serious defect on any military weapon; (5) No auxiliary iron sights; (6) Rifle insufficiently accurate.

By stretching the point of tolerance to the limit, it might be permissible to say that the M–1903 sniper job was a little better than no scope-sighted rifle at all. Even that, however, is stretching a point.

Since the gun proved on the range to be such a sad sort of a cluck we didn't make much use of it in Burma, where we finally did get it. I saw it used a few times under conditions which called for any old kind of a rifle—shooting Japanese across a fifty-yard-wide stream.

In this it did perhaps a little better than an '03, not quite so well as a Garand. The Weaver scope, plenty good enough for sporting use in the States, just wasn't the instrument to give to a sniper at the front. An M1, with its increased rate of fire, would be much better for sniping than the so-called sniper rifle.

Sniper talk was mostly lip service in this last war, anyway. With no snipers, and without the time or the will to create any, what need did we have for good sniper equipment in the field?

SNIPER RIFLE AMMUNITION

Ammunition was not such an important factor when it came to sniping in the jungle. Shooting at short ranges as we did provided no real test of accuracy and made no great demands for super-refined target type loadings. The ordinary M–2 would shoot well enough for most sniping purposes.

However there were occasions when we needed good long range performance, and there were times when we needed gilt-edged accuracy for short range shooting, as in the instance of a very small target, such as an exposed arm or helmet-top. For all-round sniping purposes the only satisfactory ammunition would have to be something like the national match ammunition we had before the war, loaded with boat tail bullets. Men in the European Theater of Operations would know more about this, where ranges were presumably longer than in the Pacific. I rather think that they would recognize target accuracy as a prerequisite for any sniper rifle and its ammunition.

But that is just the point. The rifles we were given were not up to realizing the accuracy of the ammunition we already had, so why try to improve? No one worried about getting good ammunition for such junk as we were issued to use as sniping rifles. Now that we have a pretty good sniping rifle—delivered after the war was finished—we can start to worry about developing a good load for it. I would like to see what the Garand-Alaskan combination could be made to do with the best loads we could make up. Probably the standard load of M1, in a National Match loading, would be the best we could work up. That load as used at Perry was a pretty hard one to beat for all-round accuracy.

THE .30 CALIBER CARBINE

We never saw this nice little weapon on Guadalcanal, though we had been hearing of it for more than a year. Later on it became the standard arm for all infantry officers of company grade—and a lot more in the front lines. Most of the battalion and regimental commanders, and many generals, carried carbines in place of pistols.

The carbine turned out to be an ace weapon of this war, as far as

I am concerned. It was light and handy, powerful, and reasonably accurate. If I had to make my own in hostile jungle, travelling with the lightest possible kit where I should be likely to encounter enemy at any time, the carbine is the weapon I should choose.

The little gun was okeh as issued with one exception. It had a long protruding magazine, which caused no disadvantage in use, but a slight unhandiness in carrying. I trimmed one down to six shot capacity, shortening the follower guide in the clip so that the magazine was flush with the trigger guard. With this alteration the little gun became the neatest weapon in the world, handier—as far as I am concerned—than the Colt .45 Automatic Pistol.

The development of the carbine had the effect of putting a good offensive-defensive weapon in the hands of the leader and gun crew member, thereby making him the near-equal of an M1 rifleman. The cartridge was powerful enough to penetrate several thicknesses of helmet, and to perforate the plates of the Japanese bullet proof vests, which would only be dented by .45 auto slugs. It was flat shooting enough to have practical accuracy at more than two hundred yards. It would be interesting to know how many casualties it created during the war. Certainly more than all the pistols and revolvers our military has ever used.

The great advantage was that it got a gun that could shoot into the hands of the average Infantryman. The pistol, as far as general usage is concerned, is a purely defensive weapon, accurate only when in the hands of an expert. The carbine performed moderately well in the hands of dubs. For many types of offensive fighting, such as sneak raids and infiltration tactics, it was often superior even to the M1, penetration being the only point of difference.

The greatest advantage of the carbine was its lightweight, which is the greatest advantage any Infantry weapon can have. Of all the guns we used in this war it is the only one which does not need further reduction in heft. The rest are all too heavy for the job they do.

TOMMY GUNS

We received these weapons when we first landed in New Caledonia, early in '42. They were issued initially to the drivers and later to officers, and had the immediate result of becoming prime weapons of the chase for a few mad days. Everyone in uniform—colonels, majors, privates alike—went deer hunting with Thompson Submachine guns. A few deer were killed, a few more wounded and a great number of soldiers, civilians, and deer were badly scared. Jeeps, Tommy guns, and a plentiful supply of beer, with a little rum and whiskey thrown in, proved to be the makings of an Idiot's Holiday which went on until everyone got tired.

Shortly afterward the training period began and everyone had to carry his individual weapons on the march, so the Tommy gun began to lose popularity as an officer's weapon very rapidly. The pistol became the favorite and since carbines were not available, the '03 rifle fell next in line.

After we shipped to Guadalcanal, however, the Tommy gun regained much of its lost popularity. Officers began to use them again, especially officers who lacked skill in using other weapons. By this time we had used it in both the old and the new simplified types, both of which functioned well. It was the perfect weapon for close-defense—carrying one provided perhaps the best life insurance a man could have. And you didn't need to be a skilled shot to use the thing effectively. It was one of the more successful contrivances built by Americans to take the place of human knowledge. Little specialized ability is required to simply turn on a water hose, point it at an object to be wetted, and turn it off after the object is obviously saturated. Most of our Tommy guns—often with buttstocks discarded—were fired in that manner.

They were good guns, especially for the man who couldn't shoot. And although they were much too heavy—I never wanted to carry one myself—it always made me feel good to have one or two close at hand.

This would hold true only where ranges were consistently short. The Tommy gun was never good for anything beyond fifty yards or so. Its great inaccuracy made a gamble of shooting at greater ranges at targets which were at all able to shoot back. The rough sights, poor stocking, and awkward feel made it a poor pointer, hard to align quickly on a fleeting target. A tendency to climb off the target during sustained bursts was very marked in all Tommies not fitted with compensators. In semi-auto fire it was inferior to the Reising because of the open-breech firing; the closing bolt would jar the piece and disturb the aim each time you fired.

The oft-mentioned ability of the Tommy to hit and kill at ranges up to five hundred yards is theoretical hokum. Practically speaking, the gun will always be an ultra short range weapon, good in the jungle and in street-fighting, but poor where the least measure of accuracy would be called for. Another most serious limitation was the poor penetration. Bullets that bounce off a hard wood surface at fifty yards are not good brush-rakers. Firing a Tommy into the jungle blindly was not effective because so many of the bullets would be stopped by vines and branches. The greater power of military rifle cartridges, fired from full-automatic rifles and machine guns would be preferable for such work. The standard Japanese bullet-proof vest, which would not even slow down a carbine bullet, stopped .45 slugs cold, whether fired from pistols or Tommy guns.

And because of the lumbering velocity of the .45, it had little or no "secondary effect" if fired into sand or stone emplacements. Where a .30 caliber bullet would blast into sand or stone and create a veritable explosion, sending bits of flying stone in all directions, the .45 would merely ricochet.

The advent of the carbine later on in the war eliminated, in my opinion, the last need for a Tommy gun. The carbine made a much more accurate offensive weapon, and a much quicker pointing and more accurate defensive weapon. The lighter weight and greater penetrating power of the .30 caliber carbine cartridge increased this margin of superiority even more.

THE REISING GUN

The Marines used these weapons as a substitute, I believe, for carbines. They weren't much of a gun, but they worked and they provided a timely substitute for better guns which were slower to get into the hands of men up front. Many Marines liked them and they must have been pretty effective. Henry Adams was photographed with one in his hand, and that's a good recommendation for any gun.

Several of our boys "promoted" Reisings, shot them, and kept them. I tried out two of them, managed to make both malfunction while shooting at lizards in the groves, and gave them away to friends. Being so cheaply made, it would only stand to reason that they would not be as dependable as other guns. They did possess a tremendous advantage in their very lightweight and this would have caused me to carry one as a personal weapon had I been forced to choose between a Reising and a Tommy, although I had more confidence in the latter.

All in all, I never learned much about the use of the Reising gun first hand. I know only what I've heard. The boys who served in the 1st Marine Division would know a lot more about it. Generally, however, I believe it was regarded as a good, cheaply made substitute weapon.

As far as accuracy was concerned, the Reising had it all over the Tommy. Despite its lightweight it seemed to have less tendency to climb and jump. The closed-breech firing system made it many times more accurate when fired semi-automatically. With a compensator it held steadily throughout a long burst, and because of the better stock-fit and lower axis of bolt movement it was a much more natural "pointer."

The effective range seemed to be at least twice that of the Tommy gun, because of the greater accuracy in semi-auto fire. The brush-flushing ability was slightly less, with the smaller magazine capacity of the Reising.

This Japanese rifle was probably destroyed by American action. The Japs were almost complete failures at any form of retreat tactics as far as their own weapons were concerned. They were trained and conditioned only for victory, it seemed. We came upon tons of equipment in new condition, left behind with no attempt at demolition. Rear guard activities were in this instance confined to a few booby traps and ambushes.

I suppose it wasn't until much later in the war that the Japanese High Command began to utilize any form of plans or procedures for abandoning equipment, and I rather think that they never got instructions for same down to the lowly doughboy. And the doughboys I encountered just didn't seem to have the sense to destroy the stuff they couldn't take along.

So weapons lying like this in the sand were usually the results of our own shellfire, or maybe the doings of some of our raiding parties.

The .45 Colt Pistol

I don't know if we shall ever again fight a war like this one just finished in the Pacific, with a foe who made such terrifying use of night Infantry tactics. Probably we won't; but if we do, one thing is certain: there will be a crying need for a good pistol. Every doughboy on Guadalcanal felt a need for one during each night he spent in the frontlines.

My own pistol was a constant source of comfort to me after dark, and I always had it in my hands. There is no room in a fox-hole to wield a rifle against an assailant who is inside the hole with you. The only answer is a pistol. I had one—a regular .45 auto—and was constantly thankful that I had been lucky enough to secure it.

But it was not the ideal handgun for the purpose. I would have been much happier with a good snub-nosed or belly gun—even a lighter caliber than .38 special, because the Colt was too damned heavy. It weighed a ton in either hip or shoulder holster and your wrist would even get tired holding it while you dozed.

Ordnance says that they cannot lighten the .45 ACP without ruining its accuracy. To me, that statement is laughable. The accuracy of a .45 Colt Automatic is like the virtue of Lady Hamilton. For all practical purposes, the .45 is a bayonet-distance weapon, a lot more effective than any sort of cold steel, but usable at about the same range. Accuracy for such a weapon is of little or no importance.

Ordnance should either reduce the weight—or the weight *and* caliber of the weapon—so that we have in the pistol a weapon easier to carry than the carbine. Then it could be carried as an auxiliary weapon, in lieu of the present bayonet, and used for closein protection at night. During daylight hours any smart soldier, regardless of rank, would be carrying a carbine or rifle. General Stilwell carried one at all times when he was visiting his Burma or China fronts.

For a military handgun the automatic principle is a good one. The .45 loads easily in the dark, lies flatter in a holster than a revolver, and it shoots well enough to fill the combat mission of the handgun. But the bulk and weight of our present handgun is too close to that of the much more effective carbine (which did much toward rendering all handguns obsolete in their present forms as military weapons). If the handgun is to remain as a useful Infantry weapon, it must be made lighter. The fact that the peculiar conditions of warfare in the Pacific dictated a strong need for a handgun, causing us to cherish the ones we had, is no real proof that the .45 ACP is still worth its salt as a military weapon.

The Browning Auto Rifle

At the outset of the war our old BAR had been much changed from its original person, in both appearance and function. Ordnance had thrown a lot of gadgets—buttrests and bipods and hooked buttplates—on both ends of the poor weapon so that the man carrying it looked from a distance like a traveling tin shop. This was an effort to give the weapon long range accuracy and sustained steadiness throughout long bursts: a typical American attempt to substitute gadgets for skill. The BAR as originally issued was wonderful in the hands of a good man. The gadgets worked beautifully on the range—the gun would practically fire itself and on the thousand inch targets it would hold to a burst smaller than some of our heavy machine guns fired with tripods firmly sandbagged.

Seeing this—back in 1940—we all congratulated ourselves on having such a splendid weapon, but not for long. Two weeks after we were on Guadalcanal we had thrown away all of the gadgets and were using the guns stark naked—the way old John Browning had built them in the first place. The only times when bipods and buttrests were worthwhile were in long range sniping from hilltop to beach, opportunity for which was rare in occurrence. We did, however, make good use of the guns we stripped down.

We used them for blind shooting—for taking care of surprise targets. We placed them at the head of patrols we knew would run into trouble, and we found them very valuable. We had always thought of the Tommy gun as the standard "sprayer," but we found that it lacked penetrating ability—it could not cut down brush or penetrate small treetrunks as could the rifle or BAR. The more powerful .30–06 was many times better for shooting into cover. It soon became almost standard procedure for two BARs (carried slung in the assault position) to be placed at the head and tail of all large columns moving through coconut groves or jungle.

Actually, I believe our fondness for the BAR was more concerned with the type of fire than with the weapon itself. We would have been equally pleased with the Bren gun—perhaps more so. What we yearned for was a good gun to throw a lot of lead, faster and harder than the Tommy gun. This the Browning did, moderately well.

I say "moderately" because the twenty-shot magazine of the weapon was too small, and because the gun seemed to require too much maintenance. The ones we used broke too many parts and malfunctioned just a little too often—in my experience, much more often than the British Bren.

I hesitate to say these things about the BAR because of the great esteem my friends have for it. Only a few days ago I was chatting with Colonel Wall, a veteran battalion commander in New Guinea and the Islands, about the early Solomons campaign. I had just started to relate an account of a patrol action on Guadalcanal and was describing the organization of the column when the Colonel interrupted me.

"Wait a minute," he said, "What did you use at the critical points in that column—what guns?" (I had failed to state the exact placement of my weapons.)

"BARs," I answered.

The Colonel smiled and leaned back, ready to hear the rest of the story. From that single statement he had satisfied himself that I knew what I was talking about. He was a jungle soldier, and he knew the value of rifle-calibered automatic weapons in the Pacific war.

If we can't say much for the BAR, we can say a lot for the type of fire it delivers. In my own mind I sometimes question the real effectiveness of shots fired one at a time. Such shots are deadly only if well held and accurately directed. They furnish no natural provision for human error. But with a burst of from four to twenty rounds things become very different. The chances of scoring one good hit on a man at long range are greatly increased if the long and careful aim taken by the sniper is supplemented by a shotgun pattern of bullets arriving at the target. You can get several bullets on the way at one time if the target is distant, so that they all strike before the soldier can take cover. The first four will strike before an enemy soldier can even duck his head. This gives the BAR or Bren Gun man a better chance of creating a casualty at long range than any exponent of sniping would care to concede. I have seen some awfully good long range "sniping" done with a bipod and buttrest equipped BAR.

It is food for thought to know that the ideal sniping weapon might well be a scope sighted machine rifle, with some sort of a stabilizing mount to hold the bursts to small size at longer ranges. After the sniper has located a target and gone to the trouble of accurately determining the range and wind, why should he throw all his chances away in a single shot? Why not send fifteen or twenty closely clustered bullets on their way, so that the enemy rifleman would be caught in a shotgun pattern, small enough to be dense, but big enough to make up for a lot of error? Say a shotgun pattern with a ten-foot circle, good up to 600 yards?

The biggest reason I can think of against such a weapon is that it would be too heavy, and its design would be an expensive one. But the Browning Auto Rifle has had some such application in the Pacific, especially where circumstances permitted the gunner to use it with the stabilizing attachments.

Light Machine Guns

The only standard light .30 caliber machine guns which we used on Guadalcanal were those issued to the weapons platoons of our rifle companies. Our heavy weapons companies were still using the watercooled Browning heavies, marvelous guns in the defense but very difficult to use in the jungle attack. Lights—even for the machine gun platoons—would have been better all-around guns for our purpose.

Our Lights were used for many purposes all through the show. They made excellent trail-block weapons or fine main points upon which a rifle company commander could organize the rest of his fire in a defensive setup. Being handy and easy to carry, such guns could keep up with their companies or even large patrols. Although they could not be practicably fired during movement they could be quickly mounted for action, easily dug in (because of their low profile) and easily hand-carried while fully mounted. For men who knew how to use them they were very good performers and could fire rapidly enough to burn up all of the ammunition which could be manhandled into their positions. These guns were the first real firepower which a commander could rely upon during the early stages of a fight; the heavier guns and mortars, because of their weights, could seldom be counted on for sure until the second day or so.

LMGs could be used conventionally, for firing at well defined targets or laying down protective lines, or they could be loosened and swung free to spray a Banzai charge or to flush suspect cover. They were always good guns to have around; although lacking the sustained fire ability of the watercooled Heavy, they still had a lot of firepower—certainly more than almost any other gun of their own size and weight. Two men could carry the gun and tripod, even with a couple of boxes of ammunition thrown in, much farther than four men could move the Browning Heavy at the same time Together, both the gun and tripod of the Light was an easier load than only the tripod of the Heavy.

Our LMG was the one gun we had at the outset of the war which appeared to have been designed with some concern over its weight. It was lightened wherever practicable and its tripod was constructed sparsely to make it easier to carry. In place of the usual machine gun waterjacket, it had a perforated tubular jacket and its barrel was built proportionately heavier to better resist the heat of firing.

I believe this gun replaced the Heavy, to a large degree, in almost every Infantry regiment which fought the Japs. It lacked the suitability of the Heavy for long range and support (including overhead) fire because its mount was none too stable, but the Light was portable and it got there on time. And the same old basic Browning recoil-operated action gave it dependability to go along with its lead-slinging power. The LMG was a good gun with a very good record in the Pacific-half of World War II.

THE BROWNING HEAVY MACHINE GUN

This gun was not given much chance in the Islands campaigns. Those who used it in Europe may have a different story to tell, but on Guadalcanal the Heavy machine gun did not enjoy wide employment; it was used mostly in defensive roles and generally in positions not too far up in the mountains. The M–1917 Browning HMG, like other Infantry weapons, was much too heavy to be worth its salt.

It was actually an improved development of World War I, where it was discovered that machine guns could do more than merely spray an enemy attacking in front of their very muzzles. In mounting the gun solidly it was learned that an even distribution of bullet strikes could be spread nicely over a fixed and predetermined area, making the old spray gun an excellent long range weapon. It was also discovered that by the use of fixed tripods and artillery type instruments (range finders, aiming circles) machine guns could be fired accurately at targets not in the view of the gunner—indirect fire.

Because it was so mystic, I guess, this indirect fire became the pet subject of every postwar machine gun instructor and, though it was an admittedly lesser role of the weapon, we began to find great emphasis being placed upon it. The changes in the heavy machine gun tripod after World War I tended toward improvements for such indirect fire, and ultra-long range machine gun fire was certainly the main consideration in the later design of the boat tail bullet replacing the flat base of the M–1918 ammunition. The new cartridge, designated the M1, was fitted for long range machine gun fire. Instructors began to speak of machine guns, with their new ability to reach 4000 yards, as becoming the competitor of artillery in flat terrain. Fortunately this idea did not hold for long.

The reversion to the old flat base bullet during the late thirties scotched the idea that Ordnance intended the machine gun to replace the 75mm howitzer but we kept right on practicing our indirect laying. Even after the emergency was declared in 1940 we were still firing indirect problems with the HMG at ranges of 2000 yards or more. This was a wicked waste of time—interesting to the "Brass" perhaps, because it involved a little plane geometry, but very detrimental in the long run. When we went overseas we took with us machine guns of a design too strongly influenced by what proved to be a very minor consideration. We didn't do any indirect firing at all on Guadalcanal, although I believe we could have done so with success on several occasions. The real trouble with machine gun instrument fire is that it is a technique demanding more skill than our limited training periods could possibly produce. Also, such employment of flat trajectory weapons would be an infringement on the field of artillery—an attempt, in employing a weak weapon with very great skill, to take the place of a stronger weapon, much better fitted for the same tasks. The way the United States trains and fights does not allow the development of sufficient specialized skill. It is hard enough, in the few weeks (or days) allotted for weapons training, to properly teach a man to *fire* the machine gun—much less to fire it indirectly by the use of artillery instruments.

So the full theoretical value of the heavy Browning was not utilized on Guadalcanal. It was not even used in its proper role as a medium and long range striker, much less as a long range, indirectly laid, flat-trajectory weapon. The jungle terrain would not often permit these uses. However, the gun did fine yeoman service as a defensive firepower weapon, either for fixed final protective fire or for spraying. In the earlier perimeter battles, for instance, it was the mainstay of a battalion line that held tight and killed more than 900 Japanese with negligible loss to themselves. Marines used the Heavies all along with good effect.

It would have been entertaining if some of our backhome instructors in 2000-yard indirect fire problems could have seen us digging in and sandbagging our guns in positions where they would have less than fifty yards field of fire—mere grenade distance! Now and then we were able to give support fire from a flank of a maneuvering force, but mostly it was the same old line defense. Once in a blue moon we would get a gun up on a high point and pot away at targets of opportunity. Most often though—and herein lies the worst part of the story—commanders simply did not make full use of their heavy automatics; they either rearmed their heavy weapons companies with BARs and M1 rifles and kept them in reserve or they armed the men with even lighter weapons and used them for carrying parties.

Sometimes I think we all missed a bet by not trying harder to fully employ our Heavy machine guns in offensive roles. Certainly they had some application there because they performed so beautifully on the range. I would like to hear of the employment of Heavy machine guns in Europe, especially would I like to hear the story of a good machine gun enthusiast who commanded a platoon on that theater. His story might be a good deal different from the one of men who fought in the tropics.

For us, though, the Heavy was never more than a static defense weapon—a grand gun with which to stop a Banzai charge.

FIFTY CALIBER MACHINE GUNS

Our ground mounted .50s were other guns of which we didn't make much use. They too had impressed all of us by their stellar performance on the range; they were accurate, powerful and easy to aim and fire.

They were not, however, easy to carry; we could not practicably move them inland beyond the beaches and groves. Even if we did get the guns themselves up into the mountains there would still remain the problem of ammunition supply—and for .50s that would mean tons more for the carrying parties.

So we left these guns with the outfits charged with beach defense, who were becoming perhaps the heaviest armed Infantry in the world. Every outfit moving inland would do the same—each one peeled off its heavy stuff and turned it over to the beach. Had a Jap landing been attempted in those later days, the boys at Lunga would have been more than able to receive them with plenty of both ground and anti-aircraft .50s, 40mm anti-aircraft and 37mm anti-tank guns.

However, even disregarding the weight of our .50s, we could still have permissibly left them behind on the basis of a lack of appropriate targets. These guns are primarily anti-vehicular weapons and there were few opportunities to fire at Japanese tanks or trucks. In fact, the only use of the ground .50s I know of was against the Jap force which made the big perimeter attack in October before we (the 132nd) landed—and this was an anti-personnel usage. The 164th Infantry had some of their .50s in their line to supplement their regular guns and they were very effective in cutting through treeroots and other cover to chop up the Japanese who were crawling up into the barbed wire. But this was in a fixed defensive position, within short, hand-carry distances from the truckheads.

OUR GRENADES

The grenade is another weapon which is seldom recognized as truly important until in actual combat use. Americans are very skilled grenade throwers as a rule, because of their universal backgrounds of sandlot baseball, and that very factor seemed to have a strong influence in the design of our grenades. They were principally designed for hand-throwing and, except during war years, little was done to devise launchers in any form which could be used independently or when attached to a rifle. This failure to develop such weapons can be regarded as a serious oversight, for

Hideo

Looks like a non-com or officer leading an outfit with which he has served only a short time. Casts his most nervous glances back over his shoulder from time to time to make sure that he is not advancing alone.

His fatigues have the usual bulging look; pockets are all stuffed with grenades and "K" ration, more than likely. No net on his helmet; probably his regimental commander decided to not use the things in order to simplify identification of Japs. If such is the case, anything with a net on it will draw fire in this sector.

Things around this soldier cannot be too hot; if the air close by was popping with bullets he would not be in this proud, upright posture. Most likely this is some sheltered spot, in defilade from enemy fire. If that's the case, the hind-leg stance doesn't mark this man as a greenhorn. Only a fool would ordinarily expose himself like this in a fire swept area . . .

it sent us down into the tropics without a complete battery of jungle weapons.

Our most popular grenade, the fragmentation type, was limited to hand-throwing; it could not be launched by other means; this reduced its all-around effectiveness as a weapon, despite the fact that it was reliable, surefire and powerful. It could not be accurately projected into small or distant enemy emplacements. Almost any man could easily break a third story window with some slight mechanical assistance, such as the use of a simple rubber slingshot, but this same window would become a very difficult target for hand-thrown grenades, especially under the nerve-straining conditions of street fighting.

Hand-throwing, our weapons designers should realize, is only *one* of the several means of placing grenades and is a crude and primitive method at best, acceptable only because of its universal application to many different types of targets. It is not half so accurate as any of the mechanical methods and it greatly shortens the potential range of the weapon. It is no more than logical that every soldier who carries these grenades should have at his immediate disposal some means of launching them with at least as much accuracy as longbow archery. A good sight-type, rifle attached, grenade launcher would provide this means; it would enable the soldier to place a grenade through a window at 50 yards or on top of a small roof at 200, even inside the top of a halftrack at as much as 150 yards. These targets are at present in the "very difficult" class for any type of weapon other than the rifled-rocket or ordinary rocket guns, which are not nearly so portable as a few grenades and a launching attachment.

The only alteration the present grenade itself would require to fit it for rifle launching would be the fitting of a finned tubular tail and an impact detonator, both of which could be made removable and also interchangeable with other launching adaptations. The standard line of Japanese fragmentation grenades was so designed and adapted and this made them much more versatile than anything we had.

This versatility, however, was the only good quality missing in our own grenade. In its capacity as a hand grenade and boobytrap device it was a reliable and powerful instrument; its fuses were very seldom erratic, it was safe to use, and it was of good size and weight for hand-throwing. Once in a great while we would hear of an instantaneous detonation, but not often. Most of our grenade accidents—and there were plenty—were of human rather than mechanical origin. Many were caused by incredible stupidity. Several men on frontline duty went to sleep with grenades clasped "ready" in their hands—with the safety pins pulled; as soon as fingers relaxed in sleep the levers were naturally released and the fateful grenades exploded. This explanation of the accident had to be deduced from evidence on hand; none of the careless individuals was alive to testify.

But even with all of the danger involved with their use "pineapples" proved to be an important jungle weapon—especially at night. Most of us carried one or two at all times, using the heavy tape which sealed the cardboard containers to rig the grenades to our belts or pack straps, so that they could be quickly tornoff and used. Many of the routine trail details—stretcher bearers, supply-carrying parties, anti-sniper patrols—carried grenades as almost basic weapons. Anything suspicious in the brush would be checked and blasted if it looked like enemy. Sounds at night were given the same attention.

Of course, grenade throwing at night can be overdone, and it frequently was. There were too many doughboys who tried to assure their own safety at night by keeping up a constant barrage of grenade explosions in front of their positions. In extreme cases this habit would become incurable and grenades had to be taken completely away from a few of the more rattled characters.

Our methods of using grenades, both daytime and night, were largely devised in the field. The training we had received in the States actually found little practical application at Guadalcanal. Most of the formal throwing positions taught back at training camps could not be used at all and we took to tossing sidearm and underhand more than the football-pass methods of the books. Overhand throwing always meant a fully exposed arm, which is very bad practice any time.

Throwing at maximum distances was rare in jungle fighting but accuracy and force were both needed—the former to find the small pillbox ports and holes in the treeroots and the latter to sometimes penetrate heavy screens of leaves and small twigs. This made us feel more than ever the need for a good rifle-fitted launcher; we could have used it many, many times.

"Frags" were practically the only grenade we used on Guadalcanal. We got a few "smokes" and a few "thermites," as I remember, but never used them for anything important. Perhaps they would have been more effective than the frags against pillboxes and roofed entrenchments but that required rifle-launching too. We could have used another type of grenade—a lightweight fragmentation, or "concussion" type, which could have been easily carried into remote areas, such as Hill 27; but we were never lucky enough to receive any.

More than additional types of grenades we needed better means of projecting the ones we had. Every man should have been able to launch his grenades by rifle as well as by hand and every squad should have been equipped with some sort of ground discharger— something which could talk back to the Japanese knee-mortar, using the conveniently available grenades carried by the riflemen.

OUR AMMUNITION

There are two important factors which decide, of themselves, whether or not the soldier at the front will be able to shoot good, reliable cartridges or shells in his weapons. Manufacture is the first consideration: if the shells are not well made and of good material, they cannot be expected to perform properly under the conditions of battle. Our own cartridges were well made, and their performance in the field was very good. As far as I know, we had very few complaints to make regarding the manufacture of our different cartridges, shells, and grenades.

The second and most critical factor to us was the one of delivery —the mechanics of everything connected with getting the ammunition from the manufacturers' finishing rooms to the frontlines. This would include the packaging, sealing, boxing, loading, shipping, unloading, and final distribution of boxes and bandoleers to riflemen and gunners in the fight.

These shipments would be banged about a lot in getting to us on Guadalcanal, and the original cases and containers would surely be broken in the process if they were not very well made. With the manufacturer located in the Midwest, for instance, his product would likely travel to the west coast by rail, from there to Hawaii by ship, then down under New Zealand to New Caledonia, then up to Esperito Santos and on to Guadalcanal—practically half way around the globe. After it got to Guadalcanal it would be unloaded to receive perhaps a month or more of steambath and heat-testing. Then some of it would be lost, some destroyed, and some—that all-important fraction—fired at the enemy. Of this portion, the defection of a single round—the misfire of one rifle or pistol cartridge—might well be a matter of life and death to an Infantryman.

Because the failure of a small mechanical device was on occasion such an important matter to the frontline soldier, he was very likely to feel extremely bitter against all designers, manufacturers, and even the factory hands associated with the fabric of any weapon or cartridge which had misperformed. The old frontline expression of all modern wars was often repeated, loudly and profanely: "Boy, Oh Boy!" some grimy, bearded gunner, struggling with a stubborn part on a heavy machine gun, would snarl through gritted teeth, "If I could only lay my hands on the dirty, low, rotten son-of-a-bitch who invented this thing!"

Ammunition difficulties were only a minor cause of such bitterness, however, because most of the complaints were made against particular items of weapons and equipment not too well suited for use on Guadalcanal.

As far as ammunition supplies were concerned, even the delivery factor had left small cause for complaint. Ammunition packages, especially those for small arms cartridges, had been adequately strong and weatherproofed. If there was a single phase of supply which had any claim to flawlessness, it was the packaging and handling of rifle and machine gun ammunition. The sturdy wingnut-held cases, with their hermetically sealed tin linings, were the best packing boxes ever, and they did much to see that we got our fodder delivered in good shape. These boxes would fit compactly into any shipping space—the hold of a ship, the bed of a truck, or anywhere—and they would take a very severe fall without breakage. A dunking in water, either fresh or salt, would not harm the ammunition inside, and to store them, even in the tropics one had but to stack the cases on dunnage. No covers or shields were necessary unless the storage period was to extend into years.

We did not take ammunition in cases up to the very front, of course. It was broken down into tactical containers in rear areas, and carried up in the same form—machine gun boxes, or bandoleers and loaded BAR clips. We knew that after ammunition got up to the battalions it would not be long before it would be fired away. Storage would no longer be important, but the ability of the unprotected clips and individual rounds to stand repeated dipping in mud and water would become a prime consideration. Our rifle and machine gun ammunition, in this respect, was not found to be wanting.

In the beginning on Guadalcanal we used ball ammunition, M–2. Only a few rounds of 173 grain M1 had been available to us on New Caledonia, and to my knowledge none was shipped with us. The Marines had some with them, so that a few men who wanted it for sniping purposes could have used the boat tail stuff. Ranges were generally so short that it didn't matter to me, and because I had cut the barrel of my rifle to twenty inches I found the lighter bullets a little more pleasant to shoot.

Armor-piercing ammunition was issued in great quantity on the Island, though it did not replace ball entirely as it did later on. In the jungle it didn't seem to make so much difference what we used but I can see the advantages of having the standard cartridge capable of good metal penetration. Lots of times it comes in handy. In the assaults against pillboxes it became standard procedure to have some sort of rifle or BAR fire pouring into the visible ports. The Japs invariably rigged their pillboxes so that the gun could be fired by a crouching gunner, from below the line of fire. This left the gun itself as the sole target; naturally such a metal target would be more affected by armor-piercing missiles. So, as long as no sacrifice in accuracy is involved, I would always prefer to use armor-piercing ammunition in place of ball. And recently loaded armor-piercing has proven very accurate.

It always worked—the primers were always good. I don't remember any ammunition failures on the entire island, as far as .30 and .45 caliber stuff was concerned. When you squeezed the trigger the gun always went off and something came out of the front end. Of all the thousands of rounds fired around me, none could be proven defective—not one. Fortunately for us, however, things were very different on the Japanese side of the fence. Their ammunition was not nearly so reliable as ours. Even a limited amount of firing with 6.5mm or 7.7mm stuff would reveal a few misfires, due to faulty manufacture, or later processing—I wouldn't know which. All of these processes were second rate, judging from the way the cartridges were finished and packed, so I rather suppose it was a combination of errors which put their ammunition in a quality bracket far below our own.

The greater diameter of our bullet gave many advantages over the Japanese .256. Our tracers were more reliable and our incendiaries superior in performance to anything we had shot at us. Actually I do not know that the Japs had incendiaries in their standard rifle ammunition—some of it seemed to behave that way, however. The several times that I was able to cross-section and examine .256 caliber tracers made clear to me why ours were better. There just isn't enough space in the narrow 6.5mm projectiles for the necessary amount of chemical. It would be wise, when Ordnance comes to think of adopting a smaller caliber for the sake of ballistic advantage, to bear in mind that a wider bullet is a great advantage when special fillings are used. We may—if the present trend in morality continues—use explosive bullets in the next War.

Our biggest trouble was with our heavier ammunition. Everything up to and including .50 caliber was packed beautifully, and it stored well if the cases were left with seals intact. Only when we got to using the larger-calibered stuff that came in individual cardboard tube containers did we run into trouble. Grenades and 37mm ammunition were generally okeh because they were well packed with the cardboard containers on the inside of wooden boxes, but the stuff that really gave us trouble was another type of ammunition that came packed in cardboard tube-type containers—mortar shells.

Mortar shells were well protected from natural deterioration in their very construction. The detonators and fuses were concealed in heavy metal, well moistureproofed, and the initial propelling charge was in the form of a shotgun shell fitted into a metal chamber. Surely if shotgun shells could be proofed against the dampness of duck blinds and snipe bogs, they could be waterproofed satisfactorily as a component of mortar ammunition—and they were. It was another part of the mortar round which was to cause the trouble—the relatively exposed propellant powder increments.

This propellant charge was not in a powder form at all, but in the form of celluloid strips, cut and sewn into little waferlike packets. These were attached to the fin portion of each shell and were removable in increments to permit the gunner to vary the charge. They had to be exposed on the outside of the shell in order to be so handled and they had to be attached near the tail to facilitate their ignition from the basic charge, so they were shipped out in just that way—in cardboard containers, handy but not weatherproof. There were no storehouses on the beach of Guadalcanal, so they were stacked in the open with the cardboard-tube containers exposed to tropic rains. Eventually the ammunition was delivered up front and fired, and it wasn't long afterward that reports of trouble began to leak back to the beach.

In some areas a lot of mortar rounds began to fall short, all too often with fatal results. "Shorts" on the ranges back in the States didn't matter so much because there we had generally been required, in the interests of safety, to avoid any inline positions of the mortar observation posts. The line from gun to target was always a little off to the right or left of the OP so that any shorts would fall clear of the OP crew. In war this arrangement was generally impossible, mainly because the mortar often had a more or less solid line of friendly troops across its entire front, with no time available to even permit their location on the range card or fire map. Mortars were nearly always firing directly over some of our own people.

Under these circumstances there was no choice but to go ahead and fire, taking due precautions and following carefully the instructions received from the observation post. A certain small number of shorts, due to mechanical failures and occasional human errors was expected and the Infantrymen up front took them without too much groaning. But after the first few weeks on the island these shorts began to occur too often. In some sectors round after round fell short, initially convincing the front line platoons that a lot of Japanese 90mm mortars had been moved into their sector. This impression was soon dispelled by the discovery of telltale American shell fragments and other clues and the incident lost its humor in the process. Some of the fragments were removed from the bodies of our Infantrymen.

A few commanders silenced their mortars entirely, having lost all confidence in them. Investigations were made and it was quickly learned that the whole trouble had been caused by the effect of moisture on the propellant increments. Some of them had failed to ignite—had, in fact, remained attached unburned to the shell, being discovered at the site of the short explosion. It was only a few days before Ordnance straightened the matter out and issued orders for the disposal of increments which had been darkened with moisture.

This was an excusable slip and a small one, but it had caused casualties—some of the shorts even fell into aid stations and command posts; and somehow, a casualty of this self-inflicted sort always seems ten times harder to take. In such a matter there is nothing half-way about the resentment felt by the injured. If responsibility for failure to properly wetproof those shells could have been placed on a single man and that man delivered alive to the front, there were many on hand who would have joyfully shot him—through the middle so he'd die slowly.

This difficulty with mortar ammunition was the only serious trouble of the sort which arose on the Island and although the Artillerymen may have not been pleased with the supply handling of their ammunition, the doughboys had little cause in that matter for complaint. We knew that changes could have been made to make the packaging more suitable for the tropics. For instance, packages could have been made with smaller hermetically sealed units in order to facilitate hand carrying over poor trails and rope or metal handles could have been added to the cases as a carrying aid, but such criticisms were very minor.

Air supply containers and parachutes could have been made available and would have helped a lot in getting supplies to outfits far inland or isolated, but air dropping technique was just then beginning to be developed to a point of real usefulness. Later in Burma I was to see a whole new method of supply evolved, which, had it been applied in time to the Guadalcanal operation, could have shortened the campaign by at least a month.

Naturally we complained, as soldiers always will, about the way every bit of supplies was delivered to us. We learned that service troops are service in name only because we ourselves had to furnish nearly all of the work details to unload and handle the supplies—which was an endless and a thankless job. We found that many of the rear area outfits were often allowed to be more concerned with their own comfort than with the very lives of the men up front, so pretty soon we began to take such things for granted and ceased to resent them.

We had only one great consolation in the matters of supply,

Hideo

Back in the days of 1943–44 the purported Japanese definition of the term
"American" was often expressed as "a strange animal who travels from island
to island digging holes!"

Practically speaking this definition was not far from correct. Each stop
called for the preparation of diggings of some sort. We quickly learned to halt
our columns early, so that we could be well dug in by nightfall. By that procedure we would insure our being below ground when Japanese counterassaults
would come—always after darkness.

We learned also to grab a Japanese entrenching shovel at first opportunity
and to then throw away the Woolworth toy which had been issued to us.

The Jap shovel being used by the sketched American is a good one. Maybe
not so good as the one we received later in the war, but a hundred times better
than our old model. It is made of good steel, to hold a good root-cutter edge,
and it is perforated to prevent soil from clinging to the blade. This man using
it will have all but his eyes and the top of his helmet underground in 20 minutes
—digging in soft sand.

And it is kind of amusing to see the way this man is putting his heart into
his work. Quite likely he is one of those Joes who had to be forced to dig a hole
six inches deep during the Louisiana Maneuvers. Now he digs one four feet
deep and puts a logged roof on it if he has time.

hardship, or anything else. We could always look at the poor Japanese Infantry on the same island and know that there was at least one group of people worse off than we. This was especially true in the matter of ammunition supply. Ours was good—theirs was lousy.

OUR MASTER CRAFTSMEN

Whenever an outfit goes into battle for the first time its personnel will automatically reclassify themselves as to military competence and general reliability. Some, whom the commander thought to be the finest men he had, will turn out worthless. Some whom he might have thought worthless are liable to become the heroes of the action. It is not a rare occurrence for the drunken, riotious element in a command to provide it with its very best fighting men.

But while individuals within the organization will rise and fall in the commander's opinion after he first sees them in combat, the commander's overall impression of his whole group of men is one of amazed admiration. All of the men generally do much better than could have reasonably been expected from their pre-combat records, and the shock of seeing this sometimes almost knocks the Old Man over.

That is one of the reasons that we found many officers—who kept protesting during training that "this gang of bums will never learn to fight"—later praising their units as the best ever. Such commanders often found that each man would work industriously and bravely, where he had expected to have to drive them constantly.

It brings a measure of idealism into the front lines to match the cynical and pessimistic atmosphere which one learns to expect there. It gives a new meaning to the terms used by war correspondents, lifts the word "valor" from the level of hackneyed newspaper copy and makes it a real, live thing. One soon comes to realize that, if war does not bring out the best in men, it most surely does call forth their greatest talents for sacrifice and endurance. Nothing in peace is so stimulative to will and physical strength.

I suppose that it can all be explained by the natural fusion of all effort into the one great struggle to get the important life-and-death job done. Men realize that all petty concern must be cast aside in the face of the enemy, and all strength bent to the fight. The only extraneous factor of interference left in an army in battle is in back of the front, where petty jealousies and political side-currents can find room to move. Staff officers and generals may sometimes find time to think of selfish interests, while the men doing the fighting cannot. Infantrymen in the foxholes have mind and body alike busied in defending their lives.

Still, I like to think that not all of this heroism and devotion to duty is the result of the pressure of circumstance. It seems cynical in the extreme for one to say that Infantrymen do a good job only because they have to. My own belief is that after a while in the fight the doughboy gains a new faith in his fellow soldiers and a new love for his personal ideals, far surpassing any propaganda-instilled patriotism. Wherever I have seen fighting in this war—with rare exceptions—all of the Americans involved behaved in a more than creditable manner. And in Burma, during service with Merrill's Marauders in early '44, I was privileged to see infantry actions where extreme bravery and heroism were standard, rather than exceptional. It is pretty easy for one to be proud of being an American after a few such sights. . . .

Hideo

BOOK II
BURMA

FIJI

In August of 1943 a directive from the Pentagon was sent out to all U.S. Army installations and read aloud at the formations of combat units. With a certain adjectival redundancy, it called for volunteers for "a dangerous and hazardous mission," who would be trained in living off the land and receiving supplies from the air while operating behind the enemy lines. (My friend Charlton Ogburn, who would later write the celebrated war memoir *The Marauders*, heard the directive read back in the States about the time I heard it in Fiji and asked himself how the hell a mission could be dangerous without being hazardous!)

Picture a beautiful tropical island. Soft warm breezes stirring the coastal groves, rustling the palm fronds. Grassy volcanic hills rolling up to a high divide. Gentle, smiling natives. Handsome white colonials. Even more handsome half castes, especially the females. Beauty and color and a lazy, unchallenging lifestyle that the foreign soldier could observe or join at will. Or if the soldier happened to be a sportsman, outdoor adventure: wild boar and cattle to hunt in the higher grasslands; big game fishing that millionaires had travelled half way round the globe to enjoy.

This is what we had had on New Caledonia in 1942, plus some splendid deer hunting, before we became involved in grimmer adventures on Guadalcanal. And now it was what we were offered again, in 1943, as the Navy transport *Penn* docked at a sugar mill pier near Latoka, Viti Levu Island of the Fiji group. The 2nd Battalion walked down the gangplank and entrucked for the Sambeto Valley, to a camp that lay between the towns of Nandi and Latoka.

For reasons that I've ever since been trying to explore and understand, most of us soon wanted to escape from this quite literal tropical paradise. The wonderful climate, the pervading peace and scenic loveliness, the ample food and pleasures of the place became a bore.

Years later, I think I've finally found the reasons for this perverse disaffection with paradise itself, and plan to write a separate book

419

about them. In this story I'll just ask the reader to concede or consider that such a basic uneasiness does, or might, exist inside the human male, and that it might be this that sometimes makes soldiers tend to give up peace and comfort for the severest kind of danger and hardship.

In another Pentagon missive, Memo OPD 320.2, dated 18 September 1943, the ongoing assembly of some 2,604 "personnel for the American Long Range Penetration Units for employment in Burma" was confirmed. Its second paragraph added that "a total of 674 battle-tested jungle troops from the South Pacific Area are being assembled at Noumea (New Caledonia) and will be ready for embarkation on the Lurline 1 October."

These two documents carried out a minor decision taken at the Quebec Conference of that year, where General Marshall had met the British Major General Orde C. Wingate and heard of his 77th Indian Brigade's operations behind the Japanese lines in Burma some months earlier. The decision was to create an organization unromantically designated Provisional Unit 5307, later to be known as Merrill's Marauders.

The second communication was kept under lock and key somewhere above the regimental level, so that when the first was read at a battalion formation on our cow pasture parade ground near Nandi, we knew nothing of the Burma location. But the phrases "dangerous and hazardous" and "receiving supplies from the air" were enough to stir that male restlessness in us. As what a 1970s journalist might call "combat jocks," many of us who stood in that formation listening were eager candidates. For these past few months we had been in static ("stagnant") defense dispositions on this island with the enemy hundreds of miles away, across the water, and that strange male restlessness squirmed inside us.

Not just restlessness, either. There was plain boredom and a yearning for that strange kind of infantryman's freedom that is obtained nowhere but in the front lines with the enemy within shooting distance. Here on Fiji we were badgered by the memory of that old unqualified freedom of the outflung jungle patrol or flank platoon in combat. In battle, the radio could always be made to "fail" if the orders from the rear were making no sense. Here on Fiji, every platoon and company commander had a regimental or division staff officer breathing down his neck, on the drill field or coast defense location.

So we volunteered, so many of us that lots had to be drawn to reduce the number to our regimental quota. And, being lucky in the draw, I found myself standing several days later on that sugar cane loading dock near Latoka, ready to board a Navy transport with a group of enlisted men and several other officers.

I was glancing out to sea, remembering the details of the going off party that the local British administrator and his daughters had given for us the night before, when I overheard a crisp voice behind me ask a question I'd heard before and get an answer from a sergeant nearby: "I don't know, sir, but he never lets it out of his sight."

The craggy-faced major general who had asked the question about the piece of luggage that leaned against me, four feet long and bound inside a waterproof sheet, said, "Let's see it, George," and returned my salute. So I lifted the poplin sheet off to let him see the thick leather scabbard and boot with the rifle and telescopic sight pouched inside.

"I see. Still in love with the glass-eyed Model 70? Gonna carve some more notches on it soon?"

As always, in those years, such a friendly few words from a general made me blush like a schoolgirl. This usual burst of red would be showing, I knew, even through my tan and my Atabrine yellow complexion. I dared not utter the reply that came to mind ("Thank you, General, but I don't carve notches on my rifle!"), so I merely smiled on nervously and drew myself into a more rigid position of attention, receiving his powerful handshake with a trembling young hand. As a onetime scout officer at his division (later corps) headquarters on Guadalcanal, I'd done better—speaking out my few crisp words when I had had something worthwhile to report in his G-3 tent. Hodge was a hunter and a firearms enthusiast. He had called me out on Fiji to help him sight in one of the carbines, newly issued to us there, which he would carry as a personal weapon. Many months later in Korea, on a staff officer's visit from Tokyo, I'd feel that lumberman's handshake again, and hear him tell me of the good pheasant shooting not far from his residence (as U.S. armed forces commander) in the American embassy at Seoul.

We expected a speech, but he simply walked through the cluster of officers and the ranks of enlisted men behind and shook everyone by the hand, then stood and waved to us as we walked up the gangplank.

I suppose there was every reason for it, but the lack of a better sniping weapon than this in the Marauders made life substantially easier for infantrymen of the Japanese 18th Division in Burma. I don't feel bitter about it today (after all, we had the splendid M-1 and other weapons-advantages) but it does seem a bit odd that the only first class sniper gun in our 3,000 man outfit was the Springfield that I'd modified and fitted with a Lyman Alaskan in G&H, double lever mounts. And odder still that I'd had to find and pay for that scope and mount myself.

The soldier depicted here looks reasonably real and right: clinging helmet chin strap, and canvas lace up leggings long since abandoned on the trail. Even as I, he could be aiming a shot up some hillside from some river valley trail in north Burma. Not as well equipped with scout planes as we, General Tanaka used a network of ground scouts, mobile watching and listing posts, that our Kachin scouts sometimes would spot above us as we marched along.

Nothing against this makeshift sniping equipment. It was much better than none, but I'm pleased today to know that we've got at least a small number of fine sniper M-14s and bolt guns on hand—the deadly and militarily priceless product of our NRA civilian and military marksmanship programs, along with a larger number of men who know how to use them!

THE S. S. LURLINE

With that warrior-gladiator style of handshake still tingling in our palms, we sailed to New Caledonia, where we had spent our last pre-combat months before the Army phase on Guadalcanal. Assigned on arrival to a replacement camp (the worst status that a combat soldier can endure, as a mere designated Major Occupational Specialty number) we all sought old contacts among the French and base section Americans still there. I had time to renew old deer-hunting friendships on the ranches to the north before the *Lurline* came into the harbor from the States, already loaded with the non-combat-experienced (we'd not let them forget it!) *other* troups from the American Theatre.

Aboard the *Lurline*, we victualed luxuriously on Argentine beef and other homestyle goodies. Enjoying steaks and roast beef, with pancakes, eggs and bacon for breakfast from a printed menu, we sailed south and west to Brisbane, where we picked up the rest of the combat-tested portion of this shipful of armed American males. Like us, they tended to look down on the troops who had not been in action. Because we had been through combat we were full of bragga-docio as we loitered or walked the decks, and we would gather in exclusive groups to talk of our battle experiences. Whether on New Georgia, New Guinea, or Guadalcanal, the topography had made the fighting much the same—characterized by the coconut grove and inland hilly jungle, with the combat objectives usually those grassy hilltops that commanded the narrow coastal shelves. In their campaigns, American troops demonstrated that the tenacity, brutal-ity and blind courage of the Japanese infantry and marines, could be turned to their lethal disadvantage. Pacific veterans of that time, before the Japanese had learned their lesson, shared an awesome sense of surprise that these little brown conquerers of all of Southeast Asia were so easy to mow down by the hundreds in our own barbed wire. These Americans in front of them, armed with semi-auto rifles and backed by massive mortar and artillery support, were a far cry from the Chinese or Malaysian police and militia forces, armed with a rusty antique rifle for every third man.

Within this larger group of American combat veterans—"combat infantry jocks" Tom Wolfe might call them today—was a smaller group of men and officers united by common interest. Though we bore no designation, Wolfe, I think, might well have called us "weapons jocks" because our central interest was in the well-oiled, blue-steel tools of the frontline doughboy. Our gatherings in state-rooms and along the rail were mainly to talk about these then ultra-modern artifacts of World War II.

We extolled the M-1 rifle for its semi-automatic fire, but criticized its excessive weight and its top-loading eight-shot magazine, which rendered the gun inoperative, with no round ready in the chamber, while the poor doughboy reloaded in the shadow of an enemy pill-box. We praised the Browning Automatic Rifle (BAR) as a fine weapon for a moving advance guard in the narrow-trailed palm groves and jungle. We agreed that the Winchester M-97 riot guns were also good for this purpose—*when* you could find shot shells for them that weren't swollen with moisture to jam their pump-action feeding. Many of the coarser souls among us liked Thompson .45 caliber sub-machine guns, with or without the buttstock removed. We all bemoaned the lack of a heavier machine rifle, a squad-weapon counterpart to that damned deadly Japanese Nambu.

And so on, in a kind of permanent floating seminar, we appraised not only the tools of war but the tactics and the strategy of generals as these impinged on the footslogger on the frontline jungle trail. Except for one item that I especially remember, there was no harsh and bitter criticism of our high command. As soldiers go, I think we all were hopeful, undisgruntled with the way we were being led at the top. The one point of bitterness was the frequent insistance, towards the end of a battle or a campaign that we could safely call already won, on a fiercely hurried mop-up operation to clear out the last bit of "organized enemy resistance." Those of us from Guadal-canal, for example, felt embittered that we had been ordered to move inland from our secured airstrip and our captured coastal promonto-ries, to root out the last surviving enemy from their scattered surviv-ing entrenchments in the hills still further from the coast. Cut off from supplies, these Japanese were dying of malaria and malnutri-tion one by one. We would not soon forget the practice, under an otherwise revered corps commander, of sending us out to trade man for man with these Japanese, whom we had forced into their deadliest and most effective mode of fighting—sacrificial defense from deeply dug and logged-in strong points. We knew they would have died off by themselves, and their few raids against our heavy strength along the shoreline would have done little damage.

Within the ranks of the "weapons jocks" there was yet a smaller number that met as a clique along the rail or in a stateroom. These were the "weapons jocks" who were snipers, who had hunted Japanese soldiers as one might stalk deer in the Michigan woods or coyotes on the Western deserts. Tinctured with formal competitive marksmanship, because long range accuracy was the critical element in its most refined form, these conversations about sniping were the most intense of all. The subjects of these sessions were the spotting of enemy faces and helmets in jungle cover, the stalking and lying in wait at trail bends, the careful search with binoculars down the avenues between the planted Lever Brothers palms, the rare but nonetheless widespread long-range shooting that brought telescopic sights, match-grade ammunition and even rifle range tricks of wind-doping into action.

We had heard vaguely of M-1 sniping rifles then in development, with Lyman Alaskan and other hunting telescopic sights. These had Griffin and Howe double lever mounts, offset so that clip loading was possible. The only sniper equipment we had was the "Woolworth" wartime Springfield bolt gun, fitted with a common Weaver scope. We welcomed these as better than nothing at all, but every competitive rifleman in this little weaponry sub-group itched to have a scope-sighted M-1 of this ideal sort.

This, it turned out, the original Merrill's Marauders organization would never receive. Some of us already had seen, too late to use them in the fighting we had earlier survived, the family of night aiming and viewing devices called sniperscopes and snooperscopes, and we all talked about the killings we could have made with them against the Japanese with all their suicidal emphases on night operations. For the Army, it seemed all too often that each war had to demonstrate anew the deadliness and the value of a rifle skillfully aimed.

With the Navy and the Merchant Marine, though, the material and supply situation seemed to be better. Take this fast-moving coverted liner, the *Lurline*, so fast that a Japanese sub would have to be situated right in her path to get her. Let her get by and the chance was gone: we could feel her powerfully vibrating against the waves, the speed making her plates sing, while we enjoyed (sumptuously if you were an enlisted man, luxuriously if an officer) the fine clean quartering and the lovely food and the perfect paint and maintenance that we could see above deck and below.

As she glided on through the Pacific, going down under Australia from east to west, then up into the Indian Ocean, her passengers appreciated her in different ways. No peacetime voyage with the ship lit up could ever show a man the stars and the sea in such untrammelled splendor. My old trick of setting a cot out on the deck, learned on the crudely converted *Kungsholm* that had taken me to Australia in the (northern hemisphere) winter of 1941-42, was trotted out again, and I could lie there looking up as the ship swung, and watch the

North Star and the Southern Cross without a move of my head. So there was beauty, nature in all her maritime glory. But to me, the strongest memory would be of those seminars on weaponry and sniping: a book—and a good one, I think—could have been edited out of a transcript of the collective cunning that we combat veterans had acquired on our separate battlefields.

By now we were provisionally organized into three battalions, with us combat veterans (don't you forget it, you unblooded others!) comprising the 3rd, and the remainder grouped into the 2nd and the 1st, in the order that their personnel had boarded the ship, back there in the American and Caribbean theaters. This made the lot of us into a potential regiment and therefore stirred thoughts about the artillery and engineer support units that customarily accompanied a regiment in transport and that were conspicuously missing here. But these higher-up considerations of artillery and tactical aviation were discussed only briefly. As jungle infantrymen we had learned to think intensely about our hand-carried weapons. The rifle, the carbine, the Browning automatic rifle, and the Thompson submachine gun were the artifacts most often mentioned.

Each of these weapons had its devotees. The M-1 was acknowledged to be the best all-around instrument to have in your hand in most kinds of terrain. And all of us agreed that, despite the carrying convenience of the .25 Arisaka carbine and the demonstrated deadliness of the Nambu light machine gun, and even the well-standardized Japanese grenade and grenade launcher system, we Americans were far better armed than our Pacific theater foe.

Facing the personnel of the other two battalions (when something moved us outside our clannish combat-experienced exclusivity, like a meeting of all the officers on the ship, or all the grade so-and-so sergeants), the men of the 3rd Battalion tended to be cocky. We knew there were grounds for a feeling of superiority: men did crack up totally in combat and have to be shipped back to the States; we had not. But it was also based on that knowledge that we alone, on the ship, had picked up about *ourselves*. There was nothing "classroom" or "theoretical" about our skill with hand-carried weapons. We had applied it in the field. We had seen the Japanese fall before us, often in such numbers that bulldozers were needed to carve out their mass graves. We were rid of the last shred of the Japanese superman myth. Tokyo Rose could go right on telling us of the might and invincibility of Japan, as indeed she did via shortwave radio each night in the officers' wardroom. And back on New Caledonia and in our other pre-combat waiting stations, we had listened with concern. Now she only made us laugh.

Whatever else a semi-guerrilla infantry campaign in the mountainous tropics may bring to its participants, it brings fatigue. A vast weariness, tinged with bewilderment over why it all had to happen in this strange and far away place, came over us all at one time or another. This snapshot is the nearest I came to capturing this feeling on film.

At our training camp in India. Camp meat.

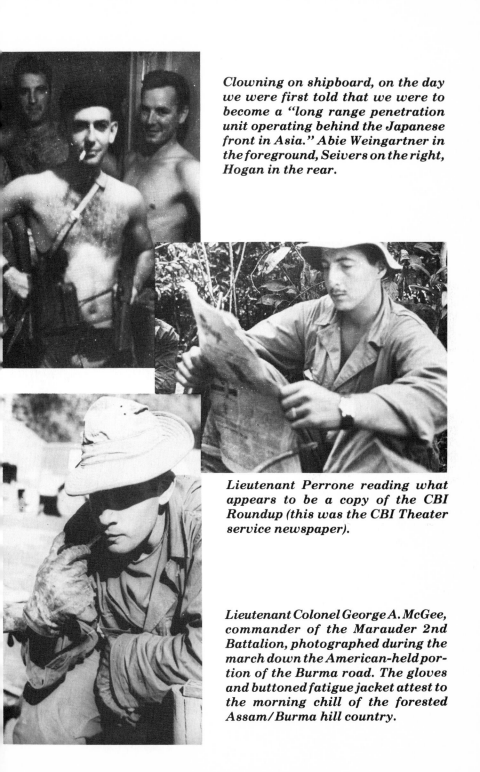

Clowning on shipboard, on the day we were first told that we were to become a "long range penetration unit operating behind the Japanese front in Asia." Abie Weingartner in the foreground, Seivers on the right, Hogan in the rear.

Lieutenant Perrone reading what appears to be a copy of the CBI Roundup (this was the CBI Theater service newspaper).

Lieutenant Colonel George A. McGee, commander of the Marauder 2nd Battalion, photographed during the march down the American-held portion of the Burma road. The gloves and buttoned fatigue jacket attest to the morning chill of the forested Assam/Burma hill country.

*Larry Lew, the celebrated com-
mander of Orange combat team,
whose penchant for practical jokes
was almost as great as his skill and
devotion as a combat leader.*

*The author in December 1943,
at the Marauders' training camp
in India.*

*Sergeant Hill, 3rd Battalion headquarters (pencil behind ear),
receives an intelligence report from a Kachin scout and a reconnaissance platoon Marauder.*

Lord Louis Mountbatten, the supreme allied commander, South East Asia (SACSEA), addresses Marauders of the 3rd Battalion at their training camp in India.

Captain, later Major, Petito holds my short-barrelled Model 70 on an informal range set up in our Indian training camp.

A Chinese-descent Marauder (Lum Pun, I believe) talks with some village OSS guerillas and scouts.

Officers of the 3rd Battalion at their mess table in our camp at Deogarh, in central India.

Training camp in central India. Lieutenant Brown, a decorated veteran of the Guadalcanal campaign who volunteered on Fiji. The smile is a knowing one: he's quite aware of all that new and shiny equipment; this is a shot for the home front and our own amusement. He's imitating the oft-storied, newly arrived second lieutenant. The packboards and machetes, not to speak of the parachutists jacket, were seldom taken into Burma.

Another Marauder wearing the shiny new gear we were issued at the training camp at Deogarh and posing, consciously, for the homefront.

Flame throwers were intended for investing enemy pillboxes and machine gun positions, especially with improved fuel that struck low and flamed up hot from ground level. But to get the equipment-bearing squirter into position usually involved a lot of bodily exposure, enough to give the waiting Japanese infantryman some clear and easy targets.

They were hardly the mainstay of our transport and evacuation fleet, but these tribally domesticated elephants often helped us get our food distributed out from the drop fields and get our wounded back to hospital. Not the severely wounded, of course. No medic who had ever ridden a pack elephant uphill and down, would ever put a badly hit casualty aboard one.

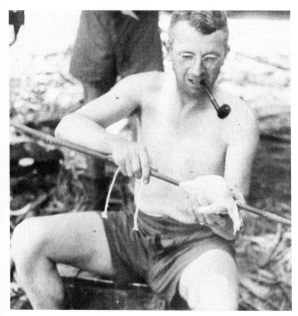

General Frank D. Merrill serving as field chief in a bivouac spot along the Tanai River.

A rare few days of leave, taken in old central provinces of India, and a primitive but successful hunt for tiger, leopard, and deer.

A column of Marauder mules on the march down the Ledo road showing the Army pack saddle (on mule in foreground) which had to be individually fitted and "settled in" during this hundred and more mile trek through Assam/Burma hill country.

When Japanese and American patrols met head on and in mutual surprise on a jungle trail the American advantage in semi-auto weapons usually let us win heavily. But where curved trajectory fire was appropriate, the Japanese had the advantage. Our own devices included a crude rifle grenade launcher and the mortar like the one shown in this picture. The mortar was too heavy to carry in its entirety —only the tube could be carried on a light patrol sortie.

Here we see mules and horses at rest, saddles and packs in the foreground, during our semi-tactical march down the Ledo road. Having these animals during the fighting that followed, we could move down onto the Japanese held extension of this same road from the broad jungle country to the east, and then back into these flanking hills with our heavy weapons along, making Japanese pursuit and counter-operations costly and exhausting.

The rocket launchers or "bazookas" in this photo are very special task weapons that required far greater body exposure on the part of our jungle infantrymen for them to be effective. Though useful for occasional assault missions, bazookas and flame throwers were best left back at the company command post.

This photograph depicts a bit of garrison tedium, applied in this case with the enemy mere hundreds of yards away. Naturally, in Marauder conversation of that time, it proved to be a bit controversial.

A Marauder column in the Hukawng Valley, early in the first mission marching. To me this snapshot is evocative: the morning mists, the men moving off unfed (or deeply grateful for the fog that hid the smoke of our morning coffee fires). The general rain forest and bamboo cover was broken here and there by grassy spaces, sometimes with barking deer or pig standing in the margins. Without the fighting the Marauders' march through north Burma could have been a scenic backpackers' idyll, a lovely tropical adventure.

Marauders on the march. Note the usage of parachute cloth, jungle boots as alternate foot-gear (some wore them all the time; most used them for the more wet and less plodding occasion). Also the odd assortment of Ghurka knives (kukris), entrenching tools, and the use of that classic infantry device, the blanket-poncho-groundsheet horseshoe roll on most of the packs.

Marauders during a break on the march. (You can be sure the so[o]
was dry, otherwise those two M-1 rifles would not be lying on it.

Here we see a river crossing. In this instance a very peaceful one,
at one of the upper curves of the Tanai with no Japanese to inter-
fere. The exposure of a column like this on sand or gravel spaces,
and wading in the water, is enough to send a chill up my spine.
Through Guadalcanal as well as Burma, the Marauder leaders
were glad to see their columns gain the far bank and thread safely
back into the cover.

One of the twin Lieutenant Higgins, (Elbert I think) marching with the headquarters section of the Marauder column in Burma.

Colonel Charles "Chuck" Hunter (in foreground), with Lieutenant Colonel Beach, CO of the 3rd Battalion.

Some men and women of the OSS Detachment 101, an American sponsored guerrilla force and intelligence net, which made our operation infinitely less difficult, along with their many other accomplishments in the winning of the war in Asia.

A common remark after a month or two in the Hukawng valley was: How could this war continue without L-5s and bamboo? L-5s, of course, were our Piper Cub aircraft, used to evacuate wounded and for liaison and personnel replacement in the field. But bamboo was yet more fundamental. We hoisted our radio antenna on its 30-foot shoots. We steam-cooked fish in its joints with native rice paddy; we poled our poncho-lean-to shelters with it. Here you see it in its very welcome form as a Kachin-built footbridge, enabling us to cross a river, this time, with dry feet and unsoaked fatigues.

DEOLALI

Suddenly our lovely shipboard idyll ended: the *Lurline* docked at Bombay (because Calcutta had no berthing deep enough), and we entrained 125 miles to a British training and replacement camp called Deolali. But for those of us who had read Kipling, another idyll immediately began: a visit to that then-still-existing world of Tommy Atkins east of Suez, slogging the Indian subcontinent with the turbanned, romanticized likes of Gunga Din.

Overly romanticized, we soon learned, but fantastically entertaining and exotic still. The enlisted barracks at Deolali were dryly, brutally austere, the officer's dining room contrastingly large and high-ceilinged, hung with ibex, sambur, chital and other Asiatic big game trophies, carpeted in the corners with tiger skins.

The Guards-mustached major who gave us our orientation lecture also told us of the historical and scenic attractions near at hand and in Bombay. During the questioning period he answered my queries about local hunting possibilities, naming the various local guides and shikaris and telling me the forests and hills further inland where reasonably good boar and leopard hunts could be laid on. But mostly I remember his words just before the question-and-answer session, ending his lecture. "For those of you who go on pass to Bombay, if you must have a woman, let me recommend 9 (I think that was the number) Grant Road."

Perhaps because of the weapons emphasis so visible within the 3rd Battalion, the days of training at Deolali were given over largely to firearms drill and training. One look along the front of a barracks or a quarters made this emphasis obvious. One could see rifles being carefully cleaned, the rifle and carbine stocks rubbed carefully with linseed oil, purchased in a local Indian shop. A glance down any barrel at inspection would reveal a well-tended, mirror-like surface: weapons were cleaned on the range, minutes after firing, to prevent rust from the chlorate-primered ammunition that was still being used at that time. Boiling soapy water or aqueous issue cleaner was used with care just after firing, and then the gun would be re-cleaned

427

outside the soldier's or officer's sleeping place at sundown.

In some odd manner of adaptation, we had all picked up the cross-legged sitting position for this purpose, a beginner's yoga position with the feet not entwined. This way we could disassemble an M-1 or carbine and lay the parts out on our fatigue-trousered thighs, avoiding the dust of the dry soil. I gave much time to the care of my two rifles and their scope sights, with the jag-tipped Parker-Hale rod and some selected trimmed flannel patches.

The case of Denver Ordnance M-2 ball that had shot so well in these rifles was still three-fourths full, and lay on its side under my cot. The English lieutenant that I was quartered with (each American officer was shoved in on one of the permanent Deolali training staff) would smile as he saw me trying boxes of that ammunition, easing each round into the chamber, lowering the bolt to feel the bullet seat against the rifling throat, and rejecting rounds that felt excessively loose or tight. By this competitive rifleman's practice, it was thought that accuracy could be much improved, and this ritual helped me to pass spare time in the evening.

The case of Denver Ordnance M-2 ball that had shot so well in these rifles was still three-fourths full, and lay on its side under my cot. The English lieutenant that I was quartered with (each American officer was shoved in on one of the permanent Deolali training staff) would smile as he saw me trying boxes of that ammunition, accuracy could be much improved, and this ritual helped me to pass spare time in the evening.

Our other evening pastimes, of course, were more in the orthodox vein of the company grade officer, circa 1943. We drank in a comradely way. We found the nearest garden party or club dance floor where the girls were. And where the girls weren't, we indulged in heavier drinking and in the high jinks prankery of younger men at war. Of the many practical jokes that this included, some of which were Anglo-American in a good-humored but uninhibited way, I'd like to recount one in particular.

Among the officers I knew best in this aggregation of combat volunteers were Pete Petito and Larry Lew, both captains who would soon be promoted. I'd known Pete since my earliest days in the 132nd Infantry, a year before the outbreak of the war. Muscular, swarthy, with a flashing smile and coal-black-hair—and known to have come from Chicago—he was humorously called "that Sicilian gangster" by the female Red Cross workers and nurses who happened to be aboard the *Lurline*. In fact, he was a high school mathematics teacher and an athletics coach, but he played up to this image with a certain glee, posing for photos with a tommy gun held in the assult-fire position and staring into the camera with a Mafia-member's leer on his Valentino-like face.

Lew was entirely different in background and appearance, being from Oregon and of Anglo-Saxon extraction. Where the two of them came close indeed was in their love of a good practical joke. Pete loved any kind of military high jinks. (He had once typed a regimental order that called for the execution of the regimental commander and the placing of his remains in the regimental trophy room, "on display as an example of senile decay," and tricked the colonel into signing it himself and ordering it posted on the bulletin board outside his office.) But, Larry Lew was a specialist. Whenever he got drunk past midnight, his eyes would suddenly go round with a sense of joyful invention. Then, grinning like a copulating racoon, he would look around at the rest of us and say, "Let's flip the colonel."

By flip he meant that three or four of us should form a mock drill team under his command, march on his shouted orders into the victim's sleeping quarters, grasp the edge of his cot and give a powerful upward heave, catapulting the sleeper up and over, tangling him in his mosquito net and bruising him in his fall to the floor.

By the third night at Deolali, Lew had instigated three such flippings, so that the rest of us slept very lightly on the fourth. I slept lightly indeed, having been a party, along with Petito, to the revenge plotted by the three victims against Lew. Pete and I had supplied the idea of rigging a huge pitcher filled with water and chunks of ice to the door of Lew's quarters with a rope and a contrived hook, with the acquiescence of his British host who would spend the night elsewhere. The contrivance functioned to perfection, so that as Larry opened the door to escape the chilly winter night, a five-inch column of ice water splashed down over face, chest and midriff, drenching him to his boot tops.

Instinct led Lew to blame us instantaneously as "those two island rats, Pete and Johnny," who had teamed up often to beat him at poker. With the uncanny guile of the happy, articulate drunk, he flashed out his plan to take revenge against the proxy avengers.

Here I must say a word about the officer Pete was quartered with, a memorable British type who wore the classic Guards mustache and who played a mean game of tennis every morning. He also loved to listen to symphonies on his Gramophone, had a signed photograph of Anthony Eden on his wall, and was a Cambridge MA. Look at him one moment and you saw a ramrod-straight infantryman; look again and he was the aesthete of aesthetes, viewing portraits in an art gallery with an appreciative gesture of the wrist and lower arm.

The Britisher I bunked with had a faint Yorkshire accent and a more practical look about him which now proved to be correct and valid. Lew, who knew the exact location of his room and that I was his guest, had soon recruited three of his fellow drunks, organized them into the required mini drill squad, and was marching them across the bachelor officers' compound.

"Detail! 'Ten-SHUN!" came the first shouted command. Then,

"Right FACE! Forward March!" followed by the various columns right and left needed to bring the four-man column of drunks, stomping time with their hobnailed boots, inside the room and alongside my cot.

I lay there resigned, smelling the booze on the breath of my four fellow officers, as Lew gave the next command, "Right FACE!" and then the final "In three counts, prepare to FLIP!" At the shout of "ONE!" each member of the detail grasped the outer rail of my cot. At "TWO!" they all heaved upward as mightily as they could. At "THREE!" they let the now empty bed fall down on top of my prostrate, bruised form on the cold concrete floor.

Now I smelled Larry's boozy breath, close up, as he bent down. "Okay, Johnny," he slurred out in the darkness. "We've taken care of you, and we're quits for that ice water gambit. Tell us where your buddy Pete sleeps and we'll spare you a bucket of beer-cooler, now. Pete might as well share the reward, don't you think?" My British host lay chuckling through it all.

Though not at my mental best (the skin had come off my shoulder against the rough brick wall, the iron-grid bedspring had gashed my left cheek and temple) a plan came to me in that instant. "Yes," I said, feigning the tone of a frightened and penitent traitor. "It was his bloody idea. He's in the far corner of the quad, two doors this way from the triangle alarm-gong. Bed's on the left as you enter. The left, with a green mosquito net."

Out they went in the same mock drill fashion. "Detail, 'Ten-SHUN! Right FACE! Forward MARCH!" and so on, their eight hobnailed boots striking sparks on the cobblestoned quad. Soon the noise was coming from that far corner, outside the designated door. One by one the commands to enter the room and to execute the bed-flip were shouted, loudly and drunkenly, and there was the rip of a mosquito net, the crash of a heavy body, and then the cot falling on top of it.

This time, though, there was a catch and a surprise. As the reader no doubt will have guessed, the victim was not my buddy Pete but the killer/aesthete Britisher with whom he was quartered. As he untangled himself from the mosquito net and sprang toward his table, the air turned blue.

"BLOODY AMERICAN BASTARDS!" he roared, in a voice two octaves lower than usual and many decibels louder. And the hasty scrambling of his assailants toward the door, their grunts as they tried to squeeze through it all at one time, were now audible and visible to me and my host, who by this time had eased out to the veranda for a starlit view.

Hard on their fleeing heels, the tennis player-symphony listener emerged from the doorway, drawing a Webley .455 revolver from its canvas holster. The light was bad for aiming and the officer was not angry enough to kill, but the sparks kicked up by the hobnails made a mark of sorts, and he was angry enough not to worry about ricochets. He aimed each shot low at the scampering feet, then nudged it a bit lower as he fired, emptying the big handgun with evenly spaced timed-fire shots.

There were distant shouts, relayed in Hindustani, and the Guard soon arrived. By this time Lew and company were safely distant, and my British host and I were back in bed, giggling and exchanging thanks and congratulations, with me full of happy conceit. The incident was closed by a few curt words by the Britisher, Webley still in hand, addressed to the Guards in their own dialect, and the otherwise peaceful Indian night, with only the jackals crying in the distance, resumed its restful course.

At the enlisted level relations were just as good, or better. Tommy Atkins got on well with GI Joe, and their cultural differences were joked about much and fought over very little. During our daily sessions out on the ranges and drill fields we were introduced to the Indian Army institution of the char wallah or tea vendor, who moved his charcoal-heated pots close to the formations and waited for the rest calls or breaks. Then, the turbanned hucksters would cry their wares: "Tea! Fine hot tea!" — and always with that enhancing adjective added: "Fine BRITISH tea! Lovely BRITISH char! Hot, hot, hot BRITISH tea! Good BRITISH brand! Best BRITISH Darjeeling!"

After three days of this, our enlisted men got together and conspired, to a man, to change this bit of vocal advertising. They named a delegation to go round the vendors and distribute a little sample baksheesh—a rupee here and there—and to offer a lot more if the vendors would change the wording of their cries just a bit.

Next day the training spaces round the Deolali compound rang with a modified series of barker-cries. "ROTTEN BRITISH TEA! NO GOOD BRITISH POISON! PISS-POOR TEA!" And finally, to emphasize the unpopularity of one of the American officers who sported a mustache of heroic proportions: "HANDLEBAR JOHNSON TEA!"

In keeping with their bargain, the GIs bought twice as much tea and tipped twice as generously. And the British in charge of the post took it in the best of humor, laughing along with us, and getting back at us right and left with their witty arsenal of Yankee Doodle jokes and comments.

From this kind of contact we learned more about the British, whom we'd learned to respect a lot in the South and Southwest Pacific theaters. The way that bed-flipped officer laughed about it afterwards, the way all ranks of Britishers accepted the char wallah prank, made their quality known to us in garrison. (We already knew they could fight like hell.) For those of us who knew it then or met it later, the high jinks that could go on in a British officer's mess on holiday occasions could make all ours look pale. Lieutenants and captains and majors could throw one another through wood-framed, third story glass windows, and nearly kill one another in mock fencing matches with foils torn off their mantlepiece display cross. Our stay at Deolali was only a few days, but we left it with sacrificial gift exchanges, letting go an only Parker pen, receiving a Britisher's only good Ghurka kurkri, razor-edged and unobtainable in the best local bazaar, and with warm handshakes and sincerest hopes that we'd meet again.

And some of us, still short of Valhalla, would be meeting again. Brewing up in Burma, being planned out on the campaign maps of General Tanaka of the 18th Japanese Division and his superiors, was a final big offensive. In the midst of it a few months later, many of us would shake hands again with a British friend, this time on some disputed riverbank or paddyfield echoing with the noise of Enfields, Brens, Nambus and M-1 rifles. . .

DEOGARH

Before these chance second meetings, though, there'd be a lot more training and rehearsing. Following this brief and earliest Asian encampment at Deolali, we entrained and rolled slowly eastward along the Great Indian Peninsular Railway. For four-and-a-half days we eyed the exotic wilderness and countryside—plains country, forest, with cultivation that seemed in no way to reduce the wild herds of blackbuck, chinkari and nilgah. Peasants seen along the way seemed as compatible with the wild herds' presence as they seemed resentful of us. The looks we received from those dark eyes were understandably hostile: the subcontinent's history had been studded with Moghul, Ayran, British and now American invasions.

I saw our new camp a week before the main body was to arrive. With haste that caused me to be separated temporarily from that case of Denver Ordnance Depot ammunition, I was sent back to Bombay to pick up a carload of carbines and other supplies and move on ahead to the campsite in central India.

The name of the place, Deogarh, served by a railway stop called Jahklann, proved to be unknown to the Bombay station agent with whom I had to clear the shipment. To find either of these names, he had to pull out a dusty small-scale map from a filing cabinet and examine it with a magnifying glass. He then filled out the forms, and I could move on with my small guard and escort detail.

Most advance assignments are a pain: this one was sheer joy. The trip to Bombay had been in a first class compartment with a bevy of WAC (I)s—officers of the Indian Army's Women's Corps, one of whom looked like a dusky Ava Gardner. The trip back past Deolali and on for those four-and-a-half days eastward, in another first class coach coupled to the cargo van (as a rail car was called there when it wasn't called a wagon), was delightfully solo. I could eye the passing scenery, enjoy the ceiling-fanned dining rooms where the train halted three times a day for plates heaped with curry or tea things, like a European nobleman on tour. There was the odd glance across these dining rooms from the local British administrator or railway

433

officer, of course. The sight of an officer carrying two scabbarded firearms everywhere he went, including the dining table, was bound to rouse curiosity. But, apart from this, I was free of all social scrutiny. I could trace back my memories, now, to that last night on the town in Bombay and the whole long journey from Fiji before, and know myself to be a damned lucky soldier.

With the usual paperwork crises, I managed to get the train to stop at Jahklann and uncouple the carload of munitions, which my detail duly guarded (against some feared act of hijacking by the anti-British underground?) until a truck column from the training camp arrived to unload it. The senior advance detail officer, a Lt. Colonel Dan Still, took pains to congratulate me on the "arduous" chore of escorting the rail car, and I managed to stifle the laugh that came up from my overfed belly.

For another week this advance detail idyll continued. Still and I were quartered in the Dak bungalo at Deogarh, a stone and red tile structure on a rise near the Betwa River, overlooking the broad space now patterned with tents in company blocks, with the three battalions clearly separated by drill field strips.

On the truck ride out, I'd seen a score of nice big game animals, from a trophy-sized gazelle (chinkari) to a nicely-antlered sambur, elk-like in size. The British liaison officer in the truck beside me just grinned when I asked him if one needed a license to shoot game here, and beside his large officer's tent I saw a nice blackbuck hanging, freshly shot, with his Ghurka batman sharpening a knife to dress it out.

Then sheer disaster. My cherished case-lot of Denver Ordnance ammo was back with the 3rd Battalion's baggage. For the two scope-sighted .30-06s, I found I had but four rounds of ammunition in the rifle cartridge belt kept in my footlocker. A search through the whole camp, the carload of carbines and carbine ammunition, plus my personal kit and Still's, turned up not one more round. Unless I used my .45 or borrowed someone else's .303, I'd have to hunt now as so many of the resident British did, with less than a pocketful of ammo in country that contained both tiger and leopard: an austerity that previous experience had never put me through.

But, that lovely week went on, with my every question about the tent camp, kitchen space and other preparations met with the answer: "It's already done," so that I had plenty of daytime to spend as I wished. It's another story, book-length if I gave every detail, so I won't describe those six remaining days in a big game hunter's paradise with so few of those cartridges at hand. Somewhere in my files I've got a folder thick with yellowing notebook paper, notes for an article with the working title of Four Cartridges. It was more than a year past those days on New Caledonia when my market hunting (shooting deer for a battalion mess twice a week) had given me material for an article on shot-placement that would be published in the American Rifleman magazine. Then as now, I am a firm believer in the nerve center shot, meaning the brain (if you don't want the trophy) as first choice aiming point and thereafter any point further down the spine, to drop the animal in its tracks either dead or totally immobile. The central boast in that article yet-to-be-written is that the four cartridges took four selected animals: a chinkara, a black-buck, a blue-bull or nilgai, and one very succulent peacock (head shot surreptitiously behind the Dak bungalo because the bird was locally sacred).

If ever a man had a love affair with a mere mechanical artifact, I had one with the little M-70 as I eked out that joyful week's hunt with those four rounds of 150 grain Denver Ordnance Depot M-2 ammo. Before I gave it to a dear friend, who shares this book's original dedication (J.K. "Makki" Atal of the Indian Civil Service) at the end of my stay in wartime south Asia, this little gun was to round out eight years of war and of peaceful sporting use to me, ending with a wonderful last hunt in Makki's company for the tiger that now hangs in my club at Princeton. But that week with only four cartridges on hand stands out in my memory.

Then the week was over, and the three battalions marched into that neat tent camp, with a British general hospital tented adjacently, and the war resumed in its most grinding and tedius form: the hurried training of a unit too quickly thrown together.

As we received further shipments of equipment, incomplete, of course, but enough to go to work with, the training became dead serious. We had been told that we'd be serving with Wingate's new Special Force, to go into Burma early the next year and tear up the enemy's rear on a scale much larger than he'd been able to do the year before, with only one British brigade. This was the way we understood it, and this was also the way Wingate and his ultimate theater superior Mountbatten understood it. General Marshall had promised us to the British back at the Quebec Conference, and that was that. But the official histories were to disclose later that others, particularly "Vinegar Joe" Stilwell, had other ideas. But no matter. Unaware of the high-up paperwork war that was being waged over our poor GI bodies, we began to train in earnest.

Accepting Wingate's truism that no military unit is ever ade-quately trained for combat, and abiding the loud advice of the combat-experienced minority of its officers, the unit's training pro-gram centered on the time proven infantry essentials: shooting and marching and marching and shooting. The only things added were the necessities of feeding and general supply, and the specialities forced upon us by the need to operate without ground supply and reinforcement, receiving these and also "artillery" support from the U.S. Air Force. It was the infantry training routine of a unit that had learned the penalties paid in combat for the traditional garrison frills of spit and polish, plus this new air-supply and evacuation business.

Oh yes, there were also the mules. To give mobility to our mortars and machine guns behind the enemy lines, and to enable us to carry heavy loads of ammunition other than on our own backs, we had been issued mules and had been provided with personnel of quarter-master pack units: mule skinners and veterinary officers who had to be integrated with the more purist type of doughboy. This proved to be easier than expected. The Texan and Okie Southwesterners, many of them Indians, got on well with us from the start. By the time General Merrill arrived to take command, we were already used to a familiar Marauder scene—the drop field at dawn with the last of the DC 3s passing over, and men and mules hurriedly picking up their litter of parachuted and free-dropped ammo and food in the morning mists, to clear the area re-victualled and re-armed before the still hypothetical enemy could catch us there like sitting ducks.

As a company commander throughout that period at Deogarh, I faced no training officer's doubts. Knowing their utter importance, I kept to these essentials. Rifle marksmanship, of course, was my specialty, and I applied with a vengeance the practical exercises that we'd found priceless on Guadalcanal and had double checked with the New Guinea and New Georgia veterans on the *Lurline:* those deep-dug single pits for the markers to crouch in, stationed at various ranges and activated in surprise-fire style by telephones in each pit, so that the cardboard silhouettes-on-poles came up without warning near the firer standing at a point or walking the course, some close, some a few out as far as 200 yards. If he failed to spot them, they went down unhit in their brief exposure times—very brief if they were close. Except for initial zeroing and occasional checking to keep them centered on a six-inch bull at 100 yards (three inches above exact point of aim) there was no known distance firing. Too far from the range sergeant to hear his whispering into the control phone, the firer would either hit or miss the target, or not see it at all, during its three to 10 seconds of exposure. There were no position require-ments beyond those of safety aflank and behind; the firer could make use of any convenient rest, could fall prone to fire the shot if he chose and the cover permitted it. As revealed during our *Lurline* seminars, this was the "trainfire" kind of course that we had all separately discovered or invented, decades before trainfire was formalized at home. The silhouette targets we innovators had used on New Gui-nea, Guadalcanal, New Caledonia, Australia and elsewhere were the same as those we were using now, made of cut saplings and the brown packing box corrugated paper with pasters improvised with flour paste and writing paper.

Among our 3,000 volunteers there were woefully few with a background in competitive target shooting—perhaps 10 who could make full use of long-range sniper rifles with high magnification scopes, had such equipment been available. But since this was an American outfit, containing its share of hunters, casual plinkers and farm boys, and since many of us had been through combat and had learned the life insurance value of quick and practical marksmanship, an intense interest in good shooting was there.

The result, which began to be demonstrated as soon as our ammunition and guns got together, was a shootin' outfit. And our Camp Deogarh became the scene of many impromptu shooting exhibitions of the sort that are never mentioned in the training manuals. As a seasoned, if young, Camp Perry veteran, I was forced against my better judgement to accept these impromptu demonstrations and exercises—because I found that there was no way for me to halt them, even in the company that I commanded. War is a cruel, bizarre game, full of trickeries that can be as successful in battle as they are unmentionable by the official historians afterwards. The gun tricks that I refer to now are best understood, I think, as a part of the makeup of what a modern journalist might call the character of "the combat infantry jock."

In his recent best selling book *The Right Stuff,* Tom Wolfe speaks of the deadlier fighter pilots of the Air Force and the Navy as "fighter jocks," and he associates this term with a catalogue of dangerous tricks: outside loops inscribing circles much too small, exaggerated victory rolls, buzzing ground installations at supersonic speeds, and other strictly non-regulation, if not criminal, disobediences; also flying without breakfast and badly hung over, and the larger pattern of risks that Wolfe describes under his heading: "Flying & Drinking & Drinking & Driving." All of it forbidden, of course, and every offender technically subject to a court-martial. But, it was done all the time by the deadliest (and therefore in wartime the best) of the fighter jocks, and viewed with a blind eye by the ex-fighter jocks in command. "It's legally and morally wrong, and stupidly dangerous gentlemen, but I remember boozy old Joe back on Henderson Field, who shot down 20 Japs on 12 takeoffs . . ."

In the 3rd Battalion at least, every company and most platoons had their one-two-three hierarchy of trick shots, ready at the opening of a beer can to put on one of these impromptu shooting exhibitions. For me, they were frightening reprises of the derring-do I'd seen earlier in the Pacific and had tried my best, for a while, to halt. A sergeant would lift his .45, take aim, and one of his squad would hold a beer can for him at 10 paces, six inches in front of his own chin. A corporal would pick up a rifle, and a comrade would hold a fired .06 cartridge between thumb and forefinger for him to hit, offhand, at 15 paces. Other such intellects would "smoke" a long cigar, or a pithy dry weed stem to simulate one, while a colleague, firing in a timed fire sequence, would shorten it to within an inch of his lips with a pistol or carbine. For a long time I had protested against this sort of thing at earlier locations, had pleaded with my men to stop it. But now, with this all-volunteer group of combat infantry jocks at Deogarh, I felt utterly defeated.

Not only did I feel defeated by this gross abuse of my cherished sport of marksmanship, but resigned. The tactical-level irrationality of war itself often pays off "irrational," aggressive and egotistical leaders with victories, while sober and cerebral types like myself lose out by trying to play it safe. So, this irrational chance-taking seemed perhaps to fit, so long as it didn't reach the stage of Russian roulette, which in my sight it never did. I had to wait several more years before I would be near a death caused by the insane abuse of firearms by a group of student drunks who knew nothing of firearms.

At Deogarh, I joined the other officers in turning a blind eye and a deaf ear to these gun "games." To the deeper unconscious selves of the men who played them, they were battle rehearsals, perhaps. They brought real danger of death, not just competitive shooting range pressure, into the challenging execution of good trigger squeeze. They tested a man's battle coolness, perhaps. And for all I could argue otherwise, in our battle days soon to come in northern Burma, the men who played these deadly games might kill hundreds of Japanese trying to storm our roadblocks set up behind their lines.

The finest shots we had, the several seasoned competitive riflemen with advanced NRA training, would never try such things, of course. They knew that the finest marksman's muscles occasionally might go into spasm, that the keenest competitor could have a shot "set off" by some extraneous noise and cause a flinch. But that mass of cruder combat jocks went on doing, or cheering as spectators, these dangerous firearms abuses. I know of no resulting fatality, but I have never felt so much the need for a team of NRA instructors and safety umpires as in my wartime combat units on the eve of another campaign. Warriors we were in that war, and deadly combat jocks, fully capable of dealing with the Japanese who were far, far more suicidal in their ways. But *soldiers* in my finest definition of the term, the cool technicians who think of the next thing to do and thus allay their fears and who don't need this macho danger drill and its irrational bravado, we never became. Perhaps there's too much of the wild animal in us still for this ideal soldier of mine to ever be.

On afterthought, perhaps, I might have been able to halt or allay risky trick shooting by being a bit less selfish. I'd made my contacts with several primitive local shikaris, hunters on the edge of native agriculture who lived by taking gazelle and larger game; and I got my firearms pleasures legitimately (if not strictly legally) as I had before on New Caledonia, Guadalcanal and Fiji. The 3rd Battalion mess was always ready for fresh meat, and the barrels of my Model 70 and my Springfield were warmed every two days or so on the tasty chinkari, blackbuck and nilgai herds along the Betwa River where it adjoined the camp. With a safe background I could also take partridge and peafowl with headshots: the service ammunition from my cherished Denver Ordnance case lot made this, plus head and spine shots on the larger animals, easy. Night hunting was entirely legal in this part of India, so "market" slaughter of chital and sambur deer species was also practiced when we needed the meat. On the rifle shooting side, considering the limitations of personnel and past NRA-type training, it is hard for me to think of a deadlier kind of preparation for our meeting with the Japanese 18th Infantry Division. Those risky tricks and that more limited hunting experience at Deogarh prepared us both technically and emotionally for deadly frontline marksmanship, especially in the jungle. Had we all been adequately grounded, as civilians or as peacetime soldiers, in NRA firearms safety training and competition, there would have been no psychological need for such silly risk taking. We'd have known guns for the fine and oftentimes essential artifacts that they are. None of us would have felt the need to treat them as ego-builders, as toys in the hands of men turned back towards boyhood by the deprivations and desperations of an infantryman's war.

Machine gun, mortar, grenade, and other crafts-training went on with equal verve. There was ammunition enough for fullscale firing exercises, and infiltration courses to introduce the combat-inexperienced to the sensual impact of a fire-fight. The importance of such exercises was known to many in the 1st Battalion, who had memories from the Infantry School at Fort Benning as well as Pacific campaign experiences. We anxiously sought out the men who had never heard a full-scale platoon and company fire-fight and let them hear one simulated. Later, they would escape the shock that many of us had felt, unprepared for it as we had been. A platoon armed with M-1s and BARs, firing their weapons as in combat— even as in a trail engagement where only the leading elements have targets—sounds to the green soldier first hearing it like a battalion or more. To know that it is a humble platoon he needs to hear it from both sides, as an infiltrator, hearing that vicious whip-snapping above and that roaring blast before, as well as the more comforting noise of his own firing and that of his buddies. By this experience (and by work in the range pits, where he hears the snap of bullets through the silhouette he holds on a pole) he learns of frightening noises that really can't hurt him, that in fact warn him not to raise his head at the wrong juncture in a fight. This guards against panic and despair later on, when the bullets are enemy instead.

As much as I'm in love with marksmanship, both as a hobby and as an assurance that the young men of a nation can become effective soldiers when this is essential, I now must pay homage to another, perhaps co-equal, talent of my *Maraduer* comrades. Toward the end of our training days at Deogarh, which had included almost as much hard marching as we Guadalcanal and other combat veterans had urged, Pete Petito and I were standing on one bank of the Betwa,

Major General Orde C. Wingate, speaking to us in our training camp of his long range penetration groups (LRPGs), paid homage to the priceless invention that he called, in British terminology, wireless. Along with air support, radio at the level depicted above made the Marauder operation possible and profitable.

Here we see two signalmen at work with an SCR at Force or Battalion levels, getting out a message to rear base. It may be a call for a supply drop, for some bombing and strafing help from the P-51 fighter squadron that supported us, or an order passed between Merrill and one of the battalions.

No one worked harder than these signalmen. Antennae wire was often raised high on bamboo uprights (bamboo shoots that were keg-thick and hard to cut through at the base. Raising these antennae, staking out guy wires to support them, getting the messages through, encoding, decoding—often under enemy artillery or mortar fire— made heroes out of these men.

watching a column strung out along a difficult rocky trail on the other side. Our view was wide angle, so that we could see a couple of hundred men moving in single file. But it also was close enough so that we could see the confidently planted feet, the sagely gradual pace as they marched uphill, the individually chosen and fitted packs (some regular, some ski-troop type, some pack-frame, some captured Japanese, and various forms of the horseshoe poncho/blanket roll tied on). We could also note, those many years before the cargo-belt came into wide backpacking use, the way that the wide pistol belt or rifle cartridge belt was fitted around each man's hips—to keep off his spinal column the heavy weight of pistols, machetes, aid-kits, one or two canteens and the basic increments of ammunition.

As unseen admirers, Pete and I were feeling the same proud and comradely thought, and as usual he could put it better. "Look at them, Johnny, not only can they shoot and get fed from the air and call down fighter planes to be their artillery for them, but those bastards can march like the best damn troops at Waterloo. We're looking at an outfit that can do 30 miles a day in this kind of country, and have strength enough left to dig in and fight when they get there!"

This, of course, had been no accident. General Merrill and our other seniors knew that the Japanese we would soon be facing were in one sense a commander's dream. They would have that "unique marching power of Japanese infantry" that military historians would extoll. Granted that the first ingredient of victory was Bedford Forrest's trick of getting there "fustest wid de mostest," General Tanaka could count on this important advantage against the average occidental army. But not against us. With our added advantage of air drop and mule transport we, too, could traverse jungle trails and other unmotorable terrain and get our firepower astride their supply routes, as the Japanese had done so often in Malaya and in China.

As we completed this training stay at Deogarh and marched back to that tiny whistle stop of Jahklann, we therefore felt ready. By the standards of the American military, which had to throw itself together afresh for each new world crisis, we were fairly well prepared (though not, of course, adequately prepared by Wingate's standards). Our only severe lack was in animal transport: one load of mules had been lost in the Arabian Sea to an enemy submarine, and the Phillips pack saddles had not been worn long enough to have "settled in". Our mule leaders were experienced and able, but they and their veterinary officers had had little time to become acquainted with their charges. In the mode of hurried improvisation that democratic non-militarism seems always to invite, though, we could feel that this time, facing a campaign in an exotic land against an undemocratic, very militaristic foe, we had the right tools and the good craftsman's skill to use them.

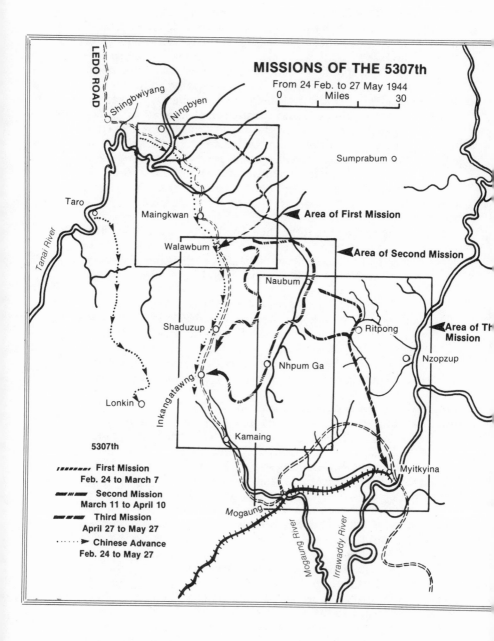

MISSIONS OF THE 5307th

From 24 Feb. to 27 May 1944

0   Miles   30

LEDO ROAD

Shingbwiyang

Ningbyen

Sumprabum ○

Taro ○

Maingkwan ○

◄ Area of First Mission

Walawbum ○

◄ Area of Second Mission

Tanai River

Naubum

Shaduzup ○

Ritpong ○

◄ Area of Th
Mission

Nzopzup ○

Inkangatawng ○

Nhpum Ga ○

Lonkin ○

Kamaing ○

Myitkyina ○

5307th

┄┄┄┄ **First Mission**
Feb. 24 to March 7

▬▬▬ **Second Mission**
March 11 to April 10

▬▬▬ **Third Mission**
April 27 to May 27

┄┄┄► **Chinese Advance**
Feb. 24 to May 27

Mogaung

Mogaung River

Irrawaddy River

ASSAM

The trip from Deogarh, India, to our assembly point in Margher-
ita, Assam, took us a week and a half. The now distinguished writer
Charlton Ogburn, then a communications platoon leader in the 1st
Battalion, would later write in *The Marauders* that the trip:

> "...could have taken a hundred (days) without my object-
> ing. After the exertions of the past two months it was bliss
> to be able to lie about all day even on wooden benches,
> eight of us to a compartment, with nothing to do but talk,
> eat, buy tea from the vendors at the stations, and look out
> across the face of India as the train sauntered on its way or
> lay up on a siding to allow the slow-paced time of the
> Orient to catch up with it..."

Bliss, indeed, I now can echo. The love for the more primitive
Indian earth and its natural beauty (that I was later to feel on
elephant-pad shikar ventures for tiger and other trophies in old
central provinces) had begun to overwhelm me. I'd felt it through
the first few miles out of Bombay, where the semi-desert landscape
was punctuated by outcrops rising out of a general flatness reaching
out spaciously to the horizon. Here and there, a small herd of gazelle,
a hairy sounder of wild pig, a larger herd of blackbuck or nilgai
would spice the scene for the hunters among us.

Now it was more of the same, with stretches of the denser Indian
forest added. As we slowly clicked along the rails I now saw sambur,
the big elk-like deer of Asia. Also enhancing the view were chital or
axis deer, dotted as adults like Virginia whitetail fawns, but with
grand symmetrical antlers spreading above the heads of the males,
some so long that when tilted back they touched the animals's back at
its extreme rear.

In the more open country it was more of the usual gazelle and
antelope herds, compatible with agriculture, obviously, since they
were grazing mostly in the paddy fields. For a man most at home in
the gamelands, walking with his rucksack and camera and rifle,

443

these views of the Indian spaces were bittersweet indeed. With the little M-70 or its companion Springfield '03 (now shortened to my preferred 20-inch barrel length for jungle usage) across my knees being oiled and rechecked, I had to fight the urge to get out at the siding halts and collect some Indian meat and trophies. My bolder compartment mates urged me to do so, or to lend them the rifles and they'd do it for me, but I stood firm and let them call me killjoy and spoilsport with many obscene adjectives. As truer and hardier combat infantry jocks, they would have delighted in the adventure: a hurried shot or two, well placed in neck or head, a scramble out of the compartment door to pick up the blackbuck or nilgai and drag it back to the door, with one of us inside to pull the emergency stop rope if the train should begin to move too soon, and then the problem of gutting the animal and distributing and cooking the meat. It was the sort of thing these Marauder types would have loved, and I felt a bit guilty as I had denied them. For me, it conjured up visions of peasant wrath, of Indians whose religion denied them the right to kill even insects, revenging themselves by tearing up rails or burning down stations.

I felt this way because I sensed hostility in half the glances from the track side—dark eyes glowing under the fez or turban above them. But like Charlton Ogburn, gathering his memories in another compartment, I did not allow these inhospitable stares to make me—

". . .feel out of place or ill at ease. It was not we, but they who were the newcomers, the interlopers, the transcients. We knew it and they knew it. We belonged to that which was older than any nation. We were the British, we were the Moguls, we were the Aryans, we were the Dravidians. We went back to the beginning of history. We were the soldiery."

The worst of this invading soldiery at points in India's history had, of course, behaved rapaciously. And, the discipline against impromptu big game shooting that I'd imposed on my compartment companions no doubt was a bit high-minded. These two points proved themselves emphatically at one of these farmland rail sidings, where the train pulled in and halted. As it did so, from one of the compartments two cars to the rear of ours, two M-1 rifles were emptied, eight shots each, and a hundred yards off three turbanned natives danced, kicking high as the bullets struck a yard or two right or left of their feet, spurting sand and ricocheting on.

We eight officers exchanged a sudden, outraged glance, and as the train drew up, sprang for our compartment door. I grabbed my .45 on the way and led our angry pack to the door of the two offending enlisted men. Their identities I established on the spot by inspecting their rifles and picking the two with hot barrels and with the oil shot out inside. In a voice totally out of control I ordered the two owners out of the train, and had them stand at attention in front of me.

Both men were known to me, members of the company I had commanded through the training period: an Apalachian farmer and a former Chicago postal employee. Not too far from shooting them both on the spot, I shouted the conventional reprimands: "You call yourselves soldiers! You fire at innocent civilians just for kicks! You disgrace us all. . ."

I became aware that their positions of attention were not all that rigid and respectful. The tallest dared to smile, and to interrupt me. "Lieutenant," he said slowly, "do you remember that smashed windshield on the Old Ranger's jeep?"

I did. An officer with this man and three other riflemen crowded in the jeep had been driving down a road near Deogarh, at some 40 miles-per-hour. We passed an Indian road gang, smoothing out the coarse crushed rock along the road's straight stretching distance. On each of the Indian faces we saw that hostility, which we attributed to Ghandi's passive resistance program against the British Raj. But for the last in this line of workers, the resistance now became active. Too late for the driver to veer away, a heaping shovelful of the crushed rock was flung, with a precision that made it hover as a clump squarely in front of the windshield on the driver's side.

Blinded by the shattered glass, though saved from permanent injury by the safety layers, the driver successfully kept the car upright, halting it 100 yards farther on the roadside grass. Then he acted automatically: a tug at the M-1 rifle in its scabbard on the jeep apron, and a casual aim at the feet of the offending Indian who was left dancing like a dervish. Then he aimed higher to bring the passing snap of the bullets closer to the Indian's ears, with the trigger pulled as the front sight went off to the right or left. Though not wanting quite to kill him, the driver didn't care much, either, if the man should happen to leap the wrong way and get hit.

The taller soldier faced me while the memory of this earlier shooting incident came back to cool my present, lofty-minded anger. One could plead a greater provocation and temptation, of course, could argue that the hurled rock was lethal as a bullet. But a shot by invading or visiting soldiery at a native, for any reason, was the poorest of public relations. Caught between the glances of the man who knew, and two officer colleagues who also knew of the jeep incident, I was given a way out by the train, which had begun to whistle and to stir up towards the engine. I about-faced and led the way back to our officers' compartment, regarding the incident as closed.

As I remember the rest of that train journey, with all those young

Americans cleaning, fondling, and talking about their weapons, I can almost hear the pseudo-liberal cry, Gun Freaks! I dare to call it pseudo-liberal because almost every liberal privilege or right that exists was bought, in part, by people with guns in their hands. Open liberal government, in the minority of nations where it exists today, can trace its very inception, usually, to the use of firearms by individuals who are today acclaimed as heroes.

We were not merely soldiers. A third of our outfit was combat veterans, and the guns we loved would help blot out a closed and extremely non-liberal government nearly four decades ago. Nevertheless our enthusiasm for the tools of our wartime-adopted craft and profession, and the sight of us riding these trains armed to the teeth, probably would have made some of my friends of more recent times, mutter that revealing epithet—at least to themselves.

We suspended our train riding at the vast Bramaputra River, after we had crossed the Ganges, at a place called Pandu. There we unloaded into a transient camp and then put up on a side-wheel river steamer for a journey of two days, going out at the sandbars and the gradually more lush and tall vegetation on the shores of the lower, sprawling reach of this river, mightier in flow than the Ganges. Finally we landed at Gauhati where we again boarded railway coaches, this time the narrow gauge rolling stock, worn and run down by military overuse, of the Bengal Assam Line.

On Feb. 6, 1944, we got off the train in the totally different environment of an Assam tea plantation area. Here, the cultivated plots were cut out of a fierce rain forest that loomed on every side, ready to move back and reclaim the captured land should the armies of dark-skinned laborers pause in their almost constant hacking at the vines, creepers and sprouting broadleaf seedlings in the shadow of their 200-foot parents all around.

To one who had read the Britisher shikar accounts from tea planter-hunters, these dark forests towards dusk seemed to have predatory eyes peering out of them. And not without reason: in a large tea estate dining room that was "papered" with tiger skins on all four walls, I heard a hospitable old colonel tell me of many adventures. He also took me out on his veranda to show me a "tree chair" that he had "invented"—an obvious improvement over the usual machaan which was improvised customarily from a native rope-and-wood frame bed. He shot all his tiger at night with a light on his Holland and Holland .470. He had never otherwise seen a tiger in the wild. That beasts so huge could be so secretive, showing a 30-year resident only their tracks and the traces of their (sometimes human) kills in daytime, made the jungle country into which we were now moving seem the more forbidding, the rifle that I held the more precious.

Here we learned a new and much-to-be-used word: basha. For the next few months we would spend our happiest few nights dry and warm on the bamboo floor of one of these long versions of a red Indian lodge. Erected on stilts made of termite-resistant tree trunks, these thatch-roofed bamboo structures varied greatly in length. Some were more than 100 yards long, I think, though I never measured them. Their floors were from four to seven feet off the ground, bamboo woven between bamboo joists, with woven bamboo walls, bamboo studs, ceiling joists and rafters. Our temporary camp at a place called Margherita was made up of pseudo bashas, really, the kind that a resentful peasantry might build for pay for a transient soldiery they wished to be uncomfortable. These had no stilts, and their studs and rafters and corner posts were made of green bamboo or any available wood. Their dirt floors when we entered were filmed with sawdust, the chewings of the termites or beetles that we could clearly hear, gnawing away, as we dozed in what to us was a grand kind of comfort in our mosquito nets on canvas cots.

Later on, we would see the real bashas, fine structures set on posts a foot or more in diameter, like the beach houses at Rehoboth and Atlantic City, near Washington D.C. Kachins and the more prosperous Nagas would own them communally: they would be dry and comfortable during the height of the rainy season, with their flat stones set on the floor (a terrible fire hazard, of course) for cooking jungle fowl, barking deer and domestic livestock on rare occasions. Bashas were to become luxurious occasional shelters for the Marauders, commandeered headquarters for battalions and the force headquarters, places for officers' meetings—the jungle equivalent of hotels, albeit with a certain danger. A form of typhus transmitted by mites was hyper-endemic in the lower parts of northern Burma, and the mites were encountered when you slept in the bashas.

I won't pretend to be able to say what or why, but this drawing of a young Kachin guerrilla of our OSS Detachment 101 and the two older tribesmen behind him, all American-armed and out — in this instance — for Japanese blood carries some sort of a message.

After my Guadalcanal contacts with Melanesians similarly armed, similarly out for Japanese blood, my later camaraderie with these fine tribesmen seemed to hint of a notion as old as Caesar's training and use of Gauls and other janissaries.

The Japanese had their collaborators, too (though many of these were reporting back to us from time to time). But despite an American's occasional misbehavior (an erring air-strike at an innocent village, for example) the most and the best, of these natives were with us and the British, their former colonial administrators. Maybe the message is simple: "We'll fight for you now because the Japanese are worse. But you behave and watch out after the Japs are gone; we don't like you so much, either."

SHINGBWIYANG

About midnight on Feb. 7, 1944, in secrecy so profound that the news of my promotion to captain two days before was whispered into my ear as we moved from a side trail onto the Ledo Road, we began to march from Assam into north Burma. The men of the 3rd Battalion were wise about combat body cargo. They would weigh every item and select a plastic instead of a heavier metal waterproof matchbox, for example. At this last halt we had been offered a further increment of the belt-hangings and pack-bulging chattels that a gadget-ridden American culture is so prone to supply its soldiers with, and at first these bright new items of home-invented "jungle equipment" were hard to throw away. Nevertheless, they decorated the roadside lavishly along the first five miles of our march, as the freshly overladen men had second thoughts.

The theme of the locale of World War II that we had now moved into was Roadbuilding and Counter-Roadbuilding. Stilwell's Allied Forces in the north and Tanaka's Japanese 18th Division to the south were each attacking and building, southward and northward, along the same stretch of muddy highway. The allies had it hardest with the terrain: the heavy-rooted rain forest and its drenched clay could stall the most powerful bulldozer, especially on the steepest possible gradients up the mountains they were carving. The road met itself so dramatically "coming back" that we learned again to be cautious—not to raise our weapons instinctively at the columns of men in the moonlight who were "coming the other way." To suddenly notice a file of dark, armed figures above or below us on the mountainside, not 30 yards away sometimes, was startling. But, after a first experience with M-1 and carbine safeties clicking off in both directions, we were glad of the reminder here in country where you knew there were no organized Japanese units of any size. Remember it when you get into real enemy country, we told ourselves. Don't panic and fire too quickly when you see those ghostly figures moving in the direction that an enemy column might logically be marching: those objects so vulnerable and close to your rifle will most likely be your own people, part of the column you're marching in now.

On the second day of the march down the road I made an equipment decision. I handed the little M-70 to a quartermaster warrant officer for storage, left the 1903 with its case and Lyman Alaskan sight (my second sniping rifle) on a mule, as part of my authorized mule-cargo as battalion intelligence officer, and from that point on carried a .30 carbine, carefully sighted in and tested for sure functioning. Others, including my friend Roy Dunlap, a firearms expert if ever there was one, have spoken out against the .30 carbine, calling its cartridge inadequately powerful. I found it to be an excellent weapon for an officer who spent most of his time with a headquarters group. It was far more accurate than a pistol. Its ammunition was lighter than an M-1's .30-06s, yet this light and handy gun could penetrate the Japanese helmets and body armor of that era with ease. With the mule moving close by, the sniping rifle could be taken out to carry when the country might seem to make it the first choice. At that point, the country we were moving through was not turnbolt rifle country. All of my experience on Guadalcanal told me that it was autoloader country, where the knowledgeable infantryman would feel more drawn to the faster firing weapons. Ideally, I thought, an officer could carry a handy carbine on the trail and trade it with some stay-behind for an M-1 and some extra bandoliers when in fixed defense or on a combat patrol. A sergeant in the battalion intelligence section had agreed to carry (as his own, until I might want to make the switch) an M-1 that I had picked out and carefully zeroed back at Deogarh. I bemoaned the eight-shot, trick rechargeable clips that made it so difficult to keep a rifle fully loaded during a fight without throwing cartridges away to do so, but I knew that if I could keep my head it would let me outshoot any five Arisaka-armed Japanese that I might meet head on, on a trail.

Others, too, made their weapons and equipment decisions, demonstrating the Yankee penchant for variety and choice. One officer in the 3rd Battalion, a bull of a man, chose to carry a stripped-down Browning Automatic Rifle with its full waist belt of ammunition as a personal weapon. Others chose tommyguns and 12-gauge M-97 Winchester riot guns; but the fact that most commissioned ranks stuck to the recommended .30 caliber carbine was notable, and, I think, no mere sign of conformity. To make the carbine more trim for carrying on the march, most of us used improvised five-round magazines. For most of us those little guns became almost a part of our bodies. When talking one would gesture with one, pointing it this way and that with a bend of the wrist; when resting, it lay lightly across the knees; when reading a map, it could be slung on a shoulder; when riding (the cavalrymen among us kept a saddle horse here and there, still) it could be slung diagonally or scabbarded quite neatly.

Like all the military combat units that I have seen or served in, this one became more polyglot, more motley as it moved closer to battle. Individual preferences in dress, in haircuts and shaving habits also became more evident. In the Marauders this variety was the greater for the 3rd Battalion's combat experience, and for the innovative attitude of Colonel Hunter and his colleagues, who had come from the Fort Benning Infantry School. Combat-tested and "school" notions of jungle warfare techniques combined in the Marauders to make them perhaps the most sophisticated unit of its kind and time.

For the 3rd Battalion, the only aspect that seemed wholly new was the animal transport. The mules and the horses, substituted for mules lost through enemy submarine action, were strange to nearly all of us, and we deferred to the veterinary officers and to a few mule-wise regulars (Colonel Hunter among them) who had operated in the Phillippines and other areas where the 75mm mountain howitzer was mule-carried over terrain too rugged for jeeps and other drive vehicles.

The novelty of it was especially evident as we began the march. To the usual humor and frustration of infantry movement on foot, we now had the braying (the mules had not been devocalized for humanitarian reasons), the kicking, the incredible stubbornness of these animals as an added attraction. Ed Rothchild, a Chicago attorney who led a platoon through the campaign while fighting off orders that would have assigned him to the judge advocate general's theatre representation, was to tell me, years later, that his memory of Burma, scenically, was of endless jungle trails, obscured in front, always, by a mule's behind. And as he spoke, he drew a huge circle in the air with his hands, then lifted his right to slice down the center. For a Marauder column on the march, this was as good a description as any from the individual marcher's most typical point of view.

Less typically, during the part of the campaign that we would be going through once we got down off this mountain road, the individual marcher's field of vision would be empty. And he would be praying for the moment when it would be filled again with a mule's bottom or with the comforting bulk of comrades marching in front of him. This less typical view, we knew as we marched towards the Japanese-held Hukawng Valley, would be assigned to everyone but a few key technicians in the battalion in turn, man by man, and timed by stop watch. Called Nambu Bait by the Guadalcanal contingent, this, of course, was the designation of one of us as lead scout in the Point—the Point of the Advance Guard, which I capitalize here because it deserves to be capitalized. As each of us marched on so casually now, labored perhaps in our breathing but still in the comfort of this mule's behind or the other men in our foreground, we thought ahead to those allotted moments when we'd be Nambu Bait.

Later on, when we got scout dogs and their trainers assigned, the dangers were reduced a great deal. But for the days we saw ahead, most of our imaginative energies were focused on our individual survival during those few moments of Point duty: our visual alertness, our readiness to fall quickly to the earth as the waiting enemy Nambu opened up on us, our tennis player's reflex to return that fire in the quickest and deadliest way, and our lying, hypocritical calmness when we would accept this share of mortal danger. This feeling, which reaches its truest intensity in the man who has "walked the Point" in an earlier campaign, wiping the sweat off his palms (if his nervous system reacts like Sammy Wilson's) and then re-grasping his gunstock, or feeling his socks drench and squash inside his shoes (if his nerves work like mine instead), had been our greatest inspiration to train in earnest with our weapons and our anxious, searching eyes back at Deogarh.

This ultimate sense of security in numbers or mass, and this private terror of being so utterly alone as Nambu Bait out in front, were two of the thoughts that occupied the more imaginative among us especially at nighttime as we marched, down that really quite secure rear area road. I also began to ponder an idea that intrigues me today. Like a growing number of paleo-anthropologists, popular writers, and professional animal watchers like Konrad Lorenz, I've tended to link man's behavior, in these post World War II years, to his increasingly proven origin as a primitive big game hunter. In its oversimplified popular utterance, this very complex idea postulates that man today goes to war and commits other violent acts because the paleolithic big game hunt that made him as a species no longer exists, to serve as the outlet for his "killer" aggressions. I've been working for the past two decades on its much less simple implications and arguments, referring often to 18 happy months that I spent, five years and more after this Assam-Burma walking trip, among African tribesmen who lived by taking elephants and other game with spears and poisoned arrows.

Far off, this wild neo-Darwinian idea, from the story of Merrill's Marauders in Burma? Perhaps. But as we marched along that road I could see along its side ditches, standing all impassive with their bows and spears and belted long knives, a varied sampling of the Naga hill tribes. These small and wiry men lived now, I knew, as all of us men had been made to live through a million and more years of evolution. Warriors they were not, primarily, although they could kill outsiders and one another with facility when provoked. They were hunters who could take elephant, buffalo and tiger with their primitive weapons and their hunter's trickery of pit-trap and deadfall. There at our trail side, holding spears with blades shaped to find the vitals of the largest land animals, they seemed a delegation from our evolutionary past. Their deep-set staring eyes seemed to challenge me, to cast doubt upon my most cherished images and ideals. Think more deeply, you pseudo-civilized hunters. Consider your deeper, truer reasons for all of this driving, striving war-making that you can explain only on the surface. Forbidden in your city lives to track and stalk and hunt, in the way of the ancient mammoth-hunters that you still are in body and in brain as well, do you trump up your excuses for this vast hunt-surrogate of war? Do you seek the lost dramatic turbulence of the caveman's bison drive, the mammoth trackdown and kill, in the mass killing of your fellow hunter-human beings?

One of these Nagas, in mien a very senior hunter and wearing a necklace made of tiger thumb-claws (betokening the deaths of eight large tigers), looked directly at me as I passed. He faintly smiled, and I leaped to the fantasy that he was inviting me, beckoning me back to my own beginnings. "Defect," he seemed to say. "Forget this imitation hunt you go on now. Turn off this unnatural tear of the earth through our wonderful elephant forests. Come with me and track the wild cattle, the buffalo, to our celebrant tribal feastings around their dead heaps of meat. Come back to the reality that made you; leave off this perverse dream that grips you now!"

It was a startling thought, this unspoken message, and one that I quickly suppressed. The war to me was a compelling necessity, a meeting of violence with its only countermeasure of a greater violence, against the evils of Hitler and Tojo. To question our side in such a war at all was ridiculous; to call it a contrived substitute for a primitive big game hunter drive that remained in our "hunter" blood was absurd. I shifted my carbine on my shoulder, snugging the sling against my neck, and told the part of my own unconscious that had fabricated this absurdity from the simple sight of a primitive tribesman's face to keep quiet for the remainder of the war. Nonetheless, I felt an almost irresistible urge to pause, to find an interpreter among our native scouts and talk to this man about his hunting ways; about the teamwork and the skills of his band, about their own keen interest in their finely made and sharpened weapons, about their tactics when taking elephant with stabbing spears. Today, the implications of the primitive big game hunt for our modern megatribes, grown in an evolutionary split-second from those tiny, brotherly teams of paleolithic hunters, have come back to haunt my old man's years, and I treasure every contact that I've had with surviving primitive big game hunters like this one. But on that march I exchanged hardly a word with these hunters. I quieted that troublesome inner voice and performed my duties with our specialists and scouts in the battalion intelligence section.

This decision to march down the Ledo Road had been controversial. Some of the senior officers involved had opposed it, arguing that the men should make their first contact with the Japanese in the freshest possible condition, should be hauled the 110-mile distance in trucks. Others, including several officers that I'd perhaps place in the "too macho" category of infantrymen, felt that the hardening and shakedown effects would be good, particularly after the long train and riverboat journey. In the end the latter won out, wrongly I think, because an outfit that had been hardened to 30-miles-a-day a month before would seem able to harden itself again in a very short time, and because we could presume a modicum at least of physical exertion in the campaign proper. As things turned out, the Marauders were going to need every ounce of tissue they had, both muscle for marching and fat to burn up when our food drops were stalled by bad weather.

Soon we crossed the highest point in the road; I remember pulling out my precious Leica to snap a photo of Pete standing by its marker sign. We halted for a moment to look down from its bald commanding height, free from the blinding forest for a mile or so, and to feel its windy coolness, so refreshing after the rain forest humidity. A few miles back, we'd had a hearty breakfast of scrambled eggs and bacon, and now our lungs were hyperventilating in our healthy young bodies, the blood pounding happily in our temples. The sense of natural beauty that Pete and I could usually share, we usually kept to ourselves, knowing others didn't seem to share it. But this time he came out with it, as he took in the sweeping panorama below, like low green clouds hazed into the distance, the tops of rain forest giants that lay like some vast green carpet under dramatic, pre-monsoonal skies.

"Breathtaking," he exclaimed, forgetting the column of mules and foot-slogging infantry moving on by. "Awesomely grand," I echoed, also forgetting the battalion column a few steps away from the roadside mound we stood on, and also being overheard.

A BAR man, sweating as he trudged along, paused to spit out a wad of tobacco. The tommygunner following him said, "Jesus Christ!" and shook his head. The mule skinner next in line took it out on his long-eared charge, which shook its huge jug head and almost jerked him off balance as he topped the rise. "Listen to me, you long-eared sonofabitch. Mah patience with youh bigmouth brayin' is just about used up. And youh stoppin to browse and watchda goddamn scenery. Keep it up an they'll think youah a goddamn officer!"

From that point in the Ledo Road march, at least two out of three steps were taken downhill. So abruptly downhill was the march that there seemed to be almost as much pressure of instep as of sole against the leather of our boots. Thirty-mile marches along those shallower rises at Deogarh had failed to develop the needed callouses on upper foot surfaces, and to exercise and harden connective tissues round the kneecaps. The trails we'd known before went up and down, instead of down, down, down for days on end. The result was near-crippling for some and punishment for all, to the point where a rare upward slope ahead would bring an audible sigh of relief along the column.

The hints of death seen earlier along the road by now were with us day and night. The trail out of Burma that this roadway now inversely followed had been a massive refugee exit-path. Seasoned British administrators who knew the hill country and their many Kachin and Shan charges had marched back along it with ease, some of them carrying infants nursing, with children walking happily along. Others, prone to panic and without the help of natives who could find food in the jungle itself, had died in droves. The stench was everywhere. Bones stripped by insects, gnawed by forest animals, were lying here and there on the surface. Once, as I spaded the earth to make an impromptu latrine near the roadside, my shovel glanced off a shallowly buried bone and the two eye sockets of a skull stared up, to constipate me for the next three days. The humor that served others on this march, and that had served me too, a bit, amid the improvised skull-and-crossbones patterns, the Christmas time bearded and red-capped Santa Claus that some Marine had made with a Japanese death's-head on Guadalcanal, was beginning to wear thin and lose its calming powers.

Besides the natural beauty of these grand, forested hills, there was another distraction for me from the death that they also contained. A halt and a careful scanning of the cover on the roadside at dawn or dusk would often reveal another, smaller beauty, and stir another kind of hunter's yearning. I'd see a small but succulent species of deer or gazelle, materialize as if by magic as I watched the cover and the spaces of cropped grass between the forest giants. I'd raise the carbine, aim for an easy head or neck shot, but, of course, I'd never fire. Despite the welcome the meat would receive at the kitchen truck, or the more selfish private cook-out for the battalion intelligence section, the cost to me could have been steep. All hell would have ensued in the quartermaster truck units or the engineer units stationed nearby; their fear of Jap infiltrators was active and, for all I knew, quite justified, and work on the road would have been halted at the point of the unauthorized firing. So the hunter that was in me even in the modern civilized context also stood frustrated, and as we marched on towards the Hukawng Valley, a true big game hunter's paradise, the perversity of my own privately-felt circumstance would seem even more perverse, even more ironic.

The ruling that my modern world had laid down for my present and ensuing behavior was exactly as I had sensed it being read, by the sensitive eyes of that eldest Naga hunter: Go on, white-man-who-thinks-he-is-no-longer-a-hunter. In that valley down there you may track and stalk and shoot in a wild and wholesale hunter's excess, but your quarries will be of your same animal species that will yield up only trinket-trophies, and you will bury the meat or leave it to rot or be eaten by jackals and vultures.

On Feb. 16, after a few miles during which the constant down-grade was a bit relieved with roller-coaster upgrades, too, we heard the artillery rumblings of the past few days overprinted by the chatter of machine guns, distant but unmistakable, and heard, louder yet, the roar of cargo aircraft—those good old Dakotas, or C-47s—in takeoff and landing. The gunfire augmented the bones we had been seeing, making the hint of death now audio-visual; but the friendly noise of the supply planes somehow also spelled life—the basic necessities of troops that still move, as Napoleon used to repeat, on their stomachs as much as their feet.

This airstrip within the sound of enemy gunfire was at a place called Shingbwiyang, on Burma soil at last, and our destination during this lengthy foot march. I suppose you could call it a forward combat base, with an Allied, multi-national flavor and those diverse bits of tentage marked with American, Nationalist Chinese and British nomenclature on little staked-out signs. And multi-service, too. Quartermaster, ordnance, and other emblems emblazoned the little signs, as well, and there was a small American hospital unit with a row of tents that seemed very different from the others. On the night that we bivouacked in the mud nearby, a self-appointed delegation of captains and lieutenants, that included Pete and I, quite literally besieged this row of tents, with their garden plots outside and their entries lined with crimson and yellow parachute cloth. We sang mock-serenades, mostly Neopolitan love songs, bawdily parodied, until this group of that particularly wonderful category of American women who were the Army Nurse Corps began to laugh and to invite us inside, where we found the gaudy parachute cloth motif carried to a comic extreme, with a kind of Bedouin sheik interior. Each of these girls held a kind of Queen of Sheba court that evening, couched on a cot with us combat-booted infantrymen seated round her on the floor. For reasons that I can only guess, no other male officers were there that night. There was joking and laughing and some rather spectacular drinking. There were even invocations of our infantry officers' code, which reads in iron characters that when such a lovely girl begins to toy with a particular officer's hair, or to otherwise indicate a single preference, the others will gracefully but expeditiously get the hell out of her tent. For some of those young Americans, that evening provided a final touch of what hunters most basically hunt for, and fighters most basically fight for, next to purest survival, and the memories continue to haunt me in a moving and bittersweet way. Whatever privileges and honors have been given to these fine girls, be they individually chaste or grossly generous to all male comers, they are too few. No better group of humans, male or female, ever served their countries in a military specialty.

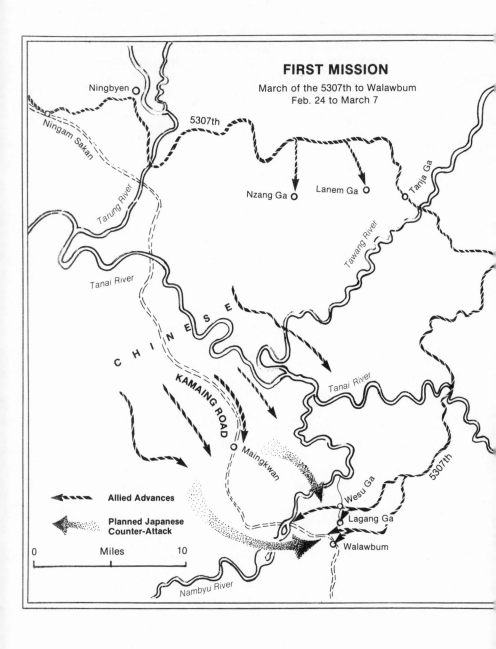

FIRST MISSION

March of the 5307th to Walawbum
Feb. 24 to March 7

Ningbyen

Ningam Sakan

5307th

Tarung River

Nzang Ga   Lanem Ga   Tanja Ga

Tawang River

Tanai River

C H I N E S E

KAMAING ROAD

Tanai River

Maingkwan

5307th

Allied Advances

Planned Japanese
Counter-Attack

Wesu Ga

Lagang Ga

Walawbum

0   Miles   10

Nambyu River

WALAWBUM

We rose with the usual old age stiffness from our bivouac that night, with my own crippled, supine writhings this time taking 15 minutes, significantly more than the usual five. We had all learned to begin with our heads, hands and feet, moving these stiffened outer points an inch each way while still against the cold ground, insulated by a sixteenth of an inch of compressed blanket, poncho, and "shirt, wool, knit" on the spaded, now re-flattened soil. If a curl-up or side-sleeper by habit, one dug a hip hole, to prevent the yet more crippling kink in the pelvic region. For all but those who had abnormally high blood pressure and metabolism there were those five minutes of tentative movement on the ground before daring to clench one's teeth, trying to rise, and slowly, arthritically, straightening up to stand. This was the procedure unless, of course, there was gunfire, and then we rose easily, without this ritual.

We got up to face the day as infantrymen, doughboys, foot sloggers, sniffing the drift of coffee aromas from the cooks' kitchen trucks, God bless them. Bless the nurses, but also, where there were good ones, bless the cooks and mess sergeants, who would, this particular morning, kiss their marmite cans and field stoves good-bye and walk along with us as riflemen, on combat field rations designated "K" and, when we were lucky, "C" or "Ten-in-One."

Rid of the mists of the hills, we now saw the even denser mists of the valley floor. They were friendly and protective as they allowed us to build fires to heat our powdered coffee and these austere rations in the hour just after dawn, without fear of enemy aircraft spotting us. As we sipped that last big-burner-heated coffee that we'd have for several months, those of us near a battalion headquarters received another and quite different kind of lift. And it was not just for the few officers but for the unit as a whole, including its backbone and flesh

459

of enlisted grades, for whom no nurses and no Japanese army comfort girls had been offered on this eve of combat.

This lift was one of almost unique recognition, from what we'd call today the media. As a single infantry regiment (in numerical strength if not in actual name) we had not even expected "mention in the dispatches." Our coming casualties and deaths would be statistics, small and unnoticed in this global war. To make the front page of even a small town newspaper we'd have to be either wiped out or spectacularly and impossibly victorious—to march into Mandalay unassisted. But this fine cool morning, here in the Himalaya foothills, we heard our new name or nickname, Merrill's Marauders, intoned by every news announcer that our shortwave radios could pick up.

This was totally unexpected, startling, and ego-inflating to the men of such a tiny probing finger of the Allied war machine. But a moment's thought, of course, explained it. This was February of '44, when the buildup of men and guns in Great Britain had become immense, and the second front had long seemed imminent in Europe. Top correspondents for *Time* magazine and all the major press services were coming and going around Merrill's headquarters. And there would be a continuing coverage, with his articles reprinted in all major news chains, by a sergeant from *Yank* magazine who would later become a distinguished international correspondent for *Time* and for *U.S. News & World Report*. There was even a film unit, armed with 35mm cameras, planning to make a film that had the tentative title *Jungle Victory*, intended to compete with the British film *Desert Victory* which extolled British units' achievements in North Africa under Field Marshall Montgomery. To the swagger and cocky air that an infantryman comes by naturally, as he passes through rear-area troops who tend to nod respectfully like circus tent peg drivers to their highwire and trapeze acrobats, there now was added this journalistic and photographic limelight, and all this mention on the international radio waves. As the three battalions moved into their final assembly areas, I'm afraid our mood and mien were not very modest or self-effacing.

The situation in this northern operational extreme of the Japanese Burma occupation, faced by the southernmost movement of the Chinese troops under Stilwell and now by these three new American battalions, was not too adverse. The Chinese divisions were now much better equipped but still notoriously slow in their movements, and the Japanese 18th Division commander General Tanaka's position astride the road, and with the railroad also behind him, made his supply and communication problems relatively simple. The Chinese had one division more or less astride the road, the others spread out on the wings, with a mission to outflank and envelop, which their ponderous and deliberate shifts of position would always betray before they could strike. By screening his own flanks with patrols (which also served as foraging parties, buying or taking fresh food-stuffs from the peasants along their way) Tanaka would always be aware of the Chinese movements. They had to be wider-circling and farther-marching than his countermoves from his dispositions along the axis of the road before they could reach and directly attack any of his important holdings. "...Though threatened by enemy envelop-ment," he decided, "we will exploit advantages of operations on interior lines, and, by utilizing every opportunity, defeat in detail the slow-moving Chinese forces. . ."

To make this strategy seem all the more wise and practical, Tanaka had in the battalions under his command that splendid Japanese capability that I've already extolled: their unique marching power. Like a duelist armed with a rapier, he could thrust right and left at his awkward broadsword-armed opponents, overweight with impedi-menta (including loot extraneous to any military need). He could strike at one at a time without fear that the unstruck one would be able to get at his back before he had downed the selected target. With the sheer walking ability of his soldiers, their characteristic aggres-siveness, plus the advantage of the shorter interior distances he would have to move them, this approach seemed bound to work. The only advantage that seemed likely to impede it was the Allied superiority in the air. Most of the avenues of troop movement were on sheltered trails, however, and the main road and railway could be used safely at night and with caution during daylight hours as well.

Tanaka's strategy had served him well against Stilwell's first two attempts, using only the Chinese, to envelop or outflank him. That it would fail him badly against a Stilwell now in command of 3,000 American infantrymen, volunteers and Rangers trained to use air drop and mule-transport, and capable of marching 30 miles a day, was perhaps quite predictable. But back to the bits of flesh and blood on the ground that would have to sweat and strain to make this "predictable" more than a staff officer theory.

A few yards windward of where I still slept, a frying pan packed by one of the men in the 3rd Battalion intelligence section began to sizzle its load of K ration pork and egg yolk, and a bank of canteen cups boiled water for coffee at the first misty peep of dawn. The smell shortened my unstiffening ritual, made me rise and limp to the fire of wood and waxed K ration boxes so quickly that I groaned with arthritic pain. Sergeant Russell Hill accepted my ration box and invited me to join in a leisurely and gluttonous breakfast before we slung our packs and marched south, with the mists that hid our fires still hiding our 3,000-strong movement to outflank and cut in far behind the Japanese dispositions along the road—this one Allied-Japanese road—where it led southward to Kamaing, some 65 miles away as the crow flies.

To find out how far we had to swerve eastward to do this, reaching towards the rising spur of the Himalayas that separates China from Burma, Merrill probed southward this day with all three of his battalion intelligence and reconnaissance platoons. Our 3rd Battalion "recce" platoon, led by one of the outstanding platoon leaders of the Pacific war, had the honor of making first contact with the enemy. Lieutenant Logan Weston, peering cautiously ahead, saw what he first thought was a neighboring Chinese unit, perhaps a small foraging party of the kind that the Kachin natives hated equally, whether Japanese or Chinese. The sight, as usual, was inconclusive: a movement in the cover, accompanied by some faint sounds.

When a small party of men in wild country encounters another small, unknown group, as I was later to learn as I trekked with native hunters in Africa, strong human feelings tend to surface. It's natural I suppose to be friendly, or to approach the strange party ahead, with an appearance of friendliness, at least. In war, therefore, a man tends, at the level of instinct, to be a bit off guard.

In their long China and south Asia experience the Japanese infantry had learned to exploit this human tendency, to convert it into a deadly advantage of shock and surprise. They knew that by a simple hand-waving, and a seemingly relaxed stance (with a weapon held below the grass or other cover), the foxy patrol leader could secure that all important period of two seconds and get his men behind him readied, weapons at aim, while he made his own quick identification and knew the men in front were enemy.

In this locale, of course, the Japanese had another advantage. For us there were friendly Kachins and Chinese moving on the same valley floor, in a war that had no fixed front line and with intra-Allied communications pretty faulty: for them any white face was a ready target, while we had to select among three kinds of brown and dark-haired varieties. These two advantages figured in this first contact.

At the moment he saw the movement at some distance ahead, Weston was covering his lead scout a few yards in front, a corporal named Warner Katz. A furrier in his civilian trade, but an adventurer by avocation, Katz had served on Guadalcanal and before that in the Spanish Civil War. Logan signalled Katz, Katz intensified his own scrutiny of the cover ahead, and then a khaki-clad figure emerged from the cover, stood in the center of the trail, and waved in a welcoming manner.

It almost worked. Katz tilted his head rearward and said, "They're Chinese. They're waving us to come on." Only the good luck of a depression at Katz's feet and the finest of reflexes, saved him. As two Japanese automatic weapons, presumably Nambu light machine guns, opened up, Katz dived into the depression.

As the fire slackened in a moment, he raised his head, felt the graze of an enemy bullet, gashing his cheek and nose, and began to worm his way back along the trail under Weston's covering fire. By firing two at a time while one man would run back, Weston, Katz, and another of his scouts managed to break contact per their instructions only to probe for the Japanese flank and to rejoin the rest of the platoon to the rear.

For Merrill, this first contact helped to decide the diameter of the large half-circle that we would have to inscribe eastward, in order to avoid a mass confrontation short of our first mission objective. This objective was the Japanese 18th Division's line of communications— the road, that is—substantially behind their foremost infantry battalions. For Weston and Katz the incident constituted another lesson. In a land where there are enemy Orientals, never let a friendly-looking Oriental use this trick to get the drop on you. For the world press, of course, with its attention abnormally centered on this tiny little operation south of the Assam-Burma border, the contact with its resulting news firsts (the first aggressive U.S. infantry action of this war in Asia; the first American soldier wounded in Asia since the Boxer Rebellion, etc.) meant something beyond the supply and troop buildup and the bombing raid statistics in Europe to write about.

For the Japanese 18th Division, we knew, this contact would hint broadly of Merrill's intent—to make that long left hook around the Japanese right flank. Speed, therefore, became important to us, to prevent the Japanese from probing out our further movements and learning exactly where we planned to hit them, at two points along the road above and opposite the tiny village of Walawbum, some 30 miles behind their front against the Chinese.

To the Japanese 18th Division commander, these moves by this American unit that had only a third of his strength would offer a grand opportunity. He would ignore the slow-moving Chinese excepting those directly astride the road in the north and would concentrate his power against the 5307th. Working from internal lines of communication, he felt that the advantage would be his. With heavy division artillery and other road-run weapons and supplies against our mule and hand-carried weapons, he could destroy us as a unit and then resume his easy defense of the Hukawng Valley against the Chinese.

General Stilwell, going on intelligence estimates prepared under his son Colonel Joseph Stilwell Jr., which were often 100 per cent or more short of the actual Japanese numbers, had a very different assessment of the situation. To him, the ensuing movements could entrap Tanaka, cutting off his rear and preventing him from escaping southward with his heavy equipment. That the Japanese commander was determined not just to defend his position, but to cripple and destroy the Chinese and us as well, seemed far from the senior Stilwell's thoughts.

With the two opposed generals both in error, each of them feeling he had an advantage over the other in his own way, the movements of the Americans were hastened. Ignoring the lesser patrol clashes the 2nd and 3rd Battalions continued their wide outflanking and encircling movement and then closed back in on their objectives. It was the usual kind of World War II action in such primitive jungle country: columns moving along trails with scouts out on alternate approaches in case of trail blocks; nighttime harboring with protection all around. A frontless, zoneless war during the movement, it was quick to become a dug-in, fixed battle when a roadblock would cut a major supply line. And both battalion objectives envisaged such a roadblock.

When the 2nd and 3rd Battalions did reach their objectives, this war of movement made this radical switchover and turned into a vicious, rearing struggle for a very small piece of real estate, a few hundred yards around or alongside a dug-in emplacement, miles and miles behind the defender's recognized front lines.

For the 3rd Battalion, whose headquarters I was a part of (the headquarters was just another part of the foot-slogging column, distinguished only by its mule and back-packed radios from any of the platoons), this digging-in was on a riverbank facing the village of Walawbum's outskirts across a narrow, hip-deep stream. With the sounds of Japanese trucks and of human voices heard through the cover on the far side, we quietly, nervously dug in. Except, that is, for the recce platoon under Logan Weston, which was across the stream to probe or, as it turned out, to stab and stir up an enemy force that vastly outnumbered us. The force was there in anticipation of our arrival, the Japanese documents later would reveal, to destroy these Americans who dared to try to turn Tanaka's flank.

Behind us, a bit farther back from the Japanese and screened from their roadside observation posts (we hoped) we had found a cleared series of paddy fields, free of the riverine brush, and large enough to serve as a dropfield and light aircraft strip for supply and the evacuation of the wounded that we now could logically expect. As we knocked down the paddy field barriers and otherwise prepared this field a few hours earlier, our battalion headquarters group had its own and personal bit of enemy action.

We were sitting, still in column, on our packs, sheltered (or half-blinded) by grass that was almost hip high all around us. Of the entire occupation force of this drop field, which might have numbered 100 or so, with the rest of the battalion under cover nearby, we were the nearest to the river and a small network of footpaths on its eastern bank. Along one of these footpaths through the high grass, moving towards us from the supposedly "safe" north, came several khaki-clad soldiers.

Since we were facing southwest, the movement was on our right, from a direction that should make these soldiers Chinese—most likely a liaison party from the Chinese 36th Division. This outfit was due to relieve us if the roadblock was successfully held and the Japanese forced to abandon their heavy gear and filtrate around us to the west.

Nonetheless, at the sight, I clicked off the safety on my carbine, and heard another click behind me, from a signal sergeant similarly eying the movement, now less than 40 yards away. The two of us were up to a kneeling position, now, viewing the oncoming figures through the heads of the high grasses.

"They're Chinese," someone muttered farther down the resting column. "No, they're Yanks," said the speaker's neighbor, out of my view also, round a curve in the trail behind.

As the figures came closer, I knew that either could be right: the American liaison groups with the Chinese battalions wore khaki shirts above their green trousers, per the style of Stilwell's combat headquarters in this area. I was ready for the usual greeting, the smiling exchanges of "Hello!" or "Okay, ding how!" that we always used, but still I kept my carbine barrel aligned, the safety thrown, and my finger lightly on the trigger, which broke clean at five pounds plus. Cheek against the stock, eye just offside the sights, I watched the man in the lead. He wasn't a Yank, I knew for sure now. His skin was brown; he'd be Chinese.

Then I noticed a shoulder patch, red if I remember correctly, and the weapon that the man was carrying diagonally across his shoulder. The weapon had a crooked offset stock and a large bulk of metal above the receiver; it was clearly a M-1922 Nambu, hopper-fed light machine gun—unmistakably Japanese, and I hadn't heard of Chinese using captured Japanese weapons in this area.

I shifted my eye to the aperture, centered the wide post of the front sight on the khaki shirt, and fired. As this soldier went down I saw more khaki shirt fronts behind that post, through the recoil and realignment of three more shots. I fired the fifth shot into the grass, guessing at the location of others behind who were falling to our fire or taking cover. This emptied my improvised five-shot magazine and sent me down to "Mother Earth" to hurriedly cram in another, a 15-rounder snatched from my belt pouch.

As I rose back to kneeling, I found that it was all over. Others in the column fore and aft of me had fired, too, so quickly that all my hits but the first one probably were shared and everything in front of us now was dead quiet. "In front of us" of course meant to the column's right; we were now a kneeling line of carbineers, ready for a squad or small patrol action to blossom into a company-strength fire fight, all nerves and anxiously waiting. Mustering a normal voice, I called out to the others—"Hold it. Keep watch. There may be others," or something of the sort. To me a situation of this kind called for extreme caution and immobility.

But not to the battalion commander, the Old Ranger, who had heard the firing from his position farther back in the column, blinded by the grass along the bending trail. Carbine held loosely in his right hand, standing fully upright, he walked up to our little rank of aimers and then turned half right, heading to where our targets had been standing. He waved for us to rise and follow, which we did with hesitation and with carefully bent knees.

Seven Japanese were lying there, spread compactly on the grass. Six of them including the Nambu light machine gunner were dead, a testimony to the effectiveness of the .30 caliber M-1 carbine. The seventh one, a Japanese lieutenant, was alive but lying helpless. His lower-down position as a litter patient had saved him; his only wound was a bone-shattering central hit in a lower leg, already bandaged round its swollen calf. The carriers had dropped him as they fell, their rifles now lay randomly across him. Shock from the shattered bone, perhaps, had kept him quiet then and now.

The confident stance of the Old Ranger, perhaps, had made me feel a bit less tense. I found myself reaching for the Leica in my pack, taking some photographs of the scene while ordering others not to congregate there, and while supervising the intelligence section men who searched the bodies and the wounded lieutenant for documents. I felt a bit in luck; we could get the Japanese lieutenant on a plane and back to Stilwell's headquarters shortly. More planes than we needed to evacuate our own wounded were on the way, and with captured Japanese so rare he'd be an intelligence officer's prize. As it turned out, though, my photographs and the documents from wallets were the sole intelligence items gained. Charlton Ogburn's account in *The Marauders* mentions that "it was later whispered that one of the Marauders had murdered the helpless litter patient by cutting his throat with a trench knife, but no one had the stomach to try to establish the facts."

Since the person concerned is dead, the eyewitnesses to his act will not be called at this late date to testify. What stings me to this day is that this person was not one of us combat veterans, not one who had known first hand of Japanese atrocities on other battlefields. Perhaps he had a brother who had been tortured to death in the Philippines. I didn't know and didn't try to find out. As one of those who lacked "the stomach to try to establish the facts," though, I've found myself less able to blame others for man's crimes against his kind, and less able to see the romance and adventure of an infantryman's kind of war.

My photography and intelligence-gathering operation was interrupted some 15 minutes later by a second bit of firing, by a Japanese platoon which Charlton's account suggests might have attacked us to avenge the shooting of the party with the litter, though the downed soldiers all were armed and none was wearing a Red Cross arm band. Freed this time from the need to identify them first as enemy, we demonstrated again the deadliness of our semi-automatic carbines. We killed 10 of them in the grass beyond the ones already dead, and the others pulled back and fired no more.

After these two incidents in the middle of the column had been explained by radio to its forward elements, who were concerned with the noise in their rear, the column got moving again. This brought us southward down the trail along the river bank, opposite the eastern edge of the village of Walawbum, which lay directly across the stream. In the cover on the opposite side Weston's recce platoon was becoming engaged with a far larger force of Japanese than Stilwell's intelligence had anticipated. We could hear the exchange of gunfire mount, with the crack of American weapons soon almost drowned out by the sounds of Japanese Arisakas and Nambus.

We were not yet officially disposed to interdict the road traffic, unseen but actually audible across the river. The Old Ranger had moved on up the column after the two shooting incidents at his headquarters were resolved, leaving Pete in charge. Hearing the noise mounting on the far bank, Pete and I exchanged a glance. "Here's as good a place as any," Pete said, reaching for his entrenching shovel. I echoed him and reached for mine as the Old Ranger nodded, and the signal to dig in where we were went up and down the column. Unlike the coral on Hill 27, which we had to heap in chunks to ward off the bullets and mortar fragments, this Burma soil dug well. In short minutes we were comparatively tiny targets, lying on our sides as we dug deeper and deeper, until we could crouch entirely protected from flat-trajectory fire. The mules were off loaded and led away from the bank and trail, into the scant defilade available here and there. Of the many unfair aspects of war, the one that leaves innocent pack animals above ground while men dig in ranks high.

Dug defensively, these foxholes that we kept improving through the next hour could also fill our aggressive intent. By doing a simple right face from our route of march, each soldier now could help to interdict the traffic on the Japanese-held road. Each shot fired into the cover across the water would go ricocheting towards the village and across the road, the supply line of the 18th Japanese Division. Our mortars could pound the road itself, and began to do so quickly now, in response to Logan's desperate calls. Badly outnumbered and running low on ammunition, he was now trying to extricate his platoon, to get back across the river with his wounded. To cut the Japanese lifeline of the road (here called the Kamaing Road for its next major village southward), we didn't need to be astride it. From the foxholes and our mortar emplacements right here we could cut Tanaka's jugular vein. Pete and I wondered if the Old Ranger would grasp this thought where he was now, up front; throughout the hour of digging we had been trying to contact him on the radio and suggest it to him, in slang or other terms, that a monitoring Japanese signalman might find confusing.

The Old Ranger, we later learned, was also on the far side of the river, trying to contact Weston and drawing his full share of the enemy fire that we were hearing. He had been unhappy with the invisibility of the foe up there, too, and had decided to make a personal reconnaissance of the ground behind the trees on the far bank. Not having been present at the scene, I can't be sure of what happened. But the colonel's own account (in a citation of his orderly Sweeney) claims that his call for volunteers to accompany him on this reconnaissance was warmly received by the men of Major Lew's column up front.

"All officers and men volunteered at once," he wrote. Only Sweeney, though, waded with him across the stream and up the opposite bank, where the fire fight was getting louder by the minute.

I suppose I should assume the move was sound, motivated by some information that the Old Ranger had received. Perhaps he had simply accepted the Stilwell assumption that Tanaka was setting out to escape when in fact, as the official histories later made clear, he was setting out to destroy us. In any case, the intrepid battalion commander and his orderly made it to the edge of the village, where they almost tripped over the body of a Japanese resting in the grass. At this point he felt satisfied, and according to the official record, he and Sweeney turned and ran (which I find hard to understand because the colonel was handy with his carbine and never lost a chance to make a kill). At the river bank they ran into an estimated platoon of enemy riflemen with two Nambu lights and waded the river in front of them, through a veritable hail of bullets. The factors that saved them here, it seems, were incredibly poor Japanese marksmanship and a fierce covering fire that an officer known well by me called down.

This officer, a Camp Perry team member, extracted a leaven of humor from the incident. Knowing the Old Ranger's exemplary concept of military combat leadership, under which the commander must take frequent and visible risks with his own life before his men, and respecting this concept a great deal less than I do, he later commented: "Missed our chance, really. Could have left those Japs alone. Let them keep their heads up and take aim, while His Nibs waded back from that damn suicide mission, up to his ass in the water. Couldn't do that, of course, but I did the next best thing. While we sprayed the bush behind that wading pair I saw three clear targets, front sight solid on three Jap shirt fronts as they fired, kneeling. As each one slumped I said out loud: 'Take that, you yellow-bellied shithead, for *missing* our colonel!'"

Such danger-seeking by a senior officer, if that's what it really was, was hardly necessary here. As Ogburn's book was to recount, "In the kind of fighting that built up for three days to the climax of the battle of Walawbum, the 5307th's commanders were not much safer than anyone else."

Besides the two countretemps already told, where enemy walked right into our 3rd Battalion headquarters, Colonel Hunter, Merrill's second in command, had had a direct duel on the trail; a Jap machine gunner was gunned down within 100 yards of Merrill's command post; and the Old Ranger—this time without an effort on his part to bring it on—was almost killed by a trail-side one-man ambush. Necessary or not, though, his bravery impressed the rank and file, and today some of the most reputable of military critics see profit in such risk-taking by commanders and believe there should be more of it in any future war.

After the Old Ranger and Weston had got back across the river, Pete's decision to interdict from the near bank with fire and semi-observed aerial bombardment was confirmed as wise, and we waited. Waited in the sense that no one but an infantryman deep in enemy territory with no protected means of escape, and still in contact with a foe that he has lightly cut and fiercely angered, can begin to understand. The unseen but much heard foe on the road beyond the streamside fields and trees in this instance was still there in large numbers, more than twice our own strength we were sure. He stayed there, too, his truck motors turning in the night, his transport under cover by day when we could call down those lovely little P-51s to dive bomb and strafe the ground across our front.

Along with the sense of insecurity that goes with waiting, such a static line of foxholes brings on intense boredom. When the enemy guns go quiet for half a day something often happens in such places. The social theorists that hold that man is by nature a crisis animal— so much so that he tends to manufacture crises when none is being handed to him—should have been watching us during those few days.

Or so my afterthoughts seem to tell me when I remember Major Larry Lew coming up to me and talking in a friendly but also a challenging way. He hunkered down beside me, where I worried over the disposition markings on a map laid on the grass, trying to plot the likely Japanese positions from the sounds and the reports of a few Kachin scouts. Lew knew all too well of the scope-sighted rifle in its scabbard on a mule, and back on the *Lurline* he'd heard me mention, too damned often, my ventures with it on Guadalcanal. He told me of abundant sniping opportunities along his part of the line, towards the head of the column that had crystallized on the march into a dug in half-a-hedgehog, plumped up against a bend of the Japanese supply route. Then, as he noticed the Old Ranger listening from his own hole eight feet distant, Lew put it bluntly to me. "If you want to go Jap hunting, Johnny, my boys up there can be your hunting guides."

This takes me back to a point that I mentioned in the introduction to this second edition. After a fragment from a Japanese 77mm battalion gun had dimpled my helmet and almost broken my neck with its impact, and a stream of tracers had pinned my head down throughout a particular night, I'd begun to lose my classic soldier's "illusion of immortality." The praise that my old battalion commander George Ferry would give me in a letter copied at the beginning of the first edition—that I had "never lost an opportunity to kill or harass the enemy"—was not really merited. In the last month on Guadalcanal I'd lost plenty of opportunities to go out and pop away with my sniping rifle, though I hadn't been invited then as Lew was inviting me now.

I glanced towards the Old Ranger, expecting him to forbid me to accept this challenge. Eyes atwinkle, he sat silent. Angry and—if you want—afraid, I said, "No thanks," and pointed to the map.

Lew and the Old Ranger then exchanged a glance, and I stared hard at each of them in turn. Several others in the battalion head-quarters group had heard the invitation and my refusal. Lew then turned and left, walking back towards his forward part of the line, farther south along the river bank. In the next half hour, while I worked on the map and provided the Old Ranger with the estimate of enemy strength across the river that he had asked for the day before (at least a reinforced battalion) I felt the pressure mounting inside me. When I had the estimate crayoned onto the acetate sheet over the map, I checked my four 15-round carbine clips to make sure they were full, ate four K ration cubes of sugar, and stood up, announcing that I was going to visit Lew's part of the line. The Old Ranger, in a way that he had, grinned. There was plenty more to be done in this headquarters, which General Merrill had said "could make more use of it's planning capacities," but the colonel wasn't going to halt me now and remind me of duties here. His notion of exemplary exposure of officers no doubt extended to his staff, and besides I hadn't said that I was picking up Lew's challenge; I could have been making a routine intelligence officer's visit.

I'd made my weapons decision before I began to move up the trail. This country was heavy in its cover; the riverine growth wasn't big trees with only grass beneath. It was tangled bush with visibility less than 50 yards, even for a shot across the river. At our part of the line there were open fields on the far side, only thinly screened by brush and trees, but along Lew's part of the line this cover was thick and nearly blind. This meant that any shots would be fired at that frightening, close stalking range that I'd known in the jungles of Guadalcanal. So the rifle and scope remained on the mule and I carried the little carbine instead.

The riverside trail was ox cart width and rutted. On my right, between it and the water, was a thin line of foxholes, weapons bristling westward, aligned at the opposite bank. Walking south, though the brush was often dense around the bends, I had no problem of guards challenging me. All eyes at these outposts faced that opposite bank, all ears strained to hear the sounds of enemy in the cultivated township space beyond. On prior walks south I had heard the sound of truck motors and the distant rattle of other military hardware. Now I heard this and hum of conversation as well. Lew had to be right. With so much going on in the cleared fields beyond it, the riverine growth on the far bank would have to hold a number of Japanese outposts and at least squad-size units on patrol. Lew hadn't used the term, but as an outdoorsman from Oregon, who had heard game wardens speak of populous elk cover, or populous deer range, he could have gilded his invitation and spoken of populous Jap jungle. Since the Old Ranger had not forbidden me to go, I knew I'd have to go through with it. But, I'd make this stupid and inappropriate exercise as brief as possible: one short venture in the view of Lew's soldiers and a trip back to my maps and my journal, hopefully on my own two feet.

Some 80 yards inside Lew's right flank, my crouching, cautious progress brought me to what I sought: a familiar face from Lew's Orange Combat Team (as our bastard half-battalion units were so incongruously called) who knew me from Guadalcanal. This sergeant was deep in his hole, and the two other foxhole inhabitants on either side joined him, in his urgent arm signal for me to take cover. Some gunfire had begun to crackle across the river behind me, its enemy portion snapping, for sure now, over the heads of the battalion foxholes I'd just left. For a moment I tried to persuade myself that this was enough, I could now go back to the command post without further ado, I'd moved to take Lew up on his offer but stopped when my own part of the line became active. Then I decided to go on and act it out, and bent down to speak to the sergeant.

I told him that I wanted to "establish the organizational identity of the Japanese across the river," and asked him if he would come with me down the river bank "to scrutinize more closely." Today these pedantic phrases clot my memory as examples of profound machismo—of that cheaply typical bravado of the front-line-visiting division staff officer. The kind of bravery that a man who eats hot meals and sleeps on a dry cot under as many blankets as he wants can muster during a one-day trip forward, making some poor frontline doughboy share the hobbyist, ostentatious danger of it. I spoke the phrases with a commander's mustered intensity, or tried to, to mask the visceral fear that I was feeling.

The sergeant looked briefly up at me, begging with his eyes for a reprieve, and then ostentatiously crossed himself though I knew he was a Protestant. He checked his M-1, signalled for the other two to cover us, and moved out of the foxhole to guide me forward down the bank.

We made the scant distance to the water's edge through blessedly dense bushes. There we found a bit of cover and began to eye the other bank microscopically, twig to twig and grass blade, with our only comfort now the two riflemen in the foxholes, higher on the bank behind us, waiting for an enemy reaction. If wise, any Jap would hesitate to fire at us: he'd give himself away with muzzle blasts and invite a reply from the M-1s which by now he surely knew were there. Without knowing, one could sense this past day as one of enemy buildup, preparing for something large scale later on.

Our legs were wet with ooze as we sat there, with only eyes and flop-brimmed jeep hats lifted in the screening brush, watching as mere hunters never have. It might have been 500 heartbeats (much less than five minutes, but seemingly a 100 years) before that violent rigidity came to the muscles of my arms, to ease the carbine upward to my shoulder. There they were!

Those khaki uniforms again! Couldn't Tanaka get the later issue green that the last japs we killed on Guadalcanal were wearing? The Japanese soldiers, several of them together, were clearly visible, if shadowy, around an edge of bushes clumped along the far bank.

And at this moment I discovered an error of my own, one that a jury of 12 John Georges would have sentenced me to death by slow torture for commiting. I had left the sleek and neat little five-round magazine in my carbine; the 15-rounders were still in the belt pouches, which I now silently unsnapped.

Anxious touch on the arm and a series of covert hand signals informed the sergeant of this problem and confirmed that he, too, had spotted our targets on the far bank. With strangely steady hands that I attribute entirely to reloading drill in rapid fire on the range (a post-war Camp Perry coach, a master sergeant named John Bartgis, would later tell me that I had the steadiest reloading hands and the steadiest offhand front sight on the Second Army team) I now carefully removed the five-shot clip and replaced it with the longer one, to give me 16 shots in magazine and chamber, and aimed.

The Japanese were doing something together, gathered round some central object that we couldn't see through the lower cover. Perhaps they were positioning a machine gun or digging an entrenchment and now resting for a moment. As I aimed I noticed my companion doing the same, and now we fired together, semi-auto but as fast as we could aim. For me, every shot, until the magazine went empty, saw the front sight recoiling upward off one of those khaki shirts, or off the writhing, moving cover into which they fell. Then I snatch-replaced the empty 15-rounder with a fresh magazine and bolted its top round up the spout.

The getaway plan was already in our minds—a quick scramble up the bank, taking the risks involved. Staying in place quietly was a poor gamble when the distance was so short from other Japanese and our cover was so thin. Our muzzle blasts would have disturbed this cover, not to mention the smoke of the first shots from oiled barrels down here at the water's edge.

The bank we had to climb back up was steep and brushy. No matter, though. We tore back up its blessedly short distance like frightened squirrels, clawing at the dirt with our hands, praying we'd reach the defilade of the road unhit. But, halfway up the climb the nightmarish inevitable began to happen.

From our direct rear where our targets now lay dead or helplessly wounded, nothing came, not a shout or a shot. But undisclosing brush to our left now came alive with muzzle blasts, all directed at us but drawing an instant return fire from our buddies up above us, from their dug-in trail-side holes.

I had never had so many bullets crack so close to me in so few split seconds, though later that day in my own foxhole I'd have more. They tore into the bank to the right, left, and rear and front of me. I know it's impossible, but I seemed to be in a hollow Nambu burst for the second half of that scramble before we were up on the trail in ample defilade, tumbling into the (fortunately large) hole that the sergeant had left to come with me. The fire continued for another minute or two, with us returning it and our farther flanking foxholes joining in, making it a platoon-strength fire exchange, I'd guess, on both sides. The lifetime that it all had lasted had to measure scant minutes on that totally irrelevant instrument, the clock.

As the firing quieted down to a shot here and there along the line, the sergeant beside me, crowded into his foxhole dug for one, said nothing. But as I climbed out our eyes met, and his told me all that he wouldn't say aloud in those less candid days of infantry officers and men in combat: "You know, Captain, that this was damn unnecessary. And crazy. And I think you did it for the usual staff officer reasons—to get yourself written up for one of those headquarter-issue Silver Stars."

I made my way back to the battalion headquarters part of the line filled with a new resolution. This was to be my last bit of voluntary combat riflery. If the word of it didn't get back to Lew in detail, I'd tell him the story myself, and likewise for the battalion CO, who was already getting the tale out of me with his not-too-solicitous questions and his readiness to grin at the more frightening parts of the tale.

At the time I felt the better for it. But, on afterthought, I felt worse. There was no sound reason for me to leave that battalion headquarters when I did, with Pete gone and only an Air Force liaison officer there to help the commander in a crisis that might last, with Pete and me pinned down elsewhere along the line. But lacking the moral courage to appear afraid, or to admit that I was afraid but insist that that didn't matter, I had left my staff and leadership responsibilities and played frontline rifleman—a role that I'd proved myself in already, and probably more often than I should have, on Guadalcanal the year before.

I paid a price for it immediately, too. As the Old Ranger asked his questions, I began to fumble with a K ration package. And the hands that had been steady enough aiming now were trembling, from the memory of that moment when I'd seemingly been centered, dead-centered, in a hollow Nambu burst. My loss of that feeling of seductive romance and adventure in infantry combat situations was a gradual thing. Get me away from this fight and safe in Delhi and it would creep back into me. In early 1945 I'd persuade Major General Merrill, then chief of staff of 10th Army, to promise me a battalion in the planned invasion of the Japanese home islands. But the stark fear that made my hands shake then had added more cold weight to other scary memories, so that by now, I no longer have to be in, or near a

A standard scene at 3rd Battalion headquarters throughout the campaign. The battalion commander (or S-3 or S-2) hears a burst of firing somewhere nearby, and gets into the platoon net forthwith to learn what the hell is happening.

After the usual voice procedure he asks, in the calmest voice he can muster, "What's up, Joe?" And the answer can be as variant as the jungle and mankind. "No problem, Pete. Scratch three nips. Just walked into us."

Or: "Get ready for something bigger. Those two looked like point men for a company!"

Or, especially if it's in the night, "Just trigger happiness. Two buffalo grazed into the first platoon's perimeter."

Or anything else, including an attack in battalion strength—the jungle screen was that protective. A life and death struggle could be going on a hundred yards away, with nothing more dangerous here than an odd stray bullet or a lost and wandering Japanese squad.

The positive point here is the SCR 300 and our other radios. Compared to the enemy gear, they were good indeed. Usually we had a better awareness of what was happening ahead on the trail, or to the other nearby friendly units because of this equipment.

fire fight to be deathly afraid of one. Sitting at my typewriter, in my house on the banks of the Potomac, I find the Wagnerian allure of warfare of the intimate infantry kind unable to suborn my love of life for even a moment.

A few days later, after the climax of the battle of Walawbum, the 1st Battalion moved on the same trail to Lagang Ga and one of its officers (Lieutenant Seivers, as I remember), congratulated me on being still alive. I thought he was referring to the sniping venture, but he went on to ask about the bullet that had "ripped through my pack." He was talking about what had happened a day later, in this unmoved 3rd Battalion headquarters as the battle of Walawbum approached this deadly climax.

Except for the absence of its commander, the Old Ranger, who continued to spend much of his time at the platoon level and was now out on one of the flanks of our extended line along the river bank, the battalion headquarters was intact, as a part of this extended line of foxholes and weapons emplacements. As the senior officers present, Major Pete Petito and I were dug in in the center of this headquarters group, which, of course, was also serving as a part of the line. To clear the radio antennae we were in the clear and on a slight rise, on the western edge of the ox cart track, which sacrificed for us a good view of the opposite bank and the surface of the water. The tactical units on either side of us had a better view, commanding the whole width of the river.

For our mission to interdict the traffic on the road, and so cut the flow of supplies and reinforcements to the 18th Japanese Division front, now undisclosed miles to the north, the 3rd Battalion's position was nearly perfect. Our flat trajectory fire was tearing through the grassfields and screened bush on the far side, ricocheting on into the traffic on the road. Our 80mm and 60mm mortars were nicely ranged in, and, with the limitations imposed by mule-carried ammunition, always in inadequate supply for a sizeable fight, they could blast right down on the travelled roadway itself. Our air liaison officer could call down, in daytime, his yet deadlier deliveries of 500-pound bombs—deadlier because these bombs required no heavy metal casings and could contain much more explosive than artillery shells. Like most of our weaponry, these P-51s performing as skip-bombers struck at their targets in long elliptical patterns, with the greatest error along their line of flight. "Keep those damn planes running parallel!" I would yell to the air liaison officer each time one crossed our thin line of foxholes. "Parallel!"

The pilots who bombed for us those two days were skilled, and they knew their bomb patterns erred mostly along their axis of flight, but they also knew something else. The Japanese had a trick of digging fugasse pits at intervals of a hundred yards or so along the road, placing blocks of picric acid (their TNT) at the bottom of the pits and heaping fist-sized stones on top to ground level. When planes came in for their passes they'd detonate these charges electrically, filling the air above the roadway with tons of these small rocks, deadly clouds that the little pursuit ships must then fly through. (Later we'd be hearing about this from a pilot named Jenkins, whose torn and crippled fighter had barely climbed to parachute altitude after one of these runs and who joined us for a while after being rescued by Lieutenant Tilly's Kachins.)

The fire and bombardment we delivered were controlled mostly by sound: the trucks moving along the roadway, voices heard across the bank, and even information from a telephone tap by the 2nd Battalion which had thrown a roadblock more dangerous than ours directly across the road further north. Having a complement of Nisi (Japanese-Americans) with us, of course, was the key, here. Japanese officers are often strident, and their noncoms even more so, in shouting commands. Henry Gosho, a splendid soldier two foxholes away from me, was feeding us a continuous translation of these distant voices, his keen ears cocked in the intervals between the gunfire and bombing towards that bush-screened road across the river. Henry had (and still has, as a foreign service officer whom I've met now and then here in Washington) an infectious, hearty laugh. He would throw back his head after each giveaway translation and chortle, "Good God. Don't those crazy Japs over there know we've got Japs over here too? Can't they shut their big mouths for a moment?" I've never seen or heard of a better demonstration of the American Army's ethnic advantages, having access to the varied—and not just linguistic—talents of so many integrated peoples.

As battalion intelligence officer, I was grateful for Henry's presence. Assigned to Logan Weston's intelligence and reconnaissance platoon, he was not always available. We were lucky that he was on hand this time, because in addition to directing our fire against the road traffic, he now began to sense a pattern of enemy preparation along that battered but unseen road. Tailgates of trucks banged, and motors accelerated for a while (unusual in the daytime), and without Gosho I'd have thought this a confirmation of the intelligence we had been given by Stilwell's headquarters. In Ogburn's postwar summary of the later historical information, Stilwell's advisors "were convinced that they had trapped General Tanaka; it did not occur to any of them that it was for the purpose of destroying the 5307th that Tanaka was getting his forces into line."

While this priceless Japanese-American in his muddy foxhole was giving us his much more correct view of the enemy situtation astride that road, the Japanese attempt to destroy us got under way, like a tiger snarling at a dog that bites it in a hindquarter. The bite felt first was at the 2nd Battalion, which had formed a block directly across the road some miles to the north. They had barely set their weapons up, in foxholes dug by the Japanese along the roadside, when a force not local in size attacked them. Their performance with rifles, carbines and sub-machine guns against charging, outflanking companies of Japanese underwrote and justified our pop-up target practice back at Deogarh. The Americans held their fire until hits were certain, so close that in the words of Captain Fred Lyons "you could see the bronze star shining dully on their bouncing little hats."

The attacking Japanese had artillery support; shelling came with these six or more attacks; but there had to have been a commendable coolness in Lieutenant Colonel McGee's 2nd Battalion headquarters. Because this was where Sergeant Roy Matsumoto, another Nisi of the stamp of Henry Gosho, began to tap in on the roadside telephone wire and intercept the 18th Division's messages. Some of these messages were remarkably explicit: one was from a Japanese sergeant in charge of an ammunition dump at the roadside, which he was now forced to defend "with only three riflemen." He gave the precise location of the dump and requested "help and advice" from his commanding officer. This was to provide our press representatives with a colorful anecdote that made the front pages of many newspapers back home during those news-hungry weeks before the Second Front opened in Europe and made everything out here seem tiny.

For some 36 hours the 2nd Battalion fought on, astride that roadway with their bodies as well as their gunfire. Its men withdrew only when food and ammunition became critically low. Since this unit had only a sprinkling of transferred combat veterans from the 3rd Battalion, this action had been, in British military parlance, its blooding. Yet, in that intimate kind of fighting that involved other arms but made the battle of Walawbum into a rifleman's and machine gunner's action, with far more enemy dead from aimed shots from hand held weapons, they had faced the Japanese and made them pay in scores for each American they killed.

The 3rd Battalion's movement south from the drop field and evacuation landing strip site at Lagang Ga into our present, and soon to be crucial, position had spared as well as exposed us. Our activity there, those two fire fights by the battalion headquarters unit with the two parties of enemy and related air drop and light plane traffic afterwards, had been too noisy not to be observed and pinpointed as an artillery target. After we had moved out the 1st Battalion had moved in, and as we dug in in our present positions some

Japanese artillery observer, binoculars to his eyes, began to direct a deadly 140mm fire onto that strip of knocked down paddy banks. Across the river from us we could hear the sounds of numerous Japanese, and I saw Henry Gosho shake his head and grin when I asked him if the Japs were pulling out. Behind us we could hear the blast of artillery shells, louder by far than any that the Chinese mules could carry, louder even than our 81mm mortar rounds, going off dead on our only escape route and avenue of supply.

But perhaps since the rounds were not actually falling on me at the time, I can remember my reaction to those not very distant ear-cracking explosions. Somehow I failed to think of the killing and maiming. It was the tropical beauty of those paddy fields that struck me then, of that scene that I'd read of again and again in the accounts of big game hunters after tiger, Asiatic buffalo and gaur, not to speak of the wild elephant that we had already spotted several times. Along with the zig-zag tread of the Japanese infantry sneakers, I'd seen tiger pug marks, wild cattle hoofprints and elephant tracks on the trails back there. Any such admiration of scenic beauty now, I knew, would soon give way to the most frantic digging, with the men who had dropped off their shovels and entrenching pick mattocks because of their weight now clawing the earth or scooping at it with their helmet rims, frantic as moles with hawks above to get below ground level. Soon the noise told us that there were badly wounded, frightened, fragment-struck mules and horses back there where we had lately sat on the trail. Why couldn't I be here now as a venturing peacetime male, with a larger caliber hunting rifle and some kit thrown into an ox cart, and nothing but wilderness time on my hands? Why?

It was meaningful to us that this artillery fire subsided. The 1st Battalion had pulled more under cover, perhaps, or those damned guns were being turned in their emplacements to shell us. I looked almost lovingly at the orchard-spaced thick and high broadleafs along our bank. They'd cause tree bursts and deflections from where those large guns had to be right now; the guns would have to displace to other positions, and even then we'd be no open field, easily observed target. We were too thin, too linear, and thank God for it, I thought, as Henry Gosho began to listen more intently and to point, and Pete and I signalled heads down (but not too far down!) along the line. There was a silence now across the river, and a silence, ever more profound, along our entire stretch of diggings between the ox cart track and the river, mostly on the high or forward bank.

Then they let drive. Crowded now with Japanese soldiers, the cover some 150 yards beyond the far bank now erupted with rifle, mortar, and machine gun fire—all of it aimed at our thin green line of earth-protruding helmets. On the higher ground where Pete, Henry and I were dug in the blast was solid. Original and ricocheting rifle and machine gun bullets ripped at the dirt on our foxhole ledges, penetrating anything left out of the holes. A pair of leather shoes on my foxhole rim was hit three times, neatly perforated by the really quite stable and "humane" .256 Arisaka bullets. Another bullet exploded inside my haversack (had it also destroyed a precious Leica?) and showered me with carbon dust from two ruptured flashlight batteries. To raise my head above the rim would be instant suicide: I feared even for the narrow carbine barrel and front sight, kept it held low though pointed upward and ready, ready, READY if ever a firearm was. Pete and Henry, nearby, did the same. A coward's choice or not, while that sheet of fire continued those inches above our sonically-battered eardrums (each shot like a low three, just over the parapet in the pits on a 200-yard range, a painful, piercing snap!), our heads remained low. To be shot by us now, our enemies would have had to brave their own fire and loom right over our holes, in that circle of light above, which the Japanese had been known to try before. Horrible as it seemed, though, we were safe from all but direct or tree-burst explosives, which, thank God, weren't coming over in quantity.

"Those bastards have tons of ammunition!" was my thought while it went on like this, for more than 20 minutes we later would agree. Then the splintering of saplings and tree bark let up a bit, the fire lulled for a moment, and I could see the sinewy, Daniel Boone figure of Logan Weston, outside his damn foxhole, by God, making his crouching way along his platoon, asking his men by name if they were all right, his tone as cheery as a Baptist preacher shaking hands at the church door. There, I thought, was a praying, practicing Christian for you, in whose personal beliefs all of the Christian absolutes were anchored firmly. I envied him his lack of fear, before the lull of some two minutes ended and the holocaust of fire drove him, even, back into the good, good earth.

A lower rear ledge of my foxhole made it possible for me to inch my head up as the fire again subsided (only slightly, damn it!) and try to read Hank Gosho's lips. He was trying to tell me something, but neither Pete nor I could read him through the noise. Reckless, now, he reached an arm above his ledge to point. "They're shouting 'Go round to the left!' " he said, and the hand duly pointed off to our right, where our lowering line of foxholes looked across the river and into the cleared, thinly-screened fields back from the river. Pete, via radio, and I by loudest yells passed on this warning, and I heard a confirming series of shouts from that lower right hand extension. "Here they come! Get ready!"

Pete and I exchanged a serious glance. The fire was being maintained as this movement was beginning. Nothing could be worse for us. Our Japanese friends gone wise at last, keeping a covering fire on us instead of getting up all along the line and providing us with easy oncoming targets and no heads-down bursts to mar our aiming. As much as we dared, we lifted our gaze, to see the leafy sky in front of our holes at least. We'd have to deal with any Japanese, now, it seemed, at little more than bayonet distance. That driving horizontal hail of bullets was still with us.

Then, harkening happily back to some of our easier Guadalcanal experience, the old Japanese error repeated itself. Almost to a round, the Japanese firing stopped; a maximun delivery of fire was now followed by a maximum movement of flesh. This meant that our deadly and frightening battlefield was converting, in a trice, into an easy and entertaining shooting gallery. With a broken cry of "Banzai!" the Japanese who had been firing at us now rose along their broad front and charged towards and down the river bank.

The fields across where droves of enemy now ran, were screened by bamboo and other riverside growth and a few of the too-eager opened up on it. The movement as a whole was clear. All our forward foxholes (forward five to seven yards, that is) had to do was to wait a few seconds, until the surge of khaki uniforms was definite, some 50 yards or less behind the screen, aim into it, and pull the trigger. This was done in a measured way, though, because the trigger-pullers knew that better targets were yet to come, nearer to, and in the waist-deep water.

At this point, Pete and I were frustrated. We could rise to firing position now but the cover and the topography kept the Japanese tide just out of our safe field of fire. The only avenue I had to the targets was a narrow lane in the shrubbery, past the left and right ears of two riflemen of Logan's platoon, with scant inches to spare. I aimed and aimed but did not fire—better spare 50 Japs than kill one American. An American spared in this outfit, we bragged, would likely kill a hundred to make up for it.

Beyond this, Pete and I could only wait until the Japs might gain this bank and try to climb up over us. But none survived to do so. The slaughter that continued for some 30 minutes longer was so easy and so exultant that the men who were doing it, from the majority of the foxholes that were not blinded as were ours, were moved from their usual shouted obscenities and insults to a chorus of what had become the 3rd Battalion's own battle cry.

When Charlton Ogburn attributed the origin of this cry to me, years later, I didn't deny it. I'm not ashamed that I among others did bring it into use. In the depths of the Indian night, during one of our

Here we see the weapons that create the bulk of enemy casualties in recent and current wars: hand held, hand thrown, or hand operated at the front by foot soldiers, with no more than a light tripod to make them steadier than human flesh and nerves.

In this setup the experienced doughboy has questions to ask. Why is the rifleman in the foreground firing a bolt gun: no M-1 available? Why doesn't the sniper, center, also have an M-1 sniper-rifle with a Lyman scope: Again, none available, produced too late for delivery to the Pacific theaters in 1944? And, finally, why the hell are all three men (and the under parts of the machine gun) so "carelessly" exposed to enemy fire?

One answer to that last one—in a sane world—has to be that there isn't any enemy return fire. These men have to be shooting (as we often did) at some target that, for the moment, is harmless to them. Perhaps some Japanese, lower down the hill on the paddy fields, who are caught in the open and trying to get away. The rifle grenades on the parapet also hint that the target is distant and visible, with no immediate ability to talk back.

Another answer to this question of why these men so "carelessly" expose themselves comes out of a Japanese tactical habit in World War II.

This habit, which was bad for them and good for us, was developed in China against Nationalist troops that had one rusty Mauser for every ten men. It was to charge our positions recklessly, coming at us across open ground without covering fire from a flank to make us keep our head down.

When they tried this on the 3rd Battalion at Walawbum, coming at us across a field and a wide waist-deep stream, many marauders felt safe enough (or became excited and frenzied enough!) to rise up like this in order to see more of the easy oncoming targets . . . .

maneuvers back at Deogarh, I had felt the need to reply in some way to the yipping, yelping choruses of the jackals and the occasional far off cry of an Asiatic wolf that made our bivouac night music for us. A canteen cupful of hot buttered rum also had something to do with it. In any case, I lifted my face to the sky and with the most wolf-like intonation that I could muster I howled these two syllables to the sky, letting them draw out operatically, trying to outdo in volume the finest tenor, the strongest bass. Then, borrowing a bit from some hog-calling contests that I'd witnessed at various Missouri county fairs, I varied the sounds, cutting them to an explosive yelp, a staccato cough, a coloratura trill, shifting the accent from first to second syllable and back again as I began to get replies to it, sounding back from the flanks of our outflung, separated battalion bivouac. Like a pack of arctic wolves, these distant platoons and squad outposts took up the call, all around our loose perimeter, until the jackals and other native noisemakers all went quiet.

Sipping the rum mix from my cup, losing the artistry of it more and more as the headquarters group began to break up with uncontrollable laughter, and getting more and more hoarse, I finally quit. But not until the whole battalion had lifted this word, or these hyphenated two words, into the very sky as a kind of 3rd Battalion battle cry.

Now as the Japanese firing went quiet and the ranks of enemy rose from their firing positions, one soldier out on our right flank howled out this obscene cry, and another far to his left, somewhere beyond Pete's and my foxholes in the center of the line, echoed it in that long, drawn out wolfish wail. As these ranks came closer, most of them at a dead run, the cry was further repeated at points intervening, until it began to sound along the entire line of American foxholes.

As the thinning horde of Japanese arrived at the opposite bank of the river, out of the foliage and into the clear, shooting gallery aim space, leaving a virtual blanket of dead and wounded on the screened-view earth behind, these long, or short and otherwise varied yells of *Ass H—o—l—e! Ah—ah—ah—ah—s Hole!* became interspersed with other graphic Anglo-Saxon terms.

Unable to fire ourselves, Pete and I now felt almost protected, and the easy laugh of Hank Gosho, as he continued to translate the many loud cries of the Japanese, seemed almost justified by this protection. We were hearing ample machine gun fire of our own, and the slower pum-pum-pum of Browning Automatic Rifles, of the sort that is aimed, with the bursts halted short as the sights climbed off visible targets. But mostly we heard the eight-round, spaced semi-auto fire of M-1s, with the long battle cry, now the 3rd Battalion's trademark for the rest of the campaign, yelled out while each rifleman reloaded.

With the Japanese fire now wholly quiet, replaced on the far bank and now on the edge of the water itself by throaty Japanese yells and shouted orders to move on, to keep going, we could almost relax. Nothing of flesh and blood could get at us through the deadly fire of that thin but heavily-armed line of American citizens now turned savage killers, yelling obscene invitations as the surviving Japanese continued to come on, the last 50 of them actually making it to the center of the stream, chest deep for some of them.

There, these last few members of the attacking force died, their bodies moving faster downstream than their already dead buddies killed just off the far bank and hung up in the roots and mud. The Americans continued to shout for several minutes more, saying, "Come on! Come on! Let's have more!" amid the other less civil words of it. As the overall sounds of the battle subsided I remember Don Hogan, in a foxhole to my left front, turning to look at Pete and me. His eyes had a look in them that it took me a while to fathom, as he nodded his head toward the right and left where the yelling was subsiding and said, of that line of foxhole occupants that we'll never forget, "Those guys! Those guys!" I can't be sure of it, of course, (Don was killed later in the campaign, in a night action that caught him exposed in his jungle hammock) but I think that the feeling that his eyes expressed was more than gratitude; it was love.

For us and for Stilwell's campaign, this was the end of the battle of Walawbum. A couple of hours later, while any of the Japanese attack force that might have been still alive moved quietly back from the bank and then marched south, the area became the quietest sector I'd known thus far in the war. The Chinese who came in to relieve us the next day walked into Walawbum without resistance, securing some 30 more miles southward on the contested Burma Road.

Historians have since had at this battle, with access to Japanese and Allied high command records that I've still not seen in the original, and they have cleared away the battle-fog and confusion that surrounded it at the time. In an ocean of military sluggishness, Walawbum was a rapier thrust, a planned use of fast-moving foot soldiery in connection with a more plodding old line division operation along the road. Students of infantry tactics in primitive, poorly roaded country have found much instruction in it. In contrast to the operations of Wingate's 77th Brigade, his original long range penetration unit that had operated farther south, 5307's gains were immediately exploited by heavier infantry units with ground supply lines dragged behind them. Tactically, it seemed very profitable.

For me, though, it carried a singular message—a kind of grass-roots lesson that all future foot soldiers would do well to hear and understand. The American military historian Brigadier General

S.L.A. Marshall has written with a special and rather new intimacy of infantry combat, basing his findings on direct battlefield observations and on interviews with participants soon after the fighting, while memory presumably is still sharp.

After many such interviews with men who fought the Germans and the Japanese in World War II, he found that no more than a quarter of all "fighting" soldiers ever use their weapons against the enemy, even in severe situations. He attributes this largely to western teaching and social conditioning against aggression, "against killing, against taking advantage." And, he calls this social conditioning a western soldier's greatest handicap when he enters combat" because it "stays his trigger finger even though he is hardly conscious that it is a restraint upon him."

This finding may have been true for the American soldier at large, and I assume that it was correct indeed, from General Marshall's fine reputation, but it did not hold true for the men of the 3rd Battalion in this action. When the Japanese were descending that river bank and trying to wade across, every American rifleman who had a visible target was firing. Not only firing, but from everything that I was able to find out when I craned my neck to see them, they were cheeking their stocks, peering through their aperture sights. Although the nearer targets were close enough for mere instinctive pointing, or sense-shooting, they were placing that front sight on enemy flesh or cloth. Most of the foxholes that had good views of the charging mass of enemy were dug as riflemen's positions, with elbow and forearm rests inside the parapet. Except for their more solid forearm support, which would have been illegal in most target competition, these soldiers might just as well have been firing through the 300-yard rapid fire stage of the national team match at Camp Perry.

Under such conditions the result is slaughter. Fewer than a dozen Japanese reached our bank alive. And this brings up General Marshall's other and more basic point: the culturally-instilled hesitancy to kill, the inhibitions against personal aggression. Here again I'm moved to argue that there is an exception, and a pronounced one, to this generalization by a fine military historian.

During 1945-47, I'd be assigned to GHQ Far East Command in Tokyo and quartered in the Dia Ichi Hotel with many of the witnesses in the war crimes trials, most of them former prisoners of war. What I heard from these survivors of Japanese imprisonment wasn't news to me. The atrocities they witnessed in camps matched those imbedded in my memory on Guadalcanal: torture, mutilation, execution by beheading or bayonetting, gang rape of local and American female prisoners, you name it. And even cannibalism. On Guadalcanal I'd seen strips of meat cut from one of our soldier's calves and stowed in a mess kit (definitely not a Japanese burial token, the leg hairs were blond and matched cuts on the American's mutilated body found nearby).

No one knows better than I that this was unrepresentative of Japanese society at large. Japanese intellectuals regarded their national ground force military as little better than a uniformed mafia gang, guilty of mass murder, and rape in China as a matter of military policy. To many Japanese civilians, the Japanese soldiery of that era were worse than vermin. So it is not surprising that Americans, shocked by their killing of wounded as well as these other sadisms, took pleasure as they aimed their M-1s and felt the triggers let off. And this revulsion and joy-in-the-killing was not a redneck or GI Joe reaction. Harvard graduates and ordained ministers, shoe clerks, and PhD's in political science felt this intense and uncompromising hatred. One might ponder philosophically about the close-up, intimate sight of a young Japanese that one has just killed, or feel pity for the wife and child in the photographs in his bloodstained wallet but, by and large, this killing was sheer joy. The dead man had become a part of an organized terrorist gang, and the fact that that organization was also an internally well-disciplined army made no emotional difference.

Perhaps this was the reason that Marshall's generalization about Americans not firing their weapons even in severe situations did not hold in our 3rd Battalion. Unless a virtual hail of fire made it suicidal to raise their heads, these Guadalcanal, New Guinea and New Georgia veterans would fire whenever they had a visible target. And, if they couldn't raise their heads, they would lean back, as Pete and I were doing, with their weapons pointed skyward, ready to perforate anything that appeared above them, and ready to rise and fire horizontally when enemy fire slackened. Logically one can say that Americans value their lives more than other soldiers; in the good life their society offers they obviously have more to lose. I have actually seen Chinese peasant soldiers opt for death when there was no real need for them to make this sacrifice. But in the 3rd Battalion, this greater love of life was matched by an intense and burning hatred of the enemy, and a determination that that enemy should lose the war it had begun.

Appropriately, Marshall does not condemn the non-firing soldiers. He recognizes the inertial factor of a body just being there, and the function that front line infantrymen often serve as bodyguards for artillery observers. By bringing forward observers for the division artillery or air liaison officers close to the enemy positions, and protecting them while they direct their batteries or squadrons in more accurate firing or bombing and strafing, they bring down a hail of death on the enemy from above. This kind of teamwork kills enemy with less danger to ourselves, and does it in an essentially American manner, by marshalling industrial power in the form of factory-produced shells and bombs against the foreign human flesh. On Guadalcanal a standard form of Japanese suicide, saving the pain of self-killing with a short sword, was to rise from his bunker and sit above the gound for the necessary few seconds! But for us in Burma then, with no division artillery, this role of artillery-observer escorts didn't exist, and the air support we had was subject to theater scarcities and to the approaching monsoon weather. To do their killing in sufficient quantity, our soldiers had to raise their heads and fire their weapons, and they did. If they didn't kill those oncoming hundreds of banzai-shouting Japanese, no lanyard-pulling artillerymen miles to the rear would do it for them.

Granted that this tendency not to fire one's weapon is an American combat fault, though, and knowing that our 3rd Battalion seemed to have a special immunity from it, I'd like to address this fault more generally and say how I think it might be countered.

Beyond the culturally-induced squeamishness about aggression and killing, there is also the plain factor of fear. Men in combat simply tend to be afraid to raise their heads to fire and thereby expose themselves to enemy counterfire. When this fire from the enemy in front is a virtual hail, as I've said earlier, no one can be expected to move his cranium and his shoulders up into it. No one really has to, because such solid flat-trajectory fire insures that no enemy will move through it to get you. Even in the closest squad operation, to invest an enemy machine gun nest, the covering fire must cease before the assault men reach the digging itself. The problem is to prevent Marshall's inert fraction of combat personnel from remaining inert throughout the action, until the enemy is literally on top of them, at bayonet distance, making the "banzai" charge thereby successful when it should have been the bloodiest kind of failure against Americans armed with semi-auto weapons. How do we do this?

One way, of course, is through a military-religious myth. If the soldier can be convinced that he'll be wafted straight up to heaven and a cloud-walled luxurious harem the moment he dies bravely, then fear is conquered. Islam had done much in this field, no doubt with some success. So did bushido and the samurai code for portions of the Japanese armed forces. Barring a few exceptions among the more fundamentalist religions, American forces do not have this option; our answer to this problem must be more rational, or at least more in accord with our basic human nature.

The first rational counter-measure against this inhibiting, paralyzing fear, might be psychological. Extensive research and observation has disclosed the infantryman's most basic motivation towards useful and rational risk-taking. This is his sense of peer respect, of not letting his small-group fellow soldiers down in a dangerous situation. Unfortunately for the American armed forces, which traditionally are thrown together anew for every national emergency, this peer-group sense of obligation is strongest when the group has been together for a long time. It is important, it should be stimulated by bonding these hastily-thrown-together units by mutual experience in training. But for American purposes, it has to be heavily reinforced by another factor.

This factor, and its importance merits repetition, is weapons skill. The deadliest soldiers I knew relied on their immediate buddies, when present, and on the wonderful loyalties that can bond a squad or platoon together with amazing speed once it gets into combat. But more fundamentally, they relied on their individual skill. Perhaps this was more visible in a jungle war, where a man's own gun and cunning more often was his only salvation, but I think it holds for all wars and all times. The man who learns to know his weapon as an almost living thing, a friend and companion that will never desert him, and who learns to use it with a deadliness approaching its designer's dreams, so that it almost becomes a part of his body, gains an instant advantage. This advantage is not bravery, perhaps not even conscious self-confidence. Some of the most Nervous Nellies I have met, men who worry and who tremble more visibly than some real, legally indictable cowards that I have identified here and there have made themselves into the deadliest of riflemen or machine gunners. It is simply drill and training. By continuous handling, dry-firing, cleaning, and practicing with their weapons they have made the acts of loading, aiming, and firing into reflex or instinctive responses. Needing neither courage nor camaraderie, these men mow the enemy down. Being Americans, they also may need that aforementioned factor of hate, or at least a conviction that their enemy is morally dangerous and wrong. But they don't have to be of hero stock. I'll even go so far as to say they can be constitutional cowards, because I know persons who have overcome their cowardice through technique. By becoming so wrapped up in the cultivation of skill they learn the art of concentration: as they aim and fire, they see only the front sight and the enemy targets, they hear only the sounds of their weapons going empty and needing to be reloaded.

Thanks to better weapons training, plus the genuine hatred and revulsion for the Japanese military enemy, these no doubt rather exceptional Marauders did fire their weapons, almost to a man, whenever a visible target or a brush movement was in front of them that day. As I fire in a rifle match today their memory often comes back to me, and I imagine the feelings, in foxholes better situated than mine and Pete's as those enemy rose from cover and ran through the meadow behind the bamboo screen and then came right out into the open in front, wading into the river itself. "Cold turkey!" I heard one rifleman shout in a joyous, incredulous voice. "Ducks in a shooting gallery!" came another cry as the heavy firing became even heavier at all this exposure of enemy flesh and khaki cloth. Throughout the hot and angry minutes of that larger Walabum fire fight, the men of the 3rd Battalion, volunteers all, were proud and joyous killers of a foe who had earned their deadliest hatred.

The Japanese casualties claimed by Stilwell at Walawbum, as I remember, were on the order of 400. I don't need to consult the files in the Pentagon to form my own estimate; I counted 350 enemy dead in sight along the river bank and floating down the stream. We have the journalistic cliche, when fighting is heavy along a water course, of "rivers running red with blood." To redden the flow of a medium-sized creek, though, would take the blood of a brigade—artificially pumped out of the bodies into the stream. But the scattered clots of corpses along both banks, hung up on the roots of the bamboos and other trees, did leave traces of crimson in the water; and scattered splotches downstream from each floating body showed a brighter crimson where the hits had been arterial.

There was little time for trophy taking. We passed the night in those same positions, trusting in a tentative way that the motor transport sounds we now heard in plenty, and searched for with our remaining mortar ammunition, were a withdrawal south. The clobbering the enemy had received from the 2nd Battalion's roadblock earlier, to the north, plus the carnage just completed by us, we dared to theorize, would cripple any brigade and would make even a Japanese division lose its stomach for another day of combat now. So the spirit of morale or whatever of the 3rd Battalion, despite our shortage of food and ammunition then in hand, was excellent.

This was not so for the other two battalions, which had not witnessed the death of so many Japanese. Earlier that day, in fact, the 1st Battalion had feared that the firing it was hearing farther south might be spelling out defeat for us. And the 2nd, though conscious of the damage it had wreaked back on the road, was also wondering about the outcome of this three-pronged, separated action.

Moving into the open fields at Lagang Ga where the 3rd Battalion had merely stirred up a hornets nest and moved on, the 1st Battalion felt especially set upon. The Japanese 150mm artillery along the road had duly noted our presence there, our killing of two of their small parties, too, no doubt, and the ongoing use of those fields for drop supply and light plane evacuation of our wounded. The fire they delivered as the 1st Battalion moved in to replace us, was hotly accurate until attack aviation was called down upon its suspected sources. And our presence farther south (the 3rd Battalion emplacing along the river bank) seems to have made the Japanese gunners worried about their southward escape route if Tanaka's plan to destroy us should fail.

Charlton Ogburn, as the 1st Battalion's signal officer, desperately digging in under this artillery fire at the drop field, reflected on his feelings in *The Marauders*, conveying his amazement, later on, when he learned that we had won instead of lost the larger battle.

"It is a cruel test of any unit's morale, for it to have to remain in enforced inaction under a pounding without being able to throw even a rock back at its assailant. In addition, knowing little of what the other battalions had been engaged in, we had a sense that the 5307th had been a failure. We were as amazed as we were relieved to hear the next day that the operation in which we had played so peripheral a part was accounted a stunning success and that the exploits of the men in the 3rd Battalion in the hours before we had pulled out of Lagang Ga were such as to warrant their looking just as they did when we saw them next—keyed up, cocky, and exuberant, their pride effectively set off by the ravages of hunger and exhaustion in their faces, their pallor, and their feverish-looking eyes."

After that fight, the Old Ranger, who may have felt again that his officers should display a degree of physical bravery that would approach his own, did not wait for daylight next morning to contact the Chinese units which were to move in and hold the ground from which we had driven the Japanese. A growing silence on the other bank, by then, had convinced us they had left; this was confirmed by word from two Kachin scouts, picked up second hand from a Kachin evacuee from farther south. The colonel sent me north along the ox cart trail, a mile and a half of which was lacking any outposts, to make this contact and insure our own withdrawal sans the frequent inter-Allied bloodshed that he knew might well occur. Sergeant Russ Hill volunteered to come with me, and hastened to learn the night's password from our right flank outposts, which turned out to be the bilingual routine greeting, "Okay ding how!"

Testily, we moved outside the battalion headquarter's night perimeter, tripping no booby traps, and onto the trail. Then very gingerly indeed we made our way northward on the splotchily moon-

Lieutenant Tilly, OSS Detachment 101, with the Tanai River behind.

Sergeant Hill, one of two Sergeants Hill in the 3rd battalion headquarters, carries three artifacts that Marauders lived by: a carbine, a map sheathed in transparent acetate, and grenades in containers.

Captain Emerick in foreground. Behind him a highly inadvisable clustering of personnel at the drop-field during the early Walawbum fighting.

*One of my snapshots of a chute drop of ammunition and food,
with that old warhorse DC-3, called the Dakota by our British
buddies, doing its routine job of keeping us fed and armed in
the field.*

*Another shot of a DC-3 dropping food. This time rice, put into
double bags that could survive the free-fall strike and rebound
from the paddyfields hard-dry surface. I'm told this sight was
a familiar one decades later in Viet Nam, where the technique
of loading a loose bag outside a more taut inner one was
repeated or re-discovered.*

The stitched individual burlap bags each contain several days of "K" rations along with added chocolate bars and other goodies. Assembled back at base, they could be ripped from their larger parachute packs after a supply drop and handed out in a manner of minutes. With no serious holdups, a battalion could be resupplied and clear of the drop field in less than half an hour.

A light plane, our main means of getting our wounded out, barely airborne in this photo. Another stands by in the foreground, engine nose visible. The improvised landing strip is near Walawbum, servicing the ongoing fight against the Japanese at that point along the road.

Major Jones and Lieutenant Higgins exchange information on the trail with two of Tilly's Kachin scouts.

A dead enemy being searched by Marauder personnel. The callous attitude apparent here came all too naturally. A few weeks experience with the vicious Japanese infantryman of World War II, whose behavior toward helpless prisoners reached new depths, made it hard to regard him as human.

Drop field at Lagang Ga, near Walawbum. Evacuation of wounded by light plane.

A Marauder wounded in the fighting at Walawbum being put on a light plane at the nearby drop-field.

*Long before the first American Indian took his first scalp, mankind's
various soldiery has had its favorite trophies. In the Marauder campaigns, where trophies had to be carried, the Japanese individual battle
flag was more treasured than a Japanese officer's sword. Following a
firefight at Walawbum, I handed Pete Petito my Leica and immodestly
posed for this snapshot.*

Elephants, sometimes used for evacuation of wounded as well as for supply and labor clearing drop fields, were often available from the natives.

Enemy dead.

*Evacuation operation by light aircraft, probably at Lagang
Ga drop field.*

*Mules, of course, were considered more sure-footed than horses. Note
the testiness with which the foremost one plants its fore-hooves on the
woven bamboo surface of this footbridge. The scene in the background,
the gravel banks, clear fast water and bordering riverine jungle, was
typical along many of our march routes.*

Col. Charles N. Hunter, whose tireless leadership of the Marauders and other troops brought him far less praise than he deserved. In this picture a Signal Corps cameraman captures the image that Hunter largely projected: the fine regular officer who could make and carry out command decisions with firmness and impartiality.

A Marauder signal officer at the radio set used by battalion and by force headquarters for longer-distance communication with these headquarters and with our supply base.

A halt on high ground, probably near Janpan, which shows some of the gear we used. Leggings that tended to be thrown away as the campaign went on. Ghurka kukri knives that were good for cutting bamboo, jungle boots worn supplementally on a pack, SCR-13 radios which served us at the platoon and company levels.

Air supply operation, probably at Janpan.

Typical march scene. Marauders move through a friendly Kachin village in the Hukawng Valley of north Burma.

Drop field crews run out to recover parachuted supplies under enemy artillery fire.

An unknown exchange of words between 3rd Battalion Marauders on a north Burma trail. Could be something official or serious, more likely a bartering of cigarettes between a smoker and a non-smoker. The burlap-sacked allotment of K rations (back of tall soldier's pack) contained little boxes of name-brand smokes, which made non-smokers many friends after each supply-drop.

A typical, if highly unmilitary looking rest scene after a highly successful jungle infantry engagement. At a streamside location, safely back from the Japanese-held road, we would take a drop of gourmet ten-in-one rations and pause to bathe, luxuriate and fatten up for the next fight.

Major Edwin Briggs, commander of Khaki combat team, and Captain Phillip Cecala, Medical Corps, and other 3rd Battalion personnel are amused by a "honey bear" which turned out to be a Himalaya black bear cub. The last time I saw this animal, back at our supply base in Assam, it weighed some two hundred pounds and was a wrestling and sparring mate for the more courageous of its human messmates.

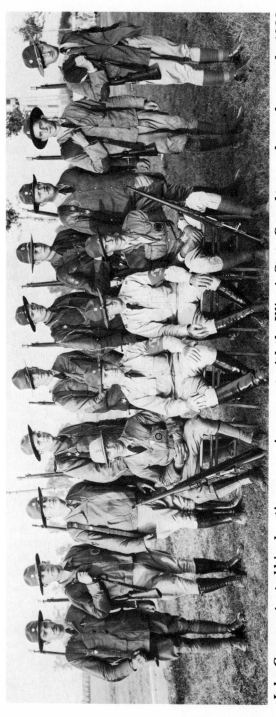

John George started his shooting career in earnest with the Illinois State Guard team, shown here at the 1938 National Matches at Camp Perry. Young George is fourth from the right in the back row. There is no substitute for training to produce an effective combat rifleman.

Author, aged 19, with trophies emblematic of the Illinois state .30 caliber rifle championship, 1938.

Colonel Hunter, left, and Lieutenant Colonel Still converse over map, while air-dropped supplies are sorted and loaded.

The author's adventuresome nature soon took him afield again after the Burma campaign. Here he has just downed his first trophy elephant in the game fields west of Lake Victoria, in the old British colony of Tanganyika, in 1950 while studying the hunting methods of nomadic African hunters.

lit ox road, through each of the remaining outposts, until we reached the lonely, hopefully non-Japanese outposted stretch of road that would lead us to the Chinese forward elements. The colonel's idea of night contact was to me a negation of everything we had learned about night warfare against the Japanese, particularly the acquired wisdom of remaining totally immobile in our foxholes at night so that we could listen and shoot or grenade everything that we might hear or see above the ground. Nevertheless, it worked out well in the end. Countless anxious halts and crouchings, carefully listening until we heard some sound or saw some movement that branded the humans ahead either Americans or Chinese; a score of breathless moments when a breech bolt or safety snicked metallically; and many agonizing decisions to finally call out the password and hope for a reply. Then, finally, the ready laugh, the toothy grin under a British-issue tin hat, and a friendly beckoning on from a sentry whom we decided to bet our lives was not Japanese. We must have looked as hungry as we were, because the squadleader of the Chinese point, at the edge of the now-silent artillery target field at Lagang Ga, took one look at us in the moonlight and reached for his belt.

When he lifted an object off his belt, one of the finest pieces of field equipment ever designed, I felt an instant warm kinship with him. It was one of those heavy aluminum Japanese mess kits with its deep cooking space and its nestling kidney-shaped plates that fit inside on the top. It was brimful of rice, still warm, with cooked fish bits and redpepper halves as tasty as anything I've ever eaten. When Russ and I looked up at him ashamed, as we sat down and took out our mess kit spoons, he raised his hands, patted his belly to indicate that he was full from earlier eating, and pointed to the mess kits of the rest of the squad, knuckling the nearest two to prove they were full. We ate on, luxuriously seated on the edge of the squadleader's foxhole, not thinking of what might have happened had we first spotted and identified the enemy origin of those large aluminum utensils with their belthooks, which were worn by the whole squad. I'd known and used one of them since Guadalcanal, lacking one at the moment because of its size and weight. I had also used the fine Japanese haversacks and water bottles when I felt brave enough to wear them in a particular situation. It was natural that the Chinese should like them too, particularly as another rice-loving people; I have never learned to cook rice as well as it cooked in those Japanese mess kits and would give a great deal for one toady.

No longer feeling like a mule driven ahead to clear booby traps on a trail, I rested on with Russ Hill and ate, then asked to be escorted to the nearest Chinese commissioned officer. I told him that the 3rd Battalion would be coming along the ox road next morning and asked him, since he understood English fairly well, to be out with his point to make sure there would be no repetition of our several false alarms and possible casualties.

The Chinese officer then escorted us to General Merrill's headquarters at the northwest corner of the drop field. As we approached the several ponchos strung to shelter the 5307th's forward staff, Merrill recognized me, got up from his rest on a groundsheet and led me a few yards aside, away from the clicking, buzzing radio and code equipment. Our conversation went much like this:

"So, you ran into it heavy down there, John?"

"Yes sir. I counted 350 dead Japs, but we lost no one."

"So your Colonel told me on the radio. He claimed 500. Either figure makes it more than NCAC estimated. We've killed more people than they say were there."

"Yes sir."

"And now some of these Light Horse Harrys here (he smiled in the moonlight and swept an arm back towards the improvised lean-tos, where Colonel Hunter and others of his command group were resting) are urging me not to pull back northeast and take a rest and an airdrop. They want us to attack south, now, cut deeper along the road, with the minimal food and ammo we've got now. What do you think?"

From an hour or so of earlier contact with this oddball general, I'd witnessed the utter informality and candor of his style. But even so, this confiding manner and this request for a young captain's opinion, within hearing of his entire command group, caught me by surprise. It also refreshed me somehow, made the tiredness seem to leave my limbs, and I felt the glaze of bewhiskered dirt on my face crack as I involuntarily grinned back in the moonlight. I rolled my eyes at the resting shapes in the cluster of lean-tos, stirring to look our way, and decided that politesse had no place in this situation. While those four flattering words—What do you think?—seemed to echo in my half-filled stomach, recalling the two days of fasting before that perfect meal of peppered rice and fish, I shook my head and looked as grim as my soft young features would let me.

It was an old enemy, here, I felt sure. God save us from that macho urge, so virulent on Guadalcanal, that seems to rise somewhere near the base of a regimental or division staff officer's spine. That urge to push your luck too far, to not know when to consolidate what you've got and rest up for the next fight, which comes from lack of exposure to front, front, frontline suffering. And thank God in this case that we had a general who could keep that urge within bounds, and rest and re-supply this outfit before sending it into action again.

I'd read the field service regulations, too, knew the profitable nature of pursuit of a damaged foe. I could have been wrong. But if anything seemed ill-advised at that moment, when we had just struck a telling blow against an obviously superior enemy force, at a point miles inside their then-held territory, an enemy who with better local intelligence and leadership could have destroyed us utterly, it was another outflanking movement now, without first resting and receiving an airdrop of food and ammo. The macho adjunct (so revered by the Japanese) that, when in doubt, a commander always should attack has it's adherents in the American army, I know. Since my later days on Guadalcanal, and particularly after that night described on pages 146-147, when my own misguided macho notion might have got a company wiped out, I've doubted that old chestnut every time I've had it thrown at me.

In any case, we didn't immediately press on with this "Light Horse Harry" notion. For the next few days we rested on our laurels, which would later be assessed "remarkable" in a publication of the War Department Armed Forces in Action series, *Merrill's Marauders*. This booklet, an official precursor of Ogburn's far more detailed *The Marauders*, concluded that "the Americans had killed 800 of the enemy, had cooperated with the Chinese to force a major Japanese withdrawal, and had paved the way for further Allied progress." And General Merrill himself, standing at rail side as we marched northwest towards his selected drop field and resting place, smiling steadily, cuffing an officer or sergeant or private on the shoulder and saying his name, more often than not, seemed to feel that this rest was well deserved.

The resting place Merrill had selected was a point on the map called Shikau Ga, far enough off the road to make raids by Japanese counter-long range penetration groups unlikely, and topographically suitable for resupply and evacuation by drop ships and light planes. This time the supply point would serve the entire three battalions and the field headquarters group, which had numbered some 2,350 as we debouched from the road march for this first mission. Only eight had been killed (one to an even 100 of Japanese, interestingly enough), and only 70 had been evacuated with wounds, malaria, and other illnesses. The rest of us remained fit enough to go on our second mission, which it was rumored would be to drive the Japanese out of their last bit of foothold in the Hukawng Valley, pushing their foremost outpost south of a hilly road pass called Jambu Bum.

Such a resting period, to a fighting unit pulled safely back from the scene of a battle with an enemy of superior numbers, has a very special flavor for the troops who enjoy it. In a sense, it's like a reprieve from death row, or like a gladiators' feast between stints in the coliseum sand. In a less remote part of the world, complete with girls and other entertainments, the theme of such a happy break is "eat, drink and be merry." And in this beautiful upper valley, a stretch of glorious wilderness only dotted with tribal habitation, this theme could still prevail.

Paddy field clearings in the primal broadleaf forest, tiny villages of one or two bashas, and a network of paths whose softer footing left tiger and leopard tracks visible, was the setting. The natives were smiling and happy, with their windfalls of parachute cloth, salt, and extra rice from our air drops, and they were so few that they seemed to fit into the wilderness scene. The pristine landscapes, so strangely underpopulated for an area that could grow good rice, would have made the 19th Century schools of landscape artists in Europe gasp with appreciation.

Back at Deogarh, in a characteristic western soldier's way, Colonel Hunter had ordered, "There will be no sunbathing." But here, as we lazed and went naked while our fatigues hung out to dry on the foliage, we let our fungus-attacked skins feel the cleansing heat. As soon as we had taken a drop, we refilled all the ammunition belts and hung two bandoliers across each haversack, re-cleaned and checked our weapons. Then we bargained with the natives for chickens and eggs and feasted hugely on the Ten-in-One rations. After taking precautions against alarm from the noise, I checked the zero of the scoped Springfield by headshooting two barking deer on the edge of the largest paddy field area, at about 100 yards. The battalion intelligence section and selected guests had two grand dinners on the fillet cuts, and the rest of the carcasses went into curries prepared by our Kachin scouts.

Rather quickly, in a strict and utterly predictable priority that I've witnessed many times before and since, the soldiers' talk of food, food, food gave way to other subjects, chiefly sex. Reclining on the earth near the luxury of open fires, chewing away at heated rations or coal-roasted chicken and game meat, letting the sun bake the fungus off their skin, the soldiers now exchanged their lurid anecdotes. They spoke of warm evenings in Sydney, Melbourne, Noumea (they'd yet to sample the flesh-pots of Calcutta), and then intoned their solemn resolutions for the future. "If I get out of this place alive," I heard a sergeant say in a braggadocio tone, "I'm going to try to bed every woman I meet!"

Two full days without food, I knew, would blot this sexual chatter completely, and get us back to talking of fine restaurant steaks and roast beef dinners, of delicatessens shelved with corned beef, potato salad, roast cold chicken. But for now, the pornographic tales poured out, through mouthfuls of food. Sex, however, never pushed aside the permanent preoccupation of every soldier in this outfit—the constant loving care of his rifle, carbine, or tommy gun. Scarcity of food could quiet all talk of sex, but this fierce interest in weapons remained strong in hunger and in plenty for these men.

Lieutenant Colonel Lloyd Osborne, the 1st Battalion commander was a veteran of the Philippines campaign, a sparely-built man of medium stature who had escaped the Japanese occupation in a small boat. Whether by temperament or because of this personal score he had to settle with the enemy, he was anxious to have more directly at the Japanese in this valley. Especially after his unit had suffered casualties from the Japanese artillery at Lagang Ga, he yearned for a more active assignment. In our next mission, Merrill would provide him with one, in which his battalion would suffer another kind of punishment and frustration, this time from the jungle and hilly terrain that had to be crossed before he could sever the Japanese-held roadway in another outflanking operation.

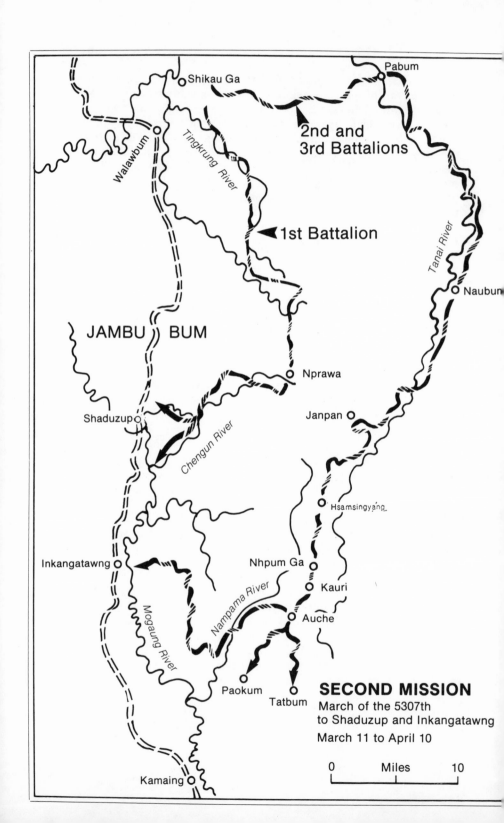

Pabum

Shikau Ga

2nd and
3rd Battalions

Walawbum

Tingkrung River

◀ 1st Battalion

Tanai River

Naubun

JAMBU) BUM

Nprawa

Shaduzup

Janpan

Chengun River

Hsamsingyang

Inkangatawng

Nhpum Ga

Nampama River

Kauri

Mogaung River

Auche

Paokum

Tatbum

SECOND MISSION

March of the 5307th
to Shaduzup and Inkangatawng

March 11 to April 10

0   Miles   10

Kamaing

NHPUM GA

When our restful, fattening few days at the paddy fields of Shikau Ga were over, Osborne's 1st moved off on the most direct path back to the enemy's holdings. His would be the northernmost prong of this second and deeper outflanking operation, intended to cut the Japanese-held road another 30 miles south of Walawbum at a place called Shaduzup.

Shaduzup lay in the Japanese rear, well behind their current defensive emplacements, along a range of hills athwart the road. Topographically speaking, our objective was now the southern, bottled-up end of the Hukawng Valley. We would be leaving a forested fastness, with its small salient of agriculture pushed northward, for the deeper foothills of the Himalayas, trying to move down into what might be called Burma proper. There, months later, the largest ground force movement in military history, the 14th Army and 15th Corps under Mountbatten and Slim, would retake Burma in the conventional ground force manner. The far-less-conventional 5307th, glorying by now in its new name Merrill's Marauders, and still front page news throughout the Allied world, would now do its much smaller, but much more romantic thing. And 1st Battalion's half of the effort would be to cut the Japanese supply road at Shaduzup.

With its trucks and tanks and artillery vans, the roadway itself made a civilized mechanical scene, but the route of the 1st Battalion to cut it was sheer primitiveness and forest. Much of the way, Osborne's men would learn how priceless a tiny footpath could be, as opposed to cutting or, rather, tunnelling, through solid growths of bamboo and other hillside vegetation. Not being with them on the way, and having Charlton Ogburn's fine account to read and commend to anyone interested, I'll turn to the less direct, and somewhat less primitive march route and mission of the 3rd Battalion.

Our march route, along with that of the 2nd Battalion until we parted some 80 miles later, led us some three times farther to reach

497

our objectives than the march of the 1st Battalion. But nearly all of it was infinitely more endurable, leading as it did along the Tanai River Valley. Paralleling the Japanese-held road some 30 miles to the east, this valley had a narrow, gently sloping floor, letting the Tanai River drain without too many rapids into the lower streams of the Hukawng. The flow was north and west, the opposite of the larger rivers it fed, so that though we moved southward, the direction that more generally led down hill in northern Burma, we were actually climbing higher into the Himalaya foothills. And since it cut through these steeper foothills, the valley seemed very deep, becoming more and more a high-walled gorge, or canyon. Yet the walking was easy compared to the route that had to be taken by the 1st Battalion, because we were following established trails and footpaths which lay in a narrow network astride the river's way. For miles and miles our walking was essentially wading: we simply forded and reforded the river, scores of times.

In such a high-walled valley or canyon, the blinding jungle cover is in a sense defeated. Though it may truly blind you to the immediate front and rear, as you walk along its stream bed or follow contours higher up, it often provides wide and beautiful vistas, giving hillside-to-hillside views of country, with promontories and cleared spaces exposed. This meant that the more classic or conventional mode of sniping, the long range type that Hubert McBride described in the World War I account *A Rifleman Went to War*, might now come into play.

As battalion intelligence officer, kept aware of local spying and counter-spying by our attached Kachin scouts and their American Office of Strategic Services (OSS) officers, I often exchanged my carbine for the mule-carried scoped '03 and a binocular. As we noticed more of the zig-zag and hobnail markings of Japanese footgear on the side paths, along with the giveaway litter of Japanese cigarette wrappings, I developed a spare-time diversion. With one or two of the Kachin scouts (from a Lieutenant Tilly's OSS unit, if I remember correctly) at my side, I would sit on a promontory during a rest halt and glass the more suspect slopes above us with great care. When not occupied with the more routine duties of a battalion intelligence officer, or the other staff tasks that our Colonel assigned, I spent much of my time in this manner, straining my eyes to try to locate the scouts or agents that General Tanaka would surely have active along this valley.

What I saw mostly, of course, was big game, largely sambar moving along the hillside trails, but also chital (axis deer), and an occasional leopard taking the morning sun on a rocky ledge. Also the smaller animals, the unbiquitous pigs and barking deer.

Six times, though, I spotted humans that were not friendly

Kachins, watching our column from some logical observation point above. Always when I had this luck, one or more of the Kachin scouts was at hand. From one of our command echelons below General Merrill, we all had orders to shoot first and ask questions afterwards whenever we should spot such a target. A restraining factor was the fear of a mis-identification that might turn the attitude of the Kachins around and make them hate us as they hated the Japanese and the Chinese. So I would make hurried gestures from where I sat, holding the binoculars to my eyes so as not to lose the suspicious object, to bring one of the senior Kachin scouts, always a responsible tribal elder, to affirm that it was an enemy soldier or agent. Three of the six were in Japanese uniform, with that characteristic peaked cap with the glint of a bronze star on it. The other three were identified as enemy by one of Tilly's or Father Stuart's Kachin elders. It was a type of shooting that recalled my first sniping adventure in the Point Cruiz groves on Guadalcanal, or, the fine long range work that Hubert McBride reported from World War I in France.

Apart from the six mentioned, I conducted academic target searches in areas where the Kachins sensed that our movement was not known to Tanaka's network of informants and therefore advised against any shooting at all. I missed the right kind of equipment, a heavy-barreled, big-scoped "bull gun" and a good wide-field spotting scope. How I longed for the fine little Zeiss that I used on the ranges in the States!

The sheer beauty of the winding stream and the steep valley walls, I'm happy to say, did not escape at least some of us. Esthetically speaking, the 2nd and 3rd Battalions, thus far on this second mission, might just as well have been on a lovely backpack excursion, along a tropical mountain stream selected for its outstanding green-and-crystal primitiveness. The minority of us who openly enjoyed it (as apart from the conventional majority who called all military combat terrain hell holes) would shake our heads in awe, pausing at a turn in the hillside trail or while fording the crystal water to let the vista imprint our memories. While some 20 miles northwest the 1st Battalion was clawing and literally tunnelling through solid growths of bamboo, so that mules and men walked under a ceiling that was patterned in those hundreds of white rings of severed shoots, Pete and I could thank our lucky stars and praise nature's glories. Also, unlike the 1st Battalion, we had no formal engagements with the Japanese along this long approach. While Osborne's men fought the jungle and the Japanese, mile by mile, our only displeasure was the knowledge that we couldn't stop in this glorious country and spend an extra lifetime.

And yet, for a soldier who was also a keen big game hunter, this "only displeasure" could at times prove a torment. For as we moved farther south and closer to the Japanese axis along the road, we entered big game hunting country par excellance. In addition to the sambur, pig, and leopard I now saw wild elephant and tiger. It was here that I first learned how elephant depend on scent, and will feed peacefully only a few yards from a standing human if he stands down wind. And years later in East Africa I'd note the reason African elephant seemed more totally fearless of other wild animals, more totally dominant in their respective wilderness.

This reason, of course, was tiger. Unlike the adult African species, who feared lions only on behalf of their young calves, the Asiatic species still suffered, eons past the demise of the sabertooth tiger, a deadly natural enemy in the big striped cat. An angry or hungry tiger was not afraid to run alongside or even under an adult Asiatic elephant, tearing upward with claw and fang to drive them away from their young. Tiger tracks in relative abundance were now found on the trails we walked, more frequently per mile than in the best of Indian tigerland where I'd later bag a huge one.

During our first-mission march in the northern Hukawng, on the trail where we stepped over the first Japanese dead we'd seen in Asia, the trio killed in Weston's and Katz's first enemy contact, I'd seen some huge pug marks in the mud and paused to read them. Two big cats had walked past two of these dead, had sniffed them both and backed away. Half seriously Jack Girsham, an OSS employee and British commissioned officer later famed as *Burma Jack* in his book with Lowell Thomas, implored me to take a day or two off from the war and stay there. He'd set up a machaan with a young domestic buffalo as bait and these two big cats, one of which he felt would go more than 10 feet "between pegs," would likely come back. We'd skin our trophies quickly and send the hide back via one of his Kachins.

This set a pattern for the two of us, during the rest of that second-mission march. With eyes aglow he'd point down at every tiger sign we saw. "Let's stop right here," he'd say. "To hell with this bloody war. These Burma cats are big. Good trophies. Let's stop and set up a damned machaan, I tell you!"

Jack walked mostly with the 5307 headquarters, close to Merrill himself, as a treasured local advisor and guide. When he varied this routine, to check his and Tilly's scouts attached to the 3rd Battalion, we would walk along the trail and talk about his hunting experiences: he'd been an elephant control officer for years before the war. I never tired of listening to him then, and was elated last year to find his book in our local library, and to see some of these wonderful adventures in print.

Scenically speaking—and that's how I most remember this march south, before all hell would break loose later—the most memorable point we passed through was Janpan, a tiny Kachin village set on the eastward heights of the Tañai gorge, as the valley could now be aptly called. After a sweaty but incredibly beautiful climb three or four thousand feet up from the river floor, our part of the column halted at an almost Alpine hilltop. Grassy, windswept, and a few hundred feet above the last bamboo and broadleaf jungle, we knew it would make a fine bivouac place, and though it was early to do so, Merrill had called a halt for the day. Near the edge of the village I took the little Springfield off the mule, stowed the carbine in the scabbard instead, and set up my usual observation point, glassing the distant wall of the gorge, where its winding gave me an almost bird's eye view through the cover. It was a commanding position, from which I could trace the feeding path of a herd of elephant on the slope and also look down at the valley floor, with the ribbon of the river flowing through the center.

Complementing more than damaging this vista was an aerial exhibition unique to me at the time. Offside from the slope with the elephant feeding on it, circling narrowly above an exposed gravel bar of the river, were three Dakotas, C-47 cargo planes. I hadn't noticed them at first, indeed I'd seen the elephants feeding before I saw the tiny, toy-like planes thousands of feet below me, at the bottom of what could almost be called a crevasse!

What pilots! What flying! These were the thoughts this sight inspired in a grateful, grateful foot soldier. To feed and re-arm us these miles behind the enemy front, these flyboys had to circle in a narrow hole, their outer wingtips banking mere yards from the hillside bamboos that almost surrounded their small-circle pattern. And to get down there to do this, they'd clearly had to fly at low altitudes down the meandering valley and to inscribe tight corkscrew patterns inside this bend of it.

To drop their free-drop rice bags and parachute their ammunition cases onto this narrow gravel bank, they had to circle more tightly than any cargo planes I'd seen before, maintaining the necessary flying speed by careful throttling, holding their lives in their own skillful fingers. Below me, visually between the toes of my shoes as I sat on an outcrop, the planes looked like wayward children's toys. As they tumbled to earth, the double rice sacks looked for all the world like fish dropped by eagles, onto the river bank because they proved too heavy.

When the drop was completed, with the colored parachutes aflower all over the gravel space below the lightened aircraft gunned their engines and spiraled up, out of this well of a drop mission,

The finesse of unconventional warfare anywhere rests in improvisation, I suppose. Here we see this rule being demonstrated by seven MARAUDERS and a Kachin-valley ox cart. Mortar and other ammunition, airborne five minutes before, has been torn from its parachute containers, tossed onto this cart in the drop zone, and is now moving quickly to the pack mules under cover in the rain forest close by.

Perhaps even more than in the hill campaigns in Italy, animal transport and man-drawn carts were occasionally more valuable than trucks. With the drop zone actually or imminently under fire, it was crucial that the supplies be secured and moved at once. Then—barring some operational "call for staticity" (an order to sit right here on our ass and take it)—we'd move off from the exposed location with all undeliberate speed, before Tanaka's artillery could really zero in on us.

straining to make it to my level, wagging their wings to acknowledge our cheering and waving from the hillcrests.

As the light faded I traded the Springfield back for the carbine in the now off-saddled scabbard by the grazing mule. As I walked back towards the 3rd Battalion headquarters I looked up at the principal basha of the village and noticed Jack Girsham, beckoning from the veranda. I walked closer and saw Merrill's handsome face glancing casually out, and heard his voice ring out through his characteristic, flashing smile.

"John" he said in that tone of recognition with which a truly gifted commander can charm his every underling, "Come in. Join us in this lovely Swiss chalet!" And as I climbed the bamboo ladder and moved through the doorway, he smiled more broadly still and said "Quite a salubrious atmosphere here; let's celebrate the change in seasons!"

On the slab rock hearth of the basha inside, a charcoal fire was glowing, a kettle was boiling, and a row of canteen cups were warming nearby. In response to Girsham's gestures as we sat down in a circle of some 12 around the hearth, I unsnapped my canteen cover and let my cup be added to the warming row. At the end of the cup row stood a bottle of British issue rum and an open tin of butter, with a trench knife, with blade already smeared and scented by its present barkeeper's usage. In the next few minutes all of the remaining cups were totted with rum, filled with boiling water, and slabbed on top with a rich slice of butter.

In my lifetime of safari and camp life I've never been a drinker by habit; the bottle I still carry in a peacetime wilderness is for guest occasions only. But to every human taboo there should be occasional exceptions; and this present all-male atmosphere, suggestive of a dozen deer hunting camps I'd known, made one for the books. The circle around the basha fire included Merrill, his half-Japanese intelligence officer, Captain Laughlin, the force intelligence officer Jones, who led a number of toasts to the homefront and to the girls left behind. Merrill toasted, "This remote and lovely valley: if we must have war it's a good place to fight it!" His words warmed my loyal insides far more than the scalding buttered rum.

This theme of beautiful North Burma then began to take hold, with Girsham as its native, holding forth. He sat forward in the circle, to hand out and refill the cups, and to tell one big game hunting story after another—of sitting night after night in a machaan for a man-eating tiger, of hunting elephant and Asiatic rhino on control. The atmosphere was that of a guerrilla hideout, strewn with green jungle cloth and worn packstrap webbing, weapons leaning against the woven bamboo wall, a map outspread on the floor with pistols laid to flatten its curl, the air permeated with the smell of alcohol and charring bamboo. In this scene, there seemed to be an inkling of the classic, the evermore of military ventures into remote and beautiful hinterlands. At the time the ambiance and the rum stirred visions of Roman legions in Gaul, of soldiery moving out from every empire in every age. We were Caesar's long right arm, Napoleon's dragoons and hussars. The theme of beautiful Burma met the deadliness of conquest, in this instance of counter-conquest and revenge.

Later on, I'd think differently about males and their abstract armed presence in a far-flung wilderness. I'd walk with native hunters who lived by taking elephant and cape buffalo with spears. I'd sit around other fires with other all-male groups and hear their hunting stories. Large-scale warfare is as old as history itself, but in the shaping of our species, hand and brain, history is but the most recent moment. What made us what we are was big game hunting, blowing our brains to their full present shape as hunting tools. Man in his present modern shape of brain, hand, and far-walking legs is a primitive big game hunter, neurophysiologically unchanged. Thirty thousand years before he farmed and fought his big, agriculturally-supported wars, his clever use of flint blades and other tools conquered the other continents and made him the arch-predator of the world. Was it not a logical thesis that right now we were basically less soldiers than hunters, acting out in these primitive surroundings our genetic nostalgia for the lost excitements of the mammoth hunt, the lost man-to-man intimacy of the hunting band? The faces round that fire belonged to the command group of a modern infantry unit, out to defeat a dictator-led enemy with our automatic weapons and our supporting aviation; but I see them also as the faces of a council of tribal hunters, planning a seasonal mass bison drive, and then exchanging their male gossip and story telling into the starry night.

In the morning I rose up from my poncho and half-blanket, back in the 3rd Battalion headquarters plot. How grand it is to be young! I had no memory of staggering back there when the party in the basha had broken up, but I had no hangover from the multiple tots of rum in buttered hot water; just my usual morning aches and stiffness. And Sergeant Russ Hill, bless him, was holding out a hot canteen cup of coffee, heated on some Sterno-type canned heat from a Japanese supply truck.

From this towering overlook at Janpan, the 2nd and 3rd Battalions continued southward, descending from these highlands gradually. And still enjoyably, scenically, while the 1st Battalion hacked and struggled through almost impenetrable jungle to our right, moving westward to cut the enemy-held road. Members of that battalion would later tell of a message dropped from a friendly aircraft, a liaison plane from Stilwell's "advance" headquarters that buzzed them during one of their rare moments of visibility, as they crossed a small, bare hilltop. The staff officer in the plane had pencilled a note inquiring when they were going to stop their leisurely scenic tour and get moving towards their objective. The plane then flew away, making no further passes to get radio contact and receive a reply. This was just as well for the sarcastic staff officer and his pilot, because the plane would quite likely have been fired at, had it dallied in the area. Had such a note been addressed to us in the 2nd and 3rd Battalions, thus far on this mission, we would have to have accepted it as a justified rebuke. For us, as we marched on up that beautiful Tanai Valley, through a Kachin paddy field village and air-drop site named Hsamsingyang, and up over a later-fateful hilltop village called Nhpum Ga, the mission remained just that: a "leisurely scenic tour." The adjective "leisurely" is accurate, because Merrill's men could move 25 miles a day with relative ease.

Southward from Nhpum Ga, we crossed a kind of small divide, leaving the north-flowing headwaters of the Tanai for a new watershed, and finding before us a spreading valley floor, hard on the rearward flank of an enemy that had motor roads to supply, fed by a rail line and river boats. Here again Tanaka could strike out from his advantageous interior lines, if he played it wisely, and destroy us. Our nervousness increased with every leveling gradient in the trails; our scenic tour was ending. We left those beautiful, sheltering hills, where it was hand-carried or mule-carried weapons and guerrilla-like tactics, to move into the backyard of a full ground-force division. As the battalion intelligence officer, reported to daily by a screen of our own and Kachin scouts, I had to be much aware of this new circumstance. And my nightly bit of earth with the hip-hole scooped out became less of a sleeping place than a worrying nail-bed.

Our entry-point onto this alluvial flat space was a village named Auche, some 30 walking miles south of Janpan, within minutes of scouting contact and sometimes within actual hearing, of mechanized enemy equipment moving in this area north of Kamaing, a Japanese stronghold on the road. The only good thing that I could see about our situation was that we had this scouting contact, provided by Kachins under Captain Curl and Lieutenant Tilly. The force that could destroy us was present, and if the weather went wrong and blinded our attack aircraft we'd have nothing with which to reply to their artillery. But, we'd know when and in what force they would be hitting us. While the 2nd Battalion moved on west-

ward, to interdict the road traffic at a point near Inkangatawng, some
20 miles north on the road from Kamaing, we in the 3rd took up
positions along the Nampana River, west of Auche. A Japanese
reaction, as angry as a lion's when a dog nips at its right rear leg, was
clearly and rapidly on its way.

Strangely, the estimates in Stilwell's headquarters continued to
downplay the word we were getting from Curl's scouts. Staff officers
back there felt that we were timorous, I suppose. But all was clarified
by the happenings of the next few days, which began, as far as I am
concerned, with three of Curl's Kachins running back into our lines
from the south, crying "Jaba! Jaba! Jaba!"

Recognizing the three natives, knowing them as men not easily
frightened, I took quick note of their sweating, nervous state, and
called them to the battalion command post. No one who spoke
Kachin was present, and any English that the three might have
known was gone for the moment. So I asked how many Jabas there
were by holding up one finger and grasping it while I uttered the
word Jaba, and then by holding out both fists and opening them,
repeatedly, to get the count by 10's.

At a count of 80 they stopped me and took over; I wasn't doing it
speedily enough. All three held out their hands, opening and closing
them as fast as they could, indicating that hundreds of enemy were on
their way northward. And in a moment a fourth Kachin, running up
from one of the companies on our left flank, brought his meager
English into play. Two Japanese battalions, or thereabouts, were
headed northward towards Auche, where they could effectively cut
our route back to the north and then clobber us at leisure.

This counting scene was witnessed by most of the 3rd Battalion
headquarters, and the chill it brought to our separate insides was easy
to read in our eyes. We could put it together with what had happened
the night before, which was not without its personal and, I suppose,
its humorous aspect as well.

I had lain down to take my rest that night with a growing feeling of
irritation, because I knew that rest would likely be interrupted at
least once by the battalion commander. For weeks now, the Old
Ranger had been plaguing me with midnight errands. "Fire discipline" was his rationale; and it was very true that ours at night had
lately been imperfect. In this outfit whose nerves had grown increasingly jangled, and in this country where leopards, pythons, and the
ubiquitous wild pig moved around noisily at night, the boys had
indeed begun to get trigger-happy.

"Bang! Bang!" the routine would begin, or "Rat-tat-tat!" if it
were a machine gun or a BAR shattering the peace of the wilderness
night.

"George! George," the Old Ranger then would call out. "What the hell is that?"

"Two shots," I'd call back from my poncho, "or a tommy gun, off to the left."

This wouldn't satisfy the colonel, and he'd say "Go check it out!" a marked variation in our policy of no unnecessary movement at night. That policy had enabled Americans throughout the war against the Japanese to shoot at anything human that moved and thereby hold a powerful advantage. Something macho in the Japanese infantryman made him think that he could move around safely, aggressively, in darkness, and it cost him thousands of casualties. After all, a quiet, waiting soldier, dug in usually, will always have the drop on a crawling, moving foe. The Old Ranger for some reason wanted to cast this advantage in the hope of satisfying his curiosity.

I hadn't taken kindly to this routine. As it continued, my checkings out became more and more hesitant, especially since I'd thus far found every such shot to be at a bit of the local fauna, wild and sometimes domestic; a wandering goat or domestic buffalo. It had become a sore point with me, and had brought me, however inconsiderately, to join the other officers in the battalion, who almost to a man disliked their commander and identified him with an ever larger part of their overall problems and inconveniences. Man needs a scapegoat in most unpleasant situations, and as our scenic tour had moved us more and more towards danger the Old Ranger tended to receive our blame even for this.

And so on the night before, sometime past midnight, a machine gun, sited to interdict anything that crossed a ford in the Nampana River along the southeast edge of our perimeter, fired a long and two short bursts, totalling perhaps 60 rounds, breaking through the purely natural jungle sounds and silencing them for some two dozen heartbeats. Everyone woke, grabbed their weapons, and looked around, but not with the utmost concern, though, because there had been no Japanese cries, no American gunner's yells. At the end of those two dozen heartbeats, as the jungle noises started up again, I heard the expected cry from the colonel's lean-to.

"George! Go check that out!"

Achingly I arose, carbine in hand. I had profited from that experience at Walawbum, and now always made sure I had a 15-round, not a five-round clip in my carbine except when on the march in a secure situation moving towards the sounds of the firing. I repeated the password as I moved, as well as my name and position—"Lilly Langtree; George; Battalion S-2." On the way to the MG site, despite precautions, I found myself four times staring into gun-muzzles, held by very competent but very nervous American soldiers. I squatted beside the foxhole of the fourth, whose intense look and fierce exhalation of breath as he lowered the aim of his M-1 from my solar plexus expressed an experienced infantryman's contempt for this impolitic and highly irregular nighttime movement inside a perimeter. I felt a need to explain, and a little angry at the same time. "You heard the colonel, didn't you?"

The man said nothing, but the look on his face, even in the faint starlight, made plain his thoughts. An order of the sort the colonel had given was more honored in the breech.

I nodded toward the MG site and the ford, the latter faintly visible as a series of gravel banks with channels ankle deep, fallen logs and many shadows. "What were they shooting at?" I asked.

"Water buffalo, probably," he shrugged.

I looked into the darkness of the far bank, saw nothing in its trees and brush. I scanned the ford itself, where water buffalo would come to cross or drink. I listened for perhaps five minutes. All I saw was a suggestive curve, low on the far bank, 60 yards away, that looked like the right horn of a buffalo now dead. Then I turned, made my whispering way back to my own sleeping place, and lay down again, hoping the colonel, a sound sleeper by nature, might be back in the arms of Morpheus. But, no such luck. "George!" he cried. "What was it?"

My reply as I remember was, "water buffalo, it seems," and we all went back to sleep, or to the soldier's recuperative rest, with a hand touching each loaded weapon.

I didn't wake until dawn was bright in the sky, and it was the colonel's boot against my toe that woke me. He was looking down at me, carbine in hand, and his voice as he spoke had that characteristic half-angry, half-supplicative tone.

"John, get up and come with me."

I struggled up, going through warm-up stretches and limped along after him, passed the four foxholes that I'd encountered and on another 60 yards to the machine gun site. There he halted, faced the ford, pointed to its far bank, and said in that strangely patient, pleading tone, "There's your goddamn water buffaloes!"

I had already seen them of course; three dead Japanese in khaki uniforms, wrapped leggings, lying there in unnatural sprawls, the water trickling around the stiffened ankles of the one nearest, the farthest with his neck bent backward, teeth visible in his gaping mouth.

I found myself, even there on the battlefield, noticing that he'd been ungrammatical. It is not uncommon for subordinates in a combat situation to be unfairly critical of their commanders, and to unfairly identify them with just about all of their miseries. I should have noticed myself doing this now. Suddenly the aches I felt from the night slept on hard earth; the three leeches, ballooned with my blood, that I'd scraped off my calf with my trench knife, seemed somehow to be the Old Ranger's doings. A bit later than his other officers but in the same unjust pattern, I now think, I was beginning to join the growing young wolfpack of detractors, which had come to include almost every officer in the battalion.

When the three frightened Kachins came across the stream, to enact their "counting scene" in the battalion headquarters, the colonel was not there. He came back from our right flank dispositions as the scene was ending, held up his hand to halt our anxious attempts to warn him, and opened a can of C rations from his grounded pack. While he sat down and began to eat from the can, using his fingers, the three Kachins almost danced in anxiety. Carried away by their concern, they kept making those fast repeated openings of their fists, counting 10 more with each unclasping, and kept exclaiming "Jaba! Jaba!" I took the liberty of interrupting his eating to say, "Colonel, they're telling us that a large force—more than two companies and perhaps two full battalions—are headed for us now, coming north from Kamaing on two trails."

Petito and I watched the colonel eating. Somehow it made me think back to a staging camp near Noumea, New Caledonia, where the personnel of this 3rd Battalion was first being gathered. Someone of the camp staff had told us that the Old Ranger would be arriving to take command of our group of volunteers, and a lieutenant named Mitchell had winced, and blurted out: "Oh no, no. It can't be him."

Mitch (we later became the best of friends and hunting companions) quickly retracted saying, "Belay that wise crack. I ought to keep my big mouth shut," or something of the kind. But the words had been said, and other officers, less kindly than Mitch, began to pass anecdotes about a major they had known on Guadalcanal who ate C rations with his fingers.

Thus from the earliest rumor that he was to command us, the officers of the 3rd Battalion began, as I then put it, to gang up on him. Charlton Ogburn tells of how we "heard of his appointment with sinking hearts. . ." how we "regarded him as slow thinking and crude although without fear—which they ascribed to his being also without imagination—and rather touching in his desire to be liked. He was one of those curious cases of a commander who while little respected by his officers is very popular with the enlisted men." And now, as I watched him continue to eat from the can of beef stew, this memory was tincturing the scene.

With a resigned feeling that now I, too, must join this ganging up, I unfolded my map and laid it on the ground in front of him. I pointed with my little finger to the tiny trail mark to our rear, the village named Auche, and moved the finger to show how the Japanese could cut us off, could nail us up against the jungle barrier that rose just north of us and then cut us into bits, in this narrow stream bed where we couldn't find an evacuation strip or a good drop site, even.

The colonel continued to eat his C rations, eyes dully aglow, no doubt in justified annoyance over the buffalo incident. I felt guilty and angry at myself, too, but this was making me definitely one of the pack, and ready even to be impolite, and to spell the danger out in terms that the lowest private would understand.

I was saved from doing so by the arrival of a signal sergeant, who had been working at decoding near the field radio setup. The sergeant handed the Old Ranger a message from Merrill. Pete and I read its block letters as the Colonel reached out for it. Less the coded addresses, it read simply: DID YOU BLOCK WARONG-AUCHE TRAIL AS I ORDERED?

Pete and I looked at one another, dumbfounded. Neither of us knew of an order to block those trails, which the Japanese would have to use on their way to us. I'd been told they were covered by other Kachin scouts, or at least outposted, as the direct avenues between the Japanese stronghold of Kamaing and us right here.

The Old Ranger pocketed the radiogram and resumed his eating, and the memory of what he did next would come back to me from that moment on, whenever I might hear mention of the question of moral versus physical courage. He finished the can of stew, picked up his own message book, and slowly pencilled his reply: WARONG-AUCHE TRAIL BLOCKED AS ORDERED.

He handed the message to the signal sergeant, called for Logan Weston to come over, and ordered him to proceed and block the Warong-Auche trail. Which, thank God or nature, he and another lieutenant named Smith did, quite handsomely, during the next few score hours.

I have no idea of why the Old Ranger might have ignored, forgotten, or perhaps never even received Merrill's order. It could have been that he wanted to keep his force together, as a hedgehog capable of a stronger self-defense around its headquarters group, accepting the risk of an open rear and left flank. One thing I did feel sure of was that Merrill's radiogram, telling or reminding him, saved the 2nd and 3rd Battalions from otherwise certain destruction. For General Tanaka, well aware of our movements up the Tanai Valley and across this southern divide, could now see his second chance to wipe us out. His one or more battalions, dragging their short ground-supply line behind them, were already marching to cut off our rear. Cork the bottle's neck at Auche, he could assure himself, and the rest would be simple. With the east-west hill range behind us to serve as his anvil, he could hammer us to bits. From his own smooth valley floor, he could hammer us with artillery, could interdict any attempt to receive an air drop, could cut our food and ammunition to zero a few hours after first contact.

But thanks to Merrill's acumen, this was not to happen. The rifle skill and the heroism of two brilliantly-led infantry platoons would thwart Tanaka's second chance to destroy us, and would spare the 5307th for another and more ambitious third mission. Unhappily, we didn't know this as the 2nd and 3rd Battalions turned back discouraged, marching for dear life back to where they had come from, that peaceful, sunny Tanai Valley across that dangerous divide.

On that 25th day of March it poured, a tropical rain that sheeted down off the trail-side broadleafs onto mules, men, packs and pack saddles, soaking everything. Out in front of us Lieutenants Weston and Smith moved on hurriedly, similarly soaked, but marching yet more anxiously to reach that narrow gateway at Auche, before the northward moving Japanese. The continued life of the men of our two battalions depended on their reaching it first—and Weston and Smith knew it as they marched through mud that was viscid and deep on those river and hillside trails, making every step an effort for their hungry and exhausted men.

Scholars of infantry weaponry, and especially the conservative ones who once even argued against the adoption of self-loading rifles, should know about the fight along those trails south of Auche. The American force numbered 90, the two platoons led by Logan E. Weston and Warren B. Smith. The Japanese force numbered 850.

In the first part of this action the two American forces operated separately. After beating the Japanese to Auche, they each turned right, but on forking trails, slanting gently apart, Smith's route led more directly south, towards Tatbum; Weston's southwest towards another village named Poakum.

At 1410 hours an estimated 30 Japanese hit Weston's platoon, and at 1025 on the following day, March 26, a company-strength unit of Japanese hit Smith's other trail defense setup.

The term hit, taken from a report of these two officers, holds meanings far beyond its simple sound, and in the context of the jungle and the Japanese and my generation of American infantrymen, tells a story on its own. To hit is to move into something, something that is by implication stationary or moving slower than the force that hits it. For men armed with semi-automatic rifles this factor of being static or slower-moving is all important. It means the faculties of the rifleman can concentrate defensively. He has no bolt to work between shots; his eyes and ears and aiming and firing reflexes are less distracted by his other body movements; as a predatory animal he can be more deadly, lying in wait. In a fairer test of Japanese and American weaponry we have the head-on collision of two patrols on a trail, with both sides equally surprised or expectant. In such cases the eight-shot M-1 semi-auto gave us a marked advantage over the clumsy, rattly turnbolt and charger-loaded Arisaka. But when the M-1 rifleman was lying in wait, or sitting, or kneeling, or even standing as his targets walked up to him, this advantage became more than "marked;" it became terrible. In the head-on collision we might expect a 10-to-one advantage—10 Japanese downed to one American.

In the lying-in-wait circumstance this advantage became awesome: the Japanese would take two-to-four shots from each of us while fully exposed, before taking to good old Mother Earth. The survivors of these several well-aimed shots (an M-1's bullet can penetrate three men if they happen to be behind one another), would return their one shot each as they hit the ground, to two or more from the Americans. And once prone or kneeling, this uneven exchange would continue, with the Japanese having to wrestle between shots to work their bolts. "Wrestling" was the word for it, too, because the Japanese, unlike the better-trained American Marines who archaically used the '03 bolt gun on Guadalcanal, never learned to operate the bolt with the butt still to the shoulder. This wrestling, plus the rattling noise of the Arisaka bolt, especially when the sliding sleeve was left in place, disturbed the cover and announced the positions of the Japanese, often making them clear and obvious targets even in cover.

Meanwhile the Americans, each man an independent base of fire with his M-1, carbine, tommygun or BAR, capable of wiping out an enemy squad without reloading, needed to make no revealing body movement other than that "gentle snatch" of the trigger as in the rapid fire stage of a competition.

The result of this American weapons superiority was hardly "fighting." Barring inexperience or poor leadership in the American unit, it was slaughter. Japanese officers had reported the even eight-shot sequence of the new American rifle with a certain respect on Guadalcanal, but both they and we were slow to realize its full deadliness. With their misleading experience against the sparsely-armed Chinese, and the resultant tactical doctrine that they could advance into superior enemy fire (unlike the inferior Occidental infantry), the Japanese had to suffer whole battalions downed before they learned. And we Americans actually had to take the contested ground and count the corpses to know how lethal our semiautomatic weapons were, and how appropriate this increased firepower was in the hands of individuals from a society that had taught them self-reliance and the ability to think for themselves under pressure.

In this action by Weston's and Smith's platoons, the advantage was fiercely demonstrated. Thanks to the informal quickfire marksmanship exercises at Deogarh and in the islands earlier, they had that dual rifle skill: (1) the instinctive two quick rounds when there was no time to aim, pointed from the hip or at some other stage in raising the weapon to the shoulder; and (2) the careful but still very quick use of the front and rear sight, the rule of thumb being point short of 25 yards and to use the sights beyond. But here again the American individualism paid off: each man would point or aim according to his self-tested, self-known skills; no need for shouted commands such as we could always hear from the Japanese side, or even for gentle counsel from a superior. As an American taught to make his own way from childhood, the average rifleman or tommy-gunner, or BAR man in this small 90-man force had learned what his weapon could do, had trained himself to make the weapon do a part of this awesome destruction, and now lay or crouched or stood behind cover in that fell, stationary way—largely unseen by his approaching enemy as he "drew a bead" in the tradition of Daniel Boone, Davy Crockett, or any hired hand back on his father's farm.

And "drawing a bead" with an M-1 rifle means letting the top of the big front sight blade, made easier to see by the huge guard-ears, center naturally in the large rear aperture, zeroed to strike within a couple inches of aim per hundred yards of range, and placing that bead against Japanese uniform (at these usually short ranges). That done, one could give the trigger a fast release, could in fact jerk it if he didn't flinch (and most men are too afraid to flinch in a fire fight) and a hit was assured.

In the jungle, these hits were largely fatal. That 150 grain bullet travelling at close to 3,000-foot seconds would impact bone, flesh and intestinal fluids with a powerful secondary effect: the exit holes (as I had first learned while deer-shooting on New Caledonia) of those bullets would be at least quarter, and often fist-sized. The tissues or fluids impacted by its supersonic passage would often literally explode.

Carbine and tommygun fire was not so terrible in its wounding, but the huge .45 slugs and the moderately super-sonic .30 caliber 110 grain bullets were also effective. And both of these could be fired full-auto with a modicum of accuracy retained because of the lighter recoil.

Thus, the reinforced Japanese platoon that hit Weston's ambush at 1020 hours was clobbered badly; it suffered 28 known dead. Despite the use of a "scout" dog, it walked right into Weston's ambush. And the hundred or so Japanese who walked into Smith's ambush on the other trail a few minutes later, took 18 known killed.

From those notable first contacts the deadly delaying tactics continued. Backing up the trail in stages, breaking contact after each successive devastation of the overly aggressive enemy, the two American platoons fought on. The ancient trick of withdrawing half at a time, with the other half keeping up a covering fire until a fresh base of fire had been set up behind them, was their principal device. By its repeated use they worked their way back to the trail fork south of Auche, where they joined forces.

Their last ambush, which they held for two hours, was a mere 100 yards south of that critical trail juncture. The performance of these two platoons, accomplished mainly with the M-1 rifle, enabled our two battalions to escape from Tanaka's trap and to fight another day. It was not the situation we had hoped for, not our ideal kind of confrontation with the Japanese. We would have much preferred a deep-dug defensive line as at Walawbum, or, better still, the pillboxed entrenchments around the perimeter of Henderson Field on Guadalcanal, where some of us saw the famed Japanese infantryman Colonel Ichiki leave 966 bodies in the two double-aprons of barbed wire in front. But it was the next best kind: lying in wait on a trail and letting them "hit" us in their brave but stupid manner.

The delaying action, however, was one tactic of the circumstance; in a larger sense our disadvantage of space and distance remained severe. For our own bold venture into this Japanese back yard, Tanaka now could make us pay a price. Reassured by the ground supply route that they dragged behind them, using vehicles, then ox carts and mules, then porterage, with their first 15 miles out of Kamaing along smooth roadway, Tanaka's brave infantrymen could take their losses and press angrily on. They knew our desperate supply state and our individual hunger and exhaustion, with most of us out of food entirely and with our cartridge belts going empty, too. They knew we'd have to receive an air drop soon or be unable to shoot back, while their mule-carried and hand-pushed artillery, brought up the trail with their foremost companies, could now set up and begin to range in.

Our trail back up to the divide was an easy target; it followed a ridge clearly contoured on their captured British maps, and it had occasional exposed stretches where bursts could be observed. With fire so easy to observe and correct, and the forward-reaching axis of their target fitting the error-pattern of their 77mm battalion guns, so that an over or a short would also be a hit on our lengthy and tired column of men and mules, almost every round would count.

What happened next made grist for all who like to debate over the various concepts of infantry organization and deployment. The 28th of March gave us an argument as heavily against, as any previous day had given us arguments for, the particular concept of the Long Range Penetration Group (LRPG) which we were now acting out. On our first mission, the long left hook 30 miles behind the enemy's front along the road had placed us perfectly, and the enemy response to this cut at his hip and thigh had played right into our hands. Our roadblocks had reaped their grisly harvest, and our replacement by the plodding Chinese let us move back to safety and rest up and re-supply. The LRPG notion had paid off.

Here things were very different. We had no space behind us for a drop field and light plane strip. No happy rain of food and ammunition could come to us, and our wounded had to be carried over muddy trails in a downpour so intense that holes had to be stabbed in the canvas litters to drain them enroute. A big price in morale is paid with every death from medical inattention or exposure of a casualty; it is small consolation at such times that 30 or 100 enemy were dead to this one of ours. The good old infantry divisional concepts with lines of ground communication give the wounded a better chance.

Another price is paid—and this one in advance—by the men who serve in LRPG units. A deadly, if insidious, gnawing at the nerves goes on all the time, from the moment one passes through that last row of friendly foxholes (in this case with smiling Chinese in them, parapets piled with plenty of grenades and extra cartridges) and into the no man's land and enemy-held ground beyond.

A question of territoriality then arises. Like his fellow mammal the wolf, man often takes his territory by force, and will savagely defend it from another would-be taker. And in this case the holder was an infantryman-enemy that had never before known retreat. The Japanese defeats on Guadalcanal and in New Georgia had been kept concealed from their other soldiers, and nearly all the regimental histories were free of defeats. The resulting sense of cockiness and invincibility now made ultimate defeat unthinkable. Japanese infantry had a superman complex that only death and more death could diminish. Killing off half a platoon in one encounter, or destroying a whole battalion, just wasn't enough, and so this savage bravery of the Japanese infantry, supplemented by a perhaps bio-genetic sense of territoriality as brutal as any in the animal kingdom, was then being felt full force by us—most specifically in that blast of artillery lengthwise along our footpath.

This fire was soon so accurate that direct hits were scored on men and mules. For men and animals walking in the trail's confining narrowness, mostly under canopies of huge bamboos that could cause even more deadly airbursts, there was only one rational act. It was to move on, to get the hell ahead of those damned blasts and airbursts. If a mule went down in the way, shoot it in the brain and roll it off the trail, and to hell with its cargo unless it was rifle ammunition.

Everybody by now was tired, going on sheer nerve and an over-drawn Adrenalin-account. The 2nd Battalion had had the worst of it, completing 70 miles of marching, a fierce engagement along the Jap-held roadside, and over 100 stream fordings to and from their objective of Inkangatawn. The 3rd had had but two days rest (a thousand years ago?) to recover from the Jap-killing but nonetheless exhausting stress at Walawbum, For seven weeks all units of the 5307th had been marching arduously by day and harboring nervously at night behind enemy lines, knowing that a superior force could hit and cut them off on briefest notice. Scariest of all, perhaps, was that lack of a ground route of supply and evacuation. Our dependence on aircraft, which in turn were dependent upon good weather, was all but total.

The tenuous evacuation factor especially could stir our soldier's imagination: the thought of being gut-shot and unable to get to a hospital, of being left in the care of Kachin villagers to be hidden from patrolling Japanese was always there.

All put together, it made for psychic exhaustion which, along with the routine privation of sleeping on cold ground, most often soaking wet, helped many of us to make up our minds. We'd have to forget any wish to harm the enemy now pursuing us and get ourselves up over that divide. We'd have to find a place where we could block the trail behind us from some bottlenecking promontory with our last few rounds of ammunition, and hastily receive a drop in a field protected by that trail block. Only then would we turn to face this aggressive, driving enemy with any hope of profit. And, more importantly still, only then could we get out an accummulating number of hospital-case wounded.

To most of us on the ground, and (in a rare coincidence of opinion) to the staff officers in Stilwell's forward headquarters, this dictated that we halt and regroup at two points farther back along the Tanai Valley trail. The first point was a high, commanding hilltop that rose astride the trail, with a few small bashas comprising the village of Nhpum Ga, some seven miles to the north of Auche. The second point was a rare space of paddy fields another six miles northward, named Hsamsingyang. The Nhpum Ga hilltop seemed the best bet for this crucial trail block, and the Hsamsingyang paddy fields would have to do as a drop field, a light plane strip for evacuating our wounded, and a location for the headquarters of all three battalions.

As the 2nd and 3rd Battalions approached and cleared their danger point of Auche, Merrill received confirmation, via a captured Japanese map and a report from intelligence agents in the Kamaing area, of Tanaka's clear intent to destroy us in the Tanai Valley. The force he had sent after us was three reinforced battalions. So, Merrill knew what he was asking for when he ordered McGee's 2nd Battalion, as it approached the Nhpum Ga hilltop in its present state of weary and artillery-damaged retreat, to dig in on the spot and block the Japanese from further northward progress.

To all of us, this was an odd-seeming change in our role as a long range penetration group. Static, fixed defense was not supposed to be our thing. General Orde Wingate wouldn't have approved; under his procedures we would likely have taken a quick drop and then harbored further north until we could come out and strike again in semi-guerrilla fashion. But the more experienced soldiers in the 2nd Battalion, were aware at the grass roots platoon level of our edge in firepower over the Japanese. With our semi-auto M-1s plus full-auto rifles and light machine guns of John Browning's invention, such static defense could truly become our thing. The order to halt and dig in represented a sound, if dreaded, decision to all of us, and it appeased a small but vocal minority in both battalions that had resented the order to march back into the Tanai Valley, "running away from the goddamn Japs again."

One could see its effect on morale from the edge of the Nhpum Ga hilltop clearing where I stood counting the late comers carrying litters and limping along at the tail end of the 3rd Battalion column. As McGee transmitted the order to his leading company, the wide-eyed dismay of retreat gave way to another infantryman's stock attitude. It wasn't a look of story book resolution or dauntless bravery; it was more the grimly professional visage of soldiers who knew they had time to get their bodies below ground level, and would show no more than their helmets and a thin slice of forehead and eye to the enemy who would die in droves, surely, when he would come on at them. From good old Mother Earth's comforting shelter they could finally be routed, perhaps, but not until they had mowed down the enemy like a field of ripe wheat.

Under Colonel McGee they quickly laid out a perimeter, an oval crown of thorns fit to the hilltop, measuring some 400 by 200 yards. Its outpointing gun muzzles commanded the brief open spaces and bamboo cover that led down to streams on either side, and insured a central space, defiladed from enemy flat trajectory fire, where the men could recover air-dropped supplies of food, ammunition, and, as it was to turn out, even plastic containers of drinking water.

To support this crucial trail block, the leading elements of the 3rd Battalion were already forming a perimeter around the much larger grassy space at Hsamsingyang, six miles downhill to the north, where larger air drops and light plane evacuation could be effected.

Bringing up the tail of the column, I rejoined the 3rd Battalion commander and the main body of the 3rd about noon.

This withdrawal without significant losses (without any loss of personnel to enemy rifle fire in the column itself), had been possible because of the stubborn operations of Smith's and Weston's patrols those two days before. And now we were in position, waiting, with our scant supplies of ammunition carefully redistributed in each platoon, and with nothing in our bellies except banana stalks and grass seeds, plucked or cut to chew for their faintly sugary taste.

A few moments past noon on March 28, 1944, the Japanese hit this capable rear guard at a cluster of huts called Kauri, some 2,000 yards short (south) of the hilltop perimeter. The Americans held for some four hours, then laid down a screen of automatic fire and retreated north to become a part of the hilltop garrison. The hilltop's crown of thorns now bristled in three directions, left weak only at its northward curve, facing the trail to the 3rd Battalion and a drop field source of supply and communication at Hsamsingyang that everyone prayed we could keep open.

The Japanese first struck frontally on the south side of the perimeter, taking their first, insanely excessive, casualties from the 2nd Battalion proper that late afternoon. Next, as they felt the line holding and getting stronger during the next few days with food and ammunition dropped at Hsamsingyang and brought up by mule train, they probed right and left of the trail, seeking weak spots. Encirclement soon became their prime objective; unable to crush they would go around and cut the lifeline of the trail behind. They kept up the frontal pressure hard, by fire and by disastrous movement of their target-bodies, making their regimental-level strength more and more obvious. But they also probed on around trying to grip the 2nd Battalion in a boa constrictor embrace, but getting cut and bled with each new reaching.

As the encirclement proceeded, with the Japanese clearly willing to pay the necessary price, McGee's orders and remarks to his soldiers were as optimistic and uplifting as the circumstances could make credible. But his communications to Colonel Hunter, now in command after Merrill's evacuation with a heart attack, gradually grew darker. One message that I remember reading spoke of a "pressure" that "had to be relieved." In the understated prose of one West Pointer addressing another, this was the ultimate note of desperation.

Hunter at this time—it must have been about the fifth day of the growing Japanese encirclement—called me into his lean-to and showed me this message. He ordered me to accompany the next of two daily patrols up the supply trail and to "talk to McGee and assess the situation there." He told me that "things up there" might look more grim to McGee than "they really are" and he'd like to have a separate opinion, from "someone who hadn't been hearing all that stuff go over his head" these past few days.

I undertook this mission with the feeling that Hunter could have picked better than he had, if he wanted an officer who would coolly assess this confrontation with a Japanese regiment miles behind the Japanese lines. And today I feel sure the feeling was correct. As it turned out, this errand would refresh and renew my intimacy with the little carbine, my routine marching weapon, that had served me well enough at Walawbum.

Had I known the future details, I would have left the carbine with Russ Hill and substituted an M-1. But this time I did remember to substitute a borrowed 15-shot magazine, and to have four loaded 15 shotters in belt pockets right and left.

The patrol moved off, each member taking that sensitive, gingerly step over the trip wires outside the Hsamsingyang perimeter, into the bamboo-shrouded trail that we used daily but could not keep defended. For a while our progress was routine, a repetition of the usual movement out of the south end of the perimeter at Hsamsingyang. The path led sharply upward, under an almost solid overarching canopy of huge bamboo. The bamboo was rooted in clumps yards thick at their base, with each shoot keg-thick where it came out of the ground and gently tapering to enormous length. From their roots the crowded shoots then spread outward in huge curves—upward, over, and then, as the shoots tapered gracefully to their points, downward. The overall result was a solid overarching ceiling with moist bare earth in between the bases, making us walk in effect through a series of cloisters up the ridge trail. On either side a lesser growth of other vegetation crowded in, but up the trail there were avenues of vision that could stretch 100 yards ahead, though visibility was usually 50 yards or less. Under these vaulted green ceilings, through which most of the time no bit of sky was visible, this 12-man patrol could move with considerable ease and speed.

The leader of the patrol was a sergeant, whose name I'm ashamed not to remember. He was heavily bearded, above medium height, broad shouldered. He had placed me behind himself, fourth in line with the two lead scouts in front, and was moving now with that economy of effort and that ready reserve of spring-like energy that marked the ideal kind of combat noncom. He also seemed to be on the best of terms with his men, as though he'd led them for awhile and gained their confidence.

The scouts set a fast pace these first miles out from the Hsamsingyang perimeter. Then suddenly, at about the third mile, they halted to examine something on the ground. They were standing upright and had waved no warning, so I moved forward with the patrol leader to join them.

There on the ground was a pattern of fresh Japanese footprints, of their zig-zag-treaded, big-toe sneakers and of hobnailed boots as well. There was also a sprinkling of used bandages, gauze wrappings that had been clotted with blood and replaced on this spot, where a number of litters had been rested on the trail side. Mixed in the rubbish was a number of cigarette butts and wrappings. Hoping this was no more than another Jap litter party gone astray, like the one that had walked into our battalion headquarters near Lagang Ga, we now moved on, but with redoubled caution and with a BAR man put up front with his weapon slung ready for assault fire. Other weapons were carried at the ready, too, fingers curled to the triggers, because the bandages and cigarette wrappings had been free of evening or morning dew, and the tracks no more than three hours old.

No more enemy sign for pehaps another 1,000 yards, then lots more, also of wounded being carried out. But didn't that mean almost certainly that the ring had now been closed? Wouldn't the use of this trail above and behind the 2nd Battalion's perimeter by Japanese litter bearers mean that they had forces on both sides of the trail, bottling the 2nd Battalion up? We looked silently at one another as we continued our move upward, almost a climb, until it reached a more gradual gradient, and straightened into a wider, clearer pathway under a broader and higher archway of bamboos that were as thick as nailkegs at the base. Then we heard and saw this question answered.

A Nambu opened up in front of us, raking the trail. All of us hit the dirt and crawled offside. I had just loosened one of the straps on the musette bag on which I had stitched regular packstraps for use instead of the regular blanket-roll carrier. As I rolled over to get out of the Nambu beaten zone, now enfilading the trail, the pack slipped out of my arm. That pack had to be a kind of magnet for enemy fire; struck twice at Walawbum, it was struck half a dozen times more during the next few minutes.

Offside safely and with a clear field of fire, I aimed one shot after another into the rhythmically-quivering ferns and other cover at the base of a trail clump some 50 yards ahead, which had to be that Nambu, firing. I put a round every six inches or so, from right to left, aimed as low as possible, knowing that a ricochet would do more damage than a bullet unmutilated by earth contact. On the sixth round or so the Nambu went silent.

Intense concentration on his target may not always be best for a soldier's survival, but it does help marksmanship. My training in shooting somehow managed to outweigh my great fear of the situation as I fired three shots more to make sure and heard that giveaway gurgling and moaning from the earth just behind that now quiet, unmoving cover.

Then I became aware of other things. All hell had broken loose behind me while I had been firing in that forward direction. Japanese yells, a burst of Nambu fire (damn those ubiquitous Yank killers!), and some hot and unusually accurate rifle fire was raking the trail from our rear, and the yells were coming also from our left, just down the hill. Mortar fire now added to the din, grenade projector or "knee mortar" slams coming from the front, as those little pineapples ripped through the bamboo overarch to tumble on the bare clay of the trail and then explode.

It was clear to me that we were under a double and possibly a coordinated attack from three sides, and the only comfort of that moment, other than the fact that the fourth side, to our right down the slope, was still quiet, was the slow chug-chug-chug of a BAR. Our rearguard BAR man, slightly offside the trail, with one foot sticking out onto its bare trodden clay, was lying prone and doing hell's own destruction along the stretch of path behind us that we had just moved along, apparently under calculating, gloating Japanese eyes. Like me a moment earlier, he might have been just concentrating. Or, maybe he was genuinely courageous and self-sacrificing, in that literal sense that only a fighting infantryman knows. And in front of me, offside my riddled pack, that bearded sergeant and two other men were similarly firing away, knocking down oncoming Japanese who were making themselves clearly visible or audible in front.

Though merely accompanying the patrol, I shouted a command whose wisdom I'm prepared to defend to the death. I think it was "Haul ass!," or something of the sort. "Pull out to the right. Now! For Christ's sake now!" And the men in front did so, breaking contact with their inviting but soon-to-be overwhelming enemy in front and rising to run at a crouch down the steep undergrown slope to our right, towards the stream bed lower to the west. It was one of those infantry actions where, as Charlton Ogburn puts it, the "film is sped up," where the stream of conscious memory records a second as a lifetime, engraving every detail, every finger move or roll of eyes for later review.

Leaving my pack in the center of the trail (What an affair I was later to have in New Delhi over the report of the loss of my identity card behind enemy lines!), to receive its further spanking of bullets, I rolled, skidded and then crawled off the knife-edge trail. There I crouched, eyes all around, and waited for the sergeant and the others in front to do likewise and get past me, down the slope. The five or six of us moved as a group, rearguard style, for perhaps another 25 yards downward.

Then we heard that now more distant chug! chug! chug! of the BAR, and I witnessed an unforgettable demonstration of infantry courage. The bearded sergeant, hearing that BAR still engaged above and behind us, froze in his tracks, shaking his head from side to side. He stood there despite increasing noise and movement on our side of the slope, abreast of the BAR man or even closer to us, that was entirely Japanese. As I turned, took aim and killed the most obvious of these downhill scramblers, I yelled "Haul out! On down! For Christ's sake pull out!" or something of the sort. But to no avail. While the rest of us moved on downward, firing now and then at the two or more squads of pursuing Japanese, he turned and moved back up to the trail. And somehow, by one of those miracles that one sees far too seldom in such jungle engagements, he managed to rejoin us in another five minutes or so, leading the still uncontrollably blood-thirsty BAR man with him by the arm. The story I heard later and would like to verify now if anyone knowledgeable happens to read this partial account, was that the sergeant regained the trail above this dedicated one-man roadblock and saw the BAR man methodically emptying his belt of clips, enfilading the trail and firing into the bush at clearly visible Japanese. Performing the most splended execution at 50 yards range and less, he apparently had no thought of any alternate or wiser thing to be doing with his time.

It took an amost knockout blow between the shoulder blades to bring him round, I was later told, and even then he had to be physically led away from his range-like firing point, littered with fired cartridges that had probably accounted for a quarter of their own number of enemy.

Whether or not this was literal truth, the next observable fact for me was the sergeant's return with this wild BAR man, which hope-fully would let us complete this disengagement as a body, yielding this goddamned bit of jungle to our pursuers for the moment and maybe a hell of a lot longer.

Our pursuers, though, were still full of that crazy aggressiveness they'd learned in China against poorly armed peasant soldiers. They just didn't seem to want us to disengage. They kept scrambling, yelling, down that slippery, fern-grown slope after us, some of them at a dead run.

In the remaining sped-up mental film of that joint American-Japanese downhill skidway I have some strangely clear Camp Perry marksman's images and recollections. In the same way that I can remember the exact position of my front sight, at the moment of letoff in a crucial rapid-fire competition, telling me I'd got a center or

slightly left or right of center bullseye, I remember the position of
that carbine front sight on Japanese khaki shirt or face or helmet at
those ranges from 30 to 100 yards or so. "Dead! Dead! Dead!" I
could say to myself. Or "Solid in the chest!" or "Through the
helmet!" These Japanese, unlike the ones on outposts and patrol,
were wearing steel helmets through which a carbine bullet slipped
quite easily. These enemy soldiers were converted into corpses and
litter cases by a marksman's skill so drilled in that it could transcend
the greatest, and I do mean the greatest, belly-felt fear and horror.
The words I grunted to myself and, I think, sometimes shouted
wildly, were of self-consolation, of fright, and of gratitude to my
saving interest in the competitive shooting sports. They were more a
prayer than a boast.

Unlike that line of riflemen in those diggings along the river near
Walawbum and unlike myself in earlier combat situations, I found
myself unable now to yell out defiance and hatred. All I wanted at
this moment was to avoid my own quite likely death. Had a delegation of Japanese generals suddenly appeared under a white flag,
ready to hand me a guarantee of personal peace and safety if I'd let
them have half of China, for example, I might have signed their
documents gladly. But not being offered this alternative, and facing
only these brave little brown-skinned infantrymen who would
neither accept nor offer surrender, I kept on moving down that hill
with a sidewise step, so that I could twist from the waist, take aim,
and kill another and another of these brave, brave foreigners who
were trying to prevent my escape with their fortunately inferior
grade of marksmanship

So much for the glory of war and John B. George, an idealized
notion and a fragile, vulnerable human being that parted company
with one another in the noisy green shade of the bamboo groves on
Nhpum Ga hill. As I've mentioned already in this Burma addendum
to my earlier text about the fight on Guadalcanal, that old romantic
seduction of combat, that old sense of adventure as one moves into
the jungle with rifle in hand, didn't fully desert me, just the thought
of war as glorious in any way. During the remaining months of the
war it was still in me to bask in the praise of a combat veteran, back in
New Delhi and Washington. And when sent back to Burma, I could
still deliver pep talks to American trainees at Ramgarh training
center. In a later assignment as aide to the Allied Land Forces
commander in chief I could still pretend to be brave: I could even
submit my body to that stupid and purposeless exposure to aimed
rifle fire when I visited a front line British unit and walked along
with British officers, looking down at the dug-in Tommies while
Japanese bullets snapped and crackled. The healthy young nerves
that I still possessed also let me accept with phony calm the risks of

jungle-hopping in light liaison aircraft, and ocean hopping in staff planes flown by 19-year-old pilots. A faint inner prayer for a formal farewell to arms, and a resolution to confine my interest in guns and shooting to the target range and the big game wildernesses of Asia and Africa, had begun to echo in my soul. I was still gung-ho; later I'd get General Merrill to promise me a battalion in the invasion of the Japanese home islands. But never again would I willingly, voluntarily, go out of my way to confront an armed enemy soldier. Not for all the tea in China, where, incidentally, I spent my final wartime months as a liaison officer with the Chinese Nationalist Honorable First Infantry Division.

This thought would not become conscious and clear to me for many years. The germ of it may have been planted earlier, during another "great fright and terror." But I'd place it here, during that running, sweating withdrawal downslope through those clumps of bamboo. Just as we gained a game path lower down, I killed a final enemy who exposed his upper body some 70 yards up to our left and rear. He seemed to be the last one coming at us, and after a few more steps on the game path, which fortuitously followed the westward stream bed back towards Hsamsingyang, we briefly regrouped to count noses. Miraculously, we found no more than scratches and a few hole in outer uniforms and a crease or two in helmets, except for one wound that would require evacuation.

When we got back through the perimeter and to the drop field I reported to Colonel Hunter, facing that taciturn, utterly composed West Pointer with the pallor of combat still greying my face, I'm sure.

I have never mastered the histrionics of the professional officer, nor fathomed the protocol that might be proper when a company-grade officer brings bad news to a regimental commander. The favored mode and mien, of course, is cool understatement. A classic beginning for the report I had to give now might have been: "Sir, the situation on that hilltop is less than ideal. . ." or some such bull. But at the moment I wasn't feeling very "classic." I told him what had happened; that our trail to McGee's battalion had been cut, that the battalion was probably completely surrounded—the truth as I saw it, without military varnish or downplay.

Hunter listened with an appearance of utter, smiling calm, for which I gave him my utter, unsmiling admiration. He was sitting in his lean-to, shirtless, cross-legged with a map on the ground before him. After I'd given him these terse facts and the news that the battalion probably was now fully besieged, he paused for a moment and then asked, "What do you think we ought to do?"

My thoughts and most of my words of the next few moments are engraved on my memory. From Colonel Hunter's lean-to I could see the bamboo slope we had just descended, misty in the distance, and the bulk of the hill itself, with its other steep slope facing the east, all now in possession of the enemy. The Japanese had hit our patrol in company strength, had closed their ring around McGee's battalion, and would now have several Nambu lights, at least, emplaced to cut that trail between us. The siege, as opposed to the earlier skirmish or battle, of Nhpum Ga had begun. I said, "Have McGee move out, shoot his way through to us here. He'll know the best way, or I can recommend the way we just came back, down that western slope and stream bed. Or he can come right down the trail, if he wants to pay the price for an easier walk down. Then we can move back north. Drag that Jap force on up into this valley. Stretch out their supply line. Let them exhaust themselves against our rear guard, and let our aviation strafe and bomb them at the fords and other points where they'll have to expose themselves. They've already been hurt by McGee, and by Weston and Smith before that. This valley is as tough on them as it is on us, and they've got no help from the air. That way they'll be petered out before we get to the north turn of the Tanai."

The colonel was nodding, but much in the way of a professor, waiting for a not-too-bright student to talk himself out. He'd asked me that unusual question, though, and the answer had come natu-rally, right off the top of my frightened head. As I shut myself up, censoring out all the detailed further arguments that I could feel coming up inside, he smiled. These arguments were all based on my sense of McGee's current fix. Nhpum Ga was too damn close to Tanaka's road-heads north of Kamaing; the trails leading up to it were too damn short. The python-like encirclement of McGee's battalion could be nourished too easily, fed more and more supplies to let it tighten ever more strongly. Remembering the Japanese on Guadalcanal, I also sensed how the Japs could now give us a dose of our own medicine. They could dig in astride the trail facing us, the 3rd Battalion here at Hsamsingyang (not yet joined by the weary, wounded 1st, still off in the jungle to the west), and make us trade them man for man if we tried to cut through and clear that trail again. They could tunnel round those rooted clumps of bamboo, could roof their Nambu pillboxes with fires interlaced. Like their colleagues on Guadalcanal, these Japanese could also learn by experience. They could learn what bull their field service regulations were, telling them they should attack, attack, attack, when the truest edge they had against us Americans was in fact a fixed, deep-dug, sacrificial defense. They could stop this new, amazingly well-armed foe from killing them in droves, and instead make us trade them man for man in a kind of warfare that could wear us out via grim attrition. I saw McGee in the position of the 2nd Battalion of the 132nd Infantry, back on Hill 27 on Guadalcanal, but lacking the 132nd's excellent ground supply line of jeeps and native porters.

While those further arguments for ordering McGee to shoot his way out and to join us in a further northward retreat raced on through my mind, Hunter continued to smile, to maintain that long silence that I didn't dare break until he had spoken. Finally he stopped smiling, let out a short breath that seemed to be the opposite of agreement or approval, and said, "Yes, George. That's one way to do it. But we're going to hold that hilltop."

Again, that cool, calm smile, which this time triggered something uncontrollable inside me, so that with no wish to say another word I heard my own voice blurting out a mixture of admiration and frustration, into this West Pointer's imperturbable face.

"Colonel, don't you see this as a nasty, bloody sweat-out? Aren't you worried about those flanks (I pointed left and right of the hilltop, where streamside paths could lead the Japanese right up to Hsamsing-yang). Don't you ever get scared?"

I was sorry the second I said this. The colonel's reply came at the end of a dismissive, steely-eyed gaze. And because I would later repeat it, and because it was overheard by sundry headquarters personnel lounging nearby, it would become a regimental anecdote, told and re-told up to this day by the veterans of the 5307th. "Wait," he said, "till you've had twins!"

At the conscious level at least, I'd like to leave it at that: a fiercely brave and cool West Pointer being fiercely brave and cool. But things that I've learned since from the official histories, and a seasoned antipathy to superman myths wherever and of whomever formed, makes me add a footnote today, as I sit at this typewriter in Washington, D.C., in the year 1980.

What I've learned since, is that Colonel Hunter at that moment had a lot of information that I did not. He knew more precisely the location of the 1st Battalion, which was then moving in to help us. Also he knew the back-up position of a Chinese Nationalist battalion, not too far back of us at the head of the Tanai River curve to our north. He also knew, in much greater detail than I did, of the location of the Japanese on either flank of McGee, through reports from Kachin scouts with whom I had no contact.

On learning this and other comforting bits of information years too late for it to give me the courage I needed then, from successively more complete historical sources, both American and Japanese, I felt a deep retroactive resentment. How dare this field grade officer, during this his first combat campaign, withhold this comforting mass of facts from frightened and discouraged me? How dare he face me with a coolness that he could have passed on, with a sense of security that he could have shared? What kind of tawdry, cheap one-upmanship was this?

But on second thought I know he had no choice. As a book soldier, a professional West Pointer without Merrill's transcendant, overriding politesse and practicality, he had to observe the rules of secrecy. The sources of all this information were heavily classified, mainly to protect the network of spies and guerrillas concerned. Except for psychological reasons (however vital and urgent they might seem to me), I had no valid need to know; like other lower officers, far forward in the fight and therefore theoretically more likely to be captured and interrogated under torture, "The Book" denied me the comforting further truths about our situation. Cynically, of course, a junior denied such comforting details by his commander can theorize about this superior's Freudian motivation. Obviously a commander can seem to be much calmer, more composed than his frightened and ignorant underlings if he knows the unit is relatively safe and his juniors do not. And in most if not all situations, it is the commander who decides who among his subordinates might have that all-important need to know. Everything that I have seen and heard of Colonel Hunter denies that he would even think of such chicanery, and attests that he was both capable and brave as the leader of our three-battalion force.

My one belated comfort from this knowledge is the slight alleviation of my deep feeling of inferiority during parts of that campaign, invoked in no small measure by Hunter's own appearance of awesome bravery and self-control. Unlike us 3rd Battalion members, Hunter was going into his first campaign, his second bit-piece of combat. His nervous system, even without the malaria in repeated bouts, had to be less frayed than mine.

Had Hunter been able to give me the comforting information, my fears would still have been there. But they would have been much easier for me to mask. I would have seen for us much more of a fighting chance, and I would have been far less ready to accept a medical officer's decision, as he read a thermometer at 103 and gave me an intravenous injection of quinine, and allow myself to be flown out to hospital. This was to happen 50 miles north and several days later, after I'd delivered Hunter's plea to that northern Chinese battalion that they march south and join us. The American medico, whom I remember as a tough-looking southwesterner (perhaps because he carried a Colt single-action Frontier Model), wrote on the evacuation tag, "It would be suicide to allow this man to return to combat." He meant "murder" of course: in the giddyness of a fever I'm always conscious of mistakes in grammar and syntax.

This was to be the end of my footslogging with an American

infantry battalion - a watershed, I'll swear, in the career of any soldier. The 3rd Battalion of course marched on, to an ultimate victory when the Myitkyina airstrip was captured by the Marauders in late May, 1944, and to a miserable anti-climax when it and the other two Marauder battalions were bogged down by a lack of ammunition and food while the Japanese reinforced the town from the south. (Through some Theater error or happenstance the first planes in carried engineer equipment and Chinese troops, and the specifically promised food and ammunition was delayed, and a long fight much akin to World War I trench warfare dragged out before the town was to fall.) In the end a Distinguished Unit Citation was awarded to the Marauders, summarizing their overall campaign:

> "After a series of successful engagements in the Hukawng and Mogaung Valleys of North Burma, in March and April 1944, the unit was called on to lead a march over jungle trails through extremely difficult mountain terrain against stubborn resistance in a surprise attack on Myitkyina. The unit proved equal to its task and after a brilliant operation on 17 May 1944 seized the airfield at Myitkyina, an objective of great tactical importance in the campaign, and assisted in the capture of the town of Myitkyina on 3 August 1944."

And while the 3rd Battalion marched on, I moved into the hospital and then out into the unfamiliar world of the staff and senior training officer. Wartime promotions and assignments would take me first to Stilwell's headquarters in New Delhi, as a field consultant regarding weapons and tactics; then to a sub-office of that headquarters and the historical branch of Army G-2 in the Pentagon to help compile a publication entitled *Merrill's Marauders;* then back to Delhi and on down to Barrackpore, outside Calcutta, to serve until the fall of Rangoon as American aide de camp to the British general then commanding Allied Land Forces, Southeast Asia, under Mountbatten; then finally to Yunan, China, to serve as a regimental liaison officer in the Chinese Nationalist Honorable First Division.

After the war—until I decided to give up active military duty in order to attend university—I served as an infantry training battalion commander at Camp Blanding, Florida, and as the China-Manchuria desk officer in the G-2 section of MacArthur's GHQ, Far East Command in Tokyo.

My journeyings in the wartime infantry had begun when I enlisted as a private in late 1940, planning to get my required year of training over quickly and return to my civilian job. The tour took five years longer than expected, but on the whole I loved, and still love, the Army. Memories of grand scenes on all the continents, thrilling events that could be calm as well as violent, and above all the friendships made it wonderful for me.

Especially the friendships. First the intimates mentioned in these two tales, of Guadalcanal and then of Burma, my buddies on the march. But also other, and generally more widely known, personalities that I met and worked with. Besides General Merrill, who remained a friend and mentor until his untimely death, there was Colonel Dean Rusk (later to become our longest serving Secretary of State) who gave me my post-Marauder job as aide de camp and who also helped me ease back into civilian existence. Professor Livingstone Wright, the former War Department chief historian who edited the Marauder history manuscript that I carried back to Washington during Christmas season, 1945, became a friend through every season. He persuaded the admissions authorities at Princeton to admit a student who certainly had one of the poorest high school academic records they had ever considered. . .me, then died at 49 before I graduated summa cum laude with the Atwater prize in politics, after only 21 months of residence. And finally there was Charlton Ogburn, not a close buddy during the campaign because he served in the 1st Battalion, but a wonderful friend ever since, whose brilliant books on subjects that range from Shakespeare through ornithology to geology and military history are monuments of admiration.

It strikes me as fantastic that access to all of this grand experience and the beginning of all these grand friendships was provided by my early love of rifle marksmanship. Not only did skill with the rifle give me access to opportunity and friendships, the use of that skill many times enabled me to avoid failure before these many friends.

Without the confidence that my rifle shooting skill provided—the sense of a clear advantage over my Japanese counterparts, the knowledge of an actual power that I could wield over those brave little brown-skinned soldiers trying to kill me—I might well have flunked out on every battlefield. With the vivid imagination that makes me afraid when I get into a commercial aircraft, I could have been one of that 75 per cent, that deadweight three-fourths of American soldiers identified by General S.L.A. Marshall, who did not fire their weapons in combat situations even when pressed. I might have kept my head down much more than I did, cowering like the anti-hero character in the film *The Americanization of Emily* on his Normandy Beach, when there were enemy targets visible in front of me. And, in a company grade officer of the 2nd Battalion, 132nd Infantry on Guadalcanal, or of Merrill's Marauders in North Burma, behavior like this wouldn't have gotten by. I might well have been labeled by kinder companions as "one of us soft Americans who loves life too goddamn much," or by colleagues less kind, as a simple coward. Thus for whatever seeming bravery that made Colonel Ferry call me "always capable and aggressive" and add that I "never lost an opportunity to kill or harass the enemy," I'm indebted to my earlier hobbyist enthusiasm for guns and shooting. And to the free society that allowed me to own and use firearms without the paperwork and thoughtless laws and bureaucratic barriers that some of our lawmakers have always misguidedly sought to impose.

From these and other plain and obvious facts, I know that no small part of my personal self-respect is due to our American constitutional right to keep and bear arms. Had my father had to beseech bureaucrats for permits and approving signatures before he could give me a .22 rifle for my seventh birthday, he might have given me some expensive toy instead. My young boy's interest in shooting might never have begun on that farm back in northern Missouri; I might never have acquired the skill that could stand in for the bravery. For me, this puts the issue of firearms ownership and use into the plainest, clearest context; the slightest curb of gun ownership and use by law-abiding citizens will inevitably increase the threat to our national security. Each piece of legislation passed that inconveniences firearms buffs and shooters can be counted on to help develop, in X number of American infantrymen, what might be called "their full potential for cowardice in the face of a military enemy."

By helping to keep our militia (this term means all men of military age, we should remember) ignorant of the weapon most basic to most battlefields still, any such law well may cause X number of our future infantrymen to keep their heads down and not fire at an oncoming foe, or to fire with no effect if they happen to be long on physical courage, if they happen to be one of that one-fourth of our manpower willing to take the dire risks even when they don't have the requisite skills.

On the other hand, every freedom that we can retain that guards the right to keep on owning and using firearms will do the reverse. It will cause X number of that militia to rise above their natural fears through craft and skill, to assess the sound of enemy fire and know when it's a good bet to take that risk. They will raise their heads and shoot because they know the deadly execution that a true marksman's skill can work on their oncoming enemy. Thus every inch that gun fanciers and shooters yield to the well-intentioned but misguided regulators and licensers in our society, every further small erosion of our remaining freedoms to pursue our chosen hobbies, will make X number of cowards out of soldiers who could otherwise seem brave, will cause X number of Americans to die, defenseless, on future battlefields, and will deprive them of that indefinable but entirely recognizable "spirit" that so marks an American that wartime U.S. intelligence agents had to be taught how to hide it, had to be schooled in walking un-proud and un-tall and in otherwise affecting the obeisant and compliant look of the male in a repressed and dictatorial society. The source of this spirit has never been scientifically defined, but most of us nonetheless sense it. A man who is free looks free. And a man who can defend himself on a battlefield, who can kill or reduce to whimpering surrender the bullies that Tojos or Hitlers can breed, can feel it deep inside as a kind of basic security, in peacetime, too.

At odd moments I've let my mind wander yet more, and have asked myself where I might be today if I'd never taken up guns and marksmanship as a serious interest and hobby. I'd be dead, most likely, for these past 40 years or living without self-respect or the respect of many of my firends. Then I think of other shooters-gone-to-war, and of guns and shooting sports today, and these thoughts connect, directly and clearly in my mind, with the abstract and hackneyed catch-words of U.S.-Soviet relations, of the Free World and Iron Curtain countries, of the overall geopolitical circumstances that might tempt this or that national leadership to move towards war and invasion.

Believe me, this connection is valid. Our potential enemies abroad are far from fools. Their agents and diplomatic representatives have travelled in this country, have read the statistics of gun use and ownership. They know the vocal moves for anti-firearms legislation, and they wish such "liberal" movements every success. They also know the broad leaven of individual skill with rifles, handguns, and shotguns in this land, manifest in the hunting fields and on the many different kinds of indoor and outdoor target ranges, that is an actual, deadly part of our military preparedness. And they, more than their counterparts in free societies, know of the recent trends in military usages; the new and crucial factors of guerrilla warfare, of urban and rural resistance to invasion, which pose serious questions to the concepts of nuclear warfare and massed movements of whole armies. Strategic weapons can cripple industry, can kill large numbers of urban residents; massed conventional armies can fan out and broadly invade a continent, perhaps. Artillery and mortars can reduce and initially occupy a village, a road junction, a railway marshalling yard. But the ground is taken and held mainly with the rifle.

All of which leads these foreign assessors of American strength to an old military truth dating from the Battle of New Orleans and before: ground and buildings and farm fields must be finally occupied and held by small groups of infantry or police, or by bands of partisans—by individuals armed primarily with rifles and pistols and light automatic weapons. The current experience of the Soviets in Afghanistan and a broader pattern of recent experience in Asia and

Africa, may be renewing this old military truth, and determining the basic character of military invasions and occupations when undertaken against the will of the local populace.

Surely a Soviet intelligence specialist today, knowing the troubles that Soviet soldiers are having in Afghanistan against tribesmen armed mostly with obsolete weapons, will have in his mind some small thought, at least, of how hard it might be to take and hold any further land grabs—in this perhaps new and changing context of warfare that is centered on this final taking and holding of ground. And, therefore, more and more, on the rifleman, the ultimate taker and holder, the ultimate defender.

Poets and philosophers and no small number of modern behavioral scientists have often tried to name the ethical, moral and material forces on earth that most favor human individual freedom. They parade grand concepts and ideas: One Man, One Vote; Parliamentary Democracy: the Dignity of Man; and so on.

It makes a grand procession, all those slogans and symbols. But behind it all, and overshadowing each one of these abstractions, I see the towering figure of the rifleman who *does* fire his weapon at the enemy, emergent today, perhaps, as the simple, grass roots, ultimately dominant factor in a changing military cosmos. The very basis of our Western belief in the overriding importance of individual freedom is symbolized for me by my memories of those individual riflemen, firing with deadly precision from their foxholes on Guadalcanal or in North Burma, defending that freedom with deadly success against a foe 10 times more experienced in war than they, but 10 times less free and less skilled with the rifle.

THE NEXT TIME

At the end of the original edition of this book, in 1947, I speculated through some three pages about *The Next Time*, meaning of course the next commitment of American infantrymen, the next shooting war, declared or otherwise, brush-fire or full scale. And we're all aware of the several commitments of American troops abroad since that date, in a world where unstable foreign governments, altering power relationships and the increasing incidence of large scale terrorism, urban and rural guerrilla operations, plus the development of ever more deadly personal weapons, have made the individual rifleman a yet more decisive factor.

How we can best defend our national and broadly Western interests in the changed world of today is no question for a single author who happens to be an ex-infantryman and a firearms enthusiast. Questions of this magnitude are for the highest elements of our national political and military leadership to face. But to the extent that our current national interests might be served by a specific defense or capture and holding of a particular piece of real estate (a threatened foreign oil field, a strategic island or an overrun U.S. Embassy or even an allied nation) the performance of our infantry battalions, companies, and platoons become the final crucial elements.

In a quantitative ground force sense, the Red Army seems to overshadow the NATO forces. For the United States to match it man for man and tank for tank would seem too costly (in social consequences if not in dollars). Not having the huge rural population of the Soviet Union to recruit from, we might have to alter our entire society and economy. Moreover, the maintenance of such a large military establishment in peace time is repugnant to many Americans. So America and the West have to think in terms of quantity in their peace time armies, plus that factor of readiness for a more general mobilization.

This moves us to considerations that are very simple: if you cannot have a large standing Army you must have a huge bank of civilian-soldiers; a trained and organized reserve, ready on a few day's notice to leave their civilian jobs and take up arms. The names of such reserve organizations can be the National Guard, the Organized

Reserves, or anything else. The important thing would be their standard of training and organization.

The greatest problem in developing such reserve forces is maintaining a good standard of training, especially weapons training; and of the weapons training the most important part is the basic and universally useful training in rifle marksmanship. Teaching civilians, especially those of military age, how to shoot the rifle, is more valuable in my opinion than any other training.

Training in itself, however, is dry. The average American wants to enjoy himself while he learns. The answer to this is to put marksmanship on a "sporting" or competitive basis, and here we can learn something from the Swiss. Let the government spend money enough to make shooting as attractive, for instance, as bowling. Let every neighborhood have its rifle range, gallery indoor and medium-range outdoor. Let evey state have several long range competition layouts for big matches. Given a rifle and ammunition every kid wants to shoot. Given good instruction and material, every kid, by present scoring standards, can become an expert rifleman. An Army of expert riflemen, with near-equality in supporting weapons, would be well nigh invincible in either defensive or aggressive combat.

Weapons can only be improved within certain limits; ours are already excellent. But with the human element it is different; not one rifleman in ten thousand can use his weapon to full advantage. The importance of skill vs weapons design is well demonstrated by the fact that a fine competitive archer can shoot better with his bow and arrow than the average Infantry rifleman armed with a rifle. Thus we find that while we have gone far in weapons design, we have not yet begun to create true weapons skill. And everything that I've seen of war and the military worldwide, convinces me that the development of that skill is vital for it will determine the ultimate effectiveness of the Infantry we send to the battlefields of the next war.

When this next war comes it may find much of our manhood in about the same shape as did the last. We may be soft from a lack of hard work and from traveling our miles in automobiles instead of on foot. We will be soft from sleeping on soft beds in warmed rooms. This will make the hardships of a campaign seem much worse to us than to the men of nations of lower standards of living, where the peasants are used to living the year round under conditions approximating military camplife. And because our country is not miserably poor or overpopulated, Americans will continue to retain an ultra-humanitarian concept of the value of human life, making us far more hesitant to take or risk the lives of our fellow human beings.

All of these can be military deterrents, working to our disadvantage during a war. To counter them we have many advantages, such as technical superiority and a higher level of mechanical education for the average man. These are qualities that help vastly in the assembly of an effective Air Corps or Navy but can only begin to make trained or hardened Infantry soldiers. We must have other capabilities developed in our militia if the average man is expected to be able to defend his country in the most elemental way.

We should teach our people how to shoot, not ordinarily, but with skill. Every man, woman and half-grown child in the country should be able to use the simpler Infantry weapons. In Afghanistan today we see the deadliness of even a modicum of firearms skill.

And in World War II, ironically, we saw a strangely similar demonstration. No one outside the Soviet Union knows how much it meant that so many of the Soviet people had learned to shoot rifles and machine guns. We all know what terrible casualties the invading German Armies suffered at the hands of armed Russian civilians. Perhaps the Russian ability to withstand the German attack was decided by that one factor. Perhaps our country's mettle will be similarly tested one day; if it is I hope we stand up as well as a heroic minority of Afghans are today, and as well as the currently misled Russians did in their dark days of 1941 and 1942.

Our victories in World War II were glorious; no one can say otherwise. The only trouble was they took too long to achieve. Advances were delayed for days because the fire against enemy positions was ineffectually delivered by men of insufficient skill. Enemy garrisons under siege were able to hold out longer. Too many enemy soldiers were able to stick their heads above ground without getting a bullet in the face—which is just another way of saying that most of our Infantrymen were lousy shots.

A good point of this experience is that most of the ex-doughboys know they were poor shots and they now know how much that lack of skill cost them. An amazing number of men whom I know of draft age are willing to learn the right way to shoot now, and kids of high school age are nearly always willing to learn how to shoot. Teach those two groups of persons to shoot well, and we will automatically be assured of a large number of good combat Infantrymen if and when we next need them.

We all have heard it said that "God is on the side with the heaviest battalions." That is an age old military truism. In my part of World War II God displayed partiality too—He always favored the side armed with semi-automatic rifles. We can secure even more of His support in wars to come if we learn how to shoot our rifles as they should be aimed and fired.

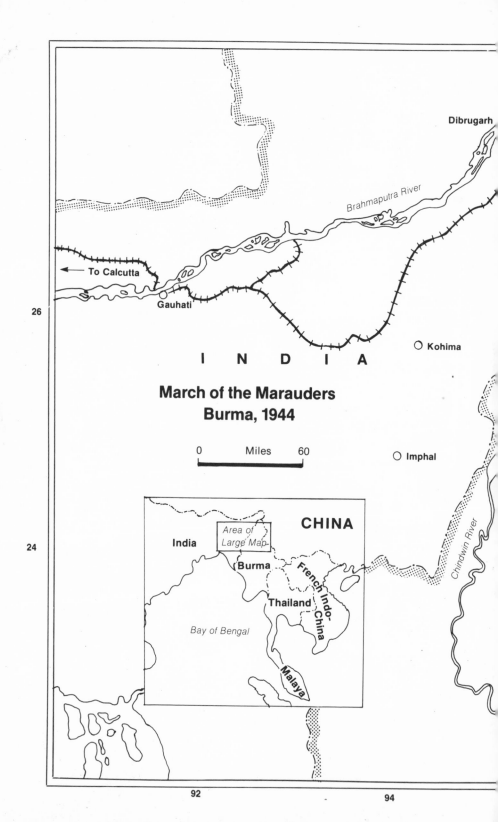

March of the Marauders
Burma, 1944

0　　　Miles　　60

Dibrugarh

Brahmaputra River

To Calcutta

Gauhati

I　N　D　I　A

○ Kohima

○ Imphal

Chindwin River

India

Area of
Large Map

CHINA

Burma

French Indo-
China

Thailand

Bay of Bengal

Malaya

26

24

92

94